WE THE PEOPLE

A CONCISE INTRODUCTION
TO AMERICAN POLITICS

Fourth Edition

Thomas E. Patterson

Bradlee Professor of Government and the Press
John F. Kennedy School of Government
Harvard University

Mc
Graw
Hill

Boston Burr Ridge, IL Dubuque, IA Madison, WI New York
San Francisco St. Louis Bangkok Bogotá Caracas Kuala Lumpur
Lisbon London Madrid Mexico City Milan Montreal New Delhi
Santiago Seoul Singapore Sydney Taipei Toronto

McGraw-Hill Higher Education ✖

A Division of The **McGraw-Hill** Companies

WE THE PEOPLE: A CONCISE INTRODUCTION TO AMERICAN POLITICS
FOURTH EDITION

Published by McGraw-Hill, a business unit of The McGraw-Hill Companies, Inc., 1221 Avenue of the Americas, New York, NY 10020. Copyright © 2002, 2000 by The McGraw-Hill Companies, Inc. All rights reserved. Previous editions © 1998, 1995 by Thomas E. Patterson. All rights reserved. No part of this publication may be reproduced or distributed in any form or by any means, or stored in a database or retrieval system, without the prior written consent of The McGraw-Hill Companies, Inc., including, but not limited to, in any network or other electronic storage or transmission, or broadcast for distance learning.

Some ancillaries, including electronic and print components, may not be available to customers outside the United States.

This book is printed on acid-free paper.

1 2 3 4 5 6 7 8 9 0 DOC/DOC 0 9 8 7 6 5 4 3 2 1

ISBN 0–07–240188–5

Editorial director: *Jane E. Karpacz*
Sponsoring editor: *Monica Eckman*
Editorial coordinator: *Shannon Morrow*
Marketing manager: *Janise A. Fry*
Senior project manager: *Marilyn Rothenberger*
Production supervisor: *Enboge Chong*
Coordinator of freelance design: *Michelle D. Whitaker*
Cover/interior designer: *Jamie A. O'Neal*
Cover image: *SuperStock, Inc.*
Senior photo research coordinator: *Carrie K. Burger*
Photo researcher: *Chris Hammond*
Supplement producer: *Brenda A. Ernzen*
Media technology producer: *Lance Gerhart*
Compositor: *GAC—Indianapolis*
Typeface: *10.5/13.5 Jansen*
Printer: *R. R. Donnelley & Sons Company/Crawfordsville, IN*

The credits section for this book begins on page C-1 and is considered an extension of the copyright page.

Library of Congress Cataloging-in-Publication Data

Patterson, Thomas E.
    We the people: a concise introduction to American politics / Thomas E. Patterson. — 4th ed.
        p. cm.
    Includes bibliographical references and index.
    ISBN 0–07–240188–5
    1. United States—Politics and government. I. Title.
JK274 .P36   2002
320.473—dc21
                                                                    2001018744
                                                                    CIP

www.mhhe.com

To My Children,
Alex and Leigh

About the Author

Thomas E. Patterson is Benjamin Bradlee Professor of Government and the Press in the John F. Kennedy School of Government at Harvard University. He was previously a distinguished professor of political science in the Maxwell School of Citizenship at Syracuse University. Raised in a small Minnesota town near the Iowa and South Dakota borders, he was educated at South Dakota State University and the University of Minnesota, where he received his Ph.D. in 1971.

He is the author of six books and dozens of articles, which focus primarily on the media and elections. His book, *Out of Order* (1994), received national attention when President Clinton said every politician and journalist should be required to read it. An earlier book, *The Mass Media Election* (1980), received a *Choice* award as Outstanding Academic Book, 1980–1981. Another of Patterson's books, *The Unseeing Eye* (1976), was selected by the American Association for Public Opinion Research as one of the fifty most influential books of the past half century in the field of public opinion.

His current research includes the Vanishing Voter Project—a study of public involvement in the 2000 presidential election campaign. He is also conducting a five-country study of the news media's political role. His work has been funded by major grants from the National Science Foundation, the Markle Foundation, the Smith-Richardson Foundation, the Ford Foundation, and the Pew Charitable Trusts.

Contents

PREFACE   xii

CHAPTER ONE   The American Heritage   1

POLITICAL CULTURE: THE CORE PRINCIPLES OF AMERICAN
GOVERNMENT   2

POLITICS: THE PROCESS OF DECIDING UPON
SOCIETY'S GOALS   12

THE CONCEPT OF A POLITICAL SYSTEM AND THE BOOK'S
ORGANIZATION   22

Summary   25

Major Concepts   25

Suggested Readings and Web Sites   26

READING 1   Presidential Inaugural Address
George W. Bush   R1-1

CHAPTER TWO   Constitutional Democracy   27

BEFORE THE CONSTITUTION: THE COLONIAL AND
REVOLUTIONARY EXPERIENCES   29

NEGOTIATING TOWARD A CONSTITUTION   34

PROVIDING FOR A LIMITED GOVERNMENT   40

PROVIDING FOR SELF-GOVERNMENT   47

CONSTITUTIONAL DEMOCRACY TODAY   55

Summary   56

Major Concepts   57

Suggested Readings and Web Sites   57

READING 2   The Mischiefs of Faction
James Madison   R2-1

CHAPTER THREE   Federalism   59

FEDERALISM: NATIONAL AND STATE SOVEREIGNTY   60

FEDERALISM IN HISTORICAL PERSPECTIVE   67

FEDERALISM TODAY   75

THE PUBLIC'S INFLUENCE: SETTING THE BOUNDARIES OF
FEDERAL-STATE POWER   85

Summary   86

Major Concepts   87
Suggested Readings and Web Sites   87
READING 3   The National Idea in American Politics
Samuel H. Beer   R3-1

CHAPTER FOUR   Civil Liberties   89

FREEDOM OF EXPRESSION   91
FREEDOM OF RELIGION   102
THE RIGHT OF PRIVACY   105
RIGHTS OF PERSONS ACCUSED OF CRIMES   107
THE COURTS AND A FREE SOCIETY   117
Summary   118
Major Concepts   119
Suggested Readings and Web Sites   119
READING 4   The Internet and Free Expression
Reno v. *ACLU (1997)*   R4-1

CHAPTER FIVE   Equal Rights   121

THE STRUGGLE FOR EQUALITY   122
EQUALITY UNDER THE LAW   138
EQUALITY OF RESULT   144
SUPERFICIAL DIFFERENCES, DEEP DIVISIONS   153
Summary   153
Major Concepts   154
Suggested Readings and Web Sites   155
READING 5   America's Racial Divide
William Jefferson Clinton   R5

CHAPTER SIX   Public Opinion and Political
Socialization   156

THE NATURE OF PUBLIC OPINION   158
POLITICAL SOCIALIZATION: HOW AMERICANS LEARN
THEIR POLITICS   165
FRAMES OF REFERENCE: HOW AMERICANS THINK
POLITICALLY   170
THE INFLUENCE OF PUBLIC OPINION ON POLICY   180
Summary   182

Major Concepts 183

Suggested Readings and Web Sites 183

READING 6   Democracy, Information, and the Rational Public
Benjamin I. Page and Robert Y. Shapiro R6-1

CHAPTER SEVEN   Voting and Participation 185

VOTER PARTICIPATION 186

CONVENTIONAL FORMS OF PARTICIPATION OTHER THAN
VOTING 201

UNCONVENTIONAL ACTIVISM: SOCIAL MOVEMENTS AND
PROTEST POLITICS 206

PARTICIPATION AND THE POTENTIAL FOR INFLUENCE 208

Summary 210

Major Concepts 211

Suggested Readings and Web Sites 211

READING 7   The Vanishing Voter
Thomas E. Patterson R7-1

CHAPTER EIGHT   Political Parties, Candidates, and Campaigns 213

PARTY COMPETITION AND MAJORITY RULE: THE HISTORY
OF U.S. PARTIES 215

ELECTORAL AND PARTY SYSTEMS 221

PARTY ORGANIZATIONS 231

THE CANDIDATE-CENTERED CAMPAIGN 239

PARTIES, CANDIDATES, AND THE PUBLIC'S INFLUENCE 244

Summary 246

Major Concepts 247

Suggested Readings and Web Sites 248

READING 8   Running for Congress
Paul S. Herrnson R8-1

CHAPTER NINE   Interest Groups 249

THE INTEREST-GROUP SYSTEM 251

INSIDE LOBBYING: SEEKING INFLUENCE THROUGH
OFFICIAL CONTACTS 260

OUTSIDE LOBBYING: SEEKING INFLUENCE THROUGH
PUBLIC PRESSURE 267

THE GROUP SYSTEM: INDISPENSABLE BUT BIASED   272

Summary   276

Major Concepts   277

Suggested Readings and Web Sites   277

READING 9   The Paralyzing Effect of Group Politics
Jonathan Rauch   R9-1

CHAPTER TEN   The News Media   279

THE DEVELOPMENT OF THE NEWS MEDIA: FROM
PARTISANSHIP TO OBJECTIVE JOURNALISM   281

FREEDOM AND CONFORMITY IN THE U.S. NEWS MEDIA   287

THE NEWS MEDIA AS LINK: ROLES THE PRESS CAN
AND CANNOT PERFORM   291

ORGANIZING THE PUBLIC IN THE MEDIA AGE   300

Summary   302

Major Concepts   302

Suggested Readings and Web Sites   303

READING 10   The Miscast Institution
Thomas E. Patterson   R10

CHAPTER ELEVEN   Congress   304

CONGRESS AS A CAREER: ELECTION TO CONGRESS   305

CONGRESSIONAL LEADERSHIP   312

THE COMMITTEE SYSTEM   319

HOW A BILL BECOMES LAW   323

CONGRESS'S POLICYMAKING ROLE   327

CONGRESS: TOO MUCH PLURALISM?   338

Summary   339

Major Concepts   340

Suggested Readings and Web Sites   340

READING 11   Tammany Hall Goes to Washington
Morris P. Fiorina   R11

CHAPTER TWELVE   The Presidency   342

FOUNDATIONS OF THE MODERN PRESIDENCY   344

CHOOSING THE PRESIDENT   350

STAFFING THE PRESIDENCY   360

FACTORS IN PRESIDENTIAL LEADERSHIP 364
Summary 378
Major Concepts 379
Suggested Readings and Web Sites 379
READING 12 The Postmodern President
Richard Rose R12-1

CHAPTER THIRTEEN The Bureaucracy 381
THE FEDERAL BUREAUCRACY: FORM, PERSONNEL, AND
ACTIVITIES 383
DEVELOPMENT OF THE FEDERAL BUREAUCRACY:
POLITICS AND ADMINISTRATION 392
THE BUREAUCRACY'S POWER IMPERATIVE 396
BUREAUCRATIC ACCOUNTABILITY 402
REINVENTING GOVERNMENT 409
Summary 411
Major Concepts 412
Suggested Readings and Web Sites 413
READING 13 Reinventing Government
David Osborne and Ted Gaebler R13-1

CHAPTER FOURTEEN The Judiciary 415
THE FEDERAL JUDICIAL SYSTEM 417
FEDERAL COURT APPOINTEES 426
THE NATURE OF JUDICIAL DECISION MAKING 429
JUDICIAL POWER AND DEMOCRATIC GOVERNMENT 438
Summary 445
Major Concepts 446
Suggested Readings and Web Sites 447
READING 14 Judicial Interpretation
William J. Brennan, Jr. R14

CHAPTER FIFTEEN Economic and
Environmental Policy 448
REGULATING THE ECONOMY 449
GOVERNMENT AS PROTECTOR OF THE ENVIRONMENT 457
GOVERNMENT AS PROMOTER OF ECONOMIC INTERESTS 460

FISCAL POLICY: GOVERNMENT AS MANAGER OF
THE ECONOMY, I   462

MONETARY POLICY: GOVERNMENT AS MANAGER OF THE
ECONOMY, II   473

Summary   478

Major Concepts   479

Suggested Readings and Web Sites   479

READING 15   Long-Term Goals for the Economy
Alice M. Rivlin   R15-1

CHAPTER SIXTEEN   Welfare and
   Education Policy   481

POVERTY IN AMERICA: THE NATURE OF THE PROBLEM   484

THE POLITICS AND POLICIES OF SOCIAL WELFARE   486

INDIVIDUAL-BENEFIT PROGRAMS   492

EDUCATION AS EQUALITY OF OPPORTUNITY:
THE AMERICAN WAY   500

CULTURE, POLITICS, AND SOCIAL WELFARE   505

Summary   508

Major Concepts   509

Suggested Readings and Web Sites   510

READING 16   Saving Social Security
Robert D. Reischauer   R16-1

CHAPTER SEVENTEEN   Foreign and
   Defense Policy   511

THE ROOTS OF U.S. FOREIGN AND DEFENSE POLICY   513

THE PROCESS OF FOREIGN AND MILITARY POLICYMAKING   519

THE MILITARY DIMENSION OF NATIONAL SECURITY POLICY   524

THE ECONOMIC DIMENSION OF NATIONAL
SECURITY POLICY   529

Summary   541

Major Concepts   542

Suggested Readings and Web Sites   542

READING 17   A Borderless World
Kenichi Ohmae   R17

THE DECLARATION OF INDEPENDENCE   A

THE CONSTITUTION OF THE UNITED STATES   A-5

NOTES   A-25

GLOSSARY   A-58

CREDITS   C-1

INDEX   I-1

Preface

ANYONE WHO WRITES an introductory American government text faces the challenge of describing and explaining a vast amount of scholarship. One way is to pile fact upon fact and list upon list. It's a common enough approach but it turns politics into a pretty dry subject. Politics doesn't have to be dry, and it certainly doesn't have to be dull. Politics has all the elements of drama, and the added feature of affecting the everyday lives of real people.

The late twentieth century has been a period of extraordinary change in America, which has raised new challenges to the practice of government. New people in the millions from Asia and Latin America have joined the American community, bringing with them cultural traditions that have made our society richer and fuller, but also more fragmented and contentious. Traditional institutions, from political parties to families, have weakened dramatically, straining the fabric of our politics but also creating the possibility of adaptive new arrangements. Minorities and women, long denied access to political and economic power, are seeking a fairer share, and sometimes getting it. America's workers and firms have built a highly productive economy but are now facing the risks and opportunities of the global marketplace. The cold war that dominated our attention in foreign policy for decades has been replaced by ethnic rivalries and localized conflicts that raise troubling new issues of world insecurity that, so far, have defied tidy solutions.

Scholars are trying to keep pace with these changes. Never before has scholarship been so closely tied to the real world. If much of what political scientists study is arcane, we have increasingly connected our work and our thinking to the everyday realities of politics. The result is a clearer and more nuanced understanding of how American government operates. I have tried in this book to convey this advancement in knowledge in an accurate and interesting way.

REACHING OUT TO THE STUDENT

This is a narrative-based text. It is the opposite of a text that piles list upon list and divides its material into narrow compartments. A narrative text provides plenty of information, but it is always part of a larger discussion.

Research indicates that the narrative form is a superior method for teaching students a "soft" science such as political science. They learn more readily because a narrative makes the subject more readable, more accessible, and more compelling. Studies also indicate that students can read attentively for a longer period of time when a text is narrative in form.

A narrative text weaves together theory, information, and examples in order to bring out key facts and ideas. The goal is to draw the students into the subject, give them a contextual understanding of major concepts and issues, and encourage them to think about the implications for themselves and society. To quicken this process, I begin each chapter by describing a situation that addresses a basic issue. The chapter on civil liberties, for example, begins with the case of the Crichton family, whose home was raided in the middle of the night by gun-toting FBI agents who suspected they were harboring a relative who was suspected of bank robbery. The suspect was not found, and the Crichtons, who were badly frightened by the intrusion, sued the FBI for wrongful search. Did the FBI have sufficient cause for a warrantless search? Or did the FBI violate the Crichtons' constitutional rights? Where should society draw the line between its public safety needs and the rights of the individual? Such questions in the context of a real-life situation immediately plunge students into the chapter's subject and into the process of thinking about its importance.

This approach is part of a second pedagogical goal of this text: helping students to think critically. Critical thinking is, I believe, the most important skill that a student can acquire from a social science education. Students do not learn to think critically by engaging in rote memorization. They acquire the skill by reflecting on what they read, by resolving challenges to their customary ways of thinking, and by confronting difficult issues. Throughout the book, I have attempted to structure the discussion in ways that ask students to think more deeply and systematically about politics. In the first chapter, for example, I discuss the inexact meanings, conflicting implications, and unfilled promise of Americans' most cherished ideals, including liberty and equality. The discussion includes the "Chinese Exclusion," a grotesque and not-well-known chapter in our history that should lead students to think about what it means to be an American.

Finally, I have attempted in this book to present American government through the analytical lens of political science but in a way that captures the vivid world of real-life politics. I regularly reminded myself while writing this book that only a tiny percentage of introductory students are interested in an academic political science career. Most of them take the course because it is required or because they enjoy politics. I have sought to write a book that will kindle political interest in the first type of student and deepen interest in the second type, while also giving them the systematic knowledge that a science of politics can provide. I had a model in mind for the kind of book that could achieve these goals. It was V. O. Key's absorbing *Politics, Parties, and Pressure Groups*, which I had read many years earlier as an undergraduate student. The late Professor Key was a masterful scholar who had a deep love of politics and who gently chided colleagues whose interest in political science was confirmed to the "science" part.

Few scholars can match Key's brilliance, but, thankfully, most political scientists share his fascination with politics. The result of their combined efforts is a body of knowledge about American government that is both precise and politically astute. This scholarship gives the text its unifying core. Political scientists have identified several major tendencies in the American political system that are a basis for a systematic understanding of how it operates, namely:

- Enduring ideals that are the basis of Americans' political identity and culture and that are a source of many of their beliefs, aspirations, and conflicts

- Extreme fragmentation of governing authority that is based on an elaborate system of checks and balances, which serves to protect against abuses of political power but also makes it difficult for political majorities to assert power when confronting an entrenched or intense political minority

- Many competing groups, which are a result of the nation's great size, population diversity, and economic complexity, and which, separately, have considerable power over narrow areas of public policy

- Strong emphasis on individual rights, which is a consequence of the nation's political traditions and which results in substantial benefits to the individual and places substantial claims on the community

- Preference for the marketplace as a means of allocating resources, which has the effect of placing many economic issues beyond the reach of popular majorities

These tendencies are introduced in the first chapter and discussed frequently in subsequent chapters. If students forget many of the points made in this book, they may at least take away from the course a knowledge of the deep underpinnings of the American political system.

CHANGES FOR THIS EDITION

The response to the first three editions of *We the People* was gratifying. The text and its full-size hardcover version *(The American Democracy)* have been used at more than five hundred colleges and universities. Accordingly, I have chosen not to tinker with the text's basic organization. Nevertheless, all chapters have been thoroughly reviewed and updated to reflect the latest scholarship and the most recent political developments at home and abroad. The role of the Internet in American politics, for example, features more prominently in this edition than in previous ones. The Internet is also part of this text's instructional content. Each chapter includes one or more worldwide web icons (identified by a globe within which WWW appears). Each icon indicates the availability of relevant supplementary material (self-quizzes, simulations, and graphics) on the text's web site.

I have tried to illustrate many of the points in this book with developments that are a remembered part of student's lives. For most of them, Vietnam is ancient history, and the fall of the Berlin Wall is, at best, a distant memory. Students need to know about, and learn from, these events. But they sometimes learn more when asked to apply the discipline of political science to events they believe they already thoroughly know. Accordingly, this text strives to deepen their understanding of the significance of the 2000 Bush–Gore election campaign and other recent developments.

To encourage students to reflect more fully on the nation's politics, each chapter has a "How the United States Compares" box and a "States in the Nation" box. The United States in many ways has the world's preeminent democracy, but it also has distinctive policies and practices. The American states, too, are quite different in their politics and policies, despite belonging to the same union. American students invariably gain a deeper understanding of their own communities when they recognize the ways in which their nation or state differs from others.

A novel feature of *We the People* is its selected readings; each chapter is followed by a reading that develops a major point of the chapter. These readings are intended to deepen the student's understanding of American politics and to add flexibility to the instructor's use of the material. For an instructor who prefers to supplement the course text with a book of readings, this text offers both. On the other hand, the instructor who wants to limit reading assignments to the text itself can simply skip the end-of-chapter readings or recommend them as optional items for students who have the time and interest. The readings, with the exception of James Madison's *Federalist* No. 10, are contemporary ones. The authors are distinguished scholars and public servants.

YOUR SUGGESTIONS ARE INVITED

I invite from instructors and students any comments and criticisms that might guide future editions of the text. The strengths and weaknesses of a text are best discovered in its use, and I hope you will share your thoughts with me. Several instructors sent me suggestions and corrections that were incorporated into this edition. Professor William E. Plants at Gallipolis College, for example, proposed changes that I have made in two chapters. You can contact me at the John F. Kennedy School of Government, Harvard University, Cambridge, MA 02138, or by e-mail: thomas_patterson @harvard.edu.

Thomas E. Patterson

SUPPLEMENTS PACKAGE

This text is accompanied by supplementary materials. Please contact your local McGraw-Hill representative or McGraw-Hill Customer Service (800-338-3987) for details concerning policies, prices, and availability, as some restrictions may apply.

For Students

Study Guide

0-07-245601-9

by Willoughby Jarrell of Kennesaw State University

Each chapter includes the following: learning objectives, focus and main points (to help direct students' attention to most critical points), chapter summary, major concepts (listed and defined), annotated Internet resources, analytical thinking exercises, and test review questions—approximately 10 true/false, 15 multiple-choice, and 5 essay topics. The answers are provided at the end of each chapter.

Interactive Study Guide CD–ROM

0-07-245598-5

This CD–ROM is a collection of multimedia and interactive tools for the student using the fourth edition of WE THE PEOPLE. It includes all of the materials included in the Student Study Guide, as well as feedback for questions, crossword puzzles, 12 interactive graphics, and 12 simulations. There are also links to historical documents, audio speeches, a photo gallery, and video clips from the newly developed McGraw-Hill American Government Video Library.

2000 Presidential Election Update

0-07-246030-X

by Richard Semiatin of American University

This 20-page supplement provides an analysis of the Millenial Election, including a detailed discussion of the events leading up to the Florida voting crisis. The Election Update also includes discussion of the context of the election, the Electoral College, the Presidential Primaries, the strategies of the Bush and Gore campaigns, results of the Senate and House races, voter turnout results, and more. This booklet can be made available shrink-wrapped free with the fourth edition of WE THE PEOPLE.

Impeachment and Trial Supplement

0-07-235127-6

by Richard Semiatin of American University

This 16-page supplement offers an overview of the impeachment and trial processes within a historical and constitutional context. It is a step-by-step examination of the foundation and progression of the process. Also, this supplement discusses the factors acting upon the case of Andrew Johnson in the 1860s and the vastly different, modern case of former President Clinton. Finally, it looks at alternatives to conviction and expulsion. This booklet can be made available shrink-wrapped free with the fourth edition of WE THE PEOPLE.

For Instructors

Instructor's Manual/Test Bank
0-07-245603-5
by Willoughby Jarrell of Kennesaw State University
For each chapter, the instructor's manual will include the following: learning objectives, focus points and main points, a chapter summary, a list of major concepts, a lecture outline, alternative lecture objectives, class discussion topics, and a list of Internet resources. The test bank consists of approximately 20 to 25 multiple-choice questions, 15 to 20 true/false questions, and 5 suggested essay topics per chapter, with answers given alongside the questions, and page references provided.

Test Bank CD–ROM
0-07-245602-7
This CD–ROM–format test bank draws on questions from the Instructor's Manual/Test Bank to assist professors in generating tests.

Instructor's Resource CD–ROM
0-07-245604-3
Tailored to the Table of Contents and format of the fourth edition, this CD integrates instructor's resources available in the Instructor's Manual/Test Bank with multimedia components, such as PowerPoint presentation, photographs, maps and charts.

McGraw-Hill American Government Video Library
This new series of 10-minute video lecture-launchers was produced for McGraw-Hill by Ralph Baker and Joseph Losco of Ball State University.

> Video # 1: Devolution within American Federalism: The Case of the Welfare System
> 0-07-303414-2
> Video #2: Public Opinion and Participation: American Students Speak
> 0-07-229517-1

Video #3: Interest Groups
0-07-234442-3
Video #4: Women in Politics
0-07-242097-9
Video #5: Civil Liberties on the Internet
0-07-244205-0
Video #6: Affirmative Action and College Enrollment
0-07-244207-7
Video #7: The 2000 Campaign
0-07-250175-8

PageOut

At www.mhhe.com/pageout, instructors can create their own course websites. PageOut requires no prior knowledge of HTML; simply plug the course information into a template and click on one of 16 designs. The process leaves instructors with a professionally designed website.

PRIMIS Online

Instructors can use this textbook as a whole, or they can select specific chapters and customize this text to suit their specific classroom needs. The customized text can be created as a hardcopy or as an e-book.

For Students and Instructors

On-Line Learning Center

This website contains distinct instructor and student areas, with numerous assets also found on the CD–ROMs. The instructor side contains the content of the Instructor's Resource CD–ROM, while the student side hosts the content of the Interactive Study Guide CD–ROM.

Web Sites

Visit our website at www.mhhe.com/patterson
For additional activities, simulations, web links, games, puzzles, and more, visit the Political Science Supersite at www.mhhe.com/socscience/polisci

PowerWeb for American Government

A special product that offers daily news updates, weekly course updates, interactive activities, the best articles from the popular press, quizzing, instructor's manuals, student support study material and more.

Acknowledgments

I am deeply thankful to the scholars whose sound advice has helped shape every page of this book. Their advice was invaluable. These scholars are:

Bob Bilodeau
South Plains College
David Dillman
Abilene Christian University
Lawrence Giventer
California State University,
  Stanialaus
Otto Feinstein
Wayne State University
Lyman Kellstedt
Wheaton College
Dennis Goldford
Drake University
Stephen Nichols
California State University,
  San Marcos
Jeff Poulet
Malone College
Brandon Rottinghaus
Northwestern University

Mort Sipress
University of Wisconsin,
  Eau Claire
Willoughby Jarrell
Kennesaw State University
Christopher Skubby
Lakeland Community College
Craig Ramsay
Ohio Wesleyan University
Robert Bradley
Illinois State University
William Pearson
Arkansas Technical University
Richard Chesteen
University of Tennessee at Martin
Ann Hildreth
University of Albany
Steve Snow
Wagner College

I also want to acknowledge those at McGraw-Hill who contributed to the fourth edition. Monica Eckman, my editor, deserves a special thanks. Her enthusiasm for the book made my work much easier, and her numerous suggestions strengthened the book considerably. Marilyn Rothenberger also contributed substantially; she carefully guided the fourth edition through the production process. Shannon Morrow also worked hard to bring this edition to life. At Harvard, I had the steady support of Melissa Ring, my faculty assistant. No one had a bigger hand in the preparation of the new material in this edition than Melissa. She did most of the research and a lot of the editing. She is enormously skilled and saved me uncounted hours of time. I am very grateful.

Thomas E. Patterson

CHAPTER ONE

The American Heritage

One hears people say that it is inherent in the habits and nature of democracies to change feelings and thoughts at every moment. . . . But I have never seen anything like that happening in the great democracy on the other side of the ocean. What struck me most in the United States was the difficulty experienced in getting an idea, once conceived, out of the head of the majority.

ALEXIS DE TOCQUEVILLE[1]

I T WAS THE CLOSEST presidential race in history. A few hundred votes in a single state, Florida, was all that separated the winner from the loser. Who would be the next president? As the uncertainty mounted, Al Gore and George W. Bush sought to assure Americans that the nation and the presidency would avert a constitutional collapse. Their statements were at times deeply partisan, but sprinkled throughout were allusions to time-honored American ideals: the will of the people, justice, fairness, rule by law.

The high-sounding ideals embedded in Bush's and Gore's statements would have been familiar to any generation of Americans. The same ideals had been used to take America to war, to declare peace, to celebrate national holidays, to declare major policies, and to assert new rights.[2] The same ideals expressed by Bush and Gore had punctuated the speeches of George Washington and Abraham Lincoln, Susan B. Anthony and Franklin D. Roosevelt, Dr. Martin Luther King, Jr. and Ronald Reagan.

The ideals were also there at the nation's beginning, when they were put into words in the Declaration of Independence and the Constitution. Of course, the practical meaning of these words has changed greatly during the more than two centuries that the United States has been a sovereign nation. When the writers of the Constitution began the document with the words, "We, The People," they did not have all Americans equally in mind. Black slaves, women, and men without property did not have the same constitutional status as propertied white men.

Yet America's ideals have been remarkably enduring. Throughout their history Americans have embraced the same set of core values. They have quarreled over the meaning, practice, and fulfillment of these ideals, but they have never seriously questioned the principles themselves. As the historian Clinton Rossiter concluded, "There has been in a doctrinal sense, only one America."[3]

This book is about contemporary American politics, not U.S. history or culture. Yet American politics today cannot be understood apart from the nation's heritage. Government does not begin anew with each generation; it builds on the past. In the case of the United States, the most significant link between past and present lies in the nation's founding ideals. This chapter briefly examines the principles that have helped shape American politics since the country's earliest years.

The chapter also explains basic concepts, such as power and pluralism, that are important in the study of government and politics, and describes the underlying rules of the American governing system, such as constitutionalism and capitalism. The main points made in this chapter are the following:

* *The American political culture centers on a set of core ideals—liberty, equality, self-government, individualism, diversity, and unity—that serve as the people's common bond.*

* *Politics is the process that determines whose values will prevail in society. The play of politics in the United States takes place in the context of democratic procedures, constitutionalism, and capitalism, and involves elements of majority, pluralist, and elite rule.*

* *Politics in the United States is characterized by a number of major patterns, including a highly fragmented governing system, a high degree of pluralism, an extraordinary emphasis on individual rights, and a pronounced separation of the political and economic spheres.*

POLITICAL CULTURE: THE CORE PRINCIPLES OF AMERICAN GOVERNMENT

The people of every nation have a few great ideals that characterize their political life, but, as James Bryce observed, Americans are a special case.[4] Their ideals are the basis of their national identity. Other people take their identity from the common ancestry that led them gradually to gather under one flag. Thus, long before there was a France or a Japan, there were French and Japanese people, each a kinship group united through blood.

U.S. politics is remarkable for its historical continuity, which is celebrated
here in a ceremony at the Capitol in Washington, D.C.

Not so for Americans. They are a multitude of peoples linked by a political
tradition. The United States is a nation that was founded in 1776 on a set
of principles that became its people's common bond.[5]

A strong bond of some kind was a necessity. Nationalities that warred
constantly in Europe had to find a way to live together in the New World.
Their search for common ground has been replayed many times during
America's history. The United States is, and always has been, a nation of
immigrants and of people struggling for a greater level of acceptance and
support (see Figure 1-1). Yet they are also one people, brought together
through allegiance to a set of commonly held ideals.

America's principles are habits of mind, a customary way of thinking
about the world. They are part of what social scientists call **political culture,** a term that refers to the characteristic and deep-seated beliefs of a
particular people.[6]

The American political culture is said to include the following beliefs in
idealized form:

- **Liberty** is the principle that individuals should be free to act and
  think as they choose, provided they do not infringe unreasonably
  on the freedom and well-being of others.

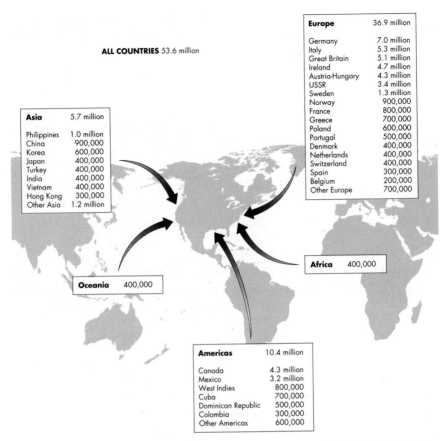

FIGURE 1-1　TOTAL IMMIGRATION TO THE UNITED STATES, BY CONTINENT AND COUNTRY OF ORIGIN (1820–1998)
America is a nation of immigrants who are joined together through a common set of ideals. Source: U.S. Immigration and Naturalization Service.

- **Self-government** is the principle that the people are the ultimate source of governing authority and that their general welfare is the only legitimate purpose of government.
- **Equality** holds that all individuals have moral worth, are entitled to fair treatment under the law, and should have equal opportunity for material gain and political influence.
- **Individualism** is a commitment to personal initiative, self-sufficiency, and material accumulation. This principle upholds the superiority of a private-enterprise economic system and includes the idea of the individual as the foundation of society.

- **Diversity** holds that individual differences should be respected and that these differences are a source of strength and a legitimate basis of self-interest.
- **Unity** is the principle that Americans are one people and form an indivisible union.

These ideals, taken together, are sometimes called "the American Creed." They have their roots in colonial America, which was shaped by European traditions and values. As Paul Gagnon noted, "The first [American] settlers did not sail into view out of a void, their minds as blank as the Atlantic Ocean. . . . Those who sailed west to America came in fact not to build a New World but to bring to life in a new setting what they had treasured most from the Old World."[7]

They brought with them a belief in reason, in progress, and in self-reliance. Most of the first settlers were Protestants who shared a belief in personal responsibility and the moral equality of each person. But their ideals were also shaped by what they discovered in the New World. America's vast wilderness and great distance from the Old World granted its settlers more liberty, equality, and self-governance than they could have envisioned. Europe's rigid aristocratic system was unenforceable in frontier America. Ordinary people had no reason to accept inferior status when greater liberty was as close as the next area of unsettled wilderness. And the vast tracts of open land enabled ordinary people to own property. It kindled their individualism, strengthened their claim to equality, and gave them a heightened sense of privacy, freedom, and self-determination.

It was this natural sense of freedom, equality, and opportunity that Thomas Jefferson captured so forcefully in the words of the Declaration of Independence: "We hold these truths to be self-evident, that all men are created equal, that they are endowed by their Creator with certain unalienable rights, that among these are life, liberty, and the pursuit of happiness." The United States, as the historian Louis Hartz said, was "born free."[8]

America's ideals have been nurtured through generations and have been a source of conflict as well as consensus. In practice, they have often meant different things to different people. Few observers would argue, however, with the proposition that *a defining characteristic of the American political system is its enduring and powerful set of cultural ideals.* The Frenchman Alexis de Tocqueville was among the first to see that the main tendencies of American politics cannot be explained without taking into account the country's core beliefs. "Habits of the heart" was Tocqueville's description of Americans' ideals.[9]

The Power of Ideals

America's ideals have had a strong impact on its politics. Ideals serve to define the boundaries of action. They do not determine exactly what people will do, but they have a marked influence on what people will regard as reasonable and desirable. If people believe, as Americans do, that politics exists to promote liberty and equality, they will attempt to realize these values through their political actions.

Why, for example, does the United States spend relatively less money on government programs for the poor and disadvantaged than do other fully industrialized democracies, including Germany, France, Switzerland, the Netherlands, Spain, Britain, Sweden, Italy, and Japan? Are Americans so much better off than these other people that we have less need for welfare programs? The answer is no. Of all these countries, the United States has in both relative and absolute terms the greatest number of hungry, homeless, and poor people. The reason the United States spends less on social welfare lies chiefly in the emphasis that American culture places on *individualism*. We have resisted giving government a larger social welfare role because of our deep-seated cultural belief that able-bodied individuals should take responsibility for themselves (see box: How the United States Compares).

Of course, social welfare policy is not simply an issue of cultural differences. The welfare issue, like all other issues, is part of the rough and tumble of everyday politics everywhere. There are always powerful interests aligned on both sides of important issues. In the United States, the Republican party, business groups, antitax groups, and others have resisted the expansion of the government's social welfare role, while liberal Democrats, unions, minority groups, and others have from time to time argued for greater intervention. Nevertheless, Americans' belief in individualism, which has no exact equivalent in European society, has played a defining role in shaping U.S. welfare policy.

The distinctiveness of this cultural belief is evident in a Times-Mirror Center survey of opinions in Europe and the United States.[10] When asked whether it is the responsibility of the government "to take care of very poor people who can't take care of themselves," only 23 percent of Americans said they completely agreed. The Germans were the closest to the Americans in their response to this question, but more than twice as many of them, 50 percent, said they believed that the state should take care of the very poor. More than 60 percent of the British, French, and Italians held the same opinion. Americans do not necessarily have less sympathy for the

HOW THE UNITED STATES COMPARES

Capitalism, Self-Reliance, and Personal Success

The United States was labeled "the country of individualism *par excellence*" by William Watts and Lloyd Free in their book *State of the Nation*. They were referring to the emphasis that Americans place on self-reliance and the trust they have in the marketplace as a basis of economic security.

Such views also prevail in European democracies but are moderated by a greater acceptance of welfare programs. The difference between the American and European cultures reflects their differing political traditions. America was an open country ruled by a foreign power, and its revolution was fought largely over the issue of personal freedom. In European revolutions, equality was also at issue, since wealth was held by hereditary aristocracies. Europeans' concern with equality was gradually translated into a willingness to use government as a means of redistributing wealth. An example is government-paid medical care for all citizens.

Even today, Europeans are more likely to feel that their social and economic status is determined by the circumstances of birth. This outlook is evident in a Times-Mirror survey that asked respondents whether "success in life is pretty much determined by forces outside our control." The percentage of Americans and Europeans agreeing with the statement is shown in the accompanying chart.

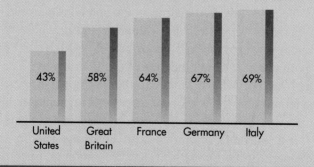

United States	Great Britain	France	Germany	Italy
43%	58%	64%	67%	69%

poor; rather, they place more emphasis on personal responsibility than Europeans do.[11]

The importance of individualism to American society is also evident in the emphasis on equal opportunity. If individuals are to be entrusted with their own welfare, they must be given a fair chance to succeed on their own. Nowhere is this philosophy more evident than in the country's elaborate system of higher education, which includes nearly three thousand two-year and four-year institutions. The system is designed to accommodate nearly every individual who wants to pursue a college education (see box: States in the Nation). More than a third of the nation's young people enter college, the world's highest rate. Even western Europe has nothing comparable to the American system; fewer than one in six young people in these countries go to college.

Of course, the idea that success is within the reach of all Americans who strive for it is far from accurate. Young people who grow up in abject poverty and without adequate guidance know all too well the limits on their lives. In some inner-city areas, teenage boys are more likely to spend time in jail than to spend time at college.

The Limits of Ideals

Cultural beliefs originate in a country's political and social practices, but they are not perfect representatives of these practices. They are mythic ideas— symbolic positions taken by a people to justify and give meaning to their way of life.[12] Myths contain elements of truth, but they are far from the full truth.

High ideals do not come with a guarantee that a people will live up to them. The clearest proof of this failing in the American case is the human tragedy that began nearly four centuries ago and continues today. In 1619 the first black slaves were brought in chains to America. Slavery lasted 250 years. Slaves in the field worked from dawn to dark (from "can see, 'til can't"), in both the heat of summer and the cold of winter. The Civil War changed the future of African Americans but did not assure their equality. Slavery was followed by the Jim Crow era of legal segregation: black people in the South were forbidden by law to use the same schools, hospitals, restaurants, and restrooms as white people. For those who got uppish with their white superiors, there were beatings, firebombings, castrations, rapes, and worse—hundreds of African Americans were lynched by white vigi-lantes in the early 1900s. Today African Americans have equal rights under the law, but in fact they are far from equal. Compared with whites, blacks are twice as likely to live in poverty, twice as likely to be unable to find a job,

★ STATES IN THE NATION ★

Percentage of Adults with College Degrees

Reflecting their cultural beliefs in individualism and equality, Americans have developed the world's largest system of college education. Every state has at least eight colleges and universities within its boundaries and eleven states have more than 100. California, with 322 colleges, and New York, with 320, are the highest-ranking states by this measure. No European democracy has as many institutions of higher education as these two states. As a result of their cultural commitment to equal opportunity through education, many Americans have college degrees. On a state-by-state basis, the range is from 16.2 percent in Arkansas to 34.0 percent in Colorado. The European average is less than 10 percent. American college graduates are concentrated in the urbanized and affluent states. Young people in these states can better afford the costs of college and are more likely to need a college degree for the work they seek.

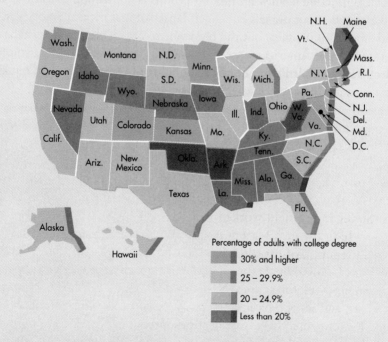

Percentage of adults with college degree

- 30% and higher
- 25 – 29.9%
- 20 – 24.9%
- Less than 20%

SOURCE: U.S. Bureau of Census, 1999. Based on percentage of adults twenty-five years of age or older with a college degree.

and twice as likely to die in infancy.[13] There have always been at least two Americas, one for whites and one for blacks.

Despite the lofty claim that "all men are created equal," equality has never been an American birthright. In 1882 Congress suspended Chinese 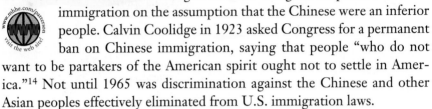 immigration on the assumption that the Chinese were an inferior people. Calvin Coolidge in 1923 asked Congress for a permanent ban on Chinese immigration, saying that people "who do not want to be partakers of the American spirit ought not to settle in America."[14] Not until 1965 was discrimination against the Chinese and other Asian peoples effectively eliminated from U.S. immigration laws.

The claim that America is a gigantic melting pot has always been as much fable as fact. When Irish, Italian, and Eastern European immigrants reached this country's shores, they encountered nativist elements that scorned their ways of life and mocked their Catholic, Orthodox, and Jewish religions. The Latinos and Asians who have come here more recently have also been made to feel less than fully welcome by many of those whose ancestors settled here in earlier times.

Discrimination against immigrant groups is not among the stories that we like to tell about ourselves.[15] Such lapses of historical memory can be found among all peoples, but the tendency to recast history is perhaps exaggerated in the American case because our beliefs are so idealistic (see Table 1-1). How could a nation that upholds the ideal of human equality

The old slave prison on Goree Island in Senegal was the last stopping place for many slaves before they were placed on ships and sent in chains to America.

TABLE 1-1 TELLING THE AMERICAN STORY TO CHILDREN
Americans' values and myths are reflected in their preferences in teaching children about the nation's history. The stories that adults regard as least important are those that reflect unfavorably on the country's idealized image.

In teaching the American story to children, how important is the following theme . . . ?	Essential/Very important	Somewhat important	Somewhat unimportant/ Very unimportant/ Leave it out of the story
With hard work and perseverance, anyone can succeed in America.	83%	14%	4%
Our founders limited the power of government, so government would not intrude too much into the lives of its citizens.	74	19	8
America is the world's greatest melting pot in which people from different countries are united into one nation.	73	21	5
America's contribution is one of expanding freedom for more and more people.	71	22	6
Our nation betrayed its founding principles by cruel mistreatment of blacks and American Indians.	59	24	17
Our founders were part of a male-dominated culture that gave important roles to men while keeping women in the background.	38	28	35

SOURCE: From James Davison Hunter and Carol Bowman, Survey of American Political Culture, Gallup Organization, 1996. Reprinted by permission. (From *The American Democracy*, Fifth Edition, by Thomas Patterson, © 2001, reproduced with permission of The McGraw-Hill Companies.)

have barred the Chinese, enslaved the blacks, betrayed the Indians, and subordinated women?

One reason America's ideals do not match reality is that they are general principles, not fixed rules of conduct. They derive from somewhat different experiences and philosophical traditions, and there are points at which they conflict. Equality and diversity, for instance, emphasize fairness and a full opportunity for all to partake of society's benefits, whereas liberty and individualism emphasize personal freedom and threats posed to it by political power. Conflict between these sets of beliefs is inevitable. Both are commendable, but the advancement of one set comes only at some cost to the other. Take the issue of affirmative action. Proponents say that only through aggressive affirmative action programs will women and minorities receive the equal treatment in the job market to which they are entitled. Opponents say that aggressive affirmative action infringes unreasonably on the liberty of the employer and the initiative of the work force. Each side can say that it has America's ideals on its side, and no resort to logic can persuade either side that the opposing viewpoint should prevail.

Despite their inexact meanings, conflicting implications, and unfulfilled promise, the ideals of Americans have had a strong impact on the nation's politics. They still do. If racial, gender, ethnic, and other forms of intolerance constitute the sorriest chapter in the nation's history, the centuries-old struggle of Americans to create a more equal society is among the finest chapters. Few nations have battled so relentlessly against the insidious hatreds that stem from superficial human differences such as the color of one's skin. High ideals are more than mere abstractions. They are a source of human aspiration and, ultimately, of political and social change.

POLITICS: THE PROCESS OF DECIDING UPON SOCIETY'S GOALS

Cultural ideals help shape what people expect from politics and how they conduct their politics. However, politics is more than the pursuit of shared ideals; it is also about getting one's own way. Commenting on the competitive nature of politics, Harold Lasswell described politics as the struggle over "who gets what, when, and how."[16]

Political conflict is rooted in two general conditions of society. One is *scarcity*. Society's resources are finite, but people's appetites are not. There is not enough wealth in even the richest of countries to satisfy everyone's desires. Conflict over the distribution of resources is the inevitable result.

This conflict is evident, for example, in policy disputes over the financing of public schools. The quality of American schools varies widely. Affluent suburban districts have better schools and teachers than poor inner-city districts, which reflects differences in their local tax base. In order to equalize quality, less affluent communities have pressed for the statewide funding of public schools, an approach that more affluent communities have resisted.

Differences in values are the other main source of political conflict. People see things in different ways. The right to abortion is freedom of choice to some and murder to others. People bring to politics a wide range of conflicting values—about abortion, about the environment, about the level of defense spending, about crime and punishment, about the poor, about the economy, about almost everything imaginable.

Politics in the United States is not the life-and-death struggle between opposing groups that typifies some countries, but there are many sources of contention. Perhaps no country has more competing interests than does the United States. Its settlement by people of many lands and religions, its enormous size and geographical diversity, and its economic complexity have made the United States a pluralistic nation. *This feature—competition for power among a great many interests of all kinds—is a major characteristic of American politics.*

It is a mistake to assume, however, that competition and conflict are the sum of politics. People must find agreeable ways of living together. Politics is not only a means of settling disputes; it is also a way of promoting collective interests. Politics is not solely about winners and losers; it is also about problem solving. Public safety and national defense are prime examples of people working together for an agreed-upon purpose. Public education is another. It reflects the older generation's willingness to tax itself for the benefit of the younger generation and ultimately for the benefit of society as a whole.

In sum, politics is a process that includes conflict *and* consensus, competition *and* cooperation. Accordingly, we shall define **politics** as, simply, the process through which a society makes its governing decisions.

Government, Power, Authority, and Policy

What is government? What is its purpose? It might be thought that the answer to these age-old questions is that government is a means by which people work together to solve their common problems. To be sure, government can serve the collective good. But it can also serve the naked interests of a few, as in the case of Stalin's Russia, Hitler's Germany, or Saddam Hussein's Iraq.

Government can be defined as the institutions, processes, and rules that are designed to facilitate control of a particular geographic area and its inhabitants.[17] There are only two things that all governments have in common. One is a capacity to raise revenues, usually in the form of taxation, to support governing activities. The other is coercion—the ability to compel inhabitants to abide by the government's rules. Without these capacities, a government would be unable to exercise control over the territory and inhabitants it claims to rule.

Those who decide issues are said to have **power,** a term that refers to the ability of persons or institutions to control policy decisions.[18] Power is a basic concept of politics. Power determines which interests will decide policy. Those who have sufficient power can impose taxes, permit or prohibit abortions, protect or take private property, provide or refuse welfare benefits, impose or relax trade barriers. With so much at stake, it is perhaps not surprising that power is widely sought and tightly guarded.

When power is exercised through the laws and institutions of government, the concept of authority applies. **Authority** can be defined as the recognized right of an individual, organization, or institution to make binding decisions. By this definition, government is not the only source of authority: parents have authority over their children; professors have authority over their students; firms have authority over their employees. However, government is a special case in that its authority is more encompassing in scope and more final in nature. Government's authority extends to all within its geographical boundaries. It can be used to redefine the authority of the parent, the professor, or the firm. Government's authority is also the most coercive. It includes the power to arrest and imprison, even to punish by death those who violate its rules.

Government needs coercive power to ensure that its laws will be obeyed. Without this power, lawlessness would prevail, as it does in Colombia, where drug lords control large areas of the country. But government power itself can be abused. In a perfect world, political power would be used in evenhanded ways for the benefit of all citizens. But the world is imperfect, and those with government power can use it for selfish ends, whether to enrich themselves or to deprive others of liberty. "Power tends to corrupt, and absolute power tends to corrupt absolutely," was how Lord Acton described the problem.

Although no governing system can assure that power will be applied fairly, the U.S. system strengthens this prospect through an elaborate system of *checks and balances.* This system, which is designed to protect against

Politics includes conflict and consensus. Women have had to struggle to be treated as equals in the workplace, but their efforts have been supported by public opinion and public policies.

abuses of power (see Chapter 2), includes the division of authority among the executive, legislative, and judicial branches of government. Each branch acts as a check on the power of the others and balances their power by exercising power of its own. Many other democratic countries have no comparable fragmentation of power. *Extreme fragmentation of governing authority is a major characteristic of the American political system. This fact, as will be seen in subsequent chapters, has profound implications for how politics is conducted, who wins out, and what policies result.*

Governments exercise authority through policy. In its most general sense, **policy** refers to any broad course of action undertaken by government. U.S. policy toward Japan, for example, consists of a wide range of activities, from trade relations to diplomatic overtures. But policy is also used more narrowly to refer to specific programs or initiatives. The Head Start program for improving the educational prospects of poor children, for example, is a policy of government. So, too, are social security and the government's student loan programs. The general view of policy is more exact, because it acknowledges that government exercises authority by not making decisions as well as by making them. In choosing not to decide, a government accepts the existing situation as well as the distribution of benefits and costs embedded in it.

The Rules of the Game of Politics

The play of politics takes place according to rules that the participants accept. The rules establish the process by which power is exercised, define the legitimate uses of power, and establish the basis for allocating costs and benefits among the participants. In the American case, the rules of the game of politics include democracy, constitutionalism, and capitalism.

DEMOCRACY　Democracy is a set of rules designed to promote *self-government*. Democracy comes from the Greek words *demos*, which means "the people," and *kratis*, meaning "to rule." In simple terms, **democracy** is a form of government in which the people govern, either directly or through elected representatives (see Chapter 2).

Democratic government is based on the idea of the consent of the governed, which in practice has come to mean majority rule. The principle of majority rule, in turn, is based on the notion that the view of the many should prevail over the opinion of the few. Implicit in the notion is the possibility that today's minority may be tomorrow's majority, which means that issues and elections are rarely completely settled. The principle also represents a form of political equality in that the vote of each citizen counts equally, a principle expressed by the phrase "one person, one vote." In practice, democracy in America works primarily through elections. There are other, more direct forms of democracy, such as the town meeting and the initiative, but ours is a mainly representative system in which people's influence is based on their votes.

As Americans discovered during the 2000 campaign, even the one person, one vote principle is not inviolate. Al Gore received a half million more votes nationally than George W. Bush but lost the election through the Electoral College. Each state has electoral votes equal in number to its representatives in Congress, and these votes are allocated to the candidate who wins its popular vote. The candidate with a majority of the electoral votes from all the states wins the presidency. Florida's electoral votes were decisive in the outcome of the 2000 election and, even in Florida, the one-person, one-vote principle did not hold completely. Thousands of Florida's ballots went uncounted because they could not be read by machine. After an effort to have them counted by hand failed, Gore conceded the election. Polls indicated that many Americans questioned the fairness of the election, but they accepted the outcome without violent protest. Bush's peaceful accession to the presidency is an indication of just how deeply Americans are committed to a system that operates by a set of rules rather than by force or dictate.

CONSTITUTIONALISM   For many Americans, *democracy* has the same meaning as *liberty*—the freedom to think, talk, and act as one chooses. However, the terms are not synonymous. The concept of democracy implies that the will of the majority should prevail over the wishes of the minority, whereas the concept of liberty implies that the minority has rights and freedoms that cannot be taken away by the majority. The democratic model of government has long been accompanied by a fear of tyranny by the majority—the concern that a majority might ruthlessly impose its will on the minority. A more general concern about all government is the possibility of abuse of power.[19]

Constitutionalism is a set of rules that restricts the lawful uses of power. In its original sense, constitutionalism in Western society referred to a government based on laws and constitutional powers.[20] **Constitutionalism** has since come to refer specifically to the idea that there are limits on the rightful power of government over citizens. In a constitutional system, officials govern according to law and citizens have basic rights that government cannot take away or deny.[21]

The constitutional tradition in the United States is at least as strong as the democratic tradition. In fact, *a defining characteristic of the American political system is its extraordinary emphasis on individual rights.* Free speech is an example. Government is prohibited by the First Amendment from interfering with the lawful exercise of free speech. No right is absolute, which means that some restrictions are allowed. No student, for example, has a First Amendment right to shout loudly and disrupt a classroom. Nevertheless, free speech is broadly protected by the courts. During the Vietnam War, there were thousands of demonstrations against U.S. policy without a single arrest and conviction for spoken words alone. There were instances where protesters were intimidated by police or jailed for destruction of property, but those who opposed the government's pursuit of the war had the opportunity to express their views freely without threat of being sent to prison. (Constitutionalism is discussed further in Chapters 2–5.)

CAPITALISM   Just as democracy and constitutionalism are systems of rules for allocating society's costs and benefits in American society, so is capitalism. Societies have adopted alternative ways of organizing their economies. One way is socialism, which assigns government a large role in the ownership of the means of production, in regulating economic decisions, and in providing for the economic security of the individual. Under the form of socialism practiced in democratic countries, such as Sweden, the government does not attempt to manage the overall economy. In communist-style socialism, the government does take responsibility for overall management.

Capitalism is an alternative method for distributing economic costs and benefits. **Capitalism** holds that the government should interfere with the economy as little as possible. Free enterprise and self-reliance are the principles of capitalism. Firms are allowed to operate in a free and open marketplace, and individuals are expected to rely on their own initiative to establish their economic security.

As is the case with the rules of democracy and constitutionalism, the rules of capitalism are not neutral. If democracy responds to numbers and constitutionalism responds to individual rights, capitalism responds to wealth. Economic power is largely a function of accumulated wealth, in the hands of either the individual or the firm. "Money talks" in a capitalist system, which means, among other things, that wealthier people will have by far the greater say in the distribution of costs and benefits through the economic system.

The United States does not have a purely capitalist system, in that the government plays a role in regulating and stimulating the economy (see Chapter 15). The term "mixed economy" is used to define this hybrid form of economic system, with its combination of socialist and capitalist elements. The United States has more elements of the capitalist model and fewer elements of the socialist model than do the countries of Europe. Because of their strong tradition of individualism, Americans tend to restrict the scope of governmental action in the area of the economy. *A major characteristic of the American system is a relatively sharp distinction between what is political, and therefore to be decided in the public arena, and what is economic, and therefore to be settled in the private realm.*

For all practical purposes, this outlook places many kinds of choices, which in other countries are decided collectively, beyond the reach of political majorities in the United States. Although Americans complain that their taxes are too high, they actually pay few taxes compared with Europeans (see Figure 1-2). This situation testifies to the extent to which Americans believe that wealth is more properly allocated through the economic marketplace than through government policy.

Theories of Power

The rules of the political game help decide who will exercise power and to what ends. The ultimate question about any political system is the issue of who governs. Is power widely shared and used for the benefit of the many?

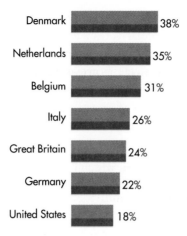

FIGURE 1-2 AVERAGE AMOUNT OF INCOME TAXES PAID
BY CITIZENS
Americans pay less taxes than Europeans do. Sources: Data from OECD, 1999.
Figure from p. 20 of *The American Democracy*, Fifth Edition, by Thomas Patterson, © 2001,
reproduced with permission of The McGraw-Hill Companies. Percentages based on taxes
paid by average worker with two children.

Or is power narrowly held and used to the advantage of the few? Although
this entire book is in some respects an answer to these questions, it is useful
here to consider what analysts have concluded about the American political
system. Three broad theories predominate (see Table 1-2). None of them
describes every aspect of American politics, but each has some validity.

RULE BY THE PEOPLE: MAJORITARIANISM A basic principle of
democracy, as discussed previously, is the idea of majority rule. **Majoritarianism** is the notion that the majority prevails not only in the counting of
votes but also in the determination of public policy.

Majorities do sometimes rule in America. Their power is perhaps most
evident in those states that offer voters the opportunity to decide directly on
policy initiatives, which then become law if they receive a majority vote.
The majority's influence is also felt indirectly through the decisions of
elected representatives. When Congress in 1996 passed a welfare reform
bill that included provisions requiring able-bodied welfare recipients to accept a job or job training after a two-year period or face a loss of their welfare benefits, it was acting in accord with the thinking of the majority of
Americans who believe that employable individuals should be self-reliant. A
more systematic assessment of the power of majorities is provided by Benjamin Page and Robert Shapiro's study of the relationship between majority

opinions and more than three hundred policy issues in the 1935–1979 period. On major issues particularly, they found that policy tended to change in the direction of change in majority opinion.[22]

Majorities do not always rule, however. There are many policy areas in which majority opinion is nonexistent or is ignored by policymakers. In these cases, other explanations of power and policy are necessary.

RULE BY GROUPS: PLURALISM   One of these explanations is provided by the theory of **pluralism,** which focuses on group activity and holds that many policies are effectively decided through power wielded by diverse (plural) interests.

Many policies are in fact more responsive to the interests of particular groups than to majority opinion. Agricultural subsidies, broadcast regulations, and corporate tax incentives are examples. In many cases, the general public has no real knowledge or opinion of issues that concern particular groups. For pluralists, the issue of whether interest-group politics serves the public good centers on whether it serves a diverse range of interests. Pluralists contend that it is misleading to view society only in terms of majorities that may or may not form around given issues. They see society as primarily a collection of separate interests. Farmers, broadcasters, and multinational corporations have different needs and desires and, according to the pluralist view, should have a disproportionate say in policies directly affecting them. Thus, as long as many groups have influence in their

TABLE 1-2   THEORIES OF POWER: WHO GOVERNS AMERICA?
There are three theories of power in America, each of which must be taken into account in any full explanation of the nation's policies.

Theory	Description
Majoritarianism	Holds that numerical majorities determine issues of policy
Pluralism	Holds that policies are effectively decided through power wielded by special interests that dominate particular policy areas
Elitism	Holds that policy is controlled by a small number of well-positioned, highly influential individuals

own area of interest, government is responding to the interests of most Americans. Pluralists such as Robert Dahl have argued that this is in fact the way the American political system operates most of the time.[23]

Some critics argue that pluralists wrongly assume that nearly all of society's interests are able to compete effectively through group politics. They see a system biased toward a small number of powerful groups. These critics are proponents of elite theory.

RULE BY A FEW: ELITISM   Elite theory offers a pessimistic view of the U.S. political system. **Elitism** holds that power in America is held by a small number of well-positioned, highly influential individuals who control policy for their own purposes. A leading proponent of elite theory was the sociologist C. Wright Mills, who argued that key policies are decided by an overlapping coalition of select leaders, including corporate executives, top military officers, and centrally placed public officials.[24] Other proponents of elite theory have defined the core group somewhat differently, but their contention is the same: America is essentially run not by majorities or a plurality of groups but by a small number of well-placed and privileged individuals.

Some theorists, including G. William Domhoff, hold a conspiratorial view of elites, contending that they consciously operate behind the scenes in

The Federal Reserve Board of Governors is a government body that through its interest-rate policies exerts a substantial influence on the American economy. The board meets in secrecy and is an example of the influence of political elites.

order to manipulate government for their selfish purposes.[25] Other theorists argue that elite influence is a result of size and complexity. Nearly a century ago, Roberto Michels articulated an "iron law of oligarchy," concluding that power inevitably gravitates toward a few people at the top, even in societies and organizations that aim to be governed more democratically.[26]

Although some of the claims about elites are exaggerated, it is clearly the case that certain policies and governing processes are effectively controlled by a tiny circle of influential people. The nation's monetary policy, for example, is set by the decisions of the Federal Reserve Board, which meets in secrecy and is highly responsive to the concerns of bankers and financiers (see Chapter 15).

WHO DOES GOVERN?　The perspective of this book is that each of these theories—majoritarianism, pluralism, and elitism—must be taken into account in any full explanation of politics and power in America. Some policies are decided by majority influence, whereas others reflect the influence of special interests and elites. The challenge is to distinguish the situations where each of these influence patterns predominates. Subsequent chapters will attempt that task.

THE CONCEPT OF A POLITICAL SYSTEM AND THE BOOK'S ORGANIZATION

As the foregoing discussion suggests, American government is based on a great many related parts. For this reason, it is useful to regard these components as constituting a **political system.** The parts are separate but they connect with one another, affecting how each performs. The political scientist David Easton, who was a pioneer in this conception of politics, said that it makes little sense to study political relations piecemeal when they are, in reality, "interrelated."[27]

The complexity of government has kept political scientists from developing a dynamic explanatory model of the full political system, but the concept of politics as a system is useful for instructional purposes. The concept emphasizes the actual workings of government rather than its institutional structures alone. This approach characterizes this book, beginning with its organizational sequence.

As Figure 1-3 indicates, the political system operates against the backdrop of a constitutional framework that defines how power is to be obtained and exercised. This framework is the focus of Chapters 1–5, which examine

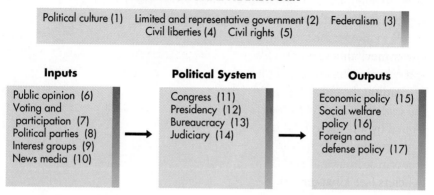

FIGURE 1-3 THE AMERICAN DEMOCRACY
The book's chapters are organized within a political systems framework.

the governmental structure and individual rights. *Inputs* are another part of the political system; these are the demands that people and groups place on government and the supports they provide for its institutions, leaders, and policies. These inputs are the subject of Chapters 6–10, which examine public opinion, political participation, voting, political parties, interest groups, and the news media. The functioning of governing officials is the focus of Chapters 11–14, which examine the nation's elective and appointive institutions: Congress, the presidency, the government bureaucracy, and the courts. Some of the discussion in these chapters is devoted simply to describing these institutions, but most of it explores their relationships and how their actions are affected by inputs and the constitutional framework. Building on all the previous units, Chapters 15–17 examine the major areas of public policy: the economy and environment, social welfare and education, and foreign affairs and national defense. These are the system's *outputs:* policy decisions that are binding on society.

The chapters are collectively designed to convey a reliable body of knowledge that will enable the reader to think broadly and systematically about the nature of the American political system. To assist in this process, this chapter has identified five encompassing tendencies of American politics that will be examined more closely in later chapters. The United States has

- Enduring cultural ideals that are its people's common bond and a source of their political goals
- Extreme fragmentation of governing authority that is based on an elaborate system of checks and balances

Democracy, an organizing principle of the U.S. political system, is based on the idea of popular rule. In practice, it means a government in which people rule through their freely elected representatives. Here, Al Gore and George W. Bush meet in a televised debate during the 2000 election.

- Many competing interests, which are the result of the nation's great size, population diversity, and economic complexity
- Strong emphasis on individual rights, which is a consequence of the nation's political traditions
- A relatively sharp separation of the political and economic spheres, which has the effect of placing many economic issues outside the reach of political majorities

Underlying this book's concern with the broad patterns of the American political system is a question that must be asked of any democracy: What is the relationship of the people to their government? The answer to this question is the foundation not only of a reasonable assessment of the state of American democracy but also of good citizenship. Responsible citizenship depends finally on an informed perspective, on a recognition of how difficult it is to govern effectively and yet how important it is to try. It cannot be said too often that the issue of governing is the most difficult issue facing any society. Nor can it be said too often that governing is a quest and a search, not a resolved issue. The Constitution's opening phrase, "We, the People," is a call to Americans to join that quest. E. E. Schattschneider said it clearly: "In the course of centuries, there has come a great deal of agreement about what democracy is, but nobody has a monopoly on it and the last word has not been spoken."[28]

SUMMARY

The United States is a nation that was formed on a set of ideals that includes liberty, equality, self-government, individualism, diversity, and unity. These ideals became Americans' common bond and today are the basis of their political culture. Although they are mythic, inexact, and conflicting, these ideals have had a powerful effect on what generation after generation of Americans have tried to achieve politically for themselves and others.

Politics is the process by which it is determined whose values will prevail in society. The basis of politics is conflict over scarce resources and competing values. Those who have power win out in this conflict and are able to control governing authority and policy choices. In the case of the United States, no one faction controls all power and policy. Majorities govern on some issues, while groups and elites each govern on other issues.

The play of politics in the United States takes place through rules of the game that include democracy, constitutionalism, and capitalism. Democracy is rule by the people, which, in practice, refers to a representative system of government in which the people rule through their elected officials. Constitutionalism refers to rules that limit the rightful power of government over citizens. Capitalism is an economic system based on a free market principle that allows the government only a limited role in determining how economic costs and benefits will be allocated.

MAJOR CONCEPTS

authority	majoritarianism
capitalism	pluralism
constitutionalism	policy
democracy	political culture
diversity	political system
elitism	politics
equality	power
government	self-government
individualism	unity
liberty	

SUGGESTED READINGS AND WEB SITES

Dahl, Robert. *On Democracy*. New Haven, Conn.: Yale University Press, 1998. A handbook on democracy by a leading advocate of pluralism.

DeLaet, Debra L. *U.S. Immigration Policy in an Age of Rights*. Westport, Conn.: Praeger Publishers, 2000. Analysis of the impact of civil rights action on the changes in U.S. immigration policy in recent decades.

Domhoff, G. William. *Who Rules America? Power and Politics in the Year 2000*. Mountain View, Calif.: Mayfield Publishing, 1998. A critical assessment of American government by a leading proponent of elite theory.

Lipset, Seymour Martin. *American Exceptionalism: A Double-Edged Sword*. New York: Norton, 1996. Argues that Americans' tendency to view society in idealized terms is a source of both alienation and progress.

McElroy, John Harmon. *American Beliefs: What Keeps a Big Country and a Diverse People United*. Chicago: I. R. Dee, 1999. An examination of the role of beliefs in Americans' political identity.

Schmidt, Ronald. *Language Policy and Identity Politics in the United States*. Philadelphia: Temple University Press, 2000. A critical assessment of language policy and its role in Americans' identity.

http://www.conginst.org A site that provides up-to-date survey data on the American political culture.

http://www.loc.gov The Library of Congress web site; it provides access to over seventy million historical and contemporary U.S. documents.

http://www.stateline.org A University of Richmond/Pew Charitable Trusts site dedicated to providing citizens with information on major policy issues.

http://www.tocqueville.org Includes biographical and other references to Alexis de Tocqueville and his writings.

READING 1

Presidential Inaugural Address
GEORGE W. BUSH

Introduction

In his inaugural address, George W. Bush repeatedly invoked America's time-honored ideals: justice, liberty, equality, self-government. The speech was delivered on January 20, 2001, but it would have made sense to any generation of Americans. Bush's speech won praise from his supporters while his opponents questioned whether his actions in office would match his words. Nevertheless, Bush's inaugural address is a contemporary reminder that the American political system is founded on a set of shared and timeless ideals.

We have a place, all of us, in a long story—a story we continue, but whose end we will not see. It is the story of a new world that became a friend and liberator of the old, a story of a slave-holding society that became a servant of freedom, the story of a power that went into the world to protect but not possess, to defend but not to conquer. It is the American story—a story of flawed and fallible people, united across the generations by grand and enduring ideals.

The grandest of these ideals is an unfolding American promise that everyone belongs, that everyone deserves a chance, that no insignificant person was ever born. Americans are called to enact this promise in our lives and in our laws. And though our nation has sometimes halted, and sometimes delayed, we must follow no other course.

Through much of the last century, America's faith in freedom and democracy was a rock in a raging sea. Now it is a seed upon the wind, taking root in many nations. Our democratic faith is more than the creed of our country, it is the inborn hope of our humanity, an ideal we carry but do not own, a trust we bear and pass along. And even after nearly 225 years, we have a long way yet to travel. While many of our citizens prosper, others doubt the promise, even the justice, of our own country. The ambitions of some Americans are limited by failing schools and hidden prejudice and the circumstances of their birth. And sometimes our differences run so deep, it seems we share a continent, but not a country.

We do not accept this, and we will not allow it. Our unity, our union, is the serious work of leaders and citizens in every generation. And this is my solemn pledge: I will work to build a single nation of justice and opportunity. I know this is in our reach because we are guided by a power larger than ourselves who creates us equal in His image. And we are confident in principles that unite and lead us onward.

America has never been united by blood or birth or soil. We are bound by ideals that move us beyond our backgrounds, lift us above our interests and teach us what it means to be citizens. Every child must be taught these principles. Every citizen must uphold them. And every immigrant, by embracing these ideals, makes our country more, not less, American. Today, we affirm a new commitment to live out our nation's promise through civility, courage, compassion and character.

America, at its best, matches a commitment to principle with a concern for civility. A civil society demands from each of us good will and respect, fair dealing and forgiveness. Some seem to believe that our politics can afford to be petty because, in a time of peace, the stakes of our debates appear small. But the stakes for America are never small. If our country does not lead the cause of freedom, it will not be led. If we do not turn the hearts of children toward knowledge and character, we will lose their gifts and undermine their idealism. If we permit our economy to drift and decline, the vulnerable will suffer most. We must live up to the calling we share. Civility is not a tactic or a sentiment. It is the determined choice of trust over cynicism, of community over chaos. And this commitment, if we keep it, is a way to shared accomplishment.

America, at its best, is also courageous. Our national courage has been clear in times of depression and war, when defending common dangers defined our common good. Now we must choose if the example of our fathers and mothers will inspire us or condemn us. We must show courage in a time of blessing by confronting problems instead of passing them on to future generations. Together, we will reclaim America's schools, before ignorance and apathy claim more young lives. We will reform Social Security and Medicare, sparing our children from struggles we have the power to prevent. And we will reduce taxes, to recover the momentum of our economy and reward the effort and enterprise of working Americans. We will build our defenses beyond challenge, lest weakness invite challenge. We will confront weapons of mass destruction, so that a new century is spared new horrors. The enemies of liberty and our country should make no mistake: America remains engaged in the world by history and by choice, shaping a balance of power that favors freedom. We will defend our allies and our interests. We will show purpose without arrogance. We will meet aggression and bad faith with resolve and strength. And to all nations, we will speak for the values that gave our nation birth.

America, at its best, is compassionate. In the quiet of American conscience, we know that deep, persistent poverty is unworthy of our nation's promise. And whatever our views of its cause, we can agree that children at risk are not at fault. Abandonment and abuse are not acts of God, they are failures of love. And the proliferation of prisons, however necessary, is no substitute for hope and order in our souls. Where there is suffering, there is duty. Americans in need are not strangers, they are citizens, not problems, but priorities. And all of us are diminished when any are hopeless.

Government has great responsibilities for public safety and public health, for civil rights and common schools. Yet compassion is the work of a nation, not just a government. And some needs and hurts are so deep they will only respond to a mentor's touch or a pastor's prayer. Church and charity, synagogue and mosque lend our communities their humanity, and they will have an honored place in our plans and in our laws. Many in our country do not know the pain of poverty, but we can listen to those who do. And I can pledge our nation to a goal: When we see that wounded traveler on the road to Jericho, we will not pass to the other side.

America, at its best, is a place where personal responsibility is valued and expected. Encouraging responsibility is not a search for scapegoats, it is a call to conscience. And though it requires sacrifice, it brings a deeper fulfillment. We find the fullness of life not only in options, but in commitments. And we find that children and community are the commitments that set us free.

Our public interest depends on private character, on civic duty and family bonds and basic fairness, on uncounted, unhonored acts of decency which give direction to our freedom. Sometimes in life we are called to do great things. But as a saint of our times has said, every day we are called to do small things with great love. The most important tasks of a democracy are done by everyone.

I will live and lead by these principles: to advance my convictions with civility, to pursue the public interest with compassion, to speak for greater justice and compassion, to call for responsibility and try to live it as well. In all these ways, I will bring the values of our history to the care of our times.

What you do is as important as anything government does. I ask you to seek a common good beyond your comfort; to defend needed reforms against easy attacks; to serve your nation, beginning with your neighbor. I ask you to be citizens: citizens, not spectators; citizens, not subjects; responsible citizens, building communities of service and a nation of character. Americans are generous and strong and decent, not because we believe in ourselves, but because we hold beliefs beyond ourselves. When this spirit of citizenship is missing, no government program can replace it. When this spirit is present, no wrong can stand against it.

After the Declaration of Independence was signed, Virginia statesman John Page wrote to Thomas Jefferson: "We know the race is not to the swift nor the battle to the strong. Do you not think angel rides in the whirlwind and directs this storm?" Much time has passed since Jefferson arrived for his inauguration. The years and changes accumulate. But the themes of this day he would know: our nation's grand story of courage and its simple dream of dignity. We are not this story's author, who fills time and eternity with his purpose. Yet his purpose is achieved in our duty, and our duty is fulfilled in service to one another. Never tiring, never yielding, never finishing, we renew that purpose today, to make our country more just and generous, to affirm the dignity of our lives and every life. This work continues. This story goes on. And an angel still rides in the whirlwind and directs this storm.

God bless you all, and God bless America.

George W. Bush is the forty-third president of the United States.

CHAPTER TWO

Constitutional Democracy

The people must be governed by a majority, with whom all power resides.
But how is the sense of this majority to be obtained?

FISHER AMES (1788)[1]

O N THE NIGHT of June 17, 1972, a security guard at the Watergate apartment-office complex in Washington, D.C., noticed that the latch on a basement door had been taped open. He called the police, who apprehended five burglars inside the National Democratic Party headquarters. As it turned out, the men had links to Republican president Richard Nixon's Committee to Re-elect the President.

Nixon called the incident "bizarre" and denied that anyone on his staff had had anything to do with the break-in. The Watergate break-in, however, was just one incident in an orchestrated campaign of "dirty tricks" designed to ensure Nixon's reelection. Funded by illegal contributions and conducted through the CIA, IRS, FBI, Secret Service, and Nixon's own operatives (called the White House "plumbers"), the dirty-tricks campaign extended to wiretaps, tax audits, and burglaries of Nixon's political opponents (the "enemies list"), who included journalists and antiwar activists in addition to Democrats. Nixon told his close advisors: "I want you all to stonewall it, let them [the Watergate burglars] plead the Fifth Amendment, cover up, or anything else."[2]

Although the Nixon White House managed for a time to hide the truth, the facts of the dirty-tricks campaign gradually became known. In early 1974 the House Judiciary Committee began impeachment proceedings, helped along, ironically, by Nixon's own words. During Senate hearings, a White House assistant revealed that Nixon had tape-recorded all his telephone calls and personal conversations in the Oval Office. At first Nixon refused to release the tapes, but then made public what he claimed were "all the relevant" ones. The House Judiciary Committee demanded additional tapes, as did the special prosecutor who had been appointed to

The Senate Judiciary Committee holds hearings on allegations of illegal acts
by President Richard Nixon. The congressional investigation led to
Nixon's resignation.

investigate criminal aspects of the Watergate affair. In late July the Supreme
Court of the United States, which included four justices appointed by
Nixon, unanimously ordered the president to supply sixty-four additional
tapes. Two weeks later, on August 9, 1974, Richard Nixon, citing a loss of
political support, resigned from office, the first president in U.S. history to
do so.

Nixon's downfall was owed in no small measure to the handiwork, two
centuries earlier, of the writers of the Constitution. They were well aware
that power could never be entrusted to the goodwill of leaders. "If angels
were to govern men," James Madison wrote in *Federalist* No. 51, "neither
external nor internal controls on government would be necessary." Madison's point, of course, was that leaders are not angels and, as mere mortals,
are subject to temptation and vice, including a lust for power—hence the
Framers' insistence on constitutional checks on power, as when they gave
Congress the authority to impeach a president and remove him from office.

The writers of the U.S. Constitution were intent on protecting *liberty*
and therefore sought to restrict the use of political power. Yet they also
wanted a government that would allow the majority to rule. The first objective was **limited government:** a government that is subject to strict limits on its lawful uses of power. The second objective was **self-government:**
a government that is subject to the will of the people as expressed through
the preferences of a majority. Self-government requires that the voters'

preferences find their way into public policy in a substantial and timely way. However, limited government requires restraints on the majority as a way of protecting the rights and interests of the minority. These considerations resulted in a constitution that has provision for majority rule but also has built-in restrictions on the exercise of majority power.

This chapter describes how the principles of self- and limited government are embodied in the Constitution and explains the tension between them. The chapter also indicates how these principles have been modified in practice in the course of American history. The main points of this chapter are the following:

* *America during the colonial period developed traditions of limited government and self-government.*
* *The Constitution provides for limited government mainly by defining lawful powers and by dividing those powers among competing institutions.*
* *The Constitution in its original form provided for self-government mainly through indirect systems of popular election of representatives.*
* *The idea of popular government—in which the majority's desires have a more direct and immediate impact on governing officials—has gained strength since the nation's beginning.*

BEFORE THE CONSTITUTION: THE COLONIAL AND REVOLUTIONARY EXPERIENCES

Early Americans' admiration for limited government was based partly on their English heritage. Other European nations of the eighteenth century implicitly acknowledged the divine right of their kings; England was an exception. British courts had developed a system of precedent known as "common law," which guaranteed trial by jury and due process of law as safeguards of life, liberty, and particularly property. These rights were defended by the courts and ordinarily respected by the king and Parliament.

This tradition of limited government was evident in the American colonies. In each colony there was a right to trial by jury. There was also freedom of expression, although of a limited kind. Religious freedom, for example, was not granted by all the colonies. Nevertheless, religious oppression of the kind that was commonplace in Europe was rare. There was also a degree of self-government in all the colonies. Each had an elected assembly and, although the assemblies were usually controlled by wealthier interests, they acted as representative bodies and grew increasingly power-ful as the number of settlers increased.

"The Rights of Englishmen"

The Revolutionary War was partly a rebellion against England's failure to respect its own tradition of limited government in the colonies. Many of the colonial charters had conferred upon Americans "the rights of English-men," but British kings and ministers showed progressively less respect for this guarantee as time went on. The period after the French and Indian War (1755–1763) was a turning point in the relationship between the colonists and Britain. Until then the colonists had viewed themselves as loyal subjects of the Crown and, although there had been occasional dis-putes, few voices argued for independence. In fact, colonists had fought alongside British soldiers to drive the French out of Canada and the West-ern territories.

At the end of the French and Indian War, however, Britain imposed burdensome taxes on the colonists. The war with France, which had also been waged in Europe, had created a severe financial crisis for the British government, which looked to the increasingly prosperous colonies for relief. The colonies were not accustomed to paying taxes to the British. The prac-tice was for Britain to raise its revenues from tariffs on imports and exports while the colonists kept any tax revenues they raised. But the British Parlia-ment in 1765 levied a stamp tax on colonial newspapers and business docu-ments, disrupting commerce and public communication. As the colonists were not represented in the British Parliament that had imposed the tax, the colonial pamphleteer James Otis declared that the Stamp Act violated the fundamental rights of the colonists as "British subjects and men." "No taxa-tion without representation" became a rallying cry for the colonists.

Although Parliament backed down and repealed the Stamp Act, it then passed the Townshend Act, which imposed taxes on all paper, glass, lead, and tea entering the colonies. When the colonists protested, King George III sent additional British troops to America and interfered with colonial legislatures. These actions served only to arouse the colonists further. En-gland then tried to placate the Americans by repealing the Townshend du-ties except for a nominal tea tax, which Britain retained in order to display its authority. The colonists viewed the tea tax as a petty insult, and in the "Boston Tea Party" of December 1773, a small band of patriots disguised as Native Americans boarded an English ship in Boston Harbor and dumped its cargo of tea overboard.

In 1774, the colonists met in Philadelphia at the First Continental Congress to define their demands of the British Crown: they called for free assembly, an end to the British military occupation, their own councils for the imposition of taxes, and trial by local juries. (British authorities had resorted to shipping "troublemakers" back to London for trial.) King George III refused their petition and, in 1775, British troops and colonial minutemen clashed at Lexington and Concord. Eight colonists died on the Lexington green in what became known as "the shot heard 'round the world."

The Declaration of Independence

Although grievances against Britain were the immediate cause of the American Revolution, ideas about the proper form of government were also on the colonists' minds. A century earlier, the English philosopher John Locke (1632–1704) had written that government must be restrained in its powers if it is to serve the common good. In his *Two Treatises of Government* (1690), Locke advanced the liberal principle that people have **inalienable rights** (or **natural rights**), including those of life, liberty, and property. In Locke's view, such rights belonged to people in their natural state before governments were created. When people agreed to come together (or, in Locke's term, entered into a "social contract") in order to have the protection that only organized government could provide, their natural rights were neither taken from them by government nor surrendered by them to government. If the government protected their natural rights, they were obliged to obey it, but if the government failed to protect their rights, they could rightfully rebel against it.[3]

Locke's ideas inspired a generation of American leaders.[4] Thomas Jefferson declared that Locke "was one of the three greatest men that ever lived, without exception," and Jefferson paraphrased Locke's ideas in key passages of the Declaration of Independence:

> We hold these truths to be self-evident, that all men are created equal, that they are endowed by their Creator with certain unalienable rights, that among these are life, liberty and the pursuit of happiness.

> That to secure these rights, governments are instituted among men, deriving their just powers from the consent of the governed.

> That whenever any form of government becomes destructive of these ends, it is the right of the people to alter or to abolish it, and to institute a new government.

A Declaration by the Representatives of the UNITED STATES
F AMERICA, in General Congress assembled.
When in the course of human events it becomes necessary for a people
ssolve the political bands which have connected them with another, and to
me among the powers of the earth the separate and equal station
hich the laws of nature & of nature's god entitle them, a decent respec
the opinions of mankind requires that they should declare the caus
hich impel them to the separation.
We hold these truths to be self evident: that all men a
eated equal, that they are endowed by their creator with
rights inherent & inalienable, among which are
e & liberty, & the pursuit of happiness; that to secure these rights, q
ernments are instituted among men, deriving their just powers from
e consent of the governed; that whenever any form of government
becomes destructive of these ends, it is the right of the people to alt
to abolish it, & to institute new government. laying it's foundation on
ch principles & organising it's powers in such form, as to them shal
em most likely to effect their safety & happiness. prudence indeed
ll dictate that governments long established should not be changed for
ght & transient causes: and accordingly all experience hath shewn tha
ankind are more disposed to suffer while evils are sufferable, than t
ght themselves by abolishing the forms to which they are accustomed bu
en a long train of abuses & usurpations [begun at a distinguished perio
pursuing invariably the same object, evinces a design to reduce
em under absolute Despotism. it is their right, it is their duty to throw off suc
vernment is to provide new guards for their future security. such ha
en the patient sufferance of these colonies & such is now the necessity
hich constrains them to [expunge] their former systems of government.
e history of the present king of Great Britain is a history of unremitting injuries and
surmations. [among which appears no solitary fact to contra
ict the uniform tenor of the rest, all of which have] in direct object th
tablishment of an absolute tyranny over these states to prove this, let facts b
ubmitted to a candid world. [for the truth of which we pledge a faith
et unsullied by falsehood]
e has refused his assent to laws the most wholesome and necessary for the pu
-lic good:
e has forbidden his governors to pass laws of immediate & pressing important
unless suspended in their operation till his assent should be obtained

This is a portion of Thomas Jefferson's handwritten draft of the Declaration of Independence, a formal expression of America's governing ideals.

The Declaration was a call to revolution rather than a framework for a new form of government, but the ideas it contained—liberty, individual rights, self-government, lawful powers—were to become the basis, eleven years later, for the Constitution of the United States. (The Declaration of Independence and the Constitution are reprinted in their entirety in the appendices of this book.)

The Articles of Confederation

The first government of the United States was based not on the Constitution, but on the Articles of Confederation. The Articles were adopted during the Revolutionary War and created a very weak national government that was subordinate to the states. This arrangement stemmed from the colonial experience. The colonies had always been governed separately, and their people considered themselves Virginians, New Yorkers, or Pennsylvanians as much as they thought of themselves as Americans. They naturally preferred a government that was constitutionally derived from the states. Moreover, they were leery of a powerful central government. The American Revolution was sparked by grievances against the arbitrary policies of King George III, and Americans were in no mood to replace him with a strong national authority of their own making.

Under the Articles of Confederation, each state retained its "sovereignty, freedom and independence." There was a national Congress, but its members were appointed and paid by their respective state governments. Each of the thirteen states had one vote in Congress, and the agreement of nine states was required to pass legislation. Moreover, any state could block constitutional change: the Articles of Confederation could be amended only by unanimous approval of the states.

The American union held together during the Revolutionary War out of necessity: the states had either to cooperate or to surrender to the British. But once the war ended, the states felt free to go their separate ways. Several states sent representatives abroad to negotiate their own separate trade agreements with foreign nations. New Hampshire, with its eighteen-mile coastline, even established its own navy. In a melancholy letter to Thomas Jefferson, George Washington wondered whether the United States deserved to be called a nation.

Congress was expected to provide for the nation's defense and establish the basis for a general economy, but it lacked the power to achieve these goals. It was not allowed to interfere in the states' commerce policies, and the states were soon engaged in ruinous trade wars. Congress also lacked the power to tax and consequently had no money with which to build a navy and hire an army.

Shays's Rebellion: A Nation Dissolving

By 1784, the nation was unraveling. Congress was so weak that its members often did not bother to attend its sessions.[5] Finally, in late 1786, a revolt in western Massachusetts prompted leading Americans to conclude that the country's government had to be changed. A ragtag army of two thousand farmers, armed with pitchforks, marched on county courthouses to prevent foreclosures on their land and cattle. Many of the farmers were veterans of the Revolutionary War; their leader, Daniel Shays, had been a captain in the Revolutionary army. They had been given assurances during the Revolution that their land, which lay fallow because they were away at war, would not be confiscated for reasons of unpaid debts and taxes. Instead, heavy new taxes were placed on farms, and many farmers faced loss of their property and even jail because they could not pay their creditors.

Although many Americans, including Jefferson, sympathized with the farmers, Shays's Rebellion scared propertied interests, and they called upon the governor of Massachusetts to put down the revolt. He asked Congress for help, but it had no army to send.[6] He finally raised enough money to hire a militia that put down the rebellion, but Shays's Rebellion made it clear that Congress and the army were weak and that mob action was increasing. At Virginia's urging, five states met at the Annapolis Convention in late 1786 to address the crisis. They did not reach agreement on a solution but urged Congress to authorize a constitutional convention of all the states, which would be held the following spring in Philadelphia. Congress did authorize the convention but placed a restriction on it: the delegates were to meet for "the sole and express purpose of revising the Articles of Confederation."

NEGOTIATING TOWARD A CONSTITUTION

The delegates to the Philadelphia constitutional convention ignored the instructions of Congress. They drafted a plan for an entirely new form of government. Prominent delegates (among them George Washington, Benjamin Franklin, and James Madison) were determined from the outset to establish an American nation built upon a strong central government.

The Great Compromise: A Two-Chamber Congress

Debate at the constitutional convention of 1787 began over a plan put forward by the Virginia delegation, which was dominated by strong nationalists. The Virginia Plan (also called the large-state plan) called for a two-chamber Congress that would have supreme authority in all areas "in which the separate states are incompetent," particularly defense and interstate trade. The

The Constitution was written in Philadelphia during the summer of 1787 in the East Room of the Old Pennsylvania State House, where the Declaration of Independence had been signed a decade earlier. George Washington presided over the Constitutional Convention but played a less active role in the debate than many of the delegates.

Virginia Plan also provided that the states would have numerical representation in Congress in proportion to their populations or tax contributions. Either way, representatives of the small states would be greatly outnumbered. Small states such as Delaware and Rhode Island would be allowed only one representative in the lower chamber, while large states such as Massachusetts and Virginia would have more than a dozen.

Not surprisingly, the Virginia Plan was roundly condemned by delegates from the smaller states. They rallied around a counterproposal made by New Jersey's William Paterson. The **New Jersey Plan** (also called the small-state plan) called for a stronger national government with the power to tax and to regulate commerce among the states; in most other respects, however, the Articles would remain in effect. Congress would have a single chamber in which each state, large or small, would have a single vote.

The debate over the New Jersey and Virginia Plans dragged on for weeks before the delegates reached what is now known as the **Great Compromise.** It provided for a bicameral (two-chamber) Congress: the House of Representatives would be apportioned among the states on the basis of population and the Senate on the basis of an equal number of votes (two) for each state. The small states would never have agreed to join a union in which their vote was always weaker than that of large states,[7] a fact reflected in Article V of the Constitution: "No state, without its consent, shall be deprived of its equal suffrage in the Senate."

The North-South Compromise: The Issue of Slavery

The separate interests of the states were also the basis for a second major agreement: the **North-South Compromise** over economic issues. The South had a slave-based agricultural economy, and its delegates feared that the North, which had a stronger manufacturing sector, would gain a numerical majority in Congress and then proceed to enact unfair tax policies. If Congress levied high import tariffs on finished goods from foreign nations in order to protect domestic manufacturers and placed heavy export tariffs on agricultural goods, the burden of financing the new government would fall mainly on the South. Its delegates also worried that northern representatives in Congress might tax or even bar the importation of slaves.

After extended debate, a compromise was reached. Congress was to be prohibited by the Constitution from taxing exports but could tax imports. In addition, Congress would be prohibited from passing laws to end the slave trade until 1808. A final bargain was the infamous "Three-Fifths Compromise": for purposes of both taxation and representation in Congress, five slaves were to be considered the equivalent of three white people; in effect, a slave was to be counted as three-fifths of a human being.

Although the Philadelphia convention has been criticized for the compromise over slavery, the southern states' dependence on slavery was a formidable obstacle to union. Northern states had no economic use for forced labor and had few slaves, whereas southern states had based their economies on large slave populations (see Figure 2-1). John Rutledge of South Carolina asked during the convention debate whether the North regarded southerners as "fools." Southern delegates declared that they would bolt the convention and form their own union rather than join one that prohibited slavery.

A Strategy for Ratification

The compromises over slavery and the structure of the Congress took up most of the four months that the convention was in session. Some of the other issues, such as the structure and powers of the federal judiciary, were the subject of surprisingly little debate.

There remained a final issue, however: Would those Americans not at the convention share the delegates' opinion of the Constitution? The

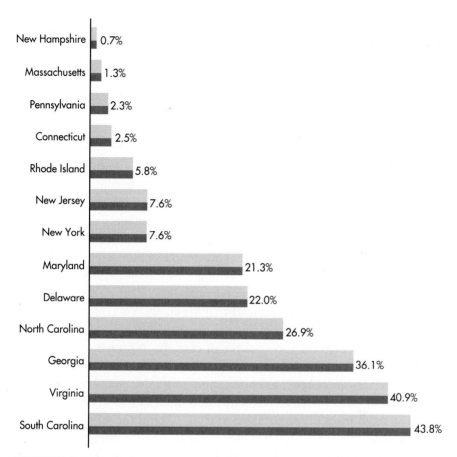

FIGURE 2-1 AFRICAN AMERICANS AS A PERCENTAGE OF STATE POPULATION, 1790. Source: U.S. Bureau of the Census, 2000.

delegates realized that ratification was not a sure thing. Congress had not authorized a wholesale restructuring of the federal government and had created a barrier to any such plan. In authorizing the Philadelphia convention, Congress had stated that any proposed change in the Articles would have to be "agreed to in Congress" and then "confirmed by [all of] the states." The delegates recognized that if they followed this procedure, which required unanimity, the Constitution had almost no chance of ratification. In a bold move, they established their own ratifying process. They instructed Congress to submit the document directly to the states, where it would become law after being approved by at least nine states in special ratifying conventions of popularly elected delegates. It was a masterful strategy: there was little hope that all thirteen state legislatures would approve the Constitution, but nine states through conventions might be persuaded to ratify it. And indeed, North Carolina and Rhode Island were steadfastly opposed to the new union and did not ratify the Constitution until the eleven other states had ratified it and begun the process of establishing the new government.

The Ratification Debate

The debate over ratification was a contentious one. The **Antifederalists** (as opponents of the Constitution were labeled) raised arguments' that still echo in American politics. They claimed that the national government would be too powerful and would threaten the sovereignty of the separate states and the liberty of the people. Many Americans had an innate distrust of centralized power and worried that the people's liberty could be eclipsed as easily by a distant American government as it had been by the British king. The fact that the Constitution contained no bill of rights heightened this concern. Did its absence indicate that the central government would be free to define for itself what the people's rights would be?

The presidency was also a source of concern. No such office had existed under the Articles, and some worried that it would lead to the creation of an American monarchy. Even the motives of the men who wrote the Constitution came under attack. They were men of wealth and education and had acted in response to debtors' riots. Would the Constitution become a tool by which the wealthy ruled over those with little or no money? And who would bear the burden of additional taxation? For Americans struggling with local and state tax payments, the creation of yet another tax agency was hardly an attractive proposal.

Most Antifederalists acknowledged a need to strengthen national commerce and defense. What they opposed was the creation of a powerful national government as the mechanism. They favored a revision of the Articles of Confederation, which in their opinion could accomplish these goals without the risk of establishing a government that could threaten their liberties, their livelihoods, and their local interests.

The **Federalists** (as the Constitution's supporters called themselves) responded with a persuasive case of their own. Their strongest arguments were set forth by James Madison and Alexander Hamilton, who, along with John Jay, wrote a series of essays during the New York ratification debate. The essays were published in a New York City newspaper under the pen name Publius and were entitled "The Federalist." (The essays are collectively referred to as *The Federalist Papers* and are widely acknowledged as a brilliant political treatise.) Madison and Hamilton argued that the government of the Constitution would correct the defects of the Articles; it would have the power necessary to forge a secure and prosperous union. At the same time, because of restrictions on its powers, the new government would endanger neither the states nor personal liberty. In *Federalist* Nos. 47, 48, 49, 50, and 51, for example, Madison explained how the separation of national institutions was designed to both empower and restrict the federal government. (The Federalist and Antifederalist arguments are discussed further in Chapter 3.)

Whether the ratification debate changed many minds is unknown. Historical evidence indicates, however, that a majority of ordinary Americans opposed the Constitution's ratification. But their voice in the state ratifying conventions was smaller than that of wealthier interests, which, in the main, supported the change. The pro-ratification forces were also bolstered by the widespread assumption that George Washington would become the first president. He was the most-trusted and popular American leader, and many historians believe that Washington's endorsement of the new government tipped the balance in favor of ratification.

Delaware was the first state to ratify the Constitution, and Connecticut, Georgia, and New Jersey followed, an indication that the Great Compromise had satisfied several of the small states. In the early summer of 1788, New Hampshire became the ninth state to ratify. The Constitution was law. But neither Virginia nor New York had ratified, and a stable union without these two major states was almost unthinkable. They were as large in area as many European countries and conceivably could survive as independent nations. They nearly did choose a separate course. In both states, the Constitution barely passed, and then only after the Federalists promised to support a bill of rights designed to protect individual freedoms from the power of the central government.

The Framers' Goals

A **constitution** is the fundamental law that defines how a government will legitimately operate: how its leaders will be chosen, the institutions through which these leaders will work, the procedures they must follow in making policy, and the powers they can lawfully exercise. The Constitution, which was written in Philadelphia in 1787, is exactly such a law. In theory, it is the highest law of the land: neither a popular majority nor a leader at the highest pinnacle of power stands above it. Its provisions define how power is to be acquired and can be used.

TABLE 2-1   MAJOR GOALS OF THE FRAMERS OF THE CONSTITUTION

1. To establish a government strong enough to meet the nation's needs—an objective sought through substantial grants of power to the federal government in areas such as defense and commerce (see Chapter 3).

2. To establish a government that would not threaten the existence of the separate states—an objective sought through federalism (see Chapter 3) and through a Congress connected to the states through elections.

3. To establish a government that would not threaten liberty—an objective sought through an elaborate system of checks and balances.

4. To establish a government based on popular sovereignty—an objective sought through provisions for the direct and indirect election of public officials.

The Constitution reflected the Framers' vision of a proper government for the American people. Its provisions addressed four broad goals (see Table 2-1). One was the creation of a national government strong enough to meet the nation's needs, particularly in the areas of defense and commerce. Another goal was to preserve the states as governing entities. The states already existed and had the loyalty of their people. Accordingly, the Framers established a system of government (*federalism*) in which power is divided between the national government and the states. Federalism is discussed at length in Chapter 3, which will also explain how the Constitution laid the foundation for a strong national government.

The Framers' other goals were to establish a national government that was restricted in its lawful uses of power (limited government) and that gave the people a voice in their governance (self-government). These two goals and how they were written into the Constitution are the focus of the rest of this chapter.

PROVIDING FOR A LIMITED GOVERNMENT

A challenge facing the Framers of the Constitution was how to control the coercive force of government. Government's unique characteristic is that it alone can legally arrest, imprison, and even kill people who break its rules.[8] Force is not the only basis of effective government, but government must be able to use force or lawless elements would take over society. The dilemma is that government itself can destroy civilized society by using its force to brutalize and intimidate its opponents. "It is a melancholy reflection," James Madison wrote to Thomas Jefferson shortly after the Constitution's ratification, "that liberty should be equally exposed to danger whether the government has too much or too little power."[9]

The men who wrote the Constitution sought to establish a government strong enough to enforce national interests, including defense and commerce among the states (see Chapter 3), but not so strong as to destroy liberty. Limited government was built into the Constitution through both grants and restrictions of political power.

Grants and Denials of Power

The Framers chose to limit the national government in part by confining its scope to constitutional **grants of power.** Congress's lawmaking powers are specifically listed in Article I, section 8, of the Constitution. Seventeen in number, these listed powers include, for example, the powers to tax, to establish an army and navy, to declare war, to regulate commerce among the states, to create a national currency, and to borrow money. Authority *not* granted to the government by the Constitution is in theory denied to it. In a period in which other governments had unrestricted powers, this was a remarkable limitation.

The Framers also used **denials of power** as a means to limit government, prohibiting certain practices that European rulers had routinely used to intimidate their political opponents. The French king, for example, could imprison a subject indefinitely without charge or trial. The U.S. Constitution prohibits such action: individuals have the right to be brought before a court under a writ of habeas corpus for a judgment as to the legality of their confinement. The Constitution also forbids Congress and the states from passing *ex post facto* laws, under which citizens can be prosecuted for acts that were legal at the time they were committed.

As a further denial of power, the Framers' powers made the Constitution difficult to amend. Those in authority would not be able to increase their lawful powers unless the change had broad and extraordinary support. An amendment could be proposed only by a two-thirds majority in both chambers of Congress or in a national constitutional convention called by the legislatures of two-thirds of the states. Such a proposal would then become part of the Constitution only if ratified by three-fourths of the state legislatures or by three-fourths of the states in a special national convention.

(The Constitution has been amended only twenty-seven times during the nation's history; in each instance, the amendment was proposed by Congress and ratified by the state legislatures.)

Using Power to Offset Power

Although the Framers believed that grants and denials of power could act as controls on government, they had no illusion that written words alone would restrain power. As a consequence, they sought to check power with power. The idea was to divide the authority of government, so that no single institution could exercise great power without the agreement of other institutions.[10]

The idea that a **separation of powers** was necessary to the preservation of liberty had been proposed decades earlier by the French theorist Montesquieu. His argument was widely accepted in America, and when the states drafted new constitutions after the start of the Revolutionary War, they built their governments around the concept of a separation of powers. Pennsylvania was an exception, and its experience only seemed to prove the necessity of separated powers. Unrestrained by an independent judiciary or executive, Pennsylvania's all-powerful legislature systematically deprived minority groups of their basic rights and freedoms: Quakers were disenfranchised for their religious beliefs, conscientious objectors to the Revolutionary War were prosecuted, and the right of trial by jury was eliminated.

In *Federalist* No. 10, Madison asked why governments often act according to the interests of overbearing majorities rather than according to principles of justice. He attributed the cause to "the mischiefs of faction." People, he argued, are divided into opposing religious, geographical, ethnic, economic, and other factions. These divisions are natural and desirable, in that free people have a right to their personal opinions and interests. Yet factions can themselves be a source of oppressive government. If a faction gains full power, it will use government to advance itself at the expense of all others. (*Federalist* No. 10 is widely regarded as the finest political essay ever written by an American. A portion of it is reprinted at the end of this chapter.)

Out of this concern came the Framers' special contribution to the doctrine of the separation of powers. They did not believe that it would be enough, as Montesquieu had suggested, to divide the government's authority strictly along institutional lines, granting all legislative power to the legislature, all judicial power to the courts, and all executive power to the presidency. This *total* separation would make it too easy for a single faction to exploit a particular kind of political power. A faction that controlled the legislature, for example, could enact laws ruinous to other interests. A better system of divided government would be one in which political power could be applied forcibly only when institutions agreed on its use. This would require a system of separated but *overlapping* powers. Since no one faction could easily gain control over all institutions, factions would have to work together, a process that would require each to moderate its demands and thus would serve many interests rather than one or a few.[11]

Separated Institutions Sharing Power: Checks and Balances

The Framers' concept of divided powers has been described by political scientist Richard Neustadt as the principle of **separated institutions sharing power**.[12] The separate branches are interlocked in such a way that an elaborate system of **checks and balances** is created (see Figure 2-2). No institution can act decisively without the support or acquiescence of the other institutions. Legislative, executive, and judicial powers in the American system are divided in such a way that they overlap; each of the three branches of government checks the others' powers and balances those powers with powers of its own. As natural as this system now might seem to Americans, most democracies are of the parliamentary type, where executive

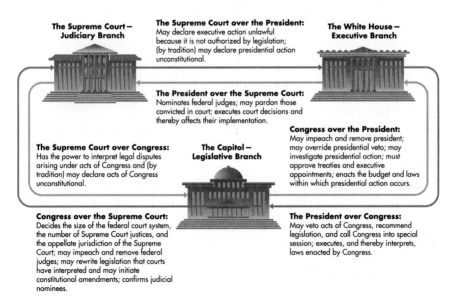

The Supreme Court — Judiciary Branch

The Supreme Court over the President: May declare executive action unlawful because it is not authorized by legislation; (by tradition) may declare presidential action unconstitutional.

The White House — Executive Branch

The President over the Supreme Court: Nominates federal judges; may pardon those convicted in court; executes court decisions and thereby affects their implementation.

Congress over the President: May impeach and remove president; may override presidential veto; may investigate presidential action; must approve treaties and executive appointments; enacts the budget and laws within which presidential action occurs.

The Supreme Court over Congress: Has the power to interpret legal disputes arising under acts of Congress and (by tradition) may declare acts of Congress unconstitutional.

The Capitol — Legislative Branch

Congress over the Supreme Court: Decides the size of the federal court system, the number of Supreme Court justices, and the appellate jurisdiction of the Supreme Court; may impeach and remove federal judges; may rewrite legislation that courts have interpreted and may initiate constitutional amendments; confirms judicial nominees.

The President over Congress: May veto acts of Congress, recommend legislation, and call Congress into special session; executes, and thereby interprets, laws enacted by Congress.

FIGURE 2-2 THE SYSTEM OF CHECKS AND BALANCES

and legislative power are combined in a single institution rather than vested in separate ones. In a parliamentary system, the majority in the legislature selects the prime minister, who then serves as both legislative leader and chief executive (see box: How the United States Compares).

SHARED LEGISLATIVE POWERS   Under the Constitution, Congress has legislative authority, but that power is partly shared with the other branches and thus checked by them. The president can veto acts of Congress, recommend legislation, and call special sessions of Congress. The president also has the power to execute—and thereby to interpret— the laws made by Congress.

The Supreme Court has the power to interpret acts of Congress that are disputed in legal cases. The Court also has the power of judicial review; it can declare laws of Congress void when it finds that they are not in accord with the Constitution.

Within Congress, there is a further check on legislative power: for legislation to be passed, a majority in each house of Congress is required. Thus the Senate or the House of Representatives can block the other from acting.

SHARED EXECUTIVE POWERS   Executive power is vested in the president but is constrained by legislative and judicial checks. The president's power to make treaties and appoint high-ranking officials, for example, is subject to Senate approval. Congress also has the power to impeach and remove the president from office. In practical terms, Congress's greatest checks on executive action are its lawmaking and appropriations powers. The executive branch cannot act without laws that authorize its activities or without the money that pays for these programs.

The judiciary's major check on the presidency is its power to declare an action unlawful because it is not authorized by the legislation that the executive claims to be implementing.

SHARED JUDICIAL POWERS   Judicial power rests with the Supreme Court and with lower federal courts, which are subject to checks by the other branches of the federal government. Congress is empowered to establish the size of the federal court system, to restrict the Supreme Court's appellate jurisdiction in some circumstances, and to impeach and remove federal judges from office. More important, Congress can rewrite legislation that the courts have misinterpreted and can initiate amendments when it disagrees with the courts' rulings on constitutional issues.

The president has the power to appoint federal judges with the consent of the Senate and to pardon persons convicted in the courts. The president is also responsible for executing court decisions, a function that provides opportunities to influence the way rulings are implemented.

The Bill of Rights

Although the delegates to the Philadelphia convention discussed the possibility of placing a list of individual rights (such as freedom of speech and the right to a fair trial) in the Constitution, they ultimately decided that such a list was unnecessary because of the doctrine of expressed powers: government could not lawfully assume powers, such as the abridgment of human rights, that were not authorized by the Constitution. Moreover, the delegates concluded that a bill of rights was undesirable because government might feel free to disregard any right that was inadvertently left off the list or that emerged at some future time. These considerations did not allay the fears of leading Americans who believed that no possible safeguard against tyrannical government should be omitted. "A bill of rights," Jefferson argued, "is what the people are entitled to against every government on earth."

Opposition to the absence of a bill of rights led to its addition to the Constitution. Madison himself introduced a series of amendments during the First Congress, ten of which were soon ratified by the states. These amendments, traditionally called the **Bill of Rights,** include such rights as free expression and due process for persons accused of crimes. (These rights, termed "civil liberties," are the subject of Chapter 4.)

The Bill of Rights is a precise expression of the concept of limited government. In consenting to be governed, the people agree to accept the authority of government in certain areas but not in others; the people's constitutional rights cannot lawfully be denied by governing officials.

Judicial Review

The writers of the Constitution both empowered and limited government. But who was to decide whether the government was operating within its constitutional powers? The Framers did not specifically entrust this power to a particular branch of government, although they did grant the Supreme Court the authority to decide on "all cases arising under this Constitution." Still, because the Constitution did not explicitly provide for judicial review, it was a principle that had to be established in practice.

Limits on Government in the U.S. Constitution

Grants of power: Powers granted to the national government by the Constitution. Powers not granted it are denied it unless they are necessary and proper to the carrying out of granted powers.

Denials of power: Powers expressly denied to the national and state governments by the Constitution.

Separated institutions sharing power: The division of the national government's power among three branches, each of which is to act as a check on the powers of the other two.

Bill of Rights: The first ten amendments to the Constitution, which specify rights of citizens that the national government must respect.

Federalism: The division of political authority between the national government and the states, enabling the people to appeal to one authority if their rights and interests are not respected by the other authority (see Chapter 3).

Judicial review: The power of the courts to declare governmental action null and void when it is found to violate the Constitution.

Elections: The power of the voters to remove officials from office.

The opportunity arose with an incident that occurred after the election of 1800, in which John Adams lost his bid for a second presidential term after a bitter campaign against Jefferson. Between November 1800, when Jefferson was elected, and March 1801, when he was inaugurated, the Federalist-controlled Congress created fifty-nine additional lower-court judgeships, enabling Adams to appoint loyal Federalists to those positions before he left office. However, Adams's term expired before the secretary of state could deliver the judicial commissions to all the appointees. Without this formal authorization, an appointee could not take office. Knowing this, Jefferson told his secretary of state, James Madison, not to deliver them. William Marbury was one of those who did not receive his commission, and he asked the Supreme Court to issue a writ of *mandamus* (a court order that directs an official to take a specific action) requiring Madison to deliver it.

Marbury v. *Madison* (1803) became the foundation for judicial review by the federal courts. Chief Justice John Marshall wrote the *Marbury* opinion, which declared that Marbury had a legal right to his commission. The opinion also said, however, that the Supreme Court could not issue him a writ of *mandamus* because it lacked the constitutional authority to do so. Congress had granted the Court the power to issue such writs in an ordinary act of legislation—the Judiciary Act of 1789. Marshall pointed out that the Constitution prohibits any extension of the Supreme Court's authority except through an amendment to the Constitution. That being the case, Marshall stated, the portion of the Judiciary Act that provided the authorization was constitutionally invalid.[13]

Marshall's decision was ingenious since it asserted the power of judicial review without creating the possibility of its rejection by either the executive or the legislative branch. In declaring that Marbury had a right to his commission, the Court in effect said that President Jefferson had failed in his constitutional duty to execute the laws faithfully. But since it did not order Jefferson to deliver the commission, he had no opportunity to refuse to comply with the Court's judgment. At the same time, the Court admonished Congress for passing legislation that exceeded its constitutional authority. And in the process of invalidating an act of Congress on constitutional grounds, the Court asserted its power of **judicial review**— that is, the power of the courts to decide whether a governmental official or institution has acted within the limits of the Constitution and, if not, to declare its action null and void.

PROVIDING FOR SELF-GOVERNMENT

"We the People" is the opening phrase of the Constitution. It expresses the idea that in the United States, the people will have the power to govern themselves. In a sense, there is no contradiction between this idea and the Constitution's provisions for limited government, since individual *liberty* is part of the process of *self-government*. In another sense, the contradiction is clear: restrictions on the power of the majority are a denial of its right to govern society as it chooses.

The Framers believed that the people deserved and required a voice in their government, but they also feared popular government. To the Framers, the great risk of popular government was **tyranny of the majority**: the people acting as an irrational mob that tramples on the rights of others. Their fear was not without foundation. The history of democracies

HOW THE UNITED STATES COMPARES

Checks and Balances

All democracies place constitutional limits on the power of government. The concept of rule by law, for example, is characteristic of democratic governments but not of authoritarian regimes. Democracies differ, however, in the extent to which political power is restrained through constitutional mechanisms. The United States is an extreme case in that its government rests on an elaborate system of constitutional checks and balances. The system employs a separation of powers among the executive, legislative, and judicial branches. It also includes judicial review, the power of the courts to invalidate actions of the legislature or executive. These constitutional restrictions on power are not part of the governing structure of all democracies.

Most democracies, for example, have parliamentary systems, which invest both executive and legislative leadership in the office of prime minister. Britain is an example of this type of system. Parliament under the leadership of the prime minister is the supreme authority in Britain. Its laws are not even subject to override by Britain's high court, which has no power to review the constitutionality of parliamentary acts.

Country	Separation of Executive & Legislative Powers?	Judicial Review?
Belgium	No	No
Canada	No	Yes
France	Yes	No
Germany	No	Yes
Great Britain	No	No
Israel	No	Yes
Italy	No	Yes
Japan	No	Yes
Mexico	Yes	Yes
United States	Yes	Yes

was filled with popular excesses, and there were even examples from the nation's brief history. In 1786, for example, debtors had gained control of Rhode Island's legislature and made paper money a legal means of paying debts, even though existing contracts called for payment in gold. Creditors were then hunted down and held captive in public places so that debtors could come and pay them in full with worthless paper money. A Boston newspaper wrote that Rhode Island should be renamed *Rogue* Island.

Democracy Versus Republic

No form of self-government could eliminate completely the threat to liberty of majority tyranny, but the Framers believed that the danger would be greatly diminished by properly structured institutions.[14] Madison summarized the Framers' intent when he said in *Federalist* No. 10 that the Constitution was "a republican remedy" for the excesses historically associated with "democratic" rule. Today the terms **democracy, republic,** and **representative democracy** are often used interchangeably to refer to a system of government in which ultimate political power rests with the majority through its capacity to choose representatives in free and open elections. To the writers of the Constitution, however, "democracy" and "republic" had different meanings. When the Framers complained about the risks of democracy, they were referring to "pure democracy," in which the public participates directly in the making of public policy. In their use of the term "republic," the Framers were referring to "representative democracy," in which elected officials meet in representative institutions to decide policy through extended debate and deliberation.[15]

The Framers' concept of a proper system of representation was similar to an idea put forth by the English theorist Edmund Burke (1729–1797). In his *Letter to the Sheriffs of Bristol,* Burke argued that representatives should act as public **trustees:** they are obliged to promote the interest of those who elected them, but the nature of this interest is for the representatives, not the voters, to decide. Burke was concerned about the ease with which society could degenerate into selfishness, and he thought it imperative for representatives not to surrender their judgment to popular whim.

Limited Popular Rule

The Constitution provided that all power would be exercised through representative institutions. There was no provision for any form of direct popular participation in the making of policy decisions. In view of the fact that the United States was much too large to be governed directly by the people in popular assemblies, a representative system was necessary. Moreover, the separation of powers meant that the majority's will, again by necessity, would be filtered through an institutional structure. The Framers went beyond what was necessary, however, and placed officials at a considerable distance from the people they represented (see Table 2-2).

The House of Representatives was the only institution that would be based on direct popular election—its members would be elected for two-year terms of office through vote of the people. Frequent and direct election of House members was intended to make government sensitive to the concerns of popular majorities.

U.S. senators would be appointed by the legislatures of the states they represented. Because state legislators were popularly elected, the people would be choosing their senators indirectly. Every two years, a third of the senators would be appointed to six-year terms. The Senate was expected to check and balance the House, which, by virtue of the more frequent and direct election of its members, would presumably be more responsive to popular opinion.

Presidential selection was an issue of considerable debate at the Philadelphia convention. Direct election of the president was twice pro-posed and twice rejected because it linked executive power directly to pop-ular majorities. The Framers finally chose to have the president selected by the votes of electors (the so-called **Electoral College**). Each state would

TABLE 2-2   METHODS OF CHOOSING NATIONAL LEADERS
Fearing the concentration of political power, the Framers devised alternative methods of selection and terms of service for national officials.

Office	Method of Selection	Term of Service
President	Electoral College	4 years
U.S. senator	State legislature	6 years (1/3 of senators' terms expire every 2 years)
U.S. representative	Popular election	2 years
Federal judge	Nomination by president, approval by Senate	Indefinite (subject to "good behavior")

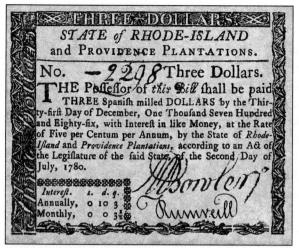

Rhode Island was nicknamed "Rogue Island" for its disregard of property rights.
Shown here is the Rhode Island three-dollar banknote, which came to be
worth no more than the paper on which it was written and yet
was used to pay off gold debts.

have as many **electoral votes** as it had members in Congress and could select them by any method it chose. The president would serve four years and be eligible for reelection.

The Framers decided that federal judges and justices would be appointed rather than elected. They would be nominated by the president and confirmed through approval by the Senate. Once confirmed, they would "hold their offices during good behavior." In effect, they would be allowed to hold office for life unless they committed a crime. The judiciary would be more of a "guardian" institution than a "representative" one.[16]

These differing methods of selecting national officeholders would not prevent a determined majority from achieving unbridled power, but control could not be attained easily or quickly. Unlike the House of Representatives, institutions such as the Senate, presidency, and judiciary would not yield to an impassioned majority in a single election. The delay would reduce the probability that government would degenerate into mob rule driven by momentary whims.

Altering the Constitution: More Power to the People

The Constitution's provisions for limited government have stood the test of time: in its structure and formal powers, the national government today has nearly the same features as the government established in 1789. This is not true, however, of the original provisions for self-government: in no other constitutional area have Americans shown a greater willingness to devise new arrangements.

A desire for change was evident nearly as soon as the Constitution was unveiled. The Framers' conception of self-government was at odds with what the average American in 1787 believed was appropriate (indeed, most historians conclude that, if George Washington had not presided over the Philadelphia convention and had not been widely expected to become the nation's first president, the Constitution would not have been ratified). It certainly was at odds with the spirit and letter of the state constitutions. Every state but South Carolina held annual legislative elections, and several states also chose their governors through annual election. And it was not long after ratification of the Constitution that Americans sought a stronger voice in their own governing.

JEFFERSONIAN DEMOCRACY: A REVOLUTION OF THE SPIRIT

Thomas Jefferson, who otherwise admired the Constitution, was among the prominent Americans who questioned its provisions for self-government. And it was Jefferson who may have spared the nation a bloody conflict over the issue of popular sovereignty. Under John Adams, the second president, the national government increasingly favored the nation's wealthy interests. Adams publicly suggested that the Constitution was designed for a governing elite, while Alexander Hamilton urged him to use force if necessary to suppress popular dissent.[17] Jefferson asked whether Adams, with the aid of a strong army, planned soon to deprive ordinary Americans of their freedoms altogether. Jefferson challenged Adams in the next presidential election and, upon defeating him, hailed the victory as the "Revolution of 1800."

Although Jefferson was a champion of the common people, he had no clear vision of how a popular government might work in practice. He believed that congressional majorities were the proper expression of popular majorities and accordingly was reluctant to use his presidency as the instrument of the people.[18] Jefferson also had no illusions about a largely illiterate population's readiness for a significant governing role and feared the ruinous consequences of inciting the masses to contest the moneyed class. Jeffersonian democracy was thus mainly a revolution of the spirit; Jefferson taught Americans to look upon the national government as belonging to all, not just to the privileged few.[19]

JACKSONIAN DEMOCRACY: LINKING THE PEOPLE AND THE PRESIDENCY   Not until Andrew Jackson was elected in 1828 did the country have a powerful president who was willing and able to involve the public more fully in government. Jackson carried out the constitutional revolution that Jeffersonian democracy had foreshadowed.

Jackson recognized that the president was the only official who could legitimately claim to represent the people as a whole. Unlike the president, members of Congress were elected from separate states and districts rather than from the entire country. Yet the president's claim to popular leadership was diminished by the existence of the Electoral College. Jackson persuaded the states to choose their presidential electors on the basis of popular voting. Jackson's reform, which is still in effect today, basically places the selection of a president in the voters' hands. The winner of the popular vote in a state is awarded its electoral votes; hence the candidate who wins most of the popular votes in the states is also most likely to receive a majority of the electoral votes. Since Jackson's time, only three candidates—Rutherford B. Hayes in 1876, Benjamin Harrison in 1888, and George W. Bush in 2000—have won the presidency after losing the popular vote. (The Electoral College is discussed further in Chapter 12.)

THE PROGRESSIVES: SENATE AND PRIMARY ELECTIONS   The Progressive era of the early 1900s brought another wave of democratic reforms. The Progressives rejected the Burkean idea (discussed earlier in this chapter) of representatives as trustees; they embraced instead the idea of representatives as **delegates**—officeholders who are obligated to respond directly to the expressed opinions of the people whom they represent.

The Progressives succeeded primarily in changing the way that state and local governments operate (see box: States in the Nation). Progressive reforms of these governments included nonpartisan local elections; recall elections, which enable citizens through petition to require a particular officeholder to submit to election before the expiration of his or her normal term of office; the initiative, which enables citizens through petition to place legislative measures on the ballot for enactment or rejection through popular voting; and the referendum, which permits legislative bodies to submit measures to the voters for enactment or rejection.

The Progressives also brought about two changes in the role of voters in national politics. One was the direct election of U.S. senators, who, before the Seventeenth Amendment was ratified in 1913, were chosen by state legislatures and were widely perceived as agents of big business (the Senate

★ STATES IN THE NATION ★

Direct Democracy: The Initiative and Referendum

The Progressive movement's reforms included the direct initiative (which allows citizens through petitions to place legislative measures directly on the ballot) and the referendum (which permits legislative bodies to submit proposals to the voters for approval or rejection). Not all states adopted these devices or have them today. The initiative and referendum are common in the Midwest and West, where the Progressive movement was strong. They are less prevalent in the Northeast, where the party machines were strong, and in the South, where political elites opposed reforms that would have enabled African Americans and poor whites to exercise more power.

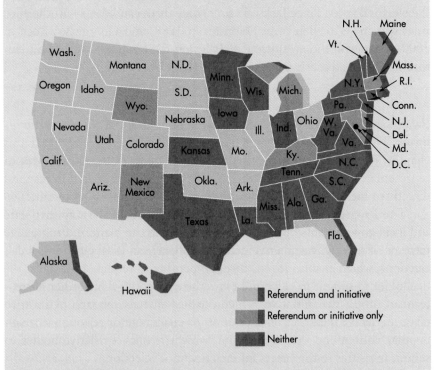

- Referendum and initiative
- Referendum or initiative only
- Neither

SOURCE: Council of State Governments, *Book of the States, 2000–2001* (Lexington, Ky.: Council of State Governments, 2000), p. 233.

was nicknamed the "Millionaires' Club"). The second was the **primary election,** which gave rank-and-file voters the opportunity to select party nominees. Nearly all states in the early 1900s adopted the primary election as a means of choosing nominees for at least some federal and state offices. Before this change, nominees were chosen by party leaders.

The Progressive era spawned attacks on the Framers. A prominent criticism was the historian Charles S. Beard's *Economic Interpretation of the Constitution.*[20] Arguing that the Constitution grew out of wealthy Americans' fears of the debtor rebellions, and noting that many of the Framers were themselves wealthy men, Beard claimed that the Constitution's elaborate systems of power and representation were devices for keeping power in the hands of the rich. Beard's thesis was challenged by other historians, and he later acknowledged that he had not taken the Framers' full array of motives into account. Their conception of separation of powers, for example, was a time-honored governing principle that had previously been incorporated in state constitutions. Although the Framers did not have great trust in popular rule, it would be a mistake to conclude they were foes of democracy. They were intent on balancing the demands of limited government with those of self-government and, in striking a balance, leaned toward the former, believing that the evil of unrestrained power was the greater danger to a civil society.

CONSTITUTIONAL DEMOCRACY TODAY

The type of government created in the United States in 1787 is today called a **constitutional democracy.** It is *democratic* in its provisions for majority influence through elections and *constitutional* in its requirement that power gained through elections be exercised in accordance with law and with due respect for individual rights.

By some standards, the American system of today is a model of *self-government.* The United States schedules the election of its larger legislative chamber (the House of Representatives) and its chief executive more frequently than any other democracy. In addition, it is the only country that relies extensively on primary elections instead of party organizations for the selection of party nominees. The principle of popular election to office, which the writers of the Constitution regarded as a prerequisite of popular sovereignty but one to be used sparingly, has been extended farther in the United States than anywhere else.

By other standards, however, the U.S. system is less democratic than many others. Popular majorities must work against the barriers to influence—the elaborate system of divided powers, staggered terms of office, and separate constituencies—that were devised by the Framers. In fact, the link between an electoral majority and a governing majority is far less direct in the American system than in nearly all other democratic systems. In the European parliamentary democracies, for example, legislative and executive power are not separated, are not subject to close check by the judiciary, and are acquired through the winning of a legislative majority in national elections. The Framers' vision was a different one, dominated by a concern with *liberty*, and therefore with controls on political power, a response to the experiences they brought with them to Philadelphia in the summer of 1787.

SUMMARY

The Constitution of the United States is a reflection of the colonial and revolutionary experiences of the early Americans. Freedom from abusive government was a reason for the colonies' revolt against British rule, but the English tradition also provided ideas about government, power, and freedom that were expressed in the Constitution and, earlier, in the Declaration of Independence.

The Constitution was designed in part to provide for a limited government in which political power would be confined to proper uses. The Framers wanted to 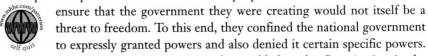 ensure that the government they were creating would not itself be a threat to freedom. To this end, they confined the national government to expressly granted powers and also denied it certain specific powers. Other prohibitions on government were later added to the Constitution in the form of stated guarantees of individual liberties: the Bill of Rights. The most significant constitutional provision for limited government, however, was a separation of powers among the three branches. The powers given to each branch enable it to act as a check on the exercise of power by the others, an arrangement that, during the nation's history, has, in fact, served as a barrier to abuses of power.

The Constitution, however, made no mention of how the powers and limits of government were to be judged in practice. In its historic ruling in *Marbury* v. *Madison*, the Supreme Court assumed the authority to review the constitutionality of legislative and executive actions and to declare them unconstitutional and thus invalid.

The Framers of the Constitution respected the idea of self-government but distrusted popular majorities. They designed a government that they felt would temper popular opinion and slow its momentum, so that the public's "true interest" (which includes a regard for the rights and interests of the minority) would guide public policy. Different methods were established to select members of the House of Representatives and of the Senate, the president, and federal judges as a means of separating political power from momentary and unreflecting majorities.

Since the adoption of the Constitution, however, the public has gradually assumed more direct control of its representatives, particularly through measures affecting the way in which officeholders are chosen. Presidential voting (linked to the Electoral College), direct election of senators, and primary elections are among the devices aimed at strengthening the majority's influence. These developments are rooted in the idea, deeply held by ordinary Americans, that the people must have substantial direct control of their government if it is to serve their real interests.

MAJOR CONCEPTS

Antifederalists

Bill of Rights

checks and balances

constitution

constitutional democracy

delegates

democracy

denials of power

Electoral College

electoral votes

Federalists

grants of power

Great Compromise

inalienable (natural) rights

judicial review

limited government

New Jersey (small-state) Plan

North-South Compromise

primary elections

representative democracy

republic

self-government

separated institutions sharing power

separation of powers

trustees

tyranny of the majority

Virginia (large-state) Plan

SUGGESTED READINGS AND WEB SITES

Beard, Charles S. *An Economic Interpretation of the Constitution.* New York: Macmillan, 1941. Argues that the Framers had selfish economic interests uppermost in mind when they wrote the Constitution.

Farrand, Max. *The Records of the Federal Convention of 1787.* New Haven, Conn.: Yale University Press, 1966. A four-volume work that includes all the important records of the Philadelphia convention.

Federalist Papers. Many editions, including a one-volume paperback version edited by Isaac Kramnick (New York: Penguin, 1987). A series of essays written by Alexander Hamilton, James Madison, and John Jay under the pseudonym Publius. The essays, published in a New York newspaper in 1787–1788, explain the Constitution and support its ratification.

Hardin, Russell. *Liberalism, Constitutionalism, and Democracy*. New York: Oxford University Press, 1999. Analysis of the great ideas that underlie the Constitution.

Levin, Daniel. *Representing Popular Sovereignty*. Albany: State University of New York Press, 1999. An analysis of how the Constitution is reflected in popular culture.

Sheldon, Garrett Ward. *The Political Philosophy of James Madison*. Baltimore: Johns Hopkins University Press, 2000. A synthesis of James Madison's political philosophy in the context of the social and political history of his day.

Tocqueville, Alexis de. *Democracy in America*, vols. 1 and 2, ed. J. P. Mayer. New York: Doubleday/Anchor, 1969. A classic analysis (originally published 1835–1840) of American democracy by an insightful French observer.

http://www.nara.gov   The National Archives site includes an in-depth look at the history of the Declaration of Independence.

http://odur.let.rug.nl/~usa/P/aj7/about/bio/jackxx.htm   A site that focuses on Andrew Jackson and his role in shaping U.S. politics.

http://www.yale.edu/lawweb/avalon/constpap.htm   Includes documents on the roots of the Constitution, the American Revolution, and the Constitutional Convention.

http://www.yale.edu/lawweb/avalon/presiden/jeffpap.htm   A site that includes the papers of Thomas Jefferson. His autobiography is among the available materials.

READING 2

The Mischiefs of Faction

JAMES MADISON

Introduction

James Madison wrote *Federalist* No. 10 during the debate over ratification of the Constitution. It has been described as the finest political essay ever written by an American. In it, Madison argues that a "republican" form of government is the surest protection against abuse of political power. He argues that people naturally and passionately pursue their self-interest and, therefore, that power placed directly in the hands of a popular majority is likely to be directed against minority interests. Madison's solution, as was described in Chapter 2, is a constitutional system where popular influence works through, and is moderated by, representative institutions.

Among the numerous advantages promised by a well-constructed Union, none deserves to be more accurately developed than its tendency to break and control the violence of faction. . . .

By a faction I understand a number of citizens, whether amounting to a majority or minority of the whole, who are united and actuated by some common impulse of passion, or of interest, adverse to the rights of other citizens, or to the permanent and aggregate interests of the community.

There are two methods of curing the mischiefs of faction: the one, by removing its causes; the other, by controlling its effects.

There are again two methods of removing the causes of faction: the one, by destroying the liberty which is essential to its existence; the other, by giving to every citizen the same opinions, the same passions, and the same interests.

It could never be more truly said than of the first remedy that it was worse than the disease. Liberty is to faction what air is to fire, an ailment without which it instantly expires. But it could not be a less folly to abolish liberty, which is essential to political life, because it nourishes faction than it would be to wish the annihilation of air, which is essential to animal life, because it imparts to fire its destructive agency.

The second expedient is as impracticable as the first would be unwise. As long as the reason of man continues fallible, and he is at liberty to exercise it, different opinions will be formed. As long as the connection subsists between his reason and his self-love, his opinions and his passions will have a reciprocal influence on each other; and the former will be objects to which the latter will attach themselves. The diversity in the faculties of men, from which the rights of property originate, is not less an insuperable obstacle to a uniformity of interest. The protection of these faculties is the first object of government. From the protection of different and unequal faculties of acquiring property, the possession of different degrees and kinds of property immediately results; and from the influence of these on the sentiments and views of the respective proprietors ensues a division of the society into different interests and parties.

The latent causes of faction are thus sown in the nature of man; and we see them everywhere brought into different degrees of activity, according to the different circumstances of civil society. A zeal for different opinions concerning religion, concerning government, and many other points, as well of speculation as of practice; an attachment to different leaders ambitiously contending for pre-eminence and power; or to persons of other descriptions whose fortunes have been interesting to the human passions, have, in turn, divided mankind into parties, inflamed them with mutual animosity, and rendered them much more disposed to vex and oppress each other than to cooperate for their common good. So strong is this propensity of mankind to fall into mutual animosities that where no substantial occasion presents itself the most frivolous and fanciful distinctions have been sufficient to kindle their unfriendly passions and excite their most violent conflicts. But the most common and durable source of factions has been the various and unequal distribution of property. Those who hold and those who are without property have ever formed distinct interests in society. . . .

The inference to which we are brought is that the *causes* of faction cannot be removed and that relief is only to be sought in the means of controlling its *effects*.

If a faction consists of less than a majority, relief is supplied by the republican principle, which enables the majority to defeat its sinister views by regular vote. . . . When a majority is included in a faction, the form of popular government, on the other hand, enables it to sacrifice to its ruling passion or interest both the public good and the rights of other citizens. To secure the public good and private rights against the danger of such a faction, and at the same time to preserve the spirit and the form of popular government, is then the great object to which our inquiries are directed.

By what means is this object attainable? Evidently by one of two only. Either the existence of the same passion or interest in a majority at the same time must be prevented, or the majority, having such coexistent passion or interest, must be rendered, by their number and local situation, unable to concert and carry into effect schemes of oppression. If the impulse and the opportunity be suffered to coincide, we well know that neither moral nor religious motives can be relied on as an adequate control. They are not found to be such on the injustice and violence of individuals, and lose their efficacy in proportion to the number combined together, that is, in proportion as their efficacy becomes needful.

From this view of the subject it may be concluded that a pure democracy, by which I mean a society consisting of a small number of citizens, who assemble and administer the government in person, can admit of no cure for the mischiefs of faction. A common passion or interest will, in almost every case, be felt by a majority of the whole, a communication and concert results from the form of government itself; and there is nothing to check the inducements to sacrifice the weaker party or an obnoxious individual. Hence it is that such democracies have ever been spectacles of turbulence and contention; have ever been found incompatible with personal security or the rights of property; and have in general been as short in their lives as they have been violent in their deaths. . . .

A republic, by which I mean a government in which the scheme of representation takes place, opens a different prospect and promises the cure for which we are seeking. Let us examine the points in which it varies from pure democracy, and we shall comprehend both the nature of the cure and the efficacy which it must derive from the Union.

The two great points of difference between a democracy and a republic are: first, the delegation of the government, in the latter, to a small number of citizens elected by the rest; secondly, the greater number of citizens and greater sphere of country over which the latter may be extended.

The effect of the first difference is, on the one hand, to refine and enlarge the public views by passing them through the medium of a chosen body of citizens, whose wisdom may best discern the true interest of their country and whose patriotism and love of justice will be least likely to sacrifice it to temporary or partial considerations. Under such a regulation it may well happen that the public voice, pronounced by the representatives of the people, will be more consonant to the public good than if pronounced by the people themselves, convened for the purpose. . . .

The other point of difference is the greater number of citizens and extent of territory which may be brought within the compass of republican than of democratic government; and it is this circumstance principally which renders factious combinations less to be dreaded in the former than in the latter. The smaller the society, the fewer probably will be the distinct parties and interests composing it; the fewer the distinct parties and interests, the more frequently will a majority be found of the same party; and the smaller the number of individuals composing a majority, and the smaller the compass within which they are placed, the more easily will they concert and execute their plans of oppression. Extend the sphere and you take in a greater variety of parties and interests; you make it less probable that a majority of the whole will have a common motive to invade the rights of other citizens; or if such a common motive exists, it will be more difficult for all who feel it to discover their own strength and to act in unison with each other. . . .

Hence, it clearly appears that the same advantage which a republic has over a democracy in controlling the effects of faction is enjoyed by a large over a small republic—is enjoyed by the Union over the States composing it.

SOURCE: James Madison, *Federalist* No. 10.
James Madison, the fourth president of the United States, has been called the "Father of the Constitution."

CHAPTER THREE

Federalism

The question of the relation of the states to the federal government is the
cardinal question of our Constitutional system. It cannot be settled by the
opinion of one generation, because it is a question of growth, and each
successive stage of our political and economic development gives
it a new aspect, makes it a new question.

WOODROW WILSON[1]

SENATE MAJORITY leader Trent Lott declared the legislation a triumph for those who believe that the answers to America's problems are more likely to be found in Albany, Sacramento, and Jackson than in Washington. Senator Daniel Patrick Moynihan, an outspoken critic of the legislation, called it "the most brutal act of social policy since Reconstruction." He claimed that within a decade the legislation would push more than a million children into poverty.[2]

At issue was the nation's program of assistance for poor families and whether the program would be directed by the national government or the states. Since the 1930s, the program had been run out of Washington as an entitlement policy, which meant that every American family who met the eligibility criteria was entitled to assistance. For many liberal Democrats, it was the cornerstone of the idea that no needy American family, wherever it resided, would be denied help. Individual states had some leeway in deciding the amount of support a needy family would receive each month, but they had to participate in the program and contribute to its funding.

The new legislation ended this federal guarantee of cash assistance, replacing it with a system of cash grants to the states, which would assume responsibility for caring for welfare recipients and getting them into jobs. The legislation fulfilled the long-held desire of conservative Republicans to reduce welfare dependency and move welfare recipients into tax-paying jobs. It also met their goal of reducing the power of the federal government. Under the new program, a state would have to support a needy family for five years but could deny benefits if, after two years, an able-bodied adult refused to accept a job or job training. And after five years, a state could unconditionally deny benefits to poor families.

The 1996 Welfare Reform Act is one of thousands of controversies during American history that have hinged on whether national or state authority should prevail. Americans possess what amounts to dual citizenship: they are citizens both of the United States and of the state where they reside. The American political system is a *federal system*, one in which constitutional authority is divided between a national government and state governments: each is assumed to derive its powers directly from the people and therefore to have sovereignty (final authority) over the policy responsibilities assigned to it. The federal system consists of nation *and* states, indivisible and yet separate.[3]

This chapter on American constitutionalism focuses on federalism. The nature of the relationship between the nation and the states was the most pressing issue when the Constitution was written in 1787, and this chapter describes how it helped shape the Constitution. The chapter's closing sections discuss how federalism has changed during the nation's history and conclude with an overview of contemporary federalism. The main points presented in the chapter are the following:

* *The power of government must be equal to its responsibilities. The Constitution was needed because the nation's preceding system (under the Articles of Confederation) was too weak to accomplish its expected goals, particularly those of a strong defense and an integrated economy.*
* *Federalism—the Constitution's division of governing authority between two levels, nation and states—was the result of political bargaining.*
* *Federalism is not a fixed principle for allocating power between the national and state governments, but a principle that has changed over the course of time in response to changing political needs.*
* *Contemporary federalism tilts toward national authority, reflecting the increased interdependence of American society. However, there is a current trend toward reducing the scope of federal authority.*

FEDERALISM: NATIONAL AND STATE SOVEREIGNTY

The delegates to the Philadelphia convention in 1787 included many of the nation's most prominent leaders, such as George Washington and Benjamin

Franklin. Not all of America's top leaders were at the convention, however, and many of them were steadfastly opposed to a strong national government. When rumors circulated that the convention would propose a new form of government rather than an amended Articles of Confederation, Patrick Henry, an ardent supporter of state-centered government, said that he "smelt a rat." After the convention had adjourned, he realized that his fears were justified. "Who authorized them," he asked, "to speak the language of 'We, the People,' instead of 'We, the States'?"

The question—"people or states?"—was dictated by the experience with the Articles of Confederation. The government of the Articles (see Chapter 2) was a union of states rather than also of people. The result was an inherently weak national government, since its strength rested entirely on the states' willingness to cooperate. If they refused to contribute to the collective effort, the national government had no sure way to make them comply. Georgia and North Carolina, for example, contributed no money at all to the national treasury between 1781 and 1786, and the national government could do nothing more than implore them to pay a fair share of

Patrick Henry was a leading figure in the American Revolution ("Give me liberty or give me death!"). He later opposed ratification of the Constitution on grounds that the national government should be a union of states and not also of people.

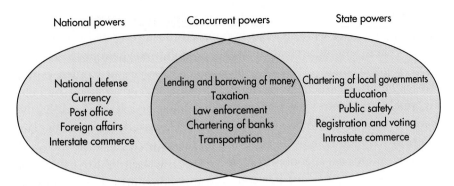

FIGURE 3-1 FEDERALISM AS A GOVERNING SYSTEM: EXAMPLES OF NATIONAL, STATE, AND CONCURRENT POWERS
The American federal system divides sovereignty between a national government and the state governments. Each is constitutionally protected in its existence and authority, even though their powers overlap in some cases.

the costs of defense, diplomacy, and other national policies. The only realistic solution was a government based on the people. If ordered to pay taxes, individuals would either do so or face consequences—imprisonment or confiscation of property—that most of them would choose to avoid.

Although the need for a national government based directly on the people was therefore a goal of the writers of the Constitution, they also wanted to preserve the states as governing bodies. When Virginia's George Mason said he would never agree to a union that abolished the states, he was speaking for virtually all the delegates. The Philadelphia convention thereby devised a governing system that came to be known as **federalism.** Federalism is the division of **sovereignty,** or ultimate governing authority, between a national government and regional (that is, state) governments. Each directly governs the people and derives its powers from them.

American federalism is basically a system for dividing authority between sovereign national and state governments (see Figure 3-1). The system gives states the power to address local matters in separate ways, thus providing for a responsiveness to local values and differences. At the same time, federalism gives the national government the power to decide matters of broad national scope on a uniform basis. In practice, there is some overlap between state and national action, but there is also a division of responsibilities. The national government has primary responsibility for national defense and the currency, among other things, while the states have primary responsibilities for such policy areas as public education and police protection. The national and state governments also have some concurrent powers (that is, powers exercised over the same areas of policy); for example, each has the power to raise taxes and borrow money.

A federal system is different from a **confederacy,** which is the type of government established by the Articles. A confederacy is a union where the states alone are sovereign. The authority of the central government is derived from the states, which can, at will, redefine the central government's authority. Federalism is also different from a **unitary system,** in which sovereignty is vested solely in the national government. In a unitary system, all regional and local governing units are subject to national authority. The people are citizens or subjects only of the national government, and the other governments derive their authority from the national government, which can, in theory at least, abolish them or redefine their authority.

In a federal system, because the national and state governments are both sovereign, each has powers that are not subject to the other's discretion. Moreover, each is protected constitutionally in its existence and from undue interference by the other in the conduct of its lawful affairs.

Federalism was invented in America in 1787. It was different not only from a confederate or unitary system but also from any form of government the world had known. The ancient Greek city-states and the medieval Hanseatic League were confederacies. The governments of Europe were unitary in form. The United States of America would be the first nation to be governed through a federal system.

The Argument for Federalism

Unlike many other decisions made at the Philadelphia convention, federalism had no clear basis in political theory. Federalism was a practical necessity: there was a need for a stronger national government and yet the states existed and were intent on retaining their sovereignty.

Nevertheless, the Framers developed arguments for the superiority of federalism. Federalism, they claimed, would protect liberty, moderate the power of government, and provide the foundation for a strong and energetic national government.

PROTECTING LIBERTY Theorists such as Locke and Montesquieu had not proposed a division of power between national and local authorities as a means of protecting liberty. Nevertheless, the Framers came to look upon federalism as a component of the Constitution's system of checks and balances (see Chapter 2). Alexander Hamilton argued in *Federalist* No. 28 that the American people could shift their loyalties back and forth between

HOW THE UNITED STATES COMPARES

Federal versus Unitary Governments

Federalism involves the division of sovereignty between a national government and subnational (such as state) governments. It was invented in 1787 in order to maintain the preexisting American states while establishing an effective central government. Since then other countries have established *federal* governments, but most countries have *unitary* governments, in which all sovereignty is vested in a national government. In some cases, countries have developed hybrid versions. Great Britain's government is formally unitary, but Parliament has granted some autonomy to regions. Mexico's system is formally federal, but in actuality power is concentrated in the national government.

Country	Form of Government
Canada	Federal
France	Unitary
Germany	Federal
Great Britain	Modified unitary
Italy	Modified unitary
Japan	Unitary
Mexico	Modified federal
United States	Federal
Sweden	Unitary

the national and state governments in order to keep each under control. "If [the people's] rights are invaded by either," Hamilton wrote, "they can make use of the other as the instrument of redress."

MODERATING THE POWER OF GOVERNMENT   To the Antifederalists (opponents of the Constitution), the sacrifice of states' power to the nation was as unwise as it was unnecessary. They argued that a distant national government could never serve the people's interests as well as the states could. Madison took issue with their argument. In *Federalist* No. 10, Madison contended that whether a government serves the common good is a function not of its size but of the range of interests that share political power. The problem with a smaller republic, Madison claimed, is that it is likely to have a dominant faction—whether it be large landholders, financiers, an impoverished majority, or some other group—that is strong enough to take full control of government, using this power to advance its selfish interests. A large republic is less likely to have such an all-powerful faction. If financiers are strong in one area of a large republic, they are likely to be weaker elsewhere, and the same will be true of other interests. By this reasoning, Madison concluded that political control in a large republic could not be won by a single interest but would require a joining of interests, each of which would be forced to limit its demands and to respect the interests of others. "Extend the sphere," said Madison, "and you take in a greater variety of parties and interests; you make it less probable that a majority of the whole will have a common motive to invade the rights of other citizens." (Madison's argument has historical support in the American case. The severest forms of repression, such as enforced slavery and segregation, have been perpetrated by the state governments.)

STRENGTHENING THE UNION The most telling argument in 1787 for a federal system, however, was that it would overcome the deficiencies of the Articles. The Articles had numerous flaws (including the lack of a strong executive and a judiciary independent of the state courts) and two of them were fatal: the government had the power neither to tax nor to regulate commerce.

Under the Articles, Congress was given responsibility for national defense but was not granted the power to tax, and so it had to rely on the states for the money to maintain an army and navy. During the first six years under the Articles, Congress asked the states for $12 million but received only $3 million—not even enough to pay the interest on Revolutionary War debts. By 1786 the national government was so desperate for funds that it sold the navy's ships and had fewer than a thousand soldiers in uniform—this at a time when England had an army in Canada and Spain occupied Florida.

Congress was also expected to shape a national economy, yet it was powerless to do so because the Articles forbade interference with the states' commerce policies. States imposed trade barriers among themselves. Connecticut placed a higher tariff on finished goods from Massachusetts than it did on the same goods shipped from England. New Jersey imposed a duty on foreign-made goods shipped from other states. New York responded by taxing goods from New Jersey shipped through New York ports.

The Articles of Confederation showed the fallacy of the adage "That government is best which governs least." The consequences of an overly weak authority were abundantly clear: public disorder, economic chaos, and inadequate defense.

The Powers of the Nation

The Philadelphia convention met to strengthen the powers of the national government. The delegates had not been sent to determine how state government should be structured. Accordingly, the U.S. Constitution focuses on the lawful authority of the national government, which is provided through *enumerated* and *implied powers*. Authority that is not in this way granted to the national government is left—or "reserved"—to the states. Thus the states have *reserved powers*.

ENUMERATED POWERS   Article I of the Constitution grants to Congress seventeen **enumerated (expressed) powers.** These powers were intended by the Framers to be the basis for a government strong enough to forge a union that was secure in its defense and stable in its commerce. Congress's powers to regulate commerce among the states, to create a national currency, and to borrow money, for example, would provide a foundation for a sound national economy. Its power to tax, combined with its authority to declare war and establish an army and navy, would enable it to provide for the common defense.

The writers of the Constitution recognized that the lawful exercise of national authority would at times conflict with the actions of the states. In such instances, national law was intended to prevail. Article VI of the Constitution grants this dominance in the so-called **supremacy clause,** which provides that "the laws of the United States . . . shall be the supreme law of the land."

IMPLIED POWERS   The Framers of the Constitution also recognized that an overly narrow definition of national authority would result in a government incapable of adapting to change. Under the Articles of Confederation, Congress was strictly limited to those powers expressly granted to it, inhibiting its ability to respond effectively to the country's changing needs after the Revolutionary War. Concerned that the enumerated powers by themselves might be too restrictive of national authority, the Framers added the **"necessary and proper" clause,** or, as it later came to be known, the **elastic clause.** Article I, section 8, gives Congress the power "to make all laws which shall be necessary and proper for carrying into execution the foregoing [enumerated] powers." This grant gave the national government **implied powers:** the authority to take action that is not expressly authorized by the Constitution but that supports actions that are so authorized.

The Powers of the States

The Framers' preference for a sovereign national government was not shared in 1787 by all Americans. Although Antifederalists recognized a need to strengthen defense and interstate commerce, they feared the consequences of a strong central government. The interests of the people of New Hampshire were not identical to those of Georgians or Pennsylvanians, and the Antifederalists argued that only state-centered government would protect and preserve this *diversity.*

The Federalists responded by asserting that the national government would have no interest in submerging the states.[4] The national government would take responsibility for establishing a strong defense and for promoting a sound economy, while the states would retain nearly all other governing functions, including oversight of public morals, education, and safety. The national government, James Madison said, would neither want these responsibilities nor have the competence to fulfill them.[5]

This argument did not persuade the Antifederalists that their fears of a powerful national government were unfounded. The supremacy and "necessary and proper" clauses were particularly worrisome, since they provided a constitutional basis for future expansions of national authority. Such concerns led to demands for a constitutional amendment that would protect the states against encroachment by the national government. Ratified in 1791 as the Tenth Amendment to the Constitution, it reads: "The powers not delegated to the United States by the Constitution, nor prohibited by it to the States, are reserved to the States." The states' powers under the U.S. Constitution are thus called **reserved powers.**

FEDERALISM IN HISTORICAL PERSPECTIVE

Since ratification of the Constitution two centuries ago, no aspect of it has provoked more frequent or bitter conflict than federalism. By establishing two levels of sovereign authority, the Constitution created competing centers of power and ambition, each of which was sure to claim disputed areas as belonging within its realm of authority.

Conflict between national and state authority was also ensured by the brevity of the Constitution. The Framers deliberately avoided detailed provisions, recognizing that brief phrases would give flexibility to the government they were creating. The document does not define what is meant by the "necessary and proper" clause, does not list any of the states' reserved powers, does not indicate whether the supremacy clause allows the states discretionary authority in areas where state and national responsibilities overlap, and does not indicate how *inter*state commerce (which the national government is empowered to regulate) differs from *intra*state commerce (which presumably is reserved for regulation by the states).

Not surprisingly, federalism has been a contentious and dynamic system, its development determined less by constitutional language than by the strength of contending interests and by the country's changing needs. Federalism can be viewed as having progressed through three historical eras, each of which has involved a different relationship between nation and states.

An Indestructible Union (1789–1865)

The issue during the first era, which lasted from the Constitution's beginnings in 1789 through the end of the Civil War in 1865, was the Union's survival. Given the state-centered history of America before the Constitution, it was inevitable that the states would dispute national policies that threatened their separate interests.

THE NATIONALIST VIEW: *McCULLOCH v. MARYLAND* A first dispute over federalism arose when President George Washington's secretary of the treasury, Alexander Hamilton, persuaded Congress to establish the First Bank of the United States, granting it a twenty-year charter. Opponents claimed the bank was unlawful since the Constitution did not explicitly authorize the creation of a national bank. Hamilton and his supporters claimed that because the federal government had constitutional authority to regulate currency, it had the "implied power" to establish a national bank.

When the bank's charter expired in 1811, Congress did not renew it, but, in 1816, Congress established the Second Bank of the United States over the objections of state and local bankers. Responding to their complaints, several states, including Maryland, attempted to drive the Second Bank of the United States out of existence by levying taxes on its operations

A first dispute over federalism was whether the Constitution allowed the creation of a Bank of the United States (shown here in an early nineteenth-century painting). The Constitution had a clause on the printing of currency but not on the establishment of a bank itself.

within their borders. Edwin McCulloch, who was head cashier of the U.S. Bank in Maryland, refused to pay the Maryland tax, and the resulting dispute reached the Supreme Court.

John Marshall, the chief justice of the Supreme Court, was, like Hamilton, a strong nationalist, and in *McCulloch* v. *Maryland* (1819) the Court ruled decisively in favor of national authority. It was reasonable, Marshall concluded, to infer that a government with powers to tax, borrow money, and regulate commerce could establish a bank in order to exercise those powers properly. Marshall's argument was a clear statement of *implied powers*—the idea that, through the "necessary and proper" clause, the national government's powers extend beyond a narrow reading of its enumerated powers.

Marshall also addressed the meaning of the Constitution's supremacy clause. The state of Maryland argued that it had the sovereign authority to tax the national bank even if the bank was a legal entity. The Supreme Court rejected Maryland's position, concluding that valid national law prevailed over conflicting state law. Because the national government had the power to create the bank, it could also protect the bank from actions by the states, such as taxation, that might destroy it.[6]

The *McCulloch* decision served as precedent for future assertions of national authority, including a second landmark decision by the Marshall Court. In *Gibbons* v. *Ogden* (1824), the Court ruled on the power of Congress to regulate commerce. The state of New York had granted a monopoly to Aaron Ogden to operate a ferry between New York and New Jersey. When Thomas Gibbons set up a competing ferry under a federal coastal licensing agreement, Ogden tried to prevent Gibbons from operating it. Marshall invalidated the New York monopoly, saying it intruded on Congress's power to regulate commerce among the states. Going further, Marshall ruled that Congress's power extended *into* a state when commerce between two or more states was at issue.[7]

Marshall's opinions asserted that legitimate uses of national power took precedence over state authority and that the "necessary and proper" clause and the commerce clause were broad grants of national power. As a nationalist, Marshall was providing the U.S. government the legal justification for expanding its power in ways that fostered the development of the nation as a nation rather than as a collection of states. This constitutional vision was of utmost significance. As Justice Oliver Wendell Holmes, Jr., noted a century later, the Union could not have survived if each state had been allowed to determine for itself the extent to which national authority restricted its actions.[8]

THE STATES'-RIGHTS VIEW: THE *DRED SCOTT* DECISION   Although John Marshall's rulings helped strengthen national authority, the issue of slavery posed a growing threat to the Union's survival. A resurgence of cotton farming in the early nineteenth century revived the South's flagging dependence on slaves and heightened white southerners' fears that Congress might move to abolish slavery. Southerners consequently did what others have done throughout American history: they devised a constitutional argument to fit their political needs. John C. Calhoun of South Carolina argued that the Constitution had created "a government of states . . . not a government of individuals."[9] This line of reasoning led Calhoun to his famed "doctrine of nullification," which declared that each state had the constitutional right to nullify a national law.

In 1832 South Carolina invoked this doctrine, declaring "null and void" a tariff law that favored northern interests. President Andrew Jackson retorted that South Carolina's action was "incompatible with the existence of the Union," a position that was strengthened when Congress authorized Jackson to use military force against South Carolina. The state backed down when Congress agreed to amend the tariff act slightly.

The clash foreshadowed a confrontation of far greater scope and consequence: the Civil War. War between the states would not break out for another thirty years, but, in the interim, conflicts over states' rights intensified.[10] Westward expansion and immigration into the northern states were tilting power in Congress toward the free states, which increasingly signaled their determination to outlaw slavery in the United States at some future time. Attempts to find a compromise acceptable to both the North and the South were fruitless.

The Supreme Court's infamous *Dred Scott* decision exemplifies the conflict. Dred Scott, a slave, applied for his freedom when his master died, citing a federal law—the Missouri Compromise of 1820—that made slavery illegal in a free state or territory. Scott had lived in the North four years, but the Supreme Court in a 7–2 decision ruled that slaves were "property" and not "citizens" under the Constitution. The Court also invalidated the Missouri Compromise, declaring that Congress had no authority to outlaw slavery in any part of the United States.[11]

The *Dred Scott* decision outraged many northerners and contributed to a sectional split in the majority Democratic party that enabled the Republican Abraham Lincoln to win the presidency in 1860 with only 40 percent of the popular vote. Lincoln had campaigned for the gradual, compensated abolition of slavery. By the time he assumed office, seven southern states had already seceded from the Union. In justifying his decision to wage civil war on these states, Lincoln said, "The Union is older than the states." In 1865 the superior strength of the Union army settled by force the question of whether national authority would be binding on the states.

Dual Federalism and Laissez-Faire Capitalism (1865–1937)

Although the Civil War preserved the Union, new challenges to federalism were surfacing. Constitutional doctrine held that certain policy areas, such as interstate commerce and defense, were the clear and exclusive province of national authority, while other policy areas, such as public health and intrastate commerce, belonged clearly and exclusively to the states. This doctrine, known as **dual federalism,** was based on the idea that a precise separation of national and state authority was both possible and desirable. "The power which one possesses," said the Supreme Court, "the other does not."[12]

American society, however, was in the midst of changes that raised questions about the suitability of dual federalism as a governing concept. The Industrial Revolution had given rise to large business firms, which

The American Civil War was the bloodiest conflict the world had yet known. It was also the bloodiest by far in American history. The death toll—360,000 from the North and 250,000 from the South— exceeded that of the American war dead in World War I, World War II, the Korean War, and the Vietnam War combined.

were using their economic power to dominate markets and exploit workers. Government was the logical counterforce to this economic power. Which level of government—state or national—would regulate business?

JUDICIAL PROTECTION OF BUSINESS   For the most part, the answer was that neither level of government would be permitted to regulate business. The Supreme Court was dominated by adherents of the doctrine of laissez-faire capitalism (which holds that business should be "allowed to act" without interference), and they interpreted the Constitution in ways that frustrated government's attempts to regulate business activity. In 1886, for example, the Court decided that corporations were "persons" within the meaning of the Fourteenth Amendment, and thus their property rights were protected from substantial regulation by the states.[13]

The Court also weakened the national government's regulatory power by narrowly interpreting its commerce power. The Constitution's **commerce clause** says that Congress shall have the power "to regulate commerce" among the states but does not spell out the economic activities included in the grant of power. When the federal government invoked the Sherman Antitrust Act (1890) in an attempt to break up a monopoly on the manufacture of sugar, the Supreme Court blocked the action, claiming that interstate commerce covered only the "transportation" of goods, not their "manufacture."[14] Manufacturing was deemed part of intrastate commerce and thus, according to the dual federalism doctrine, subject to state regulation only. However, since the Court had previously decided that the states' regulatory powers were restricted by the Fourteenth Amendment, they were relatively powerless to control manufacturing activity.

Although the national government subsequently made some headway in business regulation, the Supreme Court remained an obstacle. An example is the case of *Hammer* v. *Dagenhart* (1918), which arose from a 1916 federal act that prohibited the interstate shipment of goods produced by child labor. The act was popular because factory owners were exploiting children, working them for long hours at low pay. Citing the Tenth Amendment, the Court invalidated the law, ruling that factory practices could be regulated only by the states.[15] However, in an earlier case, *Lochner* v. *New York* (1905), the Court had prevented a state from regulating labor practices, concluding that such action was a violation of firms' property rights.[16]

In effect, the Supreme Court had denied both Congress and the states the authority to decide economic issues. As the constitutional scholars Alfred Kelly and Winifred Harbison have concluded, "No more complete perversion of the principles of effective federal government can be imagined."[17]

NATIONAL AUTHORITY PREVAILS   Judicial supremacy in the economic sphere ended abruptly in 1937. For nearly a decade, the United States had been mired in the Great Depression, which President Franklin D. Roosevelt's New Deal was designed to alleviate. The Supreme Court, however, had ruled much of the New Deal's economic recovery legislation to be unconstitutional. A constitutional crisis of historic proportions seemed inevitable until the Court suddenly reversed its position. In the process, American federalism was fundamentally and forever changed.

The Great Depression revealed clearly that Americans had become a national community with national economic needs. By the 1930s, more than half the population lived in cities (only 20 percent did so in 1860), and more than ten million workers were employed by industry (only one million were so employed in 1860). Urban workers were typically dependent on landlords for their housing, on farmers and grocers for their food, and on corporations for their jobs. Farmers were more independent, but they,

Between 1865 and 1937, the Supreme Court's rulings severely restricted national power. Narrowly interpreting Congress's constitutional power to regulate commerce, the Court forbade Congress to regulate child labor and other aspects of manufacturing.

too, were increasingly a part of a larger economic network. Their income depended on market prices and shipping and equipment costs.[18]

This economic interdependence meant that no area of the economy was immune if things went wrong. When the depression hit in 1929, its effects could not be contained. A decline in spending was followed by a drop in production, a loss of jobs, unpaid rents and grocery bills, and a shrinking market for foodstuffs, which led to a further decline in spending and so on, creating a relentless downward spiral. At the depths of the Great Depression, one-fourth of the nation's work force was unemployed.

The states by tradition had responsibility for welfare, but they were nearly penniless because of declining tax revenues and the growing ranks of poor people. The New Deal programs offered a way out of the crisis; for example, the National Industry Recovery Act (NIRA) of 1933 called for a massive public works program to create jobs and for coordinated action by major industries. However, the New Deal was opposed by economic conservatives (who accused Roosevelt of leading the nation down the road to communism) and by justices of the Supreme Court. In *Schechter* v. *United States* (1935), the Court invalidated the Recovery Act by a 5–4 vote, ruling that it usurped powers reserved to the states.[19]

Frustrated by the Court, Roosevelt in 1937 proposed his famed "Court-packing" plan. Roosevelt recommended that Congress enact legislation that would permit an additional justice to be appointed to the Court whenever a seated member passed the age of seventy. The number of justices would increase, and Roosevelt's appointees would presumably be more sympathetic to his programs. Roosevelt's scheme was resisted by Congress, but the controversy ended with "the switch in time that saved nine," when, for reasons that have never become fully clear, Justice Owen Roberts abandoned his opposition to Roosevelt's policies and thus gave the president a 5–4 majority on the Court.

Within months, the Court upheld the 1935 National Labor Relations Act, which gave employees the right to organize and bargain collectively.[20] In passing the act, Congress had argued that labor-management disputes disrupt the nation's economy and therefore can be regulated through the commerce clause. In upholding the act, the Supreme Court in effect granted Congress authority to apply its commerce powers broadly.[21] During this same period, the Court also loosened its restrictions on Congress's use of its taxing and spending powers.[22]

In effect, the Supreme Court had finally recognized the obvious: that an industrial economy is not confined by state boundaries and must be subject to some level of national regulation if it is to serve the nation's needs and interests.[23] It was a principle that business itself also increasingly accepted. The nation's banking industry, for example, was saved in the 1930s from almost complete collapse by the creation of a federal regulatory agency, the Federal Deposit Insurance Corporation (FDIC). By insuring depositors' savings against loss, the FDIC gave depositors the confidence to keep their money in banks, enabling many banks to remain solvent despite the depression.

FEDERALISM TODAY

Since the 1930s, the relation of the nation to the states has changed so fundamentally that dual federalism is no longer even a roughly accurate description of the American situation.[24]

An understanding of the nature of federalism today requires a recognition of two countervailing trends. The first is a long-term *expansion* of national authority that began in the 1930s and continued for the next half century. The national government now operates in many policy areas that were once almost exclusively within the control of states and localities. The national government does not dominate these policy areas, but it does have a significant role. Much of this influence stems from social welfare policies that were enacted in the 1960s as part of President Lyndon Johnson's Great Society program, which included initiatives in health care, public housing, nutrition, welfare, urban development, and other areas reserved previously to states and localities.

The second trend is more recent and involves a partial *contraction* of national authority. Known as "devolution," the recent trend involves "the passing down" of authority from the national government to the state and local levels. Devolution has reversed the decades-long increase in federal authority, but only in some areas and then only to a modest degree.

Stated differently, the national government's policy authority has expanded greatly since the 1930s, even though that authority has been reduced somewhat in recent years.

We will start with an explanation of the first of these trends: the expansion of federal authority since the New Deal era.

Interdependency and Intergovernmental Relations

Interdependency is a primary reason national authority has increased dramatically in the twentieth century. Modern systems of transportation, commerce, and communication transcend local and state boundaries. These systems are national, even international, in scope, which means that problems affecting Americans in one part of the country are likely also to affect Americans living elsewhere. This situation has required Washington to assume a larger policy role: national problems ordinarily require national solutions.

This situation has also encouraged national, state, and local policymakers to work together to solve policy problems. This collaborative effort has been described as **cooperative federalism.**[25] The difference between this system of federalism and the older dual federalism has been likened to the difference between a marble cake, whose levels flow together, and a layer cake, whose levels are separate.[26]

Cooperative federalism is based on shared policy responsibilities rather than sharply divided ones. An example is Medicaid, which provides health care for the poor. The program is jointly funded by the national and state governments, operates within eligibility standards set by the national government, and gives states some latitude in determining the benefits recipients receive. The Medicaid program is not an isolated example. There are literally hundreds of policy programs today that are run jointly by

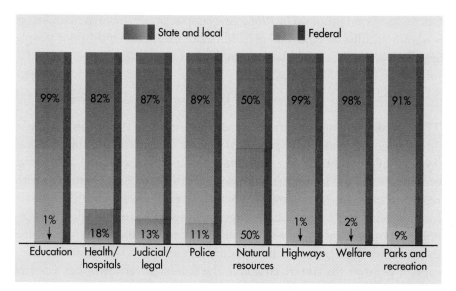

FIGURE 3-2 FEDERAL AND STATE/LOCAL GOVERNMENT EMPLOYEES, AS PERCENTAGE OF ALL GOVERNMENT EMPLOYEES WHO WORK IN SELECTED POLICY AREAS
Although federal authority has reached into areas traditionally dominated by the state governments, state and local governments still dominate many policy areas. One indicator is the high percentage of government employees in selected areas who work for state or local governments. Source: U.S. Bureau of the Census, 2000.

the national and state governments. In many cases, local governments are also involved.

Cooperative federalism should not be interpreted to indicate that the states are now powerless and dependent. States have retained most of their traditional authority. In fact, the states have a larger influence than Washington in many policy areas (see Figure 3-2). Nearly 95 percent of the funding for public schools, for example, is provided by states and localities, which also set most of the education standards, from teachers' qualifications to course requirements to the length of the school day. Moreover, the policy areas dominated by the states—such as education, law enforcement, and transportation—tend to be those that have the greatest impact on people's daily lives. Finally, contrary to what many Americans might think, state and local governments have nearly six times as many employees as the federal government.

Nevertheless, the federal government's involvement in policy areas traditionally reserved for the states has increased its policy influence and has diminished state-to-state policy differences.[27] Before the enactment of the federal Medicaid program in 1965, for example, poor people in many states were not entitled to government-paid health care. Now most poor people are eligible, regardless of where in the United States they live.

Government Revenues and Intergovernmental Relations

The interdependence of different sectors of modern American society is one of two factors that have propelled a larger federal role in domestic policy. The other is the federal government's superior taxing and borrowing capacity. States and localities are in an inherently competitive situation with regard to taxation. A state or locality cannot raise taxes very high without losing residents to a place where taxes are lower. The result is that the federal government raises more tax revenues than do all fifty states and the thousands of local governments combined (see Figure 3-3). Moreover, because it controls the American dollar, the federal government has a nearly unlimited ability to borrow money to cover its deficits.

FISCAL FEDERALISM   The federal government's revenue-raising advantage has helped make money the basis for many of the relations between the national government and the states and localities. **Fiscal federalism** refers to the expenditure of federal funds on programs run in part through state and local government.[28] The federal government provides some or all the money for certain programs through **grants-in-aid** (cash payments) to states and localities, which then administer the programs.

The pattern of federal assistance to states and localities during the last four decades is shown in Figure 3-4. Federal grants-in-aid increased tenfold

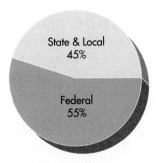

FIGURE 3-3   FEDERAL, STATE, AND LOCAL SHARES OF GOVERNMENT REVENUE
The federal government raises more revenues than all state and local governments combined. Source: U.S. Department of Commerce.

during this period. The sharpest rise occurred in the 1960s and early 1970s as a result of President Johnson's Great Society programs. Even at the height of the New Deal, federal aid had accounted for less than 10 percent of state and local spending. With Johnson's Great Society, however, the figure rose above 20 percent and has remained in that range ever since. In other words, roughly one in every five dollars spent by local and state governments in recent decades was raised not by them, but by the government in Washington.

Cash grants to states and localities have extended Washington's influence over policy.[29] Through the funds it provides and the conditions it attaches to the use of those funds, Washington affects the policy choices of state and local governments. Presidents and members of Congress have used cash grants as inducements to state and local officials to establish programs they favor. State and local governments can reject grants-in-aid, but if they accept one, they must spend it in the specified ways. And since most grants require states to contribute matching funds, the federal programs in effect determine how states will use some of their own tax dollars.

Nevertheless, federal grants-in-aid also serve the policy interests of state and local officials. They have often complained that federal grants

Texas Attorney General John Cornya speaks at a gathering of federal, state, and local law enforcement officials. Cooperative federalism brings together officials from all levels of government in joint efforts to solve common problems.

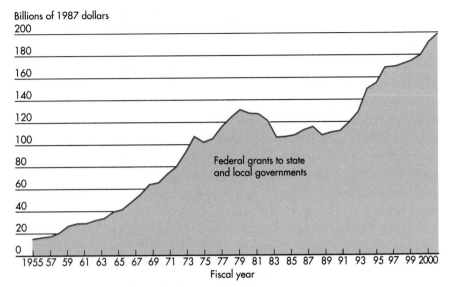

FIGURE 3-4   FEDERAL GRANTS TO STATE AND LOCAL
GOVERNMENTS IN CONSTANT (1987) DOLLARS, 1955–2000
Federal aid to states and localities has increased dramatically since the 1950s.
Source: U.S. Bureau of the Census.

contain too many restrictions and infringe too much on their authority, but
they have been eager to get the money, since it permits them to offer services they could not otherwise provide. An example is a 1994 federal grant
program that has enabled local governments to put seventy-five thousand
additional police officers on the streets.

CATEGORICAL AND BLOCK GRANTS   State and local governments
receive two major types of assistance, categorical grants and block grants,
which are differentiated by the extent to which Washington defines the
conditions of their use.

Categorical grants are the more restrictive; they can be used only for
a designated activity. An example is funds directed for use in school-lunch
programs. These funds can be used only in support of school lunches; they
cannot be diverted for other school purposes, such as the purchase of textbooks or the hiring of teachers. Block grants are less restrictive. The federal government specifies the general area in which the funds must be used,
but state and local officials select the specific projects. A block grant
targeted for the health area, for example, might give state and local officials

leeway in deciding whether to use the money on hospital construction, medical equipment, or some other health care activity.

State and local officials have naturally preferred federal money that comes with fewer strings attached, so they have favored block grants. On the other hand, members of Congress have at times strongly preferred categorical grants, since this form of assistance gives them more control over how state and local officials will spend federal funds.[30] Recently, however, officials at all levels have looked to block grants as the key to a more workable form of federalism. This tendency is part of a larger trend—that of "devolution."

A New Federalism: Devolution

Devolution is the idea that American federalism will be improved by a shift in authority from the federal government to the state and local governments. Devolution is reshaping American federalism and is attributable to both practical and political developments.

BUDGETARY PRESSURES AND PUBLIC OPINION   As a practical matter, the growth in federal assistance had slowed by the early 1980s. The federal government was facing huge budget deficits, and large new grants-in-aid to states and localities were not feasible.

As budgetary pressures intensified, relations among national, state, and local officials became increasingly strained. An increase in unfunded mandates (federal programs that require action by the states but that provide no funds to pay for it) and cuts in some grant programs had forced states and localities to pay an increasingly larger share of the costs of joint programs. As they raised taxes or cut other services to meet the costs, taxpayer anger intensified. Some of the grant programs, such as AFDC, food stamps, and housing subsidies, had not been very popular before the budget crunch and now came under even heavier criticism.

By the early 1990s, American federalism was positioned for a major change. Two decades earlier, three-fourths of Americans had expressed confidence in Washington's ability to govern effectively. Less than half of the public now held this view. A 1993 CBS News/New York Times survey indicated that 69 percent of Americans believed that "the federal government creates more problems than it solves."

THE REPUBLICAN REVOLUTION   When the Republican party scored a decisive victory in the 1994 congressional elections, Newt Gingrich declared that "1960s-style federalism is dead." The Republican

★ STATES IN THE NATION ★

Federal Grants-in-Aid as a Percentage of Total State Revenue

Federal assistance accounts for a significant share of state revenue, but the state-to-state variation is considerable. Louisiana is at one extreme: 34.6 percent of its total revenue comes from federal grants. Nevada is at the other extreme: only 14.5 percent of its revenue comes from federal assistance. Ironically, states in the South, where anti-Washington sentiment is relatively high, tend to get a larger percentage of their revenue through federal grants than most other states do. Many of the grant programs are designed to assist people with low incomes, and poverty is more widespread in the South than in other regions. Moreover, southern states have traditionally provided fewer government services, and federal grants therefore constitute a larger proportion of their state budgets.

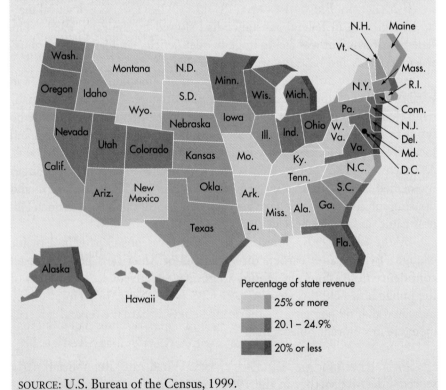

Percentage of state revenue

- 25% or more
- 20.1 – 24.9%
- 20% or less

SOURCE: U.S. Bureau of the Census, 1999.

majority called for sharp cutbacks in federal grant-in-aid programs, particularly in the welfare area. Republicans also proposed to lump dozens of categorical grants into a few block grants, thus giving states more control of how money would be spent.

That Republicans would lead the move to a more decentralized form of federalism was no surprise. Although both parties had initiated expansions of federal authority, Republicans had more often questioned the overall result. Republican presidents Richard Nixon, Ronald Reagan, and George Bush all advocated some version of a "new federalism" in which some areas of public policy for which the federal government had assumed responsibility would be returned to states and localities.[31]

Upon taking control of Congress in 1995, Republican lawmakers acted to reduce *unfunded mandates*. These are federal programs that require action by states or localities but provide no or insufficient funds to pay for it. For example, states and localities are required by federal law to make their buildings accessible to the physically handicapped, but Washington pays only part of the cost of these accommodations. In the Unfunded Mandates Reform Act of 1995, Congress eliminated some of these mandates, although under threat of a presidential veto it exempted those that deal with civil rights and liberties. The GOP-controlled Congress also took action to lump additional categorical grants into block grants, thus giving states more control over how federal money would be spent.

The most significant legislative change came a year later, when the Republican Congress enacted the sweeping 1996 Welfare Reform Act. Its key element is the Temporary Assistance for Needy Families block grant (TANF), which ended the decades-old program that granted cash assistance to every poor family with children. TANF restricts a family's eligibility for federal assistance to five years, and after two years, a family head normally has to go to work or the benefits cease. Moreover, TANF gives states wide latitude in setting benefit levels, eligibility criteria, and other regulations affecting aid for poor families. (TANF and other aspects of the 1996 welfare reform legislation are discussed further in Chapter 16.)

After passage of the 1996 Welfare Reform Act, congressional efforts to roll back federal authority declined sharply. Devolution had hardly rolled back a half century of Washington-centered federalism, nor had it blunted new federal assistance programs. Among the federal initiatives enacted recently are grants for classroom modernization and the hiring of tens of thousands of additional teachers.

Although it is uncertain how far devolution will be extended, American federalism has clearly entered a new stage, where answers to the nation's problems will be sought less in Washington than in the states and localities. Devolution has resulted in a modification of fiscal and cooperative federalism rather than their demise. The federal government will continue to be a part of the answer to problems in policy areas once reserved almost exclusively to the states. Because of the complexity of modern policy issues, and the interdependency of American society, the states will never regain the level of autonomy that they exercised in the early twentieth century. Through devolution, however, they have acquired a greater degree of discretionary authority in some policy areas.

DEVOLUTION, JUDICIAL STYLE   In the five decades after the 1930s, the Supreme Court granted Congress broad discretion in the enactment of policies affecting state and local governments. In *Garcia* v. *San Antonio Authority* (1985), for example, the Court held that federal minimum wage standards apply even to state and local governments.[32] States and localities are prohibited from paying their employees less than the federally mandated minimum wage.

In recent years, however, the Supreme Court has restricted congressional authority somewhat. Chief Justice William Rehnquist and some of the other Republican appointees on the Supreme Court believe that Congress in some instances has encroached on powers properly reserved to state and local governments. In *United States* v. *Lopez* (1995), for example, the Court struck down a federal law that prohibited the possession of guns within a thousand feet of a school. Congress had justified the law as an exercise of its commerce power, but the Court stated that the ban had "nothing to do with commerce, or any sort of economic activity."[33] Two years later, in *Printz* v. *United States* (1997), the Court struck down that part of the federal Handgun Violence Prevention Act (the so-called Brady bill) which required local law-enforcement officers to conduct background checks on prospective handgun buyers. The Court said the provision violated the "principle of separate state sovereignty," arguing that the federal government cannot "command" local officials "to administer or enforce a federal regulatory program."[34] Then, in *Kimel* v. *Florida Board of Regents* (2000), the Supreme Court held that Congress did not have the authority to require state governments to comply with the federal law that bars discrimination against older workers. Age discrimination is not among the forms of discrimination expressly prohibited by the U.S. Constitution, and the Court declared that states have the power to decide for themselves the age-related policies that will apply to their employees.[35]

Although these Court decisions have restricted federal authority, they have done so only to a limited extent. The Court has not by any means repudiated the principle established in the 1930s that Congress's commerce and spending powers are broad and substantial. In *Reno* v. *Condon* (2000), for example, the Court ruled that the states have to comply with a federal law barring them from selling to private firms or groups their databases of personal information obtained from automobile license applicants. The majority opinion, which was written by Chief Justice Rehnquist, declared that the information in these databases is "an article of commerce" and thus is subject to regulation through Congress's commerce power. The Court noted that the law also applied to "private resellers" and was aimed at regulating "the owners of databases," which in this case included the states.[36]

THE PUBLIC'S INFLUENCE: SETTING THE BOUNDARIES OF FEDERAL–STATE POWER

The ebb and flow in Washington's power in the twentieth century has coincided closely with public opinion. The American people have had a decisive voice in determining the relationship between the federal and state governments.

During the Great Depression, when it was clear that the states would be unable to help, Americans turned to Washington for relief. For people without jobs and money, the fine points of the Constitution were of little consequence. President Roosevelt's welfare and public jobs programs were a radical departure from the past but quickly gained widespread support.[37] The second great wave of federal social programs—President Lyndon Johnson's Great Society—was also driven by public demands. Income and education levels had risen dramatically after the Second World War, and Americans wanted more and better services from government. When the states were slow to respond, Americans pressured federal officials to act.[38] Public opinion is also behind the recent rollback in federal authority. The Republican takeover in 1995 was in large part a result of Americans' increased dissatisfaction with the performance of the federal government.[39]

The public's role in defining the boundaries between federal and state power would come as no surprise to the Framers of the Constitution. For them, federalism was a pragmatic issue, one to be decided by the nation's needs rather than inflexible rules. And indeed, each succeeding generation of Americans has seen fit to devise a balance of federal and state power that would serve its interests. The historian Daniel Boorstin said the true genius of the American people is their pragmatism, their willingness to try new ways when the old ones stop working.[40] In few areas of governing has this been more true than in Americans' approach to federalism.

SUMMARY

A foremost characteristic of the American political system is its division of authority between a national government and the states. The first U.S. government, established by the Articles of Confederation, was essentially a union of the states.

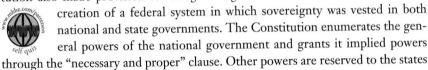

In establishing the basis for a stronger national government, the U.S. Constitution also made provision for safeguarding state interests. The result was the creation of a federal system in which sovereignty was vested in both national and state governments. The Constitution enumerates the general powers of the national government and grants it implied powers through the "necessary and proper" clause. Other powers are reserved to the states by the Tenth Amendment.

From 1789 to 1865, the nation's survival was at issue. The states found it convenient at times to argue that their sovereignty took precedence over national authority. In the end, it took the Civil War to cement the idea that the United States was a union of people, not of states. From 1865 to 1937, federalism reflected the doctrine that certain policy areas were the exclusive responsibility of the national government, while others belonged exclusively to the states. This constitutional position permitted the laissez-faire doctrine that big business was largely beyond governmental control. It also allowed the states in their public policies to discriminate against African Americans. Federalism in a form recognizable today began to emerge in the late 1930s.

In the areas of commerce, taxation, spending, civil rights, and civil liberties, among others, the federal government now has an important role, one that is the inevitable consequence of the increasing complexity of American society and the interdependence of its people. National, state, and local officials now work closely together to solve the country's problems, a situation that is described as cooperative federalism. Grants-in-aid from Washington to the states and localities have been the chief instrument of national influence. States and localities have received billions in federal assistance; in accepting that money, they have also accepted both federal restrictions on its use and the national policy priorities that underlie the granting of the money.

In recent years, the relationship between the nation and the states has again become a priority issue. Power is shifting downward to the states, and a new balance in the ever-evolving system of U.S. federalism is taking place. This change, as has been true throughout U.S. history, has sprung from the demands of the American people.

MAJOR CONCEPTS

block grants

categorical grants

commerce clause

confederacy

cooperative federalism

devolution

dual federalism

enumerated powers (expressed
    powers)

federalism

fiscal federalism

grants-in-aid

implied powers

"necessary and proper" clause
    (elastic clause)

reserved powers

sovereignty

supremacy clause

unitary system

SUGGESTED READINGS AND WEB SITES

Beer, Samuel H. *To Make a Nation: The Rediscovery of American Federalism.* Cambridge, Mass.: The Belknap Press of Harvard University Press, 1993. An innovative interpretive framework for understanding the impact of federalism and nationalism on the nation's development.

Conlan, Timothy. *From New Federalism to Devolution.* Washington, D.C.: Brookings Institution Press, 1998. A careful analysis of the changing nature of modern federalism.

Cornell, Saul. *The Other Founders: Anti-Federalism and the Dissenting Tradition in America.* Chapel Hill: University of North Carolina Press, 1999. An analysis of Antifederalist thought, its origins, and its legacy.

Elkins, Stanley, and Eric McKitrick. *The Age of Federalism: The Early American Republic, 1788–1800.* New York: Oxford University Press, 1993. An award-winning book on the earliest period of American federalism.

Ross, William G. *A Muted Fury: Populists, Progressives, and Labor Unions Confront the Courts, 1890–1937.* Princeton, N.J.: Princeton University Press, 1993. A valuable study of the political conflict surrounding the judiciary's laissez-faire doctrine in the 1890–1937 period.

Thompson, Tommy. *Power to the People: An American State at Work.* New York: HarperCollins, 1996. An argument for state-centered federalism by one of its leading practitioners, the governor of Wisconsin.

Walker, David B. *The Rebirth of Federalism,* 2d ed. Chatham, N.J.: Chatham House Publishers, 2000. An optimistic assessment of the state of today's federalism.

http://lcweb2.loc.gov/ammem/amlaw/lawhome.html   A site containing congressional documents and debates from 1774–1873.

http://www.statesnews.org   The site of the Council of State Governments. Includes current news from each of the states and basic information about their governments.

http://www.temple.edu/federalism   The site of the Center for the Study of Federalism. Located at Temple University, it offers information and publications on the federal system of government.

http://www.yale.edu/lawweb/avalon/federal/fed.htm   A documentary record of the Federalist Papers, the Annapolis Convention, the Articles of Confederation, the Madison Debates, and the U.S. Constitution.

READING 3

The National Idea in American Politics

SAMUEL H. BEER

Introduction

In his essay, Samuel Beer discusses the "national idea" as a prevailing theme of American politics. He focuses on two aspects of federalism that were discussed in Chapter 2: the distribution of power between the two levels of government and the use of power at each level. By contrasting Hamilton with Jefferson and Johnson with Reagan, he shows the persistent nature of the conflict between those Americans who favor activist national government and those who oppose what they regard as excessive centralization. Beer's accounting is a capsule summary of federalism: a system of government where sovereign power is simultaneously invested in two levels of government, resulting in a dynamic system where competing visions of America are played out.

The national idea is a way of looking at American government and American society. It embraces a view of where the authority of government comes from and a view of what it should be used for. As a concept of authority, it identifies the whole people of the nation as the source of the legitimate powers of any and all governments. As a concept of purpose, it tells us that we are one people and guides us toward what we should make of ourselves as a people. The national idea envisions one people, at once sovereign and subject, source of authority and substance of history, affirming, through conflict and in diversity, our unity of being and becoming.

Because the national idea is also a democratic idea, these concepts of authority and purpose are interdependent. Self-government is reflexive. The people who govern are also the object of government. A government of the people, therefore, gets its legitimacy both from being a government by the people and from being a government for the people.

This theory of legitimacy is national and democratic. It is also federal. In the national perspective, although we are one people who enjoy a common life as one nation, we have set up not a unitary but a dual system of government. In establishing this system, the American people authorized and empowered two sets of governments: a general government for the whole, and state governments for the parts. The constitutional authority for the two sets of government is therefore coordinate. Neither created the other, and both are subject to the same ultimate legitimating power, the sovereign people. And periodically the people in this constituent capacity amend these institutions, by which in their governing capacity they direct the day-to-day affairs of the nation.

From our revolutionary beginnings the national idea has been widely accepted as a description of historical fact and a theory of legitimacy of American federalism. The American political tradition, however, has also sustained another view. In this opposing view, one of these levels of government, the federal government, was brought into existence not by the act of a sovereign people but by a compact among sovereign states. From this compact theory inferences follow that radically contradict the conclusions of the national theory. While the national theory has, on balance, had much the greater influence on thought and action, the compact theory has survived and continues even today to show itself in the feelings of citizens, the rhetoric of politicians, and the actions of governments.

When President Reagan took office in 1981, for instance, he proclaimed a "new federalism." Its central thrust was to cut back on the activities of the federal government by reducing or eliminating a vast number of programs, the principal cuts falling on federal aid to state and local governments. The President wished to do this because he judged these activities to be inefficient, unnecessary, and sometimes positively harmful. He also claimed that they were improper under the Constitution. . . .

In his first inaugural address on January 20, 1981, accordingly, President Reagan promised to "restore the balance between levels of government." And while he did not elaborate his political philosophy, he made clear in a phrase or two his reliance upon the compact theory of the Constitution to justify his new federalism. "The Federal government," he declared at one point in his address, "did not create the states; the states created the Federal government."

This allegation did not pass without comment. In response to President Reagan's use of the compact theory, eminent academic critics counterattacked in terms of the national theory. Richard P. Morris of Columbia University called the President's view of the historical facts "a hoary myth about the origins of the Union" and went on to summarize the evidence showing that "the United States was created by the people in collectivity, not by the individual states." No less bluntly, Henry Steele Commager of Amherst College said President Reagan did not understand the Constitution, which in its own words asserts that it was ordained by "We, the People of the United States," not by the states severally. . . .

The argument between the President and the professors was not simply about history. Nor was it mainly about the constitutional authority of the federal and state governments. Their primary disagreement was over public policy, specifically, the use of federal authority in recent years to expand the social and economic programs of the welfare state, especially those dating from the "new federalism" of Lyndon Johnson. President Reagan had taken office as the champion of conservative attitudes that had been gathering force around the country for a generation. He articulated these attitudes in a distinctive vision of American society at home and abroad and in a set of strategies for realizing that vision. Expressing in a new public philosophy the old and familiar values of rugged individualism, he sought to cut back the welfare state and to restore the free market—or in the language of political economy, to shift social choice from public choice toward market choice. Declaring in his first inaugural address that the excessive growth of the public sector in recent years meant that "government is not the solution to our problem; government is the problem," he proposed to "reverse" that growth. Intrinsic to this goal was his promise of another "new federalism" which would "restore the balance between levels of government." The reduction of federal grant programs would at once help restore the federal-state balance and promote the free market.

Some critics called him insincere, claiming that when he said he wanted to restore the federal-state balance, what he really wanted to do was to cut federal spending on social and economic programs. No doubt he was mainly interested in the impact of his policies on American society. But that is no reason for saying that he was not also interested in reducing what he thought was excessive centralization of power in the federal system. In American politics, thinking about federalism has usually had those two aspects: a concern with both the pattern of authority and the pattern of purpose, with the balance of power between levels of government and with the policies for which that power is used. When President Reagan called in the compact theory to lend support to his views on public policy, he was doing what its adherents before him had often done. In their way the nationalists had done the same, right from the days when Alexander Hamilton, as Secretary of the Treasury, set the course of the first administration of George Washington. . . .

Hamilton's nationalism was expressed not only in his belief that Americans were "one people" rather than thirteen separate peoples but even more emphatically in his commitment to governmental activism. This concern that the American people must make vigorous use of their central government for the tasks of nation-building separated him sharply from Thomas Jefferson, Washington's Secretary of State, who leaned toward the compact theory. . . .

Hamilton is renowned for his statecraft—for his methods of using the powers of government for economic, political, and social ends. But that emphasis obscures his originality, which consisted in his conceptualization of those ends. . . . [E]arlier craftsmen of the modern state in Bourbon France or Hohenzollern Prussia or Whig Britain could take for granted the established authority of a monarchic and aristocratic regime. They too had their techniques for enhancing the attachment of the people to the prince. But in America the people *were* the prince. To enhance their attachment to the ultimate governing power, therefore, meant fortifying the bonds that united them as a people. If the authority of this first nation-state was to suffice for its governance, the purpose of the state would have to become the development of the nation. This was the essential Hamiltonian end: to make the nation more of a nation.

SOURCE: Reprinted by permission of the publisher from *To Make a Nation: The Rediscovery of American Federalism*, Cambridge, Mass.: The Belknap Press of Harvard University Press, Copyright © 1993 by the President and Fellows of Harvard College.
Samuel H. Beer is Eaton Professor of the Science of Government, emeritus, Harvard University.

CHAPTER FOUR

Civil Liberties

A bill of rights is what the people are entitled to against every government
on earth, general or particular, and what no just government
should refuse, or rest on inference.

THOMAS JEFFERSON[1]

R OBERT AND Sarisse Creighton and their three children were asleep
when FBI agents broke into their home in the middle of the
night. Brandishing guns, the officers searched the house for a relative of the
Creightons who was suspected of bank robbery. When asked to show a
search warrant, they said, "You watch too much TV." The suspect was not
there, and the officers abruptly left. The Creightons sued the FBI agent in
charge, Russell Anderson, for violating their constitutional right against unlawful search.

The Creightons won a temporary victory when the Eighth U.S. Court
of Appeals, noting that individuals are constitutionally protected against
warrantless searches unless officers have good reason ("probable cause") for
a search and unless they have good reason ("exigent circumstances") for
conducting that search without a warrant, concluded that the FBI's Anderson should have sought a warrant from a judge, who would have decided
whether a search of the Creightons' home was justified.

The Supreme Court of the United States overturned the lower court's
ruling. The Court's majority opinion said: "We have recognized that it is
inevitable that law enforcement officials will in some cases reasonably but
mistakenly conclude that probable cause is present, and we have indicated
that in such cases those officials . . . should not be held personally liable."
Justice John Paul Stevens sharply dissented. He accused the Court's majority of showing "remarkably little fidelity" to the Constitution.[2] Civil liberties groups also claimed that the Court's decision gave police an open
invitation to invade people's homes on the slightest pretext. However, the

Court's decision was praised by law enforcement officials, who contended that a ruling in the Creightons' favor would have made police hesitant to pursue suspects for fear of a lawsuit if a search failed to produce the person sought.

As this case illustrates, issues of individual rights are complex and political. No right is absolute. For example, the Fourth Amendment protects Americans not from all searches but from "unreasonable searches." The public would be unsafe if police could never search for evidence of a crime. Yet the public would also not be secure if police could frisk people at will or break into their homes whenever they pleased. The challenge to a civil society is to establish a proper balance between the need for public safety and the need for individual freedom.

This chapter discusses **civil liberties:** specific individual rights which are constitutionally protected against infringement by government. As we saw in Chapter 2, the Constitution's failure to enumerate individual freedoms led to demands for the **Bill of Rights.** Enacted in 1791, these first ten amendments to the Constitution specify certain rights of life, liberty, and property that the national government is obliged to respect. A later amendment, the Fourteenth, became the basis for extending these protections of individual rights to actions by state and local governments.

Rights have full meaning only as protected in law. A constitutional guarantee of free speech, for example, is worth no more than the paper on which it is written if authorities can prevent people from speaking freely. Judicial action is important in defining what people's rights mean in practice and in setting and enforcing limits on official action that may infringe on these rights. In some areas, the judiciary devises a specific "test" to determine whether government action is lawful. In the area of free speech, for example, one "test" that U.S. courts apply is whether general rules (such as restrictions on the time and place of street demonstrations) is applied fairly to all groups. Government officials do not meet this "test" if they apply one set of rules to groups that they like and a harsher set of rules to those they dislike.

Issues of individual rights have become increasingly complex and important. The writers of the Constitution could not possibly have foreseen the United States of the early twenty-first century, with its huge national government, enormous corporations, urban crowding, and the rest. These developments are potential threats to individual freedom, and the judiciary in recent decades has seen fit to expand the rights to which individuals are entitled. However, these rights are constantly being balanced against competing individual rights and society's collective interests, and it is at this juncture that issues of civil liberties arise. Should an admitted murderer be entitled to recant a confession? Should prayer be allowed in the public schools? Should extremist groups be allowed to voice their messages of prejudice and hate? Such questions are among the subjects of this chapter, which focuses on the following major points:

* *Freedom of expression is the most basic of democratic rights, but, like all rights, it is not unlimited. Individual rights are constantly being weighed against the demands of majorities and the collective needs of society.*

* *"Due process of law" refers to legal protections (primarily procedural safeguards) that are designed to ensure that individual rights are respected by government.*

* *During the last half-century, the civil liberties of individual Americans have been substantially broadened in law and given greater judicial protection from action by all levels of government. Of special significance has been the Supreme Court's use of the Fourteenth Amendment to protect these individual rights from action by state and local governments.*

FREEDOM OF EXPRESSION

Freedom of political expression is the most basic of democratic rights. Unless citizens can openly express their political opinions, they cannot properly influence their government or act to protect their other rights.

It is for such reasons that the First Amendment provides the foundation for **freedom of expression**—the right of individual Americans to hold and communicate views of their choosing. For many reasons, such as a desire to conform to social pressure or a fear of harassment, Americans do not always choose to express themselves freely. Nevertheless, the First Amendment prohibits laws that would abridge the freedoms of religion, speech, press, assembly, and petition.

Freedom of expression, like other rights, is not absolute. It does not entitle individuals to say or do whatever they want, to whomever they want. Free expression can be denied, for example, if it endangers national security, wrongly damages the reputations of others, or deprives others of their basic freedoms. An individual's private thoughts are completely free, but words and actions may not be. The Supreme Court has ruled, for example, that abortion protesters can be arrested if they violate laws or court orders that bar them from protesting within a certain distance of abortion clinics or from physically interfering with a woman's attempt to enter a clinic.[3]

Freedom of expression is widely regarded as the most basic of rights since other aspects of a free society, such as open and fair elections, are dependent on it.

In recent decades, free expression has received broad protection from the courts. Today, under most circumstances, Americans can freely verbalize their political views without fear of governmental interference. In earlier times, Americans were less free to express their political views.

The Early Period: The Uncertain Status of the Right of Free Expression

The first legislative attempt by the U.S. government to restrict free expression was the Sedition Act of 1798, which made it a crime to print false or malicious newspaper stories about the president or other national officials. Thomas Jefferson called the Sedition Act an "alarming infraction" of the Constitution and, upon replacing John Adams as president in 1801, pardoned those who had been convicted under it. As the Supreme Court did not review the sedition cases, however, the judiciary's position on free expression remained an open question. The Court also did not rule on free speech during the Civil War era, when the government severely restricted individual rights.

In 1919 the Court finally ruled on a case challenging the national government's authority to restrict free expression. Two years earlier, Congress had passed the Espionage Act, which prohibited forms of dissent deemed to be harmful to the nation's effort in World War I. Nearly two thousand Americans were convicted for such activities as interfering with draft registration and distributing antiwar leaflets. The Supreme Court upheld one of these convictions in *Schenck v. United States* (1919), ruling unanimously that the Espionage Act of 1917 was constitutional. In the opinion written by Justice Oliver Wendell Holmes, the Court said that Congress could restrict speech that was "of such a nature as to create a clear and present danger" to the nation's security. In a famous passage, Holmes argued that not even the First Amendment would permit a person to falsely yell "fire" in a crowded theater and create a panic that could kill or injure innocent people.[4]

Although the **clear-and-present-danger test** has been superceded by a more rigorous test (discussed later in the chapter in the context of *Brandenburg* v. *Ohio*), it served to place a limit on governments' authority over free expression. Political speech that did *not* pose a clear-and-present danger could *not* be restricted.

The Modern Period: Protecting Free Expression

Until the twentieth century, the tension between national security interests and free expression was not a pressing dilemma for the United States. The country's great size and ocean barriers provided protection from potential enemies, minimizing concerns of internal subversion. World War I, however, intruded upon America's isolation, and World War II brought it to an abrupt end. Since then, Americans' rights of free expression have been defined largely in the context of national security concerns.

FREE SPEECH AND ASSEMBLY   During the cold war that developed after World War II, many Americans perceived the Soviet Union as bent on destroying the United States through internal subversion and global expansion. In this period, the Supreme Court allowed government to put substantial limits on free expression; in *Dennis v. United States* (1951), for example, the Court upheld the convictions of eleven members of the U.S. Communist party who had been prosecuted under a law that made it illegal to advocate the forceful overthrow of the U.S. government.[5]

By the late 1950s, however, fear of internal communist subversion was subsiding, and the Supreme Court expanded the scope of permissible speech.[6] The Court implicitly embraced a legal doctrine first outlined by Justice Harlan Fiske Stone in 1938. Stone argued that First Amendment rights of free expression are the basis of Americans' liberty and ought to have a "preferred position" in the law. If government can control what people know and say, it can manipulate their opinions and thereby deprive them of the right to decide for themselves how they will be governed. Therefore government should be broadly prohibited from restricting free expression.[7]

This philosophy has led the Supreme Court to rule that government officials must show that national security is directly and substantially imperiled before they can lawfully prohibit citizens from speaking out or assembling. For example, during the Vietnam era, despite the largest sustained protest movement in America's history, not a single individual was convicted solely for voicing objections to the government's war policy. (Some dissenters were found guilty on other grounds, such as inciting riots and assaulting police.)

The Supreme Court's protection of **symbolic speech** (conduct that is designed to express an opinion) has been less substantial than its protection of verbal speech. For example, the Court in *United States* v. *O'Brien* (1968) upheld the conviction of a Vietnam protester who had burned his draft registration card. The Court said that government can prohibit conduct that threatens a legitimate public interest as long as the main purpose of the policy is not to restrict free expression. The Court concluded that the federal law prohibiting the destruction of draft cards was designed primarily to protect the military's need for soldiers, not to prevent people from criticizing government policy.[8]

The Supreme Court, however, has not granted the government broad power to restrict symbolic speech. In *Texas* v. *Johnson* (1989), for example, the Court ruled that the burning of the American flag is a protected form of free expression. The ruling came in the case of Gregory Lee Johnson, a member of the Communist Youth Brigade. Johnson had set fire to a U.S. flag outside the hall in Dallas where the 1984 Republican National Convention was being held. Johnson was arrested and convicted in a Texas court, but the Supreme Court rejected the state's argument that flag burning is, in every instance, an imminent danger to public safety. A year later the Court struck down a new federal statute that made it a federal crime to burn or deface the flag.[9] "If there is a bedrock principle underlying the First Amendment," the Court ruled in the *Johnson* case, "it is that the Government may

Civil rights attorney William Kunstler (*right*), with defendant Gregory Lee Johnson (*second from right*), addresses reporters outside the Supreme Court building. Kunstler defended Johnson in the celebrated case that ultimately established flag burning as a constitutionally protected form of political expression.

not prohibit the expression of an idea simply because society finds the idea itself offensive or disagreeable."[10]

Government's authority to regulate activities that are related to free speech is also subject to certain limitations. In its landmark *Buckley* v. *Valeo* (1976) decision, for example, the Supreme Court held that Congress cannot restrict the amount of their own money that political candidates can spend on their own campaigns. Any such limit, the Court concluded, would infringe on candidates' freedom of speech. Legal limits on individual and group contributions to candidates, however, were upheld on grounds that such limitations were necessary to prevent the appearance and possibly the reality that officeholders would be unduly influenced by large donors.[11]

PRESS FREEDOM AND PRIOR RESTRAINT   Freedom of the press has also received strong judicial support in recent decades. In *New York Times Co.* v. *United States* (1971) the Court ruled that the *Times*'s publication of the "Pentagon Papers" (secret government documents revealing official deception about the success of the Vietnam War policy) could not be blocked by the Department of Justice, which claimed that publication would hurt the war effort. The documents had been illegally obtained by antiwar activists, who had turned them over to the *Times* for publication. The Court ruled that "any system of prior restraints" on the press is unconstitutional unless the government can fully justify the restriction.[12]

The unacceptability of **prior restraint**—government prohibition of speech or publication before the fact—is basic to the current doctrine of free expression. The Supreme Court has said that any attempt by government to prevent expression carries "a 'heavy presumption' against its constitutionality."[13] News organizations and individuals are legally responsible after the fact for what they report or say (for example, they can be sued by an individual whose reputation is wrongly damaged by their words), but generally government cannot stop them in advance from expressing their views. An exception is coverage of military operations. During the Persian Gulf War, U.S. journalists in Saudi Arabia had to work within limits placed on them by military authorities. The courts have also upheld the government's authority to ban uncensored publications by certain past and present government employees, such as CIA agents, who have taken part in classified national security activities.

Free Expression and State Governments

In 1790 Congress rejected a proposed amendment to the Constitution that would have applied the Bill of Rights to the states. Thus the freedoms guaranteed in the Bill of Rights were initially protected only from action by the national government, a constitutional arrangement that the Supreme Court upheld in *Barron* v. *Baltimore* (1833).[14] The effect was that the Bill of Rights had little practical meaning in the lives of ordinary Americans since state and local governments carry out most of the activities, such as law enforcement, where people's rights are at issue.

Not until the twentieth century did the Supreme Court begin to protect individual rights from infringement by state and local governments. The vehicle for this change was the **due-process clause** of the Fourteenth Amendment to the Constitution.

THE FOURTEENTH AMENDMENT AND SELECTIVE INCORPORATION   Ratified in 1868, the Fourteenth Amendment includes a clause that forbids a state from depriving any person of life, liberty, or property without *due process of law* (due process refers to the legal procedures that have been established as a means of protecting individuals' rights). Six decades later, the Supreme Court in *Gitlow* v. *New York* (1925) decided that the Fourteenth Amendment applied to state action in the area of freedom of expression. The Court upheld Benjamin Gitlow's conviction for violating a New York law that prohibited advocacy of the violent overthrow of the U.S. government, but warned that the states were not completely free to limit expression:

> For present purposes we may and do assume that freedom of speech and of the press—which are protected by the First Amendment from abridgement by Congress—are among the fundamental personal rights and "liberties" protected by the due process clause of the Fourteenth Amendment from impairment by the states.[15]

There is no indication that Congress, when it passed the Fourteenth Amendment after the Civil War, meant it to protect First Amendment rights from state action. The Supreme Court justified its new interpretation in the *Gitlow* case by reference to **selective incorporation**—the absorption of certain provisions of the Bill of Rights, particularly freedom of speech and press, into the Fourteenth Amendment so that these rights would be protected by the federal courts from infringement by the states. The Court reasoned that the Fourteenth Amendment's due-process clause was largely meaningless if states could prohibit their residents from speaking freely.

Having developed in the *Gitlow* case a new interpretation of the Fourteenth Amendment, the Supreme Court proceeded during the next decade to overturn state laws that restricted expression in the areas of speech, press, religion, and assembly and petition (see Table 4-1).[16] The most famous of these judgments is *Near* v. *Minnesota* (1931). Jay Near was the publisher of a Minneapolis weekly newspaper that regularly made scurrilous attacks on blacks, Jews, Catholics, and labor union leaders. His paper was closed down on authority of a state law that banned "malicious, scandalous, or defamatory" publications. Near appealed the shutdown, and the Supreme Court ruled in his favor, saying that the Minnesota law was "the essence of censorship."[17]

LIMITING THE AUTHORITY OF STATES TO RESTRICT EXPRESSION

Since the 1930s, the Supreme Court has broadly protected freedom of expression from action by the states and by local governments, which derive their authority from the states. The Court has held that the states cannot restrict free expression except when such expression is almost certain to result in imminent lawlessness. A leading free-speech case was *Brandenburg* v. *Ohio* (1969). The appellant was a Ku Klux Klan member who, in a speech delivered at a Klan rally, said that "revenge" might have to be taken if the national government "continues to suppress the white Caucasian race." He was convicted of advocating force under an Ohio law prohibiting "criminal

TABLE 4-1   SELECTIVE INCORPORATION OF RIGHTS OF FREE EXPRESSION

In the 1920s and 1930s, the Supreme Court selectively incorporated the free-expression provisions of the First Amendment into the Fourteenth Amendment so that these rights would be protected from infringement by the states.

Supreme Court Case	Year	First Amendment Right at Issue
Gitlow v. New York	1925	First Amendment's applicability to free speech
Fiske v. Kansas	1927	Free speech
Near v. Minnesota	1931	Free press
Hamilton v. Regents, U. of California	1934	Religious freedom
DeJonge v. Oregon	1937	Freedom of assembly and of petition

syndicalism," but the Supreme Court reversed the conviction, saying the First Amendment prohibits a state from suppressing speech that advocates the unlawful use of force "except where such advocacy is directed to inciting or producing imminent lawless action, and is likely to produce such action."[18] This test—the likelihood of **imminent lawless action**—is a severe restriction on the government's power to restrict expression. It is rare when words alone immediately incite others to act lawlessly.

The Court has broadly held that "hate speech" cannot be silenced. This ruling came in a unanimous 1992 opinion that struck down a St. Paul, Minnesota, ordinance making it a crime to engage in speech likely to arouse "anger or alarm" on the basis of "race, color, creed, religion or gender." The Court said the First Amendment prohibits government from "silencing speech on the basis of its content."[19] This protection of violent *speech* does not, however, extend to violent *crimes*, such as assault, motivated by racial or other forms of prejudice. A Wisconsin law that provided for increased sentences for such crimes was challenged as a violation of the First Amendment. In a unanimous 1993 opinion, the Court said that the law was aimed at "conduct unprotected by the First Amendment" rather than the defendant's speech.[20]

In a key case involving freedom of assembly, the U.S. Supreme Court in 1977 upheld a lower-court ruling against local ordinances of Skokie, Illinois, which had been invoked to prevent a parade by the American Nazi party.[21] Skokie had a large Jewish population, including many survivors of Nazi Germany's concentration camps. The Supreme Court held that the right of free expression takes precedence over the mere *possibility* that exercising the right may have undesirable consequences. Before government can lawfully prevent a speech or rally, it must offer persuasive evidence that an evil will almost certainly result from the event and must also demonstrate the lack of alternative ways (such as assigning police officers to control the crowd) to prevent the evil from happening.

The Supreme Court has recognized that freedom of speech and assembly may conflict with the routines of daily life. Accordingly, individuals do not have the right to hold a public rally at any time or place of their choosing. The Court has held that public officials can regulate the time, place, and conditions of public assembly, provided that these regulations are reasonable and do not discriminate on the basis of who is speaking.[22] In general, the Supreme Court's position is that the First Amendment makes any government effort to regulate the *content* of a message highly suspect. In the flag-burning case, Texas was regulating the content of the message—contempt for the flag and the principles it represents. Texas could not have been regulating the act itself, for the state's own method of disposing of worn-out flags is also to burn them. But a content-neutral regulation (no public rally can be held in the middle of a busy intersection at rush hour) is acceptable as long as it is reasonable and nondiscriminatory.

Libel and Slander

The right of free expression is not a legal license to avoid responsibility for the consequences of what is said or written. If false information that greatly harms a person's reputation is published (**libel**) or spoken (**slander**), the injured party can sue for damages. The ease of winning such suits has obvious implications for free expression. Individuals and organizations are less likely to express themselves openly if they stand a good chance of subsequently losing a libel or slander suit.

Libel is the more compelling issue for the political process because it affects the news media's ability to criticize public officials. A leading decision in this area is *New York Times Co.* v. *Sullivan* (1964), in which the Court overruled an Alabama state court that had found the *Times* guilty of libel for printing an advertisement accusing Alabama officials of physically assaulting black civil rights demonstrators. The Court ruled that libel of a public official requires proof of "actual malice," which was defined as a knowing or reckless disregard for the truth.[23] It is *very* difficult to prove that a publication acted with reckless or deliberate disregard for the truth. In fact, no federal official has won a libel judgment against a news organization in the three decades since the *Sullivan* ruling. (The press has less protection against a libel judgment when its target is a "private" person rather than a "public" official. The courts regard the communication of information about private individuals as less basic to the democratic process than information about public officials, and the press must therefore take greater care in ascertaining the validity of claims about an ordinary citizen.)

The *Sullivan* decision notwithstanding, the strongest protection against a libel judgment is truthfulness. The Court has held that expressions of opinion deserve "full constitutional protection" against the charge of libel as long as they do not contain "a provably false factual connotation."[24]

Obscenity

In 1990 the director of a Cincinnati museum, Dennis Barrie, was charged with obscenity for holding an exhibit that included homoerotic art by the photographer Robert Mapplethorpe. Barrie was acquitted in a jury trial, but the incident provoked a controversy that extended to Congress. The exhibit had been funded in part by a grant from the National Endowment for the Arts (NEA), and Congress enacted a law requiring the NEA to take "decency standards" into account in granting funds. Artists claimed that the law would have a "chilling effect" on artistic expression, but the Supreme Court in 1998 upheld Congress's authority to set limits on the uses of the funds it appropriates.[25]

Obscenity is a form of expression that is not protected by the First Amendment. However, the Supreme Court has found it difficult to define which publicly disseminated sexual materials are obscene and which are not. The Court has struggled to develop a standard that gives predictability to the law without endangering First Amendment rights.

The Court's first test was established in *Roth v. United States* (1957), when the Court defined obscenity as material that "taken as a whole" appealed to "prurient interest" and had no "redeeming social significance." The perspective was to be that of "the average person, applying contemporary community standards."[26] The test proved unworkable. Even the justices, when personally examining allegedly obscene material, would argue over whether it appealed to prurient interest and was without redeeming social value. In the end, they usually concluded that it had at least some social significance.

In *Miller v. California* (1973), the Court changed the test, saying that the material had to have "serious literary, artistic, political, or scientific value." The Court also narrowed the "contemporary community standards" to the local level. The court said that what might offend residents of "Mississippi might be found tolerable in Las Vegas." But this test proved too restrictive. The Court subsequently ruled that material cannot be judged obscene simply because the "average" local resident might object to it. "Community standards" were to be judged in the context of a "reasonable person"—someone whose outlook is broad enough to evaluate the material on its overall merit rather than its most objectionable feature. The Court later also modified its content standard, saying that the material must be of a "particularly offensive type."[27] These efforts illustrate the difficulty of defining obscenity and, even more, of developing a legal standard that can be applied evenhandedly by courts when an obscenity case arises.

The Supreme Court has distinguished between obscene materials in public places and in the home. A unanimous ruling in 1969 held that what adults read and watch in the privacy of their homes cannot be made a crime.[28] The Court created an exception to this rule in 1990 by upholding an Ohio law making it a crime to possess pornographic photographs of children.[29] The Court reasoned that purchase and distribution contributed to the spread of the crime of abusing minors through pornography.

The Supreme Court in 1997 invalidated the
Communications Decency Act, which had broadly
outlawed indecent material on the Internet. The Court
held that the law was so broad and so punitive that it
would censor "a large amount of speech."

The shielding of children from the effects of sexually explicit material has also affected cable television policy. In 1996, the Supreme Court held that, although cable operators are not required to scramble the signal of channels that provide "adult" programming, they must do so for individual subscribers who request that the signal be scrambled.[30]

The Internet is also a source of indecent material. To prevent it from reaching children, Congress in 1996 passed the Communications Decency Act, which made it a federal crime to use the Internet to transmit obscene material to someone under eighteen years of age or to post material in a way that made it available to minors. In a key 1997 ruling, *Reno v. ACLU*, the Supreme Court declared the Decency Act to be unconstitutional. "We have repeatedly recognized the governmental interest in protecting children from harmful materials," the Court said. "But that interest does not justify an unnecessarily broad suppression of speech addressed to adults." The Court noted that authorities might apply too restrictive a definition of obscenity and that someone sending a targeted message on the Internet could not be sure that it would reach only its intended recipients. The Court further noted that the penalties for communicating indecent material were harsh—up to two years in jail and $200,000 in fines.

The effect of such a broad punitive law, the Court concluded, would be to have a "chilling effect" on free expression. "[The Decency Act] effectively suppresses a large amount of speech that adults have a constitutional right to receive and to address to one another."[31] (The Court's decision does not legalize child pornography on the Internet or grant immunity to pedophiles who might prey on children through the Internet; the decision only invalidates the Communications Decency Act as a basis for restricting Internet expression.)

FREEDOM OF RELIGION

Free religious expression is the precursor of free political expression, at least within the English tradition of limited government. England's Glorious, or Bloodless, Revolution of 1689 centered on the issue of religion and resulted in the Act of Toleration, which gave Protestant sects the right to worship freely and publicly. The English philosopher John Locke (1632–1704) extended this principle, arguing that legitimate government could not inhibit free expression, religious or otherwise. The First Amendment reflects this tradition, providing for freedom of religion along with freedom of speech, press, assembly, and petition.

In regard to religion, the First Amendment reads: "Congress shall make no law respecting an establishment of religion, or prohibiting the free exercise thereof." The prohibition on laws aimed at "establishment of religion" (the establishment clause) and its "free exercise" (the free-exercise clause) applies to states through the Fourteenth Amendment.

The Establishment Clause

The **establishment clause** has been interpreted by the courts to mean that government may not favor one religion over another or support religion over no religion. (This position contrasts with that of a country such as England, where Anglicanism is the official, or "established," state religion, though no religion is prohibited.) The Supreme Court's interpretation of the establishment clause has been described as maintaining a "wall of separation" between church and state, which includes a prohibition on nondenominational support for religion.[32] The Court has taken a pragmatic approach, however, permitting some establishment activities but disallowing others. The Court has permitted states to provide secular textbooks for use by church-affiliated schools, for instance, but has forbidden states to pay part of the salaries of teachers in church-affiliated schools.[33] Such distinctions follow no strict logic but are based on judgments of whether government action involves "*excessive* entanglement with religion."[34] In allowing public funds to be used by religious schools for secular

The First Amendment's protection of free expression includes religious freedom, which has led the courts to hold that government should not in most instances promote or interfere with religious practices.

textbooks but not for teachers' salaries, the courts have indicated that, whereas it is relatively easy to ascertain whether the content of a particular textbook promotes religion, it would be much harder to determine whether a particular teacher were promoting religion in the classroom.

In 2000, the Supreme Court expanded the range of permissible support in a ruling that allows federal funds to be used to buy computers and other equipment for parochial school classrooms.[35]

In *Engel v. Vitale* (1962), the Court held that the establishment clause prohibits the reciting of prayers in public schools.[36] A year later the Court struck down Bible readings in public schools.[37] Religion is a strong force in American life, and the Supreme Court's position on school prayer has evoked strong opposition, particularly from Protestant fundamentalists. An Alabama law attempted to circumvent the prayer ruling by permitting public schools to set aside one minute each day for silent prayer or meditation. In 1985, the Court declared the law unconstitutional, ruling that "government must pursue a course of complete neutrality toward religion."[38] The Court in 2000 reaffirmed the ban by extending it to include student-led prayer at public school football games.[39]

The Free-Exercise Clause

The First and Fourteenth amendments also prohibit governmental interference with the "free exercise" of religion. The idea underlying the **free-exercise clause** is clear: Americans are free to hold any religious belief they choose.

Although people are free to believe what they want, they are not always free to act on their beliefs. The courts have allowed government interference in the exercise of religious beliefs when such interference is the secondary result of an overriding social goal. An example is the legal protection of children with life-threatening illnesses whose parents refuse to permit medical treatment on religious grounds. A court may order that such children be given medical assistance because the social good of saving their lives overrides their parents' free-exercise rights.

In an important 1997 decision, the Court struck down the Religious Freedom Restoration Act, which was passed by a large congressional majority with the backing of President Clinton. The law said that government at any level could not interfere with religious practices unless a "compelling reason," such as a danger to health or safety, were involved. In striking down the law, which was challenged in a case where a city wanted to prevent a church from enlarging its building, the Court said that Congress lacked the authority through statute to redefine the meaning of the Constitution.[40] The statute placed more restraints on government (for example, denying it the power to regulate construction) than is required by the First Amendment's prohibition on government interference in the free exercise of religion.

In some circumstances, exceptions to certain laws have been permitted on free-exercise grounds. The Supreme Court ruled in 1972 that Wisconsin could not compel Amish parents to send their children to school beyond the eighth grade because this policy violates a centuries-old Amish religious practice of having children leave school and begin work at an early age.[41] In upholding free exercise in such cases, the Court may be said to have violated the establishment clause by granting preferred treatment to people who hold a particular religious belief. The Court has recognized the potential conflict between the free-exercise and establishment clauses and, as in other such situations, has tried to strike a reasonable balance between the competing claims.

When the free-exercise and establishment clauses cannot be balanced, the Supreme Court has been forced to make a choice. In 1987, the Court overturned a Louisiana law requiring that creationism (the Bible's account of how the world was created) be taught along with the theory of evolution in public school science courses. Creationism, the Court concluded, is a religious doctrine, not a scientific theory; thus its inclusion in public school curricula violates the establishment clause by promoting a religious belief. Creationists viewed the Court's decision as a violation of their right to the free exercise of religion; they argued that their children were being forced to study a theory of evolution that contradicts the biblical account of human origins.

THE RIGHT OF PRIVACY

Until the 1960s, Americans' constitutional rights were confined largely to those enumerated in the Bill of Rights. This situation prevailed despite the Ninth Amendment, which reads: "The enumeration in the Constitution, of certain rights, shall not be construed to deny or disparage others retained by the people."

In 1965, however, the Supreme Court added to the list of individual rights, declaring that Americans have "a right of privacy." This judgment arose from the case of *Griswold* v. *Connecticut*, which challenged a state law prohibiting the use of birth control devices, even by married couples. The

Supreme Court invalidated the statute, concluding that a state had no business interfering with a married couple's decision regarding contraception. The Court did not base its decision on the Ninth Amendment, but reasoned instead that the freedoms in the Bill of Rights imply an underlying right of privacy. Individuals have, said the Court, a "zone of [personal] privacy" that government cannot lawfully infringe upon.[42]

The right of privacy was the basis for the Supreme Court's ruling in *Roe v. Wade* (1973), which gave women full freedom to choose abortion during the first three months of pregnancy.[43] In overturning a Texas law prohibiting abortion except to save the life of the mother, the Supreme Court said that the right to privacy is "broad enough to encompass a woman's decision whether or not to terminate her pregnancy."

After *Roe*, antiabortion activists sought to reverse or weaken the Court's ruling. Attempts to pass a constitutional amendment that would ban abortions were unsuccessful, but abortion foes succeeded in a campaign to prohibit the use of government funds to pay for abortions for poor women. Then, in *Webster v. Reproductive Health Services* (1989), the Supreme Court upheld a Missouri law that prohibits abortions in public hospitals and by public employees.[44]

The Webster decision was followed in 1992 by a judgment in the Pennsylvania abortion case *Planned Parenthood v. Casey*. Pennsylvania's law placed a 24-hour waiting period on women who sought an abortion, required doctors to counsel women on abortion and alternatives to abortion, required a minor to have a parent's consent or a judge's approval before having an abortion, and required a married woman to notify her husband before obtaining an abortion. Antiabortion advocates saw the Pennsylvania law as an opportunity for the Supreme Court to overturn the *Roe* precedent. However, in a decision that surprised many observers, the Court by a 5–4 margin reaffirmed the "essential holding" of *Roe v. Wade:* that a woman, because of the constitutional guarantee of privacy, has a right to abortion during the early months of pregnancy. The Court also ruled, however, that states can regulate abortion as long as they do not impose an "undue burden" on women seeking abortion. The Court concluded that the 24-hour waiting period, physician counseling, and the informed-consent requirement for minors were not undue burdens and were therefore permissible. The spousal-notification requirement, however, was judged to place a "substantial obstacle" in the path of women seeking abortion and was thereby declared unconstitutional.[45]

In a controversial 2000 ruling, *Stenberg v. Carhart*, the Supreme Court ruled that states may not ban partial-birth abortion (where the fetus's life is terminated during delivery) because it is the most appropriate medical procedure for terminating some pregnancies.[46]

Although a right of privacy has been established in some areas of personal conduct, the Supreme Court has declined to extend it to other areas. In *Bowers* v. *Hardwick* (1986), for example, the Court upheld a Georgia law prohibiting sodomy, concluding that the right of privacy did not include homosexual acts among consenting adults.[47] States can choose to permit these acts, but they are not bound to do so by the Constitution of the United States.

The Court has also held that the right of privacy does not extend to the terminally ill who might want medical help in taking their own lives. This ruling came in response to New York and Washington state laws that ban physician-assisted suicide. The Court held that a state has a legitimate interest in protecting vulnerable people. Although the Court did not say so, it hinted in its ruling that a state might choose to permit physician-assisted suicide if there were proper safeguards in its use. But the Court was clear that "liberty" in the Fourteenth Amendment does not include a constitutional *right* to doctor-assisted suicide.[48]

Privacy questions are becoming increasingly important. Mandatory drug testing by employers, DNA testing by police, and the security of personal medical records are among the many privacy issues that have been raised. Privacy questions are among the most contentious in American politics because of the moral and ethical issues they raise. Physician-assisted suicide, for example, is seen as a humane act by its proponents. What is the public benefit, they ask, in forcing the dying to accept prolonged and horrible suffering? A majority of Oregon voters in a statewide referendum concluded that there was no public benefit to this suffering and enacted the first state law that permits physician-assisted suicide. Opponents argue that society's interest in preserving life outweighs a patient's desire to die. They also worry that laws allowing doctors to assist a suicide would be abused, arguing that doctors and relatives in some instances would persuade terminally ill patients to accept death against their will or that depressed patients who ask to die will be granted their wish rather than be treated for their depression, after which they might choose to live.

RIGHTS OF PERSONS ACCUSED OF CRIMES

"Due process" refers to legal protections that have been established to preserve the rights of individuals. The most significant form of these protections is **procedural due process;** the term refers primarily to procedures that authorities must follow before a person can legitimately be punished for an offense.

The U.S. Constitution provides for several procedures designed to protect a person from wrongful arrest, conviction, and punishment. According to Article I, section 9, any person taken into police custody is entitled to seek a writ of habeas corpus, which requires law enforcement officials to bring him or her into court within a reasonable time and explain the legal reason for the detention. The Fifth and Fourteenth Amendments provide generally that no person can be deprived of life, liberty, or property without due process of law. And specific procedural protections for the accused are spelled out in the Fourth, Fifth, Sixth, and Eighth Amendments:

- *The Fourth Amendment* forbids the police to conduct searches and seizures unless they have probable cause to believe that a crime has been committed.
- *The Fifth Amendment* protects against double jeopardy (being prosecuted twice for the same offense), self-incrimination (being compelled to testify against oneself), and indictment for a crime except through grand jury proceedings.
- *The Sixth Amendment* provides the right to have legal counsel, to confront witnesses, to receive a speedy trial, and to have a trial by jury in criminal proceedings.
- *The Eighth Amendment* protects against excessive bail or fines and prohibits the infliction of cruel and unusual punishment on those convicted of crimes.

These procedural protections have always been subject to interpretation. The Sixth Amendment, for example, provides the right to have legal counsel. But what if a person cannot afford a lawyer? For most of the nation's history, poor people had almost no choice but to act as their own attorneys. Today, if a person is accused of a serious crime and cannot afford a lawyer, the government must provide one. This change came about not through a constitutional amendment but through Supreme Court rulings that gave new meaning in practice to the Sixth Amendment.

Selective Incorporation of Procedural Rights

For most of the nation's history, the procedural protections in the Bill of Rights applied only to the actions of the national government; states were not bound by them. There were limited exceptions, such as a 1932

Supreme Court ruling that a defendant charged in a state court with a crime carrying the death penalty had to be provided with an attorney.[49]

Not until the 1960s did the Court broadly require states to safeguard procedural rights. Changes in public education and communication made Americans more aware of their rights, and the civil rights movement dramatized the fact that minority group members and the poor had many fewer rights in practice than other Americans. In response, the Supreme Court in the 1960s "incorporated" Bill of Rights protections for the accused in state courts by ruling that these protections are covered by the Fourteenth Amendment's guarantee of due process of law (see Table 4-2).

This selective incorporation process began with *Mapp* v. *Ohio* (1961). Dollree Mapp's home had been entered by Cleveland police, who, though they failed to find the drugs they were looking for, happened to discover some pornographic material. Mapp's conviction for its possession was

---

TABLE 4-2   SELECTIVE INCORPORATION OF RIGHTS OF THE ACCUSED

In the 1960s, the Supreme Court selectively incorporated the fair-trial provisions of the Fourth through Eighth Amendments into the Fourteenth Amendment so that these rights would be protected from infringement by the states.

Supreme Court Case	Year	Constitutional Right (Amendment) at Issue
Mapp v. *Ohio*	1961	Unreasonable search and seizure (4th)
Robinson v. *California*	1962	Cruel and unusual punishment (8th)
Gideon v. *Wainwright*	1963	Right to counsel (6th)
Malloy v. *Hogan*	1964	Self-incrimination (5th)
Pointer v. *Texas*	1965	Right to confront witnesses (6th)
Miranda v. *Arizona*	1966	Self-incrimination (5th)
Klopfer v. *North Carolina*	1967	Speedy trial (6th)
Duncan v. *Louisiana*	1968	Jury trial in criminal cases (6th)
Benton v. *Maryland*	1968	Double jeopardy (5th)

overturned by the Supreme Court on the grounds that she had been subjected to unreasonable search and seizure.[50] The Court ruled that illegally obtained evidence could not be used in state courts.

Two years later, the Court's decision in *Gideon* v. *Wainwright* (1963) required the states to furnish attorneys for poor defendants in all felony cases. Clarence Gideon, an indigent drifter, had been convicted and sentenced to prison in Florida for breaking into a poolroom. He successfully appealed on the grounds that he had been denied due process because he could not afford to pay an attorney.[51]

During the 1960s the Court also ruled that defendants in state criminal proceedings cannot be compelled to testify against themselves;[52] have the rights to remain silent and to have legal counsel when arrested;[53] have the right to confront witnesses who testify against them;[54] must be granted a speedy trial;[55] have the right to a jury trial;[56] and cannot be subjected to double jeopardy.[57] The best known of these cases is *Miranda* v. *Arizona* (1966), as a result of which police are required to inform suspects of their rights at the time of arrest. Ernesto Miranda had confessed during police interrogation to kidnapping and raping a young woman. His confession led to his conviction, but the Supreme Court overturned it on the grounds that he had not been informed of his rights to remain silent and to have legal counsel present during interrogation. Using other evidence of Miranda's crime, the state of Arizona then retried and convicted him again. He was paroled from prison in 1972 and four years later was stabbed to death in a bar fight. Ironically, Miranda's assailant was read his "Miranda rights" when police arrested him. By now the wording has become familiar: "You have the right to remain silent. . . . Anything you say can and will be used against you in a court of law. . . . You have the right to an attorney."

In a 2000 case, *Dickerson* v. *United States*, the Supreme Court reaffirmed the *Miranda* decision, saying that because it had established a "constitutional rule," it was not subject to change by legislative action.[58]

Restricting Defendants' Rights

Although the *Miranda* decision is still intact, the Supreme Court since the 1960s, as a result of political pressures and changes in its membership, has narrowed the protections afforded those accused of crime.

THE EXCLUSIONARY RULE   Since the 1980s, a shift in the Court's philosophy has been evident. The greatest change can be seen in the application of the **exclusionary rule,** which bars the use in trials of evidence

In recent decades the Supreme Court has restricted the scope of the "exclusionary rule." This rule excludes from use in court proceedings any evidence that is illegally obtained by law enforcement officials.

obtained in violation of the Fourth Amendment's protection against "unreasonable searches and seizures." The rule was formulated in a 1914 Supreme Court decision,[59] and its application was further expanded in federal cases. The *Mapp* decision extended the exclusionary rule to state trial proceedings as well. Subsequent decisions of the Supreme Court broadened its application to the point where almost any type of illegally obtained evidence was considered inadmissible in a criminal trial.

In the 1980s, the Supreme Court reversed the trend by placing restrictions on the rule's application, concluding that illegally obtained evidence can be admitted in trials if the procedural errors are small, inadvertent, or ultimately inconsequential. In a key 1984 decision, for example, the Court ruled that illegally obtained evidence can be used against a defendant if the prosecution can prove that it would have discovered the evidence anyway.[60]

Recent Supreme Court decisions have further weakened the exclusionary rule. In the 1960s, the Court developed the principle that police had to have a solid basis ("probable cause") for believing that an individual was involved in a specific crime before they could engage in search and seizure activity. This principle has been downgraded. In 1990, for example, the Supreme Court held that roadside checkpoints where police systematically stop drivers to check them for signs of intoxication do not violate their right to protection against unreasonable search.[61]

A more definitive statement of the Court's new position is *Whren v. United States* (1996), which unanimously upheld the conviction of an individual who had been found with packets of drugs in the front seat of his car after being stopped for a minor traffic infraction. The police had no evidence (no "probable cause") to believe that drugs were actually in the car but suspected the driver was involved with drugs and used the traffic infraction as a pretext to stop and check him. The Supreme Court accepted defense arguments that the police had no clear evidence on which to base their suspicion; that the traffic infraction was not the real reason the individual was stopped; and that police usually do not stop a person for the infraction in question (turning a corner without signaling). But the Court concluded that the officers' motive was irrelevant, as long as an officer in some situations might reasonably stop a car for the infraction that occurred. Thus the stop and search of the driver was deemed to meet the Fourth Amendment's reasonableness standard.[62]

The Court's objective has been to weaken the exclusionary rule without granting police unbridled discretion. This position was evident in a case that tested the legality of a Chicago anti-loitering ordinance that gave police the authority to arrest a person who refused to obey an order to leave a scene where a suspected gang member was present. In *Chicago* v. *Morales* (1999), the Court invalidated the ordinance, concluding that it gave the police too much leeway to arrest or harass innocent persons.[63] The Court has also restricted police entry into people's homes. The Court has declared, for example, that states may not exempt drug-related searches from the general requirement that, when entering a person's home with a search warrant, police must first knock and announce their presence.[64]

HABEAS CORPUS APPEALS The Supreme Court has recently restricted habeas corpus appeals to federal courts by individuals who have been convicted of crimes in state courts. (Habeas corpus gives defendants access to federal courts in order to argue that their rights under the Constitution were violated when they were convicted in a state court.) A 1960s Supreme Court precedent had assured prisoners of the right to have their petitions heard in federal court unless they had "deliberately bypassed" the opportunity to make the appeal in state courts.[65]

This precedent was overturned in 1992, when the Court held that inmates can lose the right to a federal court hearing even if, through a lawyer's mistake, they have first failed to present their appeal properly in state courts.[66] Another significant habeas corpus defeat for inmates occurred in 1993 when the Supreme Court held that federal courts cannot overturn a state conviction on the basis of constitutional error unless the prisoner can demonstrate that the error contributed to the conviction.[67]

★ STATES IN THE NATION ★

The Death Penalty

Of the rights of the accused, none has proven more difficult to define in practice than the Eighth Amendment's prohibition against "cruel and unusual punishment." A 1972 Supreme Court decision (*Furman* v. *Georgia*) struck down the death penalty, ruling that its arbitrary application amounted to cruel and unusual punishment. States then revised their death penalty statutes to specify more precisely "the aggravating circumstances" that might justify a sentence of death, and the Supreme Court in *Gregg* v. *Georgia* (1976) upheld one such law. However, the odds that a convicted murderer will be sentenced to death vary dramatically from state to state and even within states because local prosecutors differ in how aggressively they pursue the death penalty in capital cases. Texas is far and away the leader in executions; roughly a third of all executions in the United States since 1976 have taken place in that state. The uneven application of capital punishment has been a source of recent (but unsuccessful) lawsuits that have charged that the death penalty violates the Eighth Amendment.

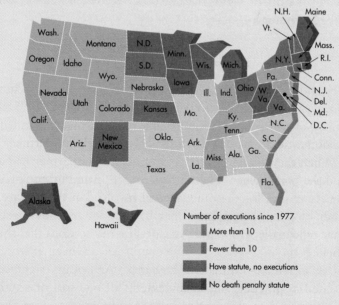

Number of executions since 1977
- More than 10
- Fewer than 10
- Have statute, no executions
- No death penalty statute

SOURCE: Bureau of Justice Statistics, 2000.

Previously, the burden of proof was on the state: it had to prove that the error did not affect the case's outcome. Then, in *Felker* v. *Turpin* (1996), the Court upheld a recent federal law that severely restricts federal habeas corpus appeals by state prison inmates who have already filed one.[68]

Through these decisions, the Supreme Court has sought to prevent frivolous and multiple federal court appeals. State prisoners had used habeas corpus appeals to contest even small issues, and some—particularly those on death row—had filed appeal after appeal. An effect was to clog the federal courts and delay other cases. A majority of Supreme Court justices concluded that a more restrictive policy toward these appeals is required. They have held that it is fair to ask inmates to first pursue their options in state courts and then, except in unusual cases,[69] to confine themselves to a single federal appeal. Civil liberties groups have objected to the change, arguing that no procedure that would protect the innocent from wrongful punishment—particularly when the death penalty is at issue—is too big a burden to place on the courts.

However, no one claims that recent decisions mark a return to the lower procedural standards that prevailed before the 1960s. Many of the vital precedents set in that decade remain in effect, including the most important one of all: the principle that procedural protections guaranteed to the accused by the Bill of Rights must be observed by the states as well as by the federal government.

Crime, Punishment, and Police Behavior

The theory and practice of procedural guarantees are often two quite different things, as Adrienne Cureton discovered on January 2, 1995. She is a plain-clothes police officer who, with a uniformed partner, was called to the scene of a domestic dispute. When a struggle ensued, her partner radioed for help. When the officers arrived, Cureton and her partner had already handcuffed the homeowner. The officers barged in and mistook Cureton, an African American, for the other person involved in the dispute. They grabbed her by the collar, dragged her by the hair onto the porch, and clubbed her repeatedly with flashlights, despite her screams that she was a police officer.[70]

There is no reliable estimate of how often Americans' rights are violated in practice, but infringements of one sort or another are commonplace. Minorities and the poor are the more likely victims. *Racial profiling* (the assumption that certain groups are more likely to commit particular crimes) is a common police practice and results

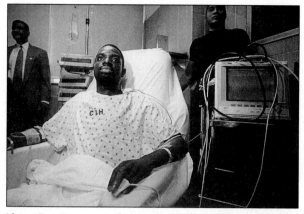

Abner Louima was sodomized with a wooden handle by a
New York City police officer after having been taken into
custody. Louima's case focused national attention on the
issue of police brutality and dramatized the difference that
can exist between the theory and the reality
of constitutional rights.

in the unequal treatment of minorities. A 1999 American Civil Liberties
Union study found that although minority and white motorists were about
equally likely to commit traffic infractions, 80 percent of the motorists
stopped and searched by Maryland State Police on Interstate 95 were minorities and only 20 percent were white, despite the fact that white motorists constituted 75 percent of all drivers. A 1999 report by the New
Jersey Attorney General's Office revealed a similar pattern in that state.

Another issue of justice in America is whether adherence to proper legal procedures produces reasonable outcomes. The Eighth Amendment
prohibits "cruel and unusual punishment" for those convicted of crime, but
judgments in this area are relatively subjective. Although the Supreme
Court has ordered officials to relieve inmate overcrowding and to improve
prison facilities in a few instances, it has concluded that inmates cannot sue
over prison conditions unless prison officials show "deliberate indifference"
to conditions.[71] The severity of a sentence can also be an Eighth Amendment issue. A divided Supreme Court in 1991 upheld a Michigan law that
mandated life imprisonment without parole for a nonviolent first-offense
conviction for possession of as little as 1.5 pounds of cocaine.[72] In general,
the Court has shied away from decisions about what constitutes cruel
and unusual punishment, preferring to leave them in the hands of legislative bodies.

How the United States Compares

Law and Order

Individual rights are a cornerstone of the American governing system and receive strong protection from the courts. The government's ability to restrict free expression is severely limited, and the individual's right to a fair trial is protected through elaborate due-process guarantees.

According to Amnesty International, a watchdog group that monitors human rights achievements and violations around the world, the United States has a good record in terms of its constitutional protection of civil liberties. Nevertheless, Amnesty International does not rank the United States as high as the countries of northern Europe in terms of respect for human rights. Among other problems, Amnesty International faults police in the United States for "excessive force" in their treatment of prisoners and faults U.S. immigration officials for the forcible return of asylum seekers to their countries of origin without granting them hearings.

Although human rights groups admire America's elaborate procedural protections for those accused of crime, they are critical of its sentencing and incarceration policies. The United States is the world leader in the number of people it places behind bars and in the length of sentences for various categories of crime. More than half of the people in prison were convicted of nonviolent offenses, such as drug use or a crime against property. Whatever the reasons, the United States is rivaled only by Russia in the proportion of its people who are in prisons.

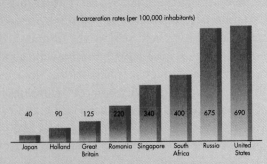

Incarceration rates (per 100,000 inhabitants)

Japan	Holland	Great Britain	Romania	Singapore	South Africa	Russia	United States
40	90	125	220	340	400	675	690

SOURCE: The Sentencing Project (U.S. and Russia), 2001; U.K. Home Office (all others), 2001.

In recent years, legislators in the United States have taken a tougher stance on crime. Congress and most states have mandated stiffer sentences, and the number of federal and state prisoners has more than doubled in the past decade. The United States has a larger proportion of its people behind bars than any country in the world (see "How the United States Compares"). America's high incarceration rate has resulted in increasingly expensive, overcrowded, and unsafe prisons, which has prompted some officials to call for more lenient sentencing, particularly for nonviolent crimes such as drug use and petty theft.

THE COURTS AND A FREE SOCIETY

A free and democratic nation has a vital stake in maintaining individual freedoms. The United States was founded on the belief that individuals have an innate right to personal liberty—to speak their minds, to worship as they choose, to be free of police intimidation. The greatest threat to individual rights in a democratic society is a popular majority backed by elected leaders determined to carry out its will. Majorities have frequently preferred policies that would diminish the freedom of those who hold minority views, have unconventional lifestyles, or simply "look different." A Time/CNN poll found, for example, that Americans were nearly as likely to say they would allow police to search anyone who merely looked suspicious as to say they would not allow it.

Greater support for individual rights exists among the political elite. Those who are most active politically, including officeholders and journalists, are more likely to express strong support for free expression and fair-trial rights. They are also better positioned than the ordinary citizen to express their beliefs. But they are not always willing to act on them. Often, the exercise of rights involves society's least savory characters—its murderers, rapists, drug dealers, and hate peddlers. Miscreants are hardly the type of people who engender public support at any level.

The courts are not isolated from the public mood. They inevitably balance society's demand for safety and order against the rights of the individual. Nevertheless, the judicial branch can normally be expected to grant more consideration to the rights of the individual, however unpopular his or her views or actions, than will the general public or elected officials. How far the courts will go in protecting a person's rights depends on the facts of the case, the existing status of the law, prevailing social needs, and the personal views of the judges. Nevertheless, the courts regard the protection of individual rights as one of their most significant responsibilities, a perspective that is owed in no small measure to the Bill of Rights. It transformed the inalienable rights of life, liberty, and property into legal rights, thus putting them under judicial protection.[73]

Nevertheless, the judiciary alone cannot provide adequate protection for individual rights. A civil society rests also on enlightened representatives and a tolerant citizenry. If, for example, politicians and the public encourage police to infringe on the rights of vaguely threatening minorities or nonconformists, the judiciary's protection of persons accused of crimes will not ensure justice. It may be said that the test of a truly civil society is not its treatment of popular ideas and of its best citizens but its willingness to tolerate ideas that the majority detests and to respect equally the rights of its least popular citizens.

SUMMARY

In their search for personal liberty, Americans added the Bill of Rights to the Constitution shortly after its ratification. These amendments guarantee certain political, procedural, and property rights against infringement by the national government. Freedom of expression is the most basic of democratic rights. People are not free unless they can freely express their views. Nevertheless, free expression may conflict with the nation's security needs during times of war and insurrection. The courts at times have allowed government to limit expression substantially for purposes of national security. In recent decades, however, the courts have protected a very wide range of free expression in the areas of speech, press, and religion.

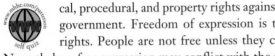

The guarantees embodied in the Bill of Rights originally applied only to the national government. Under the principle of selective incorporation of these guarantees into the Fourteenth Amendment, the courts extended them to state governments, though the process was slow and uneven. In the 1920s and 1930s, First Amendment guarantees of freedom of expression were given protection from infringement by the states. The states, however, continued to have wide discretion in criminal proceedings until the early 1960s, when most of the fair-trial rights in the Bill of Rights were given federal protection.

"Due process of law" refers to legal protections that have been established to preserve individual rights. The most significant form of these protections consists of procedures or methods (for example, the right of an accused person to have an attorney present during police interrogation) designed to ensure that an individual's rights are upheld. A major controversy in this area is the breadth of the exclusionary rule, which bars the use in trials of illegally obtained evidence. The right of privacy, particularly as it applies to the abortion issue, is also a source of controversy.

Civil liberties are not absolute but must be balanced against other considerations (such as national security or public safety) and against one another when different rights come into conflict. The judicial branch of government, particularly the Supreme Court, has taken on much of the responsibility for protecting and interpreting individual rights. The Court's positions have changed with time and conditions, but the Court has generally been more protective of and sensitive to civil liberties than have elected officials or popular majorities.

MAJOR CONCEPTS

Bill of Rights	imminent-lawless-action test
civil liberties	libel
clear-and-present-danger test	prior restraint
due-process clause	procedural due process
establishment clause	selective incorporation
exclusionary rule	slander
freedom of expression	symbolic speech
free-exercise clause	

SUGGESTED READINGS AND WEB SITES

Abraham, Henry J. *Freedom and the Court.* New York: Oxford University Press, 1998. A comprehensive analysis of the Supreme Court's work on civil rights and civil liberties.

Epstein, Lee, and Thomas G. Walker. *Constitutional Law for a Changing America,* 2d ed. Washington, D.C.: Congressional Quarterly Press, 2000. An accessible introduction to U.S. constitutional law.

Lewis, Anthony. *Gideon's Trumpet.* New York: Random House, 1964. The riveting story of Clarence Gideon and the effects of his case on the right to legal counsel.

McDonagh, Eileen. *Breaking the Abortion Deadlock.* New York: Oxford University Press, 1996. A forward look at breaking the abortion deadlock.

Nagel, Robert F. *Judicial Power and American Character.* New York: Oxford University Press, 1996. Concludes that the real protection for legal rights resides in political action rather than judicial decisions.

Perry, Michael J. *Religion in Politics: Constitutional and Moral Perspectives.* New York: Oxford University Press, 1997. A constitutional and moral look at the role of religion in politics.

Wirenius, John R. *First Amendment, First Principles.* New York: Holmes and Meier, 2000. Analysis of verbal acts and freedom of speech.

http://oyez.nwu.edu/index.html   Includes information on Supreme Court rulings; particularly useful when studying nineteenth-century cases.

http://www.aclu.org/   The American Civil Liberties Union site. It provides information on current civil liberties and civil rights issues, including information on recent and pending Supreme Court cases.

http://www.findlaw.com/casecode/supreme.html   An excellent source of information on Supreme Court and lower court rulings.

http://www.mitretek.org/business_areas/justice/cjlinks/   A site dedicated to criminal justice questions with links to many additional sites that focus on particular issues.

READING 4

The Internet and Free Expression
RENO V. ACLU (1997)

Introduction

The government has a legitimate interest in protecting children from exposure to indecent material. It also has a legitimate interest in protecting free speech rights. But what happens when these interests conflict? In its *Reno* v. *ACLU* decision, the Supreme Court ruled that provisions of the Communications Decency Act (hereafter, CDA) of 1996 were unconstitutional because they were overly broad and would suppress free speech. The CDA was intended to protect minors from "indecent" and "patently offensive" materials communicated on the Internet. In reaching its judgment, the Court did not conclude that the government was prohibited from regulating Internet content. But the Court did conclude that the CDA, as written, would serve to inhibit lawful speech on the Internet and, therefore, abridged the First Amendment right of free speech. The following is a portion of the Supreme Court's opinion (quotation marks indicate the Court's references to words used in earlier court rulings or other texts).

At issue is the constitutionality of two statutory provisions enacted to protect minors from "indecent" and "patently offensive" communications on the Internet. Notwithstanding the legitimacy and importance of the congressional goal of protecting children from harmful materials, we [conclude] that the statute abridges "the freedom of speech" protected by the First Amendment. . . .

[The two CDA provisions] are informally known as the "indecent transmission" provision and the "patently offensive display" provision. . . . The first prohibits the knowing transmission of obscene or indecent messages to any recipient under 18 years of age. . . . The second provision prohibits the knowing sending or display of patently offensive messages in a manner that is available to a person under 18 years of age. . . .

[The vague language of CDA] renders it problematic for purposes of the First Amendment. For instance, each of the two parts of the CDA uses a different linguistic form. The first uses the word "indecent," while the second speaks of material that "in context, depicts or describes, in terms patently offensive as measured by contemporary community standards, sexual or excretory activities or organs." Given the absence of a definition of either term, this difference in language will provoke uncertainty among speakers about how the two standards relate to each other and just what they mean. Could a speaker confidently assume that a serious discussion about birth control practices, homosexuality, or the consequences of prison rape would not violate the CDA? This uncertainty undermines the likelihood that the CDA has been carefully tailored to the congressional goal of protecting minors from potentially harmful materials.

The vagueness of the CDA is a matter of special concern for two reasons. First, the CDA is a content based regulation of speech. The vagueness of such a regulation raises special First Amendment concerns because of its obvious chilling effect on free speech. Second, the CDA is a criminal statute. In addition to the opprobrium and stigma of a criminal conviction, the CDA threatens violators with penalties including up to two years in prison for each act of violation. The severity of criminal sanctions may well cause speakers to remain silent rather than communicate even arguably unlawful words, ideas, and images. . . .

Given the vague contours of the coverage of the statute, it unquestionably silences some speakers whose messages would be entitled to constitutional protection. That danger provides further reason for insisting that the statute not be overly broad. The CDA's burden on protected speech cannot be justified if it could be avoided by a more carefully drafted statute. We are persuaded that the CDA lacks the precision that the First Amendment requires when a statute regulates the content of speech. In order to deny minors access to potentially harmful speech, the CDA effectively suppresses a large amount of speech that adults have a constitutional right to receive and to address to one another. That burden on adult speech is unacceptable if less restrictive alternatives would be at least as effective in achieving the legitimate purpose that the statute was enacted to serve. . . .

It is true that we have repeatedly recognized the governmental interest in protecting children from harmful materials. But that interest does not justify an unnecessarily broad suppression of speech addressed to adults. As we have explained, the Government may not "reduc[e] the adult population . . . to . . . only what is fit for children." "[R]egardless of the strength of the government's interest" in protecting children, "[t]he level of discourse reaching a mailbox simply cannot be limited to that which would be suitable for a sandbox. . . . "

In arguing that the CDA does not diminish adult communication, the Government relies on the incorrect factual premise that prohibiting a transmission whenever it is known that one of its recipients is a minor would not interfere with adult to adult communication. . . . [T]his premise is untenable. Given the size of the potential audience for most messages, in the absence of a viable age verification process, the sender must be charged with knowing that one or more minors will likely view it. Knowledge that, for instance, one or more members of a 100 person chat group will be minor—and therefore that it would be a crime to send the group an indecent message—would surely burden communication among adults. . . .

The breadth of the CDA's coverage is wholly unprecedented. Unlike the regulations upheld in [other cases], the scope of the CDA is not limited to commercial speech or commercial entities. Its open ended prohibitions embrace all nonprofit entities and individuals posting indecent messages or displaying them on their own computers in the presence of minors. The general, undefined terms "indecent" and "patently offensive" cover large amounts of nonpornographic material with serious educational or other value. Moreover, the "community standards" criterion as applied to the Internet means that any communication available to a nationwide audience will be judged by the standards of the community most likely to be offended by the message. . . . [A] parent who sent his 17-year-old college freshman information on birth control via e-mail could be incarcerated even though neither he, his child, nor anyone in their home community, found the material "indecent" or "patently offensive," if the college town's community thought otherwise. . . .

The Government . . . asserts that the "knowledge" requirement. . . , when coupled with the "specific child" element, saves the CDA from overbreadth. Because both sections prohibit the dissemination of indecent messages only to persons known to be under 18, the Government argues, it does not require transmitters to "refrain from communicating indecent material to adults; they need only refrain from disseminating such materials to persons they know to be under 18." This argument ignores the fact that most Internet fora—including chat rooms, newsgroups, mail exploders, and the Web—are open to all comers. The Government's assertion that the knowledge requirement somehow protects the communications of adults is therefore untenable. Even the strongest reading of the "specific person" requirement cannot save the statute. It would confer broad powers of censorship, in the form of a "heckler's veto," upon any opponent of indecent speech who might simply log on and inform the would be discoursers that his 17-year-old child—a "specific person . . . under 18 years of age,"—would be present. . . .

[The] CDA places an unacceptably heavy burden on protected speech. . . . [In an earlier decision], we remarked that the speech restriction at issue there amounted to "'burn[ing] the house to roast the pig.'" The CDA, casting a far darker shadow over free speech, threatens to torch a large segment of the Internet community. . . . [The] Government asserts that—in addition to its interest in protecting children—its "[e]qually significant" interest in fostering the growth of the Internet provides an independent basis for upholding the constitutionality of the CDA. The Government apparently assumes that the unregulated availability of "indecent" and "patently offensive" material on the Internet is driving countless citizens away from the medium because of the risk of exposing themselves or their children to harmful material.

We find this argument singularly unpersuasive. The dramatic expansion of this new marketplace of ideas contradicts the factual basis of this contention. The record demonstrates that the growth of the Internet has been and continues to be phenomenal. As a matter of constitutional tradition, in the absence of evidence to the contrary, we presume that governmental regulation of the content of speech is more likely to interfere with the free exchange of ideas than to encourage it. The interest in encouraging freedom of expression in a democratic society outweighs any theoretical but unproven benefit of censorship.

SOURCE: *Janet Reno, Attorney General of the United States v. American Civil Liberties Union*, No. 96-511 (1997).

CHAPTER FIVE

Equal Rights

I have a dream that one day this nation will rise up and live out the
true meaning of its creed: "We hold these truths to be self-evident:
that all men are created equal."

MARTIN LUTHER KING, JR.[1]

T HE PRODUCERS of ABC television's *Prime Time Live* put hidden
cameras on two young men, equally well dressed, and sent them
on different routes to do the same things—search for an apartment, shop
for a car, look at albums in a record store. The cameras recorded the reactions the two men received. One was greeted with smiles and was invited to
buy, sometimes at favorable prices. The other man was treated with suspicious looks, was sometimes made to wait, and was sometimes asked to pay
more. Why the difference? The explanation was simple: the young man
who was routinely well received was white; the young man who was treated
badly was an African American.

The Urban Institute had conducted a similar but more elaborate ex-
periment. It was based on pairs of specially trained white and black male
college students who were the same in all respects—education, work experience, speech patterns, physical builds—except for their race. The students
responded individually to nearly five hundred classified job advertisements
in Chicago and Washington, D.C. The black applicants got fewer interviews, had shorter interviews, and were given fewer job offers than the
white applicants. An Urban Institute spokesperson said, "The level of reverse discrimination [favoring blacks over whites] that we found was limited, was certainly far lower than many might have been led to fear, and was
swamped by the extent of discrimination against black job applicants."[2]

These two experiments suggest why some Americans are still struggling for equal rights. In theory, Americans are equal in their rights, but in
practice, they are not equal today, nor have they ever been. African Americans, women, Hispanic Americans, the disabled, Jews, Native Americans,

Catholics, Asian Americans, homosexuals, and members of nearly every other minority group have been victims of discrimination in fact and in law. The nation's creed—"all men are created equal"—has encouraged minorities to believe that they deserve equal justice and has given weight to their claims for fair treatment. But inequality is built into almost every aspect of our society. To take but one example: African Americans with a correctable heart problem are three times less likely to receive the necessary surgery than are whites with the same problem.[3]

This chapter focuses on **equal rights,** or **civil rights,** terms that refer to the right of every person to equal protection under the law and equal access to society's opportunities and public facilities. We saw in Chapter 4 that "civil liberties" refer to *individual* rights, such as freedom of speech, that are protected from infringement by government. "Equal rights" or "civil rights" have to do with whether individual members of differing *groups*—racial, sexual, and the like—are treated equally by government and, in some areas, by private parties. To oversimplify, civil liberties deal with issues of personal freedom, and civil rights involve issues of equality.

Although the law refers to the rights of individuals first and to those of groups in a secondary and derivative way, this chapter concentrates on groups because the history of civil rights has been largely one of group claims to equality. The chapter emphasizes the following main points:

* *Disadvantaged groups have had to struggle for equal rights.*
* *Americans have attained substantial equality under the law. They have, in legal terms, equal protection of the laws, equal access to accommodations and housing, and an equal right to vote.*
* *Legal equality for all Americans has not resulted in* de facto *equality. African Americans, women, Hispanic Americans, and other traditionally disadvantaged groups are given a disproportionately small share of America's opportunities and benefits.*

THE STRUGGLE FOR EQUALITY

Equality has always been the least fully developed of America's founding concepts. Not even Thomas Jefferson, who had a deep admiration for the "common man," believed that broad meaning could be given to the claim of the Declaration of Independence that "all men are created equal." To Jefferson, equality had a restricted, though significant, meaning: people are of equal moral worth and as such deserve equal treatment under the law.[4]

Even then, Jefferson made a distinction between free men, who were entitled to legal equality, and slaves, who were not.

The history of America shows that disadvantaged groups have rarely achieved a greater measure of justice without a struggle. Legal equality has rarely been bestowed by the more powerful upon the less powerful. Their gains have nearly always occurred through intense and sustained political movements, such as the civil rights movement of the 1960s, that have pressured established interests to relinquish or share their privileged status (see Chapter 7).

Disadvantaged groups have a shared history of political exclusion, struggles for empowerment, and policy triumphs, but they also have distinctive histories, as is evident by a brief look at the efforts of African Americans, women, Native Americans, Hispanic Americans, Asian Americans, and other groups to achieve a greater degree of equality.

African Americans

Of all America's problems, none has been so persistent as the white race's unwillingness to yield a fair share of society's benefits to members of the black race. The ancestors of most African Americans came to this country as slaves, after having been captured in Africa, shipped in chains across the Atlantic, and sold in markets in Charleston and other seaports.

It took a civil war to abolish slavery, but institutionalized racism did not end with the war. When Reconstruction ended in 1877 with the withdrawal of federal troops from the South, whites in the region gradually reestablished racial segregation by enacting laws that prohibited black citizens from using the same public facilities as whites.[5] In *Plessy v. Ferguson* (1896), the Supreme Court endorsed these laws, ruling that "separate" facilities for the two races did not violate the Constitution as long as the facilities were "equal." "If one race be inferior to the other socially," the Court asserted, "the Constitution of the United States cannot put them on the same plane."[6] The *Plessy* decision became a justification for the separate and *unequal* treatment of African Americans. Black children, for example, were forced into separate schools that had few teachers and had to get by with worn-out books that had been used previously in white schools.

Black leaders challenged these discriminatory state and local policies through legal action, but not until the late 1930s did the Supreme Court begin to respond favorably to their demands. The Court began modestly by ruling that where no public facilities existed for African Americans, they must be allowed to use those reserved for whites.[7]

THE *BROWN* DECISION　Substantial judicial relief for African Americans was finally achieved in 1954 with *Brown* v. *Board of Education of Topeka*, arguably the most significant ruling in Supreme Court history. The case involved Linda Carol Brown, a black child in Topeka, Kansas, who was denied admission to an all-white elementary school that she passed every day on her way to her all-black school, which was twelve blocks farther away.[8] In its decision, the Court fully reversed its "separate but equal" doctrine by declaring that racial segregation of public schools "generates [among black children] a feeling of inferiority as to their status in the community that may affect their hearts and minds in a way unlikely ever to be undone. . . . Separate educational facilities are inherently unequal."[9]

As a 1954 Gallup poll indicated, a sizable majority of southern whites opposed the *Brown* decision, and billboards were erected along southern roadways calling for the impeachment of Chief Justice Earl Warren. For their part, northern whites were neither strongly for nor strongly against school desegregation. A Gallup poll revealed that only a slim majority of whites outside the South agreed with the *Brown* decision.

THE BLACK CIVIL RIGHTS MOVEMENT　After *Brown*, the struggle of African Americans for their rights became a political movement. Perhaps no single event turned national public opinion so dramatically against segregation as a 1963 march led by Dr. Martin Luther King, Jr., in Birmingham, Alabama. An advocate of nonviolent protest, King had been leading peaceful demonstrations for nearly eight years before that fateful day in Birmingham.[10] As the nation watched in disbelief on television, police officers led by Birmingham's sheriff, Eugene "Bull" Connor, attacked King and his followers with dogs, cattle prods, and firehoses.

The modern civil rights movement peaked with the triumphant March on Washington for Jobs and Freedom of August 2, 1963, which attracted 250,000 demonstrators, one of the largest gatherings in the history of the nation's capital. "I have a dream," the Reverend Dr. King told the gathering, "that my four little children will one day live in a nation where they will not be judged by the color of their skin but by the content of their character."

A year later, after a prolonged fight in Congress that included every legislative obstacle that racial conservatives could muster, the Civil Rights Act of 1964 was enacted. The tide was turning against racial inequality. President Lyndon Johnson, who had been a decisive force in the battle to pass the Civil Rights Act, called for new legislation that would end racial barriers to voting.[11] Congress's answer was the 1965 Voting Rights Act.

Two police dogs attack a black civil rights activist (*center left of picture*) during the 1963 Birmingham demonstrations. Such images of hatred and violence shook many white Americans out of their complacency regarding race relations.

(The Civil Rights and Voting Rights acts are discussed in detail later in the chapter.)

Although the most significant progress in history toward the legal equality of all Americans occurred during the 1960s, Dr. King's dream of a color-blind society has remained elusive.[12] Studies have found, for example, that African Americans accused of crime are more likely to be convicted than white Americans on trial for comparable offenses and that they are more likely to receive stiffer sentences if convicted.[13] Federal statistics from the National Office of Drug Control Policy and the U.S. Sentencing Commission revealed that in 1997 black Americans accounted for more than 75 percent of crack cocaine convictions but only about 35 percent of crack cocaine users.

One area where African Americans have made substantial progress since the 1960s is the winning of election to public office (see "States in the Nation").[14] Although the percentage of black elected officials is still far below the proportion of African Americans in the population, it has risen sharply over recent decades, as has the rate of black voting.[15] As of 2001, there were more than twenty black members of Congress and two hundred black mayors—including the mayors of some of this country's largest cities.

★ STATES IN THE NATION ★

Black and Latino Representation in State Legislatures

For a long period, minorities were barely visible in the state legislatures. The situation began to change after passage of the 1964 Civil Rights Act and the 1965 Voting Rights Act, but minorities are still underrepresented relative to their numbers in the population. Only 8 percent of state legislators in 2000 were black and a mere 3 percent were Hispanic. Alabama and Mississippi have the highest proportion (25 percent each) of African American state legislators. New Mexico has the highest number (37 percent) of Latino lawmakers. A few states, including Maine and North Dakota, have no legislator from either of these minority groups. Of course, these states have small minority populations while states such as Alabama, Mississippi, and New Mexico have much larger ones.

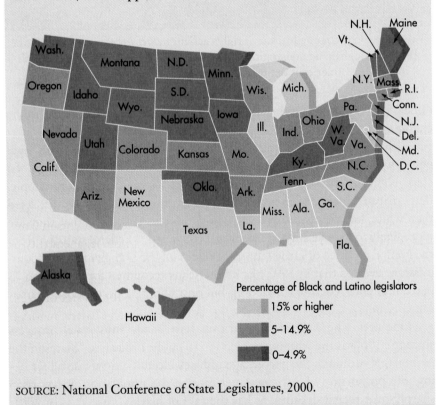

Percentage of Black and Latino legislators

15% or higher

5–14.9%

0–4.9%

SOURCE: National Conference of State Legislatures, 2000.

Women

The United States carried over from English common law a political disregard for women, forbidding them to vote, hold public office, and serve on juries. Upon marriage, a woman essentially lost her identity as an individual and could not own and dispose of property without her husband's consent. Even the wife's body was not fully hers. A wife's adultery was ruled by the Supreme Court to be a violation of the husband's property rights![16]

The first women's rights convention in America was held in 1848 in Seneca Falls, New York, after Lucretia Mott and Elizabeth Cady Stanton had been barred from the main floor of an antislavery convention. Thereafter, however, the struggle for women's rights became closely aligned with the abolitionist movement, but the passage of the post–Civil War constitutional amendments proved to be a setback for the women's movement. The Fifteenth Amendment, for example, said that the right to vote could not be abridged on account of race or color, but said nothing about sex.[17] After decades of struggle, the Nineteenth Amendment was finally adopted in 1920, forbidding denial of the right to vote "by the United States or by any state on account of sex."

WOMEN'S LEGAL AND POLITICAL GAINS   Ratification of the Nineteenth Amendment encouraged leaders of the women's movement to propose in 1923 a constitutional amendment that would guarantee equal rights for women. Congress rejected that proposal and several subsequent ones. In 1973, however, Congress approved an Equal Rights Amendment (ERA) and submitted it to the states for ratification or rejection. The ERA failed by three states to get the three-fourths majority required for ratification.[18]

Although the ERA did not become part of the Constitution, it helped bring women's rights to the forefront at a time when developments in Congress and the courts were contributing significantly to the legal equality of the sexes.[19] Among the congressional initiatives that have helped women are the Equal Pay Act of 1963, which prohibits sex discrimination in salary and wages by some categories of employers; the Civil Rights Act of 1964, which prohibits sex discrimination in programs that receive federal funding; Title IX of the Education Amendment of 1972, which prohibits sex discrimination in education; the Equal Credit Act of 1974, as amended in 1976, which prohibits sex discrimination in the granting of financial credit; and the Civil Rights Act of 1991 and the Family Leave Act of 1993 (discussed later in this chapter).

Women have made clear gains in the area of appointive and elective offices.[20] In 1981 President Reagan appointed the first woman to serve on the

Supreme Court, Sandra Day O'Connor. When the Democratic party in 1984 chose Geraldine Ferraro as its vice-presidential nominee, it was the first time a woman ran on the national ticket of a major political party.[21] The election of California's Dianne Feinstein and Barbara Boxer in 1992 marked the first time that women occupied both U.S. Senate seats from a state.

Despite such signs of progress,[22] women are still a long way from political equality with men.[23] Women occupy less than 15 percent of congressional seats and only 20 percent of statewide and city council offices[24] (see box: "How the United States Compares").

Although women are underrepresented in political office, their vote is becoming increasingly distinctive. Until the 1970s, there was almost no difference in the voting patterns of women and men. Today, there is a substantial **gender gap:** women and men differ substantially in their political attitudes and voting tendencies. Women are more supportive than men of government programs for the poor, minorities, children, and the elderly. They also have a greater tendency to cast their votes for Democratic candidates (see Figure 5-1). (The gender gap is discussed further in Chapters 6 and 8.)

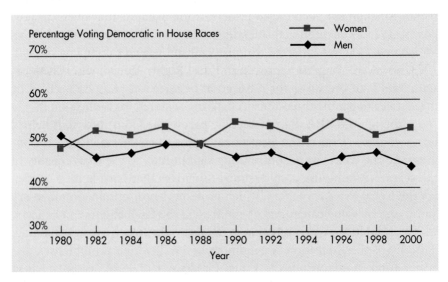

FIGURE 5-1 THE GENDER GAP IN CONGRESSIONAL VOTING
Women and men differ, on average, in their political behavior. For example, women are more likely than men to vote Democratic, as shown by the difference between the women's vote and the men's vote for Democratic candidates in U.S. House races. Source: National Election Studies (1988–1998); Exit Polls (2000).

HOW THE UNITED STATES COMPARES

Women's Inequality

The one form of inequality common to all nations is that of gender: nowhere are women equal to men in law or in fact. But there are large differences between countries. A study by the Population Crisis Committee ranked the United States third overall in women's equality, behind only Sweden and Finland. Based on five measures—jobs, education, social relations, marriage and family, and health—the study rated the status of U.S. women at 82.5 percent that of men.

The inequality of women is also underlined by their lack of representation in public office. There is no country in which women constitute as many as half the members of the national legislature. The Scandinavian countries rank highest in terms of the percentage of female lawmakers. Other northern European countries have lower levels, but the levels are higher than that of the United States. Until the 1992 election, only 6 percent of U.S. House members were women. In 1992, as a consequence of reapportionment and the retirement of an unusually large number of incumbents, the number of women in the House nearly doubled and has since risen to 13 percent. The accompanying figure, estimated from several sources, indicates the approximate percentage of seats held by women in the largest chamber of each country's national legislature.

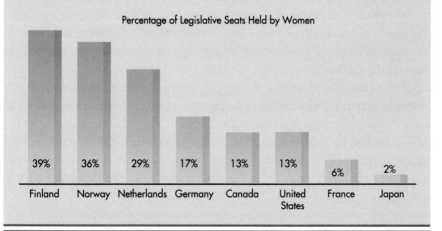

Percentage of Legislative Seats Held by Women

Finland	Norway	Netherlands	Germany	Canada	United States	France	Japan
39%	36%	29%	17%	13%	13%	6%	2%

JOB-RELATED ISSUES: FAMILY LEAVE, COMPARABLE WORTH, AND SEXUAL HARASSMENT   In recent decades, increasing numbers of women have sought employment outside the home. Government statistics indicate that three in five women worked outside the home in 2000, compared with only one in eight in 1950. Women have made gains in many traditionally male-dominated fields. For example, women now make up a third of the new lawyers who enter the job market each year. The change in women's status is also reflected in education statistics. In 1972, more white, black, and Hispanic men than women enrolled in college. Today, the reverse is true: more women than men of each race are enrolled.

The increase in the number of women in the workplace has created demands for the expansion of programs such as day care centers and parental leave. In 1993, Congress passed the Family and Medical Leave Act, which provides up to twelve weeks of unpaid leave for employees, male or female, to care for a new baby or a seriously ill family member. Upon return from leave, employees must ordinarily be restored to their original or equivalent positions with equivalent pay, benefits, and other employment terms.

Nevertheless, women are less than equal to men when it comes to job opportunities and benefits. Women increasingly occupy managerial positions, but they are less likely to receive promotions than men and rarely get the top corporate jobs. The term "glass ceiling" refers to the invisible but nonetheless real barrier to advancement that talented women encounter after having reached the middle-management level.

Women also hold a disproportionate number of the poorer-paying jobs in society. Although the situation has been improving, the average salary for full-time women employees is only about three-fourths that of full-time men employees. This situation has led to demands by women for equal pay for work that is of similar difficulty and responsibility and that requires similar levels of education and training—a concept called **comparable worth.** A comparable-worth policy would eliminate salary inequities resulting from the fact that some jobs (for example, secretarial positions) have traditionally been dominated by women and thus pay less than male-dominated jobs (for example, truck driver positions). Advocates of comparable worth gained an early victory when the Supreme Court held in 1981 that female guards at a prison had to be paid the same as male guards even if their work assignments differed.[25] In general, however, proponents of comparable worth have had only limited success in persuading public and private employers to accept their view.

Workplace discrimination against women includes sexual harassment. Lewd comments and unwelcome advances are a part of everyday life for

Employees in certain job categories dominated by
women—day care workers, secretaries, and so on—are
paid less than those in male-dominated jobs with similar
educational requirements and levels of responsibility.
The concept of comparable worth is proposed as a
remedy for such inequities.

many working women, and the courts have taken an increasingly firm stand
against firms that tolerate such behavior. In 1998, the Supreme Court held
that a firm can be held liable for sexual misconduct by supervisors even if
higher officers in the firm were unaware of it and even if the employee's
suffering did not extend to denial of job benefits, such as pay and promotion. The Court also held, however, that a firm's liability is reduced when it
has an aggressive program to guard against sexual harassment in the workplace.[26]

Federal law also bars sexual discrimination in schools. In a 1999 ruling,
the Supreme Court held that schools that ignore a pattern of persistent and
severe sexual harassment are liable for damages. However, in a controversial 2000 decision, the Supreme Court invalidated a provision of the federal
Violence Against Women Act (VAWA) that permitted victims of domestic
violence, rape, and other acts motivated by gender to sue their attackers in
federal court. The Court struck down the provision on grounds that it unlawfully infringed on the power of the states. Although the ruling was one
in a series of recent decisions that have sought to limit federal power (see
Chapter 3), the substance of the case gave it national attention. The implications of the ruling depend on whether a woman lives in a state that itself
provides an adequate civil remedy in the case of such attacks. In states that
do not provide this legal protection, women will not have an opportunity to
seek monetary damages from their attackers.[27]

Native Americans

When white settlers began arriving in America in large numbers during the seventeenth century, nearly ten million Native Americans were living in the territory that would become the United States. By 1900, the Native American population had plummeted to less than one million. Diseases brought by white settlers had taken a toll on the various Indian tribes, but so had wars and massacres. "The only good Indian is a dead Indian" is not simply a hackneyed expression from cowboy movies. It was part of a strategy of westward expansion, as settlers and U.S. troops alike mercilessly drove the eastern Indians from their ancestral lands to the Great Plains, and then took those lands as well.

Today Native Americans number more than one million, about half of whom live on or close to reservations set aside for them by the federal government. Native Americans are less than half as likely to attend college as other Americans, their life expectancy is more than ten years lower than the national average, and their infant mortality rate is more than three times higher than that of white Americans. In recent years, some Native American tribes have erected gaming casinos on reservation land. The casinos have brought jobs and income to the reservations but have also brought controversy: traditionalists argue that the casinos are destroying their tribal cultures.

The civil rights movement of the 1960s at first did not include Native Americans. Then, in the early 1970s, militant Native Americans occupied the Bureau of Indian Affairs in Washington, D.C., and later seized control of the village of Wounded Knee on a Sioux reservation in southwestern South Dakota, exchanging gunfire with U.S. marshals. These episodes brought attention to the grievances of Native Americans and may have contributed to the passage in 1974 of legislation that granted Native Americans on reservations a greater measure of control over federal programs that affected them. Native Americans had already benefited from the legislative climate created by the civil rights movement of the 1960s. In 1968, Congress had enacted the Indian Bill of Rights, which gives Native Americans on reservations constitutional guarantees that are similar to those held by other Americans.

In recent years Native Americans have filed suit to reclaim lost ancestral lands and have won a few settlements. But they stand no realistic chance of getting back even those lands that had been granted them by federal treaty but were later sold off or simply taken forcibly by federal authorities. Native Americans were not even official citizens of the United

States until an act of Congress in 1924. This status came too late to be of much help; their traditional way of life had already been seriously eroded.

Hispanic Americans

The fastest-growing minority in the United States is that of Hispanic Americans, that is, people of Spanish-speaking background. Hispanics are also one of the country's oldest ethnic groups. Some Hispanics are descendants of people who helped colonize the areas of California, Texas, Florida, New Mexico, and Arizona before they were taken over by the United States. But most Hispanics are recent immigrants or their descendants.

The 2000 census counted roughly 35 million Hispanics living in the United States, an increase of 40 percent over the 1990 census. Hispanics had surpassed African Americans as the nation's largest racial or ethnic minority group. They have emigrated to the United States primarily from Mexico and the Caribbean islands, mainly Cuba and Puerto Rico. About half of all Hispanics in the United States were born in Mexico or claim a Mexican ancestry. Hispanics are concentrated in their states of entry; thus Florida, New York, and New Jersey have large numbers of Caribbean Hispanics, while California, Texas, Arizona, and New Mexico have many immigrants from Mexico. More than half the population of Los Angeles is of Hispanic—mostly Mexican—descent.

The term *Hispanic* can be misleading if it is construed to mean a group of people who all think alike (see Table 5-1). Hispanics cover a wide political spectrum, from the conservative Republican-leaning Cuban Americans of southern Florida to the liberal Democratic-leaning Puerto Ricans of the Northeast. Hispanic Americans share a common language, Spanish, but they are not monolithic in their politics.

LEGAL AND POLITICAL ACTION   Hispanic Americans have benefited from laws and court rulings aimed primarily at protecting other groups. Thus, although the Civil Rights Act of 1964 was largely a response to the condition of black people, its provisions against discrimination apply broadly to other groups as well.

Nevertheless, Hispanics had their own civil rights movement. The most publicized actions were the farm workers' strikes of the late 1960s and the 1970s that sought basic labor rights for migrant workers. Migrants were working long hours for low pay, were living in shacks without electricity or plumbing, and were unwelcome in many local schools, and sometimes in local hospitals as well. Farm owners at first refused to bargain with the

TABLE 5-1 HISPANICS' PARTY IDENTIFICATION, BY NATIONAL ORIGIN Hispanics share a common language and ancestry but differ substantially in their political leanings.			
Party Identification	Puerto Rican Americans	Mexican Americans	Cuban Americans
Democratic	64%	60%	19%
Independent	22	24	17
Republican	14	16	64
	100%	100%	100%

SOURCE: Reported in Rudolpho O. de la Garza, Angelo Falcon, F. Chris Garcia, and John A. Garcia, "Hispanic Americans in the Mainstream of U.S. Politics," *The Public Perspective*, July/August 1992, p. 19. © The Roper Center for Public Opinion Research, University of Connecticut. Reprinted with permission.

workers, but a well-organized national boycott of California grapes and lettuce forced that state to pass a law giving migrant workers the right to bargain collectively. The strikes were led by Cesar Chavez, who himself grew up in a Mexican American migrant family.[28] Chavez's tactics were copied in other states, particularly Texas, but the results were less successful.

Hispanics face some distinctive problems. The fact that many do not speak English led to a 1968 amendment to the 1964 Civil Rights Act that funds public school programs offering English instruction in the language of children for whom English is a second language. In addition, many Hispanics are illegal aliens and do not have the full rights of citizens. In *De Canas* v. *Bica* (1976), for example, the Supreme Court upheld a state law barring illegal aliens from employment.[29]

In 1986 Congress passed the landmark Immigration Reform and Control Act, commonly known as the Simpson–Mizzoli Act, which primarily affected Hispanics. The legislation offered citizenship to illegal aliens who could prove they had lived continuously in the United States for five years. Roughly two million Hispanics received their citizenship in this way. The act also mandated fines on employers who hired aliens without work permits; it was expected that the resulting lack of job opportunities would eliminate a main incentive for aliens to enter the country illegally.

The issue of illegal aliens was also addressed through California's controversial Proposition 187. Placed on the state's ballot in 1994 through a citizen petition, Proposition 187 received the votes of a majority of

Californians even though a majority of the state's Mexican Americans voted against it. The initiative aimed to cut off public services to illegal immigrants, the great majority of whom are Mexicans. They would no longer receive state-funded food stamps, welfare, and medical care except in life-threatening circumstances, and they would no longer be eligible for public schooling at any level. Supporters of the initiative claimed it would save the state from bankruptcy (for example, 10 percent of California's primary and secondary school students are illegal aliens, and their education costs the state more than $1 billion annually).[30] To many of the state's Mexican Americans, the initiative was a thinly disguised attempt to keep additional people from Mexico—legal and illegal aliens alike—out of the state. The implementation of Proposition 187 was delayed pending a court ruling on its constitutionality, and most of its key provisions were subsequently judged to be unconstitutional.

GROWING POLITICAL POWER Hispanic Americans are an important political force in several states, and their influence is likely to increase substantially in the future. Hispanics are projected to become the largest

U.S. Congresswoman Loretta Sanchez (D-Calif.) represents a part of Orange County, California. Hispanic Americans are growing in political and cultural influence as their numbers increase in California, Arizona, New Mexico, Texas, and other states.

single population group in California in the current century. Their political involvement, like that of other immigrant groups, can be expected to increase as they become more deeply rooted in the society and economy. At present, nearly half of all Hispanic adults are not registered to vote, and only about a third actually vote, which limits the group's political power. Nevertheless, the sheer size of the Hispanic population in states such as Texas and California makes the group a potent political force, as was evident in the 2000 presidential campaign when both parties mounted a massive effort to woo Hispanic voters.

More than four thousand Hispanic Americans nationwide hold public office. In 1974 Arizona and New Mexico elected governors of Spanish-speaking background. New Mexico elected its second Hispanic governor in 1982. About twenty Hispanic Americans currently serve in the House of Representatives.

Asian Americans

Chinese and Japanese laborers were the first Asians to come to the United States in large numbers. They were brought into western states during the late 1800s to work in mines and to build railroads. When the need for this labor declined, Congress in 1882 ordered a temporary halt to Chinese immigration. Over the next three decades, informal agreements kept all but a few Asians out of the country. In 1921 the United States ended its traditional policy of unlimited immigration and established immigration quotas based on country of origin. Western European countries were given large quotas and Asian countries tiny ones. About 150 Japanese a year were allowed to immigrate until 1930, when Congress excluded them entirely.[31]

Discrimination against Asians did not ease substantially until 1965, when Congress enacted legislation that adjusted the immigration quotas to favor those who had previously been disadvantaged. This change in the law was a product of the 1960s civil rights movement, which, as we have indicated, sensitized national leaders to all forms of discrimination. About half a million people now emigrate to the United States each year, and a majority come from Asian and Latin American countries. Asian Americans numbered about twelve million in the 2000 election, roughly 4 percent of the total U.S. population. Most Asian Americans live on the West Coast, particularly in California.

The rights of Asian Americans have been expanded primarily by court rulings and legislation, such as the Civil Rights Act of 1964, that were responses to the problems of other minorities. In a few instances, however, the rights of minorities have been defined by actions of Asian Americans. For example, in *Lau v. Nichols* (1974), a case involving Chinese Americans, the Supreme Court ruled that public schools with a large proportion of children for whom English is a second language must offer English instruction in the children's first language.[32]

In 1998, the second-language issue arose in the form of Proposition 227, a California ballot measure that called for a ban on bilingual education in the state's public schools. The measure received the support of a majority of voters despite opposition from teachers' groups and many within California's Hispanic and Asian communities. Children for whom English is a second language would have to take their courses in English after their first year in school. The constitutionality of Proposition 227 was challenged unsuccessfully in the courts, but some teachers have said they would not abide by its provisions.

Asian Americans are an upwardly mobile group. The values of most Asian cultures include a commitment to hard work, which, in the American context, has included an emphasis on academic achievement. For example, Asians make up a disproportionate share of the students at California's leading public universities, which base admission primarily on high school grades and standardized test scores. However, Asian Americans are still underrepresented in certain areas of the workplace. According to U.S. government figures, Asian Americans account for about 5 percent of professionals and technicians, nearly the same as their percentage of the population. Yet they hold less than 2 percent of managerial jobs; past and present discrimination has kept them from obtaining their fair share of top business positions. They are also underrepresented politically. It was not until 1996, for example, that the first Asian American was elected governor of a state other than Hawaii.

Other Groups and Their Rights

Although civil rights efforts have been directed mainly at women and racial and ethnic minorities, other groups are also involved.

One such group is the more than thirty million Americans who have a physical or mental disability that prevents them from performing a critical function, such as seeing, hearing, or walking. A goal of the disabled is equal access to society's opportunities, which was facilitated by the 1990 Americans with Disabilities Act. It grants the disabled the same employment and other protections enjoyed by other disadvantaged groups. In addition, the Education for All Handicapped Children Act of 1975 mandates that all children, however severe their disability, receive a free, appropriate education. Before the legislation, four million disabled children were getting either no education or an inappropriate one (as in the case of a blind child who is not taught Braille). Government must actively take steps to ensure the education of such children. However, government and employers are not required to honor the disability claims of those with correctable impairments, such as nearsightedness or high blood pressure.[33]

The government has also acted to protect the elderly from discrimination. The Age Discrimination Act of 1975 and the Age Discrimination in Employment Act of 1967 outlaw discrimination against older workers in hiring for jobs in which age is not clearly a crucial factor in job performance. More recently, mandatory retirement ages for most jobs have been eliminated by law. Forced retirement for reasons of age is permissible only if justified by the nature of a particular job or the performance of a particular employee.

A group that until very recently had not received substantial legal protection is homosexuals. In *Bowers* v. *Hardwick* (1986), the Supreme Court upheld a state law banning sexual acts between consenting homosexual adults, ruling that the constitutional right of privacy does not extend to such acts. Gay rights also were dealt a setback when the Supreme Court in 2000 ruled that the Boy Scouts, as a private organization that has a right to freedom of association, can ban gays because homosexuality is prohibited by the Scouts' creed.[34] Gays are also prohibited from serving in the military but can be dismissed only if they engage in overt verbal or behavioral displays of homosexuality (the so-called "don't ask, don't tell" policy).

However, gays gained a significant legal victory when the Supreme Court in *Romer* v. *Evans* (1996) struck down a Colorado constitutional amendment that nullified all existing and any new legal protections for homosexuals. In a 6–3 ruling, the Court said the Colorado law violated the Constitution's guarantee of equal protection since it subjects individuals to employment and other forms of discrimination simply because of their sexual preference. The Court concluded that the law had no reasonable purpose but was motivated instead by "animus" (hostility) toward homosexuals.[35]

EQUALITY UNDER THE LAW

The catchphrase of nearly any group's claim to a more equal standing in American society has been "equality under the law." The importance that people attach to legal equality is understandable. Once secure in their legal rights, people are in a stronger position to seek equality in other arenas, such as the economic sector. Once encoded in law, a claim to equality can also force officials to take positive action on behalf of a disadvantaged group. Americans' claims to legal equality are contained in a great many laws, a few of which are particularly noteworthy.

Equal Protection: The Fourteenth Amendment

The Fourteenth Amendment, which was ratified in 1868, declares in part that no state shall "deny to any person within its jurisdiction the equal protection of the laws." Through this **equal-protection clause,** the courts have protected such groups as African Americans and women from discrimination by state and local governments.

The Fourteenth Amendment's equal-protection clause does not require government to treat all groups or classes of people the same way in all circumstances. In fact, laws routinely treat people unequally. By law, for example, twenty-one-year-olds can drink alcohol but twenty-year-olds cannot. The judiciary allows such inequalities because they are held to be "reasonably" related to a legitimate government interest. In applying this **reasonable-basis test,** the courts give the benefit of doubt to government. It need only show that a particular law has a sound rationale. For example, the courts have held that the goal of reducing fatalities from alcohol-related accidents involving young drivers is a valid reason for imposing a twenty-one-year minimum drinking age requirement. (The *Romer* decision discussed earlier provides an example of a law that failed the reasonable-basis test. The Supreme Court concluded that Colorado's law affecting gays had "no legitimate government purpose.")

The reasonable-basis test does not apply, however, to racial or ethnic classifications, particularly when these categories serve to discriminate against minority group members (see Table 5-2). Any law that posits a racial or ethnic classification is subject to the **strict-scrutiny test,** under which such a law is unconstitutional in the absence of an overwhelmingly convincing argument that it is necessary. The strict-scrutiny test has virtually eliminated race and ethnicity as permissible classifications when the effect is to put members of a minority group at a disadvantage. The Supreme Court's position is that race and national origin are **suspect classifications**—that such classifications have invidious discrimination as their purpose and therefore any law containing such a classification is in all likelihood unconstitutional.

The strict-scrutiny test emerged after the 1954 *Brown* ruling and became a basis for invalidating laws that discriminated against black people. As other groups, especially women, began to organize and press for their rights in the late 1960s and early 1970s, the Supreme Court gave early signs that it might expand the scope of suspect classifications to include gender.[36] In the end, however, the Court announced in *Craig* v. *Boren* (1976) that sex classifications were permissible if they served "important governmental objectives" and were "substantially" related to the achievement of those objectives.[37] The Court thus placed sex distinctions in an "intermediate" (or "almost suspect") category, to be scrutinized more closely than some other classifications (for example, income levels) but, unlike racial classifications, justifiable in some instances. In *Rostker* v. *Goldberg* (1980), for example, the policy of male-only registration for the military draft was upheld on grounds that the exclusion of women from involuntary combat duty serves a legitimate and important purpose.[38]

The inexactness of the **intermediate-scrutiny test** has led some scholars to question its validity as a legal principle. Nevertheless, when evaluating claims of sex discrimination, the judiciary applies a stricter level of scrutiny than is required by the reasonable-basis test. Rather than giving government broad leeway to treat men and women differently, the Supreme Court has recently invalidated most of the laws it has reviewed that contain sex classifications. A leading case is *United States* v. *Virginia* (1996), in which the Supreme Court determined that the male-only admissions policy at Virginia Military Institute (VMI), a 157-year-old state-supported college, was unconstitutional. The state had developed an alternative program for women at another college, but the Court concluded it was no substitute for the unique education and other opportunities that resulted from attending VMI. (The VMI decision also had the effect of ending the all-male admissions policy of the Citadel, a state-supported military college in South Carolina.)[39]

Equal Access: The Civil Rights Acts of 1964 and 1968

The Fourteenth Amendment applies only to action by government. It does not prohibit discrimination by private parties. As a result, for a long period in the nation's history, owners could legally bar black people from restaurants, hotels, and other accommodations, and employers could freely discriminate in their job practices. Since the 1960s private firms have had much less freedom to discriminate for reasons of race, sex, ethnicity, or religion.

TABLE 5-2 LEVELS OF COURT REVIEW FOR LAWS THAT TREAT AMERICANS DIFFERENTLY

Test	Applies to	Standard Used
Strict-scrutiny	Race, ethnicity	Suspect category—assumed unconstitutional in the absence of an overwhelming justification
Intermediate-scrutiny	Gender	Almost suspect category—assumed unconstitutional unless the law serves a clearly compelling and justified purpose
Reasonable-basis	Other categories (such as age and income)	Not suspect category—assumed constitutional unless no sound rationale for the law can be provided

ACCOMMODATIONS AND JOBS   The Civil Rights Act of 1964, which is based on the commerce power of Congress under the Constitution, entitles all persons to equal access to restaurants, bars, theaters, hotels, gasoline stations, and similar establishments serving the general public. The legislation also bars discrimination in the hiring, promotion, and wages of employees of medium-sized and large firms. A few forms of job discrimination are still lawful under the Civil Rights Act of 1964. For example, an owner-operator of a small business can discriminate in hiring his or her coworkers, and a religious school can take the religion of a prospective teacher into account.

The Civil Rights Act of 1964 has nearly eliminated the most overt forms of discrimination in the area of public accommodations. Some restaurants and hotels may provide better service to white customers, but outright refusal to serve African Americans or other minority group members is rare. Such a refusal is a violation of the law and could easily be proved in many instances. It is harder to prove discrimination in job decisions; accordingly, the act has been less effective in rooting out employment discrimination—a subject that will be discussed in detail later in the chapter.

HOUSING   In 1968, Congress passed civil rights legislation designed to prohibit discrimination in housing. A building owner ordinarily cannot

Deacon John Hodge stands at the charred remains of Rising Star Baptist Church in Greensboro, Alabama. His church is one of several dozen predominantly black churches that were torched by arsonists in 1996 alone. The burnings are an ugly reminder that racism—"America's curse," in the words of the sociologist Gunnar Myrdal—is still the nation's most conspicuous shortcoming.

refuse to sell or rent housing because of a person's race, religion, ethnicity, or sex. An exception is allowed for owners of small multifamily dwellings who reside on the premises.

Despite legal prohibitions on discrimination, housing in America remains highly segregated. Less than a third of all African Americans live in a neighborhood that is mostly white. One reason is the fact that the annual income of most black families is substantially below that of most white families. Another reason is banking practices. At one time, banks contributed to housing segregation by refusing to grant mortgage loans in certain neighborhoods, thus driving down their housing prices and leading to an influx of African Americans and an exodus of whites. This banking practice, known as "redlining," is prohibited by the 1968 Civil Rights Act. However, a recent study by the U.S. Conference of Mayors makes it clear that race is still a factor in the lending practices of many banks.[40] Among applicants with average or slightly higher incomes relative to their communities, Hispanic and African Americans were twice as likely as whites to be denied a mortgage (see Figure 5-2).

Percentage of applicants denied mortgages

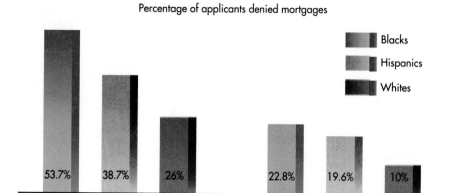

FIGURE 5-2   MORTGAGE APPLICATION REJECTIONS
Blacks and Hispanics are more likely than whites to be rejected for a mortgage,
even among applicants with similar incomes. Source: U.S. Conference of Mayors, 1998.

Equal Ballots: The Voting Rights Act of 1965, as Amended

Free elections are perhaps the foremost symbol of American democracy, yet
the right to vote has only recently become a reality for many citizens, particularly African Americans.

The Nineteenth Amendment, which in 1920 gave women the right to
vote, effectively ended resistance to women's suffrage; paradoxically, resistance to black suffrage was intensified by the Fifteenth Amendment, which
in 1870 gave black persons the right to vote. Southern whites invented a series of devices, including whites-only primaries, poll taxes, and rigged literacy tests, to keep African Americans from registering and voting.[41] For
example, almost no votes were cast by African Americans between 1920 and
1946 in North Carolina.[42]

Barriers to black participation in elections began to crumble in the
mid-1940s, when the Supreme Court declared that whites-only primary
elections were unconstitutional.[43] Two decades later, through the Twenty-
fourth Amendment, poll taxes were outlawed.

The major step toward equal voting rights for African Americans was
passage of the Voting Rights Act of 1965, which forbids discrimination in
voting and registration. Black voting rose sharply after enactment of the
legislation, which empowers federal agents to register voters and to oversee
participation in elections. The Voting Rights Act, as interpreted by the
courts, also eliminated literacy tests: local officials can no longer deny

registration and voting for reasons of illiteracy. In fact, in communities where a language other than English is widely spoken, officials are now required by law to provide ballot materials in that language.

Congress renewed the Voting Rights Act in 1970, 1975, and 1982. The 1982 extension is noteworthy because it renews the act for twenty years and requires states and localities to clear with federal officials any electoral change that has the effect, intended or not, of reducing the voting power of a minority group. When congressional district boundaries were redrawn after the 1990 census, the 1982 extension became the basis for the creation of districts that included a majority of Hispanic or African American voters. The result was the election of an unprecedented number of minority group members to Congress in 1992; Hispanic and African American representatives increased from ten and twenty-five to seventeen and thirty-eight, respectively.

In two 1996 decisions, however, the Supreme Court declared unconstitutional the redistricting of four congressional districts in Texas and North Carolina because race had been the "dominant" factor in their creation. The states were directed to redraw the districts. A year earlier, the Court had invalidated a Georgia redistricting plan, holding that the state's Eleventh Congressional District violated the rights of white voters under the Fourteenth Amendment's equal-protection clause. The Georgia district stretched from Savannah to Atlanta and had all sorts of twists and turns designed to exclude white residential areas. However, these rulings have not necessarily settled the issue of racial redistricting. The 1996 cases were each decided by a 5–4 majority, and three of the justices in the majority indicated that there might be instances in which race, along with other factors, could be taken into account in redistricting decisions. But the Court's majority made it clear that race could not be the *deciding* factor in redistricting arrangements.[44]

The Court demonstrated its flexibility in a 1999 decision, *Hunt v. Cromartie,* when it unanimously upheld the redistricting of North Carolina's Twelfth Congressional District, even though race had been a consideration in the redistricting. The Court held that the heavily Democratic district was created primarily for partisan political reasons and was therefore acceptable.[45]

EQUALITY OF RESULT

America's disadvantaged groups have made significant progress toward equal rights, particularly during the past few decades. Through acts of Congress and rulings of the Supreme Court, most forms of government-

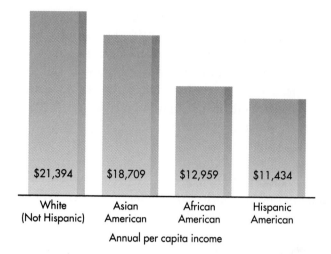

| $21,394 | $18,709 | $12,959 | $11,434 |
| White (Not Hispanic) | Asian American | African American | Hispanic American |

Annual per capita income

FIGURE 5-3 U.S. PER CAPITA INCOME, BY RACE AND ETHNICITY
The average income of white Americans is substantially higher than that of most other Americans. Source: U.S. Bureau of the Census, 2000.

sponsored discrimination—from racially segregated public schools to gender-based pension plans—have been banned.

However, civil rights problems involve deeply rooted conditions, habits, and prejudices and affect whole categories of people. For these reasons, a new civil rights policy rarely produces a sudden and dramatic change in society. Despite their greater equality in law, America's traditionally disadvantaged groups are still substantially unequal in their daily lives. Consider the issue of income disparity (see Figure 5-3). The average Asian American's income is about 90 percent of the average white person's income. But the average falls to 60 percent for African Americans and 55 percent for Hispanic Americans.

Such figures reflect *de facto* **discrimination,** which is discrimination that is a consequence of social, economic, and cultural biases and conditions. This type of discrimination is different from *de jure* **discrimination,** which is discrimination based on law, as in the case of segregation in southern public schools during the pre-*Brown* period. *De facto* discrimination is difficult to root out because it is embedded not in the law but in the very structure of society. **Equality of result** is the aim of policies intended to reduce or eliminate *de facto* discriminatory effects so that members of disadvantaged groups may obtain the same benefits as members of advantaged groups. Such policies are inherently more controversial because many

Americans believe that government's responsibility extends no further than the removal of legal barriers to equality. This attitude reflects the cultural emphasis on *individualism* and is a major reason for the lack of any large-scale government effort to reduce the economic and social gaps between Americans of varying racial and ethnic backgrounds. Nevertheless, a few policies—notably affirmative action and busing—have been implemented to achieve equality of result.

Affirmative Action

The difficulty of making newly acquired legal rights a part of everyday reality is evident in the fact that with passage of the 1964 Civil Rights Act, which prohibited discrimination in employment, women and minorities did not suddenly find it easier to obtain jobs for which they were qualified. Many employers maintained a deliberate though unwritten preference for white male employees, while other employers adhered to established employment procedures that continued to keep women and minorities at a disadvantage; membership in many union locals, for example, was handed down from father to son. Moreover, the Civil Rights Act placed the burden of proof on the woman or minority group member who had been denied a particular job, and discrimination was costly and often difficult to prove in court. In addition, a victory in court affected only the individual in question; such case-by-case settlements were no remedy for a situation in which established hiring practices kept millions of women and minority group members from competing on an equal basis for job opportunities.

A broader remedy was obviously required, and the result was the emergence during the late 1960s of affirmative action programs. **Affirmative action** is a deliberate effort to provide full and equal opportunities in employment, education, and other areas for women, minorities, and individuals belonging to other traditionally disadvantaged groups. Affirmative action requires corporations, universities, and other organizations to establish programs designed to ensure that all applicants are treated fairly. Affirmative action also places the burden of proof on the providers of opportunities; to some extent, they must be able to demonstrate that any disproportionate granting of opportunities to white males is not the result of discriminatory practices.

OPINIONS ON AFFIRMATIVE ACTION   Few issues in recent years have provoked more controversy than has affirmative action.[46] Although most Americans say they believe that minorities and women deserve a truly equal chance at jobs and other opportunities, they also say they worry that aggressive affirmative action programs will discriminate against more qualified males, an outcome that is called *reverse discrimination.*

Although opposition to affirmative action has increased in recent years, it is marked by ambivalence. Americans oppose the making of hiring and admission decisions on the basis of race, yet a majority also indicates that diversity in the workplace and in college is a desirable goal and that special efforts to enable the historically disadvantaged to compete on more equal footing should be made. In a 1997 New York Times/CBS News Poll, for example, a majority of whites said no to the question: "Do you believe that where there has been job discrimination against blacks in the past, preference in hiring or promotion should be given to blacks today?" But, in the same poll, a majority of whites said yes to the question: "Do you believe there should be special educational programs to assist minorities in competing for college admissions?" These opinions are in line with traditional American attitudes (see Chapter 1). Americans generally endorse the idea of equal opportunity and thus tend to support programs that would give people a chance to compete for success. But they oppose policies that would give someone preferential treatment once the competition is under way.

AFFIRMATIVE ACTION IN THE LAW   Most issues that pit individuals against each other in a struggle over society's benefits eventually end up in the courts, and affirmative action is no exception (see Table 5-3). The policy was first tested before the Supreme Court in *University of California Regents* v. *Bakke* (1978). Alan Bakke, a white man, had twice been denied admission to a University of California medical school, even though his admission test scores were higher than those of several minority group students who had been accepted. Bakke sued, claiming the school had a "quota" system for minorities that discriminated against white males. The Court ruled in Bakke's favor but did not invalidate affirmative action per se. The Court said only that rigid racial quotas were an impermissible form of affirmative action in determining medical school admissions.[47]

Bakke was followed by two rulings in favor of affirmative action programs, one of which—*Fullilove* v. *Klutnick* (1980)—upheld a quota system that required 10 percent of federal public works funds to be set aside for minority-owned firms.[48]

In the 1980s, the appointment of more conservative justices to the Supreme Court narrowed the scope of affirmative action policy. The Court held, for example, that preferential treatment of minorities could normally be justified only in cases where discrimination had been severe and that

TABLE 5-3 KEY DECISIONS IN THE HISTORY OF AFFIRMATIVE ACTION POLICY	
Year	*Action*
1969	Nixon Administration's Department of Labor initiates affirmative action policy
1978	Supreme Court in *Bakke* invalidates rigid quotas for medical school admissions but does not invalidate affirmative action
1980	Supreme Court in *Fullilove* upholds a quota system for minority-owned firms in granting of federal contracts
1980s	Supreme Court in a series of decisions narrows situations in which preferential treatment of minorities will be permitted
1995	Supreme Court in *Adarand* eliminates fixed quotas in the granting of government contracts
1996	California voters enact Proposition 209, which bans public employment, education, and contracting programs based on race, ethnicity, or sex

affirmative action could be applied only in a way that did not infringe on the rights of white employees to keep their jobs (thus restricting the use of race as a basis for determining which employees would be terminated in the case of job layoffs).[49]

In a key 1995 decision, *Adarand* v. *Pena*, the Supreme Court sharply curtailed the federal government's affirmative action authority. The case arose when Adarand Constructors filed suit over a federal contract that was awarded to a Hispanic-owned company even though Adarand had submitted a lower bid. The Court in a 5–4 ruling said that the government had to prove that a preference program for minorities was a response to specific past acts of discrimination, not just discrimination in a historic sense. This decision essentially reversed earlier precedents that allowed the federal government to give a preference to minority applicants. The Court said that Washington cannot set aside contracts for minority applicants unless, through costly and conclusive studies, it can demonstrate past discrimination particular to a situation; and even then, it must devise a program "narrowly tailored" to the problem that is being remedied.[50] In other words, the government cannot issue general requirements (such as a 10 percent set-aside) as a means of remedying past discrimination.

Another blow to affirmative action proponents is the California Civil Rights Initiative, which bans in California any public employment, education, or contracting program that is based on race, ethnicity, or sex. Known as Proposition 209, the initiative was placed on the 1996 ballot by citizen petition and approved 54–46 percent by California voters. The vote divided along racial, ethnic, and gender lines, with white males most strongly in favor and blacks and Hispanics most strongly opposed. The constitutionality of Proposition 209 was challenged by opponents, but the Supreme Court upheld it in 1997.

The Board of Regents of the University of California had earlier voted an end to affirmative action in university admissions, a policy that was also instituted at the University of Texas Law School and some other academic institutions. The effect was a dramatic decline in minority enrollment at these institutions. The entering classes at the Berkeley and Los Angeles campuses of the University of California in the fall of 1998, for example, had 50 percent fewer African Americans than the previous class. Hispanic enrollment also declined, although less dramatically.

Further restrictions on affirmative action are possible in the future, inasmuch as even some of its supporters believe that it is now heightening white resistance to other civil rights measures and that it is diminishing the accomplishments of women and minorities who would have gotten ahead even without the policy. It is unlikely, however, that affirmative action will be eliminated entirely. Statistical indicators show that women and minorities, as groups, are still at a substantial disadvantage to white males in terms of job hiring, pay, and promotion. In a few occupations, most of them in the professions, well-qualified women and minority group members are in high demand. In most settings, however, they are at a substantial disadvantage, a situation that creates pressure on policymakers to maintain affirmative action in some form.

In 1998, the state of Texas devised an innovative response to the problem of equal opportunity. Recognizing the disparity in the quality of its public schools and other factors that result in lower average scores on standardized tests for minorities, the state established a policy that guarantees admission at the public university campus of his or her choice to any Texas high school student who graduates in the top 10 percent of the class. The 10 percent rule has met with little opposition from even the most outspoken critics of affirmative action, and those who favor affirmative action support this program "because it eliminates suspicion that students may have been admitted solely on the basis of race."[51]

Social Integration: Busing

In 1944 the Swedish sociologist Gunnar Myrdal gained fame for his book *An American Dilemma*, whose title referred to deep-rooted racism in a country that proclaimed itself to be the epitome of an equal society.[52] Since then, legal obstacles to the mixing of the races have been nearly eliminated. Public opinion has also changed significantly in the past half-century. In the early 1940s a majority of white Americans believed that black children should not be allowed to go to school with white children; today only 5 percent of white Americans express this belief.

However, the majority of black people still live largely apart from white people. The reality of American life today is racial segregation. More than two-thirds of African Americans live in neighborhoods that are all or mostly black; more than two-thirds of black children go to schools that are mostly black; and one-third attend schools that are more than 90 percent black.

THE *SWANN* DECISION   In 1971 the Supreme Court took the controversial step of requiring the busing of children in some circumstances. Affirming a lower-court decision, the Supreme Court held in *Swann* v. *Charlotte–Mecklenburg County Board of Education* that the busing of children from one neighborhood to another was a permissible way for courts to compel the integration of public schools in instances where past years of official segregation had created residential patterns that had the effect of keeping the races in separate schools.[53]

Few policies of recent times provoked so much controversy as the introduction of forced busing. There were angry demonstrations lasting weeks in Charlotte. When busing was ordered in Detroit and Boston, the protests turned violent. A 1972 University of Michigan survey indicated that more than 80 percent of white Americans disapproved of forced busing, and the proportion has not changed significantly since then.

Despite the widespread protests, busing became a part of national policy. Each school day, thousands upon thousands of children were bused out of their neighborhoods to attend school with children of a different color. Busing's application was narrowed, however, by court-imposed restrictions on its use. The Supreme Court in 1974—perhaps in response to the protests over busing—held that it could be applied *across* school districts only in situations where it could be shown that school district boundaries were purposely drawn so as to segregate the races.[54] Because school districts in most states coincide with community boundaries, the effect of this position was to insulate most suburban schools from integration plans.

Students at a California state university demonstrate against Proposition 209. The initiative proposed to end all racial, ethnic, and gender preferences in the awarding of university admissions, jobs, and government contracts in the state. The initiative passed by a 54 to 46 percent vote margin in 1996.

DOES BUSING WORK?   Studies indicate that busing has contributed to more positive racial attitudes among children. Studies also show that the performance of black children on standardized tests improves when they attend white-majority schools and that the test performance of the white children is not adversely affected.[55]

However, busing has contributed to whites' departure from public schools, which, along with population and residential shifts, has made it increasingly difficult to achieve diversity in city schools. In Boston, for example, less than 20 percent of public school children today are white, compared with more than 50 percent when busing began there in 1974.

Busing also fragmented neighborhoods and forced children into long bus rides to and from school. Many black and white families alike were affected by what came to be called "busing fatigue." Parents asked, in effect, whether busing was worth the costs. That debate led the Prince George's County (Maryland) school board, which had a black majority, to abandon busing in 1998 and replace it with improved funding for neighborhood schools. Alvin Thornton, chair of the Prince George's County school board and a Howard University professor, argued that the change would increase "the sense of community" among the county's African Americans.[56]

DIVERSITY AND AMERICA'S SCHOOLS Prince George's County is among dozens of communities—including Seattle, Jacksonville, Minneapolis, Mobile, and Boston—that have dismantled their school busing programs in recent years. In 1999, the school district where busing policy began—Charlotte-Mecklenburg—joined the list. Federal judge Robert Potter ruled in an anti-busing lawsuit that the school district could no longer take race into account in "assigning" children to its schools. Potter's decision followed a series of Supreme Court rulings in the 1990s that had held that busing was intended as a temporary, not permanent, solution to the problem of segregated schools;[57] that the performance of black students could not be the criterion for continuation of a busing program;[58] and that communities could devise alternative programs to replace their busing programs.[59]

The cutback in busing contributed to a decrease in school integration. Nationwide, integration peaked in the late 1980s and has declined steadily since then (see Figure 5-4). Only about a third of black children today

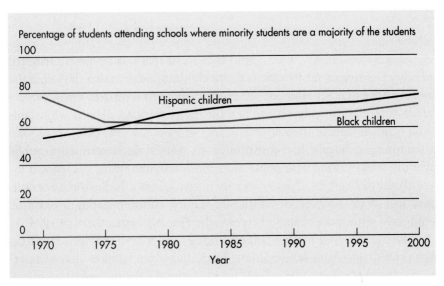

FIGURE 5-4 INCREASE IN DE FACTO SCHOOL SEGREGATION
Busing contributed to a decrease in the percentage of black children attending predominantly minority schools, but the percentage has increased since the late 1980s, and the percentage of Hispanics in predominantly minority schools has increased steadily for three decades. Source: U.S. Department of Education, 1999.

attend a predominantly white school, which is about the same proportion as in 1970, before busing was initiated. The proportion is even higher for Hispanic children—only about a fourth of them attend a predominantly white school.

As busing recedes, the focus has shifted to parity in school financing. In comparison with predominantly white schools, those schools with mostly minority children have significantly larger classroom sizes, fewer certified teachers, and fewer resources, including library materials, computers, and science laboratories.[60] In Prince George's County and other communities that have dismantled busing programs, local and state governments have promised to increase the funding for predominantly minority schools. The NAACP is among the minority-group organizations that are fearful this promise will not be kept. "We can't go back to where we were before school desegregation," says Maxine Waters, chair of the NAACP's National Education Committee. "Resources have always followed the white child. If we go back to separate facilities, that will happen again."[61]

SUPERFICIAL DIFFERENCES, DEEP DIVISIONS

Discrimination has been called America's curse. In a country that is otherwise bountiful and generous, superficial differences—sex, skin color, country of origin—are sources of deep divisions and stark contrasts. To cite but one example: a black child born in the United States has more than twice the chance of dying before reaching his or her first birthday than a white child. The difference in the infant mortality rates of whites and African Americans reflects differences in their nutrition, medical care, and education—in other words, differences in their access to the most basic resources of a modern society.

America's professed commitment to equality for all has a decidedly narrow focus—on equality under the law but not on the opportunity to share fully in all that American society has to offer. No greater challenge faces America in the twenty-first century than the rooting out of disadvantages related to race, sex, and ethnicity.

SUMMARY

During the past few decades, the United States has undergone a revolution in the legal status of its traditionally disadvantaged groups, including African Americans, women, Native Americans, Hispanic Americans, and Asian Americans. Such groups are now provided equal protection under the law in areas such as education, employment, and voting. Discrimination by race, sex, and ethnicity has not been eliminated from American life but is no longer substantially backed by the force of law.

Traditionally disadvantaged Americans have achieved fuller equality primarily as a result of their struggle for greater rights. The Supreme Court has been an important instrument of change for minority groups. Its ruling in *Brown* v. *Board of Education* (1954), which declared racial segregation in public schools to be an unconstitutional violation of the Fourteenth Amendment's equal-protection clause, was a major breakthrough in equal rights. Through its busing, affirmative action, and other rulings, the Court has also mandated the active promotion of integration and equal opportunities.

However, because civil rights policy involves large issues of social values and the distribution of society's resources, questions of civil rights are politically explosive. For this reason, legislatures and executives as well as the courts have been deeply involved in such issues, siding at times with established groups and sometimes backing the claims of underprivileged groups. Thus Congress, with the support of President Lyndon Johnson, enacted the landmark Civil Rights Act of 1964; but Congress and recent presidents have been ambivalent about or hostile to busing for the purpose of integrating public schools.

In recent years affirmative action programs, designed to achieve equality of result for African Americans, women, Hispanic Americans, and other disadvantaged groups, have been a civil rights battleground. Affirmative action has had the strong support of civil rights groups and has won the qualified endorsement of the Supreme Court but has been opposed by those who claim that it unfairly discriminates against white males. Busing is another issue that has provoked deep divisions within American society.

MAJOR CONCEPTS

affirmative action	equality of result
comparable worth	gender gap
de facto discrimination	intermediate-scrutiny test
de jure discrimination	reasonable-basis test
equal-protection clause	strict-scrutiny test
equal rights (civil rights)	suspect classifications

SUGGESTED READINGS AND WEB SITES

Armor, David. *Forced Justice: School Desegregation and the Law.* New York: Oxford University Press, 1995. An evaluation that concludes that the federal courts have overstretched their legal mandate by requiring school integration rather than simply school desegregation.

Bergmann, Barbara A. *In Defense of Affirmative Action.* New York: Basic Books, 1997. An economist's analysis of affirmative action that concludes that the policy is necessary for women and broadly beneficial to society.

Howard, John R. *The Shifting Wind.* Albany: State University of New York Press, 1999. A review of the Supreme Court and civil rights from Reconstruction to the *Brown* decision.

McClain, Charles J. *In Search of Equality: The Chinese Struggle Against Discrimination in Nineteenth-Century America.* Berkeley: University of California Press, 1994. A careful study of how Chinese in nineteenth-century California used the legal system to fight racism and injustice.

Nagel, Joane. *American Indian Ethnic Renewal: Red Power and the Resurgence of Identity and Culture.* New York: Oxford University Press, 1996. Explores the meaning of activism for Native Americans' ethnic identification.

Reeves, Keith. *Voting Hopes or Fears? White Voters, Black Candidates, and Racial Politics in America.* New York: Oxford University Press, 1997. A critical assessment of race and politics in American society.

Skrentny, John David. *The Ironies of Affirmative Action: Politics, Culture, and Justice in America.* Chicago: University of Chicago Press, 1996. An empirical analysis of affirmative action and its impact.

Stavans, Ilan. *The Hispanic Condition: Reflections on Culture and Identity in America.* New York: HarperPerennial, 1996. An analysis of the behavioral and cultural differences and similarities among the major Hispanic groups.

http://www.airpi.org/   The American Indian Policy Center was established by Native Americans in 1992. Its site includes a political and legal history of Native Americans and examines current issues affecting them.

http://www.naacp.org   The web site of the National Association for the Advancement of Colored People (NAACP). Its site includes historical and current information on the struggle of African Americans for equal rights.

http://www.nclr.org   The web site for the National Council of La Raza (NCLR), an organization dedicated to improving the lives of Hispanics. Contains information on public policy, immigration, citizenship, and other subjects.

http://www.rci.rutgers.edu/~cawp   The web site of the Center for the American Woman and Politics (CAWP) can be found at Rutgers University's Eagleton Institute of Politics.

READING 5

America's Racial Divide

WILLIAM JEFFERSON CLINTON

Introduction

America's racial divide was a subject of President Bill Clinton's first
Inaugural Address in 1993 and also of his Farewell Address in 2001.
In between, he spoke often on the issue of race relations. In the speech
that is the basis for this reading, Clinton is addressing the race issue
against the backdrop of the "Million Man March." Held on the Mall in
Washington, D.C., the march was organized by black men to signify
their commitment to social change, both within and outside the
African American community. Clinton used the occasion to argue that
America's racial problem today owes to habits of the mind rather than
limits of the law.

The rift . . . that is tearing at the heart of America exists in spite of
the remarkable progress black Americans have made in the last generation, since Martin Luther King swept America up in his dream, and
President Johnson spoke so powerfully for the dignity of man and the
destiny of democracy in demanding that Congress guarantee full voting
rights to blacks. The rift between blacks and whites exists still in a very
special way in America, in spite of the fact that we have become much
more racially and ethnically diverse, and that Hispanic Americans—
themselves no strangers to discrimination—are now almost 10 percent of
our national population.

The reasons for this divide are many. Some are rooted in the awful
history and stubborn persistence of racism. Some are rooted in the different ways we experience the threats of modern life to personal security,
family values, and strong communities. Some are rooted in the fact that
we still haven't learned to talk frankly, to listen carefully, and to work together across racial lines.

Almost 30 years ago, Dr. Martin Luther King took his last march
with sanitation workers in Memphis. They marched for dignity, equality,
and economic justice. Many carried placards that read simply, "I am a

man." The throngs of men marching in Washington today, almost all of them, are doing so for the same stated reason. But there is a profound difference between this march today and those of 30 years ago. Thirty years ago, the marchers were demanding the dignity and opportunity they were due because in the face of terrible discrimination, they had worked hard, raised their children, paid their taxes, obeyed the laws, and fought our wars.

Well, today's march is also about pride and dignity and respect. But after a generation of deepening social problems that disproportionately impact black Americans, it is also about black men taking renewed responsibility for themselves, their families, and their communities. It's about saying no to crime and drugs and violence. It's about standing up for atonement and reconciliation. It's about insisting that others do the same, and offering to help them. . . .

Today we face a choice—one way leads to further separation and bitterness and more lost futures. The other way, the path of courage and wisdom, leads to unity, to reconciliation, to a rich opportunity for all Americans to make the most of the lives God gave them. This moment in which the racial divide is so clearly out in the open need not be a setback for us. It presents us with a great opportunity, and we dare not let it pass us by.

In the past when we've had the courage to face the truth about our failure to live up to our own best ideals, we've grown stronger, moved forward and restored proud American optimism. At such turning points America moved to preserve the union and abolished slavery; to embrace women's suffrage; to guarantee basic legal rights to America without regard to race, under the leadership of President Johnson. At each of these moments, we looked in the national mirror and were brave enough to say, this is not who we are; we're better than that. Abraham Lincoln reminded us that a house divided against itself cannot stand. When divisions have threatened to bring our house down, somehow we have always moved together to shore it up. My fellow Americans, our house is the greatest democracy in all human history. And with all its racial and ethnic diversity, it has beaten the odds of human history. But we know that divisions remain, and we still have work to do.

The two worlds we see now each contain both truth and distortion. Both black and white Americans must face this, for honesty is the only gateway to the many acts of reconciliation that will unite our worlds at last into one America.

White America must understand and acknowledge the roots of black pain. It began with unequal treatment first in law and later in fact. African Americans indeed have lived too long with a justice system that in too many cases has been and continues to be less than just. The record of abuses extends from lynchings and trumped up charges to false arrests and police brutality. The tragedies of Emmett Till and Rodney King are bloody markers on the very same road. . . .

And blacks are right to think something is terribly wrong when African American men are many times more likely to be victims of homicide than any other group in this country; when there are more African American men in our corrections system than in our colleges; when almost one in three African American men in their 20s are either in jail, on parole or otherwise under the supervision of the criminal justice system—nearly one in three. And that is a disproportionate percentage in comparison to the percentage of blacks who use drugs in our society. Now, I would like every white person here and in America to take a moment to think how he or she would feel if one in three white men were in similar circumstances.

And there is still unacceptable economic disparity between blacks and whites. It is so fashionable to talk today about African Americans as if they have been some sort of protected class. Many whites think blacks are getting more than their fair share in terms of jobs and promotions. That is not true. . . . The truth is that African Americans still make on average about 60 percent of what white people do; that more than half of African American children live in poverty. . . .

On the other hand, blacks must understand and acknowledge the roots of white fear in America. There is a legitimate fear of the violence that is too prevalent in our urban areas; and often by experience or at least what people see on the news at night, violence for those white people too often has a black face. It isn't racist for a parent to pull his or her child close when walking through a high-crime neighborhood, or to wish to stay away from neighborhoods where innocent children can be shot in school or standing at bus stops by thugs driving by with assault weapons or toting handguns like old west desperados. . . .

The great potential for this march today, beyond the black community, is that whites will come to see a larger truth—that blacks share their fears and embrace their convictions. . . . White racism may be black people's burden, but it's white people's problem. We must clean our house.

Long before we were so diverse, our nation's motto was E Pluribus Unum—out of many, we are one. We must be one—as neighbors, as fellow citizens; not separate camps, but family—white, black, Latino, all of us, no matter how different, who share basic American values and are willing to live by them. When a child is gunned down on a street in the Bronx, no matter what our race, he is our American child. When a woman dies from a beating, no matter what our race or hers, she is our American sister. And every time drugs course through the vein of another child, it clouds the future of all our American children. Whether we like it or not, we are one nation, one family, indivisible. And for us, divorce or separation are not options.

Here, on the edge of the 21st century, we dare not tolerate the existence of two Americas. . . . The great divides of the past called for and were addressed by legal and legislative changes. They were addressed by leaders like Lyndon Johnson, who passed the Civil Rights Act and the Voting Rights Act. And to be sure, this great divide requires a public response by democratically-elected leaders. But today we are really dealing, and we know it, with problems that grow in large measure out of the way all of us look at the world with our minds and the way we feel about the world with our hearts.

And therefore, while leaders and legislation may be important, this is work that has to be done by every single one of you. And this is the ultimate test of our democracy, for today the house divided exists largely in the minds and hearts of the American people. And it must be united there in the minds and hearts of our people. . . .

William Jefferson Clinton was the forty-second President of the United States. His speech on race relations was delivered on October 16, 1995 in Austin, Texas.

CHAPTER SIX

Public Opinion and Political Socialization

To speak with precision of public opinion is a task not unlike coming
to grips with the Holy Ghost.

V. O. KEY, JR.[1]

W HEN AMERICAN bombs started falling on Serbia in 1999, most
Americans were ill-equipped to pass judgment on what was
happening. They had been hearing for months about the war between the
Serbs and the ethnic Albanians in Serbia's Kosovo province, but polls indicated they had only a vague idea of the nature of the conflict. One poll
found that most Americans were unable to say where Kosovo was located.

Surveys taken before the bombing began showed only limited support
for U.S. involvement. Asked in a February 1999 Gallup poll whether they
thought "the United States needs to be involved in Kosovo in order to protect its own interests," only 37 percent said that it did. An NBC News poll
taken four months earlier showed that only a minority of Americans would
support the bombing of Serb targets by the United States and its allies if Serb
forces refused to end their aggressive action against the ethnic Albanians.

Once the bombs started falling, President Clinton went on national
television to ask Americans to support the attack. He appealed to their conscience, saying that the intervention was necessary to stop the "ethnic
cleansing" campaign that the Serbs were waging in Kosovo. There was an
eerie familiarity to the speech. Three years earlier, Clinton had made a similar speech in reference to air strikes aimed at deterring Serb aggression
in Bosnia.

Public opinion quickly shifted. A *Newsweek* poll showed that 53 percent
of Americans supported President Clinton's decision to commit U.S. jets
and cruise missiles to the NATO operation. Within a few days, polls
showed that more than 60 percent of Americans approved of the military

intervention and less than 30 percent were opposed. The change occurred despite the public's worries about the outcome. In the *Newsweek* poll, 44 percent said they doubted that the NATO forces could avoid significant casualties, and 59 percent said the attacks were likely to result in a long-term U.S. military commitment in the region. They also believed that the air strikes would not stop Serb aggression, and only 47 percent said they would support a decision to send U.S. ground troops into the fighting.

The unfolding of the intervention in Serbia is a revealing example of the influence of public opinion on government. Public opinion rarely compels officials to take a particular course of action. Clinton was not forced by public opinion to order U.S. planes to bomb Serbia, nor did public opinion erupt into widespread protest when he did. The public, somewhat reluctantly, was willing to follow Clinton's lead, at least until, and if, the conflict turned sour.

Public opinion has an important place in democratic societies because of the idea that democratic government springs from the will of the people. However, public opinion is a far more elusive phenomenon than conventional wisdom suggests. It is widely assumed that there is a conclusive

U.S. soldiers have been deployed to the Balkans twice in recent years in an effort to stop Serb aggression in the region. Their deployment occurred despite the public's ambivalence about the policy.

public opinion on major issues, but in fact, as the Kosovo situation illustrates, public opinion is seldom fixed when it comes to questions of how to resolve policy problems. Political leaders typically have leeway in deciding a course of action. They may be held accountable by the public for the results, but the action itself is often theirs to choose.

This chapter discusses public opinion and its influence on the U.S. political system. A major theme is that public opinion is a powerful and yet inexact force in American politics. The policies of the U.S. government cannot be understood apart from public opinion; at the same time, public opinion is not a precise determinant of public policy. The main points made in this chapter are the following:

* *Public opinion consists of those views held by ordinary citizens that are publicly expressed.*
* *The process by which individuals acquire their political opinions is called political socialization. This process begins during childhood and continues into adulthood.*
* *Americans' political opinions are shaped by several frames of reference, the most important of which are political culture, ideology, group attachments, and partisanship.*
* *Public opinion has an important influence on government but works primarily to channel and impose limits on the choices made by officials.*

THE NATURE OF PUBLIC OPINION

Public opinion is a relatively new concept in the history of political ideas. Not until democracy arose in the eighteenth century did the need arise to obtain some idea of what the people were thinking on political issues. If democracy is truly to be a government of and for the people, then the public's opinions must be a central concern.

Defining Public Opinion

Today, "public opinion" is a widely used term. It is typically applied in ways that suggest that the people have a common set of concerns. In fact, however, it is not very meaningful to lump all citizens together as if they constituted a single coherent public.[2] There is, to be sure, an occasional issue of such power and breadth that it captures the attention of nearly all citizens. The large majority of issues, however, attract the attention of some citizens but not most citizens. Agricultural conservation programs, for example, are of intense interest to some farmers, hunters, and environmentalists, but of little interest to other people. The tendency is so pervasive that opinion analysts have described America as a nation of *many* publics.[3]

There are many issues about which there is literally no majority opinion. On issues such as agricultural conservation programs, a form of *pluralist* democracy usually prevails. Government responds to the views of an intense minority. In other cases, *elitist* opinion prevails. On the question of U.S. relations with Finland, for example, there is little likelihood that ordinary citizens would know or care what the U.S. government does. In such instances, the policy opinions of an elite group of business and policy leaders ordinarily prevail. *Majority* opinion also can be decisive, but its influence is normally confined to a few broad issues that elicit widespread attention and concern, such as social security and employment. Although this situation may suggest a limited role for popular majorities, such issues, although few in number, typically have the greatest impact on society as a whole.

Hence, in defining "public opinion" we cannot assume that all citizens, or even a majority, are actively interested and have a preference about all aspects of political life. We will define **public opinion** as those opinions held by ordinary citizens that they are willing to express openly.[4] This expression need not be verbal. It could also take the form, for example, of a protest demonstration or a vote for one candidate rather than another. The crucial point is that a person's private thoughts on an issue become public opinion when expressed openly.

How Informed Is Public Opinion?

There are practical obstacles to government by public opinion in all instances. One obstacle is that people have differing opinions; in responding to one side of an issue, government is compelled to reject other preferences. Public opinion is also contradictory in many cases. Polls indicate, for example, that Americans would like better schools, health care, and other public services while they also favor a reduction in taxes (see Figure 6-1). A significant increase in the quantity and quality of social services cannot be accomplished without additional taxes. Which opinion of the people should govern—their desire for more services or their desire for lower taxes?

Another limitation on the role of public opinion is the public's relatively low level of political information. Some citizens pay close attention to politics, but most do not. Most citizens would "flunk" a current affairs test. In 1993, for example, a Times Mirror survey asked a cross-section of

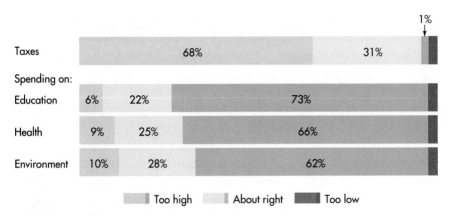

FIGURE 6-1   OPINIONS ON TAXING AND SPENDING
People's opinions are sometimes contradictory. Americans say, for example, that taxes are too high and yet also say government is spending too little in areas such as health, education, and the environment. Source: Used by permission of National Opinion Research Center, University of Chicago.

Americans five simple questions on people and events that were currently at the top of the news about international affairs. Only 6 percent of the respondents answered all five questions correctly, and 9 percent knew four answers. A total of 21 percent correctly answered only one question, and 37 percent could answer none of the questions. In other words, a majority of citizens knew little or nothing when asked relatively simple questions about world affairs. (Citizens in other countries were also asked the same five questions; the results are summarized in the box How the United States Compares.)

The public's lack of information restricts the role it can play in policy disputes. Public opinion can direct government toward certain goals, but it rarely provides a detailed guide to the way these goals are to be accomplished. The choice of one course of action over another requires knowledge of the likely consequences of the various alternatives. The average citizen typically lacks this knowledge.

Measuring Public Opinion

Woodrow Wilson once said he had spent nearly all of his adult life in government and yet had never seen a "government." What Wilson was saying, in effect, was that government is a system of relationships. A government is not a building or a person; it is not tangible in the way that an automobile

HOW THE UNITED STATES COMPARES

Citizens' Awareness of Public Affairs

Americans' knowledge of public affairs is relatively low. Even the simplest facts sometimes elude the average citizen's grasp. A 1994 Gallup poll found, for example, that a third of Americans were unable to name the vice-president of the United States.

Low levels of public information are characteristic of most countries, but Americans rank lower than citizens of other Western democracies by some indicators. In a seven-country survey conducted in 1993 by the Times-Mirror Center for the People and the Press, Americans ranked next to last in terms of their ability to respond correctly to five questions about world leaders and events. Americans did their best on a question that asked them to name the president of Russia: 50 percent said Boris Yeltsin, but this was far lower than the 94 percent of Germans who named Yeltsin. In light of America's leading role in the world, its citizens might be expected to be uniquely well informed about international affairs. However, they are less knowledgeable in this area than Europeans, who live in closer proximity to other countries and who thus may be more attentive to world politics.

Information About World Events and Leaders:
Percent Answering Two or More of Five Questions Accurately

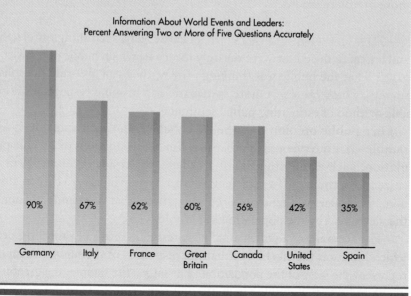

Germany	Italy	France	Great Britain	Canada	United States	Spain
90%	67%	62%	60%	56%	42%	35%

or a computer is. So it is with public opinion. No one has ever seen a "public opinion," and thus it cannot be measured directly. It must be assessed indirectly.

A time-honored method of judging public opinion is the interpretation of election returns. The vote is perceived by the press and politicians as an indicator of the public's mood—whether liberal or conservative, angry or satisfied, quiet or intense. Letters to the editor in newspapers, e-mail messages to elected officials, and the size of crowds at mass demonstrations are other indicators of how the public feels on an issue. Yet another device is the activity of lobbyists who bring the concerns of their constituents to government's attention.

All these indicators of public opinion are important and deserve the attention of those in power. These indicators, however, have shortcomings as a guide to what is on the minds of the people. Elections offer the people only a yes-or-no choice between candidates, and different voters will make the same choice for quite different reasons. The winning candidate may claim that the public has based its choice on a particular issue or inclination, but election returns almost always mask a much more complex reality.

As for letter writers and demonstrators, they are not at all representative of the general population. Less than 1 percent of Americans participate each year in a mass demonstration, and fewer than 10 percent write to the president or a member of Congress. Studies have found that the views of letter writers and demonstrators are more intense and more extreme than those of other citizens.[5]

PUBLIC OPINION POLLS   In an earlier day, such things as elections and letters to the editor were the only means by which public officials could gauge what the public was thinking. Today, they can also rely on polls or surveys, which provide a more systematic and in some respects more reliable method of estimating public sentiment.

In a **public opinion poll** a relatively small number of individuals—the **sample**—are interviewed in order to estimate the opinions of a whole **population,** such as the students of a college, the residents of a city, or the citizens of a country. If a sufficient number of individuals are chosen at random, their views will tend to be representative—that is, roughly the same as the views held by the population as a whole.

The accuracy of a poll is usually expressed in terms of **sampling error,** which indicates the likelihood that the responses of the sample accurately represent the view of the population. The larger the sample, the greater the likelihood that the sample's opinions will represent those of the population

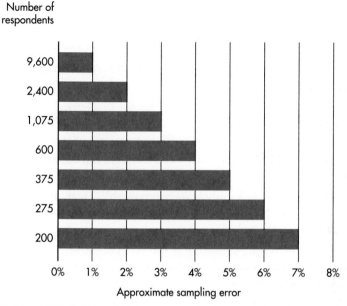

Number of respondents

0% 1% 2% 3% 4% 5% 6% 7% 8%

Approximate sampling error

FIGURE 6-2 RELATIONSHIP BETWEEN SAMPLE SIZE AND
SAMPLING ERROR
The larger a poll's sample is, the smaller is the error in estimating the population
from which the sample is taken. These figures are based on a 95 percent
confidence level, which means that for a given sample size (e.g., 600), the chances
are 19 in 20 (95 percent) that the sample will produce results that are within the
sampling error (e.g., ±4 percent) of the results that would have been obtained if
the whole population had been interviewed.

(see Figure 6-2). Many people assume that a poll of the United States, with
its 250 million people, must have a much larger sample than, say, a poll of
Massachusetts or Arizona in order to achieve the same degree of accuracy. In
fact, the mathematics of polling are such that sample size is the critical factor.[6] Thus, a sample of one thousand people will have nearly the same level
of accuracy whether the population is that of a city, a state, or the nation.

A properly drawn sample of one thousand individuals has a sampling
error of plus or minus 3 percent, which is to say that the proportions of the
various opinions expressed by the people in the sample are likely to be
within 3 percent of those of the whole population. For example, if 55 percent of a sample of one thousand respondents say that they intend to vote
for the Republican candidate for president, then the chances are high that
52 to 58 percent (55 percent plus or minus 3 percent) of the whole population plan to vote for the Republican.

The impressive record of the Gallup poll in predicting the outcomes of presidential elections indicates that the theoretical accuracy of polls is likely to be matched in practice. For example, the Gallup poll predicted a 52–41 percent victory for Bill Clinton over Bob Dole in 1996. The actual margin was 49–41. The Gallup organization has erred badly only once: it stopped polling several weeks before the 1948 election and missed a late trend that carried Harry Truman to victory over Thomas E. Dewey.

Problems with Polls   Mathematical estimations of poll accuracy require a **probability sample:** a sample in which each individual in the population has a known probability of being selected at random for inclusion. In practice, pollsters can only approximate this ideal. Because pollsters rarely have a list of all individuals in a population from which to draw a random sample, they usually base their sample on telephones or locations. Random-digit telephone sampling is the most commonly used technique. Pollsters use computers to pick random telephone numbers, which are then dialed by interviewers to reach respondents. Because the computer is as likely to pick one telephone number as any other and because 95 percent of U.S. homes have a telephone, a sample selected in this way is usually assumed to be representative of the population.[7]

Some polls are not based on probability sampling. For example, news reporters sometimes conduct "people-in-the-street" interviews to obtain individual responses to political questions. Although a reporter may imply that the views of those interviewed are representative of the general public's, the fallacy of this reasoning should be readily apparent. The sample will be biased by where and when the reporter chooses to conduct the interviews. For example, interviews conducted on a downtown street at the noon hour will include a disproportionate number of business employees who are taking their lunch breaks. Housewives, teachers, and factory workers, not to mention farmers, are among the many groups that would be underrepresented in such a sample.

Polls can also be misleading if they include poorly worded questions or ask people about remote topics. For example, a Roper poll received national attention when it found that a third of Americans expressed doubt about whether the Holocaust had actually happened. However, the poll question was a double negative ("Does it seem possible or does it seem impossible to you that the Nazi extermination of the Jews never happened?"), and some analysts suggested that the survey respondents may have been confused by the wording of the question. In fact, they were. A follow-up poll that asked a straightforward question found that less than one in ten Americans said they doubted the Holocaust had occurred.

Despite these and other sources of error, the poll or survey is the most relied-upon method of measuring public opinion. More than one hundred 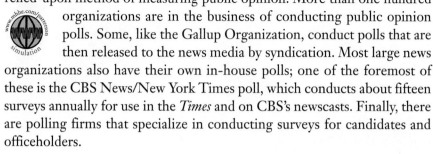 organizations are in the business of conducting public opinion polls. Some, like the Gallup Organization, conduct polls that are then released to the news media by syndication. Most large news organizations also have their own in-house polls; one of the foremost of these is the CBS News/New York Times poll, which conducts about fifteen surveys annually for use in the *Times* and on CBS's newscasts. Finally, there are polling firms that specialize in conducting surveys for candidates and officeholders.

POLITICAL SOCIALIZATION: HOW AMERICANS LEARN THEIR POLITICS

Analysts have long been interested in the process by which public opinion is formed. The learning process by which people acquire their political opinions, beliefs, and values is called **political socialization.** Just as a language, a religion, or an athletic skill is acquired through a learning process, so too are people's political orientations. Our political beliefs are not drawn from a hat; they are acquired. We are socialized to see the political world in certain ways. For most Americans, the socialization process starts in the family with exposure to the political loyalties and opinions of the parents. The schools later contribute to the process, as do the mass media, friends, and other influences. Political socialization is thus a lifelong process.

The Process of Political Socialization

The process of political socialization in the United States has several major characteristics. First, although socialization continues throughout life, most people's political outlook is substantially influenced by their childhood learning. The **primacy tendency** refers to the fact that what is learned first is often lodged most firmly in one's mind.[8] Most people do not reflect deeply on how they acquired their political preferences. Basic ideas about race, gender, and political party, for example, are often formed uncritically in childhood, much in the way that belief in a particular religion, typically the religion of one's parents, is acquired.

A second characteristic of political socialization is that it is cumulative. The **structuring tendency** refers to the tendency of earlier learning to structure later learning.[9] This tendency is less a function of age itself than of an accumulated attachment to particular ideas or values. Of course, the

Students in a North Carolina school reciting the Pledge of Allegiance.
Such childhood socialization experiences can have a profound impact on
an individual's basic political beliefs.

fact that the United States is a diverse and mobile society makes a basic
change in a person's political views possible, especially when previous and
current experiences are at odds with one another. However, individuals
have psychological defense mechanisms that protect their ingrained beliefs.
When faced with situations that might challenge their original views, they
can readily muster reasons for clinging to them because these views are
deeply ingrained.

Dramatic political transformation is uncommon, and when it has occurred on a large scale, it has always been preceded by an extraordinary event. In such instances, it is usually younger people who are more
responsive. Their beliefs are less firmly rooted in past experiences and
are therefore more easily changed. The **age-cohort tendency** holds that
a significant break in the pattern of political socialization is almost always concentrated among younger citizens. Democratic president Franklin
Roosevelt's New Deal initiatives, which sought to alleviate the economic
hardship of the Great Depression, resulted in a substantial increase in
Democratic loyalties among first-time voters but not among older ones.
Most of these new loyalists retained their Democratic preference throughout their lives.

The Agents of Political Socialization

As we have noted, the socialization process takes place through a variety of influences, including family, schools, peers, the mass media, and political leaders and events. It is helpful to consider briefly some ways in which these so-called **agents of socialization** affect people's opinions. Although these agents will be discussed separately, it should be kept in mind that, by and large, their influences overlap. Many of the same political values that people acquire at home and in school, for example, are emphasized regularly by the mass media and political leaders.[10]

THE FAMILY   The family is a powerful agent of socialization because children begin with no political attitudes of their own and tend to accept uncritically those of their parents.[11] By the time the child is a teenager and is less likely to listen to a parent, many of the beliefs and values that will stay with the child throughout life are already in place.

Some of these orientations are overtly political. Many adults are Republicans or Democrats today largely because they accepted their parents' party loyalty.[12] They now can give all sorts of reasons for preferring their party to the other. But the reasons come later in life; the loyalty comes first, during childhood. The family also contributes to basic orientations that, while not directly political, have political significance. For example, the American family tends to be more egalitarian than families in other nations, and American children often have a voice in family decisions. Such basic American values as equality, individualism, and personal freedom have their roots in patterns of family interaction.[13]

SCHOOLS   The school, like the family, has its major impact on children's basic political beliefs and values rather than on specific issues of policy. Teachers at the elementary level describe the exploits of national heroes like Abraham Lincoln and Martin Luther King, Jr., and extol the superiority of the country's economic and political systems.[14] While students in the middle and high school grades may encounter a more critical perspective in the classroom, they still receive a somewhat fabled version of the country's history and politics (see Chapter 1). U.S. schools are probably more instrumental in building support for the nation than the schools in other democracies. The Pledge of Allegiance, which is recited daily in many U.S. schools, has no equivalent in European countries.

Schools also contribute to Americans' sense of social equality. Most American children, regardless of family income, attend public schools and study a fairly standard curriculum. Today, because of the increase in private school enrollment and the sharp contrast between suburban and inner-city districts, the school plays a smaller role in maintaining a sense of equality.

PEERS   Members of peer groups—friends, neighbors, and coworkers—tend to have similar political views. Belonging to a peer group usually reinforces what a person already believes. One reason is that most people trust the views of their friends and associates. Another is that they may be reluctant to deviate too far from what their peers think. In her book *The Spiral of Silence*, Elisabeth Noelle-Neumann contends that individuals fear social isolation and hence are reluctant to speak out against a dominant opinion.[15] The effect, she argues, is to make a prevailing opinion appear to be much stronger than it actually is, which can lead public officials to give it more attention than it may deserve.

THE MASS MEDIA   The mass media are another powerful socializing agent. The media's influence, although diffuse and difficult to measure, is nonetheless substantial. While experts disagree, for example, on the extent to which violence on television contributes to violence in American society, few hold it entirely blameless.

The media's socializing influence is also felt through its news coverage. Studies indicate that the way in which news stories are "framed" affects people's political perceptions.[16] For example, the press in recent years has increasingly framed political leaders in the context of their tactics and mistakes (rather than their policy goals and accomplishments), with the result that the public thinks less highly of the candidates than it did at an earlier time.[17] (The media's influence is examined more fully in Chapter 10.)

POLITICAL LEADERS AND POLITICAL INSTITUTIONS   People look to political leaders and institutions, particularly the presidency and the political party, as guides to opinion. The level of public approval of a nuclear arms limitation agreement with the USSR rose in 1987 after President Ronald Reagan endorsed the idea. In broader terms, political leaders play a significant role in shaping political debate and opinion through the symbols and slogans they use.[18]

Their ability to mold opinion, however, has limits. When President Bill Clinton in 1993 proposed to Congress a policy that would have given nearly every American either government- or employer-provided health care, his plan quickly gained the support of 70 percent of the public. Within a year, however, support for the plan had fallen below 40 percent. Opponents had convinced most Americans that the plan was too complicated, was too costly, and would jeopardize both the quality of their medical care and their access to a personal physician. Support for the plan was so weak that it did not even come up for a floor vote in either the House or the Senate.

As the Clinton health plan illustrates, people look to leaders for guidance but tend to judge the options in the context of their own lives and values. Clinton's plan was not supported in the end by most Americans because it conflicted with their view of how medical care should be provided. (Chapters 8, 11, and 12 discuss further the impact of political leaders and institutions on public opinion.)

CHURCHES   From the seventeenth-century Puritans to today's Islamic Nation, churches have long been a powerful force in shaping Americans' basic social opinions. Most Americans say they believe in God, most attend church regularly or at least occasionally, and most adhere to a religion that teaches beliefs about the proper nature of society. Moreover, most Americans believe that religion can provide answers to many of today's problems (see Figure 6-3). In all these respects, churches and religion are a more powerful force in the United States than in other Western societies.

Scholars have not studied the impact of church attendance and religious instruction on political socialization as closely as they have studied other influences, such as the schools and the media, but churches are an important source of politically relevant attitudes, including society's obligations to the poor, the unborn, and children. (The impact of religion is discussed further in a later section of the chapter.)

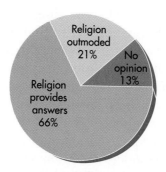

FIGURE 6-3   OPINIONS ON RELIGION AS AN ANSWER TO TODAY'S PROBLEMS
Most Americans say that religion can answer all or most of today's problems; only a minority believe religion is old-fashioned and out of date. Source: Gallup poll, March 17-19, 2000. Used with permission.

FRAMES OF REFERENCE: HOW AMERICANS THINK POLITICALLY

What are the frames of reference that guide the political thinking of Americans? The question is important in at least two respects. First, the way in which citizens think politically provides clues about the way in which public opinion is likely to affect government. The government in a democratic system is expected to act more often in accordance with public opinion than against it.

A second reason it is important to understand how the people think politically is that a shared frame of reference can bring citizens together in the pursuit of a common goal. The opinions of millions of Americans would mean almost nothing if each of these opinions were different from all the others. If enough people think the same way, however, they may be able to exert political power.

The subject of how Americans think politically fills entire books; here we will outline four of the major frames of reference through which Americans evaluate political alternatives. The first tends to unite Americans; the other three give rise to differences of opinion among them.

Cultural Thinking: Common Ideas

As we indicated in Chapter 1, Americans are unusual in their commitment to a common set of ideals that define the nature of the American political experience. Such principles as individualism, equality, and self-government have always meant somewhat different things to different people but nonetheless are a source of opinion consensus.[19] For example, government programs aimed at redistributing wealth from the rich to the poor are common in western Europe but are less appealing for Americans, who have a deeper commitment to individualism.

There are limits, of course, to the degree to which Americans' basic beliefs shape their policy opinions. For nearly two centuries African Americans were inferior by law to white Americans, despite the American creed that "all men are created equal." Such inconsistencies speak to the all-too-human capacity to voice one idea and live another.

Nevertheless, Americans' political ideals are a powerful influence on public opinion. They affect the way in which disputes are argued and affect what people regard as reasonable and desirable. Americans' ideals serve to define the boundaries of acceptable political action and opinion (see Chapter 1).

Ideological Thinking: The Outlook for Some

Commentators on public opinion in the United States often use such terms as "liberal" and "conservative" to describe how people think politically. When Republicans dominated the 1994 midterm elections, for example, analysts claimed that a "conservative tide" was sweeping the country.

Liberal and conservative are ideological terms. So, too, are such terms as populist, progressive, libertarian, communist, and fascist. An **ideology** is a consistent pattern of opinion on particular issues that stems from a core or basic belief. Communism, for example, is rooted in a belief in material equality, and a communist therefore would be expected to support wage and welfare policies designed to spread wealth more evenly across society.

Although ideological terms are often used to describe mass publics, they do not accurately describe how most people think about politics. Nearly everyone has basic beliefs that affect their opinions, but most people do not apply them consistently across a wide range of issues. They may say, for example, that they favor free trade among nations, but then oppose it in particular cases where it works to the disadvantage of U.S. firms or workers. Research indicates that no more than a third of Americans, and perhaps as few as a tenth, have a pattern of opinions on issues that is consistent enough to be described as a manifestation of a true ideology.[20] Further, most Americans are relatively pragmatic in their political judgments. Rather than applying an ideological framework, they tend to judge policies by whether they appear to be working or seem likely to work.

Nevertheless, analysts sometimes find it useful to measure the public's ideological tendencies. A standard method is to ask survey respondents whether they think of themselves as liberal, moderate, or conservative. The problem with this approach is that, although people readily label themselves by these terms, many individuals are unable to say what the terms mean or provide inexact or inappropriate definitions. For this reason, pollsters have recently developed an alternative and less direct method. They ask respondents two questions: Do you support or oppose an activist role for government in determining the distribution of economic benefits in society? Do you support or oppose activist government as a means of promoting a particular set of social values? This method does not require that respondents know the meaning of ideological terms, and yet provides a measure of people's general beliefs about government action in the broad areas of economic and social policy.

Responses to the two questions have been the basis for identifying four ideological types: conservatives, liberals, populists, and libertarians (see Figure 6-4). **Conservatives** are defined as individuals who oppose an activist

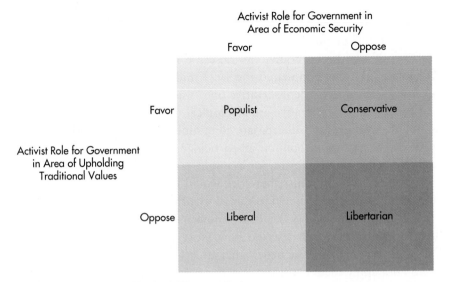

FIGURE 6-4   TYPES OF IDEOLOGIES
Americans can be classified as liberals, conservatives, populists, or libertarians, depending on their attitudes toward the government's role in the areas of economic security and social values.

role for government in providing economic benefits but look to government to uphold traditional social values. In contrast, **liberals** favor activist government as an instrument of economic redistribution but reject the notion that government should favor a particular set of social values. True liberals and conservatives could be expected to differ, for instance, on the issues of homosexual rights (a social values question) and government-guaranteed health care (an economic distribution question). Liberals would view homosexuality as a private issue and believe that government should ensure that everyone has access to adequate medical care. Conservatives would oppose government-mandated access to health care and favor government policies that actively discourage homosexual lifestyles. **Populists** are defined as individuals who share with conservatives a concern for traditional values but, like liberals, favor an active role for government in providing economic security. **Libertarians** are opposed to government intervention in both the economic and the social spheres.[21]

In sum, libertarians are the most committed to individual freedom, and populists are the most committed to government activism. Conservatives and liberals are committed to individual freedom in one area (the economic sphere for conservatives, the social sphere for liberals) but to government activism in the other (the social sphere for conservatives, the economic sphere for liberals). Of these ideological types, conservatives are the largest group. A recent Gallup poll, for example, estimated that 31 percent of Americans are conservatives, 24 percent are libertarian, 17 percent are populist, and 13 percent are liberal.[22]

Group Thinking: The Outlook of Many

For most Americans, groups are a more important frame of reference than is ideology. Many people see politics through the lens of a group to which they belong or with which they identify. These individuals nearly always pay closer attention to issues that affect the group's interests than to more remote issues. Farmers, for example, are more likely to follow agricultural issues than they are labor-management issues.

Because of the country's great size, settlement by various immigrant groups, and economic pluralism, Americans are a very diverse people. Later chapters will examine group tendencies more fully, but it is useful here to mention a few of the major group orientations.

RELIGION   Religious differences have always been a source of solidarity within a group and conflict with outsiders. At an earlier time, religion was a bitterly divisive force, as newly immigrant Catholic and Jewish immigrants encountered widespread hostility and discrimination from entrenched Protestant groups. Today, Catholics, Protestants, and Jews share similar opinions on most policy issues.

Nevertheless, some important religious differences remain. The most powerful religious force in contemporary American politics is the so-called religious right, which consists primarily of individuals who see themselves as born-again Christians and view the Bible as the infallible truth. Their views on such issues as homosexual rights, abortion, and school prayer differ significantly from those of the population as a whole. A Time/CNN survey found, for example, that born-again Christians are 37 percent more likely than other Americans to agree that "the Supreme Court and the Congress have gone too far in keeping religious and moral values like prayer out of our laws, schools, and many areas of our lives."

CLASS   Economic class has less influence on political opinion in the United States than in Europe, but it is nevertheless related to opinions on certain economic issues. For example, lower-income Americans are more supportive of social welfare programs, business regulation, and progressive taxation than are those in higher-income categories. An obstacle to class-based politics in the United States is that people with similar incomes but differing occupations do not share the same opinions. Support for collective bargaining, for example, is substantially higher among factory workers than among small farmers, service workers, and those in the skilled crafts. The interplay of class and opinion will be examined more closely in Chapter 9, which discusses interest groups.

REGION   Region has declined as a basis of political opinions. The increased mobility of the U.S. population has resulted in the relocation of millions of Americans from the Northeast and Midwest to the South and West. Their beliefs on issues such as social welfare tend to be more liberal than those of people who are native to these regions. Nevertheless, regional differences are still evident in the areas of social welfare, civil rights, and national defense. Conservative opinions on these issues are more prevalent in the southern and mountain states than elsewhere (see box: States in the Nation).

RACE AND ETHNICITY   Race and ethnicity, as we saw in Chapter 5, have a significant influence on opinions. Whites and African Americans, for example, differ on issues of integration: black people are more in favor of affirmative action, busing, and other measures designed to promote racial equality and integration. Racial and ethnic groups also differ on many pocketbook issues, largely as a result of the differences in their economic situations: African Americans and Hispanics are more supportive of social welfare programs and government-backed job and training programs. The crime issue is another area where opinion differences are pronounced and predictable: minorities are less trusting of police and the judicial system. A 1999 poll conducted for the American Bar Association found, for example, that only 26 percent of non-whites believe that "law enforcement officials and police try to treat whites and minorities alike."

GENDER   Although male-female differences of opinion are small on most issues, gender does affect opinion on some questions. Perhaps surprisingly, these issues are not primarily those that touch directly on gender or sexual equality. Men and women have generally similar views on issues such as abortion rights and affirmative action.

There are two areas, however, where men's and women's opinions diverge significantly: social welfare and the use of force by the state.[23] Women are more supportive of government spending on social welfare (such as for education and poverty programs) and more opposed to state-sponsored

★ STATES IN THE NATION ★

Conservatives and Liberals

Half of all Americans describe themselves as moderates. Of the rest, the majority are self-identified conservatives. According to a 2000 poll, liberals outnumber conservatives in only six states and the District of Columbia, although they are equal or nearly equal in number to conservatives in six other states. The concentration of conservatives is especially high in the southern, plains, and mountain states where traditionalism and individualism are more widely embraced than in the northeast and coastal West.

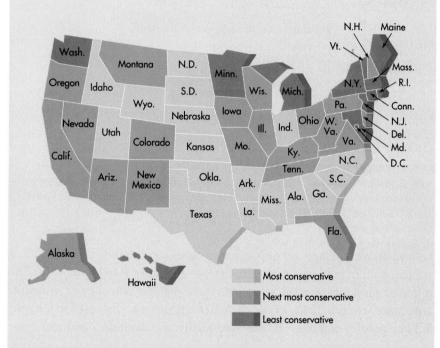

SOURCE: CNN exit polls, 2000. Classification based on the difference in the proportions of self-identified conservatives and liberals in each state.

force (for example, military power as an instrument of foreign policy). Some analysts have suggested that such differences reflect women's heightened sense of compassion and community responsibility. Men are said to

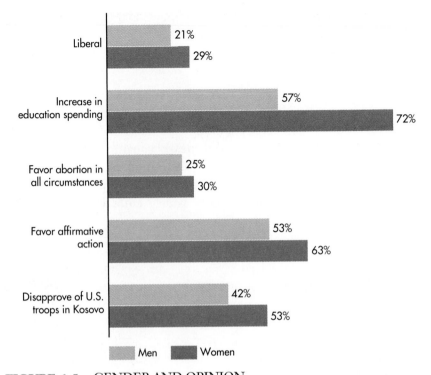

FIGURE 6-5   GENDER AND OPINION
Compared with men, women are less conservative, more supportive of social
welfare services, and more opposed to the use of military force. Sources (polls, from
top to bottom): Gallup, 2000; Washington Post/ABC News, 2000; Gallup, 2000; Gallup,
2000; Washington Post/ABC News, 1999.

believe more strongly in self-reliance and accountability. In any case,
women tend to hold less conservative views than men (see Figure 6-5). This
difference is a factor in the so-called *gender gap* (the tendency of women to
vote more strongly Democratic than men), which was discussed in Chapter
5. (The politics of gender is discussed further in Chapters 9 and 16.)

AGE   Another division of growing importance is the "age gap." Young
and old have always had somewhat divergent opinions as a consequence of
differences in their ages and socialization experiences, but their disagreements are becoming greater. In her book *Young* v. *Old*, the political scientist
Susan MacManus notes that the elderly tend to oppose increases in public
school funding while supporting increases in social security and Medicare
(government-assisted medical care for retirees). Such acts are at least somewhat at odds with the interests of younger adults, who may have children in

the public schools and who, through payroll deductions, pay the taxes that fund the social security and Medicare programs.[24]

MacManus predicts that issues of age will increasingly dominate American politics and that the elderly have the political clout to prevail. They vote at a much higher rate than young people, are better organized politically (through groups such as the powerful American Association of Retired Persons), and are increasing in number as a result of lengthened life spans (the so-called graying of America). (The politics of age is also discussed in Chapters 9 and 16.)

CROSS-CUTTING CLEAVAGES   Although group loyalties can have a powerful impact on people's opinions, their influence is diminished when identification with one group is offset by identification with other groups. In a pluralistic society such as the United States, groups tend to be "cross-cutting"—that is, each includes individuals from a range of other groups. Cross-cutting cleavages tend to produce moderate opinions. Faced with conflicting feelings arising out of identification with several groups, most people seek a balance between them when forming an opinion. However, in societies such as Northern Ireland where group loyalties are reinforcing rather than cross-cutting (Catholics tend to have much lower incomes, Protestants much higher ones), opinions are intensified by group identifications and deep hatreds among the opposing camps can result. In America, Catholics and Protestants are not at each other's throats, largely because each group includes people of varying income, education, region, and so on. *Diversity* is a source of differences; it can also be a basis for harmony.

Partisan Thinking: The Line That Divides

In the everyday play of politics, no source of opinion more clearly divides Americans than that of their partisanship. Figure 6-6 provides examples, but they indicate only a few of the differences. On nearly every major issue of economic, social, and foreign policy, Republicans and Democrats have views that are at least somewhat different. In many cases, such as spending programs for the poor, the differences are substantial.

The term **party identification** refers to a person's ingrained sense of loyalty to a political party. Party identification is not formal membership in a party but rather an emotional attachment to a party—the feeling that "I am a Democrat" or "I am a Republican." Scholars and pollsters have typically measured party identification with a question of the following type:

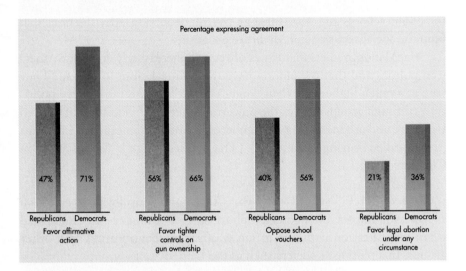

FIGURE 6-6 PARTISANSHIP AND ISSUE OPINIONS
Republicans and Democrats differ significantly in their opinions on many policy issues. Source: In order of questions: Washington Post/ABC News, 2000; Washington Post/ABC News, 1999; Gallup, 2000; Gallup, 2000.

"Generally speaking, do you think of yourself as a Republican, a Democrat, an Independent, or what?" About 65 percent of adults call themselves Democrats or Republicans. Of the 35 percent who prefer the label "Independent," most say they lean toward one party or the other. Indeed, these "independent partisans" are more loyal to their preferred party than people who say they are "weak" Democrats or Republicans.

Early studies of party identification concluded that partisan attitudes were highly stable and seldom changed over the course of adult life.[25] Subsequent studies have shown that party loyalties are more fluid than originally believed; they can be influenced by the issues and candidates of the moment.[26] Nevertheless, most adults do not switch their party loyalties easily, and a substantial proportion never waver from an initial commitment to a party, which can often be traced to childhood influences.

Once acquired, partisanship affects how people perceive and interpret events. For example, when the U.S. Supreme Court ruled against a manual recount of Florida votes, which decided the 2000 presidential election in George W. Bush's favor, the responses of Democrats, Independents, and Republicans differed sharply. A national poll indicated that 53 percent of Democrats and 25 percent of Independents but only 12 percent of Republicans had "less respect" for the Court because of its action.

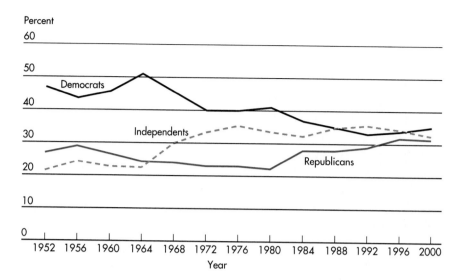

FIGURE 6-7 PARTISAN IDENTIFICATION
Party loyalties weakened in the late 1960s, and the proportion of Independents increased. Source: Compiled from multiple sources.

For most people, partisanship is not simply a "blind" faith in the party of their choice. Some Republicans and Democrats know very little about their party's traditions, policies, or group commitments and unthinkably embrace its candidates. However, party loyalties are not randomly distributed across the population, but follow a pattern that would be predicted from the parties' traditions. The Democratic party, for example, has been the driving force behind social welfare and workers' rights policies, while the Republican party has been the spearhead for pro-business and tax reform policies. The fact that most union workers are Democrats and most businesspeople are Republicans is not mere coincidence. Their partisanship is rooted in their different life circumstances and the different policy traditions of the two parties.

Partisanship is obviously a strong force in American politics, but its influence is declining. In recent decades, the proportion of voters who identify with the Democratic or Republican party has declined and the proportion of Independents has increased (see Figure 6-7). As a result, elections are more volatile than in the past. People are less likely to vote on the basis of a long-standing party loyalty and more likely to base their choice on the issues and candidates of the moment. This and other issues of partisanship are examined in depth at various points later in this book, particularly in Chapters 7, 8, 11, and 12.

THE INFLUENCE OF PUBLIC OPINION
ON POLICY

Yet unanswered in the discussion is the central question about public opinion: What impact does it have on government?

The fundamental principle of democracy is that the *majority* ought to prevail on public issues. It is difficult, however, to put this principle into practice. In any society of appreciable size, it is simply not possible for the people directly to formulate public policies and programs. However, democracy can be said to exist when officials take the majority's views into account when making policy decisions and when the people have recourse to free and fair elections when they believe their opinions are being ignored.[27]

Some analysts argue that the majority's views do not count for enough; the *elites*, it is claimed, are so entrenched and remote that they pay little attention to the preferences of ordinary citizens.[28] The most comprehensive study ever conducted of the relationship between public opinion and policy, however, concluded otherwise. In a study spanning fifty years of trends,

Bags containing the bodies of American soldiers killed in the Vietnam War await shipment back to the United States. The large numbers of American casualties during the war helped to turn public opinion against U.S. involvement in Vietnam. As public opinion turned, U.S. policymakers had little choice but to plan a phased withdrawal from Vietnam.

Benjamin Page and Robert Shapiro found a substantial relationship between changes in public opinion and subsequent changes in public policy, particularly on highly visible issues. More often than not, policy changed in response to opinion rather than the reverse. In addition, the more important the issue was, the more likely it was that policy adapted to changes in public opinion. Page and Shapiro concluded that U.S. officials are reasonably responsive to majority opinion.[29]

Not all scholars have interpreted the evidence on public opinion and policy so favorably,[30] but there is little question that the public's views do have an impact. Public opinion is rarely powerful enough to force officials into a specific course of action, but public opinion does serve as a guiding force in public policy. There are many actions, for example, that officials dare *not* take for fear of public retribution. No politician who wants to stay in office is likely to say, for example, that social security for the elderly should be abolished. And there are many actions that politicians willingly take in order to appeal to the public.[31] In late 1999, for example, the GOP-controlled Congress passed a budget that included funding to hire thousands of new public school teachers. Congressional Republicans had opposed the measure, but education ranked near the top in polls of Americans' policy priorities and the 2000 election was just around the corner. Republicans, reluctant to hand the Democrats a potent campaign issue, enacted the funding measure.

Such examples, however, do not provide an answer to the question of whether government is *sufficiently* responsive to public opinion. This question, as was discussed in Chapter 2, is a normative one; the answer to it rests on assumptions about the proper relationship between people's everyday opinions and what government does. The question is also complicated by the fact that politics includes a battle over the control of public opinion. People's views are neither fixed nor simply a product of personal circumstances. Public opinion is dynamic and can be changed, activated, and crystallized through political action.

In fact, one of the best indicators of the power of public opinion is the effort of political leaders to harness it in support of their goals. In American politics, popular demand for a policy is a powerful argument for it. For this reason and others, great effort is made to organize and represent public opinion through elections (Chapter 7), political parties (Chapter 8), interest groups (Chapter 9), the news media (Chapter 10), and political institutions (Chapters 11 to 14). Later chapters will also examine the direct impact of public opinion in particular policy areas: the economy (Chapter 15), social welfare (Chapter 16), and foreign affairs (Chapter 17).

SUMMARY

Public opinion can be defined as those opinions that citizens express openly through words or actions. Public officials have many ways of assessing public opinion, using such indicators as the outcomes of elections, but have increasingly come to rely on public opinion polls. There are many possible sources of error in polls, and surveys sometimes present a misleading image of the public's views. However, a properly conducted poll can provide an accurate indication of what the public is thinking and can dissuade political leaders from thinking that the views of the most vocal citizens (such as demonstrators and letter writers) are also the views of the broader public.

The process by which individuals acquire their political opinions is called political socialization. During childhood the family and schools are important sources of basic political attitudes, such as beliefs about the parties and the nature of the U.S. political and economic systems. Many of the basic orientations that Americans acquire during childhood remain with them in adulthood, but socialization is a continuing process. Major shifts in opinion during adulthood are usually the consequence of changing political conditions; for example, the Great Depression of the 1930s was the catalyst for wholesale changes in Americans' opinions on the government's economic role. There are also short-term fluctuations in opinion that result from new political issues, problems, and events. Individuals' opinions in these cases are affected by prior beliefs, peers, political leaders, and the news media. Events themselves also have a significant short-term influence on opinions.

The frames of reference that guide Americans' opinions include cultural beliefs, such as individualism, which result in a range of acceptable and unacceptable policy alternatives. Opinions can also stem from ideology, although most citizens do not have a strong and consistent ideological attachment. In addition, individuals develop opinions as a result of group orientations, notably religion, income, occupation, region, race, gender, or age. Partisanship is perhaps the major source of political opinions; Republicans and Democrats differ in their voting behavior and views on many policy issues. However, party loyalty has declined in importance in recent decades as a frame of reference for people's opinions.

Public opinion has a significant influence on government but seldom determines exactly what government will do in a particular instance. Public opinion serves to constrain the policy choices of officials. Some policy actions are beyond the range of possibility because the public will not accept change in existing policy or will not seriously consider policy that seems clearly at odds with basic American values. Evidence indicates that officials are reasonably attentive to public opinion on highly visible and controversial issues of public policy.

MAJOR CONCEPTS

age-cohort tendency	populists
agents of socialization	primacy tendency
conservatives	probability sample
ideology	public opinion
liberals	public opinion poll
libertarians	sample
party identification	sampling error
political socialization	structuring tendency
population	

SUGGESTED READINGS AND WEB SITES

Delli Carpini, Michael X., and Scott Keeter. *What Americans Know About Politics and Why It Matters.* New Haven, Conn.: Yale University Press, 1996. A synthesis of the American public's knowledge about politics.

Dunn, Charles W., and J. David Woodard. *The Conservative Tradition in America.* Lanham, Md.: Rowman & Littlefield, 1996. A study of the philosophical and political roots of conservatism from its origins to the present.

Jacobs, Lawrence, and Robert Shapiro. *Politicians Don't Pander.* Chicago: University of Chicago Press, 2000. An analysis that concludes politicians are not driven by polls.

MacManus, Susan A. *Young v. Old: Generational Combat in the Twenty-First Century.* Boulder, Colo.: Westview Press, 1996. A study of the emerging conflict in the political self-interest of younger and older Americans.

Noelle-Neumann, Elisabeth. *The Spiral of Silence.* 2d ed. Chicago: University of Chicago Press, 1993. An intriguing theory of how public opinion is formed and muted.

Sobel, Richard. *The Impact of Public Opinion on U.S. Foreign Policy since Vietnam.* New York: Oxford University Press, 2001. A study of the relationship between public opinion and foreign policy.

Traugott, Michael W., and Paul J. Lavrakas. *The Voter's Guide to Election Polls,* 2d ed. Chatham, N.J.: Chatham House, 2000. A clear guide to survey methods and analysis with an emphasis on election polling.

Zaller, John R. *The Nature and Origins of Mass Opinion.* New York: Cambridge University Press, 1992. A superb analysis of the nature of public opinion.

http://www.gallup.com/   The web site of the renowned Gallup Organization; includes the results of recent Gallup polls.

http://www.policy.com/   A nonpartisan site that provides a wealth of information about current public issues.

http://www.princeton.edu:80/~abelson/index.html   The Princeton Survey Research Center's site offers results from surveys conducted by a variety of polling organizations.

http://www.publicagenda.org/   The nonpartisan Public Agenda's site; it provides opinions, analyses, and educational materials on current policy issues.

READING 6

Democracy, Information, and the Rational Public
BENJAMIN I. PAGE AND ROBERT Y. SHAPIRO

Introduction

In their essay, Benjamin Page and Robert Shapiro confront a question that underpinned Chapter 6: Do Americans know enough and think clearly enough to have "reasonable" and "responsible" opinions on policy issues? Drawing mainly upon findings of their own research, Page and Shapiro conclude that the major threat to a rational and informed public is not citizens' disinterest in or inability to comprehend policy issues but the inadequacies of America's systems of public information and civic education.

The suggestion that ordinary citizens are simply too ignorant to know their own or their country's interests lies at the heart of many objections to majoritarian democracy. The authors of the Federalist Papers, for example, worried not merely that public opinion vacillated but that it erred. John Stuart Mill, considered a father of democratic theory, nonetheless advocated a severely limited suffrage and favored public rather than secret ballots, extra votes for the prosperous and the educated, "merit" appointment rather than election of most officials, no pledges by representatives to their constituents, and very limited functions for the elected body—all on the grounds that common people, especially the working class, were not competent to rule and were likely to demand class legislation.

In more recent times . . . Walter Lippmann issued scathing denunciations of the public's capabilities, maintaining that reality differs sharply from the "stereotypes" or "pictures" in people's heads. Joseph Schumpeter declared that individuals' opinions are not "definite" or "independent" or "rational" and that on most political matters individual volition, command of fact, and method of inference are defective.

Early survey research seemed to bear out these low estimates of public capacity. Surveys indicated that most Americans knew little about politics, cared little, and apparently made their voting decisions on the basis of demographic characteristics or party loyalties, which scholars (perhaps too quickly) took to indicate lack of rational deliberation. Converse's demonstration of weak ideological structure and unstable individual survey responses seemed, for a while, to close the case.

The result was a wholesale revision of democratic theory. Schumpeter's weak procedural definition of democracy, in which elite leadership competes for voters' acquiescence but does not necessarily respond to their policy preferences, influenced more than a generation of scholars. Dahl cast doubt on the desirability of "populistic" democracy. Berelson et al. speculated that citizens' passivity might function as a useful buffer for system stability. Most of the leaders of the political science and sociology professions rejected majoritarian democracy, embracing some form of pluralistic or "polyarchical" system in which organized interest groups play an important part and in which participation by, and responsiveness to, the general public is limited.

We agree with Walker, Kariel, Pateman, Barber, and others that this revisionism mistakenly blamed the citizen victims, ignoring system-level influences upon peoples' behavior (apathy about elections, for example, may result from legal restrictions, repression, or lack of attractive candidates and parties rather than from defects of the citizenry); that it abandoned a worthy normative ideal and turned democratic theory into little more than a conservative ratifier of the status quo; and that it neglected the possibility that broader participation could promote political education and human development.

In particular, we believe that the revisionists misinterpreted survey research results and gave up too quickly on the public. This should have been clear even before research contrasting the 1960s with the 1950s cast a more favorable light on citizens' capacities by showing that people displayed more interest, knowledge, and ideological thinking when the political environment was more lively. The original findings that most Americans did not live up to "classical democratic theory"—a construct of dubious provenance, which called for citizens to have unrealistically and unnecessarily high levels of political knowledge and sophistication—never really had much relevance to the desirability or feasibility of majoritarian democracy.

People probably do not need large amounts of information to make rational voting choices. Cues from like-minded citizens and groups (including cues related to demographic characteristics and party labels) may be sufficient, in an environment where accurate information is available, to permit voters to act as if they had all the available information.

Much the same reasoning applies to our own topic, policy preferences. (We have had nothing new to say about voting, though we suspect that similar principles apply.) Using their underlying beliefs and values, together with cues from leaders and like-minded citizens they trust, people can come up with reasonable opinions (i.e., opinions consonant with their basic beliefs and values) about a wide variety of issues. . . .

Our research has led us to a view of collective public opinion that justifies the use of terms like "reasonable," "responsible," and "rational." Without claiming that we have any unique knowledge of what people's true interests are, we are convinced by the general stability, differentiation, and coherent patterning of collective policy preferences, and by their responsiveness to new situations and new information, that characterizations of public opinion as ignorant fall very wide of the mark. . . .

It is simply not the case that the collective policy preferences of the U.S. public are nonexistent, unknowable, capricious, inconsistent, or ignorant. Instead, they are real, meaningful, well measured by polls, differentiated, coherent, and stable. They react understandably and predictably to events and new information. The classic justifications for ignoring public opinion do not hold up. . . .

Thus our research provides little reason for anyone to fear or oppose majoritarian democracy in the United States. There is no need to sneer at politicians who "read the Gallup polls," so long as they do so correctly. In our view, in fact, government should pay more attention to what the public wants. More democratic responsiveness, rather than less, would be all to the good, and institutional changes to that end (reducing the role of money in politics, easing voter registration, strengthening political competition, broadening electoral accountability) should be encouraged.

At the same time, we have suggested that political education—in the broad sense of providing useful political experience and information and moral guidance to the citizenry—is not what it could be; that concealment of (or failure to provide) relevant information sometimes permits government to pursue unpopular policies, outside of public view; and that the public's policy preferences may sometimes be manipulated by deceptive leaders and by flows of information subject to various biases or distortions.

There is some truth to the epigram of V. O. Key, Jr., that "(t)he voice of the people is but an echo." The public has a remarkable collective capacity for reasonable political thought, even in the face of misleading or downright false counsel from its leaders. But information inputs do matter; they can have substantial effects on policy preferences, bending them away from citizens' true interests or conceptions of the common good.

A chief focus for improvement, we believe, should be the political information system. The public deserves better political education, more opportunities for participation, and access to better information about public policy. Thomas Jefferson expressed the point neatly, in a famous passage from his letter of September 28, 1820, to William C. Jarvis:

> I know of no safe depository of the ultimate powers of the society but the people themselves, and if we think them not enlightened enough to exercise their control with a wholesome discretion, the remedy is not to take it from them but to inform their discretion by education.

SOURCE: Benjamin I. Page and Robert Y. Shapiro, "Democracy, Information, and the Rational Public," *The Rational Public: Fifty Years of Trends in Americans' Policy Preferences.* Copyright © 1992. Reprinted by permission of The University of Chicago Press.

Benjamin I. Page is Gordon Scott Fulcher Professor of Decision Making at Northwestern University. Robert Y. Shapiro is professor of political science at Columbia University.

CHAPTER SEVEN

Voting and Participation

We are concerned in public affairs, but immersed in our private ones.
WALTER LIPPMANN[1]

A T STAKE in the 2000 elections was control of the White House and Congress. Which party would have the leading voice on issues and education, health, welfare, and the environment? Which party would have the greater say in how America responded to the challenges and opportunities of the domestic and global economies? Which party would be entrusted with national security? With so much at stake, it might be thought that Americans would have been eager to cast their ballots for the party of their choice. But, in fact, nearly half of American adults did not vote in the 2000 elections. Despite a concerted get-out-the-vote campaign by the news media and public service groups, the number of people who did not vote was far greater than the number of votes the winning party received in either the presidential or the congressional races.

Voting is a form of **political participation:** a sharing in activities designed to influence public policy and leadership. Political participation involves other activities in addition to voting, such as joining political parties and interest groups, writing to elected officials, demonstrating for political causes, and giving money to political candidates.

Democratic societies are distinguished by their emphasis on citizen participation. The concept of self-government rests on the idea that ordinary people have a right, even an obligation, to involve themselves in the affairs of state. A political system that claims to represent the public's interest is not necessarily a truly democratic system; citizens must also be given meaningful opportunities to participate in the process. From this perspective, the extent of political participation—how much and by whom—is a measure of how fully democratic a society is.[2]

The question of participation also extends to the reasons people are politically involved or not involved. It is one thing if political participation

185

is like attendance at a rock concert, which is mostly a matter of individual taste and proximity, and quite another if participation is like attendance at an elite prep school, which is mostly a matter of social privilege. A democratic political system implies that society will not place substantial barriers in the way of those who want to participate. As we will see in this chapter, differences in the extent of political participation among Americans are explained by both individual and systemic factors, although the latter are more influential in the United States than in most other Western democracies. One result is that the participation rate in U.S. elections is less than that of other countries, particularly among citizens of lower income and less education. The major points made in this chapter are the following:

* *Voter turnout in U.S. elections is low in comparison with that in other democratic nations, which is due to differences in registration requirements, the frequency of elections, and the nature of political parties.*

* *Although most Americans do not participate actively in politics in areas other than voting, Americans are more active in these areas than citizens of other democracies.*

* *Most Americans make a sharp distinction between their personal lives and political life, which reduces their incentive to participate politically.*

VOTER PARTICIPATION

At the nation's founding, **suffrage**—the right to vote—was restricted to property-owning males. Tom Paine ridiculed this policy in *Common Sense*. Noting that a man whose only item of property was a jackass would lose his right to vote if the jackass died, Paine asked, "Now tell me, which was the voter, the man or the jackass?" It was not until 1840 that all states extended suffrage to propertyless white males, a change made possible by their insistence on the vote and by the realization on the part of the wealthy that the nation's abundant opportunities offered a natural defense against attacks on property rights by the voting poor.

Women did not secure the vote until 1920, with the ratification of the Nineteenth Amendment. By then, men had run out of excuses for denying women the vote. Senator Wendell Phillips expressed the prosuffrage view: "One of two things is true: either woman is like man—and if she is, then a ballot based on brains belongs to her as well as to him. Or she is different, and then man does not know how to vote for her as she herself does."[3]

After a hard-fought, decades-long campaign, American women finally won the right to vote in 1920.

African Americans had to wait nearly fifty years longer than women to be granted full suffrage. They seemed to have won the right to vote with passage of the Fifteenth Amendment after the Civil War, but they were effectively disenfranchised in the South by a number of electoral tricks, including poll taxes, literacy tests, and whites-only primary elections. The poll tax was a fee of several dollars that had to be paid before one could register to vote. Since most blacks in the South were too poor to pay the poll tax, it barred them from voting. Not until the ratification of the Twenty-fourth Amendment in 1964 was the poll tax outlawed in national elections. Supreme Court decisions and the Voting Rights Act of 1965 swept away other legal barriers to fuller participation of African Americans.

In 1971, the Twenty-sixth Amendment extended voting rights to include those eighteen years of age or older. Previously, nearly all states had restricted voting to those twenty-one years of age or older.

Today virtually any adult American—rich or poor, man or woman, black or white—who is determined to vote can legally and actually do so. Americans attach great importance to the power of their votes. They claim that voting is their greatest source of influence over political leadership and their strongest protection against an uncaring or corrupt government.[4]

They also rank voting as one of the most essential obligations of citizenship (see Table 7-1). In view of this attitude and the historical struggle of various groups to gain voting rights, the surprising fact is that Americans are not active voters. Millions of them choose not to vote regularly, a tendency that sets them apart from citizens of most other Western democracies.

TABLE 7-1   OPINIONS ON OBLIGATIONS OF CITIZENS
Americans rank voting as one of the essential obligations of citizenship.

	Essential Obligation	Very Important Obligation	Somewhat Important	Personal Preference
Treating all people equally regardless of race or ethnic background	57%	33%	6%	4%
Voting in elections	53	29	9	9
Working to reduce inequality and injustice	41	42	12	6
Being civil to others with whom we may disagree	35	45	14	6
Keeping fully informed about the news and other public issues	30	42	19	10
Donating blood or organs to help with medical needs	20	37	18	26
Volunteering time to community service	16	42	26	16

SOURCE: James Davison Hunter and Carol Bowman, Survey of American Political Culture, Gallup Organization, 1996. Reprinted by permission. From *The American Democracy*, Fourth Edition, by Thomas Patterson, ©1999, reproduced with permission of The McGraw-Hill Companies.

Factors in Voter Turnout:
The United States in Comparative Perspective

Voter turnout is the proportion of persons of voting age who actually vote in a given election. Since the 1960s the turnout level in presidential elections has not reached 60 percent (see Figure 7-1). In 2000, only about half of all adults cast a vote for president.

Turnout is even lower in the midterm congressional elections that take place between presidential elections. Midterm election turnout has not reached 50 percent since 1920, nor made it past the 40 percent mark since 1970. After a recent midterm election, the cartoonist Rigby showed an election clerk eagerly asking a stray cat that had wandered into a polling place, "Are you registered?"[5]

Nonvoting is far more prevalent in the United States than in nearly all other democracies (see box: How the United States Compares). In recent decades, turnout in major national elections has averaged less than 60 percent in the United States, compared with more than 90 percent in Belgium, more than 80 percent in France and Denmark, and more than 70 percent in Great Britain and Germany.[6] The disparity in turnout between the United States and other nations is not so great as these official voting rates indicate, however. Some nations calculate turnout solely on the basis

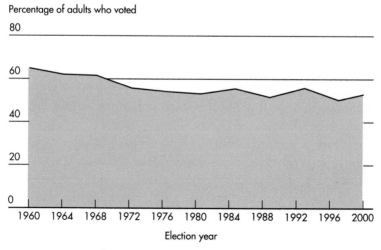

FIGURE 7-1 VOTER TURNOUT IN PRESIDENTIAL ELECTIONS, 1960–2000
Voter turnout has declined substantially since the 1960s. Source: U.S. Bureau of the Census.

of eligible adults, while the United States bases its figures on all adults, including noncitizens and other ineligible groups (e.g., convicted felons). The United States also ranks high on "spoiled" ballots—ones that are cast but not counted for reasons of human or machine error. Nevertheless, even when such statistical disparities are corrected, turnout in U.S. elections remains low in comparison with that of nearly every other Western democracy.

Voting does not require vast amounts of time. It takes most people longer to go to a video store and select a movie than it takes them to go to the neighborhood polling place and cast a ballot. Thus the explanation for the relatively low turnout rate of Americans must entail other considerations: registration requirements, the frequency of elections, and the lack of clear-cut differences between the political parties.

REGISTRATION REQUIREMENTS   Before Americans are allowed to vote, they must be registered—that is, their names must appear on an official list of eligible voters. **Registration** began around 1900 as a way of preventing voters from casting more than one ballot during an election.

Although other democracies also require registration, they place this responsibility on government. In European nations, public officials have the duty to enroll citizens on registration lists. The United States—in keeping with its individualistic culture—is the only democracy in which registration is the individual's responsibility.[7] In addition, registration laws have traditionally been established by the state governments, and some states make it relatively difficult for citizens to qualify. Registration periods and locations are usually not highly publicized, and many citizens simply do not know when or where to register. Eligibility can also be a problem. In most states, a citizen must establish legal residency by living in the same place for a minimum period, usually thirty days but sometimes as long as fifty days, before becoming eligible to register.

States with a tradition of lenient registration laws generally have a higher turnout level than other states. Idaho, Maine, Minnesota, New Hampshire, Wisconsin, and Wyoming allow people to register at their polling place on election day, and these states rank high in voter turnout. Those states that have erected the most barriers are in the South, where restrictive registration was originally intended to prevent black people from voting. These historical differences continue to be reflected in state voter turnout levels (see box: States in the Nation).

In 1993, in an effort to increase registration levels nationwide, Congress enacted a voting registration law known as "motor voter." Its supporters

HOW THE UNITED STATES COMPARES

Voter Turnout

The United States ranks near the bottom among the world's democracies in the percentage of eligible citizens who participate in national elections. One reason for the low voter turnout is that individual Americans are responsible for registering to vote, whereas in most other democracies, voters are automatically registered by government officials. In addition, unlike some other democracies, the United States does not encourage voting by holding elections on the weekend or imposing penalties, such as fines, on those who do not participate.

Another factor affecting the turnout rate in the United States is the absence of a major labor or socialist party, which would serve to bring lower-income citizens to the polls. In democracies where such parties exist, the turnout difference between upper- and lower-income groups is relatively small. In the United States, however, lower-income persons are much less likely to vote than higher-income persons are.

Country	Approximate Voter Turnout	Automatic Registration?	Social Democrat, Socialist, or Labor Party?	Election Day a Holiday or Weekend Day?
Belgium	90%	Yes	Yes	Yes
Italy	90	Yes	Yes	Yes
Denmark	85	Yes	Yes	No
Austria	80	Yes	Yes	Yes
France	80	No	Yes	Yes
Germany	80	Yes	Yes	Yes
Great Britain	70	Yes	Yes	No
Canada	65	Yes	No	No
Japan	60	Yes	Yes	Yes
United States	50	No	No	No

SOURCE: Foreign embassies, except data on United States, which are based on Federal Elections Commission information. At times, Canada has had a social democratic party alternative.

★ STATES IN THE NATION ★

State-by-State Voter Turnout in Presidential Elections

Southern states have a tradition of more restrictive registration laws, and even today they tend to have lower rates of voter turnout. States with large recent immigrant populations, such as California and New York, also have lower turnout. Categories are based on turnout average in recent presidential elections.

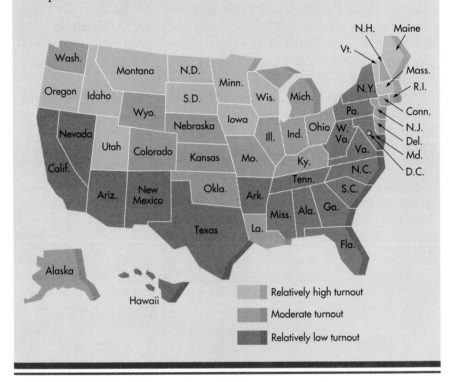

Relatively high turnout

Moderate turnout

Relatively low turnout

predicted that the legislation, so named because it requires states to permit people to register to vote when applying for a driver's license (it also requires states to provide registration through the mail and at certain state welfare offices), would add as many as 50 million new voters to registration rolls by the end of the century. The prediction seemed optimistic, since state agencies cannot compel applicants to register. Congressional Republicans made their support of the legislation contingent upon this nonmandatory provision. They had blocked the bill for several years, fearing that it would help the

Democrats by adding mainly lower-income Americans to the registration rolls. For the same reason, Republican governors in several states, including California and South Carolina, delayed putting the law into effect. Partisan concerns have always played a role in shaping registration laws, but in this case they appear miscalculated. Registrations under the motor-voter law were about evenly divided between the Republican and Democratic parties.

By the time of the 2000 presidential election, more than thirty million people had been registered as part of the motor-voter law.[8] Yet the increase did not result in a higher turnout rate; the number of voters actually declined between 1992 and 2000. Clearly, registration may be only one of the factors underlying America's low turnout rate.

FREQUENCY OF ELECTIONS   Another factor that reduces voter turnout is the frequency with which Americans are asked to vote. No other democracy has elections for the lower chamber of its national legislature (the equivalent of the U.S. House of Representatives) as often as every two years or elects its chief executive as often as every four years. In addition, elections of state and local officials in the United States are often scheduled separately from national races. Two-thirds of the states elect their governors in nonpresidential election years, and 60 percent of U.S. cities hold elections of municipal officials in odd-numbered years.

The frequency of U.S. elections reduces turnout by increasing the effort required to participate in all of them.[9] Most European nations have less frequent elections, and the responsibility of voting is thus less burdensome. Many European nations also schedule their elections on Sundays or declare election day to be a national holiday, thus making it more convenient for working people to vote. In the United States, elections are traditionally held on Tuesdays, and most people must vote before or after work.

The contrast with European practice is especially marked in the case of primary elections. The United States is the only democratic nation in which party nominees are commonly chosen by voters through primary elections rather than by party leaders. Consequently, Americans are asked to vote twice to fill a single office. Many voters skip the primaries, preferring to vote just once, in the general election. In contested statewide and presidential primaries, the average voter turnout is less than half that for the general elections.

PARTY DIFFERENCES   A final explanation for low voter turnout in the United States has to do with voters' perception that there is not much

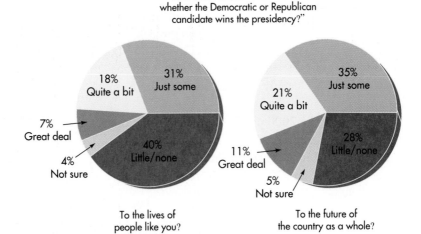

"How much difference will it make whether the Democratic or Republican candidate wins the presidency?"

To the lives of people like you?

To the future of the country as a whole?

FIGURE 7-2 THE PERCEIVED EFFECT OF ELECTING A REPUBLICAN OR DEMOCRATIC PRESIDENT (2000)
Most Americans believe that their lives and the country as a whole will not be greatly affected by whether the Republican or Democratic candidate wins the presidency. Source: Used by permission of the Shorenstein Center Poll for the Vanishing Voter Project.

difference between the major political parties (see Figure 7-2). More than half of Americans claim that it does not make a big difference whether the Republicans or the Democrats gain control of government.[10] This belief is not entirely unfounded. The two major American political parties do not normally differ greatly in most of their policies. Each party depends on citizens of all economic interests and social backgrounds for support; consequently, neither party can afford to take an extreme position that would alienate any sizable segment of the electorate. For example, both parties share a commitment to the private enterprise system and to social security for the elderly (see Chapter 8).

Parties in Europe divide more sharply over policies. In European elections, the choice between a conservative party and a socialist party has at times meant a choice between private and government ownership of major industries. Turnout is higher when political parties represent clear-cut alternatives, particularly when religious or class divisions are involved.[11] European parties, particularly those on the left, are also more closely tied to other organizations, such as labor unions, which assist in the mobilization of the electorate.[12]

Why Some Americans Vote and Others Do Not

Even though turnout is lower in the United States than in other democracies, some Americans do vote in all or nearly all elections. But other Americans seldom or never vote. What accounts for such *individual* differences?

The factors that account for differences in public opinion (see Chapter 6) are not in all cases related to turnout differences. The turnout rates of men and women, for example, are nearly the same.[13] Race was once a very significant predictor of turnout but has become less important. African Americans have nearly the same turnout rate as whites in presidential elections, compared with the 40 percent difference that existed before legal barriers to African American participation were lowered in the 1960s.

Large differences in voter turnout are associated with citizens' sense of civic involvement, age, education, and economic class.

FEELINGS OF CIVIC DUTY, ALIENATION, AND APATHY Regular voters are characterized by a strong sense of **civic duty**—that is, they regard participation in elections as one of the main responsibilities of citizenship. A sense of civic duty is an attitude that most individuals acquire during their political socialization in childhood and adolescence. When parents vote regularly and take an interest in politics, their children are likely to grow up believing that voting is an obligation of citizenship.

Many citizens do not have a strong sense of civic duty, and some of them display almost no interest in politics. **Apathy** is a general lack of interest in or concern with politics. Just as some people would not attend the Super Bowl even if it were free and being played across the street, some people would not bother to vote even if a ballot were delivered to their door. As with civic duty, a sense of apathy is often the consequence of childhood socialization. When parents disparage voting and other forms of political participation, their children are likely to hold a similar view when they reach voting age.

Alienation is a sense of personal powerlessness that includes the notion that government does not care about the opinions of people like oneself.[14] It might be thought foolish for people to withdraw from politics when they believe government is inept and uncaring. Yet for some individuals, the vote is as much an affirmation of citizenship as it is an opportunity to influence the direction of government. Most people know that their single vote is unlikely to affect the outcome of an election. When disgusted with government, they may choose simply to retreat from politics.

TABLE 7-2 OPINIONS ON ELECTION POLITICS
Americans are generally dissatisfied with election politics.

	Agree	Disagree	Don't Know
Political candidates are more concerned with fighting each other than with solving the nation's problems.	70%	26%	4%
Most political candidates will say almost anything in order to get themselves elected.	78	18	4
Political campaigns today seem more like theater or entertainment than like something to be taken seriously.	65	30	5
Interest groups and donors who give large sums of money to political campaigns have way too much influence on what candidates do once they are elected.	80	16	4

SOURCE: National poll by The Vanishing Voter Project, Joan Shorenstein Center on the Press, Politics, and Public Policy, John F. Kennedy School of Government, Harvard University, October 20-24, 2000. Used by permission of the Director, Vanishing Voter Project.

Americans have grown increasingly alienated and apathetic in recent decades, at least in relation to voting. Turnout in U.S. presidential elections dropped by almost 10 percent between 1960 and 1980, a period in which Americans' trust in government dropped sharply under the onslaught of the Vietnam War, the Watergate scandal, economic stagnation, and other national problems. Since then, the public's confidence in government has risen somewhat, but at no time has it come close to reaching the level of the 1950s and early 1960s. Americans today are also broadly dissatisfied with election politics. Most Americans believe, for example, that candidates will say almost anything to get themselves elected and that money plays too big a role in the outcome of elections and in what candidates do once they take office (see Table 7-2). Discouraged by the way in which elections are conducted, Americans have increasingly questioned whether voting is a worthwhile activity.

Young adults have the lowest voter turnout rate of any major demographic group. Efforts to increase their participation include MTV's "Rock the Vote" campaign, which often features celebrity participants. Pictured here are (from left to right) humorist Bill Maher and singers Macy Gray and Moby.

AGE When viewers tuned in MTV at various times during the most recent presidential campaign, they might have thought at first that they had selected the wrong channel. Rather than a video of their favorite rock star, they saw the presidential candidates urging young people to vote.

The candidates had targeted the right audience. Young adults are much less likely to vote than middle-aged citizens. Even senior citizens, despite the infirmities of old age, have a far higher turnout rate than voters under the age of thirty. Young people are less likely to have the political concern that can accompany such lifestyle characteristics as home ownership, a permanent career, and a family.[15] In fact, citizens under the age of thirty have a lower turnout rate than any other demographic group of comparable size.

Young voters have also contributed disproportionately to the decline in voter turnout in recent decades. Of the eligible eighteen- to twenty-four-year-olds, about half voted in 1972, compared with less than a third in 2000. On the other hand, turnout among those forty-five years of age and older declined only a few percentage points during this period.

EDUCATION What does your college education mean?[16] One thing it means is that you have a greater likelihood of becoming an active citizen. The difference is striking. Persons with a college education are about 40 percent more likely to vote than persons with a grade school education. Researchers have concluded that education generates a greater interest in politics, a higher level of political information, a greater confidence that one can make a difference politically, and peer pressure to participate—all of which are related to the tendency to vote.[17] Education, in fact, is the single best predictor of voter turnout.

ECONOMIC CLASS   Turnout is also strongly related to economic status. Americans at the bottom of the economic ladder are much less likely to vote than those at the top.[18] In presidential elections, for example, the turnout rate of low-income citizens is only about half that of high-income citizens (see Figure 7-3).

In contrast, low-income citizens in Europe have a turnout rate only slightly lower than that of high-income citizens. Europe's political traditions and institutions—its strong socialist and labor parties, its politically oriented trade unions, and its class-based political ideologies—encourage lower-class participation in ways that the U.S. political system does not.[19] For example, the United States does not have, and has never had, a major socialist or labor party. The interests of lower-income Americans have been

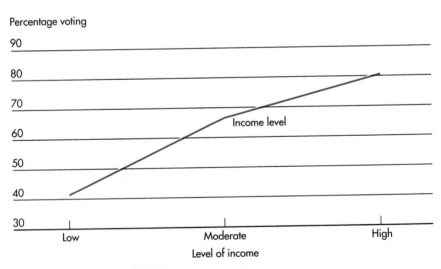

FIGURE 7-3   VOTER TURNOUT AND INCOME
Lower-income Americans are much less likely to vote than higher-income Americans, which is different from the situation in European democracies, where income level has only a marginal impact on turnout level. Source: U.S. Bureau of the Census.

addressed primarily through the Democratic party, but, like the Republican party, it focuses primarily on the interests of middle-class voters.

The Impact of the Vote

Through their votes, the people choose the representatives who will govern in their name. But what is the relationship between the vote and the actions of government? What influence does the vote have on public policy? Fuller answers to these questions will be provided later (see Chapters 8, 11, and 12), but it is useful to consider at least a partial response at this point.

Elections do *not* ordinarily produce a popular mandate for the policies advocated by the winning candidate. A mandate requires voters to consciously choose between candidates on the basis of the promises they make during the campaign. A difficulty with this interpretation of election results is that voters are not usually well informed about candidates' policy positions. In U.S. House campaigns, fewer than half the voters can recall on their own the names of the two major-party nominees in their district and even fewer can identify these candidates' positions on major issues.[20] In presidential races, the voters are better informed, but most of them cannot readily recall more than a few of the differences in the candidates' platforms.

Several influences combine to limit the voters' awareness of issues. The candidates do not always make their positions altogether clear, either because they fear that taking a firm stand will lose them votes or because they do not have specific policies in mind. Many candidates have dodged the abortion issue in recent years by expressing personal opposition to it while at the same time promising to uphold a woman's right to choose as long as the courts permit it. Additionally, the news media have increasingly focused their election coverage not on issues but on the strategic aspects of the candidates' pursuit of office. By covering campaigns as if they were a strategic game, the media deemphasize substantive issues of policy, thereby making it more difficult for the voters to discover where the candidates stand. Finally, voters can hardly be aware of issues if they are personally inattentive to politics. Most citizens do not follow campaigns closely and do not necessarily gain knowledge of even highly publicized issues.[21]

There are, to be sure, some voters who are highly informed on the issues and cast their ballots on this basis. Prospective voting describes this forward-looking type of voting. **Prospective voting** occurs when voters know the issue positions of the candidates and choose the candidate whose proposals best match their own issue preferences.

Voters in New York City's Harlem turned out in record numbers during the Great Depression. The elections of this period are classic examples of retrospective voting. In 1932, voters repudiated President Herbert Hoover for his handling of the crisis and, in 1936, they rewarded Franklin Roosevelt with a second term in office for his new approach to economic policy.

A more prevalent form of voting is **retrospective voting,** which is the situation in which voters support the incumbent party or candidate when they are pleased with its performance, and reverse their position when they are displeased. Bill Clinton's victories in 1992 and 1996 illustrate the importance that voters attach to past governmental performance. The U.S. economy in 1992 was in its longest recession since World War II, and the situation soured voters on the incumbent president George Bush. Three-fourths of the American public expressed dissatisfaction with his handling of the economy, and their dissatisfaction translated into Bush's defeat. He lost by a substantial margin to Clinton, who, despite widespread reservations about his personal character, represented the prospect of change. According to the National Election Studies survey, about 80 percent of the voters who supported Bush in 1988 but who deserted him in 1992 believed that the economy was the nation's most important problem.

In 1996, the nation's economy had recovered. Economic growth was strong, jobs were plentiful, and consumer confidence was high. Clinton's opponent, Bob Dole, tried to persuade voters that Clinton's personal character was reason enough to deny him a second term. But voters were satisfied with Clinton's handling of the economy and returned him to office.

As in these cases, economic conditions are usually the key factor in the electorate's retrospective judgments. When voters' confidence in the in-party's handling of the economy has been high, its nominee has usually won the presidential election. Conversely, its nominee has usually lost when the voters are dissatisfied with the state of the economy.[22] Congressional elections are also affected by national conditions but to a lesser degree because these races often hinge on local issues and incumbents' superior funding and name recognition (see Chapter 11).

Retrospective voting is a somewhat weaker form of public control than prospective voting, because it occurs after the fact: government has already acted, and nothing can change what has taken place. Nevertheless, retrospective voting can be an effective form of popular control over policy because it forces public officials to anticipate the voters' likely response in the next election. The fear that they might be voted out of office by an electorate upset with their policies is a powerful constraint on elected representatives.[23]

CONVENTIONAL FORMS OF PARTICIPATION OTHER THAN VOTING

In one sense, voting is an unrivaled form of citizen participation and influence. Free and open elections are the defining characteristic of democratic government, and hence voting is regarded as the most basic duty of citizens.[24] Voting is also the only form of citizen participation engaged in by a majority of adults in every democratic country.[25]

In another sense, however, voting is a restricted form of participation.[26] Citizens have the opportunity to vote only at a particular time and place, and only on those predetermined items listed on a ballot. Voting takes up less than an hour a year for most citizens, and there is no guarantee that candidates will be able or willing to keep the promises they made to the voters during the campaign. There are other forms of participation that offer a greater opportunity for personal influence or involvement. These may be divided into campaign activities, community activities, lobbying group activities, and attentiveness to the news.

Campaign Activities

A citizen may engage in such campaign-related activities as working for a candidate or a party, attending election rallies or meetings, contributing money, and wearing a candidate's campaign button. The more demanding of these activities, such as doing volunteer work for a candidate or a party, require a lot more time and effort than voting. These activities are also less imbued with notions of civic duty than is voting.[27] Not surprisingly, the proportion of citizens who engage in these activities is relatively small. For example, less than one in twenty adult Americans claim that they worked for a party or a candidate within the past year. Most of these citizens are strong partisans with a keen interest in politics.

Nevertheless, campaign participation is higher in the United States than in Europe. A five-country comparative study found that Americans ranked ahead of citizens of Germany, Austria, the Netherlands, and Great Britain in such activities as volunteering to work for a party or a candidate during an election campaign.[28]

One reason Americans, even though they vote at a lower rate than Europeans, are more likely than Europeans to work in a campaign is that they have more opportunities to do so.[29] Elections take place more often in the United States, and citizens can become involved in an election campaign by volunteering to work for either a party or a candidate (see Chapter 8). In Europe, campaigns are organized through the parties, and participation opportunities for those who are not party members are restricted. Moreover, the United States is a federal system, which results in campaigns for national, state, and local offices. A citizen who wishes to participate is almost certain to find an opportunity at one level of office or another. Most of the governments of Europe are unitary in form (see Chapter 2), which means that there are fewer elective offices and thus fewer campaigns in which to participate.

Community Activities

Many Americans participate in public affairs not through campaigns and political parties but through local organizations such as parent-teacher associations, neighborhood groups, Rotary clubs, church-affiliated groups, and hospital auxiliaries. Apart from their other purposes, these organizations also serve as a means to influence the public life of the community.

The actual number of citizens who fully participate in community affairs is difficult to estimate, but the number is surely in the millions. The United States has a tradition of community participation that goes back to colonial days. Moreover, compared with local communities in Europe, those in the United States have more authority over policy issues, which is an added incentive to participation. Due to increased mobility and other factors, Americans may be less tied to their local communities than in the

Youthful volunteers work to fix up a children's playground. Americans are
more likely than citizens of other democracies to take part in voluntary
community activities.

past and therefore less involved in community action. Nevertheless, a third
of Americans claim that they frequently or sometimes participate in a group
effort to solve a community problem, compared with about 15 percent in
most European countries.[30]

In a widely publicized book entitled *Bowling Alone*, Harvard's Robert
Putnam claims that America is undergoing a decline in its **social capital**
(the sum of the face-to-face civic interactions among citizens in a society).[31]
There has been, Putnam says, a broad and continuing erosion of civic en-
gagement. The relationships fostered by this participation are the foundation of democratic life. They bring citizens together, broaden and deepen
people's understanding of other points of view, and provide the skills
that foster continued participation in public affairs. Putnam attributes
the decline to television and other factors that are drawing people inward
and away from participation in civic and political groups. Not all scholars
accept Putnam's interpretation of trends in civic participation (some indicators point toward a rise in certain types of participation),[32] but no one
challenges his assumption about the importance of high levels of civic
participation.

Lobbying Group Activities

Increasingly, Americans are involved in public affairs through membership
in lobbying groups. This form of participation seldom consists of more

than the contribution of annual dues that enable a national organization to pressure government officials or otherwise attempt to influence public policy. Examples of these groups are the National Organization for Women, Common Cause, the Christian Moral Government Fund, the American Civil Liberties Union, and the National Conservative Political Action Committee. Chapter 9 discusses lobbying groups more fully.

Following Politics in the News

Campaign work and community participation are active forms of political involvement. There is also a passive form of participation: following politics by reading newspapers and newsmagazines and by listening to news reports on television or radio. It can safely be said that no act of political participation takes up more of people's time than does news consumption. The news is important to citizen participation: if people are to participate effectively and intelligently in politics, they must be aware of what is taking place in their communities, in their nation, and in the world.

News about politics is within easy reach of nearly all Americans. More than 95 percent of U.S. homes have a television set, and about 50 percent of Americans receive a daily newspaper. However, the regular audience for news is much smaller than these figures suggest. The mere fact of having a television or getting a daily paper does not mean that a person pays close attention to the news these media provide. If the regular audience for politics is defined as those who read a newspaper's political sections or watch television newscasts on a regular basis, then about a third of Americans can be classified as closely attentive to the news. Another third follows the news intermittently, catching an occasional newscast or scanning a paper's news sections somewhat often. The final third pays no appreciable attention to the news either on television or in a newspaper.

Television is the medium through which most Americans get most of their news (see Figure 7-4). In recent decades, citizens who say television is their main source of news have substantially outnumbered those who rely mainly on a newspaper. Radio and magazines account for even smaller proportions. The figures are somewhat misleading in that people are asked where they get "most" of their news, not how much news they actually get. Some of the people who say they get "most" of their news from television do not necessarily watch the news a lot. They may not read a newspaper at all, so that even a little exposure to television news makes it their leading news source. Since almost every American home has a television set but only half receive a daily newspaper, television has the edge.[33]

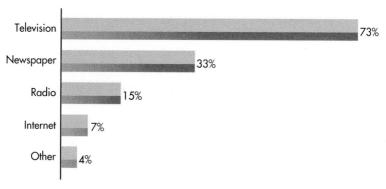

FIGURE 7-4 AMERICANS' MAJOR NEWS SOURCES
When Americans are asked where they get most of their news, they mention
television most often. Source: Pew Research Center for the People and the Press,
February 2000. Asked in context of presidential campaign. Adds to more than 100% due to
multiple responses.

The news audience has shrunk considerably in size in recent years.
Newspapers have lost audience to television newscasts, which in turn have
lost audience to television entertainment programs. Before cable television
was widely available, many television viewers had no alternative to a newscast
during the dinner hour. With cable, viewers always have a wide variety of
choices, and many viewers, as many as 40 percent by some estimates, choose
to ignore the news unless a sensational event occurs, such as the Oklahoma
City bombing in 1995 that killed more than one hundred people. To be sure,
cable has also fostered a core of news "junkies" who immerse themselves in
the Cable News Network (CNN), C-SPAN, and other news and public affairs programming. The more significant effect of cable, however, has been
to contribute to a substantial decrease in the size of the news audience.

Young Americans in particular are ignoring the news. A survey by the
Pew Center for the People and the Press found that Americans under thirty
years of age know less and care less about politics than any generation of
the last half-century and pay less attention to newspapers. They are inclined toward television use generally but do not pay much attention to
television news. Many young people apparently cannot be bothered with
news in any form.[34]

Virtual Participation

The prospect of an entire generation of politically inattentive citizens is
a disturbing one to many observers. Yet there is a glimmer of hope: the

Internet. It is used more heavily by younger people and is packed with political information and participation possibilities.

Nevertheless, it is unclear whether the Internet will actually serve as an entry into the world of politics for large numbers of citizens. Most people use it primarily for entertainment, school assignments, shopping, and personal and business communication. On the other hand, there are thousands of chat rooms where politics and public affairs are discussed. In addition, nearly every major interest group has its own website, and many groups have developed a capacity to inform and activate their membership through e-mail. Finally, candidates for public office have developed web sites to promote their campaigns; in the 2000 presidential election, the candidates used their sites to raise funds and enlist campaign volunteers.

Reliable data are not available on the extent of political participation through the Internet, but, according to a recent survey, 7 percent of Americans claimed they get most of their news of public affairs from the Internet. The full impact of this new medium on citizen participation, however, is not likely to be known until its technological capacity is fully developed and today's "computer-literate" generation reaches adulthood.

UNCONVENTIONAL ACTIVISM: SOCIAL MOVEMENTS AND PROTEST POLITICS

Before mass elections became prevalent, the public often rioted as a way of expressing dissatisfaction with government. The advent of elections allowed the masses to communicate their views in an institutionalized and less disruptive way. Elections are double-edged, however. Although they are commonly viewed as a means by which the people control the government, *elections are also a means by which the government controls the people.*[35] Because representatives have been freely chosen by popular vote, they can claim that their policies reflect the will of the majority and therefore ought to be obeyed. It is a claim that most citizens accept.

Voting in elections is also limited to the options listed on the ballot. America's voters effectively have only two choices: they can back the Democratic or the Republican party. No other party has much chance of victory, and any citizen who is dissatisfied with the major parties realistically has no way to express a policy preference through the ballot.

Social movements are an alternative method of influence. **Social movements,** or **political movements,** as they are sometimes called, are broad efforts to achieve change by citizens who feel that government is not

properly responsive to their interests.[36] Their efforts are sometimes channeled through traditional forms of participation, such as political lobbying,
but citizens can also take to the streets in protest against government. Perhaps the most dramatic recent example occurred in late 1999 when a host
of activists—trade unionists, environmentalists, and others—engaged police in what became known as the "Battle in Seattle." The World Trade
Organization (WTO) was meeting in Seattle to discuss global economic issues, and the activists were protesting the weak environmental and labor
provisions that had marked earlier trade agreements. Their actions disrupted the WTO's meeting and earned a promise that, somehow, their
views would be incorporated in future WTO deliberations.[37]

Social movements do not always succeed, but they sometimes assist
otherwise politically weak groups to force government to respond to their
desires. For example, the timing and scope of the landmark 1964 Civil
Rights Act and 1965 Voting Rights Act can be explained only as a response
by Congress to the pressure created by the civil rights movement. The
movement was in great part nonviolent, but it existed outside established
channels—civil disobedience was one of its techniques—and it challenged
existing power structures.

Protest politics in America goes back to the Boston Tea Party and earlier, but it has taken on new forms in recent years. Protest was traditionally
a desperate act that began, often spontaneously, when a group lost hope of
succeeding through more conventional methods. Today, however, protest is
usually a calculated act—a means of bringing added attention and impetus
to a cause.[38] These tactical protests often involve a great deal of planning,
including, in some instances, the busing of thousands of people to Washington for a rally staged for television. Civil rights, environmental, fundamentalist Christian, agricultural, gay rights, and pro- and antiabortion
groups are among those that have staged tactical protests in Washington in
recent years.

Most citizens, however, believe that the proper way to express disagreement over public policy is through voting, not through protesting, despite the First Amendment's guarantee of the right "peaceably to assemble."
In a 1972 University of Michigan survey, only 15 percent of those interviewed expressed approval of the Vietnam War protests. Public opinion
about demonstrations against the Gulf War was also negative, although less
so than for protests against the Vietnam War, perhaps because U.S. involvement in the Gulf was briefer and more successful. A Gallup poll in
early 1991 indicated that by a 2-to-1 margin Americans believed it was "a
bad thing for Americans to be demonstrating against the war when U.S.

Police and protestors face off in 1999 at the World Trade Organization (WTO) meeting in Seattle. Although protest movements are an American tradition, they rarely receive strong public support.

troops are fighting overseas." This view was particularly pronounced among women, older persons, Republicans, and persons with lower education levels.

Citizens who participate in social movements tend to be younger than nonparticipants, which is a reversal of the situation with voting. In fact, age is the best predictor of protest activity.[39] Participants in social movements also tend to emphasize nonmaterial values more than do nonparticipants. Social movements often develop in response to real or perceived injustices and thus attract idealists.[40]

PARTICIPATION AND THE POTENTIAL FOR INFLUENCE

Although Americans claim that political participation is important, most of them do not practice what they preach. As we have seen, most citizens take little interest in participation except to vote, and a significant minority cannot be persuaded to do even that. Americans are obviously not completely apathetic: many millions of them give their time, effort, and money to political causes, and roughly one hundred million go to the polls in presidential elections.

Yet sustained political activism does not engage a large proportion of the public. Moreover, many of those who do participate are drawn to politics by a habitual sense of civic duty rather than by an intense concern with current issues. The emphasis that American culture places on individualism tends to discourage a sense of urgency about political participation. "In the United States, the country of individualism *par excellence*," William Watts and Lloyd Free write, "there is a sharp distinction in people's minds between their own personal lives and national life."[41] Although wars and severe recessions can lead the American public to turn to government, most people under most conditions expect to solve their own problems. This is not to say that Americans have a disdain for collective action. In their communities particularly, citizens frequently take part in collective efforts to support local hospitals, improve their neighborhoods, and the like. But most Americans do not see their material well-being as greatly dependent on their active involvement in politics.

This tendency contributes to a class bias in American politics. For one thing, it helps maintain a relatively sharp distinction between that which is properly public (political) and that which is properly private (economic). The private component, which includes most economic relationships, is largely beyond the realm of political debate and action. Americans, says political scientist Robert Lane, have a preference for market justice rather than political justice.[42] They prefer to see benefits distributed primarily through the economic marketplace rather than through the policies of government. The nation's health care system is an example. Unlike the systems of Europe, which provide government-paid coverage for everyone, access to medical care in the United States is to some degree based on a person's ability to pay for it. There are about thirty-eight million Americans who do not have access to adequate health care because they cannot afford health insurance.

America's individualistic culture also contributes to a class bias by its effect on the participation level of lower-income groups. As we have seen, citizens of lower economic status are substantially less involved politically than those of higher status. The difference is much greater in the United States than in other Western democracies. These countries assist the participation of poorer citizens by placing the burden of registering voters on government and by fostering class-based political organizations. By comparison, the poor in the United States have to arrange their own registration and have a choice limited to major political parties that are attuned primarily to the middle and upper classes. The experiences of democratic countries make it clear that the poor, who have fewer personal skills and resources to take part in politics on their own, need supportive structures to foster their participation. "The rich have the capacity to participate with or without assistance," Benjamin Ginsberg writes. "When assistance is given it is primarily the poor who benefit."[43]

The relatively high participation rate of the country's middle-class citizens, who constitute the bulk of the population in any case, tends to direct public policies to their benefit. Representatives are typically more responsive to the demands of participants than to those of nonparticipants,[44] although it must be kept in mind that participants do not always promote only their own interests. It would be a mistake, however, to conclude that large numbers of people regularly support policies that impose great costs on themselves.

In sum, the pattern of individual political participation in the United States parallels the distribution of influence that prevails in the private sector. However, the issue of individual participation is only one piece of the larger puzzle of who rules America and for what purposes. Subsequent chapters will provide additional pieces.

SUMMARY

Political participation is an involvement in activities designed to influence public policy and leadership. A main issue of democratic government is the question of who participates in politics and how fully they participate.

Voting is the most widespread form of active political participation among Americans. Yet voter turnout is significantly lower in the United States than in other democratic nations. The requirement that Americans must personally register in order to establish their eligibility to vote is one reason for lower turnout among Americans; other democracies place the burden of registration on government officials rather than on the individual citizen. The fact that the United States holds frequent elections also discourages some citizens from voting regularly. Finally, the major American political parties, unlike many of those in Europe, do not clearly represent the interests of opposing economic classes; thus the policy stakes in American elections are correspondingly lower. Some Americans do not vote because they think that policy will not change greatly regardless of which party gains power.

Prospective voting is one way the people can exert influence on policy through their participation. It is the most demanding approach to voting: voters must develop their own policy preferences and then educate themselves about the candidates' positions. Most voters are not well-enough informed about the issues to respond in this way. Retrospective voting demands less from voters: they need to decide only whether the government has been performing well or poorly in terms of the goals and values they hold. The

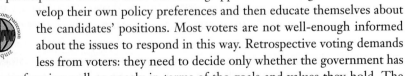

evidence suggests that the electorate is, in fact, reasonably sensitive to past governmental performance, particularly in relation to economic prosperity.

Only a minority of citizens engages in the more demanding forms of political activity, such as work on community affairs or on behalf of a candidate during a political campaign. The proportion of Americans who engage in these more demanding forms of activity exceeds the proportion of Europeans who do so. Nevertheless, only about one in every four Americans will take an active part in a political organization at some point in their lives. Most political activists are individuals of higher income and education; they have the skills and material resources to participate effectively and tend to take greater interest in politics. More than in any other Western democracy, political participation in the United States is related to economic status.

Social movements are broad efforts to achieve change by citizens who feel that government is not properly responsive to their interests. These efforts sometimes take place outside established channels: demonstrations, picket lines, and marches are common means of protest. Protesters are younger and more idealistic on average than other citizens, but they are a very small proportion of the population. In addition, protest activities do not have much public support, despite the country's tradition of free expression.

Overall, Americans are only moderately involved in politics. They are concerned with political affairs but mostly immersed in their private pursuits, a reflection in part of our culture's emphasis on individualism. The lower level of participation among low-income citizens has particular significance in that it works to reduce their influence on public policy and leadership.

MAJOR CONCEPTS

alienation	retrospective voting
apathy	social capital
civic duty	social (political) movements
political participation	suffrage
prospective voting	voter turnout
registration	

SUGGESTED READINGS AND WEB SITES

Conway, M. Margaret, Gertrude A. Steuernagel, and David Ahern. *Women and Political Participation: Cultural Change in the Political Arena.* Washington, D.C.: Congressional Quarterly Press, 1997. An analysis of women and political participation.

Neuman, W. Russell, Marion R. Just, and Ann N. Crigler. *Common Knowledge: News and the Construction of Political Meaning.* Chicago: University of

Chicago Press, 1992. An assessment of how citizens interpret and use the news they receive.

Putnam, Robert. *Bowling Alone*. New York: Simon and Schuster, 2000. A provocative analysis of the trend in civic participation.

Rimmerman, Craig A. *The New Citizenship: Unconventional Politics, Activism, and Service*. Boulder, Colo.: Westview Press, 1997. A provocative assessment of citizenship in the modern age.

Schudson, Michael. *The Good Citizen: A History of American Civic Life*. New York: Free Press, 1998. A thoughtful history of civic participation in America.

Tate, Katherine. *From Protest to Politics: The New Black Voters in American Elections*, enlarged ed. Cambridge, Mass.: Harvard University Press, 1994. A study of the transformation of a social movement into a conventional form of political participation.

Verba, Sidney, Kay Schlozman, and Henry Brady. *Voice and Equality*. Cambridge, Mass.: Harvard University Press, 1995. A careful study of political attitudes and participation.

http://www.rockthevote.org/　Rock the Vote is an organization dedicated to helping young people realize and utilize their power to affect the civic and political life of their communities.

http://www.umich.edu/~nes/　The University of Michigan's National Election Studies (NES) site provides survey data on voting, public opinion, and political participation.

http://www.vanishingvoter.org/　Harvard University's election study site provides data and analysis of public involvement in the 2000 presidential campaign.

http://www.vote-smart.org/　Project Vote Smart includes information on Republican and Democratic candidates and officials; also has the latest in election news.

READING 7

The Vanishing Voter
THOMAS E. PATTERSON

Introduction
In this reading, Thomas Patterson describes the downward spiral in election turnout. Voting rates have declined steadily for four decades, despite registration reforms and other changes that were expected to boost turnout. By some indicators and in some parts of the country, the voting rate is now at its lowest level in nearly two centuries.

Citizen regret was widespread as the outcome of the 2000 presidential campaign hung by the thread of a few hundred votes in Florida. Nearly half of adult Americans had not voted, and a CNN poll indicated that two-thirds of nonvoters wished they had. Many of them undoubtedly plan to vote in 2004. Perhaps they will. Voter turnout might increase sharply next time. But the long-term prospects are anything but bright. Voter turnout has been falling almost steadily for four decades. There was an increase of 4 percent in 1992, when economic recession and Ross Perot's strong third-party bid stirred interest. But turnout plunged to 49 percent in 1996, the first time in the modern era that it had fallen below 50 percent.

Some analysts predicted that turnout would rise sharply in 2000 because of the tight race between George W. Bush and Al Gore. The political parties and labor unions were waging massive get-out-the-vote drives. The election looked to be the closest since John F. Kennedy had defeated Richard Nixon by the slim margin of one hundred thousand votes in 1960. It appeared as if every vote might count. As it turned out, nearly every vote did count, even those that went uncounted. Yet barely more than half of adult Americans voted in 2000. Bush was elected president with the support of less than a fourth of the American public.

Turnout in 2000 was a far cry from what it had been in 1960. Then, nearly 65 percent of adult Americans voted. It was not recognized at the time, but 1960 would become the high mark of postwar turnout and the election against which turnout in all subsequent elections would be compared. In 1964, turnout fell by a few points. It fell by a few more points in 1968. In 1972, turnout dropped below 60 percent. In 1988, it fell through the 55-percent barrier. And in 1996, it dropped to the point where more Americans stayed home on Election Day than voted. The period between 1960 and 2000 is the longest stretch of turnout decline in the nation's history.

There are many mystifying aspects of American politics, but few as puzzling as the Vanishing Voter. For one thing, Americans say one thing and then do another. Americans also do one thing and then say another. Although only about 50 percent will have actually voted on Election Day, upwards of 75 percent in postelection polls will claim they did.

The turnout issue becomes even more puzzling when social change is taken into account. In the 1960s, when a sizeable majority did vote, political scientists identified education as the key factor in turnout. College-educated Americans were much more likely to vote than those who had not finished high school. With the number of college graduates increasing at a steady rate, the future looked promising. College graduates are today a much larger proportion of the population than they were in 1960. Yet, turnout has fallen.

The puzzle deepens when the voting rate of African Americans is examined. Only 20 percent of adult black Americans voted in the presidential election of 1960. The rate was much lower throughout the South. The white South had erected a whole set of barriers—poll taxes, rigged literacy tests, and courthouse intimidation—to keep African Americans from voting. The civil rights movement swept these impediments aside. The Twenty-Fourth Amendment, ratified in 1964, prohibited states from requiring citizens to pay "any poll tax or any other tax" before they could vote in federal elections. The Voting Rights Act of 1965 empowered federal registrars to go into county courthouses to enroll black citizens who had been denied registration. The Supreme Court struck down the use of literacy tests.

Black participation surged. The voting rate of African Americans nearly doubled within the decade of the 1960s and has continued to rise. Today, it is virtually identical to that of white citizens. Yet, despite the huge increase in black voting, the overall turnout rate has declined.

The Vanishing Voter puzzle deepens further when changes in election registration are considered. Unlike countries in Europe, where governments automatically register all eligible adults, the United States places the burden on the individual citizen. For a long period, states manipulated the registration system in order to make it hard for renters, the poor, and other weaker members of the community to participate. People typically had to live at the same address for a full year before they were eligible to register, and they had to reregister if they moved even a few doors away. Registration offices were often open only for limited hours and were sometimes located in remote or inconvenient places. Some states even closed their registration books a full year before the next election. By the time unregistered voters became aware of a pending election, the registration deadline had long since passed.

On the basis of a comprehensive study of nonvoters, the political scientists Ray Wolfinger and Steve Rosenstone said in 1986 that simplified and less restrictive registration requirements would boost turnout significantly. Their judgment was shared by voting analysts and by groups such as the League of Women Voters. Registration hurdles have now been largely eliminated. No state today has a residency requirement that exceeds thirty days for a federal general election. A few states, including Maine, Minnesota, and North Dakota, even permit residents to register at the polls on Election Day. Registration has also been made easier by the so-called Motor-Voter Law, which Congress enacted in 1993. It requires states to allow citizens to register when applying for a vehicle or driver's license. Roughly forty million Americans have been registered in this way. Yet, even though registration hurdles have now been largely removed, turnout has declined.

Some analysts question whether the Vanishing Voter problem is as severe as it might appear. They point out that the U.S. Census Bureau calculates turnout on the basis of the total adult population, including noncitizens, convicted felons, and others who are ineligible to vote. They further note that "ineligibles" are a larger proportion of the U.S. population today than in 1960. Noncitizens have increased as a percentage of the adult population as a result of relaxed immigration quotas. The number of persons ineligible to vote for reasons of a felony conviction has also increased sharply. America's war on drugs has made the United States the prison capital of the world. Nearly one in every hundred Americans is currently behind bars—the highest per capita incarceration rate anywhere on the globe.

When ineligible persons are excluded from the calculations, the turnout picture does improve somewhat. The turnout drop is closer to 10 percent than to 15 percent, and most of it is concentrated in the 1960s and early 1970s. But in human terms, it is still a big drop. If the turnout rate in 2000 had been equal to that of 1960, roughly 12 million more Americans would have voted in the Bush-Gore race.

The idea that the turnout decline is a small issue also requires that the influx of African Americans into the electorate be ignored. The overall turnout rate in 1960 was artificially depressed by the fact that southern blacks were counted in the total U.S. adult population even though the great majority of them had no opportunity to vote. When the South is excluded from the calculations, turnout in the 1960 presidential election changes to a whopping 75 percent. Since then, turnout outside the South has fallen by a third. It stands today at barely 50 percent. In fact, as Walter Dean Burnham has shown, turnout outside the South is now at its lowest level since the early 1800s, a period when many eligible voters could not read or write and had to travel by foot or horseback for hours to get to the nearest polling place. Americans, quite simply, are losing their appetite for voting.

Thomas E. Patterson is Bradlee Professor of Government and the Press at Harvard University's Kennedy School of Government. During the 2000 campaign, he directed the Vanishing Voter Project, which monitored citizen involvement in the election. This reading is an excerpt from a draft of his forthcoming book, The Vanishing Voter.

CHAPTER EIGHT

Political Parties, Candidates, and Campaigns

> Political parties created democracy and . . . modern democracy is
> unthinkable save in terms of the parties.
>
> E. E. SCHATTSCHNEIDER[1]

N OPPOSITE coasts and two weeks apart, the two parties faced off, each offering its own plan for a better America.

The Republicans met first, in Philadelphia. Their 2000 platform included a steep cut in personal income taxes, a limit on abortions, parental choice of schools, business deregulation, a partial privatization of the social security system, and a delegation of authority to state and local governments. The Republicans chose Texas governor George W. Bush, the son of former President George Bush, as their presidential nominee.

The Democrats met in Los Angeles, the same city where thirty-two years earlier Robert F. Kennedy had been assassinated at the end of a bitter Democratic nominating campaign that had nearly torn the party apart over the issue of the Vietnam War. This time, however, the Democrats were a united party. The Democrats chose Vice President Al Gore as their presidential nominee. The Democrats' lengthy platform included tax benefits for low- and middle-income families, restrictions on handguns, protection of social security, reproductive freedom for women, and pledges to strengthen the nation's environmental, educational, and health systems.

The political parties, as their nominees and platforms illustrate, are in the business of offering the voting public a choice. Each party seeks to define itself in a way that will attract majority support.

Competition between political parties is the foundation of the public's influence through elections. The party is the one institution that develops broad policy and leadership choices and then presents them to the voting public to accept or reject. This process is what gives the citizens an opportunity, through elections, to influence how they will be governed. "It is the competition of political organizations that provides the people with an opportunity to make a choice," the political scientist E. E. Schattschneider once wrote. "Without this opportunity popular sovereignty amounts to nothing."[2]

A **political party** is an ongoing coalition of interests jointed together in an effort to get its candidates for public office elected under a common label.[3] As such, a party is actually three election parties in one. There is, first, the *party in the electorate*, which consists of the voters who identify with it and support its candidates. This component of the party was discussed in Chapter 6 and is also addressed briefly in this chapter. The main subjects of this chapter, however, are the other two components: the *party as organization*, staffed and led by party activists, and the *party as candidates*, which consists of those individuals who run for public office under its label.[4]

A theme of this chapter is that party organizations are alive and well in America but are also secondary to candidates as the driving force in contemporary campaigns. **Party-centered politics** is an important dimension of U.S. elections, but much of what goes on in the campaign is better described by the term **candidate-centered politics.** For the most part, candidates for the presidency and Congress raise their own funds, form their own campaign organizations, and choose for themselves the issues on which they will run. Parties still play an important, indeed an indispensable, role in these elections, but their campaign role is secondary to that of the candidates.

This chapter will explain this development and also explore the history of U.S. parties, the patterns of party politics, and the conduct of modern campaigns. The following points are emphasized in this chapter:

* *Political competition in the United States has centered on two parties, a pattern that is explained by the nature of America's electoral system, political institutions, and political culture.*

* *To win an electoral majority, candidates of the two major parties must appeal to a diverse set of interests; this necessity normally leads them to advocate moderate and somewhat overlapping policies.*

* *U.S. party organizations are decentralized and fragmented. The national organization is a loose collection of state organizations, which in turn are loose associations of autonomous local organizations.*

* *The ability of America's party organizations to control nominations and election to office is weak, which in turn enhances the candidates' role.*

★ *Candidate-centered campaigns are based on the media and utilize the skills of professional consultants. Money, strategy, and televised advertising are key components of today's presidential and congressional campaigns.*

PARTY COMPETITION AND MAJORITY RULE: THE HISTORY OF U.S. PARTIES

Political parties give direction and strength to the people's votes. Through their numbers, citizens have the potential for great influence, but that potential cannot be realized unless they have the capacity to act together. Parties give them that capacity. When Americans go to the polls, they have a choice between the Republican and Democratic parties. This **party competition** narrows their options to two and in the process enables people with different opinions to render a common judgment. In electing a party, the voters choose its candidates, its philosophy, and its policies over those of the opposing party.

The history of democratic government is virtually synonymous with the history of parties. When the countries of eastern Europe gained their freedom a few years ago, one of their first steps toward democracy was the legalization of parties. When the United States was founded two centuries ago, the formation of parties was also a first step toward the erection of its democracy. The reason is simple: it is the competition between parties that gives popular majorities a chance to determine how they will be governed.

The First Parties

America's early leaders mistrusted parties. George Washington in his farewell address warned the nation of the "baneful effects" of parties, and James Madison likened parties to special interests. However, Madison's initial misgivings about parties gradually gave way to a grudging admiration; he recognized that they provided a way for like-minded people to jointly promote their vision of how the new nation should be governed.

America's parties originated in the rivalry within George Washington's administration between Thomas Jefferson, a supporter of states' rights and small landholders, and Alexander Hamilton, who promoted a strong national government and commercial interests (see Chapter 2). When Hamilton's ideas prevailed in Congress, Jefferson and his followers formed a political party, the Republicans, as a means of advancing their goals (see Figure 8-1).

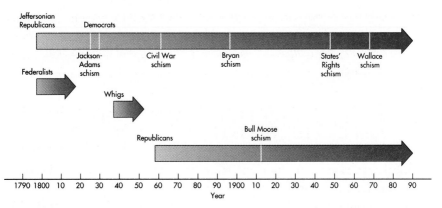

FIGURE 8-1 A GRAPHIC HISTORY OF AMERICA'S MAJOR PARTIES

Hamilton responded by organizing his supporters into a formal party—the Federalists—and in the process created America's first competitive party system. However, Federalist policies fueled Jefferson's claim that his opponents were bent on establishing a government for the rich and wellborn. After John Adams's defeat by Jefferson in the election of 1800, the Federalists were finished as a political force of any consequence.

During the so-called Era of Good Feeling, when James Monroe ran unopposed in 1820 for a second presidential term, it appeared as if the nation might exist without parties. Yet by the end of Monroe's second term, policy differences had split the Republicans. The dominant faction, led by Andrew Jackson, retained Jefferson's commitment to the interests of small farmers, tradesmen, and shopkeepers. To better reflect its base among ordinary citizens, this faction called itself Democratic Republicans, later shortened to Democrats. Thus the Republican party of Jefferson is the forerunner of today's Democratic party rather than today's Republican party.

Andrew Jackson and Grass-Roots Parties

For all its shortcomings, competition between parties is the only system that can regularly mobilize collective influence on behalf of the many who are individually powerless against those few who have extraordinary wealth and prestige.[5]

This realization led Jackson during the 1820s to develop a **grass-roots party.** Whereas Jefferson's party had been well organized only at the leadership level, Jackson sought a party that was built from the bottom up.

Jackson's Democratic party consisted of committees and clubs at the national, state, and local levels, with membership open to all eligible voters. These organizational activities, along with more liberal suffrage laws, contributed to a nearly fourfold rise in voter turnout during the 1830s.[6] At the peak of Jacksonian democracy, Alexis de Tocqueville wrote, "The People reign in the American political world as the Deity does in the universe."[7] Although Tocqueville exaggerated the people's true power, he caught the spirit of popular government that was behind the development of grassroots parties under Andrew Jackson.

In this period, a new opposition party, the Whigs, emerged to challenge the Democrats. The Whigs were a residual party of sorts. Its followers were united not by a coherent philosophy of their own but by their opposition for one reason or another to the philosophy and policies of the Jacksonian Democrats.

Competition between the Whigs and the Democrats was relatively short-lived. During the 1850s the slavery issue began to tear both parties apart. In 1860, the Democratic party's northern faction nominated for president Stephen A. Douglas, who held that the question of whether a new territory permitted slavery was for a majority of its voters to decide, while the southern faction nominated John C. Breckinridge, who called for the legalization of slavery in all territories. The Democratic vote in the fall election was split sharply along regional lines between these two candidates—with the result that the Republican nominee, Abraham Lincoln, was able to win the presidency with only 40 percent of the popular vote. The Republicans had eclipsed the Whigs and become America's other major party. However, the U.S. party system essentially collapsed in 1860, for the only time in the nation's history.[8] The issues of slavery and union were too powerful to be settled peaceably through political compromise and competition between political parties.

Republicans versus Democrats: Realignments and the Enduring Party System

After the Civil War, the nation settled into the pattern of competition between the Republican and Democratic parties that has prevailed ever since. The durability of these two parties is due not to their ideological consistency but to their remarkable ability to adapt during periods of crisis. By abandoning at these crucial times their old ways of doing things, the Republican and Democratic parties have essentially remade themselves—with new bases of support, new policies, and new public philosophies.

These periods of great political change are known as "realignments." A **party realignment** involves four basic elements:

1. The disruption of the existing political order because of the emergence of one or more unusually powerful and divisive issues
2. An election contest in which the voters shift their support strongly in favor of one party
3. A major change in policy through the action of the stronger party
4. An enduring change in the party coalitions, which works to the lasting advantage of the dominant party

Realignments are rare. They do not occur simply because one party wrests control of government from the other. They involve deep and lasting changes in the party system that affect not just the most recent election but later ones as well.

The Civil War realignment, for example, brought about a thorough change in the party system. The Republicans replaced the Democrats as the nation's majority party. The Republicans were the dominant party in the larger and more populous North; the Democratic party was left with a stronghold in what became known as "the Solid South." For the next three decades, the Republicans held the presidency except for Grover Cleveland's two terms of office.

The 1896 election resulted in a further realignment of the Republican-Democratic party system. Three years earlier, an economic panic following a bank collapse had resulted in a severe depression. The Democrat Cleveland was president when the panic broke out, and that circumstance worked to the advantage of the Republicans. During the four decades between the 1890s realignment and the next one in the 1930s, the Republicans held the presidency except for Woodrow Wilson's two terms, and had a majority in Congress for all but six years.

The Great Depression of the 1930s triggered a thoroughgoing realignment of the American party system. The Republican Herbert Hoover was president when the stock market crashed in 1929, and many Americans blamed Hoover, his party, and its business allies for the economic catastrophe that followed. The Democrats became the country's majority party, and their political and policy agenda favored a significant social and economic role for the national government. Franklin D. Roosevelt's presidency was characterized by unprecedented policy initiatives in the areas of business regulation and social welfare (see Chapters 3, 15, and 16). His election in 1932 began a thirty-six-year period of Democratic presidencies that was

The new order begins: Franklin D. Roosevelt rides
to his inauguration with outgoing president Herbert
Hoover after the realigning election of 1932.

interrupted only by Dwight D. Eisenhower's two terms in the 1950s. In this
period, the Democrats also dominated Congress, losing control only in
1947–1948 and 1953–1954.

The reason realignments have such a substantial effect on future elections is that they affect voters' *party identification* (see Chapter 6). Young
voters in particular are likely to identify with the newly ascendant party, and
they tend to maintain that identity, giving the party a solid base of support
for years to come. In the 1930s, for example, the Democratic party's image
as the party of the common people, jobs, and social security was vastly more
appealing to young voters than the Republican party's image as the party of
business and wealthy interests. First-time voters in the 1930s came to identify by a 2-to-1 margin with the Democratic party, which established it as
the nation's majority party and enabled it to dominate national politics for
the next three decades.[9]

A New Realignment or a Dealignment?

A party realignment inevitably loses strength over time, because the issues
that gave rise to it cannot remain dominant indefinitely. By the late 1960s,
when the Democratic party was divided over the Vietnam War and civil
rights, it was apparent that the era of New Deal politics was over.[10]

A realignment affecting part of the nation was soon evident. The
South, which had been solidly Democratic at all levels, was becoming

staunchly Republican in presidential elections and increasingly competitive at the state and local levels. As the Democratic party became increasingly identified as the party of civil rights and social change, it had less and less appeal to conservative white southerners.[11]

Yet Republican inroads were otherwise less dramatic or temporary. After 1968, the Republicans held the presidency for more years than the Democrats, and in 1994, they won a landslide midterm election victory that gave the GOP control of both houses of Congress for the first time in four elections. But at no time has the GOP been able to dominate presidential and congressional elections time after time the way that Democrats did during the height of the New Deal era. Nor has the GOP succeeded in gaining a decisive edge in terms of party identification. The proportion of Americans who call themselves Democrats has typically equaled or exceeded that of those who say they are Republicans. A lasting realignment favorable to the Republican party could be taking place, but, if so, it is unlike past ones—slower, more fitful, and less encompassing. And if such a realignment is taking place, it will be evident only after Republicans enjoy a period of sustained dominance.

An alternative explanation for what has been happening in American elections is put forth by advocates of the dealignment thesis. They suggest that the U.S. electoral system, rather than undergoing a realignment favorable to one party, has been in the process of **dealignment,** a partial but enduring movement of voters away from partisan loyalties.[12] The process is characterized by an electorate that wavers in its support of the parties.

Parties, in fact, do have a weaker hold on the voters than in the past. As we noted in Chapter 6, the number of voters who describe themselves as Independents has increased significantly in recent decades. Moreover, people who today identify with a party are more likely to say it is only a weak attachment. These changes are reflected in increased **split-ticket voting,** where the voter selects candidates of both parties for different offices when casting a ballot. A few decades ago, the large majority of voters engaged in **straight-ticket voting,** supporting candidates of one party only.

The decline of partisanship began during the 1960s and 1970s, when divisive issues arose and disrupted existing loyalties. The civil rights issue, for example, was unsettling not only to many southern Democrats but also to some white northern Democrats, particularly blue-collar workers from newer immigrant groups who felt that African Americans were making progress at their expense.[13] Vietnam, abortion, social welfare, and a host of other issues also divided followers of each party. Americans' trust in their elected representatives declined, as did their faith in parties.

Party loyalties have been weak ever since, and some analysts see little likelihood of a dramatic reversal. For one thing, voters of today are better educated and more likely to believe they can judge the candidates for themselves, on the basis of what they hear through the media rather than on the basis of party labels. Moreover, people today are protected by programs like social security and Medicare from the economic hardships that in the past fueled party realignments. Finally, Americans today want higher incomes and lower taxes, but they also want a cleaner environment, services for the elderly, and better schools. As a result, they are less likely to be drawn fully to either the Republican argument for a less active government or the Democratic argument for a more active one.[14]

If advocates of the dealignment thesis are correct, neither party will enjoy the prolonged success of the type the Democratic party had from the 1930s on. The predicted scenario is one of shifting support, with the Republicans prevailing at some times and the Democrats doing so at other times.

ELECTORAL AND PARTY SYSTEMS

The United States traditionally has had a **two-party system:** Federalists versus Jeffersonian Republicans, Whigs versus Democrats, and Republicans versus Democrats. These have not been the only American parties, but they have been the only ones with a realistic chance of acquiring political control. A two-party system, however, is the exception rather than the rule (see box: How the United States Compares). Most democracies have a **multiparty system,** in which three or more parties have the capacity to gain control of government, separately or in coalition. Why the difference? Why three or more major parties in most democracies but only two in the United States?

The Single-Member-District System of Election

A chief reason for the persistence of America's two-party system is the fact that the nation chooses its officials through plurality voting in **single-member districts.**[15] Each constituency elects a single candidate to a particular office, such as U.S. senator or representative; only the party that gets the most votes (a plurality) in a district wins the office. This system discourages minor parties. Assume, for example, that a minor party received exactly 20 percent of the vote in each of the nation's 435 congressional races. Even though one in five voters nationwide backed the minor party, it would not win any seats in Congress because none of its candidates had placed first in any of the 435 single-member-district races. The winning candidate in each case would be the major-party candidate who received the larger proportion of the remaining 80 percent of the vote.

By comparison, most European democracies use some form of **proportional representation,** in which seats in the legislature are allocated according to a party's share of the popular vote. This type of electoral system provides smaller parties an incentive to organize and compete for power. In the 1998 German elections, the Green party won slightly more than 5 percent of the national vote and received a proportionate number of the seats in the Bundestag, the German parliament. If the Greens had been competing under American electoral rules, they would not have won any seats and would have had no chance of exercising a share of legislative power. In this case, the Greens even gained a share of executive power. The Social Democratic party won the most legislative seats in the 1998 German election but failed to gain an outright majority. The Social Democrats formed a coalition with the Green party, which received cabinet posts in return for its backing of a Social Democrat–led government.

Policies and Coalitions in the Two-Party System

The overriding goal of a major American party is to gain power by getting its candidates elected to office. Because there are only two major parties, however, the Republicans or the Democrats can win consistently only by attracting majority support. In Europe's multiparty systems, a party can hope for a share of power if it has the firm backing of a minority faction. Not so in the United States. If either party confines its support to a narrow segment of society, it forfeits its chance of gaining control of government.

SEEKING THE CENTER, USUALLY   This situation encourages both parties to stay near the center of the political spectrum and to avoid the minority position on deeply divisive issues. American parties, Clinton Rossiter said, are "creatures of compromise."[16] The two parties typically try to develop stands that have broad appeal, or at least will not alienate significant blocs of voters. Any time a party makes a pronounced shift toward either extreme, the middle is left open for the opposing party. Barry Goldwater, the Republican presidential nominee in 1964, proposed the elimination of mandatory social security and said he would consider the tactical use of small nuclear weapons in such wars as the Vietnam conflict—extreme positions that cost him many votes.

HOW THE UNITED STATES COMPARES

Party Systems

Electoral competition in the United States centers on the Republican and Democratic parties. By comparison, most democracies have a multiparty system, in which three or more parties receive substantial support from voters. The difference is significant. In a two-party system, the parties tend to have overlapping coalitions and programs, because each party must appeal to the middle-of-the-road voters who provide the margin of victory. In multiparty systems, particularly those with four or more strong parties, the parties tend to separate themselves, as each tries to secure the enduring loyalty of voters who have a particular viewpoint.

Whether a country has a two-party or a multiparty system depends on several factors, but particularly the nature of its electoral system. The United States has a single-member plurality district system that is biased against smaller parties; even if they have some support in a great many races, they win nothing unless one of their candidates places first in an electoral district. By comparison, in proportional representation systems, each party gets legislative seats in proportion to its share of the total vote. All the countries in the chart that have four or more parties also have a proportional representation system of election.

Number of Competitive Parties		
Two	*Three*	*Four or More*
United States	Canada (at times)	Belgium
	Great Britain	Denmark
		France
		Germany
		Italy
		Netherlands
		Sweden

It is impossible to understand the dynamics of the U.S. party system without a recognition that the true balance of power in American elections rests with America's pragmatic and moderate voters rather than with those who hold more extreme views. When congressional Republicans mistook their 1994 election victory as a mandate to trim assistance programs for the elderly, the poor, and children, they alienated many of the moderate voters who had contributed to their 1994 victory. These voters wanted "less" government, but not a government that neglected society's most vulnerable citizens. After weak showings in the 1996 and 1998 elections, congressional Republicans shifted course. They unseated Speaker Newt Gingrich, replacing him with a more pragmatic conservative, Dennis Hastert. "We still need to prove that we can be conservative without being mean," was how one Republican member of Congress described the change in strategy.[17] The change in Republican outlook was also apparent in GOP presidential candidate George W. Bush's 2000 campaign slogan: "compassionate conservatism." These adjustment reflect a basic truth about U.S. politics: party ideology is acceptable, as long as it is tinged with moderation.

Nonetheless, the Republican and Democratic parties do offer somewhat different alternatives, and at times, a clear choice. When Roosevelt was elected president in 1932, Johnson in 1964, and Reagan in 1980, the parties were relatively far apart in their priorities and programs. Roosevelt's New Deal, for example, was an extreme alternative within the American political tradition and caused a decisive split along party lines. A lesson of these periods is that the center of the American political spectrum can be moved. Candidates risk a crushing defeat by straying too far from established ideas during normal times, but they may do so with some chance of victory during turbulent times.

Another lesson of such periods is that public opinion is the critical element in partisan change. Critics who say that the Democratic and Republican parties fail to offer the voters a real choice ignore the parties' tendency to tailor their appeals to majority opinion.[18] When the public's mood shifts, the parties usually also shift. The Republicans' Contract with America in 1994, for example, was a response to public discontent with the federal government's taxing and spending policies. When the Republicans won in 1994, many Democratic officeholders also embraced cutbacks in federal power, thus shifting the entire party system toward the right. If GOP leaders misjudged just how far right the public was willing to go, they nonetheless redirected the nation's politics. President Clinton, a Democrat, summed up the change in his 1996 State of the Union address when he said: "The era of big government is over."

PARTY COALITIONS   The groups and interests that support a party are collectively referred to as the **party coalition.** In multiparty systems, each party is supported by a relatively narrow range of interests. European parties tend to divide along class lines, with the center and right parties drawing most of their votes from the middle and upper classes and the left parties drawing theirs from the working class. By comparison, America's two-party system requires each party to accommodate a wide range of interests in order to gain the voting plurality necessary to win elections.[19] The Republican and Democratic coalitions are therefore very broad. Each includes a substantial proportion of voters of nearly every ethnic, religious, regional, and economic grouping.

Although the Republican and Democratic coalitions overlap, they are hardly identical (see Figure 8-2). Each party likes to appear to be all things

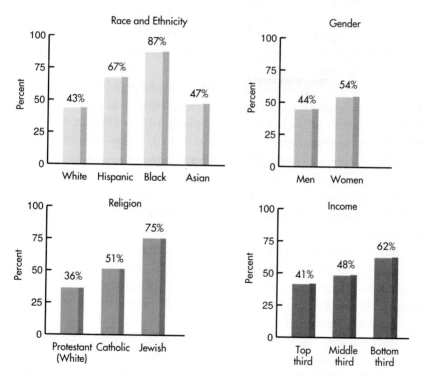

FIGURE 8-2   THE VOTE OF SELECTED DEMOGRAPHIC GROUPS IN RECENT PRESIDENTIAL ELECTIONS
Although the Democratic and Republican coalitions overlap substantially, there are important differences, as illustrated by the Democratic party's percentage of the two-party vote among some major demographic groups in recent elections.
Source: Compiled by author from various sources.

to all Americans, but in fact each builds its coalition through a process of both unification and division. If a party did not stand for something—if it never took sides—it would lose all support.

Since the 1930s, the major policy differences between the Republicans and the Democrats have involved the national government's role in solving social and economic problems. Each party has supported government action to promote economic security and social equality, but the Democrats have consistently favored a greater degree of governmental involvement. Virtually every major assistance program for the poor, the elderly, and low-wage workers has been initiated by the Democrats. To some extent, the Democratic coalition draws support disproportionately from society's "underdogs"—blacks, union members, the poor, city dwellers, Hispanics, Jews, and other "minorities."[20] For a long period, the Democratic party was also the clear choice of the nation's elderly as a result of its support for old-age assistance programs and because the basic political loyalties of the elderly were acquired during the New Deal era, a period favorable to the Democrats. Recently, however, elderly voters have split their vote more evenly between the parties.

The Democratic party's biggest gains recently have been with women, who traditionally had a voting pattern very similar to that of men. In recent elections, however, there has been a "gender gap" (see Chapter 6). Women have voted disproportionately for the Democratic party, apparently as a result of its positions on issues such as abortion rights, education spending, employment policies, and gun control.

The Republican coalition consists mainly of white middle-class Protestants. The GOP has historically been the party of tax cuts and business incentives. The GOP has also been more supportive of traditional values, as reflected, for example, in its support of school prayer and its opposition to abortion. Not surprisingly, the GOP has generally been the stronger party in the suburbs and other areas, such as the West and Midwest, where traditional values and a desire for lower taxes and less government regulation of economic activity are more pronounced.

The GOP has made big gains in recent decades among white fundamentalist Christians. The party's positions on abortion, school prayer, affirmative action, and other social issues have drawn them to the GOP. In recent presidential elections, the Republican nominee has garnered the votes of roughly 70 percent of fundamentalist Christians.

The differences in the party coalitions was clearly evident in the 2000 presidential vote. Women, minorities, and lower-income Americans cast a majority of their votes for the Democratic nominee Al Gore, while men, whites, and higher-income Americans aligned primarily with the Republican nominee George W. Bush.

There is a self-limiting feature to the party coalitions. The larger a party becomes, the greater is the likelihood that conflict among the groups within it will occur. The New Deal, for example, brought black Americans into the Democratic coalition, where they coexisted with the white southern conservatives who had sided with the Democratic party since the Civil War. However, when the Democratic party in the 1950s and early 1960s began to respond to the civil rights issues of its black constituents, it alienated many white southerners, who then gravitated to the GOP. More recently, the growing number of fundamentalist Christians in the GOP has been a source of division within that party. Their strong views on issues such as abortion and school prayer are not shared by many traditional Republicans, which has enabled Democratic candidates in some races to attract support from these voters.

Minor Parties

Although the U.S. electoral system discourages the formation of third parties, the nation has always had minor parties—more than a thousand during the nation's history.[21] Most of them have been short-lived, and only a few have had a lasting impact. Only one minor party, the Republican party, has ever achieved majority status.

Minor parties in the United States have formed largely to advocate positions that their followers believe are not being adequately represented by either of the two major parties. When a minor party gains a large following, as has happened a few times in history, the major parties are inevitably transformed by its influence. They are forced to pay attention to the problems that are driving people to look outside the two-party system for leadership. Strong support for a minor party has typically encouraged the major parties to try to capture its supporters.

Minor parties may be formed in response to the emergence of a single controversial issue, as a result of a rift within one of the major parties, or out of a commitment to a certain ideology.

SINGLE-ISSUE PARTIES Some minor parties form around a single issue of overriding concern to their supporters, such as the present-day Right-to-Life party, which was formed to oppose the legalization of abortion. Some single-issue parties have seen their policy goals enacted into law. The Prohibition party contributed to the ratification in 1919 of the Eighteenth

Republican presidential nominee George W. Bush reaches out to shake a voter's hand during the 2000 campaign. Bush sought to reverse Republican losses in recent elections by positioning the GOP closer to the political center.

Amendment, which prohibited the manufacture, sale, and transportation of alcoholic beverages (but was repealed in 1933). Single-issue parties usually disband when their issue is favorably resolved or fades in importance.[22]

FACTIONAL PARTIES   The Republican and Democratic parties are relatively adept at managing internal divisions. Although each party's support is diverse, the differences among its varying interests normally can be reconciled. However, there have been times when factional conflict within the major parties has led to the formation of minor parties.

The most successful of these factional parties at the polls was Theodore Roosevelt's Bull Moose party. In 1908 Roosevelt, after having served eight years as president, declined to seek a third term and handpicked William Howard Taft for the Republican nomination. When Taft as president showed neither Roosevelt's enthusiasm for a strong presidency nor his commitment to the goals of the Progressive movement, Roosevelt unsuccessfully challenged Taft for the 1912 Republican nomination. Roosevelt led a Progressive walkout to form the Bull Moose party (a reference to Roosevelt's claim that he was "as strong as a bull moose"). Roosevelt won 27 percent of the presidential vote to Taft's 25 percent, but the split within Republican ranks enabled the Democratic nominee, Woodrow Wilson, to win the presidency.

The States' Rights party in 1948 and George Wallace's American Independent party in 1968 are other examples of strong factional parties. These parties were formed by southern Democrats who were angered by northern Democrats' support of racial desegregation.

Deep divisions within a party give rise to factionalism and can lead eventually to a change in its coalition. The conflict over civil rights that began within the Democratic party during the Truman years continued for the next quarter-century, leading many southern whites to shift their party loyalty to the Republican party.

IDEOLOGICAL PARTIES   Other minor parties are characterized by their ideological commitment, or belief in a broad and radical philosophical position, such as redistribution of economic resources. Modern-day ideological parties include the Citizens party, the Socialist Workers party, and the Libertarian party, each of which operates on the fringe of American politics.

One of the strongest ideological parties in the nation's history was the Populist party. Its candidate in the 1892 presidential election, James B. Weaver, gained 8.5 percent of the national vote and won twenty-two electoral votes in six western states. The party began as an agrarian protest movement in response to an economic depression and the anger of small farmers over low commodity prices, tight credit, and the high rates charged by railroad monopolies to transport farm goods. The Populists' ideological platform called for government ownership of the railroads, a graduated income tax, low tariffs on imports, and elimination of the gold standard. The Populist party in 1896 endorsed the Democratic presidential nominee, William Jennings Bryan, but its support probably hurt the Democrats nationally. Large numbers of eastern Democrats abandoned their party's nominee in fear of the western Populists' radical ideas.[23]

The strongest minor party today is the Green party, an ideological party that holds liberal positions on the environment, labor, taxation, social welfare, and other issues. Its 2000 presidential nominee, consumer-rights advocate Ralph Nader, received 3 percent of the national vote. According to polls, Nader's support came primarily from voters who otherwise would have supported Democrat Al Gore, which tipped the election to the more conservative Republican nominee, George W. Bush. This outcome stirred a debate within Green party ranks. Some argued that the party should concentrate on local and state races, concluding that its participation in the 2000 presidential campaign served to elect the candidate whose policy goals were opposite its own. Others said that the Green party should continue to contest the presidential election so as to force the Democratic party toward more liberal policy positions.

Before the 2000 presidential election, the Reform party was America's strongest minor party. It originated in the 1992 independent candidacy of Ross Perot, who gained 19 percent of the presidential vote (second only to Roosevelt's 1912 percentage among candidates who were not major-party nominees). Perot's campaign was based on middle-class discontent with the major parties, was conducted almost entirely on television, and was funded by more than $60 million of his own money. Perot ran again in 1996 but as the nominee of the Reform party, which he had founded. This time, Perot accepted public funds for his campaign, which limited his spending to roughly $30 million (see Chapter 12). He ran a media-based campaign that attracted 8 percent of the vote, which qualified the Reform party for public funding again in 2000. When Perot chose not to run in 2000, however, the Reform party nomination became a contest between its party regulars and supporters of conservative Pat Buchanan. Buchanan's nomination splintered the party, and he received less than 1 percent of the presidential vote. It appears doubtful that the Reform party will recover from its 2000 debacle, which included the defection of its most prominent officeholder, Jesse Ventura, a former professional wrestler who had been elected governor of Minnesota in 1998. Ventura renounced the Reform party and said he would campaign as an independent if he ran for reelection in 2002.

ARE CONDITIONS RIPE FOR A STRONG THIRD PARTY? The Perot and Nader candidacies are the first substantial third-party presidential candidacies in a quarter-century. Do they indicate that a strong third party will soon emerge in American politics?

The long history of the American party system would be enough to discourage almost anyone who is hoping that a strong third party will surface and remain strong for more than an election or two. The obstacles are substantial. As we have seen, the U.S. electoral system frustrates smaller parties by denying them anything but a symbolic victory in national politics. In addition, most Americans identify with either the Republican or the Democratic party, and the large majority of them regularly support their party's nominee.

Nevertheless, Americans are increasingly dissatisfied with the way the two major parties are operating. According to a 2000 Harvard survey, about 30 percent of Americans believe that a third party is needed, even if they would not necessarily vote for its presidential candidate (see Figure 8-3). Americans are disgruntled by the partisan bickering that they think

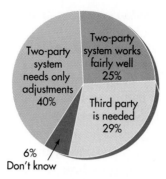

FIGURE 8-3   AMERICANS' OPINIONS ABOUT THE NEED FOR A STRONG THIRD PARTY
Most Americans say the two-party system works well or needs only some adjustments, but some believe that a strong third party is needed if the party system is to work effectively. Source: Vanishing Voter Project National Survey, Joan Shorenstein Center on the Press, Politics, and Public Policy, Harvard University, 2000.

increasingly defines the relationship between Republican and Democratic officeholders. They also believe that money has come to play too large a role in Republican and Democratic politics and that their candidates' campaign promises are too often broken once they take office. Disenchantment of this kind fueled the Progressive movement of a century ago (see Chapter 2) and contributed to an era when third parties, including the Progressive party, were relatively vibrant. They were not so strong as to threaten the hold on government of the Republican and Democratic parties. But they had the strength to force the two major parties to respond to their issues. It could be that America is again entering a period in which third parties will play a significant role in defining the national political debate.

PARTY ORGANIZATIONS

The Democratic and Republican parties have organizational units at the national, state, and local levels. These **party organizations** engage in a variety of activities, but their main purpose is the contesting of elections.

A century ago, party organizations were in control of nominations and elections. The party organizations still perform all the activities they formerly engaged in. They recruit candidates, raise money, develop policy positions, and canvass for votes. But they do not control these activities as completely as they once did.[24] For the most part, these activities are now dominated by the candidates themselves.[25]

The Weakening of Party Organizations

Nomination refers to the selection of the individual who will run as the party's candidate in the general election. Until the early twentieth century, nominations were entirely the responsibility of party organizations. To be nominated, an individual had to be loyal to the party organization, a requirement that included a willingness to share with it the spoils of office: government jobs and contracts. The situation allowed party organizations to acquire campaign workers and funds, but also enabled unscrupulous party leaders to extort money from those seeking political favors. Reform-minded Progressives argued for *party democracy*, claiming that party organizations should operate according to the same principle that governs elections: power should rest with ordinary voters rather than with the party bosses (see Chapter 2).

The most serious assault of the Progressives on the party organizations was the introduction of the **primary election** (or **direct primary**) as a method of choosing nominees. In place of party-designated nominees, the primary system placed nomination in the hands of voters (see Chapters 2 and 12).

Primaries are the severest impediment imaginable to the strength of the party organizations. If primaries did not exist, candidates would have to work through party organizations in order to gain nomination, and they could be denied renomination if disloyal to the party's goals. Because of primaries, however, candidates have the option of seeking office on their own, and, once elected (with or without the party's help), they can build an independent electoral base that effectively places them beyond the party's direct control.

Party organizations also lost influence over elections because of a decline in patronage. When a party won control of government a century ago, it also gained control of public jobs, which were doled out to loyal party workers. However, as government jobs in the early twentieth century shifted from patronage to the merit system (see Chapter 13), the party organizations lost control of many of these positions. Today, because of the expanded size of government, thousands of patronage jobs still exist. These government employees help staff the party organizations (along with volunteers), but most of them are more indebted to an individual politician than to a party organization. The people who work for members of Congress, for example, are all patronage employees, but they owe their jobs and their loyalty to their senator or representative, not their party.

In the process of taking control of nominations, candidates have also acquired control of most campaign money. At the turn of the century, when party machines were at their peak, most campaign funds passed through the hands of party leaders. Today, more than 80 percent of the money spent on congressional and presidential campaigns goes to the candidates without first passing through the parties.

In Europe, where there are no primary elections, the situation is very different. Parties control their nominations and, because of this, they also control campaign money and workers. Popular leaders in Europe are given fairly wide latitude by their party, but it is the parties, not the candidates, who are at the center of elections.

The Structure and Role of Party Organizations

Although the influence of party organizations has declined, parties are not about to die out. Political leaders and activists need stable organizations through which they can work together, and the parties serve that purpose. Moreover, certain activities, such as voter registration drives and get-out-the-vote efforts on election day, benefit all of a party's candidates and are therefore more efficiently conducted through the party organization. Indeed, parties have staged a comeback of sorts.[26] National and state party organizations in particular have developed the capacity to assist candidates with fund-raising, polling, research, and media production, which are essential ingredients of a successful modern campaign.

Structurally, U.S. parties are loose associations of national, state, and local organizations (see Figure 8-4). The national party organizations cannot dictate the decisions of the state organizations, which in turn do not control the activities of local organizations. However, there is communication between the levels, which have a common interest in strengthening the party's position.[27]

LOCAL PARTY ORGANIZATIONS   In a sense, U.S. parties are organized from the bottom up, not the top down. There are about 500,000 elective offices in the United States, of which fewer than five hundred are contested statewide and only two—the presidency and the vice-presidency—are contested nationally. All the rest are local offices; not surprisingly, at least 95 percent of party activists work within local organizations.

It is difficult to generalize about local parties because they vary greatly in their structure and activities. Today only a few local parties, including the Democratic organizations in Albany, Philadelphia, and Chicago, bear any resemblance to the fabled old-time party machines. But local parties tend to be strongest in urban areas and in the Northeast and Midwest, where

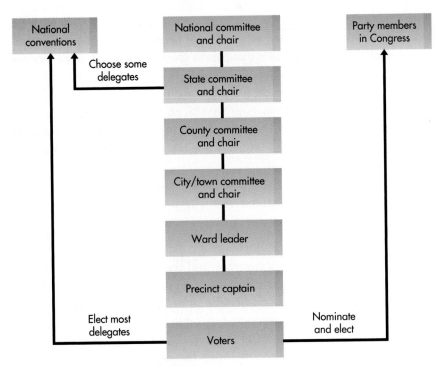

FIGURE 8-4   ORGANIZATION OF THE POLITICAL PARTY
U.S. parties today are loosely structured alliances of national, state, and local organizations.

parties traditionally have been more highly organized. In any case, local parties tend to specialize in elections that coincide with local electoral boundaries. Campaigns for mayor, city council, state legislature, county offices, and the like motivate most local parties to a greater degree than do congressional, statewide, and national contests.

In most urban areas, the party organizations today do not have enough workers to staff even a majority of local precincts (voting districts) on an ongoing basis. However, they do become active during campaigns, when they open campaign headquarters, conduct voter registration drives, send mailings or deliver leaflets to voters, and help get out the vote. These activities are not trivial. Most local campaigns are not well funded, and the party's backing of a candidate can make a vital difference.

In most suburbs and towns, the party's role is less substantial. The parties exist organizationally but typically have little money and few workers; hence they cannot operate effectively as electoral organizations. The individual candidates must carry nearly the entire burden.

STATE PARTY ORGANIZATIONS   At the state level, each party is headed by a central committee made up of members of local party organizations and local and state officeholders. These state central committees do not meet regularly, and they provide only general policy guidance for the state organizations. Day-to-day operations and policy are directed by a chairperson, who is a full-time, paid employee of the state party. The central committee appoints the chairperson, but it often accepts the individual recommended by the party's leading politician, usually the governor or a U.S. senator.

In recent decades the state parties have expanded their budgets and staffs considerably and, therefore, have been able to play a more active electoral role.[28] In contrast, thirty years ago about half of the state party organizations had no permanent staff at all. The increase in state party staff is largely due to improvements in communication technology, such as computer-assisted direct mail, which have made it easier for political organizations of all kinds, parties included, to raise funds. Having acquired the ability to pay for permanent staffs, state parties have used them to expand their activities, which range from polling to issues research to campaign management.

State party organizations concentrate on statewide races, including those for governor and U.S. senator,[29] and also focus on races for the state legislature. They play a smaller role in campaigns for national or local offices, and in most states, they do not endorse candidates in statewide primary contests.

NATIONAL PARTY ORGANIZATIONS   The national party organizations are structured much like those at the state level: they have a national committee, a national party chairperson, and a support staff. The national headquarters for the Republican and Democratic parties are located in Washington, D.C. Although in theory the national parties are run by their committees, neither the Democratic National Committee (DNC) nor the Republican National Committee (RNC) has great power. The RNC (with more than 150 members) and the DNC (with more than 300 members) are too cumbersome to act as deliberative bodies. They meet only periodically, and their power is largely confined to setting organizational policy, such as determining the site of the party's presidential nominating convention and the rules governing the selection of convention delegates. They have no power to decide nominations or to determine candidates' policy positions.

The national party's day-to-day operations are directed by a national chairperson chosen by the national committee, although it defers to the

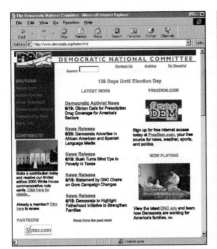

The home pages of the web sites of the Democratic National Committee (DNC)
and the Republican National Committee (RNC).

president's choice when the party controls the White House. The national
chairperson is supported by a permanent staff that concentrates on providing assistance in presidential and congressional campaigns.

This focus began in the 1970s when Republican leaders decided that a
revamped national party organization could play a contributing role in today's campaigns. The RNC developed campaign-management "colleges"
and "seminars" for candidates and their staffs, compiled massive amounts of
computer-based electoral data, sent field representatives to assist state and
local party leaders in modernizing their operations, and established a media
production division. The range of services the RNC provides is substantial.
For example, the RNC tapes and catalogues C-SPAN's televised coverage
of congressional debate and can instantly retrieve the statement of any
speaker on any issue. Republican challengers use this material to create attack ads directed at Democratic incumbents, while Republican incumbents
use it to show themselves acting forcefully on issues of concern to their
constituents.

The DNC in the early 1980s followed the Republicans' example, but
its later start and less affluent followers have kept the Democrats behind.
Modern campaigns, as David Adamany notes, are based on a "cash economy," and Democrats are relatively cash-poor.[30] The Republican model has
also filtered down to the state Republican and Democratic party committees, which, in varying degrees, provide the types of media, data-research,
and educational services that the national committees offer.

THE PARTIES AND MONEY   The national parties' major role in campaigns is the raising and spending of money. The RNC and the DNC are major sources of campaign funds, as are the party campaign committees in the House and the Senate: the Democratic Congressional Campaign Committee (DCCC), the National Republican Congressional Committee (NRCC), the Democratic Senatorial Campaign Committee (DSCC), and the National Republican Senatorial Committee (NRSC).

These party units had a relatively small fund-raising role until a loophole developed in the 1970s campaign finance laws. A court ruling gave the parties a nearly unlimited opportunity to raise and spend campaign funds, provided the funds are not channeled directly to a party's candidates.

A party can legally give $10,000 directly to a House candidate and $17,500 to a Senate candidate. This funding, along with the money a candidate receives from individual contributors ($1,000 is the maximum per contributor) and interest groups ($5,000 is the maximum per group), is termed **hard money,** since it goes directly to the candidate and can be spent as he or she chooses.

The 1970s campaign finance laws had a loophole that opened the door for what is known as "soft money." Although the law limited how much an individual could give directly to a candidate, it did not restrict party contributions. Thus, whereas a wealthy contributor could legally give a candidate only $1,000, that same contributor could give $1 million or more to the candidate's party. This **soft money** could only be spent on party activities, such as registration drives and party advertising, but, in reality, could be spent in ways that pimarily benefited a particular candidate. Soft money contributions from corporations, unions, and individuals accounted for nearly $500 million of the money spent during the 2000 elections. The Democratic and Republican parties each raised nearly $250 million through the loophole.

In 2001, Senator John McCain led a fight in Congress to ban the use of soft money in federal elections. McCain said that soft money threatened the integrity of the entire system of campaign finance regulation and gave wealthy contributors far too much influence over the electoral process. He had plenty of examples to support his case. During the 1996 presidential election, for instance, the Democratic party spent nearly $100 million on "issue" advertising that paralleled the "candidate" advertising of the Clinton campaign. The party ads did not directly urge voters to support Clinton, but his picture appeared in the ads, which featured his accomplishments as president. After the election, the Justice Department launched an investigation into whether the Democratic party ads were, in effect, Clinton ads, and therefore, in violation of the law.

In any event, money is now the greatest source of power for the national parties. The sums involved are enormous. During the last week alone of the 1998 congressional elections, for example, the GOP spent more than $20 million on "issue" ads for its candidates; most of the money was spent on races where Republican candidates were locked in a close fight with their Democratic opponents.

Although campaign fund-raising and spending is a source of power for the party, its alliance with the candidates is more of a **service relationship** than a power relationship.[31] The party offers help to virtually any of its candidates who have a chance of victory. Without the ability to control the nominating process, the party has little choice but to embrace nearly all candidates who run under its banner. At a minimum, this approach increases the likelihood that the party will gain a congressional majority and thus acquire control of the committees and top leadership positions in the House and Senate (see Chapter 11). The party may also acquire some additional loyalty from officeholders as a result of the contributions it makes to their campaigns. But, since the party is more or less willing to support any candidate, whatever his or her policy positions, its money does not give it much control over how party members conduct themselves after they take office.

No presidential first lady had run for elective office until Hillary Clinton did so in 2000. She moved to New York and won the state's U.S. Senate race. Clinton is shown here campaigning on the streets of New York City.

THE CANDIDATE-CENTERED CAMPAIGN

Although competition between the Republican and Democratic parties provides the backdrop to today's campaigns, the campaigns themselves are largely controlled by the candidates, particularly in congressional, statewide, and presidential races. Each candidate has a personal organization, created especially for the campaign and disbanded once it is over.

Running for Office

Today's candidates tend to be self-starters. Some candidates still rise through the ranks of the party or are drafted because no other qualified persons are willing to run. But most candidates seek high office because they aspire to careers in politics. They are entrepreneurs who play what the political consultant Joe Napolitan called "the election game."[32] The game begins with money, lots of it.

SEEKING FUNDS: "THE MONEY CHASE" Campaigns for high office are expensive, and the costs keep rising. In 1980, about $250 million was spent on all Senate and House campaigns combined. The figure had jumped to $425 million by 1990 and topped $700 million in 1998.

Because of the high cost of campaigns, candidates are forced to spend much of their time raising funds, which come primarily from individual contributors, interest groups (through PACs, discussed in Chapter 9), and political parties. The **money chase** is relentless.[33] It has been estimated that a U.S. senator must raise $10,000 a week on average throughout the entire six-year term in order to raise the $3 million or so that it takes to run a competitive Senate campaign in most states. A Senate campaign in a large state can cost several times that amount. In 2000, Representative Rick Lazio and First Lady Hillary Clinton raised over $55 million for the New York Senate race. House campaigns are less costly, but expenditures of $500,000 or more are commonplace.[34] As for presidential elections, even the nominating race is expensive. It is generally thought that a candidate needs at least $20 million to have a realistic chance of gaining nomination, but even that figure may need revising. In 2000, Texas governor George W. Bush raised $75 million for his nominating campaign. (In presidential races, but not congressional ones, candidates are eligible to receive federal funds, a topic discussed in Chapter 12.)

As might be expected, incumbents have a distinct advantage in fundraising. They have contributor lists from past campaigns and have acquired

★ STATES IN THE NATION ★

Party Control of State Legislatures

The strengths of the major parties vary substantially among states. An indicator of party dominance is whether one party has a majority in both chambers of the state legislature. As of 2001, the Democrats had a slight edge: 19 states to 17 states. In the other 14 states, control of the two chambers was split between the parties or there was a tie on one chamber (except for Nebraska, which has a unicameral nonpartisan legislature).

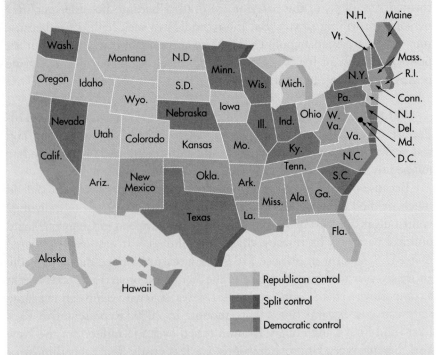

SOURCE: *The American Democracy*, Fourth Edition, by Thomas Patterson, © 1999, reproduced with permission of The McGraw-Hill Companies.

the public visibility and political clout that donors like. In recent House and Senate races, incumbents have outspent their challengers by more than 2 to 1.[35]

CREATING ORGANIZATION: "HIRED GUNS"   The "old politics" emphasized party rallies and door-to-door canvassing, which required organizations built around campaign volunteers. The "new politics" is based on the mass media and requires a much different kind of organizational structure. The key operatives are campaign consultants, pollsters, media producers, and fund-raising specialists. They are **hired guns** who charge hefty fees for their services. The "new king-makers" is the way the writer David Chagall characterized these "pros."[36]

Some of them are specialists in campaign management. Inexperienced candidates often think that campaigns are simple to run and entrust the job to an amateur, who is often a relative or friend. They soon discover that their campaign is headed nowhere. At this point, if they have the money, they hire a seasoned professional. Over the years, some of these operatives, like James Carville, Joe Napolitan, Ed Rollins, Dick Morris, and Roger Ailes, have developed almost legendary reputations.

Fund-raising specialists are also part of the new politics. Direct mail operators have developed contributor lists for every state and nearly every type of candidacy, and they flood the mail with computer-generated letters. There are also numerous specialty mailing lists, such as EMILY's List (*early money is like yeast*, "it makes the dough rise"). EMILY's List was started in the 1980s to provide seed money for liberal women candidates. Effective fund-raisers also know how to tap into the networks of large contributors and interest groups who give to election campaigns (see Chapter 9).

Polling is another essential component of the modern campaign. Although candidates make use of the public polls conducted by Gallup, the news media, and other organizations, they also hire their own pollsters.[37] They also rely on focus groups, which are small groups of voters assembled to talk at length about the issues and candidates and, in some instances, to evaluate proposed themes and materials, such as televised political ads. Polls and focus groups enable candidates to identify messages that are likely to resonate with the voters. At one point in the 1996 presidential race, for example, Bob Dole shifted from attacks on Bill Clinton's character to issues of taxes and economic growth after his polls and focus groups indicated that voters were more concerned about their disposable income than about the president's personal history.

Media consultants are another staple of the modern campaign. These experts are adept at producing televised political advertising and creating the "photo-ops" and other staged events that attract news coverage. They also "teach" the candidates how to use the media properly. Inexperienced candidates soon discover that they cannot "just be themselves" when talking with journalists or participating in televised debates. They have to conform to the demands of the media, such as the preference of television journalists for "sound bites": short, pithy statements that add zest and zing to a news story.[38]

DEVISING STRATEGY: "PACKAGING THE CANDIDATE"   In the old days, candidates were nearly prepackaged. They were labeled as Democrats or Republicans, which was about all the guidance most voters wanted or needed. Party labels are still meaningful, but today's campaigns are also based on media "images."

Often depicted as hollow deceptions, images are more typically rooted in factual arguments.[39] They are constructed by placing aspects of the candidate's partisanship, policy positions, record, and personality in the context of the voters' "ideal" candidate, a process known as the **packaging** of a candidate.[40] The voters want a representative who is honest, able, straightforward, resolute, and responsive to their interests, but there are limits on the claims a candidate can reasonably make. It would be difficult, for example, for Democratic incumbents who have been long-time advocates of welfare spending to convincingly portray themselves as fiscal conservatives. Instead, they would base their images as responsive legislators on other issues, such as education or social security. In any case, officeseekers try to create a favorable portrayal of their candidacy that is also plausible. In a way, this type of packaging is as old as politics itself. Andrew Jackson's self-portrayal as "the champion of the people" is an image that any modern candidate could appreciate. What is new is the need to fit the image to the requirements of a media campaign. It must conform to a world of sound bites, thirty-second ads, and televised debates.

GOING PUBLIC: "AIR WARS" AND "SPIN"   The battleground of the modern campaign is the mass media. Televised advertising in particular enables candidates to communicate directly, and on their own terms, with the voters.[41] Candidates spend heavily on the production and airing of televised ads, which account for more than half the expenditures in every presidential campaign and most congressional races. Indeed, televised ads are usually cited as the main reason for the high cost of U.S. campaigns. In most democracies, televised campaigning takes place through parties, which receive *free* air time to make their pitch. Many democracies even prohibit the purchase of televised advertising time by candidates (see Table 8-1).

Air wars is the term that the political scientist Darrell West applies to candidates' use of televised ads. Candidates increasingly play off each other's ads, seeking to gain the strategic advantage.[42] Modern production techniques enable well-funded candidates to get new ads on the air within a few hours' time, which allows them to rebut attacks and exploit fast-breaking developments. "Rapid-response" was the term used by the Clinton campaign in 1992 and 1996 for its capacity to counter Republican charges. For example, when Bush ads in the 1992 campaign accused Clinton of having

TABLE 8-1   TELEVISION CAMPAIGN PRACTICES
IN SELECTED DEMOCRACIES

In many democracies, free television time is provided to political parties and candidates are not allowed to buy advertising time. The United States provides no free time to parties and allows candidates to purchase air time. Television debates are also a feature of many U.S. campaigns.

Country	Paid TV Ads Allowed?	Unrestricted Free TV Time Provided?	Are TV Debates Held?
Canada	Yes	Yes	Yes
France	No	Yes	Yes
Germany	Yes	Yes	Yes
Great Britain	No	Yes	No
Italy	No	Yes	Yes
Netherlands	No	No	Yes
United States	Yes	No	Yes

SOURCE: *The American Democracy*, Fourth Edition, by Thomas Patterson, © 1999, reproduced with permission of The McGraw-Hill Companies.

raised taxes when governor of Arkansas, Clinton aired an immediate rebuttal based on his interpretation of his tax record.[43] Rapid-response has become a standard tactic in high-profile contests; both the Bush and the Gore campaigns employed the tactic in 2000.

The media campaign also takes place through news vehicles, but coverage varies depending on the race and location. Many House candidates are nearly ignored by their local news media. The New York City media market, for example, includes more than a score of House districts in New York, New Jersey, Pennsylvania, and Connecticut, and candidates in these districts get little or no coverage from the New York media. The presidential campaign, in contrast, gets daily coverage from both national and local media. Between these extremes are Senate races and House races in less populated areas; they always get some news coverage and, if hotly contested, may get heavy coverage.

Candidates try to put a positive "spin" on their news coverage. They also try to campaign in ways that will lessen the negative "spin" they have come to expect from journalists. The news is mostly critical in tone, and a candidate's blunder or misstatement can result in a torrent of bad news.[44] As a result, candidates rely increasingly on scripted statements rather than spontaneous remarks when dealing with the press.

The media campaign also includes debates and talk-show appearances. Debates are particularly important since they often attract a large and attentive audience. But they are also risky encounters, since they provide a chance to directly compare the candidates. A weak or bumbled performance can seriously damage a candidate's chances in a close race. To reduce the risks, candidates often spend the day or two before a debate "rehearsing" their presentation.

INTERNET POLITICS: "IN THE WEB"   New communication technology usually makes its way into campaign politics, and the Internet is no exception. Every presidential candidate in 2000 had a web site. Each site was packed with information, but its main purposes were to generate public support, to raise money, and to attract and organize volunteers. Republican candidate John McCain raised more than $1 million for his campaign through Internet contributions.

Although television is still the principal mechanism of election politics, some observers believe that the Internet may eventually replace it, particularly in congressional races. E-mail is much cheaper than television advertising (or, for that matter, traditional mail), and can be more easily directed at supporters and swing voters. Because it is a targeted medium, the Internet may become the channel through which candidates attack each other with charges they feel are not adequately voiced through other channels. This tactic was used, for example, by Republican hopeful Steve Forbes in his unsuccessful effort to derail George W. Bush's nominating campaign. In one instance, the Forbes campaign e-mailed subscribers a copy of a newspaper column that mocked a Bush speech to teenagers that described "a drunken college escapade when he [Bush] stole a Christmas wreath." The message claimed that the "real lesson" in Bush's remarks was that "the criminal justice system works for rich, white men."[45]

PARTIES, CANDIDATES, AND THE PUBLIC'S INFLUENCE

Candidate-centered campaigns have some distinct advantages. First, they lend flexibility to and infuse new blood into electoral politics. When political conditions and issues change, self-directed candidates quickly adjust, bringing new ideas into the political arena. Strong party organizations are rigid by comparison. Until recently, for example, the British Labour party was controlled by old-line activists who refused to concede that changes in the British economy called for changes in the party's trade unionist and economic policies. The result was a series of humiliating defeats to the Conservative party that ended only after Tony Blair and other proponents of "New Labour" successfully rebuilt the party's image.

Second, candidate-centered campaigns encourage national officeholders to be responsive to local interests. In building personal followings among their state and district constituents, members of Congress respond to local needs. Nearly every significant domestic program enacted by Congress is adjusted to accommodate the interests of states and localities that would otherwise be hurt by the policy. Members of Congress are not obliged to support the legislative position of their party's majority, and they often extract favors for their constituents as the price of their support. Where strong national parties exist, national interests take precedence over local concerns. In both France and Britain, for example, the pleas of representatives of underdeveloped regions have often gone unheeded by their party's majority.

In other respects, however, candidate-centered campaigns have some real disadvantages. Often, they degenerate into mere personality contests and are fertile ground for powerful special interest groups, which contribute much of the money that underwrites the candidates' campaigns. Many groups give large sums of money to incumbents of both parties, which enables them to insulate themselves from an election's outcome. Whether the Republicans win or the Democrats win, they are assured of having friends in high places.

Candidate-centered campaigns also blur the connection between electing and governing by making it easier for officeholders to deny responsibility for government's actions. If national policy goes awry, an incumbent can always say that he or she is only one vote out of many and that the real problem resides with the president or with "others" in Congress.[46] By comparison, lawmakers in a party-centered system cannot easily evade responsibility for what the government has done; in such systems, public dissatisfaction with the performance of government often leads to the majority party's defeat in the next election.

The problem of accountability in the U.S. system is illustrated by surveys that have asked Americans about their confidence in Congress. Although most citizens have a low opinion of Congress as a whole, most citizens also say they have confidence in their own representative in Congress. This paradoxical attitude prevails in so many districts that the net result in most elections is a Congress whose membership is not greatly changed from the previous one (see Chapter 11). In the 2000 elections, despite a widespread view that Congress was bogged down in narrow-minded partisanship, less than 3 percent of incumbents seeking reelection were defeated.

Candidate-centered campaigns also make it difficult for voters to act in unison. Candidates of the same party in different constituencies stand for different things; this deprives the national electorate of an opportunity to elect a lawmaking majority pledged to a common platform. Of course, U.S. elections produce lawmaking majorities, and it is safe to assume that most elected officials of a particular party share certain ideas even when they run and win on their own.[47] But this is a far cry from a system in which voters in all districts choose among candidates who are committed to sharply defined party platforms.

In sum, candidate-centered campaigns strengthen the relationship between the voters and their individual representative while, at the same time, weakening the relationship between the full electorate and their representative institutions. Whether this arrangement serves the public's interest is debatable. Most citizens are not even sure. A 2000 Harvard poll found that 68 percent of Americans agreed with the statement that today's politics "seem more like theater or entertainment than like something to be taken seriously." Nevertheless, it is clear that Americans do not want truly strong parties. Parties survived the shift to candidate-centered campaigns and will persist, but their heyday has passed. (Congressional and presidential campaigns are discussed further in Chapters 11 and 12, respectively.)

SUMMARY

Political parties serve to link the public with its elected leaders. In the United States, this linkage is provided by a two-party system; only the Republican and Democratic parties have any chance of winning control of government. The fact that the United States has only two major parties is explained by several factors: an electoral system—characterized by single-member districts—that makes it difficult for third parties to compete for power; each party's willingness to accept differing political views; and a political culture that stresses compromise and negotiation rather than ideological rigidity.

Because the United States has only two major parties, each of which seeks to gain majority support, their candidates normally tend to avoid controversial or extreme political positions. Candidates typically pursue moderate and somewhat overlapping policies. Nonetheless, the Democratic and Republican candidates sometimes do offer sharply contrasting policy alternatives, particularly in times of political unrest.

America's parties are decentralized, fragmented organizations. The national party organization does not control the policies and activities of the state organizations, and they in turn do not control the local organizations. Traditionally the local organizations have controlled most of the party's work force because most elections are contested at the local level. Local parties, however, vary markedly in their vitality. Whatever their level, America's party organizations are relatively weak. They lack control over nominations and elections. Candidates can bypass the party organization and win nomination through primary elections. Individual candidates also control most of the organizational structure and money necessary to win elections. Recently the state and national party organizations have expanded their capacity to provide candidates with modern campaign services. Nevertheless, party organizations at all levels have few ways of controlling the candidates who run under their banners. They assist candidates with campaign technology, workers, and funds, but cannot compel candidates' loyalty to organizational goals.

American political campaigns, particularly those for higher-level office, are candidate centered. Most candidates are self-starters who become adept at "the election game." They spend much of their time raising campaign funds, and they build their personal organizations around "hired guns": pollsters, media producers, and election consultants. Strategy and image-making are key components of the modern campaign, as is televised political advertising, which accounts for roughly half of all spending in presidential and congressional races.

Because America's parties cannot control their candidates or coordinate their policies at all levels, they are unable to consistently present the voters with coherent, detailed platforms for governing. The national electorate as a whole is thus denied a clear choice among policy alternatives and has difficulty exerting a decisive and predictable influence through elections.

MAJOR CONCEPTS

air wars

candidate-centered politics

dealignment

grass-roots party

hard money

hired guns

money chase

multiparty system

nomination

packaging (of candidates)

party-centered politics

party coalition

party competition

party organizations

party realignment

political party

primary election (direct primary)

proportional representation

service relationship

single-member districts

soft money

split-ticket voting

straight-ticket voting

two-party system

SUGGESTED READINGS AND WEB SITES

Aldrich, John H. *Why Parties? The Origin and Transformation of Political Parties in America*. Chicago: University of Chicago Press, 1995. An insightful analysis of what parties are and how they emerge and develop.

Flanigan, William H., and Nancy H. Zingale. *Political Behavior of the American Electorate*. 9th ed. Washington, D.C.: Congressional Quarterly Press, 1998. An analysis of the political behavior of the American electorate.

King, Anthony. *Running Scared: The Victory of Campaigning over Governing in America*. New York: Free Press, 1997. An analysis of why America's leaders have succumbed to the pressure of the permanent campaign.

Lijphardt, Arend. *Electoral Systems and Party Systems: A Study of Twenty-Seven Democracies, 1945–1990*. New York: Oxford University Press, 1994. A comprehensive study of the relationship between electoral systems and party systems.

Patterson, Kelly D. *Political Parties and the Maintenance of Liberal Democracy*. New York: Columbia University Press, 1996. A systematic look at the effects of political parties on American government and politics.

Rosenstone, Steven J., Roy L. Behr, and Edward H. Lazarus. *Third Parties in America*. 2d ed. Princeton, N.J.: Princeton University Press, 1996. An analysis of America's third parties and their impact on the two-party system.

West, Darrell M. *Air Wars: Television Advertising in Election Campaigns, 1952–1992*. 2d ed. Washington, D.C.: Congressional Quarterly Press, 1997. A thorough study of the role of televised advertising in election campaigns.

http://www.democrats.org/　The Democratic National Committee's site; it provides information on the party's platform, candidates, officials, and organization.

http://www.greenparties.org　The Green party's web site; it contains information on the party's philosophy and policy goals.

http://www.rnc.org/　Home page of the Republican National Committee; it offers information on Republican leaders, policy positions, and organizations.

http://www.vote-smart.org/　This site provides a link to U.S. national political parties with additional links to each organization's web page.

READING 8

Running for Congress

PAUL S. HERRNSON

Introduction

In his essay, Paul Herrnson discusses a pattern that was emphasized in Chapter 8—that candidates rather than political parties dominate the modern campaign. From the decision to run to the raising of money, candidates are the initiators. Herrnson also describes how the modern system undermines true competition between the parties. Once elected, officials use their position and resources to solidify their hold on office. Large numbers of them succeed in insulating themselves from the broad political trends that in a party-centered system would result in periodic purges of elected officials and major shifts in political power.

In order to win a congressional election or even to be remotely competitive, candidates must compete in two campaigns: one for votes and one for resources. The campaign for votes is the campaign that generally comes to mind when people think about congressional elections. It requires a candidate to assemble an organization and to use that organization to target key groups of voters, select a message they will find compelling, deliver that message, and get the candidate's supporters to the polls on election day.

The other campaign, which is based largely in Washington, D.C., requires candidates to convince the party officials, political action committee (PAC) managers, political consultants, and political journalists who are the leaders of the nation's political community that their races will be competitive and worthy of support. Gaining the backing of these leaders is a critical step in attracting the money and campaign services that are available in the nation's capital and in other major urban centers. These resources enable the candidate to run a credible campaign back home. Without them, most congressional candidates would lose their bids for election. . . .

Candidates, not political parties, are the major focus of congressional campaigns, and candidates, not parties, bear the ultimate responsibility for election outcomes. These characteristics of congressional elections are striking when viewed from a comparative perspective. In most democracies, political parties are the principal contestants in election campaigns, and the campaigns tend to focus on national issues, ideology, and party programs and accomplishments. In the United States, parties do not actually run congressional campaigns nor do they become the major focus of elections. Instead, candidates run their own campaigns, and parties may contribute money or election services to them. A comparison of the terminology commonly used to describe elections in the United States and that used in Great Britain more than hints at the differences. In the United States, candidates are said to *run* for Congress, and they do so with or without party help. In Great Britain, on the other hand, candidates are said to *stand* for election to Parliament, while their party runs most of the campaign. The difference in terminology only slightly oversimplifies reality.

Candidates are the most important actors in American congressional elections. Most of them are self-selected rather than recruited by party organizations. All of them must win the right to run under their party's label through a participatory primary, caucus, or convention. Only after they have secured their party's nomination are major-party candidates assured a place on the general election ballot. Independent and minor-party candidates can get on the ballot in other ways, usually by paying a registration fee or collecting several thousand signatures from district residents.

The nomination process in most other countries, on the other hand, usually begins with a small group of party activists pursuing the nomination through a "closed" process that allows only formal, dues-paying party members to participate. While the American system amplifies the input of caucus participants and primary voters, these other systems respond more to the input of local party activists and place more emphasis on peer review.

The need to win a party nomination forces congressional candidates to assemble their own campaign organizations, formulate their own election strategies, and conduct their own campaigns. The images and issues that they convey to voters in trying to win the nomination carry over to the general election. The efforts of individual candidates and their campaign organizations have a bigger impact on election outcomes than the activities of party organizations and other groups. . . .

Potential candidates survey the local political scene to determine whether conditions are ripe for a competitive election. Often they are not, and the result is that most congressional incumbents face weak challengers and many win by large margins. Between 1950 and 1990, House incumbents enjoyed reelection rates of better than 90 percent; the 1988 and 1990 elections returned to Congress 98.3 percent and 96 percent, respectively, of those who sought to keep their jobs. Most potential challengers find these success rates discouraging and choose to wait until a seat becomes vacant rather than run against an incumbent. Consequently, many House seats go uncontested, and a substantial portion fail to attract meaningful two-party competition.

Senate elections have been more competitive. Senate reelection rates ranged from 55.2 percent to 96.9 percent between 1946 and 1992. Between 1986 and 1990 only 5 percent of all Senate incumbents had no major-party opponent, and 58 percent of those involved in contested races won by 60 percent or more of the two-party vote. Fourteen percent of all senators seeking reelection during this six-year span were defeated. . . .

The desire of incumbents to retain their seats has changed Congress in ways that help discourage electoral competition. Most who are elected to Congress quickly come to terms with the fact that they will probably never hold a higher office because there are too few of these to go around. Like most people, they do everything in their power to hold on to their jobs. Congress has adapted to the career aspirations of its members by providing them with resources that can be used to increase their odds of reelection. Members use free mailings, WATS lines, district offices, and subsidized travel to gain visibility among their constituents. Federal "pork-barrel" projects also help incumbents gain popularity and visibility among voters. Congressional staffs help members write speeches, respond to constituent mail, resolve problems that constituents have with executive branch agencies, and follow the comings and goings in their bosses' districts. These "perks" of office give incumbents tremendous advantages over challengers. They also work to discourage those experienced politicians who could put forth a competitive challenge from taking on an entrenched incumbent.

The dynamics of campaign finance have similar effects. Incumbents have tremendous fund-raising advantages over challengers, especially among PACs. Many incumbents build up large war chests to discourage potential challengers from running against them. Those challengers who decide to contest a race against a member of the House or Senate typically find they are unable to raise the funds needed to mount a viable campaign.

Given that the cards tend to be so heavily stacked in favor of congressional incumbents, most electoral competition takes place in open seats, especially those that are not dominated by one party. Open-seat contests draw a larger than usual number of primary contestants. They also attract significantly more money and election assistance from party committees, PACs, and individuals than do challenger campaigns. Special elections are a form of open-seat contest that tend to be particularly competitive and unpredictable. They bring out even larger numbers of primary contenders than normal open-seat elections, especially when the seat that has become vacant was formerly held by a long-time incumbent.

The concentration of competition in open-seat elections and the decennial reapportionment and redistricting of House seats have combined to produce a ten-year, five-election cycle of political competition. Redistricting leads to the creation of many new House seats and the redrawing of the boundaries of numerous others. It encourages an increase in congressional retirements, leads more nonincumbents than usual to run for the House, and thereby increases competition in many House elections. Competition in the four election cycles that follow redistricting generally decreases as incumbents shore up their electoral support and work to discourage challenges by potentially strong opponents.

SOURCE: Adapted from Paul S. Herrnson, *"Running for Congress," Congressional Elections: Campaigning at Home and in Washington* (Washington, D.C.: Congressional Quarterly Press, 1995 pp. 2-17). Used by permission of Congressional Quarterly Press.
Paul S. Herrnson is a professor of government and politics at the University of Maryland.

CHAPTER NINE

Interest Groups

The flaw in the pluralist heaven is that the heavenly chorus sings
with a strong upper-class bias.

E. E. SCHATTSCHNEIDER[1]

THEY LAUNCHED their attack within hours of the announcement
that congressional Republicans had included Medicare in their
balanced-budget proposal. The GOP lawmakers planned a $1.1 trillion re-
duction in federal spending over seven years, including a $270 billion cut in
health care for the elderly. Senior-citizen groups assailed the plan and
quickly organized a mass demonstration outside the Capitol building. The
next step was an orchestrated campaign of thousands of angry calls, letters,
telegrams, and faxes from retirees to their congressional representatives.

President Clinton sided with the seniors' lobby, promising to veto the
Republican bill, which led to a showdown between Congress and the White
House that forced a temporary shutdown of the federal government. In January 1996, after a six-week battle and with their poll ratings dropping almost
daily, Republican lawmakers shelved their balanced-budget proposal.

The campaign against the Republicans' Medicare initiative suggests
why interest groups are both admired and feared. On the one hand, groups
have a legitimate right to express their views on public policy issues. It is
entirely appropriate for senior citizens or any other group—whether farmers, consumers, business firms, or college students—to actively promote
their interests through collective action.

In fact, the *pluralist* theory of American politics (see Chapter 1) holds that
society's interests are most effectively represented through the efforts of
groups. An extreme statement of this view is Arthur F. Bentley's claim in 1908
that society is "nothing other than the complex of groups that compose it."[2]
Although modern pluralists make far less sweeping claims, they do contend
that the group process, on balance, is open to a great range of interests, nearly
all of which benefit from organized activity in one significant way or another.

249

Yet groups can wield too much power. If a group gets its way at an unreasonable cost to the rest of society, the public interest is harmed. When the Republican budget package was prepared in Congress, polls indicated that most Americans wanted a balanced federal budget and were willing to bear a fair share of the costs. Did the senior-citizen lobby, in pursuit of its own narrow interest, derail a sound budgetary proposal? Or did the Republican package, which also included tax cuts for upper-income Americans, place on the elderly too much of the burden of a balanced budget?

Opinions on these questions differ widely, but there is no doubt that the special interest in some cases wrongly prevails over the general interest. Indeed, most observers are of the opinion that groups have achieved too much influence over public policy in recent decades. Some analysts describe the situation as the triumph of **single-issue politics:** separate groups organized around nearly every conceivable policy issue, with each group pressing its demands and influence to the utmost, at whatever cost to the broader society. The structure of the American political system provides fertile ground for group influence, particularly when a group seeks to protect government benefits it already receives. The system's elaborate checks and balances make it relatively easy for a group, if it has support even within a single institution, to block efforts to cut its benefits. (This "Madisonian dilemma" will be explored more fully in the chapter's concluding section.)

An **interest group** can be defined as a set of individuals who organize to promote a shared political interest. Also called a "faction" or "pressure group" or "special interest," an interest group is characterized by its formalized organization and by its pursuit of policy goals that stem from its members' shared interest. Thus, a bridge club or an amateur softball team is not an interest group because it does not seek to influence the political process. Organizations such as Common Cause, the National Organization for Women, the World Wildlife Fund, the National Rifle Association, and the Anti-Defamation League of B'nai B'rith are interest groups because, despite their differences, they all meet the definition's two criteria: each is an organized entity and each seeks to further its members' interests through political action.

Interest groups promote public policies, encourage the political participation of their members, support candidates for public office, and work to influence policymakers. Interest groups are thus similar to political parties in certain respects, but the two types of organizations differ in important ways. Major political parties address a broad range of issues so as to appeal to diverse blocs of voters. Parties exist to contest elections. They change their policy positions as the voters' preferences change; for the party, winning is almost everything. In comparison, interest groups focus on specific issues of immediate concern to their members; farm groups, for example, concentrate on agricultural policy. A group may involve itself in elections, but its purpose is to influence public policy.

This chapter examines the degree to which various interests in American society are represented by organized groups, the process by which interest groups exert influence, and the costs and benefits of group politics in regard to the public good. The main points made in the chapter are the following:

* *Although nearly all interests in American society are organized to some degree, those associated with economic activity, particularly business enterprises, are by far the most thoroughly organized.*
* *Lobbying and electioneering are the traditional means by which groups communicate with and influence political leaders.*
* *When public policy is decided solely by group demands, the group process does not serve the collective interest, regardless of the number of separate interests that benefit from the process.*

THE INTEREST-GROUP SYSTEM

In the 1830s the Frenchman Alexis de Tocqueville wrote that the "principle of association" was nowhere more evident than in America.[3] Organized groups have always flourished in the United States. The country's tradition of free association has always made it easy for Americans to join together for political purposes, and their diverse interests have given them reason to seek influence through specialized groups. Few nations have as many separate economic, ethnic, religious, social, and geographic interests as the United States (see box: How the United States Compares).

The extraordinary number of groups in the United States does not suggest, however, that these various interests are all fully organized. Some groups are inherently more attractive to potential members than others and thus find it easier to build large or loyal followings.[4] Organizations also differ in their access to financial resources and thus in their capacity for political action.

Therefore, a first consideration in regard to group politics in America is the issue of how thoroughly various interests are organized. Group politics is the politics of organization. Interests that are highly organized stand a good chance of having their views heard by policymakers. Poorly organized interests run the risk of being ignored.

How the United States Compares

Groups: "A Nation of Joiners"

"A nation of joiners" is how the Frenchman Alexis de Tocqueville described the United States during his visit to this country in the 1830s.

Even today, Americans are more actively involved in groups and community causes than are Europeans. The American tradition of group activity is only one reason. Another is the structure of the U.S. political system. Because of federalism and the separation of powers, the American system offers numerous points at which groups can try to influence public policy. If unsuccessful with legislators, groups can turn to executives or the courts. If thwarted at the national level, groups can turn to state and local governments. By comparison, the governments of most other democratic nations are not organized in ways that facilitate group access and influence. France's unitary government, for example, concentrates power at the national level.

Such differences are reflected in citizens' participation rates. Americans are more likely to belong to groups than Europeans, as the accompanying figures from the World Values Survey indicate.

	No group	1 – 3 groups	4 or more
United States	18%	63%	19%
Germany	33%	60%	7%
Great Britain	46%	45%	9%
Italy	59%	40%	1%
France	61%	35%	4%

Percentage belonging to: No group ▮ 1 – 3 groups ▮ 4 or more

SOURCE: *The American Democracy*, Fifth Edition, by Thomas Patterson, © 2001, reproduced with permission of The McGraw-Hill Companies.

Economic Groups

No interests are more fully or effectively organized than those that have economic activity as their primary purpose. An indication of their advantage is the fact that their Washington lobbyists outnumber those of other groups by more than 2 to 1.

Economic groups include corporations, labor unions, farm groups, and professional associations. They exist primarily for economic purposes: to make profits, provide jobs, improve pay, or protect an occupation. For the sake of discussion, such organizations will be called **economic groups,** although it is important to recognize that their political goals can include policies that transcend the narrow economic interests of their members. Thus the AFL-CIO concentrates on labor objectives, but it also takes positions on broader issues of foreign and domestic policy.

One reason for the abundance of economic groups is their access to financial resources. Political activity does not come cheap. If a group is to make its views known, it normally must have a headquarters, an expert staff, and communication facilities. Economic groups can obtain the requisite money and expertise from their economic activities. Corporations have the greatest natural advantage. They do not have to charge membership dues or conduct fund-raisers to get money to support their lobbying. Their political money comes from the goods and services they produce and sell.

Some economic groups do depend on dues for their support, but they can offer prospective members a powerful incentive to join: **private (individual) goods,** which are the benefits that a group can grant directly to the individual member. For example, workers in the state of Michigan cannot hold automobile assembly jobs unless they belong to the United Auto Workers (UAW). The UAW has a **material incentive**—the economic lure of high wages—to attract potential members. Economic groups are highly organized in part because they serve the individual economic needs of potential members. The predominance of economic interests was predicted in *Federalist* No. 10, in which James Madison declared that property is "the most common and durable source of factions." Stated differently, nothing seems to matter quite so much to people as their pocketbooks and livelihoods.

BUSINESS GROUPS Writing in 1929, E. Pendleton Herring noted, "Of the many organized groups maintaining offices in [Washington], there are no interests more fully, more comprehensively, and more efficiently represented than those of American industry."[5] Although corporations do not dominate the group system to the degree they did in the past, Herring's general conclusion still holds: more than half of all groups formally registered to lobby Congress are business organizations. Nearly all large corporations and many smaller ones are politically active. They concentrate their activities on policies that directly affect business interests, such as tax, tariff, and regulatory decisions.

Business firms are also represented through associations. Some of these associations, such as the U.S. Chamber of Commerce, which represents roughly three million medium-sized and small businesses, seek to advance the general interests of business and to articulate a business perspective on broad policy issues.[6] Other business associations, such as the American Petroleum Institute, are confined to a single industry. Because each trade association represents a single industry, it can promote the interests of member corporations even when these interests conflict with those of business generally. Thus, while the Chamber of Commerce promotes a free trade policy, some trade associations seek protective tariffs because their member firms want barriers against foreign competition.[7]

LABOR GROUPS   Since the 1930s, organized labor has been politically active on a large scale. Its goal has been to promote policies that benefit workers in general and union members in particular. Although some independent unions, such as the United Mine Workers, lobby actively, the dominant labor group is the AFL-CIO, which maintains its national headquarters in Washington, D.C. The AFL-CIO has more than thirteen million members in its ninety-seven affiliated unions, which include the International Brotherhood of Electrical Workers, the Sheet Metal Workers, the Communication Workers of America, and, as of 1987, the giant International Brotherhood of Teamsters.

At one time about a third of the U.S. work force was unionized, but today only about one-seventh of all workers belong to unions. Skilled and unskilled laborers have been the core of organized labor, but their numbers are decreasing while professionals, technicians, and service workers are increasing in number. Professionals have shown little interest in union organization, perhaps because they identify with management or see themselves as economically secure. Service workers and technicians are also more difficult for unions to organize than traditional laborers because they work closely with managers, often in small offices.

However, unions have made some important inroads in recent decades in their efforts to organize public employees. Teachers, postal workers, police, firefighters, and social workers are among the public-employee groups that have become increasingly unionized. Today, the nation's largest unions are those that represent service and public employees rather than skilled and unskilled laborers.

AGRICULTURAL GROUPS Farm organizations represent another large economic lobby. The American Farm Bureau Federation is the largest of the farm groups, with more than four million members. The National Farmers Union, the National Grange, and the National Farmers Organization are smaller farm lobbies. Agricultural groups do not always agree on policy issues. For instance, the Farm Bureau sides with agribusiness and owners of large farms, while the Farmers Union promotes the interests of smaller, "family" farms.

There are also numerous specialty farm associations, including the Association of Wheat Growers and the Associated Milk Producers. Each association acts as a separate lobby to try to obtain policies beneficial to its members' narrow agricultural interests.

PROFESSIONAL GROUPS Most professions have lobbying associations. Perhaps the most powerful of these groups is the American Medical Association (AMA), which, with roughly three hundred thousand members, represents about half of the nation's physicians. The AMA has consistently opposed any government policy that would substantially limit physicians' autonomy. Other professional groups are the American Bar Association and the American Association of University Professors, each of which maintains a lobbying office in Washington.

Citizens' Groups

Although economic interests are the best organized groups, they do not have a monopoly on group activity. The group system also includes **citizens' (noneconomic) groups.** The members of such groups are drawn together not by the promise of direct economic gain but by **purposive incentives:** opportunities to promote a cause in which they believe.[8] Whether a group's goal is to protect the environment, reduce the threat of nuclear war, return prayer to the public schools, feed the poor at home or abroad, or whatever, there are citizens who are willing to participate simply because they believe the policy goal is a worthy cause.[9]

In comparison with economic groups, citizens' groups have a harder time gathering the resources necessary for organized political activity. These groups do not generate profits or fees that can be used for lobbying.

Jody Williams won the Nobel Peace Prize in 1997 for organizing a
worldwide lobby of citizens' groups in a successful campaign to
ban the use of land mines. The Internet was her primary
means of organization.

Moreover, the incentives they offer prospective members are not exclusive. Unlike the private, or individual, goods provided by many economic groups (such as the jobs that firms and unions provide), citizens' groups typically offer **collective (public) goods** as an incentive to potential members. Collective goods are, by definition, benefits that must be shared; they cannot be allotted on an individual basis. The air we breathe and the national forests we visit are examples of collective goods; they are available to one and all, those who pay dues to a clean-air group or a wilderness group and those who do not.

This characteristic of collective goods creates what is called the **free-rider problem,** which refers to the fact that individuals will receive the good even if they have not contributed to the group's finances. In a purely economic sense, it is not rational for individuals to pay dues to such a group since they can obtain the benefit without paying for it.[10] Moreover, the dues paid by any single member are too small to affect the group's success one way or another. Why pay dues to a clean-air group when any improvement in air quality from its lobbying efforts is available to everyone and when one's contribution is too small to make a real difference? Although many people do join such groups anyway,[11] there is no doubt that the free-rider problem is a reason citizens' groups are less highly organized than economic ones.

Citizens' groups try to surmount the free-rider problem by creating individual benefits, akin to those offered by economic groups, to make membership more attractive.[12] Organizational newsletters and social activities are among the individual benefits that citizens' groups offer as a lure to membership. Computer-assisted direct mail has also helped citizens' groups attract members. Group organizers buy mailing lists and flood the mails with computer-typed "personal" letters asking recipients to pay a small annual membership fee. For some individuals, a fee of $25 to $50 annually represents no great sacrifice and offers the personal satisfaction of supporting a cause in which they believe. Until the computer era, citizens' groups had great difficulty in identifying and contacting potential members, which is a reason why the number of such groups was so much smaller in the past than is true today. On the whole, however, the organizational advantages rest with economic groups. In nearly all respects, they have the edge on citizens' groups (see Table 9-1).

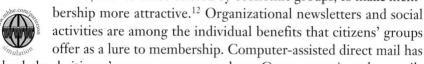

One area where citizens' groups have gained an edge is the Internet, which has made it easier for them to contact their members. Nearly every citizen group of any size has its own web site, and many have developed the capacity to reach individual members with urgent and periodic messages. One of the most successful citizen campaigns in history was conducted largely through the Internet. It was a global campaign aimed at the elimination of land mines, and its chief organizer, Jody Williams, received the Nobel Peace Prize in 1997 for her work. Through the Web, she linked together activists and groups throughout the world and, in the end, succeeded in getting one hundred countries to agree to an international treaty that bans the use of land mines and the destruction of those already in the ground.

Most citizens' groups are of three general types: public interest groups, single-issue groups, and ideological groups.

PUBLIC INTEREST GROUPS   Public interest groups are those that claim to represent the broad interests of society as a whole. Despite their label, public interest groups are not led by people elected by the public at

TABLE 9-1   ADVANTAGES AND DISADVANTAGES HELD
BY ECONOMIC AND CITIZENS' GROUPS
Compared with economic groups, citizens' groups have
fewer advantages and more disadvantages.

Economic Groups	*Citizens' Groups*
Advantages Economic activity provides the organization with resources necessary for political action. Individuals are encouraged to join the group because of economic benefits they individually receive (e.g., wages). *Disadvantages* Persons within the group may not support leaders' political efforts because they did not join the group for political reasons.	*Advantages* Members are likely to support leaders' political efforts because they joined the group in order to influence policy. *Disadvantages* The group has to raise funds, especially for its political activities. Potential members may choose not to join the group because they get collective benefits even if they do not join (the free-rider problem).

large, and the issues they target are ones of their own choosing, not the public's. Moreover, people often disagree over questions of what constitutes "the public interest."

Nevertheless, there is a basis for distinguishing the so-called public interest groups from economic groups: the latter seek direct material benefits for their members, while the former seek benefits that are less tangible and more broadly shared. For example, the National Association of Manufacturers, an economic group, seeks policies favorable to large corporations, while the League of Women Voters, a public interest group, seeks policies—such as simplified voter registration—that can benefit the public in general.

The League of Women Voters has existed for many decades, but more than half of the currently active public interest groups have been formed since 1960. One of the more visible of these newer organizations is Common Cause, which has more than two hundred thousand members; Common Cause describes itself as "a national citizens' lobby" and concentrates on political reform in such areas as campaign finance.

SINGLE-ISSUE GROUPS   A single-issue group is organized to influence policy in just one area. Notable current examples are the National Rifle Association (NRA) and the various right-to-life and pro-choice groups that have formed around the issue of abortion. The number of single-issue groups has risen sharply in the past two decades, and they now lobby on almost every conceivable issue, from nuclear arms to day care centers to drug abuse.

Environmental groups are sometimes classified as public interest groups, but they may also be considered single-issue organizations in that most of them seek to influence public policy in a specific area, such as pollution reduction, wilderness preservation, or wildlife protection. The Sierra Club is one of the oldest of such groups; it was formed in the 1890s to promote the preservation of scenic areas. Between 1960 and 1970, membership in environmental groups tripled in response to increased public concern about the quality of the environment.[13] Since then, membership in environmental groups has continued to grow. Greenpeace USA, founded in 1978, has rapidly become one of the largest and best-known environmental groups in the country.

IDEOLOGICAL GROUPS   Single-issue groups have a narrowly focused policy agenda. Other groups take a broader view, usually from the perspective of a general philosophical or moral stance. These groups have been labeled ideological groups. An example is the Christian Coalition, which was organized to restore "Christian values" to American life and politics.[14] Americans for Democratic Action (ADA) is another example; the ADA supports liberal positions on a wide range of social, economic, and foreign policy issues. Ideological groups on both the left and the right have increased substantially in numbers since the 1960s.

Groups such as the National Organization for Women (NOW) and the National Association for the Advancement of Colored People (NAACP) can also be classified as ideological groups. Their aim is to promote the general interests of a particular demographic segment of society.

A Special Category of Interest Group: Governments

While the vast majority of organized interests in the United States represents private concerns, a growing number of interest groups represents governments, both foreign and subnational.

The U.S. government's policies affect the economic development, political stability, and security of nations throughout the world. Arms sales, foreign aid, immigration, and trade practices have a great impact on foreign

Environmental activists protest against automobile and
truck emissions, which are a leading cause of air pollution.
Although environmental groups have been quite
successful in attracting public support, they still confront
the so-called free-rider problem: the fact that people will
gain the benefit of a group's effort even if they
do not contribute to it.

nations. For this reason, most foreign nations supplement the political efforts made through their embassies with the services of paid lobbying
agents in Washington.[15] Foreign governments are prohibited, however,
from contributing to U.S. election campaigns.

States, cities, and other governmental units within the United States
also lobby heavily in Washington. While most major cities across the
United States and two-thirds of the states have their own Washington lobbyists, these entities also work together through such groups as the Council of State Governments, the National Governors Conference, the
National Association of Counties, the National League of Cities, and the
U.S. Conference of Mayors.

INSIDE LOBBYING: SEEKING INFLUENCE THROUGH OFFICIAL CONTACTS

Modern government provides a supportive environment in which interest
groups can seek to achieve favorite policies. First, government today is involved in so many issue areas—business regulation, income maintenance,
urban renewal, cancer research, and energy development, to name only a
few—that hardly any interest in society could fail to benefit significantly
from having influence over federal policies.

Second, modern government is oriented toward action. Officials are inclined to look for policy solutions to problems rather than to let problems linger. For example, when forest fires raged throughout the West in 2000, Washington immediately granted assistance and loans to local governments and residents that had incurred property losses and cleanup costs.

Groups seek support through **lobbying,** a term that refers broadly to efforts of groups to influence public policy through contact with public officials. According to Norman Ornstein and Shirley Elder, the two main lobbying strategies may be labeled as "inside lobbying" and "outside lobbying."[16] Each strategy involves communication between public officials and group lobbyists, but the strategies differ in what is communicated, who does the communicating, and who receives the communication.

Inside lobbying is based on group efforts to develop and maintain close ("inside") contacts with policymakers. Inside lobbying is designed to give a group direct access to officials in order to influence their decisions. Unless a group can get the attention of officials, it has little chance of affecting their decisions. Access is not the same as influence, which is the capacity to affect policy decisions. But access is a critical first step in the influence process.[17]

Inside lobbying once depended significantly on tangible inducements, sometimes including indirect or even outright bribes. This type of lobbying survives, but modern lobbying generally involves more subtle and sophisticated methods than providing money or personal favors to officials. It focuses on supplying officials with information and indications of group strength that will persuade them to adopt the group's perspective.[18]

For the most part, inside lobbying is directed at policymakers who are inclined to support the group rather than those who have opposed it in the past. This tendency reflects both the difficulty of persuading opponents to change long-held views and the advantage of having trusted allies who will actively support the group's position in policy deliberations. Thus, union lobbyists work mainly with pro-labor officials, just as corporate lobbyists work mainly with policymakers who support business interests.

Money is the essential ingredient of inside lobbying efforts. The American Petroleum Institute, for example, with its abundant financial resources, can afford a downtown Washington office staffed by lobbyists, petroleum experts, and public relations specialists who help the oil companies to maintain access to and influence with legislative and executive leaders.[19] Many groups spend $1 million or more annually on lobbying. Other groups survive with much less, but it is hard to run an effective lobbying effort on less than $100,000 a year. Given the costs of maintaining a Washington lobby, the domination by corporations and trade associations is understandable. They have the money to retain high-priced lobbyists, while many other interests do not.

The targets of inside lobbying are officials of all branches—the legislative, executive, and judicial.

Lobbying Congress

The benefits of a close relationship with members of Congress are substantial. With support in Congress, a group can obtain the legislative help it needs to achieve its policy goals. By the same token, members of Congress also gain from working closely with lobbyists. The volume of legislation facing Congress is enormous, and members rely on trusted lobbyists to identify bills that deserve their attention and support. Lobbyists also provide research reports, polling data, and strategic policy advice. When Republican lawmakers took control of Congress in 1995, they invited corporate lobbyists to participate directly in drafting legislation affecting business. Congressional Democrats complained loudly, but Republicans said they were merely getting help from those who best understood business's needs.

Lobbyists' effectiveness with members of Congress depends in part on their reputation for fair play. Congressional action ordinarily requires compromise among contending interests, and a group that is adamant in its demands—"my way or no way"—is likely to end up with nothing. Lobbyists are also expected to play it straight. Said one congressman: "If any [lobbyist] gives me false or misleading information, that's it—I'll never see him again."[20] Arm-twisting is another unacceptable practice. During the debate over the North American Free Trade Agreement (NAFTA) in 1993, the AFL-CIO threatened retaliation against congressional Democrats who supported the legislation. The backlash from these Democrats was so intense that the union backed down on its threat. The safe lobbying strategy is the aboveboard approach: provide information, rely on long-time allies among members of Congress, and push steadily but not too aggressively for legislative goals.

Lobbying Executive Agencies

As the scope of the federal government has expanded, lobbying of the executive branch has grown in importance. Bureaucrats make key administrative decisions and develop policy initiatives that the legislative branch later enacts into law. By working closely with government agencies, groups can influence policy decisions at the implementation and initiation stages. In return, groups assist government agencies by providing information and lending support when their programs are reviewed by Congress and the president.[21]

Nowhere is the link between groups and the bureaucracy more evident than in the regulatory agencies that oversee the nation's business sectors. For example, the Federal Communications Commission (FCC), which regulates the nation's broadcasters, uses information provided by broadcast organizations to decide many of the policies governing their activities. The FCC is sometimes cited as an example of agency "capture." The capture theory suggests that regulatory agencies pass through a series of phases that constitute a "life cycle." Early in an agency's existence, it regulates an industry on the public's behalf, but as the agency matures, its vigor declines until at best it protects the status quo and at worst it falls captive to the very industry it is supposed to regulate.[22] In the 1950s, the commercial networks successfully lobbied the FCC in a campaign against the establishment of a strong public sector television system. For example, public stations were assigned UHF frequencies, while commercial stations held the more powerful VHF frequencies, which were also the only ones that most television sets of the 1950s were programmed to receive. Without the support of a large audience, public television was in a weak position to request additional funding from Congress. Without more funds, it had to struggle to develop the type of programming that would attract a larger audience. The consequences of this vicious circle linger today. Compared with Europe, where public broadcasting was established early and on a solid footing, the United States has a very weak system.

Research has shown that the capture theory describes only some agencies—and then only some of the time.[23] Agencies selectively cooperate with or oppose interest groups, depending on which strategy better suits agency purposes.[24] Agency officials are aware that they can lose support in Congress, which controls agency funding and program authorization, if they show too much favoritism toward an interest group.

Although instances of favoritism occur, the U.S. bureaucracy ranks high in comparison with other national bureaucracies in terms of its efficiency and honesty.[25] Its dealings with lobbying groups are important to effective administration, which includes an understanding of the impact of programs on affected interests. From the viewpoint of the interest group, of course, the bureaucracy's need for information is a lobbying opportunity.

Lobbying the Courts

Recent rulings by the courts in areas such as education and civil rights have made interest groups recognize that the judiciary, too, can help them reach their goals.[26] Interest groups have several judicial lobbying options, including efforts to influence the selection of federal judges. Right-to-life groups pressured the Reagan administration to make opposition to abortion a prerequisite for nomination to the federal bench. When Bill Clinton took office, pro-choice groups pressured his administration to select nominees who would support freedom of choice on abortion.

Groups typically try to influence public policy through the courts by filing lawsuits. For some organizations, such as the National Association for the Advancement of Colored People (NAACP) and the American Civil Liberties Union (ACLU), legal action is the primary means of lobbying government. The NAACP has emphasized legal action since its founding in 1909 because it recognizes that minorities often lack influence with elected officials. The NAACP financed the 1954 *Brown* case, in which the Supreme Court declared that racial segregation of public schools is unconstitutional. Had the NAACP tried to achieve the same result by lobbying state legislators in the South, it almost certainly would have failed.

As interest groups increasingly resort to legal action, they often find themselves facing one another in court. Such environmental litigation groups as the Sierra Club Legal Defense Club, the Environmental Defense Fund, and the Natural Resources Defense Council have frequently sued oil, timber, and mining corporations.

Webs of Influence: Groups in the Policy Process

Lobbying efforts provide an incomplete picture of how groups obtain influence. It is also necessary to consider two policy processes, iron triangles and issue networks, in which many groups are enmeshed.

IRON TRIANGLES   An **iron triangle** consists of a small and informal but relatively stable set of bureaucrats, legislators, and lobbyists who seek to develop policies beneficial to a particular interest.[27] The three "corners" of one such triangle are the Department of Veterans Affairs (bureaucrats), the veterans' affairs committees of Congress (legislators), and veterans' groups such as the American Legion and the Veterans of Foreign Wars (lobbyists), which together determine many of the policies affecting veterans. Of course, the support of others, including the president and a majority in

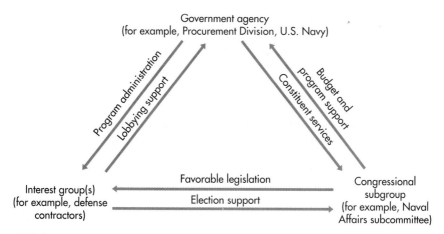

FIGURE 9-1 HOW AN IRON TRIANGLE BENEFITS ITS PARTICIPANTS

An iron triangle works to the advantage of each of its participants: an interest group, a congressional subgroup, and a government agency.

Congress, is needed to enact new programs. However, they often defer to the views voiced by the veterans' triangle, whose members are intimately familiar with the policy needs of veterans.

A group in an iron triangle has an inside track to those legislators and bureaucrats who are in the strongest position to promote its cause. And because it can offer something of value to each of them in return, the relationship tends to be ironclad. The group provides lobbying support for the agency's programs and gives campaign contributions to its congressional allies. The American Dairy Association, for example, contributes hundreds of thousands of dollars each election year to the campaigns of members of the House and Senate agriculture committees. Figure 9-1 summarizes the benefits that flow to each member of an iron triangle.

ISSUE NETWORKS Iron triangles represent the pattern of influence only in certain policy areas and are less dominant than in the past. A more common pattern of influence today is the **issue network,** which is an informal grouping of officials, lobbyists, and policy specialists (the "network") who are brought together temporarily by their shared interest and expertise in a particular policy area (the "issue").

Issue networks are a result of the increasing complexity and interconnectedness of policy problems. The complexity of modern issues often makes it essential that a participant have specialized knowledge of the issue

The policy issues surrounding the technological revolution are extraordinarily complex, and issue networks tend to form when policy issues of this type arise.

at hand in order to join in the debate. Thus, unlike iron triangles, where one's position is everything, an issue network is built around specialized interests and information. On any given issue, the participants might come from a variety of executive agencies, congressional committees, interest groups, and institutions, such as universities or "think tanks." And, compared to iron triangles, issue networks are less stable and less clearly defined. As the issue develops, new participants may join the debate and old ones drop out. Once the issue is resolved, the network disbands.[28]

An example of an issue network is the set of participants who would come together over the issue of whether a large tract of old forest should be opened to logging. A few decades ago, that issue would have been settled in an iron triangle consisting of the timber companies, the U.S. Forest Service, and some members of the House and Senate agriculture committees. But as forest lands have diminished and environmental concerns have grown, such issues can no longer be contained within the cozy confines of an iron triangle. Today, an issue network would form that included logging interests, the U.S. Forest Service, House and Senate agriculture committee members, research scientists, and representatives of environmental groups, the housing industry, and animal-rights groups. Unlike the old iron triangle, which was confined to like-minded interests, this issue network would include opposing interests (for example, the loggers and the environmentalists). And unlike an iron triangle, the issue network would dissolve once the issue was resolved; after it was settled, the separate parties would go their separate ways.

Issue networks, then, differ substantially from iron triangles. In an iron triangle, it is a shared interest that brings the participants together in a stable, long-lasting, and mutually beneficial relationship. In an issue network, it is an immediate issue that brings the participants together in a temporary network that is based on their ability to address the issue in a sophisticated way and where they play out their separate interests before disbanding once the issue is settled. Iron triangles and issue networks, however, do have one thing in common. They are arenas in which organized interests operate. The interests of the general public may be taken into account in these webs of influence, but its direct role is ordinarily a small one.

OUTSIDE LOBBYING: SEEKING INFLUENCE THROUGH PUBLIC PRESSURE

Although an interest group may rely solely on Washington lobbying, this approach is not likely to be successful unless it can demonstrate that its concerns reflect those of a vital constituency. Accordingly, groups make use of constituency connections when it is advantageous to do so. They engage in **outside lobbying,** which involves bringing public ("outside") pressure to bear on policymakers.[29] The "outside" approach typically takes the form of either *constituency advocacy* or *electoral action* (see Table 9-2).

Constituency Advocacy: Grass-roots Lobbying

Some groups depend heavily on **grass-roots lobbying**—that is, pressure designed to convince government officials that a group's policy position has broad public support. To mobilize constituents, groups can mount advertising and public relations campaigns through the media. They can also encourage their members to write or call their elected representatives, or even see their representatives personally.

No group illustrates this better than the American Association of Retired Persons (AARP). With more than thirty million members and a staff of 1,600 employees, AARP has been a powerful lobby on issues affecting the elderly. Pressure from the AARP is a major reason that social security and Medicare are politically explosive issues whenever proposals to reduce the federal budget are discussed. AARP members are so responsive to policies affecting them that they generate more mail to Congress than any other group.[30]

TABLE 9-2   TACTICS USED IN INSIDE AND OUTSIDE LOBBYING STRATEGIES

Inside lobbying and outside lobbying are based on different tactics.

Inside Lobbying	Outside Lobbying
Developing contacts with legislators and executives	Encouraging group members to write or phone their representatives in Congress
Providing information and policy proposals to key officials	Seeking favorable coverage by news media
Forming coalitions with other groups	Encouraging members to support particular candidates in elections
	Targeting group resources on key election races
	Making PAC contributions to candidates

As with other forms of lobbying, the precise impact of grass-roots campaigns is usually difficult to assess. Some members of Congress downplay its influence, but all congressional offices monitor letters and phone calls from constituents as a way of tracking their views. Most members receive hundreds of letters and phone calls each week from constituents, not counting fax messages, computer-generated mail, and organized grassroots postcard campaigns.

Electoral Action: Votes and PAC Money

"Reward your friends and punish your enemies" is a political adage that loosely describes how interest groups view election campaigns. As part of an "outside" strategy, organized groups work to elect their supporters and defeat their opponents. The possibility of electoral opposition from a powerful group can keep an officeholder from openly obstructing its goals. For example, opposition from the three-million-member National Rifle Association (NRA) is a major reason the United States has lagged behind other Western societies in its handgun control laws, although polls show that most Americans favor such laws.

The principal way in which interest groups try to gain influence through elections is by contributing money to candidates' campaigns. As one lobbyist said, "Talking to politicians is fine, but with a little money they hear you better."[31] Money does not literally "buy" votes in Congress, but it does buy access. Members of Congress listen to the groups that fund their campaigns.

The vehicle for group contributions is the **political action committee (PAC)**.[32] A group cannot give organizational funds (such as corporate profits or union dues) to candidates; but through its PAC, a group can raise money for election campaigns by soliciting voluntary contributions from members or employees. A PAC is legally limited in the amount it can contribute to the campaign of a candidate for federal office. As of 2000, the ceiling was $10,000 per candidate—$5,000 in the primary campaign and $5,000 in the general election campaign; there was no legal limit on the number of candidates a PAC could support. These financial limits do not apply to candidates for state and local office. Their campaigns are regulated by state laws, and many states allow PACs to make unlimited campaign contributions (see box: States in the Nation).

PACs mushroomed in the 1970s as a result of favorable changes in campaign finance laws. There are now roughly four thousand PACs, and PAC contributions account for roughly a third of total contributions to congressional campaigns. Because PAC money can be raised earlier and more quickly than money from individual contributors, PACs have become a critical factor in getting congressional campaigns off the ground. Their role is less significant in presidential campaigns, which are larger in scale and publicly funded in part and therefore less dependent on PAC contributions.

PACs target most of their support to congressional incumbents. PACs are well aware of the fact that incumbents are likely to win and thus to remain in a position to make policy. One PAC director, expressing a common view, said, "We always stick with the incumbent when we agree with them both."[33] In House and Senate elections, PACs typically contribute more than five times as much money to incumbents as to their challengers (see Chapter 11).

The tendency of PACs to back incumbents has to some extent blurred longstanding partisan divisions in campaign funding. Business interests are the most pragmatic. Although they generally favor Republican candidates and strongly supported them in 1994 when it became clear the GOP would sweep the congressional elections, business groups are reluctant to anger Democratic incumbents. The result is that Democratic incumbents, particularly in House races, have received substantial support over the years from

★ STATES IN THE NATION ★

Limits on PAC Contributions in State Elections

Elections for state office are regulated by the states, which in some cases limit how much a PAC can contribute to a candidate. Of the states that limit contributions, only New York and Nevada allow contributions in excess of $10,000.

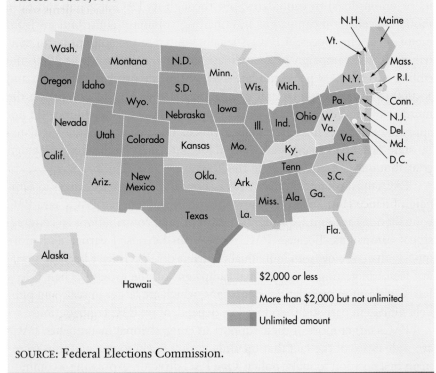

$2,000 or less

More than $2,000 but not unlimited

Unlimited amount

SOURCE: Federal Elections Commission.

business-related PACs.[34] Other PACs, especially those organized to promote a particular public policy or ideology, are less pragmatic. The Christian Moral Government Fund, for example, backs only candidates who take conservative stands on issues such as school prayer and abortion.

More than 40 percent of all PACs are associated with corporations (see Figure 9-2). Examples include the Ford Motor Company Civic Action Fund, the Sun Oil Company Political Action Committee (Sunpac), and the Coca-Cola PAC. The next largest group of PACs consists of those linked to citizens' groups (that is, public interest, single-issue, and ideological groups), such as the liberal People for the American Way and the conservative NCPAC (National Conservative Political Action Committee). Ranking third are PACs tied to trade and professional associations, such as AMPAC (American Medical Association) and R-PAC (National Association of Realtors). Labor unions were once the major source of group contributions, but they now rank fourth.

Among the largest PAC contributors in recent elections have been tobacco firms. As lawsuits against the industry mounted, tobacco firms sought a congressional settlement that would grant them immunity from class-action suits and protection against punitive damages. The industry was willing to pay a high price for a settlement—$300–500 billion spread over twenty-five years—in return for legal immunity. But many in Congress opposed the grant, at least without legislative provisions that would have the effect of sharply reducing smoking, particularly among the young. In its efforts to gain a favorable settlement, the tobacco industry in the 1995–1998 period spent more than $50 million on congressional lobbying and gave more than $12 million in PAC and soft-money contributions to congressional candidates and the national political parties. Its lobbying team included Haley Barbour, former chair of the Republican National Committee, and Howard Baker, a retired lawmaker who was Senate majority leader in the 1980s.[35]

Advocates of PACs claim that groups have a right to be heard, which includes the right to express themselves with money. Advocates also say that a campaign finance system based on pooled contributions by individuals is superior to one in which candidates rely on a few wealthy donors.[36]

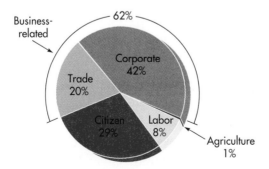

FIGURE 9-2 PERCENTAGE OF PACS BY CATEGORY
Most PACs represent business; corporate and trade association PACs make up 62 percent of the total. Source: Federal Election Commission figures, 2000.

Critics argue, however, that PACs give interest groups altogether too much influence over public officials.[37] The opposition to PACs has increased in the last few years, as citizens have come to associate the influence of interest groups with what they see as costly federal programs. Although members of Congress deny that they are unduly influenced by PAC contributions, there has been a growing sentiment within Congress to place some restrictions on PACs. Agreement on the changes, however, has been difficult to achieve because of differences between Democrats and Republicans in the way they would reform the process, and also because some incumbents are unwilling to support any change that would significantly alter the advantage they have under the present system.

THE GROUP SYSTEM: INDISPENSABLE BUT BIASED

As we noted in the introduction to this chapter, pluralist theory holds that organized groups provide for the representation of society's many and diverse interests. On one level, this claim is beyond dispute. Without groups to carry the message, most of society's interests would find it difficult to gain government's attention and support. Yet the issue of representation is also a question of whether all interests in society have a fair chance to succeed, and here the pluralist argument is less compelling.

The Contribution of Groups to Self-Government: Pluralism

Group activity is an essential part of self-government. A major obstacle to popular sovereignty is the many difficulties that public officials encounter in trying to discover what the people want from government. To determine their wishes, lawmakers consult public opinion polls, meet with constituents, and assess the meaning of recent elections. Organized groups are an additional means of determining popular sentiment, as they provide policymakers with a better picture of the policy concerns of various interests in society.[38] On any given issue, the policy positions that are likely to be expressed most clearly and intensely are those held by organized interests.

Moreover, government does not exist simply to serve majority interests. The fact that most people are not retirees or labor union members or farmers or college students or Hispanics does not mean that the special needs and concerns of such "minorities" are undeserving of attention. And what better instrument exists for promoting the interests of such "minorities" than organizations formed around them? Groups are not antithetical to the democratic process: they are basic to it.

Some pluralists even question whether such terms as "the common good" and "the collective interest" are very useful. If people disagree on society's goals and priorities, as they always do, how can it be said that people have a "common" or "collective" concern? As an alternative, pluralist theory would substitute the sum of people's varied (that is, plural) interests as a rough approximation of society's collective interest. The logic of this proposition is that because society has so many interests, the common good is ultimately served by a process that enables a great many interests to gain favorable policies. Thus, if manufacturing interests prevail on one issue, environmentalists on another, farmers on a third, minorities on a fourth, and so on until a wide range of particular interests is served, the collective interest of society will have been promoted.[39]

Finally, interest groups often take up issues that are neglected by the party system. Party leaders typically shy from issues, such as affirmative action and abortion, on which the party's voters disagree. Such issues would get less notice if not for the groups that promote them. And when groups succeed in drawing attention to these issues, the parties are nearly compelled also to address them. In this sense, as the political scientist Jack L. Walker, Jr., noted, the party and group systems "are complementary and together constitute a much more responsive and adaptive system than either would be if they somehow operated on their own."[40]

Flaws in Pluralism: Interest-Group Liberalism and Economic Bias

Although pluralist theory offers some compelling arguments, it also has questionable aspects. In a direct attack on pluralism, Theodore Lowi argues that there is no concept of society's collective interest in a system that allows special interests to determine for themselves which policy benefits they receive, regardless of how many interests are served.[41] When each group makes its own choice, the basis of decision in each case is not majority (collective) rule but minority (special-interest) rule.

It is seldom safe to assume that what a popular majority favors is what a special-interest group wants. Consider the case of the federal law that required auto dealers to list the known defects of used cars on window stickers. The law was repealed after an extensive lobbying campaign financed by contributions of more than $1 million by the National Association of Automobile Dealers to the reelection campaigns of nearly two hundred members of the U.S. House of Representatives.[42] Although an overwhelming majority of the general public would surely have favored retention of the law, the car dealers' view prevailed.

Lowi uses the term **interest-group liberalism** to describe the tendency of officials to support the policy demands of the interest group or groups that have a special stake in a policy. Interest-group liberalism constitutes a partial abdication by government of its authority over policy. In practical terms, it is the group, as much as the government, that decides policy. The adverse effects include a weakening of majoritarian institutions and an inefficient use of society's resources: groups get what they want, whether or not their priorities match those of society as a whole.

Another flaw in the pluralist argument resides in its claim that the group system is representative. Pluralists recognize that better-organized interests have more influence, but argue that the group process is relatively open and that few interests are at a serious disadvantage. These claims contain an element of truth but are far from the complete truth.

Sometimes the interests of a group clearly diverge from majority opinion, as when the National Association of Auto Dealers lobbied successfully against legislation that would have required automobile dealers to inform customers about any defects in used cars.

As we have seen, organization is a political resource that is distributed unequally across society. Economic interests, particularly corporations, are the most highly organized, and some analysts argue that group politics works almost entirely to the advantage of business.[43] This generalization is less valid today. In fact, many of the public interest groups formed in the past three decades were created to check and balance the influence of existing groups, particularly corporate lobbies.[44]

Big government has also brought the group political system into closer balance. Groups form not only to influence policy but also in response to policy. When new programs were created in the 1960s for the benefit of less advantaged interests in society, these interests mobilized to protect their newly acquired benefits. The National Welfare Rights Organization was formed during the 1960s after new welfare programs were established.[45] Many of the newer interest groups have had a significant impact in areas such as civil rights, the environment, social welfare programs for the elderly and the poor, public morality, national security, and business regulation. Moreover, policy today is less often decided by the actions of one or a few groups. The group system is thus not closed and rigid; it is open to new interests and new patterns of influence.

Nevertheless, interests differ significantly in their level of organization. Well over half of all lobbying groups in Washington are still business-related. The interest-group system is biased toward America's economically oriented groups, particularly its corporations.

The group system is also slanted toward upper-middle-class interests.[46] Studies indicate that individuals of higher socioeconomic status are disproportionately represented among group members and even more so among group leaders. These tendencies are predictable. Educated and affluent Americans have the skills and money that give organizational form to special-interest politics. Less advantaged Americans lack the money, information, contacts, and communication skills to participate even when they desire to do so. The poor, minorities, women, and the young are greatly underrepresented in the group politics system. A lack of organization does not ensure an interest's failure, just as the existence of organization does not guarantee success. However, organized interests are obviously in a better position to make their views known.

The business and class bias of the group system is especially significant because the most highly organized interests are, in a sense, those least in need of political clout. Corporations and affluent citizens already benefit from the distribution of society's material resources.

A Madisonian Dilemma

James Madison recognized the dilemma inherent in group activity. Although he worried that government would fall under the control of a dominant interest, whether of the majority or of the minority, he realized that a free society is obliged to permit the advocacy of self-interest. Unless people can promote the separate opinions that stem from differences in their talents, needs, values, and possessions, they do not have liberty.

Ironically, Madison's constitutional solution to the problem of factions has become part of the problem. The American system of checks and balances, with a separation of powers at its core, was designed primarily to prevent a majority faction from trampling on the interests of others. Indeed, throughout the nation's history, majorities have been frustrated in their efforts to gain full power by America's elaborate system of divided government.

This same system, however, makes it relatively easy for minority factions—or, as they are called today, special-interest groups—to protect the government benefits they receive. Benefits are hard to eliminate, since concerted action by the executive and both houses of Congress is usually required. If a group has strong support in even a single institution, it can usually fend off attempts to terminate its benefits. This support is ordinarily easy to acquire, since the group can provide resources—money or votes—in return. Jonathan Rauch uses the term "demosclerosis" to describe the debilitating effect on government: its resources are increasingly absorbed by entrenched interests and it consequently undergoes a progressive loss in its ability to respond to new needs. Like the arteriosclerosis that slowly deprives the human body of the oxygen-laden blood it needs to survive, demosclerosis slowly robs government of its capacity to respond.[47] Chapters 11 and 13 will discuss further the issue of interest-group power.

SUMMARY

A political interest group is a set of individuals organized to promote a shared political concern. Most interest groups owe their existence to factors other than politics. They form for economic reasons, such as the pursuit of profit, and maintain themselves by making profits (in the case of corporations) or by providing their members with private goods, such as jobs and wages. Such interest groups include corporations, trade associations, labor unions, farm organizations, and professional associations. Collectively, economic groups are by far the largest set of organized interests. The group system tends to favor interests that are already economically and socially advantaged.

Citizens' groups do not have the same organizational advantages as economic groups. They depend on voluntary contributions from potential members who may lack interest and resources, or who recognize that they will get the collective good from a group's activity even if they do not participate (the free-rider problem). These citizens' groups include public interest, single-issue, and ideological groups. Their numbers have increased dramatically since the 1960s despite their organizational problems.

Organized interests seek influence largely by lobbying public officials and contributing to election campaigns. Using an "inside strategy," lobbyists develop direct contacts with legislators, government bureaucrats, and members of the judiciary in order to persuade them to accept their group's perspective on policy. Groups also use an "outside strategy," seeking to mobilize public support for their goals. This strategy relies in part on grassroots lobbying—encouraging group members and the public to communicate their policy views to officials. "Outside" lobbying also includes efforts to elect officeholders who will support group aims. Through political action committees (PACs), organized groups now provide nearly a third of all contributions received by congressional candidates.

The policies that emerge from the group system bring benefits to many interests, and in some instances these benefits also serve the general interest. But when groups can essentially dictate policies, the common good is not served. The majority's interest is subordinated to group (minority) interests.

MAJOR CONCEPTS

citizens' (noneconomic) groups

collective (public) goods

economic groups

free-rider problem

grass-roots lobbying

inside lobbying

interest group

interest-group liberalism

iron triangle

issue network

lobbying

material incentive

outside lobbying

political action committee (PAC)

private (individual) goods

purposive incentive

single-issue politics

SUGGESTED READINGS AND WEB SITES

Berry, Jeffrey M. *The New Liberalism: The Rising Power of Citizen Groups.* Washington, D.C.: Brookings Institution Press, 1999. An exploration of the influence that citizen groups exercise.

Browne, William P. *Cultivating Congress: Constituents, Issues, and Interests in Agriculture Policymaking.* Lawrence: University Press of Kansas, 1995. An analysis of the limits of "iron triangles" as a description of congressional policymaking.

Cigler, Allan J., and Burdett A. Loomis. *Interest Group Politics.* 5th ed. Washington, D.C.: Congressional Quarterly Press, 1998. A comprehensive analysis of interest group politics.

Gatz, Thomas L. *Improper Influence: Campaign Finance Law, Political Interest Groups, and the Problem of Equality.* Ann Arbor: University of Michigan Press, 1996. An analysis of how PACs have changed the process of representation through groups.

Herrnson, Paul S., Ronald G. Shaiko, and Clyde Wilcox, eds. *The Interest Group Connection: Electioneering, Lobbying and Policymaking in Washington.* Chatham, N.J.: Chatham House Publishers, 1998. Essays and commentaries on groups and officials and the linkages between them.

Lowi, Theodore J. *The End of Liberalism.* 2d ed. New York: Norton, 1979. A thorough critique of interest groups' influence on American politics.

Olson, Mancur, Jr. *The Logic of Collective Action.* Rev. ed. Cambridge, Mass.: Harvard University Press, 1971. A pioneering analysis of why some interests are more fully and easily organized than others.

http://www.fec.gov/   The Federal Election Commission site; it offers information on elections, voting, campaign finance, parties, and PACs. It also includes a citizens' guide to campaign contributions.

http://www.pirg.org   The Public Interest Research Group (PIRG) site. PIRG has chapters on many college campuses and the site provides state-by-state policy and other information.

http://www.sierraclub.org/   The Sierra Club, one of the oldest environmental protection interest groups, promotes conservation. Its web site provides information on its activities.

http://www.townhall.com/   The web site of the American Conservative Union (ACU) includes policy and political information and has a lively chat room.

READING 9

The Paralyzing Effect of Group Politics

JONATHAN RAUCH

Introduction

In his essay, Jonathan Rauch describes a process that he labels "demosclerosis": the growing inability of government to respond to policy needs because its resources are already consumed by programs that benefit entrenched groups. These groups exploit the U.S. system's division of powers to protect the government programs that benefit them; a moderate level of support within even a single institution will normally enable a group to defeat efforts to trim its benefits. Rauch contends that neither conservatives nor liberals should be happy with this process—conservatives because the effect is excessive government spending, liberals because the government's capacity to respond to emerging needs is reduced.

As the reality of demosclerosis [group-dominated policy] sinks in, it is bound to make many traditional liberals uncomfortable. American liberals tend to believe that government's problem-solving capacity is large and expandable. Programs solve problems; more problems require more programs. Many liberals have long assumed that government can do almost anything it puts its mind to, if only the right people are in charge.

Demosclerosis says otherwise. It posits, instead, a necessary trade-off between what government tries to do and what it *can* do. By creating programs that create lobbies that lock in programs, government can choke itself on its own output. And this problem can't be wished away. Programs, like medicines, can do good things, but if you don't take the inherent side effects into account you can wind up dead. Like a careful doctor meting out drugs carefully, government needs to stay constantly aware of the limits on how much it can do. Too often, liberals have failed to do that.

Some liberals will dismiss demosclerosis as conservative cant: just another attack on government (and on liberals). That would be unfortunate, a counterproductive act of denial. Another, more common, form of denial is "Yes, but never mind." A few weeks before Bill Clinton took office, I met with a Clinton adviser who advocated a fistful of targeted federal investment programs and industrial policies. Demosclerosis implies that it's almost impossible to insulate such programs from interest groups that capture the benefits and then hoard them. How, I asked, would you get around that problem? He said he had no firm answer, instead saying, "We *have* to make this kind of thing work."

That's "Yes, but never mind": "Yes, organized interests take over programs and engrave them in stone, but we'll keep acting as though they didn't." Demosclerosis means that "Yes, but never mind" won't do. It means that liberals who want to start a new program or expand an old one ought, at least, to offer along with it a mechanism to protect it from calcification. I'm not sure that such an insulating mechanism is possible, but it might be. Maybe a program could be designed to end automatically if it didn't achieve specified goals in a specified period. (The problem, of course, would be seeing that the program actually died, given that organizations and political patrons would spring up to protect it.) Or maybe a program could measure its own performance and phase itself out. Given the difficulty, probably impossibility, of stopping lobbies and politicians from defending programs that are dear to them, I'm not hopeful that anyone will soon invest a reliable mechanism to keep programs flexible. But if one can be found, liberals, who care about making government work, are the best people to find it.

Until they do, their hope of using government in ever cleverer ways is fanciful and, ultimately, self-defeating. Visions of sharp-eyed government entrepreneurs making cutting-edge investments, or of agile officials fine-tuning innovative social programs, are mirages. That isn't to say that government needs to be dismantled. It is to say that government's effectiveness is naturally self-limiting, and that those who deny or defy government's natural limits are making its situation worse, not better.

Demosclerosis spells the end, not of liberalism, but of liberalism without limits. If politicians and the public pick their shots carefully, they can solve a handful of problems pretty well. But if they try to solve every problem at once—which is what they have done—they energize every possible lobby and every potential group, thus feeding the very process that destroys government's ability to adapt. My own frustration is that too few liberals are yet ready to understand this. They cling to a kind of unlimited governmentalism which, for example, undertakes to restore rural economies, revitalize inner cities, and shore up suburbs all at once.

In a sense, they're loving government to death, which really means they're loving liberalism to death, because liberalism relies on government to solve problems. When government fails, liberalism fails. And that is the story of the last twenty years.

Conservatives, who dislike government to begin with, will be happier than liberals with the government-limiting implications of demosclerosis. But they won't be all that happy. Demosclerosis, if it goes on unchecked, turns government into more and more of a rambling, ill-adapted shambles which often gets in the way but can't be gotten rid of. From a conservative point of view, demosclerotic government just sits there, like a big boulder in the middle of the road. If it fails to serve a liberal agenda, it is equally likely to block a conservative one. Liberals may not get new poverty programs that work, but conservatives also can't get rid of archaic banking regulations.

Conservatives would thus be foolish to think that demosclerosis is a victory for them. They, too, need to fight it. That means raising taxes and throwing coddled business lobbies out into the cold. It means saying no to financiers and insurance executives and manufacturers and Farm Bureau members and many other subsidized interests who are important parts of the conservative political base—and who don't at all mind subsidies and cozy deals that benefit themselves.

Most of all, it means cutting benefits to (among other people) the broad portion of the American middle class that votes for conservatives, grouses about "big government," and yet reaps a golden harvest of tax breaks and subsidies. The message for those people is: this means you. Government transfer payments are now a sum equivalent to a quarter of all wages and salaries earned by Americans—and that's before counting such massive tax breaks as the deduction for interest on mortgages. "As far as federal expenditures are concerned," writes Herbert Stein, a former chairman of the Council of Economic Advisers, "[the] welfare state for the not-poor is about five times as big as the welfare state for the poor." Tax breaks and regulatory protections are even more heavily skewed toward the not-poor. In 1991, notes former commerce secretary Peter G. Peterson, an average household whose income was over $100,000 collected almost twice as much in government entitlement and tax benefits as did a household earning less than $10,000. (If the government's goal is to equalize incomes, he says, "it would do a better job if it ... simply scattered all the money by airplane over every population center, to be gathered at random by passersby.") No one is off the gravy train—certainly not conservatives.

Conservatives have talked a good game about "limiting spendthrift government," but the Reagan years showed clearly that they are more interested in talk than action. Real countermeasures against demosclerosis imply real attacks on real subsidies defended by real interest groups and enjoyed by real voters. So far, conservatives haven't had the stomach.

Can either side adjust? It's not easy, partly because their ideologies stymie each other. Conservatives hate to say no to their subsidized friends, or yes to tax increases, because they believe that liberals will just take the money and spend it on new benefits for big-city mayors and welfare bureaucrats. Liberals hate to say yes to program reductions because they believe that conservatives will just take the money and spend it on tax cuts for the rich. So neither side gets anywhere. Government stays too big for conservatives and too inflexible for liberals. It neither solves problems nor goes away.

SOURCE: Jonathan Rauch, "The Paralyzing Effect of Group Politics," from *Demosclerosis*. Published by Public Affairs Books. Reprinted with permission of the author.
Jonathan Rauch is a writer and a contributing editor of the National Journal.

CHAPTER TEN

The News Media

> The press in America . . . determines what people will think and talk about—
> an authority that in other nations is reserved for tyrants, priests,
> parties and mandarins.
>
> THEODORE H. WHITE[1]

EARLY ON the morning of April 22, 2000, CNN interrupted its coverage to report a breaking story from Miami. Federal agents had just broken into the home where six-year-old Elian Gonzalez was staying and had taken him to a waiting plane that would fly him to Washington to be reunited with his father. Video pictures of the armed seizure followed almost immediately, and the story was soon playing on nearly every television news program in the country. As the day unfolded, viewers were to see Elian arriving in Washington while crowds of Cuban Americans gathered in Miami to protest the Justice Department's actions. For the next week, Elian's seizure and reactions to it filled the airwaves and front pages.

The seizure was the latest episode in a running news story that had begun months earlier when Elian was rescued at sea after his mother had drowned while trying to escape Cuba by boat. The young boy became the object of a political tug-of-war between Florida's Cuban American community and Cuba's Fidel Castro. Every move and countermove provoked a torrent of news coverage.

Not all developments receive such intensive news coverage. More new immigrants have arrived in the United States in the past two decades than during any comparable period in the nation's history. Their sheer number has strained the capacity of schools and other public organizations. In some communities, trailer houses have been converted into makeshift schoolrooms simply to get a roof over all students' heads. The impact of this great wave of immigration has been enormous and will affect the United States for years to come. Yet this development has only occasionally been mentioned in the news, let alone emblazoned in the headlines month after month.

Federal agents seize Elian Gonzalez from the home of his Miami relatives. The Gonzalez story was one of the most heavily covered news events of recent years.

Although the news has been compared to a mirror held up to society, it is actually a highly selective portrayal of reality. The **news** is mainly an account of overt, obtruding events, particularly those that are *timely* (new or unfolding developments rather than old or static ones), *dramatic* (striking developments rather than commonplace ones), and *compelling* (developments that arouse people's concerns and emotions as opposed to remote ones).[2] These characteristics of the news have a number of origins, not the least of which is that the news is a business. News organizations seek to make a profit, which leads them to prefer news stories that will attract and hold an audience. Thus, Elian Gonzalez became headline news the instant he was plucked from the sea, and he remained newsworthy while the political and legal process surrounding his status unfolded. The larger issue of the influx of immigrants into the United States during the past two decades is not considered particularly newsworthy, because it is a slow and steady process, dramatic only in its long-term implications. The columnist George Will notes that a development requires a defining event before it can become big news.[3] Without such an event, reporters have no peg on which to hang their stories.

News organizations and journalists, of either the print media (newspapers and magazines) or the broadcast media (radio and television), are referred to collectively as the **press** or the **news media.** The press is an increasingly important political actor. New technology, from television to cable to satellites, has dramatically increased the reach and speed of communication. In addition, the press has filled some of the void created by the decline in political parties and other political institutions.

Like political parties and interest groups, the press is a key link between the public and its leaders. On a daily basis, Americans connect to politics more through the news that is produced by the media than through the activities of parties or groups.

This chapter argues, however, that the news media are a very different kind of intermediary than either parties or interest groups, and that problems arise when the press is asked to perform the same functions as these institutions. The chapter begins with a review of the media's historical development and the current tendencies in reporting; it concludes with an analysis of the roles the news media can and cannot perform adequately in the American political system. The main ideas presented in this chapter are the following:

* *The American press was initially tied to the nation's political party system (the partisan press) but gradually developed an independent position (the objective press).*

* *Although the United States has thousands of separate news organizations, they present a common version of the news which reflects journalists' shared view of what the news is.*

* *In fulfilling its responsibility to provide public information, the news media effectively perform three significant roles—those of signaler (the press brings relevant events and problems into public view), common carrier (the press serves as a channel through which political leaders can address the public), and watchdog (the press scrutinizes official behavior for evidence of deceitful, careless, or corrupt acts).*

* *The press cannot do the job of political institutions, even though it increasingly tries to do so.*

THE DEVELOPMENT OF THE NEWS MEDIA: FROM PARTISANSHIP TO OBJECTIVE JOURNALISM

Democracy requires a free flow of information. Communication enables a free people to keep in touch with one another, with their leaders, and with important events.

America's early leaders were quick to see the advantages of newspapers. At Alexander Hamilton's urging, the *Gazette of the United States* was founded by John Fenno to promote the policies of George Washington's administration. Hamilton was secretary of the treasury and supported Fenno's paper by granting it the Treasury Department's printing contracts. Thomas Jefferson, who was secretary of state and Hamilton's adversary, complained that the newspaper's content was "pure Toryism." Jefferson persuaded Philip Freneau to start the *National Gazette* as the opposition Democratic Republican party's publication and supported it by granting Freneau authority to print State Department documents.[4] Early newspapers were printed on hand presses, a process that limited production and kept the cost of each copy beyond the reach of ordinary citizens—most of whom were illiterate anyway. Leading papers such as the *Gazette of the United States* had fewer than 1,500 subscribers and could not have survived without party support. Not surprisingly, the "news" they printed was a form of party propaganda.[5] In this era of the **partisan press**, publishers openly took sides on partisan issues. President James K. Polk once persuaded a leading publisher to fire an editor who had attacked Polk's policies.[6]

From a Partisan Press to an "Objective" One

Technological changes helped bring about the decline of America's partisan press. After the invention of the telegraph in 1837, editors could receive timely information on developments in Washington and the state capital, and they had less reason to fill their pages with partisan harangues.[7] Another major innovation was the high-speed rotary press (invented in 1815), a breakthrough that enabled publishers to print their newspapers rapidly and cheaply and thus to increase their profit potential.[8] Increased circulation and revenues gradually freed newspapers from their dependence on government and parties.

By the late nineteenth century, several American newspapers were printing 100,000 or more copies a day and were getting rich from advertising revenues. The period marked the height in newspapers' power and the nadir in their sense of public responsibility.[9] A new style of reporting—"yellow journalism"—had emerged as a way of boosting circulation.[10] The "yellow" press—so called because some of these newspapers were printed on cheap yellow paper—emphasized "a shrieking, gaudy, sensation-loving, devil-may-care kind of journalism which lured the reader by any possible means."[11] A circulation battle between William Randolph Hearst's *New York Journal* and Joseph Pulitzer's *New York World* is believed to have contributed to the outbreak of the Spanish-American War through sensational (and largely inaccurate) reports about the cruelty of Spanish rule in Cuba. A young Frederic Remington (who later became a noted painter and sculptor), working as a news artist for Hearst, planned to return home because Cuba appeared calm and safe; but Hearst cabled back, "Please remain. You furnish the pictures and I'll furnish the war."[12]

The excesses of yellow journalism led some publishers to consider how the news could be reported more responsibly. One step they took was to separate the newspaper's advertising department from its news department, thus reducing the influence of advertisers on news content. A second development was a new model of reporting called **objective journalism,** which was based on the reporting of "facts" rather than opinions and was "fair" in that it presented both sides of partisan debate.[13]

A chief advocate of this new form of journalism was Adolph Ochs of the *New York Times.* Ochs told his reporters that he "wanted as little partisanship as possible . . . as few judgments as possible."[14] The *Times's* approach to reporting appealed particularly to educated readers, and by the early twentieth century it had already acquired its reputation as the country's best newspaper. Objective reporting was also promoted through newly formed journalism schools. Among the first of these professional schools were those at Columbia University and the University of Missouri. The Columbia School of Journalism opened in 1912 with a grant of $2 million from Pulitzer.

Objective journalism is still a component of news coverage. Although most newspapers have a partisan bias on their editorial pages, nearly all of them accord the Republican and Democratic parties nearly equal treatment on their news pages. From another perspective, however, the influence of objective journalism is waning. Newspapers increasingly rely on an **interpretive style of reporting,** in which the journalist's job is to analyze, evaluate, and explain developments rather than merely report them. As a result, newspaper coverage has become increasingly opinionated. The older form of objective journalism (called **descriptive reporting,** because of its straightforward description of events) required that reporters stick to the "facts." The newer interpretive style allows them to speculate on what the facts mean. As we will see later in the chapter, interpretive reporting has greatly increased journalists' ability to shape the news to fit their own views, including their skeptical opinion of politicians' motives and accomplishments.

The Development of the Broadcast Media

RADIO AND TELEVISION: THE TRULY NATIONAL MEDIA   Until the early twentieth century, the print media were the only form of mass communication. Within a few decades, however, there were hundreds of

★ STATES IN THE NATION ★

In the News, or Out?

A few major media outlets dominate news production in the United States. The stories they carry tend to set the news agenda for other media. *The New York Times* is generally regarded as the most powerful of these agenda setters. Not surprisingly, since it is based in New York City, the *Times* includes a disproportionate amount of coverage of New York and surrounding states, such as New Jersey and Connecticut. But what about other states? How much attention do they receive in the *Times*? The fact is, coverage varies with events of the moment. The news highlights events that are colorful, sensational, or significant. A natural disaster can bring a state into the national media spotlight, but it may fade from view as soon as the crisis has passed. The map indicates the relative frequency with which the states were mentioned in the *Times* during the first month of 2000. It was the period of the first presidential primaries and caucuses, and thus New Hampshire and Iowa were among the most newsworthy states, even though they ordinarily do not get close attention from the national media.

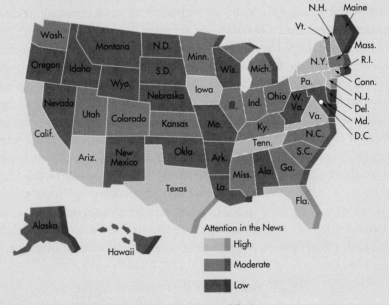

SOURCE: Data compiled by author from Lexis-Nexis.

radio stations throughout the nation. Radio represented a revolutionary change in communication. It allowed political leaders to bypass journalists and communicate directly with the people. Radio was also the first truly *national* mass medium. Newspapers had a local audience, whereas the newly formed radio networks (such as NBC) could reach millions of citizens across the country simultaneously.

Television followed radio, and by the late 1950s more than 90 percent of American homes had a television set. The political potential of television was evident as early as 1952, when seventeen million homes tuned in to the national Republican and Democratic party conventions.[15] However, television newscasts of the 1950s were brief, lasting no more than fifteen minutes, and relied on news gathered by other organizations, particularly the Associated Press and other wire services. In the early 1960s, the three commercial networks—CBS, NBC, and ABC—expanded their evening newscasts to thirty minutes, and their audience ratings increased.[16] Simultaneously, they increased the size and funding of their news divisions, and television soon became the principal news medium of national politics.

Today, television provides a twenty-four-hour forum of political news and information. The advent of the Cable News Network (CNN) and C-SPAN in the late 1970s brought Americans round-the-clock public affairs communication. Television talk shows, such as *Larry King Live*, have broadened the range of choices available to politically interested viewers. A parallel development is the emergence of radio talk shows. Nearly a sixth of the American public claims to listen regularly to a politically oriented radio talk show, most of which are conservative in orientation. The most renowned of the radio talk-show hosts is Rush Limbaugh, who is famous for his blistering attacks on liberal politicians and policies.

Even more so than their newspaper counterparts, television journalists rely on an interpretive style of reporting. The reason is that television journalists use a narrative or storytelling mode in order to appeal to an audience accustomed to entertainment programming. "Facts" alone do not tell a story; they have to be interpreted in a way that makes them into a story. Reuven Frank, a network executive and pioneer in television journalism, once told his correspondents: "Every news story should . . . display the attributes of fiction, of drama. It should have structure and conflict, problem and denouement, rising action and falling action, a beginning, a middle and an end."[17]

GOVERNMENT LICENSING AND REGULATION OF BROADCASTERS

At first the government did not carefully regulate broadcasting. The result was chaos. Nearby stations often used the same or adjacent radio frequencies, interfering with each other's transmissions. Finally, in 1934, Congress passed the Communications Act, which requires that broadcasters be licensed and meet certain performance standards. The Federal Communications Commission (FCC) was established to administer the act and to develop regulations pertaining to such matters as signal strength, advertising rates and access, and political coverage.

The principle of scarcity justifies the licensing and regulation of broadcast media. Because the number of available broadcasting frequencies is limited, those few individuals who are granted broadcasting licenses are expected to serve the public interest in addition to their own. In principle, licensing is a means of controlling broadcasting. If a station fails to comply with federal broadcast regulations, the FCC can withdraw its license. However, the FCC seldom even threatens revocation, for fear of being accused of infringing on freedom of the press. A broadcast station can apply for renewal of its license by postcard and is virtually guaranteed FCC approval, which covers seven years for radio and five for television.

Because broadcast frequencies are a scarce resource, licensees are required by law to be somewhat evenhanded during election campaigns. Section 315 of the Communications Act imposes on broadcasters an "equal-time" restriction, which means that they cannot sell or give airtime to a political candidate without granting equal opportunities to other candidates running for the same office. (Election debates are an exception; broadcasters can sponsor them and limit participation to nominees of the Republican and Democratic parties only.) During campaigns broadcasters are also required to make airtime available for purchase by candidates at the lowest rate charged to commercial advertisers.

The Emergence of the Internet

Although the First Amendment protects each individual's right to press freedom, the right in practice has been reserved for a tiny few. The journalist A. J. Liebling wrote that freedom of the press belongs to those with the money to own one.[18] Even a modest-sized broadcast station or daily newspaper costs millions to buy; the largest media conglomerates are multibillion-dollar enterprises.

Access to the Internet is no substitute for ownership of a major news outlet, but it provides ordinary citizens at least the opportunity to exercise their free-press rights. By creating a web site, the ordinary citizen can post information about public affairs, harangue officials, argue for public policies, and attempt to mobilize the support of others. There is no assurance of a wide audience and, in fact, most citizens do not have a personal web

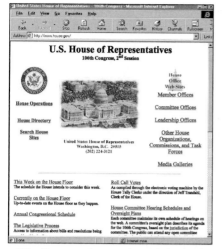

The Internet has weakened the traditional news media's control of the political information that Americans receive. Through the Internet, citizens and political leaders alike can communicate widely without having their messages filtered by the news media. Pictured here are the home pages of the U.S. House and Senate.

site; if they do, it is unlikely to have a large following. But the Internet has reduced the barriers to citizen communication to a level not seen since the colonial days, when citizen-produced pamphlets were the major form of political expression.

The Internet has also somewhat reduced the traditional media's capacity to control the news agenda. Editors and reporters are "gatekeepers" who decide what will make the news and what will not. Although they still play this role, Internet communication has in some instances virtually forced "stories" upon them. The best-known web outlet is likely the "Drudge Report," which was created by Matt Drudge and has become a prime source of information for enterprising reporters. The Monica Lewinsky scandal, for example, surfaced in the "Drudge Report" four days before it appeared in the mainstream press.

FREEDOM AND CONFORMITY IN THE U.S. NEWS MEDIA

Some democracies impose significant legal restraints on the press. The news media in Britain are barred from reporting on anything that the government has labeled an "official secret," and the nation's tough libel laws inhibit the press from publishing unsubstantiated allegations about an individual.

In the United States, as we saw in Chapter 4, the First Amendment gives the press substantial protection. The courts have held that government cannot block publication of a news story unless it can convincingly demonstrate in court that the information would jeopardize national security. U.S. libel laws also strongly protect the press. A public figure who is attacked through the media cannot collect libel damages unless it can be demonstrated that the news organization was false in its accusations and knowingly or recklessly careless in its search for the truth.

Moreover, the U.S. government provides the news media with substantial economic support. Newspapers and magazines have a special postal rate that helps them keep their circulation costs low, and broadcasters pay only a few dollars annually in license fees. Such policies have contributed to the development of a truly enormous news industry in the United States: 1,600 daily newspapers, 8,500 weeklies, 9,500 radio stations, 6 national television news networks, 850 local television stations, and 10,500 cable television systems.[19]

The audience reach of leading news organizations is substantial. Each weekday evening, more than twenty million Americans tune into a network newscast. *Time* and *Newsweek*, and *U.S. News & World Report* magazines each reach several million readers a week. The *New York Times*, the *Wall Street Journal*, *USA Today*, and the *Los Angeles Times* have daily circulations exceeding one million readers. Another three dozen newspapers have circulations in excess of 250,000 readers. The average daily circulation of America's newspapers is roughly fifty million; on Sunday, newspaper circulation jumps to more than sixty million.[20]

In view of the great number and the freedom of news organizations in the United States, it might be expected that Americans would have a lot of choice in the news they receive. However, the opposite is true. Each day, newspapers and broadcast stations from coast to coast tend to highlight the same national news stories and to interpret them in similar ways. Any number of terms—pack journalism, groupthink, media concentration—have been used to describe the fact that news reporting is fairly homogeneous.

The basic reason the news is pretty much the same everywhere is that America's reporters, unlike their counterparts in some European democracies, do not take sides in partisan disputes. They do sometimes differ on which facts, events, and issues are more important than others, but these polite disagreements are a far cry from the disputes and diversity that characterized the nineteenth-century partisan press.

Of course, today's news organizations differ in the way they tell a given story. Broadcast news tends to be, in effect, headline news with pictures. A thirty-minute network news broadcast typically presents a dozen or so stories in the twenty-two minutes allotted to news content (the other eight minutes being devoted to commercials). Newspapers have the space to present news developments in greater depth; some, like the *New York Times* (which labels itself "the newspaper of record"), provide substantial detail. The reporting styles of news organizations also vary. Although most of them present the news in an understated way, others tend toward sensationalism. For example, when Jeffrey Dahmer, a convicted murderer who had cannibalized his victims, was himself murdered in a Wisconsin prison in 1994, the *New York Post* gave its whole front page to the headline: "Death of a Monster." The *New York Times*, in contrast, gave the story a standard-sized front-page headline: "Jeffrey Dahmer, Multiple Killer, Is Bludgeoned to Death in Prison." Such differences in approach, however, do not change the fact that most news organizations tell their audiences the same stories each day.

Domination of News Production

Another reason for the lack of diversity in national news reporting is that a small number of news organizations generate most of it. The quintessential case of concentrated news production is radio, with its "canned" network-provided news; almost no local radio station in the country produces its own national news reports.

The Associated Press (AP) is the major producer of news stories. It has three hundred full-time reporters stationed throughout the country and the world to gather news stories, which are relayed by satellite to subscribing newspapers and broadcast stations. More than 95 percent of the nation's dailies are serviced by AP, and some also subscribe to other wire services, such as Reuters and the New York Times.[21] Smaller dailies lack the resources to gather news outside their own localities and thus depend on wire service reports for most of their national and international coverage.

Television news production is similarly dominated by just a few organizations.[22] Six networks—ABC, CBS, NBC, PBS, Fox, and CNN—generate most of the news coverage of national and international politics. Local stations rely on video transmissions fed to them by these networks.

News Values and Imperatives

Competitive pressures also lead the producers of news to report the same stories. No major news organization wants to miss an important story that the others are reporting.[23] The networks, wire services, and a few elite dailies, including the *New York Times, Washington Post, Wall Street Journal, Los Angeles Times,* and *Chicago Tribune,* establish a national standard of story selection. Whenever one of them highlights an important story, others jump on the bandwagon. The chief trendsetter among news-gathering organizations is the *New York Times,* which has been described as "the bulletin board" for other major newspapers, newsmagazines, and television networks.[24]

The imperatives of the fast pace of daily journalism also tend to make the news homogeneous.[25] Journalists have the task each day of filling a newspaper or broadcast with stories. Their job is to produce an edition every twenty-four hours. Thus editors assign reporters to such beats as the White House and Congress, which can be relied on for a steady supply of news. On these beats the reporters of various news organizations see and hear the same things, exchange views on what is important, and, not surprisingly, produce similar news stories.

Finally, shared professional values guide journalists in their search for news.[26] Reporters are on the lookout for aspects of situations that lend themselves to interesting news stories—novel, colorful, and compelling developments. Long practice at storytelling leads journalists to develop a common understanding of what the news is. After the White House press corps has listened to a presidential speech, for example, nearly all of the journalists in attendance are in agreement on what was most newsworthy about the speech, often only a single statement within it.

"Megamedia": Mergers, Profits, and the News

Over the past two decades and at an accelerating pace, media ownership has become increasingly concentrated. The trend reflects the high profitability of the media business and the economies of scale: the larger the media organization, the more it can leverage advertisers and achieve efficiencies in the production of news and entertainment. The net result has been the emergence of huge media conglomerates. Although The *New York Times* remains a family-controlled paper, nearly all other major news organizations have been absorbed into larger corporate entities. The ABC network and its news division, for example, is part of the Disney corporation, while CNN is part of AOL/Time Warner. The list could be extended, but the point would be the same: U.S. news is largely in the hands of what the political scientist Dean Alger calls the "megamedia."

One issue that surrounds this development is whether it is healthy to a democracy to have concentrated ownership of the means of public communication. Should so few entities control so much of what Americans see and hear through the mass media? Some observers say that the change is not all that significant because there is still competition between news organizations and because there is a degree of independence for news organizations within their corporate structures. Alger is not convinced: "It is . . . vital for democracy to have a truly diverse set of media sources present in the public arena, a variety of alternative information and perspectives representing a real competition of approaches to news definitions and thoughts on the direction in which society should head. The continued advance of megamedia and their increasing domination of the prime mass media spell a profound constriction of that diversity and a severe diminution of the marketplace of ideas, and thus a danger to democracy."[27]

Another issue is the impact of media conglomerates on the quality of news content. As news organizations have become a part of larger corporations, they have increasingly had to adapt to the demands of the economic market. The news organization or division is only one part, and usually a relatively small part, of a very large corporation. A result has been a cutback in news-gathering capacity. ABC, CBS, and NBC News, for example, have closed many of their overseas news bureaus; the assumption is that international news is not of great interest to Americans and, therefore, that its production is not a high priority. News divisions have also been directed to compete more aggressively for audiences, because audience size determines advertising revenues. As a consequence, the news has become increasingly entertainment oriented. Critics say it is "infotainment" rather than real news. A study of network evening newscasts found that, over the past decade, the amount of news time devoted to government, politics, and public affairs has declined significantly, while the amount given to lifestyle issues, celebrities, and human-interest subjects has risen sharply.[28]

Although this programming is popular with television audiences, it has contributed to a growing disenchantment with the news media. The public believes that journalists are now less professional and less moral, that the news is now more biased and less accurate, and that the news media's contribution to a healthy democracy has declined (see Figure 10-1).

THE NEWS MEDIA AS LINK: ROLES THE PRESS CAN AND CANNOT PERFORM

When the objective model of reporting came to dominate American news coverage, the relationship between the press and the public was fundamentally altered. The nineteenth-century partisan press gave its readers overt

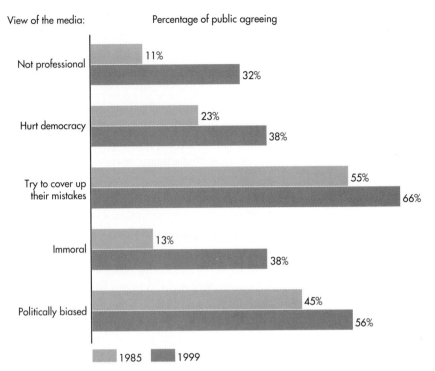

View of the media: Percentage of public agreeing

Not professional — 11% (1985), 32% (1999)

Hurt democracy — 23% (1985), 38% (1999)

Try to cover up their mistakes — 55% (1985), 66% (1999)

Immoral — 13% (1985), 38% (1999)

Politically biased — 45% (1985), 56% (1999)

1985   1999

FIGURE 10-1   THE PUBLIC'S VIEW OF THE "NEW" NEWS
In recent years as news organizations have competed more aggressively to attract an audience, the news has become more sensational, more personal, and more negative. In the process, the public's view of the news has become less favorable. Source: Pew Research Center for the People and the Press, February 25, 1999. Used by permission.

cues as to how to evaluate political issues and leaders. In the presidential election campaign of 1896, the *San Francisco Call* devoted 1,075 column-inches of photographs to the Republican ticket of McKinley-Hobart and only 11 inches to the Democrats, Bryan and Sewell.[29] Many European newspapers still function in this way, guiding their readers by applying partisan or ideological values to current events. The *Daily Telegraph*, for example, is an unofficial but fiercely loyal mouthpiece of Britain's Conservative party (see box: How the United States Compares).

In contrast, U.S. news organizations do not routinely and consistently take sides in partisan conflict. Their main task is to report and analyze events. The media are thus very different from political parties and interest groups, the other major links between the public and its leaders. The media are driven by the search for interesting and revealing stories; parties and interest groups exist to articulate political positions.

HOW THE UNITED STATES COMPARES

Partisan Neutrality as a News Value

In the nineteenth century, the United States had a partisan press. Journalists were partisan actors, and news was a blend of reporting and advocacy. This type of reporting gradually gave way to a model of journalism that emphasizes the "facts" and covers the two parties more or less equally.

European news organizations are less committed to partisan neutrality. Many European newspapers are aligned with specific parties, and although they focus on events, their coverage has a partisan component. In Great Britain, for example, the *Daily Telegraph* often serves as a voice of the Conservative party, while the *Guardian* favors the liberal side. Broadcasters in most European countries are politically neutral by law and practice, but there are exceptions, as in the case of the French and Italian broadcasters.

The difference between the U.S. and the European media is evident in a five-country survey that asked journalists whether they agreed or disagreed with the statement: "Journalists should *not* try to influence the outcome of party conflict."

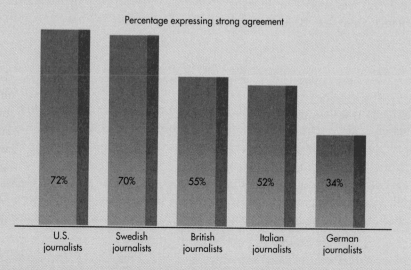

Percentage expressing strong agreement

U.S. journalists	Swedish journalists	British journalists	Italian journalists	German journalists
72%	70%	55%	52%	34%

SOURCE: Thomas E. Patterson, Media and Democracy Project, in progress.

Through their signaler role, the news media alert the public to developments in the nation and the world. Shown here are U.S. journalists taking pictures of a refugee in war-torn Kosovo.

This distinction provides a basis for determining what roles the media can and cannot be expected to perform. The press is capable of fulfilling only those public responsibilities that are compatible with journalistic values: the signaler role, the common-carrier role, and the watchdog role. The media are less successful in their attempts to perform a fourth, politically oriented role: that of public representative.

The Signaler Role

As journalists see it, one of their responsibilities is to play the **signaler role,** alerting the public to important developments as soon as possible after they happen: a state visit to Washington by a foreign leader, a bill that has just been passed by Congress, a change in the nation's unemployment level, a terrorist bombing in a foreign capital.

The signaler role is one that the American media perform relatively well. The press is poised to converge on any fast-breaking major news event anywhere in the nation and nearly anywhere in the world. For instance, as the United States prepared to intervene forcefully in Haiti in 1994, dozens of U.S. journalists went to that trouble-ridden Caribbean nation to report from the scene. The NBC and CBS networks even sent their news anchors, Tom Brokaw and Dan Rather, despite a possible risk to their personal safety.

The media are particularly well suited to signal developments from Washington. More than half of all reported national news emanates from the nation's capital, most of it from the White House and Congress. Altogether, more than ten thousand people in Washington work in the news business. The key players are the leading correspondents of the television networks and major newspapers, the heads of the Washington news bureaus, and a few top editors.[30]

The press, in its capacity as signaler, has the power to focus the public's attention. The term **agenda setting** has been used to describe the media's ability to influence what is on people's minds. By covering the same events, problems, issues, and leaders—simply by giving them space or time in the news—the media place them on the public agenda. The press, as Bernard Cohen notes, "may not be successful much of the time in telling people what to think, but it is stunningly successful in telling them what to think about."[31] This influence is most obvious in such situations as the Kosovo conflict, an event that quickly received widespread attention. When the NATO allies started their air raids on Serbia, the broadcast networks quickly expanded their news programming. News of the war was almost inescapable.

The Common-Carrier Role

Journalists base many of their news stories on the words of public officials. The press thus plays what is labeled a **common-carrier role,** providing a channel through which political leaders can reach the public. The importance of this role to officials and citizens alike is obvious. Citizens cannot very well support or oppose a leader's plans and actions if they do not know about them. And leaders need news coverage if they are to get the public's attention.

Not surprisingly, political leaders make a great effort to get coverage. They hold news conferences, issue press releases, and stage events in an effort to garner the media's attention.[32] Indeed, national news is mainly about the actions of political leaders and institutions, as is reflected in the hundreds of reporters who station themselves regularly at the Capitol and White House.

Officials try to get the most favorable news coverage they can. For example, the White House Press Office and the White House Office of Communication try to shape information in a way favorable to the president. Sometimes they succeed in placing their "spin" (that is, the president's interpretation) on the media's coverage of events.

However, the press today is less deferential to political leaders than in the past. Even though the president and Congress can expect coverage, the press increasingly places its own "spin" on these stories. Because of their increased celebrity status, their heightened skepticism of politicians since Vietnam and Watergate, and the greater latitude afforded them by the interpretive style of reporting, journalists have become accustomed to not only covering what newsmakers say, but having their own say as well.

In fact, the news today is more journalist-centered than it is newsmaker-centered. For every minute that the presidential candidates spoke on the network newscasts during coverage of the 2000 campaign, for example, the journalists who were covering them talked for five minutes.[33] It was once the case that a candidate's "sound bite" (the length of time within a television story that the candidate speaks without interruption) was about forty-five seconds in length on average. In recent campaigns, the average sound bite has been less than ten seconds long, which is barely enough time for the candidate to utter a full sentence.

The Watchdog Role

Traditionally, the American press has accepted responsibility for protecting the public from deceitful, careless, incompetent, and corrupt officials. In this **watchdog role,** the press stands ready to expose any official who violates accepted legal, ethical, and performance standards.

The most notable exercise of the watchdog role in recent decades took place during the Watergate scandal. Bob Woodward and Carl Bernstein of the *Washington Post* spent months uncovering evidence that high-ranking officials in the Nixon White House were lying about their role in the burglary of the Democratic National Committee's headquarters and in the subsequent cover-up. Virtually all of the nation's media picked up on the *Post*'s revelations. Nixon was forced to resign, as was his attorney general, John Mitchell. The Watergate episode is a dramatic reminder that a vigilant press is one of society's best safeguards against abuses of political power.

There is an inherent tension between the watchdog role and the common-carrier role. The watchdog role demands that the journalist maintain a skeptical view of political leaders and keep them at a 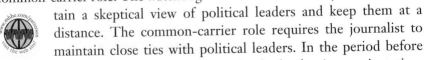 distance. The common-carrier role requires the journalist to maintain close ties with political leaders. In the period before Watergate, the common-carrier role was clearly the dominant orientation. It perhaps still is, but journalists have become increasingly critical of political leaders and institutions.

Some of this criticism revolves around scandals, such as the Iran-Contra affair (President Reagan) and the Whitewater affair, Paula Jones, and Monica Lewinsky allegations (President Clinton). Most of the criticism, however, is leveled at the day-to-day conduct of politics. Journalists are intent on publicizing the missteps of political leaders. Given the enormous size of the U.S. government, there is plenty to criticize if journalists want to focus on it. The media's preference for "bad news" can be seen, for example, in the fact that negative coverage of presidential candidates has risen steadily in recent decades and now exceeds their positive coverage (see Figure 10-2).

"Bad news" characterizes the coverage of Democrats and Republicans alike. Although surveys indicate that most journalists lean toward the Democratic party in their personal beliefs, studies have found partisan bias to be a relatively small factor in political coverage.[34] Other influences, including the norm of objectivity, counterbalance the effect of partisanship on journalists' news decisions. On the other hand, journalists' skeptical view of politicians is not offset by other factors. There is no rule that limits negativity, and thus the real bias of American journalists is a tendency to be critical of nearly everything and everybody.[35] Coverage of the Democratic-controlled Congress of 1993–1994 by the national media was nearly 70 percent negative; when the Congress shifted to Republican hands in 1995–1996, its coverage, too, was nearly 70 percent negative in tone.[36]

Critics argue that the press has gone too far in its search for bad news, claiming that it now faults nearly everything that politicians say and do, thereby undermining the public trust upon which effective leadership is built. Critics also complain that the press no longer has any respect for public officials' private lives—that everything from their bedroom behavior to decades-old "skeletons in the closet" are grist for news stories. Journalists claim that they are merely doing their job—that the public is better served by a highly skeptical and intrusive press than by a compliant one. CNN correspondent Bob Franken said, "We historically are not supposed to be popular, and it's almost our role to be bearer of bad news."[37]

The public is ambivalent about the news media's skepticism. Although most Americans believe that press skepticism is a factor in keeping politicians from abusing public office, most people also say that the press gets in the way of efforts to solve society's problems. The press skepticism is thus seen as both an obstacle to effective governance and a form of protection against wayward politicians. Yet the press may actually be undermining its watchdog role by its zealous pursuit of scandal. When the public is deluged day after day with stories of wrongdoing in high places, its expectations of

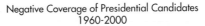

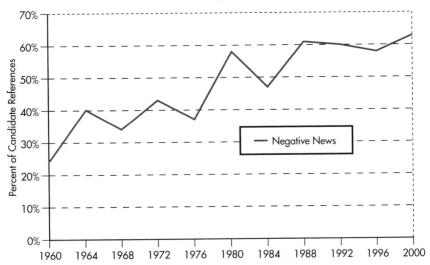

FIGURE 10-2 NEGATIVE COVERAGE OF PRESIDENTIAL CANDIDATES, 1960–2000
In the 1960s, candidates received largely favorable news coverage. Today, their coverage is mostly negative.
Source: Thomas E. Patterson, *Out of Order,* (New York: Vintage, 1994), 20, for 1960–1992; Center for Media and Public Affairs, for 1996, 2000.

public officials decline and its trust in the media's judgment diminishes. The public may then reject the media's outcries, as it did in the case of the Clinton-Lewinsky scandal. The news coverage was so negative that it created a backlash. Clinton's public support rose while the media's declined.

The Public Representative Role

Traditionally, the **public representative role**—that of spokesperson for and advocate of the public—has belonged to political leaders, political institutions, and political organizations. Today, however, many reporters believe they also have a mandate to represent the public. "[Our] chief duty," newscaster Roger Mudd claims, "is to put before the nation its unfinished business."[38]

Although the press has to some degree always acted as a stand-in for the people, the desire of journalists to play the role of public advocate has increased significantly since the 1960s.[39] As journalists' status rose, they became more assertive, a tendency sharpened by the trend toward interpretive reporting. Vietnam and Watergate also contributed to the change; these events convinced many journalists that their judgments were superior to those of political leaders.

Nevertheless, there are at least two basic reasons for concluding that journalists are not nearly so well suited as political leaders to the role of public representative. First, the news media are not subject to the level of public accountability required of a public representative. Political institutions are made responsible to the public by a formal mechanism of accountability: elections. The vote gives officeholders a reason to act in the majority's interest, and it offers citizens an opportunity to boot from office anyone they feel has failed them. Thousands of elected officials have lost their jobs this way. The public has no comparable hold over the press. Journalists are neither chosen by the people nor removable by them. Irate citizens can stop watching a news program or buying a newspaper that angers them, but no major daily newspaper or television station has gone out of business as a result.

A second obstacle to journalists' attempts to play the role of public representative is that representation requires a point of view. Politics is essentially the mobilization of bias—that is, it involves the representation of particular values and interests. Political parties and interest groups, as we saw in Chapters 8 and 9, exist to represent particular interests in society. But what political interests do the media represent? CBS News executive Richard Salant once said that his reporters covered stories "from nobody's point of view."[40] What he was saying in effect was that journalists do not consistently represent the political concerns of any segment of society. They respond to news opportunities, not to political interests. Above all, they prize good stories.

The O. J. Simpson murder trial is a prime example. The former football star's trial received more news coverage in 1994–1995 than any public policy issue, foreign or domestic. Judged by the media's priorities, Simpson's fate was more important than health care, unemployment, Haiti, drug abuse, education, and every other national problem. The Clinton-Lewinsky-Starr saga is another example. In the first month, January 1998, the scandal filled a third of the news time on the network evening newscasts. It had to compete for time with the Winter Olympics, a papal visit to Cuba, the possibility of renewed war with Iraq, and the ravaging effects of the El Niño weather system.[41] Yet it received more coverage than all these developments combined. And it remained the top news story every month thereafter, even in periods when there were no new revelations or when more pressing issues arose, such as a financial crisis in Asia that threatened to weaken the U.S. economy.

Underlying the press's search for the dramatic story is the media's quest for profits. The bottom line, rather than the public interest, increasingly drives news coverage. Audience competition has intensified with the spread of cable television, and the news has become increasingly sensational. "All Monica All the Time" was how some critics described the press's coverage of the Lewinsky scandal. One network, MSNBC, even chose to make the scandal nearly the sole focus of its programming, hoping that higher audience ratings and correspondingly higher advertising revenues would be the result.

The relentless search for attention-getting stories weakens the press's ability to provide citizens a clear understanding of what is broadly at issue in politics. It is a difficult job to formulate society's problems in a way that allows citizens to understand and act upon them. The news media cannot do the job consistently well. The journalist Walter Lippmann put it plainly when he said this:

> The press is no substitute for [political] institutions. It is like the beam of a searchlight that moves restlessly about, bringing one episode and then another out of darkness into vision. Men cannot do the work of the world by this light alone. They cannot govern society by episodes, incidents, and interruptions.[42]

ORGANIZING THE PUBLIC IN THE MEDIA AGE

Lippmann's point was not that news organizations are somehow inferior to political organizations, but that each has a different role and responsibility in society. Democracy cannot operate effectively without a free press that acts effectively in its signaler, common-carrier, and watchdog roles. To keep in touch with one another and with the government, citizens must have access to timely and uncensored news about public affairs. In other words, the media must do their job well if democratic government is to succeed. However, the media cannot also be asked to do the job of political institutions. For reasons already noted, the task is beyond the media's capacity.

As previous chapters have emphasized, the problem of citizen influence is the problem of organizing the public so that people can act together effectively. The news media merely appear to solve this problem. The fact that millions of people each day receive the same news about their government

Presidential politics is a favorite topic of the press. Here, Republican presidential nominee George W. Bush is surrounded by reporters during a 2000 campaign stop.

does not mold them into an organized community. The news creates a pseudo-community: citizens feel they are part of a functioning whole until they try to act upon their news awareness. The futility of media-centered democracy was dramatized in the movie *Network* when its central character, a television anchorman, became enraged at the nation's political leadership and urged his viewers to go to their windows and yell, "I'm mad as hell and I'm not going to take it anymore!" Citizens heeded his instructions, but the main effect was to raise the network's ratings. It was not clear what officials in Washington were expected to do about several million people leaning out their windows and shouting a vague slogan at the top of their lungs. The film vividly illustrated the fact that the news can raise public consciousness as a prelude to action, but the news itself cannot organize the public in any meaningful way. When public opinion on an issue is already formed, the media can serve as a channel for the expression of that opinion. But when society's choices are in their formative stage, the media are not an adequate guide to the actions that should be taken or the priority they should be given.

SUMMARY

In the nation's first century, the press was allied closely with the political parties and helped the parties mobilize public opinion. Gradually the press freed itself from this relationship and developed a form of reporting, known as objective journalism, that emphasizes the fair and accurate reporting of newsworthy developments. The foundation of modern American news rests on the presentation and evaluation of significant events, not on the advocacy of partisan ideas. The nation's news organizations do not differ greatly in their reporting; broadcast stations and newspapers throughout the country emphasize many of the same events, issues, and personalities, following the lead of the major broadcast networks, a few elite newspapers, and the wire services.

The press performs four basic roles in a free society. In their signaler role, journalists communicate information to the public about events and problems that they consider important, relevant, and therefore newsworthy. The press also serves as a common carrier, in that it provides political leaders with a channel for addressing the public. Third, the press acts as a public protector or watchdog, by exposing deceitful, careless, or corrupt officials. The American media can and, to a significant degree, do perform these roles adequately.

The press is less well suited, however, to the other role it plays, that of public representative. This role requires a consistent political viewpoint and public accountability, neither of which the press possesses. The media cannot be a substitute for effective political institutions. The press's strength lies ultimately in its capacity to inform the public, not in its attempts to serve as their representative.

MAJOR CONCEPTS

agenda setting

common-carrier role

descriptive (style of) reporting

interpretive (style of) reporting

news

objective journalism

partisan press

press (news media)

public representative role

signaler role

watchdog role

SUGGESTED READINGS AND WEB SITES

Bagdikian, Ben H. *The Media Monopoly.* 6th ed. Boston: Beacon Press, 2000. An examination of the growing power of the press, including tendencies toward monopolies of ownership and news production.

Cook, Timothy E. *Governing with the News: The News Media as a Political Institution.* Chicago: University of Chicago Press, 1997. An analysis of the news media as a political institution.

Kurtz, Howard. *Spin Cycle: Inside the Clinton Propaganda Machine.* New York: Free Press, 1998. A look at the Clinton White House's attempts to manage its news coverage.

Maltese, John Anthony. *Spin Control: The White House Office of Communications and the Management of Presidential News.* Chapel Hill: University of North Carolina Press, 1994. An assessment of how presidents attempt to manage news coverage.

Patterson, Thomas E. *Out of Order.* New York: Vintage, 1994. An analysis of how election news coverage has changed in recent decades.

Sabato, Larry J., Mark Stencel, and S. Robert Lichter. *Peep Show: Media and Politics in the Age of Scandal.* Lanham, Md.: Rowman & Littlefield, 2000. A penetrating critique of today's news.

Sparrow, Bartholomew H. *Uncertain Guardians.* Baltimore, Md.: Johns Hopkins University Press, 1999. A systematic assessment of the news media's political role and tendencies.

http://www.cmpa.com   The Center for Media and Public Affairs (CMPA) is a nonpartisan organization that analyzes news coverage on a continuing basis. Its web site provides analyses of news content that are useful for anyone interested in the media's political coverage.

http://www.drudgereport.com   The web site through which Matt Drudge (The Drudge Report) has challenged the traditional media's control of the news.

http://www.fcc.gov   The Federal Communications Commission (FCC) web site provides information on broadcasting regulation and current issues.

http://www.newslink.org/   Provides access to more than a thousand news organizations, including most U.S. daily newspapers.

READING 10

The Miscast Institution

THOMAS E. PATTERSON

Introduction

In his essay, Thomas Patterson examines the way in which Americans elect their president and concludes that it is rooted in a faulty assumption: the widespread belief that the news media have the capacity to organize the public's choices in a coherent way. His conclusion is based on an argument raised in Chapter 10, namely, that journalistic values and imperatives lead the press to emphasize "the new, the unusual, and the sensational" rather than the deeper and more substantial issues of politics.

The United States is the only democracy that organizes its national election campaign around the news media. Even if the media did not want the responsibility for organizing the campaign, it is theirs by virtue of an election system built upon entrepreneurial candidacies, floating voters, free-wheeling interest groups, and weak political parties.

It is an unworkable arrangement: the press is not equipped to give order and direction to a presidential campaign. And when we expect it to do so, we set ourselves up for yet another turbulent election.

The campaign is chaotic largely because the press is not a political institution and has no capacity for organizing the election in a coherent manner. The news can always be made better. Election coverage in 1992 was a marked improvement over 1988, and in a few respects the best coverage ever. The journalist Carl Bernstein, reflecting a widely shared opinion among members of the press, declared that 1992 coverage closely approximated "the ideal of what good reporting has always been: the best obtainable version of the truth."

Yet news and truth are not the same thing. The news is a highly refracted version of reality. The press magnifies certain aspects of politics and downplays others, which are often more central to issues of governing. During the last six weeks of the 1992 campaign, the economy got a lot of attention from the press, but it still received less coverage than campaign-trail controversies, including disputes over Clinton's draft record, Perot's on-again, off-again candidacy and spats with the press, and Bush's wild charges ("the Ozone Man," "bozos").

The attention that Clinton's trip to the Soviet Union while a graduate student at Oxford received in the closing weeks of the campaign was in itself revealing of the gap between news values and the nation's real concerns. When Bush questioned Clinton's trip on CNN's "Larry King Live," it exploded into the headlines in a way that policy issues seldom do. News of Clinton's Moscow visit overshadowed such October issues as developments on the North American Free Trade Agreement, CIA revelations on the U.S. government's role in the arming of Iraq, and a change in Clinton's healthcare proposal.

The press's restless search for the riveting story works against its intention to provide the voters with a reliable picture of the campaign. It is a formidable job to present society's problems in ways that voters can understand and act upon. The news media cannot do the job consistently well. Walter Lippmann put it plainly when he said that a press-based politics "is not workable. And when you consider the nature of news, it is not even thinkable."

Lippmann's point was not that news organizations are somehow inferior to political organizations but that each has a different role and responsibility in society. Democracy cannot operate successfully without a free press that is acting effectively within its sphere. The problem arises when the press is expected to perform the job of political institutions as well. . . .

The belief that the press can substitute for political institutions is widespread. Many journalists, perhaps most of them, assume they can do it effectively. Scholars who study the media also accept the idea that the press can organize elections. Every four years, they suggest that the campaign could be made coherent if the media would only report it differently.

However, the press merely appears to have the capacity to organize the voters' alternatives in a coherent way. . . . The press is in the news business, not the business of politics, and because of this, its norms and imperatives are not those required for the effective organization of electoral coalitions and debate. Journalistic values and political values are at odds with each other.

The proper organization of electoral opinion requires an institution with certain characteristics. It must be capable of seeing the larger picture—of looking at the world as a whole and not in small pieces. It must have incentives that cause it to identify and organize those interests that are making demands for policy representation. And it must be accountable for its choices, so that the public can reward it when satisfied and force amendments when dissatisfied.

The press has none of these characteristics. The media has its special strengths, but they do not include these strengths.

The press is a very different kind of organization from the political party, whose role it acquired. A party is driven by the steady force of its traditions and constituent interests, which is why the Democratic leadership in 1952 chose Stevenson, a New Deal liberal, over Kefauver, a border-state populist. The press, in contrast, is "a restless beacon." Its concern is the new, the unusual, and the sensational. Its agenda shifts abruptly when a new development breaks.

The party has the incentive—the possibility of acquiring political power—to give order and voice to society's values. Its raison d'être is to articulate interests and to forge them into a winning coalition. The press has no such incentive and no such purpose. Its objective is the discovery and development of good stories. Television-news executive Richard Salant once said that his reporters covered stories from "nobody's point of view." What he was saying, in effect, was that journalists are driven by news opportunities, not by political values.

The press is also not politically accountable. The political party is made accountable by a formal mechanism—elections. The vote gives officeholders a reason to act in the majority's interest, and it offers citizens an opportunity to boot from office anyone they feel has failed them. Thousands of elected officials have lost their jobs this way. The public has no comparable hold on the press. Journalists are neither chosen by the people nor removable by them. . . .

Other democracies have recognized the inappropriateness of press-based elections. Although national voting in all Western democracies is media-centered in the sense that candidates depend primarily on mass communication to reach the voters, no other democracy has a system in which the press fills the role traditionally played by the political party. Journalists in other democracies actively participate in the campaign process, but their efforts take place within an electoral structure built around political institutions. In the United States, however, national elections are referendums in which the candidates stand alone before the electorate and have no choice but to filter their appeals through the lens of the news media.

SOURCE: Thomas E. Patterson, "The Miscast Institution" (from *Out of Order* by Thomas E. Patterson). Copyright © 1993 by Thomas E. Patterson. Reprinted by permission of Alfred A. Knopf, Inc.
Thomas E. Patterson is the Bradlee Professor of Government and the Press at Harvard University.

CHAPTER ELEVEN

Congress

There are really two Congresses, not just one. Often these two Congresses are
widely separated; the tightly knit, complex world of Capitol Hill is a long way
from the world of [the member's district or state]—not only in miles,
but in perspective and outlook as well.

ROGER DAVIDSON AND WALTER OLESZEK[1]

THE CONGRESSIONAL action in 1998 on the $200 billion transportation bill revealed a lot about the institution. For the first
time in a generation, the federal government had the luxury of a
budget surplus. How would it be used? To cut taxes? To safeguard the future of the social security system? To provide a cushion against some future
day when the economy turned sour and federal expenditures exceeded
revenues?

As it happened, a first use of the surplus was to help fund the most expensive transportation bill in the nation's history. It was hard to argue that
it was a bad use of the money. The nation's transportation infrastructure
had been neglected for years, and there were plenty of bridges, roads, and
mass transit systems in need of repair and expansion. Yet the $200 billion
transportation bill was attractive to Congress in part because it provided
public works projects and jobs for virtually every state and every congressional district in the nation. It was good policy, but it was also very good
politics in an election year.

The story of the 1998 transportation bill illustrates the dual nature of
Congress: it is both a lawmaking institution for the country and a representative assembly for states and districts.[2] Members of Congress have both an
individual duty to serve the interests of their separate constituencies and a
collective duty to protect the interests of the country as a whole. Attention
to constituency interests is the common denominator of a national institution in which each member must please the voters back home in order to
win reelection.[3]

This chapter examines Congress, beginning with congressional election and organization, and concluding with congressional policymaking. The following points are emphasized in this chapter:

* *Congressional elections tend to have a strong local orientation and to favor incumbents, who (particularly House members) have a substantial advantage in election campaigns.*

* *Although party leaders in Congress provide collective leadership, the work of Congress is done mainly through its committees and subcommittees, each of which has its separate leadership and policy jurisdiction.*

* *Congress lacks the direction and organization required for the development of comprehensive national policies, but it is well organized to handle policies of relatively narrow scope. At times, Congress takes the lead on broad national issues, but ordinarily it does not do so.*

* *Congress's policymaking role is based on three major functions: lawmaking, representation, and oversight.*

CONGRESS AS A CAREER: ELECTION TO CONGRESS

In the nation's first century, service in the Congress was not a career for most of its members. Before 1900 at least a third and sometimes as many as half of the seats in Congress changed hands at each election. Most members left voluntarily. Because travel was slow and arduous, serving in the nation's capital required them to spend months away from their families. And because the national government was not the center of power and politics that it is today, many politicians preferred to serve in state capitals.

The modern Congress is very different. Most of its members are professional politicians, and a seat in the U.S. Senate or House is as far as most of them can expect to go in politics. The pay (about $135,000 a year) is reasonably good, and the prestige of their office is substantial, particularly if they serve in the Senate. An extended stay in Congress is what most of its members aspire to attain.[4]

Incumbents have a good chance of being reelected (see Figure 11-1). They are not a sure bet to win again, but the odds are heavily on their side.[5] In the last decade, the reelection rate of House incumbents seeking another term has exceeded 90 percent, as has the reelection rate of Senate incumbents.[6]

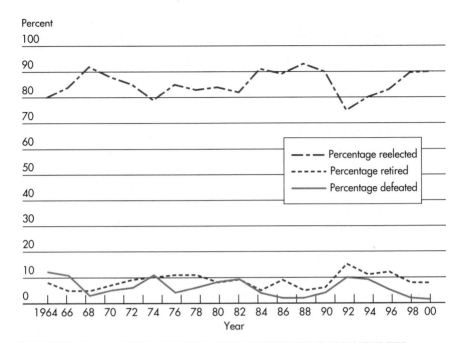

FIGURE 11-1 REELECTION RATES OF HOUSE INCUMBENTS
U.S. House incumbents have a very high rate of reelection. Source: From
Congressional Quarterly Weekly Report, various dates. Reprinted by permission of
Congressional Quarterly, Inc.

These figures overestimate somewhat an incumbent's chances of reelection. Some incumbents retire from Congress when faced with a campaign they fear they will lose. Moreover, incumbents must stand for
reelection again and again if they intend to make Congress a career; a single loss will halt or interrupt this goal. Over the period of a few elections, a
substantial number of congressional seats can change hands. The 1992 and
1994 congressional elections are an extreme example: the turnover in
House membership in these two elections was a combined 188 seats, the
highest total of any two consecutive elections since World War II.

On balance, however, incumbents have a clear edge over their opponents, as their margin of victory indicates. In recent elections, most House
incumbents and nearly half of Senate incumbents seeking reelection have
received 60 percent or more of the vote. Even when voters are convinced
that Congress as an institution is performing badly, they reelect a large majority of its members. One reason is that many congressional districts and a
few states are so lopsidedly Democratic or Republican that the candidate of
the weaker party has no realistic chance of victory. In recent congressional

elections, more than 10 percent of House incumbents have run unopposed for reelection. All incumbents, however, gain important election advantages from the offices they hold, a subject to which we now turn.

Using Incumbency to Stay in Congress

An incumbent promotes his or her reelection prospects by responding to the **constituency:** the body of citizens eligible to vote in their state or district. Members of Congress pay close attention to constituency opinions when casting their votes on legislation,[7] and they work hard to get their share of **pork barrel projects** (a term referring to legislation that funds a special project for a particular locale, such as a new highway or hospital).

Members of Congress also boost their reelection chances by catering to their constituents' individual needs, a practice known as the **service strategy.** When constituents seek information about a government program, express an opinion about pending legislation, or want help in obtaining a federal benefit, their representative usually responds.[8] This assistance is made possible by the staff resources that are provided to members of Congress. Each House member receives an office allowance of $500,000 a year, which supports a personal staff of about twenty full-time staff members.[9] Senators have larger budgets depending on the population size of the state they represent. Senators' personal staffs average about forty employees.[10] Congressional staffers spend the bulk of their time not on legislative matters but on constituency relations, which includes publicity efforts, such as newsletters and press releases designed to enhance their legislator's image.[11] Each member of Congress is permitted several free mailings annually to constituent households, a privilege known as the *frank.*

Finally, incumbents have a decided advantage when it comes to raising campaign funds. The cost of running for Congress has risen sharply in recent decades as campaign techniques, such as televised advertising and polling, have become increasingly sophisticated and costly (see Figure 11-2). Today, a successful Senate campaign costs millions of dollars, and a successful House campaign will often cost $500,000 or more. A study by the *Congressional Quarterly* found that only 10 percent of incumbents said they had trouble raising enough money to conduct an effective campaign, compared with 70 percent of challengers.[12] In 2000 House incumbents outspent their opponents by a ratio of 4 to 1. Many challengers are able to raise only enough money for a token campaign.[13]

Incumbents obtain a fund-raising advantage from their past campaigns and constituent service, which enables them to create mailing lists of potential contributors. Individual contributions, most of which are $100 or

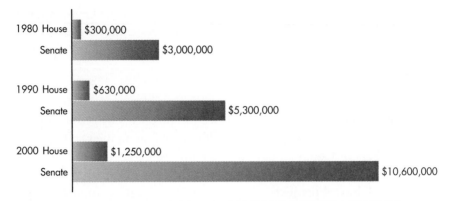

FIGURE 11-2 CONGRESSIONAL CAMPAIGN EXPENDITURES
The cost of running for congressional office has risen sharply as campaign techniques—television advertising, opinion polling, and so on—have become more elaborate and sophisticated. The increase in spending can be seen from a comparison of the approximate median spending level by both candidates per House or Senate seat at ten-year intervals, beginning in 1980.
Source: Federal Election Commission; 2000 figures based on preliminary projections.

less, account for about 50 percent of all campaign funds and are obtained mainly through direct-mail solicitation. Incumbents also have an edge with interest groups. Through their political action committees (PACs, discussed in detail in Chapter 9), groups provide about 30 percent of campaign funds. Incumbents are well positioned to help groups achieve their legislative goals. In recent elections, incumbents have received more than 85 percent of PAC contributions; their challengers, in other words, have received less than 15 percent (see Figure 11-3).

The Pitfalls of Incumbency

Incumbency is not without its liabilities. The potential problems are several: troublesome issues, personal misconduct, variation in turnout, strong challengers, and, for some House members, redistricting.[14]

TROUBLESOME ISSUES   Disruptive issues are a potential threat to incumbents. Although most elections are not waged against the backdrop of strong issues, those that are tend to produce the largest turnover in Congress. In the 1992–1994 period, when the public was angry over economic and social conditions and believed Congress was performing badly, the number of incumbents who were defeated exceeded 10 percent. After that, the economy improved and the percentage dropped below 5 percent.

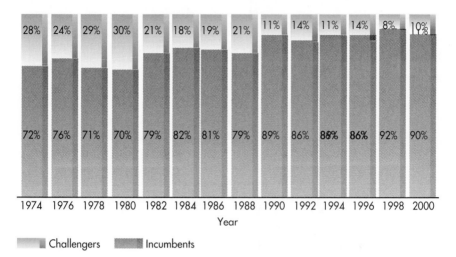

FIGURE 11-3 ALLOCATION OF PAC CONTRIBUTIONS BETWEEN INCUMBENTS AND CHALLENGERS IN CONGRESSIONAL RACES THAT INCLUDED AN INCUMBENT, 1972–2000
In allocating campaign contributions, PACs favor incumbent members of Congress over their challengers by a wide margin.
Source: Federal Elections Commission.

PERSONAL MISCONDUCT   Members of Congress can also fall prey to scandal. Life in Washington can be fast paced, glamorous, and expensive, and some members of Congress get caught up in influence peddling, sexual promiscuity, and other forms of personal misconduct. These acts receive close attention from the news media and are a major threat to the reelection of incumbents. Roughly a fourth of House incumbents who lost their bids for reelection in the last decade were shadowed by ethical questions. "The first thing to being reelected is to stay away from scandal, even minor scandal," says the political scientist John Hibbing.[15] Even the top leaders are not immune, as illustrated by the experience of former House Ways and Means Committee Chairman Dan Rostenkowski. Accused of gross misuse of congressional funds, he lost his House seat in 1994, despite having won by 20 percentage points two years earlier and outspending his 1994 opponent by more than 10 to 1.

TURNOUT VARIATION: THE MIDTERM ELECTION PROBLEM
Historically, the party holding the presidency loses seats in the midterm congressional elections, particularly in the House of Representatives. The 1998 midterm elections, when the Democrats had Bill Clinton in the White House and gained five House seats, was a rare exception. The president's party nearly always suffers a net loss.

Constitutional Qualifications for Serving in Congress

Representatives: "No person shall be a Representative who shall not have attained to the age of twenty-five years, and been seven years a citizen of the United States, and who shall not, when elected, be an inhabitant of that State in which he shall be chosen" (Article I, section 2).

Senators: "No person shall be a Senator who shall not have attained to the age of thirty years, and been nine years a citizen of the United States, and who shall not, when elected, be an inhabitant of the State for which he shall be chosen" (Article I, section 3).

The pattern is attributable largely to a dropoff in turnout for midterm elections.[16] The voters who go to the polls only during presidential election years tend to have weaker party loyalties and are therefore more responsive to the issues of the moment. In any given election, these issues tend to favor one party, which contributes to the success of its congressional candidates as well as its presidential nominee. Most of the party's congressional candidates who win narrowly owe their margin of victory to these voters. However, these voters stay home during midterm elections. Thus, unless these incumbents can make inroads among midterm voters who backed their opponent two years earlier, they stand a good chance of losing. Since many of these voters are strong partisans, they are not easily swayed, and the typical result is the midterm defeat of a significant number of these incumbents.

STRONG CHALLENGERS: A PROBLEM FOR SENATORS   Incumbents are also vulnerable to strong challengers. Senators are particularly likely to face formidable opponents: after the presidency, the Senate is the top rung of the political ladder. Governors and House members are frequent challengers for Senate seats, and they have the electoral base, reputation, and experience to compete effectively. Moreover, the U.S. Senate lures wealthy challengers. Maria Cantwell spent $10 million of her own money to defeat Senator Slade Gorton for the state of Washington's Senate seat in 2000. Cantwell made her fortune as an executive with RealNetworks, a high-tech company.

House incumbents have less reason to fear strong challengers. A House seat is often not attractive enough to induce prominent local politicians, such as mayors or state legislators, to risk their political careers in a challenge to an incumbent.[17] This situation leaves the field open to weak opponents with little or no governmental or political experience.[18]

REDISTRICTING: A PROBLEM FOR HOUSE MEMBERS   Every ten years, after each population census, the 435 seats in the House are reallocated among the states in proportion to their population. States that have gained population since the last census may acquire additional House seats, while those that have lost population may lose seats. This reallocation process is called **reapportionment.** (The Senate is not affected by population change, since each state has two senators regardless of its size.)

The responsibility for redrawing House election districts after a reapportionment—a process called **redistricting**—rests with the state governments. States are required by law to make their districts as nearly equal in population as possible. There are many ways, however, to divide a state into districts of nearly equal size, and the party in power in the state legislature will do so in a way that favors candidates of its party. A common method is to create some districts that contain overwhelming numbers of voters of the opposing party, which results in "wasted" votes in these districts and thus makes the opposing party less competitive in the other districts. The process by which one party draws district boundaries to its advantage is called **gerrymandering.** The courts have placed some limits on gerrymandering (for example, districts that are very oddly shaped may be ruled unacceptable), but it is a common practice.

Reapportionment, redistricting, and gerrymandering are a potential threat to House incumbents. Turnover in House elections is typically higher after a new census than in previous elections. The newly redrawn districts include voters who are unfamiliar with the incumbent, thereby diminishing an advantage that incumbents typically have over their challengers. Moreover, when a state loses congressional seats, there are fewer districts than there are incumbents, who may end up running against each other. Finally, incumbents of the party that does not control the state legislature may find themselves having to compete in redrawn districts that are stacked with opposing voters.

Safe Incumbency and Representation

Although the obstacles to an incumbent's reelection can be substantial, the advantage in most congressional races clearly rests with the incumbent. As a result, Congress is not highly responsive to political change. The Republicans gained a decisive victory in 1994 on the strength of voters' anger at

Washington, but a similar public mood in 1980 failed to translate into GOP control of the House of Representatives. In nearly every other Western democracy, the conditions underlying the 1980 election would have produced a change in power. It is worth noting that national legislators in other democracies do not have the large personal staffs and the substantial travel and publicity budgets that members of Congress have. Elsewhere, incumbents tend to win or lose on the popularity of their political party, not on their capacity to generate public support through constituent service.

Safe incumbency weakens the public's influence on Congress. Democracy depends on periodic shifts in power between the parties to bring public policy into closer alignment with public opinion. Research indicates that changes in congressional voting patterns occur primarily around the replacement of defeated or retiring lawmakers with new members. Incumbents tend to hold relatively stable policy positions during their time in office.[19]

Safe incumbency is also a reason Congress has relatively few women among its members. They now account for about 13 percent of the membership, which is twice that of a decade ago but less than that of many other national legislatures. Women have been no more successful than other challengers in dislodging congressional incumbents. In state and local elections, where incumbency is less important, women have made greater inroads.[20]

CONGRESSIONAL LEADERSHIP

The way in which Congress works is related to the way in which its members win election. Because of their independent power base in their state or district, members of Congress have substantial independence within the institution they serve. The Speaker of the House and the other top leaders in Congress are crucial to its operation, but, unlike their counterparts in European legislatures, they cannot demand the loyalty of the members they lead. There is a tension in Congress between the institution's need for strong leadership at the top and the individual member's need to exercise power on behalf of constituents. The result is an institution where power is widely dispersed, although not evenly; the top party and committee leaders exercise more power than the other members.

Party Leadership in Congress

The House and Senate are organized along party lines. When members of Congress are sworn in at the start of a new two-year term, they automatically are members of either the Republican or the Democratic **party caucus** in their chamber. The caucuses are critical bodies within the Congress. Through them, the Democrats and Republicans in each chamber meet periodically to plan strategy and to air their differences in the process of settling upon the party's legislative program. The caucuses also select the **party leaders** who represent the party's interests in the chamber and give direction to the party's goals.

THE HOUSE LEADERSHIP   The main party leaders in the House are the Speaker, the majority leader, the majority whip, the minority leader, and the minority whip. The Constitution provides only for the post of Speaker, who is to be chosen by a vote of the entire House. In practice, this means that the Speaker is selected by the majority party's members, since only they have enough votes to choose one of their own.

The Speaker is often said to be the second most powerful official in Washington, after the president. The Speaker has the right to speak first on legislation during House debate and has the power to recognize members—that is, give them permission to speak from the floor. Since the House places a time limit on floor debate, not everyone has a chance to speak on a bill, and the Speaker can sometimes influence legislation simply by exercising the power to decide who will speak and when.[21] The Speaker

House Speaker Dennis Hastert bangs his gavel during the opening session of the 106th Congress. Because of the House's large size and restrictive rules, the Speaker's position is a relatively powerful position. Ultimately, however, the power of the Speaker and other party leaders in the House and Senate rests on the trust placed in them by members of their party.

also chooses the chairperson and majority-party members of the powerful House Rules Committee, which controls the scheduling of bills for debate. Legislation the Speaker wants passed is likely to reach the floor under conditions favorable to its enactment; for example, the Speaker may ask the Rules Committee to delay sending a bill to the floor until there are enough votes for its passage. The Speaker has other ways of directing the work of the House. The Speaker assigns bills to committees, places time limits on the reporting of bills out of committees, and assigns members to conference committees. (The importance of these powers over committee action will become apparent later in this chapter.)

The Speaker is assisted by the House majority leader and the House majority whip, who are elected by the majority party's members. The majority leader acts as the party's floor leader, organizing the debate on bills and working to line up legislative support. The whip has the important job of soliciting votes from party members and of informing them when critical votes are scheduled. As voting is getting under way on the House floor, the whip will sometimes stand at a location that is easily seen by party members and let them know where the leadership stands on the bill by giving a thumbs-up or thumbs-down signal.

The minority party has its own leaders in the House. The House minority leader heads the party's caucus and policy committee and plays the leading role in developing the party's legislative positions. The minority leader is assisted by a minority whip.

THE SENATE LEADERSHIP In the Senate, the most important party leadership position is that of the majority leader, who heads the majority-party caucus. The majority leader formulates the majority's legislative policies and strategies and seeks to develop influential relationships with colleagues. Like the Speaker of the House, the Senate majority leader chairs the party's policy committee and acts as the party's voice in the chamber.[22] The majority leader is assisted by the majority whip, who sees to it that members know when important votes are scheduled and ensures that the party's strongest advocates on a legislative measure are present for the debate. The Senate also has a minority leader and minority whip, whose roles are comparable to those performed by their counterparts in the House.

Unlike the Speaker of the House, the Senate majority leader is not the chamber's presiding officer. The Constitution assigns this responsibility to the vice-president of the United States. However, since the vice-president is allowed to vote in the Senate only to break a tie, the vice-president does not ordinarily preside over Senate debates. The Senate has a president *pro tempore*, who, in the absence of the vice-president, has the right to preside over the Senate. President *pro tempore* is largely an honorary position that by tradition is usually held by the majority party's senior member. The presiding official has limited power, since each senator has the right to speak at any length on bills under consideration.

The Senate's tradition of unlimited debate derives from its relatively small size (only 100 members, compared with the House's 435 members). Moreover, senators like to view themselves as being equals and are thus less subject to leadership. For such reasons, the Senate majority leader's position is weaker than that of the Speaker of the House.

The position of majority leader acquired unusual attention after the 2000 campaign because the Senate was divided equally between the parties; there were 50 Democrats and 50 Republicans. Although the Democrats asked for co-majority leaders, Republicans relied on Vice President Dick Cheney's tie-breaking Senate vote to claim the majority leader's position for their party. Nevertheless, Senate Republicans made significant concessions in other areas. For example, although they retained the committee chair positions, they gave the Democrats equal membership on Senate committees. (Committees are discussed in detail in a later section of the chapter.)

PARTY LEADERS AND FOLLOWERS   The power of all party leaders, in the Senate and House alike, rests largely on the trust placed in them by members of their party. They do not have the strong formal powers of parliamentary leaders, but they are expected to lead. If they are adept at promoting ideas and building coalitions, they can exercise considerable power within their chamber.

They also are positioned to influence national debate. They are recognized by the news media as their party's chief spokespersons within the House and Senate, a role that is magnified when their party does not control the White House. In that circumstance, they are the closest thing to an opposition leader (a mainstay of European parliamentary politics) that the U.S. system has. They are pressed by journalists to respond to White House initiatives and to lay out the plans of their own party. When they are of the same party as the president, however, they are of less interest to the press. It sees the president, not the party's leaders in Congress, as the party's national voice.

Party leaders are in a stronger position today than they were a few decades ago as a result of changes in the composition of the congressional parties. The GOP once had a substantial progressive faction within it, but this faction has been eclipsed by its conservative wing. At the same time, the Democratic party's conservative wing, represented by its southern lawmak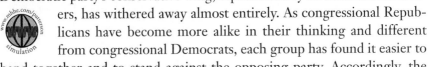ers, has withered away almost entirely. As congressional Republicans have become more alike in their thinking and different from congressional Democrats, each group has found it easier to band together and to stand against the opposing party. Accordingly, the party leaders through the party caucus have found it easier to bring their party's lawmakers together on legislative issues.

At the same time, House and Senate members are less deferential to their leaders than they were in the past. Until a few decades ago, congressional folkways dictated that newer members, particularly on the House side, would mostly listen and learn, awaiting the day when through seniority they were positioned to assume a larger role in the institution. There were always a few mavericks who were unwilling to respect this unwritten norm, but most new members willingly took a back seat. Of course, a back seat in the Senate was not the same as one in the House. Because the Senate is a small body and operates on rules that are more egalitarian, a junior senator could rise to prominence more quickly than a junior House member. Nevertheless, the Senate, too, had a tight inner circle dominated by its more senior members.[23]

Today, junior House and Senate members pursue their own agendas more aggressively. They were elected in a system that rewards self-starters and encourages them to pursue a constant reelection campaign. They seek the visibility that attends a more active legislative role. They also are increasingly likely to have forged close ties with the special interests that support their campaigns, and they are expected by these groups to vigorously pursue legislative goals. Moreover, because the two parties have become more polarized at the activist level, the newer members of Congress have been more ideological and less pragmatic in their beliefs and thus more eager to express their views.[24] Finally, television has provided a path to prominence for junior members who are articulate and engaging. The visibility they obtain outside Congress through the media magnifies their voice within the institution. The old axiom that junior members, particularly in the House, "should be seen and not heard" is hardly an accurate description of today's Congress.

Committee Chairpersons: The Seniority Principle

Party leaders are not the only important leaders in Congress. Most of the work of Congress takes place in the meetings of its thirty-nine standing (permanent) committees and their numerous subcommittees, each of which

HOW THE UNITED STATES COMPARES

Unity and Fragmentation in National Legislatures

The U.S. House and the U.S. Senate are separate and coequal chambers, each with its own legislative structure and rules. This type of legislative structure is not found in most democracies. Although many of them have a bicameral legislature like the U.S. Congress, nearly all power is vested in just one of the two chambers. In such a situation, legislative power is more concentrated and easier to exercise.

However, legislative power depends heavily on party unity. All democratic legislatures are organized by party, but they differ greatly in the degree of control exercised by parties. At one extreme (for example, in Great Britain and Germany), a single legislative chamber dominates, one party has a majority in that chamber, and the members of the majority party are united behind the party leadership. Party control of the U.S. Congress is less pronounced. For one thing, Republicans may control one chamber while the Democrats control the other. For another, Congress is not characterized by unbending party unity. Members sometimes vote against their party's position on important legislation. This lack of a reliable party majority weakens the ability of Congress and its party leaders to control the nation's policy agenda.

Country	Form of Legislature
Canada	One house dominant
France	One house dominant
Germany	One house dominant (except on regional issues)
Great Britain	One house dominant
Israel	One house only
Italy	Two equal houses
Japan	One house dominant
Mexico	Two equal houses
United States	Two equal houses

is headed by a chairperson. A committee chair schedules committee meetings, determines the order in which committee bills are considered, presides over committee discussions, directs the committee's majority staff, and can choose to lead the debate when a committee bill reaches the floor of the chamber for a vote by the full membership.

Committee chairs are always members of the majority party, and they nearly always have the most **seniority:** the most consecutive years of service on a particular committee.

Seniority is based strictly on time served on a committee, not on time spent in Congress. If a member switches committees, the years spent on the first committee do not count toward seniority on the second one. The seniority principle was instituted in the Senate in the mid–nineteenth century but was not formally applied in the House until the early twentieth century. The seniority principle remained virtually absolute until the House Democratic majority decided in the early 1970s that committee chairs would henceforth be chosen by secret ballot. Abuses by some committee chairs had led to the change. Virginia's Howard Smith, who chaired the House Rules Committee in the 1950s and 1960s and was opposed to racial change, would sometimes leave Washington for his Virginia farm when civil rights legislation reached his committee. Because the Rules Committee could not meet unless he called it into session, Smith's absence was sometimes enough to persuade the full committee to "table" a bill, or set it aside. A committee chair now has less power; for example, a majority of the committee members can vote to convene meetings in the chair's absence.

Although the seniority principle is no longer absolute, the congressional majorities usually abide by it.[25] The 107th Congress (2001–2002) is a recent exception. House Republicans had earlier placed a three-term limit on the committee chairs, and many of these positions came open after the 2000 election. Rather than following a strict seniority rule, the Republicans invited candidates to interview for the posts. Representative Bill Thomas of California was appointed chair of the House Ways and Means Committee even though he had less seniority than Representative Phil Crane of Illinois, who also sought the position.

The seniority system persists because it has several important advantages: it reduces the number of bitter power struggles that would occur if the chair were decided by open competition, provides experienced and knowledgeable committee leadership, and enables members to look forward to the reward of a position as chair after years of committee service. A drawback of the seniority system is that it places the committee chairs largely outside the power of the House or Senate's elected leaders.[26]

Congressional organization and leadership extend into subcommittees, which are smaller units within each committee formed to conduct specific aspects of the committee's business. Altogether there are about two hundred subcommittees in the House and Senate, each with a chairperson who decides its order of business, presides over its meetings, and coordinates its staff. In both chambers, a subcommittee chair is often the most senior member on the panel, but seniority is not as important in these appointments as it is in the designation of committee chairs.

Oligarchy or Democracy: Which Principle Should Govern?

In 1995, House Republicans gave committee chairs the power to select the chairs of their subcommittees and to appoint all majority-party staff members, including those who work for the subcommittees. The changes were designed to give committee chairs more control over legislation.[27] The changes reversed House reforms of the 1970s that gave subcommittees and their chairs greater authority in order to make the House "more democratic" in its organization.[28]

The opposing forces embedded in the 1970s and 1995 reforms have played themselves out many times in the history of Congress. The institution is at once a place for conducting the nation's business and a place for promoting constituency interests. At times, the positions of senior leaders have been strengthened. At other times, the positions of less senior members have been enhanced. At all times, there has been an attempt to create a workable balance of the two. The result is an institution very different from European parliaments, where power is thoroughly concentrated at the top (an arrangement reflected even in the name for rank-and-file members: "backbenchers"). The distinguishing feature of congressional power is its dispersion across the membership, with provision for added power at the top.

THE COMMITTEE SYSTEM

As indicated earlier, most of the work in Congress is conducted through **standing committees,** which are permanent committees with responsibility for a particular area of public policy. At present there are nineteen standing committees in the House and sixteen in the Senate (see Table 11-1). Each chamber, for example, has a standing committee that specializes in foreign policy issues. Other important standing committees are those that deal with agriculture, commerce, the budget, the interior (natural resources

TABLE 11-1 THE STANDING COMMITTEES OF CONGRESS	
House of Representatives	*Senate*
Agriculture	Agriculture, Nutrition, and Forestry
Appropriations	Appropriations
Armed Services	Armed Services
Budget	Banking, Housing, and Urban
Education and the Workforce	Affairs
Energy and Commerce	Budget
Financial Services	Commerce, Science, and
Government Reform	Transportation
House Administration	Energy and Natural Resources
International Relations	Environment and Public Works
Judiciary	Finance
Resources	Foreign Relations
Rules	Governmental Affairs
Science	Health, Education, Labor
Small Business	and Pensions
Standards of Official Conduct	Judiciary
Transportation and Infrastructure	Rules and Administration
Veterans' Affairs	Small Business
Ways and Means	Veterans' Affairs

and public lands), defense, government spending, labor, the judiciary, and taxation. House committees, which average about thirty-five to forty members each, are about twice the size of the Senate committees. Each standing committee has legislative authority in that it can draft and rewrite proposed legislation and can recommend to the full chamber the passage or defeat of the legislation it considers.

Each standing committee in Congress has its own staff, which, altogether, totals about 1,000 employees in the Senate and 1,300 in the House. Unlike the members' personal staffs, which concentrate on constituency relations, the committee staffs perform an almost entirely legislative function. They help draft legislation, prepare reports, organize hearings, and participate in altering bills within committee.

In addition to its standing committees, Congress also has a number of *select committees*, which are created to perform specific tasks and are disbanded after they have done so; *joint committees*, composed of members of both houses, which perform advisory or coordinating functions for the House and the Senate; and *conference committees*, which are joint committees formed temporarily to work out differences in House and Senate versions of particular bills. The role of conference committees is discussed more fully later in this chapter.

Congress could not possibly handle its workload without the help of its standing committees and their staffs. About ten thousand bills are introduced during each two-year session of Congress; the sheer volume of this legislation would paralyze the institution if it did not have a division of labor. Yet the very existence of standing committees and their subcommittees helps to fragment Congress: each of these units is relatively secure in its power, jurisdiction, and membership.[29]

Committee Membership

Each committee includes Republicans and Democrats, but the majority party holds the majority of seats on each committee and subcommittee. The ratio of Democrats to Republicans on each committee is approximately the same as the ratio in the full House or Senate, but there is no fixed rule on this matter, and the majority party sets the proportions as it chooses (mindful that at the next election it could become the chamber's minority). Members of the House typically serve on only two committees. Senators often serve on four, although they can sit on only two major committees, such as Foreign Relations and Finance. There are also limits on subcommittee assignments; no House member, for example, can serve on more than five subcommittees.

Each standing committee has a fixed number of members, and a committee must have a vacancy before a new member can be appointed. These vacancies usually occur at the start of a new congressional session, when the committee positions of members who have retired or been defeated for reelection are reallocated. On nearly all committees, members retain their seats unless they decide to relinquish them or are forced to do so by changes in party ratios or committee size. The biggest change in committee memberships comes when a party loses control of the House or Senate; several Democrats had to relinquish committee assignments when the Republicans took control of Congress in 1995.

Each party has a special committee in each chamber with responsibility for deciding who will fill vacancies on standing committees. Several factors influence these decisions, including the preferences of the legislators themselves. Most newly elected members of Congress receive a committee assignment that they have requested.[30] New members usually ask for assignment to a committee on which they can serve their constituents' interests and at the same time increase their reelection prospects.[31] For example,

The U.S. Capitol in Washington, D.C., with the House wing in the foreground. The Senate meets in the wing to the right of the central rotunda (under the dome). The offices of the House and Senate party leaders—Speaker, vice-president, majority and minority leaders and whips—are located in the Capitol building. Other members of Congress have their offices in nearby buildings.

when Hillary Clinton was elected to the Senate in 2000 from New York, a state that depends heavily on human services programs, she asked for and received an appointment on the Senate Health, Education, Labor, and Pensions Committee.

Members of Congress also prefer membership on one of the most important committees, such as Foreign Relations or Finance in the Senate and Ways and Means or Appropriations in the House. Such factors as members' intelligence, experience, party loyalty, ideology, region, length of congressional service, and work habits weigh heavily in the determination of appointments to these prestigious committees.[32]

Subcommittee assignments are handled differently. The members of each party on a committee decide who among them will serve on each of its subcommittees. The members' preferences, seniority, and personal backgrounds and the interests of their constituencies are key influences on subcommittee assignments.

Committee Jurisdiction

The 1946 Legislative Reorganization Act requires each bill introduced in Congress to be referred to the proper committee. An agricultural bill introduced in the Senate must be assigned to the Senate Agriculture Committee, a bill dealing with foreign affairs must be sent to the Senate Foreign Relations Committee, and so on. This requirement is a major source of each committee's power. Even if its members are known to oppose certain types of legislation, bills clearly within its **jurisdiction**—the policy area in which it is authorized to act—must be sent to it for deliberation.

However, policy problems are increasingly complex, and jurisdiction has accordingly become an increasingly contentious issue, particularly on major bills. Which House committee, for example, should handle a major bill addressing the role of financial institutions in global trade? Is it the Banking Committee? Or the Commerce Committee? Or the International Relations Committee? Since all committees seek legislative influence and since each is jealous of its jurisdiction, bills that overlap committee boundaries provoke conflict. The political scientist David King describes these conflicts as "turf wars." They also involve the party leaders, who are in charge of assigning bills to committees. The party leaders can take advantage of these situations by shuttling a bill to the committee that is most likely to handle it in the way they would like. But party leaders depend on the committee chairs for support, so they cannot regularly ignore a committee that has a strong claim to a bill. At times, party leaders have responded by dividing up a bill, handing over some of its provisions to one committee and other provisions to a second committee.

House subcommittees have secure jurisdictions like those of the committees: bills must be referred to the appropriate subcommittees within two weeks of their arrival in committee. The Senate has a similar policy. Thus responsibility in Congress is thoroughly divided, with each subcommittee having formal authority over a small area of public policy.

HOW A BILL BECOMES LAW

Parties, party leaders, and committees are critical actors in the legislative process. Their role and influence, however, vary with the nature of the legislation under consideration.

Committee Hearings and Decisions

The formal process by which bills become law is shown in Figure 11-4. A **bill** is a proposed legislative act. Many bills are prepared by executive agencies, interest groups, or other outside parties, but members of Congress also draft bills, and only they can formally submit a bill for consideration by their chamber. Once a bill is introduced by a member of the House or *[handwritten: no order for the bill]* *[handwritten: except budget bills (according to Constitution)]*

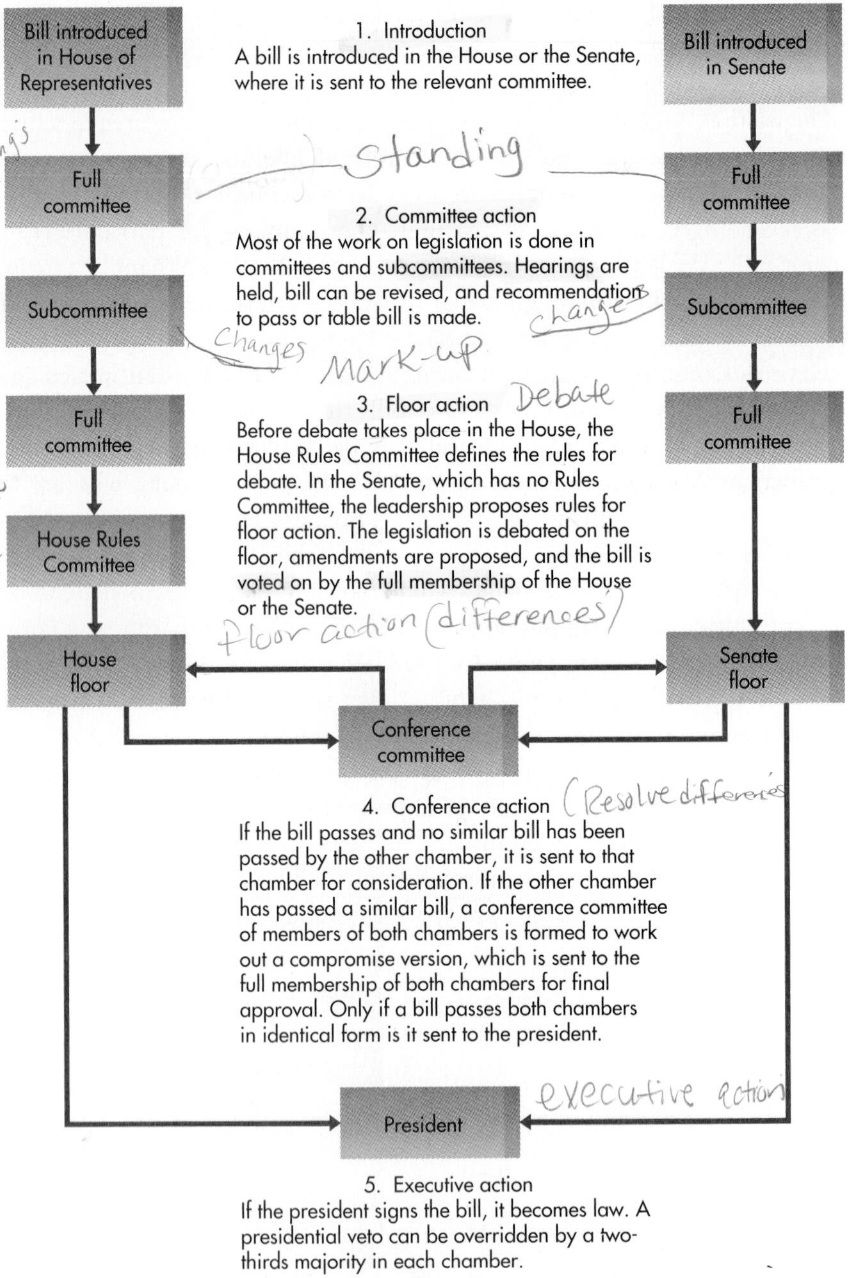

Bill introduced in House of Representatives

1. Introduction
A bill is introduced in the House or the Senate, where it is sent to the relevant committee.

Bill introduced in Senate

[handwritten: hearings]

Full committee

[handwritten: standing]

Full committee

2. Committee action
Most of the work on legislation is done in committees and subcommittees. Hearings are held, bill can be revised, and recommendation to pass or table bill is made. *[handwritten: change]*

Subcommittee

Subcommittee

[handwritten: changes] *[handwritten: Mark-up]*

Full committee

3. Floor action *[handwritten: Debate]*
Before debate takes place in the House, the House Rules Committee defines the rules for debate. In the Senate, which has no Rules Committee, the leadership proposes rules for floor action. The legislation is debated on the floor, amendments are proposed, and the bill is voted on by the full membership of the House or the Senate.

Full committee

[handwritten: not in Senate X]

House Rules Committee

[handwritten: floor action (differences)]

House floor

Senate floor

Conference committee

4. Conference action *[handwritten: (Resolve differences)]*
If the bill passes and no similar bill has been passed by the other chamber, it is sent to that chamber for consideration. If the other chamber has passed a similar bill, a conference committee of members of both chambers is formed to work out a compromise version, which is sent to the full membership of both chambers for final approval. Only if a bill passes both chambers in identical form is it sent to the president.

President *[handwritten: executive action]*

5. Executive action
If the president signs the bill, it becomes law. A presidential veto can be overridden by a two-thirds majority in each chamber.

FIGURE 11-4 HOW A BILL BECOMES A LAW
Although the legislative process can be short-circuited in many ways, this diagram describes the most typical way in which a bill becomes law.

Senate, it is given a number and a title and is then sent to the appropriate committee, which assigns it to one of its subcommittees. Most bills that reach a subcommittee are tabled on the grounds that they are not worthwhile. Only about 10 percent of the bills that committees consider reach the floor for a vote; the others are "killed" when committees decide that they do not warrant further consideration and table them. The full House or Senate can overrule these committee rejections, but this seldom occurs.

The fact that committees "kill" 90 percent of the bills submitted in Congress does not mean that committees exercise 90 percent of the power in Congress. A committee rarely decides fully the fate of legislation that is important to the majority party or its leadership. Most bills die in committee because they are of little interest to anyone other than a few members of Congress or are so poorly conceived that they lack merit. Some bills are not even supported by the members who introduce them. A member may submit a bill to appease a powerful constituent group and then quietly inform the committee to ignore it.

If a bill seems to have merit, the subcommittee will schedule hearings on it. The subcommittee invites testimony on the proposed legislation by lobbyists, administrators, and experts, who inform members about the suggested policy, provide an indication of the support the bill has, and disclose possible weaknesses in the proposal. After the hearings, if the subcommittee still feels that the legislation is warranted, members recommend the bill to the full committee, which can hold additional hearings. In the House, both the full committee and a subcommittee can "mark up," or revise, a bill; in the Senate, markup is usually reserved for the full committee.

From Committee to the Floor

If a majority of the committee votes to recommend passage of the bill, it is referred to the full chamber for action. In the House, the Rules Committee has the power to determine when the bill will be voted on, how long the debate on the bill will last, and whether the bill will receive a "closed rule" (no amendments will be permitted), an "open rule" (members can propose amendments relevant to any of the bill's sections), or something in between (for example, only certain sections of the bill will be subject to amendment). The Rules Committee has this scheduling power because the House is too large to operate effectively without strict rules for the handling of legislation by the full chamber. The rules are also a means by which the majority party controls legislation. House Democrats employed closed rules to prevent Republicans from proposing amendments to major bills, a tactic

House Republicans said they would forgo when they took control in 1995. Once in control, however, the Republicans applied closed rules to a number of major bills. The tactic was too effective to ignore.

The Senate has no Rules Committee, relying instead on the majority leader to schedule bills. All Senate bills are subject to unlimited debate unless a three-fifths majority of the full Senate votes for **cloture,** which limits debate to thirty hours. Cloture is a way of thwarting a Senate **filibuster,** a procedural tactic whereby a minority of senators prevent a bill from coming to a vote by holding the floor and talking until other senators give in and the bill is withdrawn from consideration. The Senate also differs from the House in that its members can propose *any* amendment to *any* bill. Unlike House amendments, those in the Senate do not have to be germane to a bill's content. For example, a senator may propose an antiabortion amendment to a bill dealing with defense expenditures. Such an amendment is called a **rider,** and they are frequently introduced.

Leadership and Floor Action

Committee action is decisive on bills that address small issues. If a majority of committee members favor such a bill, it normally is passed by the full chamber, often without amendment. In a sense, the full chamber merely votes to confirm or modify decisions made previously by committee and subcommittees. Of course, committees do not operate in a vacuum. In making its decisions, a committee takes into account the fact that its action can be reversed by the full chamber, just as a subcommittee recognizes that the full committee can overrule its decision.[33]

On major bills, the party leaders are the critical actors. They will have worked closely with the committee during its deliberations and may assume leadership of the bill when it clears the committee. (In the case of "minor" bills, leadership during floor debate is normally provided by committee members.)

In her book *Unorthodox Lawmaking: New Legislative Processes in the U.S. Congress,* Barbara Sinclair notes that the majority party's leaders (particularly in the House) have increasingly set the legislative agenda and defined the debate on major bills.[34] They shape the bills' broad outlines and set the boundaries of the floor debate. In these efforts, they depend on the support of party's members. To obtain it, they consult their members informally and through the party caucus. **Party discipline**—the willingness of a party's House or Senate members to act together as a cohesive group—is increasingly important in congressional action and is the key to party leaders' ability to shape major legislation. (The role of parties in Congress is discussed further in a later section of the chapter.)

Conference Committees and the President

For a bill to pass, it must receive the support of a simple majority (50 percent plus one) of the House or Senate members voting on it. To become a law, however, a bill must be passed in identical form by both the House and the Senate. About 10 percent of all proposals that are approved by both chambers—the proportion is larger for major bills—differ in important respects in their House and Senate versions and are referred to conference committees to resolve their differences. Each **conference committee** is formed temporarily to handle a particular bill; its members are usually appointed from the House and Senate standing committees that worked on the bill originally. The conference committee's job is to bargain over the differences in the House and Senate versions and to develop a compromise version. It then goes to the House and Senate floors, where it can be passed, defeated, or returned to conference, but not amended.

Legislation that is passed by the House and the Senate is not assured of becoming a law. The president also has a role. If the president signs the bill it becomes a **law.** If the president exercises the **veto,** a refusal to sign a bill, it is sent back to its originating chamber with the president's reasons for the veto. Congress can override a veto by a two-thirds vote of each chamber; the bill then becomes law. If the president fails to sign a bill within ten days (Sundays excepted) and Congress has remained in session, the bill automatically becomes law anyway. If the president fails to sign a bill within ten days and Congress has adjourned for the term, the bill does not become law. This last situation is called a *pocket veto* and forces Congress in its next session to start from the beginning: the bill must again pass both chambers and is again subject to presidential veto.

CONGRESS'S POLICYMAKING ROLE

The Framers of the Constitution expected Congress to be the leading branch of the national government. It was to the legislature—the embodiment of representative government—that the people were expected to look for policy leadership. During most of the nineteenth century, Congress, not the president, was clearly the dominant national institution. Aside from a few strong leaders such as Jackson and Lincoln, presidents did not play a major legislative role (see Chapter 12). However, as national and international forces combined to place greater leadership and policy demands on the federal government, the president became a vital part of the national legislative process. Today Congress and the president substantially share the legislative effort, although their roles differ greatly.[35]

Congress's policymaking role revolves around its three legislative functions: lawmaking, representation, and oversight. In practice, the three functions overlap, but they are conceptually distinct.

The Lawmaking Function of Congress

Under the Constitution, Congress is granted the **lawmaking function:** the authority to make the laws necessary to carry out the powers granted to the national government. However, whether Congress takes the lead in the making of laws depends heavily on the type of policy at issue.

BROAD ISSUES: THE LIMITS OF FRAGMENTATION ON CONGRESS'S ROLE   Congress is structured in a way that makes agreement on large issues difficult to obtain. Congress is not one house, but two, each with its own authority and constituency base. Neither the House nor the Senate can enact legislation without the other's approval, and they are hardly two versions of the same thing. California and North Dakota have exactly the same representation in the Senate, but in the House, which is apportioned by population, California has fifty-two seats compared to North Dakota's one (see box: States in the Nation).

Congress also includes a lot of people: 100 members of the Senate and 435 members of the House. They come from different constituencies and represent different and sometimes opposing interests. Since each member has a separate power base, and depends on it for reelection, the members can be expected to take different positions on legislative issues, even when they agree on the general goal. Nearly every member of Congress, for example, supports the principle of global free trade. When it comes to specific trade provisions, however, they often disagree. Foreign competition means different things to manufacturers that produce automobiles, computer chips, and underwear; it means different things to farmers who produce corn, sugar, and grapes; and it means different things to firms that deal in international finance, home insurance, and student loans. And because it means different things to different people in different parts of the country, members of Congress who represent these areas have conflicting views on what the nation's trade policy should be.

★ STATES IN THE NATION ★

One Person, One Vote? Not in the Election of Senators

The U.S. Congress is a true bicameral legislature. Yet the House and Senate are hardly twin institutions; they differ not only in size and procedures but also, most importantly, in their method of apportionment. The Senate is apportioned by geography: each state, regardless of population, has two U.S. senators. The House is apportioned by population. Thus, California, the largest state, has a much larger number of representatives in the House than, say, Vermont, which has only one. In fact, California has more House members (fifty-two) than all twenty-one of the least populated states combined (see map for the identity of these states, which together have a total of forty-nine House members). Yet, these same twenty-one states have a total of forty-two U.S. senators compared to just two for California. The "one-person, one-vote" concept that otherwise characterizes U.S. elections clearly does not apply to Senate elections. Vermont's six hundred thousand people have the same power in voting for senators as do California's thirty-three million voters. In other words, one Vermont voter is equal to fifty-five California voters when it comes to choosing a U.S. senator.

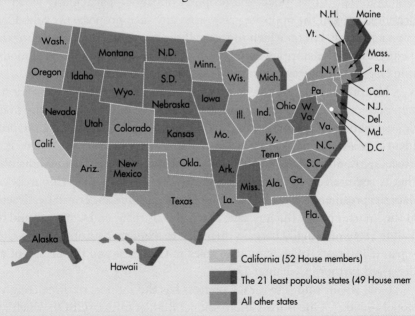

California (52 House members)

The 21 least populous states (49 House mem

All other states

For such reasons, Congress often has difficulty taking the lead on broad issues of national policy. A legislative institution can easily lead on such issues only if it assigns this authority to its top leadership. Although the rise in party discipline in Congress has strengthened leaders' role, the fact remains that House and Senate members are relatively free to go their separate ways if they so choose. For this reason, Congress often struggles when faced with the task of developing comprehensive policies that address broad national problems.

The fragmented nature of Congress enables the president to assume leadership of many of these issues. The presidency is better suited to the task. First, whereas Congress's authority is divided, the presidency's authority is not.[36] Executive power is vested constitutionally in the hands of a single individual—the president. As a result, the presidency is capable of a degree of policy planning and coordination that is far beyond the normal capacity of Congress. Second, whereas members of Congress see issues mainly from the perspective of their state or district, the president has a national outlook. The president cannot ignore specific state and local interests, but must concentrate on broad national ones in order to retain power.

Presidential leadership means that Congress will normally pay attention to White House proposals, not that it will adopt them. Congress typically accepts a presidential initiative only as a starting point in its deliberations. It may reject the proposal outright—particularly when the president is from the opposite party—but any such proposal provides Congress a tangible bill on which to focus. If the proposal is at all close to what a congressional majority would regard as acceptable, Congress will modify it in large or small ways to fit the demands of its membership.

The president's leverage is greatest when prompt legislative action is imperative. When Congress must act or face the public's wrath, the presidential veto comes into play. Congress is nearly forced into taking the president's position into account in shaping the legislation, since it is exceedingly difficult to muster the two-thirds majority in each chamber that is required to override a presidential veto. Of course, Congress can dare the president to veto the bill, hoping that public anger will be directed at the White House. But any such showdown is risky, and Congress and the White House normally bargain their way to a bill that accommodates their separate interests. (The legislative roles of Congress and the president are discussed further in Chapter 12.)

In its lawmaking activities, Congress has the support of three congressional agencies. One is the Congressional Budget Office (CBO), which was created as part of the Budget Impoundment and Control Act of 1974.

Before this time, the president, through the Office of Management and Budget (OMB), had a significant advantage in budgetary matters. Congress had no independent way to systematically assess the president's budgetary proposals or their projected impact. The CBO gives Congress this capacity. Its two hundred employees provide Congress with general economic projections, overall estimates of government expenditures and revenues, and specific estimates of the costs of proposed programs. Since the CBO's inception, its calculations have often been at odds with those of the OMB. For example, the OMB's estimates of the cost of presidential initiatives are usually optimistic, and the CBO's figures have been a basis by which Congress has trimmed or rejected these proposals. (The budgetary process, and the CBO's role in it, are described more fully in Chapter 15. The OMB is discussed further in Chapters 12 and 13.)

A second congressional agency is the General Accounting Office (GAO). With 3,500 employees, the GAO is the largest congressional agency. Formed in 1921, it has the primary responsibility of overseeing executive agencies' spending of money that has been appropriated by Congress.[37] The third congressional agency is the Congressional Research Service (CRS). It is the oldest congressional agency, has a staff of 1,000 employees, and operates as a nonpartisan reference agency. If a member of Congress wants information on a bill or other matter, the CRS will provide it.

CONGRESS IN THE LEAD: FRAGMENTATION AS A POLICYMAKING STRENGTH   Congress occasionally does take the lead on large issues. Except during Roosevelt's New Deal, Congress has been a chief source of major labor legislation. Environmental legislation, federal aid to education, and urban development are other areas in which Congress has played an initiating role.[38] The Republicans' Contract with America that was introduced during the 1994 election is yet another example of congressional policy leadership. The contract included broad fiscal, regulatory, and social initiatives. In 1996, for example, the Republican-controlled Congress led the way on legislation that fundamentally changed the nation's welfare system (see Chapter 16). Nevertheless, Congress does not routinely develop broad policy programs and carry them through to passage. "Congress remains organized," James Sundquist notes, "to deal with narrow problems but not with broad ones."[39]

As it happens, the great majority of the hundreds of bills that Congress considers each session deal with narrow issues. The leading role in the disposition of these bills falls not on the president but on Congress and, in most cases, on a relatively small number of its members. The same fragmentation that makes it difficult for Congress to take the lead on a broad issue makes it easy for Congress to tackle scores of narrow issues simultaneously. Most of the legislation passed by Congress is "distributive"— that is, it distributes benefits to a particular group while spreading the costs among the general public. Veterans' benefits and business tax incentives are examples.[40]

Such legislation, because it directly benefits a constituent group, is the type of policy that members of Congress are most inclined to support. It is also the type of policy that Congress, through its committee system, is organizationally best suited to handle. Most committees parallel a major constituent interest, such as agriculture, commerce, and labor.

The Representation Function of Congress

In the process of making laws, the members of Congress represent various interests within American society, giving them voice and attention in the national legislature. The proper approach to the **representation function** has been debated since the nation's founding. A recurrent issue has been whether the primary concern of a representative should be the interests of the nation as a whole or those of his or her own constituency. These interests overlap to some degree but rarely coincide. Policies that are of benefit to the full society are not always equally advantageous to particular localities and can even cause harm to some constituencies.

REPRESENTATION OF STATES AND DISTRICTS   The choice between national and local interests is not a simple one, even for a legislator who is inclined toward either orientation. To be fully effective, a member of Congress must be reelected time and again, a necessity that compels him or her to pay attention to local demands. Yet, as part of the nation's legislative body, no member can easily put aside his or her judgment as to the nation's needs. In making the choice, most members of Congress, it appears, tend toward a local orientation. They are particularly reluctant to oppose local sentiment on issues of intense concern. Support for gun control legislation, for example, has always been much lower among members of Congress from rural areas where sporting guns are part of the fabric of everyday life.

Nevertheless, representation of constituency interests has its limits. A representative's constituents have little interest in most issues that come before Congress and even less information about them. Whether the government should appropriate a few million dollars in foreign aid for Bolivia or should alter patent requirements for copying machines is not the sort of issue that local people are likely to know or care about. Moreover, members of Congress often have no choice but to go against the wishes of a significant portion of their constituency. The interests of small and large farmers in an agricultural state, for example, can differ considerably.

REPRESENTATION OF THE NATION THROUGH PARTIES   When a clear-cut and vital national interest is at stake, members of Congress can be expected to respond to that interest. The difficulty of using the common good as a routine basis for thinking about representation, however, is that Americans often disagree on what constitutes the common good and what government should do to further it.

Most Americans believe, for example, that the nation's education system requires strengthening. The test scores of American schoolchildren on standardized reading, math, and science examinations are significantly below those of children in many industrial democracies. This situation creates pressure for political action. But what action is necessary and desirable? Does more money have to be funneled into public schools, and which level of government—the federal, state, or local—would provide it? Or does the problem rest with teachers? Should they be subject to higher certification and performance standards? Or is the problem a lack of competition for excellence? Should schools be required to compete for students and the tax dollars they represent? Should private schools be part of any such competition, or would their participation wreck the public school system? There is no general agreement on such issues. The quality of America's schools is of vital national interest, and quality schools would serve the common good. But the means to that end are subjects of endless dispute.

In Congress, debates over national goals occur primarily along party lines.[41] Republicans and Democrats have different perspectives on national issues because their parties differ philosophically and politically. In the end-of-the year budget negotiations in 1998 and 1999, for example, Republicans and Democrats were deadlocked on the issue of new funding to hire thousands of public schoolteachers. The initiative had come from President Clinton and was supported by congressional Democrats but opposed by congressional Republicans, who objected to spending federal (as opposed to state and local) funds for that purpose, and who also objected to the proposed placement of the new teachers (they would be placed in overcrowded schools, most of which are in Democratic constituencies). Democrats and Republicans alike agreed that more teachers were needed, but they disagreed on how that goal should be reached. In the end, through concessions in other areas, Clinton and the congressional Democrats obtained federal funding for new teachers, but it was obtained through an intensely partisan process.

Partisanship is the main source of division within Congress.[42] There are real and substantial differences between members of the two parties, such that they often vote on the opposite sides of legislative issues (see Figure 11-5). Party-line voting has increased in recent decades, reflecting the rise of party discipline in Congress and the widening gap between the Democrats and Republicans who serve there. There are now in Congress fewer liberal Republicans and fewer conservative Democrats, as well as fewer moderates of both parties.

Partisanship also affects the president's relationship with Congress. Presidents serve as legislative leaders not so much for the whole Congress as for members of their own party. More than half the time, opposition and support for presidential initiatives divide along party lines. Accordingly, the president's legislative success can depend on which party controls the Congress. After Republicans took control of Congress from the Democrats in 1995, President Clinton's legislative victories declined sharply (see Chapter 12).

In short, any accounting of representation in Congress that minimizes the influence of party is faulty. If constituency interests drive the thinking

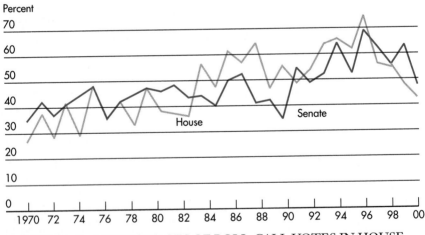

FIGURE 11-5   PERCENTAGES OF ROLL-CALL VOTES IN HOUSE AND SENATE IN WHICH A MAJORITY OF DEMOCRATS VOTED AGAINST A MAJORITY OF REPUBLICANS, 1970–2000

Democrats and Republicans in Congress are often on opposite sides of issues; party-line voting has increased in recent decades, although it has fallen somewhat in the past few years.

Source: From *Congressional Quarterly Weekly Report*, various dates. Reprinted by permission of Congressional Quarterly, Inc.

of many members of Congress, so do partisan values. In fact, constituent and partisan influences are often difficult to separate in practice. In the case of conflicting interests within their constituencies, members of Congress naturally side with those that align with their party. When local business and labor groups take opposing sides on issues before Congress, for example, Republican members tend to back business's position, while Democratic members tend to line up with labor.

The Oversight Function of Congress

Although Congress enacts the nation's laws and appropriates the money to implement them, the administration of these laws is entrusted to the executive branch. Congress has the responsibility to see that the executive carries out the laws faithfully and spends the money properly, a supervisory activity that is referred to as the **oversight function** of Congress.[43]

Oversight is carried out largely through the committee system of Congress and is facilitated by the parallel structure of the committees and the executive bureaucracy: the House International Relations and Senate Foreign Relations committees oversee the work of the State Department, the House and Senate Agriculture committees look after the Department of Agriculture, and so on. The Legislative Reorganization Act of 1970 spells out each committee's responsibility for overseeing its parallel agency:

> Each standing committee shall review and study, on a continuing basis, the application, administration, and execution of those laws, or parts of laws, the subject matter of which is within the jurisdiction of that committee.

However, oversight is easier to mandate than to carry out. If congressional committees were to try to monitor all the federal bureaucracy's activities, they would have no time or energy to do anything else. Most members of Congress are more interested in working out new laws and looking after constituents than in laboriously keeping track of the bureaucracy. Although Congress is required by law to maintain "continuous watchfulness" over programs, committees have little incentive to take a hard look at programs that they have enacted or upon which their constituent groups depend. Oversight normally is not pursued aggressively unless members of Congress are annoyed with an agency, have discovered that a legislative authorization is being grossly abused, or are reviewing a program for possible major changes.[44]

When an agency is suspected of serious abuses, a committee is likely to hold hearings. Except in cases involving "executive privilege" (the right to withhold confidential information affecting national security), executive-branch officials are compelled to testify at these hearings. If they refuse, they can be cited for contempt of Congress, which is a criminal offense. Congress's investigative power is not listed in the Constitution, but the judiciary has not challenged the power, and Congress has used it extensively.

Most federal programs must have their funding renewed every year, a requirement that gives Congress crucial leverage in its ongoing oversight function. If an agency has acted improperly, Congress may reduce the agency's appropriation or tighten the restrictions on the way its funds can be spent. A major difficulty is that the House and Senate Appropriations committees must review nearly the entire federal budget, a task that limits the amount of attention they can give any particular program.

Oversight conducted after the bureaucracy has acted has an obvious drawback: if a program has been administered improperly, some damage has already been done. For this reason, Congress in recent years has developed ways of limiting the bureaucracy's discretion in advance. One method is to include detailed instructions in appropriations bills. Such instructions serve to limit bureaucrats' flexibility when they spend funds on programs and provide a firmer basis for holding them accountable if they disregard the intent of Congress. Another oversight device is the **sunset law,** which fixes a date on which a program will end (or "fade into the sunset") unless it is renewed by Congress. Sunset provisions help to prevent a program from outliving its usefulness, because once its expiration date is reached, Congress can reestablish it only by passing a new law. The "legislative veto" is a more intrusive and controversial oversight tool. It requires that an executive agency have the approval of Congress before it can take a specified action. Legislative vetoes are under challenge as an unconstitutional infringement on executive authority, and their future is unclear.

The biggest obstacle to effective oversight is the sheer magnitude of the task. With its hundreds of agencies and thousands of programs, the bureaucracy is beyond comprehensive scrutiny. Even some of Congress's most publicized oversight activities are relatively trivial when viewed against the sheer scope of the bureaucracy. For example, congressional investigations into the Defense Department's purchase of small hardware items, such as wrenches and hammers, at many times their market value do not begin to address the issue of whether the country is overspending on the military. Overpriced hand tools represent pocket change in a defense budget of billions of dollars. The real oversight question is whether the defense budget as a whole

Newt Gingrich and three hundred Republican congressional candidates stand in front of the Capitol to dramatize their Contract with America. After their stunning victory in the 1994 elections, they launched an aggressive attempt to reduce the scope of the federal government, illustrating that, in some instances, Congress can take the lead on broad national issues.

provides cost-effective national security. It is a question that Congress has neither the capacity nor the determination to investigate fully.

Congress's zeal for oversight changes dramatically when allegations of scandal or wrongdoing engulf the presidency. Then, members of the opposing party in Congress can be expected to use the oversight process to embarrass, pressure, or rebuke the president. When independent counsel Kenneth Starr's report was submitted to Congress in late 1998, Republican lawmakers quickly approved a formal impeachment inquiry. House Republicans refused to strike a compromise with congressional Democrats and voted unanimously for an inquiry that would be unlimited by time or subject. This procedure would give the House the chance to weigh any and all charges against Clinton, but also was designed to give congressional Republicans leeway in their efforts to criticize the President. Although formal presidential impeachment inquiries are rare (there have been only three), the opposing party in Congress has seldom ignored an opportunity to use the oversight process to seek political advantage over the incumbent administration. (Chapter 12 describes the impeachment process in detail.)

CONGRESS: TOO MUCH PLURALISM?

Congress is an institution divided between service to the nation and service to the separate constituencies within it. Its members have responsibility for the nation's laws. Yet they depend for reelection on the voters of their states and districts and are highly responsive to constituency interests. This focus is facilitated by the committee system, which is organized around particular interests. Agriculture, labor, education, banking, and commerce are among the interests represented through this system. It is hard to conceive of a national legislature structured to respond to special interests more closely than the Congress of the United States. It is even harder to conceive of a national legislature that gives as much real power to these interests through committees as Congress.

Pluralists admire this feature of Congress. They argue that the United States has a majoritarian institution in the presidency and that Congress is a place where a *diversity* of interests are represented. Critics of this view say that Congress is sometimes so responsive to particular interests that the overall national interest is neglected. This criticism is blunted from time to time by a strong majoritarian impulse in Congress. The current period is one of these moments. The high level of party discipline in recent years, coupled with a widening ideological gap between the parties, has placed Congress at the center of many national policy debates, including the issue of the balance of power between Washington and the states.

The fact is, Congress cannot at once be an institution that is highly responsive both to diverse interests and to the national interest. These interests often conflict, as the rise and fall of Speaker Gingrich illustrates. He sought to make the Republican congressional majority into the driving force in American national politics, but lost his position when the conflicts generated by this goal began to weaken the GOP's support in the states and districts, thereby threatening the reelection chances of Republican incumbents. This inherent tension between Congress's national role and local base has replayed itself many times in U.S. history. In a real sense, the strengths of Congress are also its weaknesses. The features of congressional election and organization that make Congress responsive to separate constituencies are often the very same ones that make it difficult for Congress to act as a strong instrument of a national majority. The perennial challenge for members of Congress is to find a workable balance between what Roger Davidson and Walter Oleszek call the "two Congresses": the one embodied by the Capitol in Washington and other embodied by the members' separate districts and states.[45]

SUMMARY

Members of Congress, once elected, are likely to be reelected. Members of Congress can use their office to publicize themselves, pursue a "service strategy" of responding to the needs of individual constituents, and secure pork barrel projects for their states or districts. House members gain a greater advantage from these activities than do senators, whose larger constituencies make it harder for them to build close personal relations with voters and whose office is more likely to attract strong challengers. Incumbency does have some disadvantages. Members of Congress must take positions on controversial issues, may blunder into political scandal or indiscretion, must deal with changes in the electorate, or may face strong challengers; any of these conditions can reduce their reelection chances. By and large, however, the advantages of incumbency far outweigh the disadvantages, particularly for House members. Incumbents' advantages extend into their reelection campaigns. Their influential positions in Congress make it easier for them to raise campaign funds.

Congress is a fragmented institution. It has no single leader; the House and Senate have separate leaders, neither of whom can presume to speak for the other chamber. The principal party leaders of Congress are the Speaker of the House and the Senate majority leader. They share leadership power with committee and subcommittee chairpersons, who have influence on the policy decisions of their committee or subcommittee.

It is in the committees that most of the day-to-day work of Congress is conducted. Each standing committee of the House or the Senate has jurisdiction over congressional policy in a particular area (such as agriculture or foreign relations), as does each of its subcommittees. In most cases, the full House and Senate accept 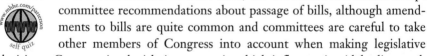 committee recommendations about passage of bills, although amendments to bills are quite common and committees are careful to take other members of Congress into account when making legislative decisions. Congress is a legislative system in which influence is widely dispersed, an arrangement that suits the power and reelection needs of its individual members. However, partisanship is a strong and binding force in Congress. It is the basis for party leaders' ability to build support for major legislative initiatives. On this type of legislation, party leaders and caucuses rather than committees are the central actors.

The major function of Congress is to enact legislation. Yet the role it plays in developing legislation depends on the type of policy involved. Because of its divided chambers and committee structure, as well as the concern of its members with state and district interests, Congress, through its party leaders and caucuses, occasionally takes the lead on broad national issues. Congress also looks to the president for this leadership; nevertheless, presidential initiatives are passed by Congress only if they meet its members' expectations and usually only after a lengthy process of compromise and negotiation. Congress is more adept at handling legislation dealing with problems of narrow interest. Legislation of this sort is decided mainly in congressional committees, where interested legislators, bureaucrats, and groups concentrate their efforts on issues of mutual concern.

A second function of Congress is the representation of various interests. Members of Congress are highly sensitive to the state or district on which they depend for reelection. Members of Congress do respond to overriding national interests, but for most of them, local concerns generally come first. National and local representation often work through party representation, particularly on issues that divide the Democratic and Republican parties and their constituent groups.

Congress's third function is oversight, the supervision and investigation of the way the bureaucracy is implementing legislatively mandated programs. Although oversight is a difficult process, it is an important means of control over the actions of the executive branch.

MAJOR CONCEPTS

bill

cloture

conference committee

constituency

filibuster

gerrymandering

jurisdiction

law

lawmaking function

oversight function

party caucus

party discipline

party leaders

pork barrel projects

reapportionment

redistricting

representation function

rider

seniority

service strategy

standing committees

sunset law

veto

SUGGESTED READINGS AND WEB SITES

Herrnson, Paul S. *Congressional Elections: Campaigning at Home and in Washington.* Washington, D.C.: Congressional Quarterly Press, 1995. A thorough study of the changing nature of congressional campaigns.

Hibbing, John R., and Elizabeth Theiss-Morse. *Congress as Public Enemy: Public Attitudes toward American Political Institutions.* New York: Cambridge University Press, 1995. An analysis through survey and focus group data of Americans' attitudes toward Congress.

King, David C. *Turf Wars: How Congressional Committees Claim Jurisdiction.* Chicago: University of Chicago Press, 1997. An innovative study on how congressional committees claim jurisdiction.

Krasno, Jonathan S. *Challenges, Competition, and Reelection: Comparing Senate and House Elections.* New Haven, Conn.: Yale University Press, 1995. A comparison of the competitiveness of House and Senate races that uses National Election Study (NES) data as evidence.

Sinclair, Barbara. *Unorthodox Lawmaking: New Legislative Processes in the U.S. Congress.* Washington, D.C.: Congressional Quarterly Press, 1997. A detailed analysis of the American legislative process.

Witt, Linda, Karen M. Paget, and Glenna Matthews. *Running as a Woman: Gender and Power in American Politics.* New York: Free Press, 1993. A comprehensive study of the problems faced by women candidates.

http://congress.nw.dc.us/rollcall   The online version of *Roll Call*, the newspaper of Capitol Hill. The site provides an insider's view of current developments within Congress.

http://thomas.loc.gov   Named after Thomas Jefferson, this Library of Congress site provides information about the congressional process, including the status of pending legislation.

http://www.house.gov   The U.S. House of Representatives' web page has information on party leaders, pending legislation, and committee hearings. It has links to each House member's office and web site.

http://www.senate.gov   The U.S. Senate's web site is similar to that of the House and provides links to each senator's web site.

READING 11

Tammany Hall Goes to Washington

MORRIS P. FIORINA

Introduction

In his essay, Morris Fiorina contrasts Congress's lawmaking role with its members' reelection needs. He notes that although Congress as a whole is a lawmaking body, the individual member's greatest concern is staying in office. The enactment of laws can force the member to make controversial choices. On the other hand, special favors for constituents and pork barrel projects nearly always work to the member's advantage. Not surprisingly, as was noted in Chapter 11, most members of Congress pursue a service strategy; they devote enormous energy and staff resources to casework and seek opportunities to obtain pork barrel projects for their districts.

For most of the twentieth century, congressmen have engaged in a mix of three kinds of activities: lawmaking, pork barreling, and casework. Congress is first and foremost a lawmaking body, at least according to constitutional theory. In every postwar session Congress "considers" thousands of bills and resolutions, many hundreds of which are brought to a record vote. Naturally the critical consideration in taking a position for the record is the maximization of approval in the home district. If the district is unaffected by and unconcerned with the matter at hand, the congressman may then take into account the general welfare of the country. (This sounds cynical, but remember that "profiles in courage" are sufficiently rare that their occurrence inspires books and articles.) Abetted by political scientists of the pluralist school, politicians have propounded an ideology which maintains that the good of the country on any given issue is simply what is best for a majority of congressional districts. This ideology provides a philosophical justification for what congressmen do while acting in their own self-interest.

A second activity favored by congressmen consists of efforts to bring home the bacon to their districts. Many popular articles have been written about the pork barrel, a term originally applied to rivers and harbors legislation but now generalized to cover all manner of federal largesse. Congressmen consider new dams, federal buildings, sewage treatment plants, urban renewal projects, etc. as sweet plums to be plucked. Federal projects are highly visible, their economic impact is easily detected by constituents, and sometimes they even produce something of value to the district. The average constituent may have some trouble translating his congressman's vote on some civil rights issue into a change in his personal welfare. But the workers hired and supplies purchased in connection with a big federal project provide benefits that are widely appreciated. The historical importance congressmen attach to the pork barrel is reflected in the rules of the House. That body accords certain classes of legislation "privileged" status: they may come directly to the floor without passing through the Rules Committee, a traditional graveyard for legislation. What kinds of legislation are privileged? Taxing and spending bills, for one: the government's power to raise and spend money must be kept relatively unfettered. But in addition, the omnibus rivers and harbors bills of the Public Works Committee and public lands bills from the Interior Committee share privileged status. The House will allow a civil rights or defense procurement or environmental bill to languish in the Rules Committee, but it takes special precautions to insure that nothing slows down the approval of dams and irrigation projects.

A third major activity takes up perhaps as much time as the other two combined. Traditionally, constituents appeal to their Congressman for myriad favors and services. Sometimes only information is needed, but often constituents request that their congressman intervene in the internal workings of federal agencies to affect a decision in a favorable way, to reverse an adverse decision, or simply to speed up the glacial bureaucratic process. On the basis of extensive personal interviews with congressmen, Charles Clapp writes:

> Denied a favorable ruling by the bureaucracy on a matter of direct concern to him, puzzled or irked by delays in obtaining a decision, confused by the administrative maze through which he is directed to proceed, or ignorant of whom to write, a constituent may turn to his congressman for help. These letters offer great potential for political benefit to the congressman since they affect the constituent personally. If the legislator can be of assistance, he may gain a firm ally; if he is indifferent, he may even lose voters. . . .

From the standpoint of capturing voters, the congressman's lawmaking activities differ in two important respects from his pork-barrel and casework activities. First, programmatic actions are inherently controversial. Unless his district is homogeneous, a congressman will find his district divided on many major issues. Thus when he casts a vote, introduces a piece of nontrivial legislation, or makes a speech with policy content he will displease some elements of his district. . . .

In contrast, the pork barrel and casework are relatively less controversial. New federal projects bring jobs, shiny new facilities, and general economic prosperity, or so people believe. Snipping ribbons at the dedication of a new post office or dam is a much more pleasant pursuit than disposing of a constitutional amendment on abortion. Republicans and Democrats, conservatives and liberals, all generally prefer a richer district to a poorer one.

Casework is even less controversial. Some poor, aggrieved constituent becomes enmeshed in the tentacles of an evil bureaucracy and calls upon Congressman St. George to do battle with the dragon. . . . Practicing politicians will tell you that word of mouth is still the most effective mode of communication. News of favors to constituents gets around and no doubt is embellished in the process.

In sum, when considering the benefits of his programmatic activities, the congressman must tote up gains and losses to arrive at a net profit. Pork barreling and casework, however, are basically pure profit.

A second way in which programmatic activities differ from casework and the pork barrel is the difficulty of assigning responsibility to the former as compared with the latter. No congressman can seriously claim that he is responsible for the 1964 Civil Rights Act, the ABM, or the 1972 Revenue Sharing Act. . . . Even committee chairmen have a difficult time claiming credit for a piece of major legislation, let alone a rank-and-file congressman. Ah, but casework, and the pork barrel. In dealing with the bureaucracy, the congressman is not merely one vote of 435. Rather, he is a nonpartisan power, someone whose phone calls snap an office to attention. . . . The constituent who receives aid believes that his congressman and his congressman alone got results. Similarly, congressmen find it easy to claim credit for federal projects awarded their districts. The congressman may have instigated the proposal for the project in the first place, issued regular progress reports, and ultimately announced the award through his office. Maybe he can't claim credit for the 1965 Voting Rights Act, but he can take credit for Littletown's spanking new sewage treatment plant.

Overall then, programmatic activities are dangerous (controversial), on the one hand, and programmatic accomplishments are difficult to claim credit for, on the other. While less exciting, casework and pork barreling are both safe and profitable. For a reelection-oriented congressman the choice is obvious. . . .

SOURCE: From Morris P. Fiorina, "Tammany Hall goes to Washington," *Congress: Keystone of the Washington Establishment*, Second Edition. Copyright © 1989. Reprinted by permission of Yale University Press.
Morris P. Fiorina is professor of political science at Stanford University.

CHAPTER TWELVE

The Presidency

[The president's] is the only voice in national affairs. Let him once win the
admiration and confidence of the people, and no other single voice
will easily overpower him.

WOODROW WILSON[I]

A L GORE and George W. Bush campaigned feverishly toward Election Day, each seeking a victory that would enable him to assume
the full power of the presidency. The outcome was expected to be close, but
the winner would be able to claim a popular mandate for his leadership and
programs.

All of that changed as the election results were tabulated. The election
had turned into a nightmare for the loser, but was hardly the full blessing
that the winner had expected. The ballot situation in the crucial state of
Florida was so flawed that both sides could contend they had won and
thereby could rightfully claim the presidency. A winner finally emerged, but
George W. Bush's claim to the spoils was diminished by the Florida debacle and the Supreme Court's decision to block a Florida recount. Gore's
popular-vote victory nationwide had already caused some Americans to
question the legitimacy of a Bush presidency. The notion that Bush might
not even have had the support of a majority of Florida's voters further
weakened his position. In any event, the nature of his victory forced Bush
to pursue a different kind of presidency than he had sought—one that offered him somewhat less freedom to follow a course of his own choosing.
He would have to reach out to his opponents on some issues or face entrenched resistance to almost any action he took.

The Bush story is but one in the saga of the ups and downs of the modern presidency. Lyndon Johnson's and Richard Nixon's dogged pursuit of
the Vietnam War led to talk of "the imperial presidency," an office so powerful that constitutional checks and balances were no longer an effective
constraint on it. Within a few years, because of the undermining effects of

Watergate and of changing international conditions during the Ford and Carter presidencies, the watchword was "the imperiled presidency," an office too weak to meet the nation's demands for executive leadership. Reagan's policy successes before 1986 renewed talk heard in the Roosevelt and Kennedy years of "a heroic presidency," an office that is an inspirational center of American politics. After the Iran-Contra scandal in 1986, Reagan was more often called a lame duck. George Bush's handling of the Gulf crisis—leading the nation in 1991 into a major war and emerging from it with the highest public approval rating ever recorded for a president—bolstered the heroic conception of the office. A year later, Bush was on his way to being removed from office by the voters. Bill Clinton overcame a fitful start to his presidency to become the first Democrat since Franklin D. Roosevelt in the 1930s to win reelection. As Clinton was launching an aggressive second-term policy agenda, however, he got entangled in an affair with a White House intern, Monica Lewinsky, that led to his impeachment by the House of Representatives and weakened his claim to national leadership.

No other political institution has been subject to such varying characterizations as the modern presidency. One reason is that the formal powers of the office are somewhat limited, and thus presidential power changes with national conditions, political circumstances, and the personal capacity of the office's occupant.[2] The American presidency is always a central office in that its occupant is a focus of national attention. Yet the presidency is not an inherently powerful office in the sense that presidents routinely get what they want. Presidential power is conditional. It depends on the president's own abilities, but even more on the circumstances—on whether the situation demands strong leadership and whether the political support for that leadership exists. When conditions are favorable, the president will seem powerful. When conditions are adverse, the president will seem vulnerable.

This chapter will examine the roots of presidential power, the presidential selection process, the staffing of the presidency, and the factors associated with the success and failure of presidential leadership. The main ideas of this chapter are these:

* *Changing national and world conditions have required the presidency to become a strong office; underlying this development are the Constitution's flexibility regarding the presidency and the public support that the president acquires from being the only nationally elected official.*
* *The modern presidential election campaign is a marathon affair in which self-selected candidates must plan for a strong start in the nominating*

contests and center their general election strategies on media and a base-line of party support.

★ *The modern presidency could not operate without a large staff of assistants, experts, and high-level managers, but the sheer size of this staff makes it impossible for the president to exercise complete control over it.*

★ *The president's election by national vote and position as sole chief executive ensure that others will listen to his ideas; to succeed, however, the president must get others to back these ideas.*

FOUNDATIONS OF THE MODERN PRESIDENCY

The writers of the Constitution knew what they wanted from a president—national leadership, statesmanship in foreign affairs, command in time of war or insurgency, enforcement of the laws—but could devise only general phrases to describe the president's constitutional authority. Compared with Article I, which enumerates Congress's specific powers, Article II of the Constitution contains relatively vague statements on the president's powers. This constitutional ambiguity, James W. Davis says, gives presidents "wide latitude in defining their presidential duties."[3]

Over the course of American history, each of the president's constitutional powers has been extended in practice beyond the Framers' intention. For example, the Constitution grants the president command of the nation's military, but only Congress can declare war. In *Federalist* No. 69, Alexander Hamilton wrote that a surprise attack on the United States was the only justification for war by presidential action. Nevertheless, the nation's presidents have sent troops into military action abroad more than two hundred times. Of the twelve wars included in that figure, only five were declared by Congress.[4] All of America's most recent wars—the Korean, Vietnam, Persian Gulf, and Kosovo conflicts—have been undeclared.

The Constitution also empowers the president to act as diplomatic leader with the authority to receive ambassadors and the power to initiate diplomatic relations with other nations. The president is further empowered to appoint U.S. ambassadors and to negotiate treaties with other countries, subject to approval by the Senate. The Framers anticipated that Congress would have responsibility for developing foreign policy, while the president's job would be to oversee its implementation. However, the president has become the principal architect of U.S. foreign policy and has even acquired the power to make treatylike arrangements with other nations, in

George W. Bush speaks to the nation shortly after he
was declared president-elect. Like all presidents of
the modern era, Bush gained authority through
two features of the presidential office: singular
authority and national election.

the form of executive agreements. In 1937 the Supreme Court ruled that
such agreements, signed and approved only by the president, have the same
legal status as treaties, which require approval by a two-thirds vote of the
Senate.[5] Since World War II, presidents have negotiated more than ten
thousand executive agreements, as compared with fewer than one thousand
treaties ratified by the Senate.[6]

The Constitution also vests "executive power" in the president. This
includes the responsibility to execute the laws faithfully and to appoint major administrators, such as heads of the various departments of the executive branch. In *Federalist* No. 76, Hamilton indicated that the president's
real authority as chief executive was to be found in this appointive capacity.
Presidents have indeed exercised substantial power through their appointments, but they have found their administrative authority—the power to
execute the laws—to be of even greater value, because it enables them to
determine how laws will be interpreted and applied. President Ronald Reagan used his executive power to *prohibit* the use of federal funds by family-
planning clinics that offered abortion counseling. President Bill Clinton
exerted the same power to *permit* the use of federal funds for this purpose.
The *same* act of Congress was the basis for each of these actions. The act

authorizes the use of federal funds for family-planning services, but it neither requires nor prohibits their use for abortion counseling, which enables the president to make this decision.

Finally, the Constitution provides the president with legislative authority, including use of the veto and the opportunity to recommend proposals to Congress. The Framers expected this authority to be used in a limited and largely negative way. George Washington acted as the Framers anticipated: he proposed only three legislative measures and vetoed only two acts of Congress. Modern presidents have a different, more activist view of their legislative role. They routinely submit legislative proposals to Congress and often veto legislation they find disagreeable.

The presidency is a more powerful office than the Framers envisioned for many reasons, but two features of the office in particular—*national election* and *singular authority*—have enabled presidents to make use of changing demands on government to claim the position of leader of the American people. It is a claim that no other official can routinely make, and it is a key to understanding the role and power of the president.

Asserting a Claim to National Leadership

The first president forcefully to assert a claim to popular leadership was Andrew Jackson, who had been swept into office in 1828 on a tide of public support that broke the hold of the upper classes on the presidency. Jackson used his popular backing to challenge Congress's claim to national policy leadership, contending that he was "the people's tribune."

Jackson's view of the presidency, however, was not shared by most of his successors during the nineteenth century, because national conditions did not routinely call for strong presidential leadership. The prevailing conception of the presidency was the **Whig theory,** which held that the presidency was a limited or constrained office whose occupant was confined to the exercise of expressly granted constitutional authority. The president had no implicit powers for dealing with national problems but was primarily an administrator, charged with carrying out the expressed will of Congress. "My duty," said President James Buchanan, a Whig adherent, "is to execute the laws . . . and not my individual opinions."[7]

Theodore Roosevelt rejected the Whig tradition when he took office in 1901; he attacked the business trusts, pursued an aggressive foreign policy, and pressured Congress to adopt progressive domestic policies. Roosevelt embraced the **stewardship theory,** which calls for a strong, assertive presidential role that is confined only at points specifically prohibited by law, not by undefined inherent restrictions. As "steward of the people," Roosevelt said, he was permitted "to do anything that the needs of the Nation demanded unless such action was forbidden by the Constitution or by the laws."[8]

Roosevelt's image of a strong presidency was shared by Woodrow Wilson, but his other immediate successors reverted to the Whig notion of the limited presidency.[9] Herbert Hoover's restrained conception of the presidency prevented him from taking decisive action even during the economic devastation that followed the Wall Street crash of 1929. Hoover argued that he lacked the constitutional authority to establish public relief programs for jobless and penniless Americans.

Hoover's successor, Franklin D. Roosevelt, shared the stewardship theory of his distant cousin Theodore Roosevelt, and FDR's New Deal signaled the end of the limited presidency. Today the presidency is an inherently strong office.[10] The modern presidency becomes a more substantial office in the hands of a persuasive leader such as Lyndon Johnson or Ronald Reagan, but even a less forceful person such as Jimmy Carter or the first George Bush is now expected to act assertively. This expectation not only is the legacy of former strong presidents but also stems from changes that have occurred in the federal government's national and international policy responsibilities.

The Need for Presidential Leadership of an Activist Government

During most of the nineteenth century the United States did not need a strong president. The federal government's policymaking role was small, as was its bureaucracy. Moreover, the nation's major issues were of a sectional nature (especially the North-South split over slavery) and thus suited to action by Congress, which represented state and local interests. The U.S. government's role in world affairs was also small.

Today the situation has greatly changed. The federal government has such broad national and international responsibilities that strong leadership from presidents is essential.

FOREIGN POLICY LEADERSHIP   The president has always been the nation's foreign policy leader, but the role was initially a rather undemanding one. The United States avoided getting entangled in the turbulent politics of Europe, and though it was involved in foreign trade, its major preoccupation was its internal development. By the end of the nineteenth century, however, the nation was seeking to expand the world market for its goods, and the size and growing industrial power of the United States was attracting more attention from other nations. President Theodore Roosevelt advocated an American economic empire, looking south toward Latin America and west toward Hawaii, the Philippines, and China (the "Open Door" policy) for new markets. However, the United States' tradition of isolationism remained a powerful influence on national policy. The United States fought in World War I but immediately thereafter demobilized its armed forces. Over President Woodrow Wilson's objections, Congress then voted against the entry of the United States into the League of Nations.

World War II fundamentally changed the nation's international role and the president's role in foreign policy. In 1945 the United States emerged as a global superpower, a giant in world trade, and the recognized leader of the noncommunist world. The United States today has a military presence in nearly every part of the globe and an unprecedented interest in trade balances, energy supplies, and other international issues affecting the nation.[11]

The effects of these developments on America's political institutions have been largely one-sided.[12] Because of the president's constitutional authority as chief diplomat and military commander and the special demands of foreign policy leadership, the president, not Congress, has taken the lead in addressing the United States' increased responsibilities in the world. Foreign policy requires singleness of purpose and, at times, fast action. Congress—a large, divided, and often unwieldy institution—is poorly suited to such a response. In contrast, the president, as sole head of the executive branch, can act quickly and can speak authoritatively for the nation as a whole in its relations with other nations.

This capacity was evident during the cold war, when the threat of Soviet communism bolstered presidential leadership of U.S. foreign policy. Since then, global economic issues have become increasingly important, and Congress has been less deferential to the president. In 1998, for example, Congress refused to extend the president's authority to negotiate comprehensive trade agreements with other countries; members of Congress wanted a stronger say over these agreements, since they have implications for U.S. firms and workers. It is also the case that America's traditional allies have been less willing to let the president define their foreign policy agendas. During the cold war, they regularly deferred to the United States, since its military might was the foundation of their national security. But as global economic issues have risen to the fore, their interests compete with those of the United States. Nevertheless, the president remains the dominant force in U.S. foreign policy and the leader to whom many countries

The White House contains, on the first floor, the president's Oval Office, other offices, and ceremonial rooms. The First Family's living quarters are on the second floor.

turn when global problems surface. (The changing shape of the world and its implications for presidential leadership are the subject of the reading at the end of this chapter.)

DOMESTIC POLICY LEADERSHIP The change in the president's domestic leadership has also been substantial. Throughout most of the nineteenth century Congress jealously guarded its constitutional powers, making it clear that domestic policy was its business. James Bryce wrote in the 1880s that Congress paid no more attention to the president's views on legislation than it did to the editorial positions of prominent newspaper publishers.[13]

By the early twentieth century, however, the national government was taking on regulatory and policy responsibilities imposed by the nation's transition from an agrarian to an industrial society, and stronger presidential leadership was becoming necessary. In 1921 Congress conceded that it lacked the centralized authority to coordinate the growing national budget and enacted the Budget and Accounting Act, which provided for an executive budget.[14] Federal departments and agencies would no longer submit their annual budget requests directly to Congress. The president would oversee the initiation of the budget, developing the various agencies' requests into a comprehensive budgetary proposal, which would then be submitted to Congress as a starting point for its deliberations.

During the Great Depression of the 1930s, Franklin D. Roosevelt's New Deal responded to the public's demand for economic relief with a broad program that involved a level of policy planning and coordination that was beyond the capacity of Congress. In addition to initiating public works projects and social welfare programs aimed at providing immediate relief, the New Deal made the government a partner in nearly every aspect of the nation's economy. If economic regulation was to work, unified and continuous policy leadership was needed, and only the president could routinely provide it.

Presidential authority has continued to grow since Roosevelt's time. In response to pressures from the public, the national government's role in such areas as education, health, welfare, safety, and protection of the environment has expanded greatly, which in turn has created additional demands for presidential leadership.[15] Big government, with its emphasis on comprehensive planning and program coordination, has favored executive authority at the expense of legislative authority.

Executive authority was also strengthened when Americans looked increasingly to the national government for solutions to their common problems. Senators and representatives are chosen by voters within a single state or district, a limitation that diminishes the claim of any one of them to national leadership. The president, in contrast, is a nationally elected official and the sole chief executive. These features of the office enabled presidents, as the policy demands on the national government increased during the twentieth century, to assume powers and leadership that helped to transform the presidency into a permanently more powerful office.

CHOOSING THE PRESIDENT

As the president's policy and leadership responsibilities changed during the nation's history, so too did the process of electing presidents. The changes do not parallel each other exactly, but they are related politically and philosophically. As the presidency drew ever closer to the people, their role in selecting the president grew ever more important.[16] The United States in its history has had four systems of presidential selection, each more "democratic" than its predecessor (see Table 12-1). The justification for each new electoral system was **legitimacy,** the idea that the choice of a president should be based on the will of the people as expressed through their votes.

TABLE 12-1 THE FOUR SYSTEMS OF PRESIDENTIAL SELECTION		
Selection System	*Period*	*Features*
1. Original	1788–1828	Party nominees are chosen in congressional caucuses. Electoral College members act somewhat independently in their presidential voting.
2. Party convention	1832–1900	Party nominees are chosen in national party conventions by delegates selected by state and local party organizations. Electoral College members cast their ballots for the popular-vote winner in their respective states.
3. Party convention, primary	1904–1968	As in system 2, except that a *minority* of national convention delegates are chosen through primary elections (the majority still being chosen by party organizations).
4. Party primary, open caucus	1972–present	As in system 2, except that a *majority* of national convention delegates are chosen through primary elections.

Toward a More "Democratic" System of Presidential Election

The delegates to the constitutional convention of 1787 were steadfastly opposed to popular election of the president. They feared that popular election would make the office too centralized and too powerful, which would undermine the principles of federalism and separation of powers. The Framers devised a novel system, which came to be called the Electoral College. Under the Constitution, the president is chosen by a vote of electors who are appointed by the states; the candidate who receives the majority of electoral votes is elected president. Each state is entitled to as many electors as it has senators and House members of Congress.

In choosing the nation's first presidents, electors acted somewhat independently, exercising their own judgment in casting their votes. This pattern changed after the election in 1828 of Andrew Jackson, who believed the people's will had been denied four years earlier, when he placed first in the popular voting but failed to gain an electoral majority. Jackson could not persuade Congress to support a constitutional amendment that would have eliminated the Electoral College, but did obtain the next-best alternative: he persuaded the states to tie their electoral votes to the popular vote. Under Jackson's reform, which is still in effect today, each party in a state has a separate slate of electors who gain the right to cast a state's electoral votes if their party's candidate places first in the state's popular voting. Thus the popular vote for the candidates directly affects their electoral vote, and one candidate is likely to win both forms of the presidential vote. Since Jackson's time, only Rutherford B. Hayes (in 1876), Benjamin Harrison (in 1888), and George W. Bush (in 2000), have won the presidency after having lost the popular vote.

Jackson also championed the national convention as a means of nominating the party's presidential candidate (before this time, nominations were made by party caucuses in Congress and in state legislatures). The parties had their strength at the grass roots, among the people, and Jackson saw the convention process as a means of bringing the citizenry and the presidency closer together. Since Jackson's time, presidential nominees have been formally chosen at national party conventions. Each state party sends delegates to the national convention, and these delegates select the nominee.

Jackson's system of presidential nomination remained fully intact until the early twentieth century, when the Progressives devised the primary election as a means of curbing the power of the party bosses (see Chapter 2). State party leaders had taken control of the nominating process by handpicking their states' delegates. The Progressives sought to shift control to the voters by allowing them to select the delegates. Such a process is called an *indirect primary*, since the voters are not choosing the nominees directly (as they do in House and Senate races), but rather are choosing delegates who in turn select the nominees.

However, the Progressives were able to persuade only a minority of states to change to the new system. Most states stayed with the older system in which the delegates were chosen through the party organizations. As a result, party leaders continued to control a majority of the convention delegates who selected the presidential nominees.

Through 1968, a strong showing in the primaries enabled a candidate to demonstrate popular support but did not guarantee nomination. In 1952, for example, Senator Estes Kefauver beat President Harry Truman in New Hampshire's opening primary and went on to win twelve of the thirteen primaries he entered; however, Kefauver was denied nomination by party leaders, who believed that his views were inconsistent with the party's traditions.

In 1968, the Democratic nomination went to Vice President Hubert Humphrey, who had not entered a single primary and was closely identified with the Johnson administration's Vietnam War policy. After Humphrey narrowly lost the 1968 general election to Richard Nixon, reform-minded Democrats forced changes in the nominating process. The new rules gave rank-and-file party voters more control by requiring that states choose their delegates through either primary elections or **open party caucuses** (meetings open to any registered party voter who wants to attend). Although the Democrats initiated the change, the Republicans were also affected by it. Most states that adopted a presidential primary in order to comply with the Democrats' new rules also required Republicans to select their convention delegates through a primary.

Today it is the voters in state primaries and open caucuses who play the decisive role in the selection of the Democratic and Republican presidential nominees.[17] A state's delegates are awarded the candidates in accordance with how well they do in the state's primary or caucus. Thus, to win the majority of national convention delegates necessary for nomination, a candidate must place first in a lot of states and do at least reasonably well in most of the rest. (In recent presidential elections, about three-fourths of the states have chosen their delegates through a primary election, while one-fourth have used a caucus system.)

In sum, the presidential election system has changed from an elite-dominated process to one that is based on popular support. The voters in effect choose both the president and the presidential nominees. This arrangement has strengthened the presidency by providing the office with the reserve of power that popular election confers upon democratic leadership.

The Campaign for Nomination

The fact that the voters pick the nominees has made the nominating races more competitive than ever before.[18] The system is basically open to any politician with the energy and resources to run a major national campaign. Nominating campaigns, except those in which an incumbent president is seeking reelection, typically attract a half-dozen or more candidates. The 2000 Republican race, for example, at one time included nearly a dozen contenders, including a governor (Bush), a former governor (Alexander), a former vice-president (Quayle), two U.S. senators (McCain and Hatch), a former cabinet member (Dole), a former ambassador (Keyes), a political advocate (Bauer), and a millionaire publisher (Forbes).

A key to success in the nominating campaign is **momentum**—a solid showing in the early contests that leads to a buildup of public support in subsequent ones. If candidates start off strongly, the press will cover them more heavily, contributors will provide them more funding, and voters will give more thought to supporting them. For these reasons, presidential contenders now give extraordinary attention to the early contests, particularly the first caucuses in Iowa and the first primary in New Hampshire.[19]

Money is a critical factor in the nominating races. Money has long been a key to success in presidential politics, and its importance has grown in the last decade as states have moved their primaries and caucuses to the early weeks of the nominating period in order to increase their influence on the outcome. To compete effectively in so many contests in such a short period, candidates need money—lots of it. A candidate can only be in one place at a time, which requires that the campaign be carried to other voters through televised political advertising. Ads are expensive to produce and air, and analysts claim that it takes at least $25 million to run a competitive nominating campaign. George W. Bush raised more than $70 million in 2000 for his successful nominating campaign, far more than any of his Republican rivals.

Candidates in primary elections are assisted by the Federal Election Campaign Act of 1974 (as amended in 1979). This act provides for federal "matching funds" to be given to any candidate who raises at least $5,000 in individual contributions of up to $250 in each of twenty states. Candidates who accept matching funds must agree to limit their expenditures for the nominating phase to a set amount (more than $40 million in 2000), which is adjusted each election year to account for inflation. (Because Bush exceeded the spending limit in 2000, he was ineligible for matching funds.)

After the state primaries and caucuses have been held, the national party conventions occur. These were once tumultuous affairs during which lengthy, heated bargaining took place before a presidential nominee was chosen. An extreme case was the Democratic convention of 1924, at which delegates took 103 ballots and ended up nominating an unknown "dark horse," John W. Davis. Today's conventions are relatively tame; not since 1952 has a nomination gone past the first ballot. The leading candidate has usually acquired enough delegates in the primaries and caucuses to lock up the nomination before the convention even begins. Nevertheless, the party convention is a major event. It brings together the delegates elected in state caucuses and primaries, who then vote to approve a party platform and to nominate the party's presidential and vice-presidential candidates.

By tradition, the choice of the vice-presidential nominee rests with the presidential nominee. Critics have argued that the vice-presidential nomination should be decided in open competition, since the vice-president stands a good chance of becoming president someday. The chief argument for keeping the existing system is that the president needs a trusted and like-minded vice-president.

The Campaign for Election

The winner in the November general election is almost certain to be either the Republican or the Democratic nominee. A minor-party or independent candidate, such as George Wallace in 1968, Ross Perot in 1992 and 1996, or Ralph Nader in 2000, stands almost no chance of victory. A major-party nominee has the critical advantage of support from the party faithful. Although party loyalty has declined in recent decades (see Chapters 6 and 8), two-thirds of the nation's voters still identify themselves as Democrats or Republicans, and a substantial majority of them support the party's presidential candidate. Even Democrat George McGovern, who had the lowest level of party support among recent nominees, was backed in 1972 by 60 percent of his party's voters. To overcome this inherent disadvantage, a minor-party candidate would have to win the support of nearly all independent voters, many of whom have a latent Democratic or Republican preference. It is an impossible task for a candidate even as strong as Ross Perot was in 1992. He gained just 30 percent of the independent vote—an extraordinary showing for a third-party candidate, but far short of what was required for victory.

On the other hand, a third-party candidate can draw enough votes away from a major-party nominee to tip the balance in a close election. The Green party's presidential nominee Ralph Nader got only 3 percent of the national vote in the 2000 election, but it came primarily at the expense of the Democratic nominee Al Gore (see Figure 12-1). If Nader had not been on the ballot, Gore would have received enough votes in the decisive state of Florida to beat his Republican rival George W. Bush in the presidential race.

ELECTION STRATEGY   The candidates' strategies in the general election are shaped by many considerations, including the constitutional provision that each state shall have electoral votes equal in number to its representation in Congress. Each state thus gets two electoral votes for its

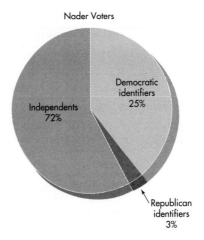

Nader Voters

FIGURE 12-1 SUPPORT FOR RALPH NADER'S 2000
PRESIDENTIAL CANDIDACY
Although Ralph Nader drew most of his 3 percent of the presidential vote from
independents, he fared better with Democrats than Republicans, which
contributed to the Democratic presidential candidate Al Gore's defeat in 2000.
Source: The Vanishing Voter Project, Joan Shorenstein Center on the Press, Politics, and
Public Policy, John F. Kennedy School of Government, Harvard University, 2000.
Published by permission of The Vanishing Voter Project.

Senate representation and a varying number of electoral votes depending
on its House representation. Altogether, there are 538 electoral votes (including 3 for the District of Columbia, even though it has no voting representatives in Congress). To win the presidency, a candidate must receive at
least 270 votes, an electoral majority. (If no candidate receives a majority,
the election is decided in the House of Representatives. No president since
1824 has been elected in this way. The procedure is defined by the Constitution's Twelfth Amendment, which is reprinted in this book's appendix.)

The importance of the electoral votes is magnified by the existence of
the **unit rule;** all the states except Maine and Nebraska grant all their electoral votes as a unit to the candidate who wins the state's popular vote. For
this reason, candidates are particularly concerned with winning the most
populous states, such as California (with 54 electoral votes), New York (33),
Texas (32), Florida (25), Pennsylvania (23), Illinois (22), and Ohio (21). Victory in the eleven largest states alone would provide an electoral majority,
and presidential candidates therefore spend most of their time campaigning
in those states.[20]

In 2000, Bush was elected with 271 electoral votes, one more than required. Bush finished second in the popular voting, receiving 50.5 million

Should the Electoral College Be Abolished?

As the votes in the 2000 election were counted, the country was thrown into turmoil by the existence of the electoral vote system. The president is chosen by an indirect system of election. Voters cast ballots for candidates but their votes choose only each state's electors, whose subsequent ballots then result in the actual selection of the president. Electoral votes are apportioned by states based on their representation in Congress, which creates the possibility that the candidate who gets the most popular votes will not get the most electoral votes and thus not be elected president. The 2000 election renewed calls for the abolition of the electoral system.

Yes: Only the President and Vice President of the United States are currently elected indirectly by the Electoral College—and not by the voting citizens of this country. All other elected officials, from the local officeholder up to United States senator, are elected directly by the people. Our bill will replace the complicated electoral college system with the simple method of using the popular vote to decide the winner of a presidential election. By switching to a direct voting system, we can avoid the result of electing a President who failed to win the popular vote.

—U.S. Representative Ray LaHood (R-Illinois)

No: [The electoral college has outgrown its usefulness] only if we think the states as semi-sovereign entities have outgrown their usefulness, which many people believe but many do not. Wyoming with its 479,000 people gets the same two senators as California with its 33 million. The electoral college is designed to reflect the same idea. And it is an idea that is also reflected in the way in which each country gets one vote in the General Assembly of the United Nations and [in] the system of representation of the European Union. The electoral college recognizes the equal status of the states, regardless of their population.

—Frederick Schauer, Harvard University professor

popular votes to Gore's 51.0 million. Bush is the first president since Harrison in 1888 to win the presidency despite losing the popular vote. The 2000 election was decided by the Florida vote. Bush received Florida's 25 electoral votes by a virtue of a 930-vote margin that excluded ballots that could not be read by voting machines. The U.S. Supreme Court blocked a count of these ballots (see Chapter 14).

MEDIA AND MONEY   The modern presidential campaign is a media campaign. At one time, candidates relied heavily on party organization and rallies to carry their messages to the voters, but now they depend on the media, particularly television.[21] Candidates strive to produce the pithy ten-second "sound bites" that the television networks prefer to highlight on the evening newscasts. They also rely on the power of the "new media," making frequent appearances on such programs as *Larry King Live* and creating their own Internet web sites.

Television is the forum for the major confrontation of the fall campaign: the presidential debates. The first televised debate took place in 1960 between Kennedy and Nixon, and an estimated one hundred million people saw at least one of their four debates.[22] Televised debates resumed in 1976 and have become an apparently permanent fixture of presidential campaigns. Elections are sometimes decided by a small margin, and the debates can make a difference. In 2000, Gore had an edge in the polls before the first debate. He was also the more experienced debater and had a firmer grasp of policy issues. But Gore drew a negative response from viewers when he huffed and grimaced while Bush was talking. Meanwhile, Bush gave a stronger performance than pundits had expected, which led them to conclude he had helped his candidacy. Gore was unable in the second and third debates to overcome fully the image created by his performance in the first debate, which some analysts believe was a key turning point in the 2000 campaign.

The television campaign includes political advertising. Televised commercials are by far the most expensive part of presidential campaign politics. Since 1976, political commercials on television have accounted for about half the candidates' expenditures in the general election campaign. Although candidates typically emphasize their own candidacies in their ads, they do not shrink from attacking their foes. Media consultants have perfected what is called the "attack ad," a blistering assault on the opponent. Such advertising may do more than turn voters away from a candidate. Recent research suggests that it may discourage some people from voting on election day.[23]

The Republican and Democratic nominees are each eligible for federal funding of their general election campaigns even if, as in Bush's case in 2000, they did not accept it during the primaries. The amount for the general election was set at $20 million in 1975 and has been adjusted for inflation in succeeding elections. The major-party nominees in the 2000 presidential election each received about $65 million. The only string attached to this money is that candidates who accept it can spend no additional funds on their campaigns (although the party can spend additional money on their behalf; see Chapter 8).

Candidates can choose not to accept public funding, in which case the amount they spend is limited only by their ability to raise money privately. However, all major-party nominees since 1976 have accepted public funding. Other candidates for the presidency qualify for federal funding if they receive at least 5 percent of the vote and do not spend more than $50,000 of their own money on the campaign. Such candidates receive an amount of funds equal to the proportion of their vote to the average of that of the two major-party nominees. Thus, if a third-party candidate received 20 percent of the national vote and the major-party nominees averaged 40 percent apiece, the third-party candidate would receive half the funds allocated to each of the major-party nominees.

THE WINNERS   The Constitution specifies only that the president must be at least thirty-five years old, a natural-born U.S. citizen, and a U.S. resident for at least fourteen years. Yet the holding of high public office is nearly a prerequisite for gaining the presidency. Except for four Army generals, all presidents had previously served as vice-presidents, members of Congress, state governors, or top federal executives. The vice-presidency in particular has been the inside track to the presidency; roughly a third of the nation's presidents first served as vice-president.

The presidency has been monopolized by white males, but it is likely only a matter of time before the nation has its first minority-group president or its first woman president. Until the early 1950s, a majority of Americans in polls said they would not vote for a woman for president. By the 1990s, however, fewer than 10 percent held this view. A similar change of opinion preceded John Kennedy's election to the presidency in 1960. Kennedy was the nation's first Catholic president and only the second Catholic to have received a major party's nomination. Anti-Catholic sentiment was once a barrier to presidential election but no longer is.

STAFFING THE PRESIDENCY

When Americans go to the polls on election day, they have in mind the choice between two individuals, the Democratic and the Republican presidential nominees. In effect, however, they are choosing a lot more than a single executive leader. They are also picking a secretary of state, the director of the FBI, the chair of the Federal Reserve Board, and a host of other executives, all of whom are presidential appointees.

Presidential Appointees

Newly elected presidents gain important advantages from their appointment powers. First, their appointees are a source of policy information. Modern policymaking requires a detailed understanding of policy issues, and this knowledge is a source of considerable power in Washington. Second, these appointees extend the president's reach into the huge federal bureaucracy, exerting influence on the day-to-day workings of the agencies they head. Not surprisingly, presidents have tended to appoint individuals who share their political and policy goals.

THE EXECUTIVE OFFICE OF THE PRESIDENT   The key staff organization is the Executive Office of the President (EOP), which Congress created in 1939 to provide the president with the staff necessary to coordinate the activities of the executive branch.[24] The EOP has since become the command center of the presidency.[25] It currently consists of ten organizations (see Figure 12-2). They include the White House Office (WHO), which consists of the president's closest personal advisers; the Office of Management and Budget (OMB), which consists of experts who formulate and then administer the federal budget; the National Security Council (NSC), which advises the president on foreign and military affairs; and the Council of Economic Advisers (CEA), which advises the president on the national economy.[26] The Office of the Vice-President is also part of the EOP.

The Vice-President   Although the vice-president works in the White House, no constitutional policy authority comes along with this office. Accordingly, the president decides the role the vice-president will play. Earlier presidents often refused to assign any significant duties to their vice-president, which diminished the office's appeal. Nomination to the vice-presidency was refused by many leading politicians, including Daniel

FIGURE 12-2 EXECUTIVE OFFICE OF THE PRESIDENT (EOP)
The EOP helps the president to manage the rest of the executive branch and promotes the president's policy and political goals. Source: From *The American Democracy*, Fourth Edition, by Thomas Patterson © 1999, reproduced with permission of The McGraw-Hill Companies.

Webster and Henry Clay. Said Webster, "I do not propose to be buried until I am really dead."[27] Recent presidents, however, have assigned important duties to their vice-presidents. George W. Bush, for example, chose Dick Cheney as his running mate in part because Cheney had ably served as White House chief of staff during the presidency of Bush's father. Once in office, Bush relied on Cheney for policy advice and for guidance in the day-to-day operations of the presidency.

The White House Office Of the EOP's ten organizations, the White House Office serves the president most directly and personally. The WHO consists of the president's personal assistants, including close personal advisers, press agents, legislative and group liaison aides, and special assistants for domestic and international policy. They work in the White House, and the president can hire and fire them at will. The personal assistants do much of the legwork for the president and serve as a main source of advice. Most of them are skilled at developing political strategy, recognizing political opportunities, and communicating with the public, Congress, key groups, and the news media. Because of their closeness and loyalty to the president, they are among the most powerful individuals in Washington.

Policy Experts The president is also served by the policy experts in the EOP's other organizations, who include economists, legal analysts, national security specialists, and others. The president is advised on economic issues, for example, by the National Economic Council (NEC). The NEC gathers information to develop indicators of the economy's strength and applies economic theories to various policy alternatives. Modern policymaking cannot be conducted in the absence of such expert advice and knowledge.

THE PRESIDENT'S CABINET   The heads of the fourteen executive departments, such as the Department of Defense and the Department of Agriculture, constitute the president's **cabinet.** They are appointed by the president, subject to confirmation by the Senate. Although the cabinet once served as the president's main advisory group, it has not played this role since Herbert Hoover's administration. As national issues have become increasingly complex, the cabinet has become outmoded as a policymaking forum: department heads are likely to understand issues only in their respective policy areas.[28] Cabinet meetings have been largely reduced to gatherings at which only the most general matters are discussed.

Although the cabinet as a collective decision-making body is a thing of the past, the cabinet members, as individuals who head major departments, are important figures in any administration. The president chooses them for their prominence in politics, business, government, or the professions. Many of them also bring to their office a high level of experience in public affairs.[29] For example, George W. Bush's Secretary of State, Colin Powell, had earlier served as chairman of the Joint Chiefs of Staff.

OTHER PRESIDENTIAL APPOINTEES   In addition to cabinet secretaries, the president appoints the directors and top deputies of federal agencies, members of federal commissions, and heads of regulatory agencies. Altogether, the president appoints more than five thousand executive officials. However, most of these appointees are selected at the agency level or are part-time workers. This still leaves nearly seven hundred appointees who serve the president more or less directly, a much larger number than the chief executive of any other democracy appoints.[30]

The Problem of Control

Although the president's appointees are a valuable asset, they also pose a problem: because they are so numerous, the president has difficulty controlling them. Most appointees are not under the president's direct supervision and have considerable freedom to act on their own initiative—not necessarily in accord with the president's wishes. President Truman had a wall chart in the Oval Office listing more than one hundred officials who reported directly to him and often told visitors, "I cannot even see all of these men, let alone actually study what they are doing."[31] Since Truman's time, the number of bureaucratic agencies has more than doubled, compounding the problem of presidential control over subordinates.[32]

The nature of the control problem varies with the type of appointee. The advantages of having the advice of policy experts, for example, is offset somewhat by the fact that they often have little political experience and tend to exaggerate the importance of their particular policy interests. As a result, their proposals are sometimes impractical or politically unacceptable. On the other hand, top political appointees, while adept at politics, have a tendency to act too independently. WHO assistants tend naturally to skew information in a direction that supports the course of action they favor.[33] At times they even presume to undertake important actions without first obtaining clearance from the president or a chief assistant, leading others to question the president's authority or performance.[34] In 1996, for example, President Clinton found himself embroiled in controversy when it became known that a low-ranking White House assistant, Craig Livingstone, had unlawfully requested hundreds of personnel files from the FBI, many of them on top Republicans who had served in the Reagan and Bush administrations. "Filegate," as the incident came to be called, resulted in congressional hearings and news stories that were highly critical of Clinton's administrative oversight.

The problem of presidential control is even more severe in the case of appointees who work outside the White House, in the departments and agencies. The loyalty of agency heads and cabinet secretaries is often split between a desire to help the president with his goals and an interest in boosting themselves or the agencies they lead.[35] Lower-level appointees within the departments and agencies pose a different type of problem. The president rarely, if ever, sees them, and they are typically political novices (most have fewer than two years of government experience) and not very knowledgeable about policy. These appointees are often "captured" by the agency in which they work because they depend for advice on the agency's career bureaucrats. (Chapter 13 examines further the relationship between presidential appointees and career bureaucrats.)

In sum, the modern presidency is a double-edged sword. Presidents today have greater responsibilities than their predecessors, and the increase in responsibilities expands their opportunities to exert power. At the same time, the range of these responsibilities is so broad that they must rely on staffers who may or may not act in the best interests of the president. The modern president's recurring problem is to find some way of making sure that aides serve the interests of the presidency above all others. (The subject of presidential control of the executive branch will be discussed further in Chapter 13.)

FACTORS IN PRESIDENTIAL LEADERSHIP

The president operates within a system of separate institutions that share power (see box: How the United States Compares). Significant presidential action normally depends on the approval of Congress, the cooperation of the bureaucracy, and sometimes the acceptance of the judiciary. Since other officials have their own priorities, presidents do not always get their way. Congress in particular—more than the courts or the bureaucracy—holds the key to presidential success. Without congressional authorization and funding, most presidential proposals are nothing but ideas, empty of action. Theodore Roosevelt expressed a wish that he could "be the president and Congress, too," if only for a day, so that he would have the power to adopt as well as propose programs.

Given that presidents must elicit support from others if they are to succeed, what is the record of presidential success? One way to judge is to measure the extent to which Congress backs legislative initiatives developed by the White House. No president has come close to getting enactment of all the programs that he has placed before Congress. The average success rate is just below 50 percent, but there has been wide variation.[36] Johnson saw 69 percent of his 1965 initiatives enacted, whereas Nixon attained only 20 percent in 1973. Moreover, presidents have had markedly less success on their more ambitious proposals than on lesser ones.[37]

Whether a president's initiatives are likely to succeed or fail depends on several factors, including the force of circumstance, the stage of the president's term, the nature of the issue, the president's support in Congress, and the level of public support for the president's leadership. Let us examine each of these factors.

How The United States Compares

Systems of Executive Policy Leadership

The United States instituted a presidential system in 1789 as part of its constitutional checks and balances. This form of executive leadership was copied in Latin America but not in Europe. European democracies adopted parliamentary systems, in which executive leadership is provided by a prime minister, who is a member of the legislature. In recent years some European prime ministers have campaigned and governed as if they were a singular authority rather than the head of a collective institution. In the 1960s, France created a separate chief executive office but retained its parliamentary form of legislature.

The policy leadership of a president can differ substantially from that of a prime minister. As a singular head of an independent branch of government, a president does not have to share executive authority, but nevertheless depends on the willingness of the legislative branch to support his leadership. By comparison, a prime minister shares executive leadership with a cabinet, but once agreement within the cabinet is reached, he or she is almost assured of the legislative support necessary to carry out policy initiatives.

Presidential System	Presidential/ Parliamentary System	Parliamentary System
Mexico	Finland	Australia
United States	France	Belgium
Venezuela		Canada
		Germany
		Great Britain
		Italy
		Japan
		Netherlands
		Sweden

The Force of Circumstance

During his first months in office and in the midst of the Great Depression, Franklin D. Roosevelt accomplished the most sweeping changes in domestic policy in the nation's history. Congress moved quickly to pass nearly every New Deal initiative he proposed. In 1964 and 1965 Lyndon Johnson pushed landmark civil rights and social welfare legislation through Congress on the strength of the civil rights movement, the legacy of the assassinated President Kennedy, and large Democratic majorities in the House and Senate. When Ronald Reagan assumed the presidency in 1981, high unemployment and inflation had greatly weakened the national economy and created a mood for significant change, which enabled Reagan to persuade Congress to support some of the most notable taxing and spending changes in history.

From presidencies such as these has come the popular impression that presidents single-handedly decide national policy. However, each of these periods of presidential dominance was marked by a special set of circumstances: a decisive election victory that gave added force to the president's leadership, a compelling national problem that convinced Congress and the public that bold presidential action was needed, and a president who was mindful of what was expected and who vigorously advocated policies consistent with those expectations.

When conditions are favorable, the power of the presidency appears awesome. The problem for most presidents is that conditions are not normally conducive to strong leadership. The political scientist Erwin Hargrove suggests that presidential influence depends largely on circumstance.[38] Some presidents serve in periods when resources are scarce or when important problems are surfacing in American society but have not yet become critical. Such a situation, Hargrove contends, works against the president's efforts to accomplish significant policy change. In 1994, reflecting on the constraints of budget deficits and other factors beyond his control, Bill Clinton said he had no choice but "to play the hand that history had dealt him."

The Stage of the President's Term

If conditions conducive to great accomplishments occur infrequently, it is nonetheless the case that nearly every president has favorable moments. Such moments tend to come during the first months in office. Most newly elected presidents enjoy a **honeymoon period** during which Congress, the press, and the public anticipate initiatives from the Oval Office and are more predisposed than usual to support these initiatives.

Not surprisingly, presidents have put forth more new programs in their first year in office than in any subsequent year. James Pfiffner uses the term "strategic presidency" to refer to a president's need to move quickly on priority items to take advantage of the policy momentum that is gained from the election.[39] Later in their terms, presidents tend to do less well in presenting initiatives and getting them enacted. They may run out of good ideas or, more likely, deplete their political resources: the momentum of their election is gone and sources of opposition have emerged. Furthermore, if they blunder or if conditions turn sour—and it is hard for any president to serve for any length of time without a serious setback of one kind or another—they will lose some of their credibility and public support. Even highly successful presidents like Johnson and Reagan tend to have weak records in their final years. Franklin Roosevelt began his presidency with a remarkable period of achievement—the celebrated "Hundred Days"—but during his last six years in office, few of his major domestic proposals were enacted.

An irony of the presidency, then, is that presidents are most powerful when they are least knowledgeable—during their first months in office. These months can, as a result, be times of risk as well as times of opportunity. An example is the Bay of Pigs fiasco during the first year of John Kennedy's presidency, in which a U.S.–backed invasion force of anticommunist Cubans was easily defeated by Fidel Castro's army.

The Nature of the Issue: Foreign or Domestic

In the 1960s, the political scientist Aaron Wildavsky wrote that although the nation has only one president, it has two presidencies: one domestic and one foreign.[40] Wildavsky was referring to Congress's greater tendency to defer to presidential leadership on foreign policy issues than on domestic policy issues. Wildavsky's thesis is now regarded as a somewhat time-bound conception of presidential influence. He wrote before the Vietnam War had weakened congressional support for presidential leadership in foreign affairs. Today, many of the same factors, that affect a president's success on domestic policy, such as the partisan composition of Congress, also affect success on foreign policy.[41]

Nevertheless, presidents are still somewhat more likely to get what they want when the issue is foreign policy, because they have more authority to act on their own and are more likely to get support from the opposite party in Congress.[42] The clash between powerful interest groups that occurs on many domestic issues is less prevalent in the foreign policy area. Moreover, foreign policy often springs from negotiations between nations. The

★ STATES IN THE NATION ★

Divided Power in the Executive

The president operates in a system of divided power where joint action by Congress is often required for the president's programs to be adopted. The chief executives in the American states are the governors, and nearly all of them must contend with a further division: a separation of power within the executive itself. Maine and New Jersey are the only states where executive power is vested solely in a governor. Five other states have separately elected and (unlike the vice-president) constitutionally empowered lieutenant governors. In most of the other states, other major executive officials, such as the attorney general and secretary of state, are also elected. Finally, there are twelve states in which even minor executive officials, such as commissioner of education, are chosen by the voters. In the case of the federal government, these other major and minor officials are appointed by the president.

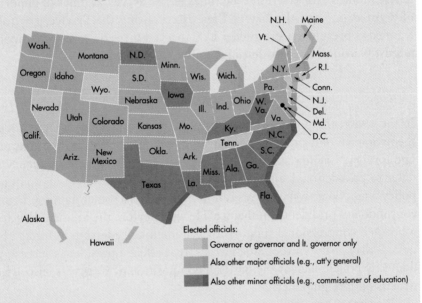

Elected officials:

Governor or governor and lt. governor only

Also other major officials (e.g., att'y general)

Also other minor officials (e.g., commissioner of education)

SOURCE: From *The American Democracy*, Fourth Edition, by Thomas Patterson, © 1999, reproduced with permission of The McGraw-Hill Companies.

president is recognized by other nations as America's voice in world affairs, and even when members of Congress disagree with the president's position, they sometimes accept it out of a concern for America's credibility abroad. In some cases, Congress effectively has no choice but to accept presidential action. When President Bush secretly ordered a military invasion of Panama in 1989, even those members of Congress who might have opposed the invasion had little choice but to express their support for U.S. troops and, by implication, for Bush's policy.

During the cold war, the threat of Soviet military power strengthened the president's hand in foreign affairs.[43] Congress was reluctant to contest presidential initiatives for fear that it would be seen as a sign of national weakness. And for most of the cold war period, public opinion would predictably rally around presidential action whenever there was an appearance that the national interest was threatened by the Soviet Union or another communist state. Since the end of the cold war, however, Congress has been less deferential to presidential leadership and at times has even tried to assume leadership on foreign policy in areas such as military spending, human rights, and international trade.

The president still retains an advantage, however, in the foreign policy area. Some of that advantage can be traced to the increased importance of the global economy. As the chief executive of the nation's most powerful economic nation, the president is expected by the American people and other nations to provide leadership on international economic issues. When Asian economies went into a tailspin in 1998 and threatened to drag down the world economy, President Clinton led the U.S. response, which included a proposed $18 billion grant to the International Monetary Fund. Although the grant was delayed for months by congressional opponents, Congress eventually relented in the face of mounting pressures from the White House, the international financial community, and foreign governments. But the global economy does not give a president the leverage that the cold war provided. Economic issues often engage opposing domestic interests. Business and labor, for example, have been sharply at odds over trade policy (see Chapter 17). Moreover, whenever domestic interests are divided, Congress usually is also divided, which compounds the problems of presidential leadership.

Relations with Congress

Although the presidency is not nearly so powerful as most Americans assume, the capacity of presidents to influence the agenda of national debate is unrivaled, reflecting their unique claim to represent the whole country. Whenever the president directs attention to a particular issue or program, the attention of others usually follows. But will those others follow the president's lead? As we have noted, a president's support varies with conditions, some of which clearly cannot be controlled. Yet presidents are not entirely at the mercy of circumstance. As sole chief executive, a president is an active participant in his fate and can increase the chance of success by striving to build support in Congress and with the American people.

SEEKING COOPERATION FROM CONGRESS   As the center of national attention, presidents can easily start to believe that their ideas should prevail over those of Congress. This line of reasoning invariably gets any president into trouble. Jimmy Carter had not held national office before he was elected in 1976, so he had no clear understanding of how Washington operates.[44] Soon after taking office, Carter deleted from his budget nineteen public works projects that he believed were a waste of taxpayers' money, ignoring the importance that members of Congress attach to obtaining federally funded projects for their constituents. Carter's action set the tone for a conflict-ridden relationship with Congress.

In order to get the help of members of Congress, the president must respond to their interests as they respond to his. The presidential scholar Fred Greenstein concludes that "whatever else his qualities, the president needs to be a working politician who can work with or otherwise win over the Washington community."[45]

The use of the presidential veto illustrates the point. Presidents can sometimes force Congress to accommodate their views through the use or threatened use of the veto. Congress can seldom muster the two-thirds majority in each chamber required to override a presidential veto, and so the threat of a veto can make Congress more responsive to the president's demands.[46] When a major civil rights bill was being debated in Congress in 1991, George Bush said flatly that he would veto any bill that imposed hiring "quotas" on employers; his ultimatum forced Congress to alter provisions of the bill. Yet the veto is more effective as a presidential restraint on Congress than as a device by which Congress can be forced to take positive action on the president's proposals. The presidential scholar Richard Neustadt argues that the veto is more a sign of presidential weakness than of strength, because it usually comes into play when Congress has refused to go along with the president's ideas.[47]

In 1996, Congress enacted legislation that gave the president a line-item veto of spending bills. The president could void (subject to override by a two-thirds vote of the House and Senate) specific spending items without vetoing the entire bill. But in 1998, the Supreme Court voided the line item veto on grounds that it violated both the constitutional separation of powers and the constitutional procedural requirements for enacting legislation.[48]

THE PRESIDENT'S PARTISAN SUPPORT IN CONGRESS   The fact that they represent separate state or district constituencies can place individual members of Congress at odds with one another as well as with the president, whose constituency is a national one. Representatives of urban and rural areas, wealthier and poorer constituencies, and different regions of the country often have very different views of the national interest. To obtain majority support in Congress, the president must find ways to overcome these differences.

No source of unity is more important to presidential success than partisanship. Presidents are more likely to succeed when their own party controls Congress (see Figure 12-3). Between 1954 and 1992, each Republican president—Eisenhower, Nixon, Ford, Reagan, and Bush—had to contend with a Democratic majority in one or both houses of Congress. Congress passed a smaller percentage of the initiatives proposed by each of these presidents than of those by any Democratic president of the period: Kennedy, Johnson, or Carter.[49] In his first two years in office, backed by Democratic majorities in the House and Senate, Clinton had a high proportion of his initiatives enacted into law. After Republicans took control of Congress in 1995, Clinton's legislative success rate sank to the lowest of any recent Democratic president, a dramatic illustration of the way presidential power is affected by whether the president's party controls Congress.

COLLIDING WITH CONGRESS   On rare occasions, presidents have pursued their goals so zealously that Congress has been compelled to take steps to curb their use of power.

The ultimate sanction of Congress is its constitutional power to impeach and remove the president from office. The House of Representatives decides whether the president should be impeached (placed on trial), and the Senate conducts the trial and then votes on the president's guilt, with a two-thirds vote required for removal from office. In 1868 Andrew Johnson was impeached and came within one Senate vote of being removed from office for his opposition to Congress's harsh Reconstruction policies after the Civil War. In 1974 Richard Nixon's resignation halted congressional proceedings on the Watergate affair that would almost certainly have ended in his impeachment and removal from office.

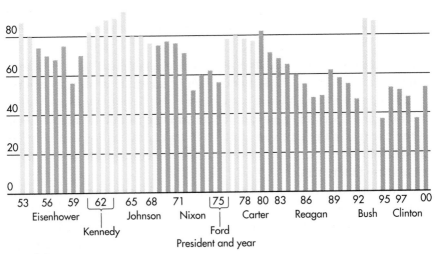

Percentage of bills on which Congress
supported president's position

Control of Congress

President's party
Other party (1 or both houses)

FIGURE 12-3 PERCENTAGE OF BILLS PASSED BY CONGRESS ON WHICH THE PRESIDENT ANNOUNCED A POSITION, 1953–2000
In most years, presidents have been supported by Congress on a majority of policy issues on which they have taken a stand. Presidents fare better when their party controls Congress. Source: *Congressional Quarterly Weekly Report*, January 6, 2001, p. 54. Reprinted by permission of Congressional Quarterly, Inc.

The prospect of impeachment was raised again in 1998 when the House of Representatives by a vote of 258 to 176 authorized an investigation of President Clinton's conduct. He was accused of lying under oath about his relationship with Monica Lewinsky and of obstructing justice by trying to conceal the affair. The gravity of the allegations was leavened by the circumstances. The charges had grown out of an extramarital affair rather than a gross abuse of executive power and were tied to a controversial five-year $40 million investigation by independent counsel Kenneth 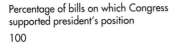 Starr. For their part, the American people were ambivalent about the whole issue. Most people approved of Clinton's handling of the presidency and did not believe his actions warranted removal from office, but they were also sharply critical of his relationship with Lewinsky. Not surprisingly, congressional Republicans and Democrats differed sharply on the impeachment issue. At all formal stages of the process—the House vote to authorize an inquiry, the House vote on the articles of impeachment, and the Senate vote on whether to convict the president—the vote divided largely along party lines. In the end, Clinton was acquitted by the Senate, but his legacy will forever be tarnished by his impeachment by the House.

The gravity of impeachment action makes it an unsuitable basis for curbing presidential power except in rare instances. More often, Congress has responded legislatively to executive abuses. An example is the Budget Impoundment and Control Act of 1974, which prohibits a president from refusing to release funds that have been appropriated by Congress. The legislation was enacted in response to the Nixon administration's practice of withholding funds from programs it disliked.

Congress's most significant effort in history to curb presidential power, however, is the War Powers Act. During the Vietnam War, presidents Johnson and Nixon repeatedly misled Congress, supplying it with intelligence estimates that painted a falsely optimistic picture of the military situation. This information contributed to the willingness of Congress to appropriate the funds necessary for continuation of the war. However, congressional support changed abruptly in 1971 with *The New York Times's* publication of classified documents (the so-called Pentagon Papers) that revealed the Vietnam situation to be much worse than portrayed by Johnson and Nixon.

To prevent future presidential wars, Congress in 1973 passed the War Powers Act. Nixon vetoed the measure, but Congress overrode his veto. The act requires the president to notify Congress of the reason for committing combat troops within forty-eight hours of their deployment; requires that hostilities must end within sixty days unless Congress extends the period; gives the president an additional thirty days to withdraw the troops from hostile territory, although Congress can shorten the period; and requires the president to consult with Congress whenever feasible before dispatching troops into a hostile situation.

Every president since Nixon has claimed that the act infringes on his constitutional power as commander in chief, and each has refused to accept it fully. Nevertheless, since Vietnam, Congress has shown no willingness to give the president anything approaching a free hand in the use of military force.

Thus the effect of executive efforts to circumvent congressional authority is heightened congressional opposition. Even if presidents gain in the short run by acting on their own, they undermine their capacity to lead in the long run by failing to keep in mind that Congress is a coequal branch of the American governing system.

Impeaching, Convicting, and Removing the President

In October 1998, for only the third time in American history, the Congress authorized an official impeachment investigation of the president. Bill Clinton joined Andrew Johnson and Richard Nixon as presidents whose legacy will be forever linked with the word "impeachment."

Although "impeachment" technically applies only to the indictment stage of congressional action, it is commonly used to refer also to the conviction stage. But these are constitutionally separate stages. The House is granted under Article I, section 2 of the Constitution the power to impeach (indict) the president. The Senate under Article I, section 3 has the power to try, convict, and remove the president.

Article II, section 4 of the Constitution states that impeachable acts are "Treason, Bribery, or Other High Crimes and Misdemeanors" but does not spell out what these other high crimes and misdemeanors shall include. Nevertheless, it is clear from the historical record that the Framers deliberately created a process that would make it difficult to remove the president from office in order to discourage Congress from seeking to get rid of a president for purely political reasons.

The steps that Congress would take in removing the president from office are the following:

1. The House of Representatives by simple majority vote would authorize an investigation of the president.
2. The House Judiciary Committee would conduct the inquiry and submit its findings to the full House.
3. The House through simple majority vote would indict the president on one or more charges (thus "impeaching" the president).
4. The Senate would hold a trial on the charges; the Chief Justice of the Supreme Court would preside over the trial.
5. The Senate through a two-thirds majority would convict, causing the president's removal from office.

The Clinton impeachment process ended with step four; the Senate did not vote to convict. The course of Andrew Jackson's impeachment was the same, although the Senate, in his case, came within one vote of conviction. Nixon resigned shortly before the House vote (step three) on impeachment.

Nurturing Public Support

Public support has a powerful effect on presidents' ability to achieve their policy goals.[50] Much of their power rests on a claim to national leadership, and the legitimacy of that claim is roughly proportional to public support of the president's performance. As long as the public is behind him, the president's leadership cannot easily be dismissed by other Washington officials. If public support sinks, they are less inclined to accept his leadership.[51]

Every recent president has had the public's confidence at the very start of the term of office. When asked in polls whether they "approve or disapprove of how the president is doing his job," a majority has expressed approval during the first months of the term. Sooner or later, however, all **presidential approval ratings** have slipped below this high point, and fewer than half of recent presidents have left office with a final-year average higher than 50 percent.

EVENTS AND ISSUES   The public's support for the president is affected by national and international conditions. Threats from abroad tend to produce a patriotic "rally 'round the flag" reaction that initially creates widespread support for the president. Every foreign policy crisis in the past four decades has fitted this pattern. Yet ongoing crises usually erode a president's support. Within a month after Iranian extremists invaded the U.S. embassy in Teheran in November 1979 and took fifty-nine Americans hostage, Carter's public approval rating jumped by twenty points.[52] As months passed without a resolution of the hostage situation, however, Carter's popularity began to sink and his hold on the presidency began to slip. He lost the 1980 election, partly because the hostage crisis remained unresolved.

Economic downswings tend to sharply reduce the public's confidence in the president.[53] Ford, Carter, and Bush experienced precipitous declines in popularity in conjunction with deepening economic problems. A poor economy probably cost Ford a second term and was clearly the key factor in the failed bids for reelection of both Presidents Carter and Bush. In contrast, Clinton's popularity rose in 1995 and 1996 as the economy strengthened, contributing to his reelection in 1996, just as an improving economy had carried Reagan to reelection in 1984. Apparently the best thing that a president can do to ensure political success is to preside over a healthy economy. It was no surprise that George W. Bush declared early in 2001 that tax cuts and other policies designed to keep the economy from faltering would be his administration's highest priority.

The irony, of course, is that presidents do not actually have all that much control over the economy. If they did, it would always be strong. Nevertheless, their popularity moves up and down with the economy, and so does the strength of their claim to national leadership.

THE TELEVISED PRESIDENCY   A major advantage that presidents enjoy in their efforts to nurture public support is their guaranteed access to the media, particularly television.[54] The television medium exalts personality, and the president is ordinarily the most compelling and familiar figure in the American political system. Only the president can expect the television networks to provide free airtime on demand, and in terms of the amount of news coverage, the president and his top advisers receive half again as much coverage as all members of Congress combined.

The political scientist Samuel Kernell calls it "going public" when the president bypasses inside bargaining with Congress and promotes "himself and his policies by appealing to the American public for support."[55] Such appeals are at least as old as Theodore Roosevelt's use of the presidency as a "bully pulpit," but have increased substantially in recent years.[56] As the president has moved from the role of administrative leader to that of policy advocate and agenda setter, public support has become increasingly important to presidential success.[57] Television has made it easier for presidents to

Clinton press secretary Mike McCurry held his daily briefings for reporters in the cramped space of the White House Briefing Room. Effective communication is an indispensable part of the modern presidency.

go public with their programs. Ronald Reagan was called the "Great Communicator" in part because of his ability to use television to generate public support for his initiatives.

However, the press is also adept at putting its own spin on events, and this spin is typically a negative one. The press is often very critical of politicians and of the process within which they operate. During Clinton's first year, for example, the press roundly criticized him for reneging on his campaign promises. This for a president who according to a Knight-Ridder summary had kept or was actively pursuing in Congress 75 percent of the promises he had made during his election campaign; included were major legislative battles already won, such as a tax increase on upper incomes, gun control, an end to the ban on abortion counseling in federally funded clinics, and budget-deficit reduction. The press's version of reality was based on broken promises on a couple of problems that would not go away. Clinton had backed away from a pledge to open the nation's shores to the Haitian boat people, and each tide of immigrants produced additional stories on his broken promise. In contrast, the promises he kept were in the news only a day or two and then not mentioned again. Kept promises are not nearly so newsworthy as broken ones. The media's interpretation of Clinton's presidency had a substantial impact. Every rise in the press criticism of Clinton was followed soon thereafter by a drop in his public approval rating.

Scandal is the biggest threat to the president's ability to control the news agenda. When scandal strikes, a media "feeding frenzy" ensues, and power shifts from the White House to the press and the president's political opponents. The Lewinsky scandal, for example, was initially fueled by news reports based on unidentified and anonymous sources, as well as journalistic analysis (the most prevalent theme: "Clinton is in big trouble") without reference to any source. It was not until the frenzy began to abate that the White House could even attempt to recapture the agenda. And then it was not very successful. During ensuing months, the White House tried to refocus the nation's attention through dramatic events, such as a presidential speech at the UN on the global financial crisis shortly after the Starr Report was released. Clinton's appearance prompted a standing ovation at the UN, a nearly unprecedented show of support by the world community for an American president. But most of these events received only fleeting news coverage. The Lewinsky story was what the press wanted to report.

THE ILLUSION OF PRESIDENTIAL GOVERNMENT   Presidents have no choice but to try to counter this type of press coverage with their own version of their accomplishments. A public relations effort can carry a president only so far, however. National conditions ultimately determine the level of public confidence in the president. Indeed, presidents run a risk by trying to build up their images through public relations. Through their frequent television appearances and claims of success, presidents contribute to the public's belief that the president is in charge of the national government, a perception that the political scientist Hugh Heclo calls "the illusion of presidential government."[58]

Because the public expects so much from its presidents, they get too much credit when things go well and too much blame when things go badly. Therein lies an irony of the presidential office. More than from any constitutional grant, more than from any statute, and more than from any crisis, presidential power derives from the president's position as the sole official who can claim to represent the whole American public. Yet because presidential power rests on a popular base, it erodes when public support declines. The irony is that the presidential office typically grows weaker as problems mount: just when the country could most use effective leadership, that leadership is often hardest to achieve.[59]

SUMMARY

The presidency has become a much stronger office than the Framers envisioned. The Constitution grants the president substantial military, diplomatic, legislative, and executive powers, and in each case the president's authority has increased measurably. Underlying this change is the president's position as the one leader chosen by the whole nation and as the sole head of the executive branch. These features of the office have enabled presidents to claim broad authority in response to the increased demands placed on the federal government by changing world and national conditions.

During the course of American history, the presidential selection process has been altered in ways that were intended to make it more responsive to the preferences of ordinary people. Today, they have a vote not only in the general election, but also in the selection of nominees. To gain nomination, a presidential hopeful must gain the support of the electorate in state primaries and open caucuses. Once nominated, the candidates receive federal funds for their general election campaigns, which are based on televised appeals.

Although the campaign tends to personalize the presidency, the responsibilities of the modern presidency far exceed any president's personal capacities. To meet their obligations, presidents have surrounded themselves with large staffs of advisers, policy experts, and managers. These staff members enable the president to extend control over the executive branch while providing the information necessary for policymaking. All recent presidents have discovered, however, that their control of staff resources is incomplete, and that some things that others do on their behalf actually work against what they are trying to accomplish.

www.mhhe.com/patterson
self quiz

As sole chief executive and the nation's top elected leader, the president can always expect that his policy and leadership efforts will receive attention. However, other institutions, particularly Congress, have the authority to make this leadership effective. No president has come close to winning approval of all the programs he has placed before Congress, but the presidents' records of success have varied considerably. The factors in a president's success include the presence or absence of national conditions that require strong leadership from the White House and whether the president's party has a majority in Congress.

To retain an effective leadership position, the president depends on the backing of the American people. Recent presidents have made extensive use of the media to build support for their programs. Yet they have had difficulty maintaining that support throughout their terms of office. A major reason is that the public expects far more from its presidents than they can deliver.

MAJOR CONCEPTS

cabinet	presidential approval rating
honeymoon period	stewardship theory
legitimacy	unit rule
momentum	Whig theory
open party caucuses	

SUGGESTED READINGS AND WEB SITES

Cohen, Jeffrey E. *Presidential Responsiveness and Public Policymaking: The Publics and the Policies that Presidents Choose.* Ann Arbor: University of Michigan Press, 1997. An accounting of presidential responsiveness and public policymaking.

Jones, Charles. *Separate But Equal Branches.* New York: Chatham House, 1999. An insightful analysis of presidential power in a system of divided powers.

Kernell, Samuel. *Going Public: New Strategies of Presidential Leadership.* 3d ed. Washington, D.C.: Congressional Quarterly Press, 1997. An examination of presidential use of going public to gain support.

Kraus, Sydney. *Televised Presidential Debates and Public Policy.* 2nd ed. Mahwah, N.J.: Lawrence Erlbaum Publishers, 2000. An analysis by one of the leading presidential debate experts.

Neustadt, Richard E. *Presidential Power and the Modern Presidents: The Politics of Leadership from Roosevelt to Reagan.* New York: Free Press, 1990. The classic analysis of the limitations on presidential power.

Pfiffner, James P. *The Strategic Presidency: Hitting the Ground Running.* 2d ed. Chicago: Dorsey Press, 1996. An analysis of the way a newly elected president can convert electoral support into power in office.

Walch, Timothy, ed. *At the President's Side: The Vice Presidency in the Twentieth Century*. Columbia: University of Missouri Press, 1997. An assessment of the vice-presidency and its twentieth-century occupants.

Walcott, Charles E., and Karen M. Hult. *Governing the White House: From Hoover through LBJ*. Lawrence: University Press of Kansas, 1995. An innovative study of how the organization of the White House affects presidential performance.

http://sunsite.unc.edu:80/lia/president This site has general information on specific presidents and links to the presidential libraries.

http://www.ipl.org/ref/POTUS Profiles of the nation's presidents, their cabinet officers, and key events during their time in office.

http://www.vote-smart.org/executive Information on the presidency and the Executive Office of the President as well as links to key executive agencies and organizations.

http://www.whitehouse.gov The White House's home page has an e-mail guest book and includes information on the president, the vice-president, and current White House activities.

READING 12

The Postmodern President

RICHARD ROSE

Introduction

In his essay, Richard Rose expands on an argument introduced in
Chapter 12: that the powers of the presidency are inadequate to the
demands placed upon the office. Rose notes that the Soviet threat
during the cold war encouraged America's allies to support the foreign policies of U.S. presidents. With the threat removed and economic rather than military issues at the forefront of international
affairs, the president is in a weaker position to gain support abroad
for U.S. objectives. The president has always had to contend with
an independent Congress in pursuit of domestic policy goals. Now
the president also has to contend with allies whose global economic
goals may compete with those of the United States.

In two centuries, America has had three different Presidencies: a traditional President who had little to do; a modern President who had a lot
to do at home and abroad; and a postmodern President who may have
too much expected of him. As the world changes, our ideas must change,
or we will become confused by applying the standards of one era to a different one. . . .

The traditional Presidency was designed two centuries ago to protect the American people against the abuses of an autocratic monarch
and to guard against the emergence of an elected despot. For a century
and a half, the White House was an office in a system of separated powers in which Congress and the Supreme Court each acted as a check on
the Presidency and Congress was the leading branch. The traditional
Presidency was not a driving force in government; with occasional exceptions, it was a dignified office of state.

The modern Presidency was created by Franklin D. Roosevelt's response to the depression of the 1930s. Although Roosevelt was not the
first occupant of the Oval Office of the White House to believe in an active Presidency, he was the first to be an active leader in peacetime. To

support his leadership, Roosevelt began the practice of appealing to the public for support through the new medium of radio broadcasting. Few Americans ever saw or heard the voice of Abraham Lincoln or Woodrow Wilson, but FDR's fireside chats made his voice familiar to every voter. America's involvement in World War II made President Roosevelt an international leader too. President Harry Truman placed America's world role on a permanent basis, deciding to drop the atomic bomb on Japan, and after 1945, committing American troops to the defense of places as far apart as Berlin and Korea. Because other nations were then devastated by war or had never been industrial powers, the modern President's eminence was at first a solitary eminence.

The military and economic eminence of America after 1945 resulted in American *hegemony* in the international system, that is, the United States was the dominant nation influencing what happened around the globe. The mobilization of American arms to contain the Soviet Union had a great impact because of America's vast population, double that of Japan and four times that of Britain, France, or Germany. The impact was enhanced by the development of new and increasingly sophisticated weapons systems. Whereas the Soviet Union is also a military superpower and Japan is also an economic superpower, only the United States has been both a military and economic superpower. American money stimulated the economies of Europe and Asia, and products such as IBM computers, Xerox machines, and Coca-Cola penetrated every corner of the earth. U.S. policies sought to secure mutual defense and worldwide economic growth: "For Americans it was the ideal outcome: one could do well by doing good."

The difference between the modern and the postmodern Presidency is that a postmodern President can no longer dominate the international system. President Carter and President Reagan have each appeared as helpless victims of forces abroad: oil-exporting nations, foreign armies, small bands of terrorists, and bankers and businessmen profiting from problems of the American economy. *Interdependence* characterizes an international system in which no nation is the hegemonic power. The President is the leader of a very influential nation, but other nations are influential too. In an interdependent world, what happens in the United States depends on what happens in other countries as well as what happens at home. For example, if America is to increase its exports, then other countries must increase their imports. The line between domestic and international politics is dissolving.

While the White House is accustomed to influencing foreign nations, the postmodern President must accept something less appealing: Other nations can now influence what the White House achieves. Whereas the Constitution made Congress and the Supreme Court the chief checks on the traditional and the modern President, the chief constraints on the postmodern President are found in other nations. The White House depends on the cooperation of the Kremlin to deter nuclear war and for agreement in arms-control negotiations. It makes a big difference to the White House whether the Soviet Union pursues a policy of *glasnost* or aggression. The White House looks to the Japanese government to act to reduce the American trade deficit, and it looks to the German central bank, the Bundesbank, to boost demand in Europe for American exports. . . .

Although America remains a world power, it is no longer the dominant power that it once was. The White House has not lost Britain or Germany or Japan, for these independent countries never belonged to the United States. Each remains an ally, but the terms of the relationship have changed. . . .

In an interdependent world a President cannot always do what he wants, because policies cannot always be stamped *Made in America.** A ruler with unchallenged authority could assume that to govern is to choose. A postmodern President must start from the assumption: *To govern is to cooperate*. A President has always needed to cooperate with Congress in order to succeed in a constitutional system that separates powers. What is novel is that a postmodern President must cooperate with foreign governments to achieve major economic and national security goals. Cooperation requires a mutuality of interests between nations. If this is lacking, then a postmodern President can face stalemate abroad, just as he can face stalemate in Congress. . . .

*Presidents are referred to as he, since every President has been a male, while countries as diverse as Britain, India, Israel, and Norway have had women as national leaders. To refer to Presidents by the phrase "he or she" would convey a misleading impression of gender equality.

The leading contemporary scholar of the Presidency, Richard E. Neustadt, has asked: "Is the Presidency possible?" His answer is not encouraging: "Weakness is what I see." The standard for presidential success that Neustadt offers is challenging but not impossible: A "minimally effective" President should match the achievements of President Truman; he adds that there is "nothing high-and-mighty about that." If Truman's achievement is taken as the standard for the Presidency, three-quarters of the country's leaders fall below this mark, in the judgment of historians. It is particularly worrisome that historians do not rate any occupant of the White House as having reached this standard since Truman left office in 1953.

It is right to worry about the capacity of the President, for the man in the White House is not an ordinary officeholder. The President is unique in his claim to political authority; he alone is elected by the nation as a whole. Lincoln's idea of government by the people is simply not practical. When America has a population of 240 million people, big decisions about the economy and foreign policy cannot be taken in a New England–style town meeting. Nor can 535 congressmen give clear and coherent direction to government, individually or collectively. The job of a congressman is to represent his or her district in Washington. The job of the President is to represent the whole of the nation in an uncertain and sometimes hostile world.

. . . To look back longingly to a world in which the President stood as a colossus is to default on our obligations to the future. We are much closer to the twenty-first century than we are to the days of George Washington, Franklin D. Roosevelt, or John F. Kennedy. . . . Reading history forward is a challenge to understand under what conditions and to what extent a postmodern President can succeed in an international system in which he is not the only leader who counts, because America is not the only nation that counts.

SOURCE: From Richard Rose, "The Postmodern President," *The Postmodern President*, 1991. Reprinted by permission of Chatham House Publishers.
Richard Rose is professor and director of the Centre for the Study of Public Policy at the University of Strathclyde, Glasgow, Scotland.

CHAPTER THIRTEEN

The Bureaucracy

[No] industrial society could manage the daily operations of its public affairs
without bureaucratic organizations in which officials play a
major policymaking role.

NORMAN THOMAS[1]

EARLY ON the morning of September 7, 1993, a truck pulled up to
the south lawn of the White House and unloaded pallets stacked
with federal regulations.[2] The mountainous display was the backdrop for a
presidential speech announcing the completion of the National Performance Review, or, as it is commonly called, NPR. The federal regulations
piled atop the pallets symbolized bureaucratic red tape, and NPR was a
statement of the Clinton administration's effort to make government more
responsive. "Our goal," said Clinton, "is to make the entire federal government both less expensive and more efficient, and to change the culture of
our national bureaucracy away from complacency and entitlement toward
initiative and empowerment. We intend to redesign, to reinvent, to rein-
vigorate the entire national government."[3]

The origins of the National Performance Review were plain enough.
For years, the federal bureaucracy had been derided as too big, too expensive, and too intrusive. These charges gained weight as federal budget
deficits increased and the public became increasingly dissatisfied with the
performance of the government in Washington. Reform attempts in the
1970s and 1980s had some success but did not stem the tide of the federal
deficit or markedly improve the bureaucracy's performance. Clinton campaigned on the issue of "reinventing government" and acted swiftly on the
promise. During the transition phase, Vice President–elect Al Gore was
placed in charge of the National Performance Review. Once in office, Gore
assembled more than two hundred career bureaucrats who knew firsthand
how the bureaucracy operated and organized them into "reinventing teams"
that would recommend ways of improving government administration. The

NPR's report included 384 specific recommendations, which were grouped into four broad imperatives: reducing red tape, putting customers first, empowering administrators, and downscaling to basics.

NPR is the latest in a list of major twentieth-century proposals to remake the federal bureaucracy. NPR was different in its particulars, but its claim to improve administration while saving money is consistent with the claims of earlier reform panels, including the Brownlow, Hoover, and Volcker commissions. Like them, NPR addressed an enduring issue of American politics: the bureaucracy's efficiency, responsiveness, and accountability.

Modern government would be impossible without a bureaucracy. It is the government's enormous administrative capacity that makes it possible for the United States to have such ambitious programs as space exploration, social security, environmental protection, interstate highways, and universal postal service. Yet the bureaucracy is also a problem. Even those who work in federal agencies bemoan its rigidity and costliness. Both these elements, the need for bureaucracy and the problems associated with it, must be taken into account in any effort to understand the bureaucracy's place in modern American politics.

This chapter describes the nature of the federal bureaucracy and the politics that surrounds it. The discussion initially aims to clarify the bureaucracy's responsibilities, organizational structure, and management practices. But the chapter also shows that the bureaucracy is very much a part of the play of politics. Bureaucrats necessarily and naturally take an

As one of thousands of services provided by the federal bureaucracy, the National Hurricane Service monitors hurricane activity and provides early warning to affected coastal areas.

"agency point of view," seeking to promote their agency's objectives. The three constitutional branches of government impose a degree of accountability on the bureaucracy; but the sheer size and fragmented nature of the U.S. government confound the problem of control and make efforts to reform the bureaucracy a high priority. The main points discussed in this chapter are the following:

* *Modern government could not function without a large bureaucracy; through hierarchy, specialization, and rules, the bureaucratic form is the only practical way of organizing large-scale government programs.*

* *The bureaucracy is expected simultaneously to respond to the direction of partisan officials and to administer programs fairly and competently; these conflicting demands are addressed through a combination of personnel management systems: the patronage, merit, and executive leadership systems.*

* *Bureaucrats naturally take an "agency point of view," which they promote through their expert knowledge, support from clientele groups, and backing by Congress or the president.*

* *Although agencies are subject to scrutiny by the president, Congress, and the judiciary, bureaucrats are able to achieve power in their own right.*

THE FEDERAL BUREAUCRACY: FORM, PERSONNEL, AND ACTIVITIES

For many Americans, the word "bureaucracy" brings to mind waste, mindless rules, and rigidity. This image is not unfounded, but it is one-sided. Bureaucracy is also an effective method of organization. Although Americans tend to equate bureaucracy with government, bureaucracy is found wherever there is a need to manage large numbers of people and tasks. Bureaucracy alone facilitates the coordination of a large work force. All large-scale, task-oriented organizations—public and private—are bureaucratic in form. General Motors is a bureaucracy. So, too, is every large university. The state governments are also every bit as "bureaucratic" as the federal government (see box: States in the Nation).

In formal terms, **bureaucracy** is a system of organization and control that is based on three principles: hierarchical authority, job specialization, and formalized rules. **Hierarchical authority** refers to a chain of command, whereby the officials and units at the top of a bureaucracy have authority over those in the middle, who in turn control those at the bottom. In a system of **job specialization,** the responsibilities of each job position are explicitly defined and there is a precise division of labor within the organization. **Formalized rules** are the standardized procedures and established regulations by which a bureaucracy conducts its operations.

These features are the reason that bureaucracy, as a form of organization, is the most efficient means of getting people to work together on tasks of great magnitude and complexity. Hierarchy speeds action by reducing conflict over the power to make decisions: the higher an individual's position in the organization, the more decision-making power he or she has. Specialization yields efficiency because each individual is required to concentrate on a particular job: workers acquire specialized skills and knowledge. Formalized rules enable workers to make quick and consistent judgments because decisions are made on the basis of preestablished guidelines rather than by deliberation and personal inclination.

These organizational characteristics are also the cause of bureaucracy's pathologies. Administrators perform not as whole persons but as parts of an organizational entity. Their behavior is governed by position, specialty, and rule. At its worst, bureaucracy grinds on, heedless of the feelings and special needs of its members or their clients. Fixed rules come to dominate everything.[4]

If bureaucracy is an indispensable condition of large-scale organization, gross bureaucratic inefficiency and unresponsiveness are not, or at least that is the assumption underlying current efforts to reform the administration of government, a topic that will be examined later in this chapter.

The Federal Bureaucracy in Americans' Daily Lives

The U.S. federal bureaucracy has roughly 2.5 million employees, who have responsibility for administering thousands of programs. The president and Congress may get far more attention in the news, but it is the bureaucracy that has the more immediate impact on the daily lives of Americans. The federal bureaucracy performs a wide range of functions; for example, it delivers the daily mail, maintains national parks, administers social security, enforces environmental protection laws, develops the country's defense systems, provides foodstuffs for school-lunch programs, and regulates the stock markets.

Types of Administrative Organizations

The chief organizational feature of the U.S. federal bureaucracy is its division into areas of specialization. One agency handles veterans' affairs, another specializes in education, a third is responsible for agriculture, and

★ STATES IN THE NATION ★

The Size of State Bureaucracies

Although the federal bureaucracy is often criticized as being "too big," it is actually smaller on a per capita basis than even the smallest of the state bureaucracies. There are 1.0 federal employees for every 100 Americans. California, with 1.2 state employees for every 100 residents, has the smallest state bureaucracy on a per capita basis. Hawaii, with 5.0 state employees per 100 residents, has the largest. In general, the least populous states, and especially those that are larger geographically, have the largest bureaucracies on a per capita basis. This pattern reflects the fact that a state, whatever its population, has basic functions (such as highway maintenance and policing) that it must perform.

Number of State Employees
- 1.5 or fewer employees/100 residents
- 1.6–2.0 employees/100 residents
- 2.1 or more employees/100 residents

SOURCE: U.S. Bureau of the Census, 1999.

so on. No two units are exactly alike. Nevertheless, most of them take one of five general forms: cabinet department, independent agency, regulatory agency, government corporation, or presidential commission.

Cabinet Departments   The major administrative units are the fourteen **cabinet (executive) departments** (see Figure 13-1). Except for the Department of Justice, which is headed by the attorney general, the top official in each department is its secretary (for example, the secretary of defense), who serves as a member of the president's cabinet and is responsible for establishing the department's general policy and overseeing its operations.

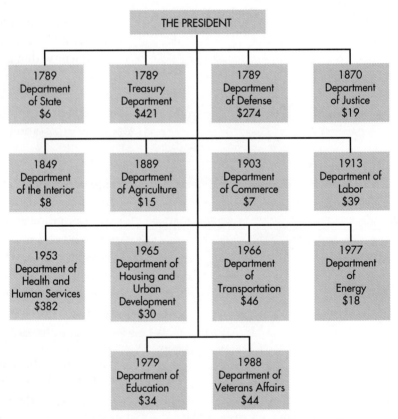

FIGURE 13-1   CABINET (EXECUTIVE) DEPARTMENTS
Each executive department is responsible for a general policy area and is headed by a secretary, who serves as a member of the president's cabinet. Shown are each department's year of origin (above the title) and annual budget in billions of dollars (below the title). Source: U.S. Office of Management and Budget, FY2000.

Cabinet departments vary greatly in their visibility, size, and importance. The Department of State is one of the oldest and most prestigious departments, but it is also one of the smallest, with approximately 25,000 employees. The Department of Defense has the largest work force, with roughly 700,000 civilian employees (apart from the roughly 1.3 million uniformed members of the armed services). The Department of Health and Human Services has the largest budget; its activities account for about a third of all federal spending, much of it for social security benefits.

INDEPENDENT AGENCIES **Independent agencies** resemble the cabinet departments, but most of them have a narrower area of responsibility. They include such organizations as the Central Intelligence Agency (CIA) and the National Aeronautics and Space Administration (NASA). The heads of these agencies are appointed by and report to the president but are not members of the cabinet. In general, the independent agencies exist apart from cabinet departments because their placement within a department would pose symbolic or practical policy problems. NASA, for example, could conceivably be located in the Department of Defense, but this positioning would suggest that the space program is intended for military purposes and not also for civilian purposes, such as space exploration and satellite communication.

REGULATORY AGENCIES **Regulatory agencies** are created when Congress recognizes the importance of close and continuous regulation of an economic activity. Because such regulation requires more time and expertise than Congress can provide, the responsibility is delegated to a regulatory agency. The Securities and Exchange Commission (SEC), which oversees the stock and bond markets, is a regulatory agency. So is the Environmental Protection Agency (EPA), which works to monitor and control industrial pollution. Table 13-1 lists some of the regulatory agencies and other noncabinet units of the federal bureaucracy.

Beyond their executive functions, regulatory agencies have certain legislative and judicial functions. They issue regulations, implement them, and then judge whether individuals or organizations have followed them. For example, the SEC can impose fines on a corporation that violates the rules for the trading of stocks and can compel it to comply with the rules or face further penalties, including even the suspension of the sale of its stocks.

Some regulatory agencies, particularly the older ones such as the SEC, are "independent" by virtue of their relative freedom from ongoing political control. They are headed by a commission of several members who are

TABLE 13-1   SELECTED U.S. REGULATORY AGENCIES, INDEPENDENT AGENCIES, GOVERNMENT CORPORATIONS, AND PRESIDENTIAL COMMISSIONS

Central Intelligence Agency
Commission on Civil Rights
Consumer Product Safety
    Commission
Environmental Protection
    Agency
Equal Employment Opportunity
    Commission
Export-Import Bank of the U.S.
Farm Credit Administration
Federal Communications
    Commission
Federal Deposit Insurance
    Corporation
Federal Election Commission
Federal Emergency Management
    Agency
Federal Maritime Commission
Federal Reserve System, Board of
    Governors of the
Federal Trade Commission
General Services Administration
National Aeronautics and Space
    Administration
National Archives and Records
    Administration

National Foundation on the Arts
    and the Humanities
National Labor Relations Board
National Railroad Passenger
    Corporation (Amtrak)
National Science Foundation
National Transportation Safety
    Board
Nuclear Regulatory Commission
Occupational Safety and Health
    Review Commission
Office of Personnel Management
Peace Corps
Securities and Exchange
    Commission
Selective Service System
Small Business Administration
Tennessee Valley Authority
U.S. Arms Control and
    Disarmament Agency
U.S. Information Agency
U.S. International Development
    Cooperation Agency
U.S. International Trade
    Commission
U.S. Postal Service

SOURCE: *The U.S. Government Manual.*

nominated by the president and confirmed by the Senate but are not subject to removal by the president. Commissioners serve a fixed term, a legal stipulation intended to free their agencies from political interference. The newer regulatory agencies such as the EPA lack this autonomy; most are headed by a presidential nominee who can be removed at the president's discretion. (Regulatory agencies are discussed more fully in Chapter 15.)

GOVERNMENT CORPORATIONS **Government corporations** are similar to private corporations in that they charge clients for their services and are governed by a board of directors. However, government corporations receive federal funding to help defray operating expenses, and their directors are appointed by the president with Senate approval. The largest government corporation is the U.S. Postal Service, with roughly 800,000 employees. Other government corporations include the Federal Deposit Insurance Corporation (FDIC), which insures savings accounts against bank failures, and the National Railroad Passenger Corporation (Amtrak), which provides passenger rail service.

PRESIDENTIAL COMMISSIONS Some **presidential commissions** are permanent commissions that provide ongoing recommendations to the president in particular areas of responsibility. Two such commissions are the Commission on Civil Rights and the Commission on Fine Arts. Other presidential commissions are temporary and disband after making recommendations on specific issues. An example is the commission on racial reconciliation that was appointed by President Clinton in 1997 and concluded its work in 1998.

Federal Employment

The roughly 2.5 million civilian employees of the federal government include professionals who bring their expertise to the problems of governing a large and complex society, service workers who perform such tasks as the typing of correspondence and the delivery of mail, and middle and top managers who supervise the work of the various federal agencies.

More than 90 percent of federal employees are hired by merit criteria, which include educational attainment, employment experience, and performance on competitive tests (such as the civil service and foreign service examinations). The merit system is intended to protect the public from the inept or discriminatory administrative practices that can result if partisanship is the employment criterion. A 1990 Supreme Court ruling prohibits patronage in all personnel operations (hiring, firing, transfers, promotions, training, and so on) unless the government can demonstrate that party affiliation will improve performance in a particular position.[5] This can be demonstrated in some cases (for example, a staff assistant to the president) but not in the large majority of personnel operations, which are thereby off limits to partisan politics.

The U.S. Postal Service, the largest government corporation, moves more mail, and does so more cheaply and reliably than do the postal bureaucracies of most other industralized nations. Yet the U.S. Postal Service, like most other federal agencies, has a poor public image.

Federal employees are underpaid in comparison with their counterparts in the private sector. The large majority of federal employees has a GS (Graded Service) job ranking. The rankings range from GS-1 (the lowest rank) to GS-18 (the highest). College graduates who enter the federal service usually start at the GS-5 level, which provides a salary of about $22,000 for a beginning employee. With a master's degree, the level is GS-9, at a $33,000 salary. Federal employees' salaries increase with rank and length of service. Public employees receive substantial fringe benefits, including full health insurance, liberal retirement plans, and generous vacation time and sick leave.

Public service has its drawbacks. Federal employees have few rights of collective action.[6] They can join labor unions, but their unions by law have limited authority: the government maintains full control of job assignments, compensation, and promotion. Moreover, the Taft-Hartley Act of 1947 prohibits strikes by federal employees and permits the firing of workers who do go on strike. There are also some limits on the partisan activities of civil servants. The Hatch Act of 1939 prohibited them from holding key positions in election campaigns. In 1993, Congress relaxed this prohibition, but retained it for certain high-ranking career bureaucrats.

The Federal Bureaucracy's Policy Responsibilities

The Constitution mentions executive departments but does not grant them any powers. Their authority derives from grants of power to the three constitutional branches: Congress, the president, and the courts. Nevertheless, the bureaucracy is far more than an administrative extension of the three branches. It never merely follows orders. The primary function of administrative agencies is **policy implementation,** which is to say that they carry out the policy decisions of Congress, the president, and the courts.

Although implementation is sometimes described as "mere administration," it is a highly significant and creative function.[7] For example, many ideas for legislative programs are initiated by the bureaucracy. In the course of their work, administrators come up with policy ideas that are then brought to the attention of the president or members of Congress. Administrative agencies also develop public policy in the process of implementing it. The decisions of Congress, the president, and the courts typically need to be fleshed out by the bureaucracy. Most legislative acts specify general goals, which bureaucrats then develop into specific programs. The Telecommunications Act of 1996, for example, had the stated goal "to promote competition and reduce regulation in order to secure lower prices and higher quality services for American telecommunication consumers and encourage the rapid deployment of new telecommunications technologies." Although the act included specific provisions, its implementation was left in large part for the Federal Communications Commission (FCC) to decide. The FCC decided, for example, that regional telephone companies (the Bell companies) had to open their networks to AT&T and other competitors at wholesale rates that were far below what they were charging their retail customers. The purpose was to enable AT&T and other carriers to compete with the Bell companies for local phone customers; in other words, the FCC was responding to its legislative mandate to promote "competition." But it was the FCC, not Congress, that determined the wholesale rates and many of the interconnection rules. This development of policy—often through *rule making*—is perhaps the chief way that administrative agencies exercise real power. To an important degree, they decide how the law will operate in practice.

Agencies are also charged with the delivery of services: carrying the mail, processing welfare applications, approving government loans, and the like. Such activities are governed by rules, and in most instances the rules decide what gets done. But some services allow agency employees enough discretion that laws end up being applied arbitrarily, a situation that Michael Lipsky describes as "street-level bureaucracy."[8] For example, FBI agents are more diligent in their pursuit of organized crime than of white-collar crime, even though the law does not designate white-collar crime as somehow deserving of more lenient treatment.

In sum, administrators necessarily exercise discretion in carrying out their policy responsibilities. They initiate policy, develop it, evaluate it, apply it, and determine whether others are complying with it. The bureaucracy does not simply administer policy; it also *makes* policy.

DEVELOPMENT OF THE FEDERAL BUREAUCRACY: POLITICS AND ADMINISTRATION

The organization and staffing of the bureaucracy have been administrative and political issues throughout the country's history. Agencies are responsible for carrying out programs that serve the society, and yet each agency was created and is maintained in response to partisan interests. Each agency thus confronts two simultaneous but conflicting demands: that it administer programs fairly and competently and that it respond to partisan claims.

Historically, this conflict has worked itself out in ways that have made the organization of the modern bureaucracy a blend of the political and the administrative. This dual line of development is clearly reflected in the mix of management systems that characterizes the bureaucracy today—the *patronage, merit,* and *executive leadership* systems.

Small Government and the Patronage System

The federal bureaucracy was originally small (three thousand employees in 1800, for instance). Under the U.S. Constitution, the states retained responsibility for nearly all domestic policy areas. The federal government's role was confined mainly to defense and foreign affairs, currency and interstate commerce, and the delivery of the mail. The nation's first six presidents, from George Washington through John Quincy Adams, believed that only distinguished men should be entrusted with the management of the national government. Nearly all top presidential appointees were men of education and political experience, and many of them were members of socially prominent families. They often remained in their jobs year after year.

The nation's seventh president, Andrew Jackson, did not share his predecessors' admiration for the elite. In Jackson's view, government would be more responsive to the people if it were administered by ordinary citizens of good sense. Jackson also believed that top administrators should remain in office for short periods, so that there would be a steady influx of fresh ideas.

Jackson's version of the **patronage system** was popular with the public, but critics labeled it a **spoils system**—a device for placing political cronies in government office as a reward for partisan service. Although Jackson was motivated as much by a concern for democratic government as by his desire to reward his campaign supporters, later presidents were often more interested in distributing the spoils of victory. Jackson's successors extended patronage to all levels of administration.[9]

Growth in Government and the Merit System

Because the government of the early nineteenth century was relatively small and limited in scope, it could be managed by employees who had little or no administrative training or experience. As the century advanced, however, the nature of the bureaucracy changed rapidly, as did the bureaucracy's personnel needs.

An impetus for change was the Industrial Revolution, which was creating a truly national economy and prompting economic groups to pressure Congress to protect and promote their interests. Farmers were one of the groups that looked to the federal government for market and price assistance; in response, Congress created the Department of Agriculture in 1889. Business and labor interests also pressed their claims, and in 1903 Congress established the Department of Commerce and Labor to "promote the mutual interest" of the nation's firms and workers. (The separate interests of business and labor proved stronger than their shared concerns, and so in 1913 Labor became a separate department.)[10]

Because of the increased need for continuous administration of government, an ever-larger bureaucracy was required (see Figure 13-2). By 1930 federal employment had reached 600,000, a sixfold increase over the level of the 1880s.[11] During the 1930s, as a result of President Franklin Roosevelt's New Deal, the federal work force increased enormously, to 1.2 million.

The assassination of President James A. Garfield in
1881 by Charles Guiteau, a disappointed office
seeker, did much to end the spoils system of
distributing government jobs.

A large and active government requires skilled and experienced personnel. In 1883, Congress passed the Pendleton Act, which established a **merit (civil service) system** whereby certain federal employees were hired through competitive examinations or by virtue of having special qualifications, such as a degree in a particular field, such as engineering, law, or medicine. The transition to a career civil service was slow. Only 10 percent of federal jobs in 1885 were filled on the basis of merit. But the pace accelerated when the Progressives promoted the merit system as a way of eliminating partisan graft and corruption in the administration of government (see Chapter 2). By 1920, as the Progressive era was concluding, more than 70 percent of federal employees were merit appointees. Since 1950, the proportion of merit employees has not dipped below 80 percent.[12]

The Pendleton Act created a Civil Service Commission to establish job classifications, administer competitive examinations, and oversee merit employees. The commission was replaced by two independent agencies in 1978. The Merit Service Protection Board handles appeals of personnel actions, and the Office of Personnel Management (OPM) supervises the hiring and classification of federal employees.[13]

The administrative objective of the merit system is **neutral competence.**[14] A merit-based bureaucracy is "competent" in the sense that

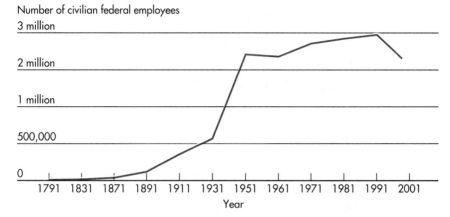

Number of civilian federal employees

FIGURE 13-2 NUMBER OF PERSONS EMPLOYED BY THE FEDERAL
GOVERNMENT, 1791–2001
The federal bureaucracy grew slowly until the 1930s, when an explosive growth
began in programs that required ongoing administration by the federal
government. Source: U.S. Office of Personnel Management, 2001.

employees are hired and retained on the basis of their skills, and it is "neutral" in the sense that employees are not partisan appointees and thus are
expected to do their work on behalf of everyone, not just those who support
the incumbent administration.

Although the merit system contributes to the impartial and proficient
administration of government programs, it has its own sources of bias and
inefficiency. Career bureaucrats tend to place their agency's interests ahead
of those of other agencies and typically oppose substantial efforts to trim
their agency's activities. They are not partisans in the sense of Democratic
or Republican politics, but they are partisans when it comes to protecting
their own positions and agencies, as will be explained more fully later in
the chapter.

Big Government and the Executive Leadership System

As problems with the merit system surfaced after the early years of this century, reformers looked to a strengthened presidency—an **executive leadership system**—as a means of coordinating the bureaucracy's activities to
increase its efficiency and responsiveness.[15] The president was to provide
the general leadership that would overcome agency fragmentation and
provide a common direction. As we saw in Chapter 12, Congress in 1939
provided the president with some of the tools needed for improved coordination of the bureaucracy. The Office of Management and Budget (OMB)

was created to give the president the authority to coordinate the annual budgetary process; agencies would be required to prepare their budget proposals under the direction of the president, who would then submit the overall budget to Congress for its approval and modification. The president was also empowered to reorganize the bureaucracy, subject to congressional approval, in order to reduce duplication of activities and strengthen the chain of command from the president to the agencies. Finally, the president was authorized to develop the Executive Office of the President, which oversees the agencies' activities on the president's behalf, assisting in the development and implementation of policy programs.

Like the merit and patronage systems, the executive leadership system has brought problems as well as improvements to the administration of government. The executive leadership concept, if carried too far, can threaten the balance between executive power and legislative power on which the U.S. constitutional system is based, and it can make the president's priorities, not fairness, the criterion by which provision of services is determined. Richard Nixon abused the system, for example, by ordering the OMB to impound (that is, fail to spend) more than $40 billion in appropriated funds of programs he disliked. (The courts ruled that Nixon's action was an unlawful infringement on Congress's constitutional authority over spending. To prevent a recurrence of the problem, Congress in 1974 passed legislation that gives the president the authority to withhold funds for only forty-five days unless Congress passes legislation to rescind the appropriation.)

Though not a panacea, the executive leadership system is, along with the patronage and merit systems, a necessary component of any effective strategy for managing the modern federal bureaucracy.[16] The federal bureaucracy today embodies aspects of all three systems, a situation that reflects the tensions inherent in governmental administration. The bureaucracy is expected to carry out programs fairly, but it is also expected to respond to political forces and to principles of effective management. The first of these requirements is addressed primarily through the merit system, the second through the patronage system, and the third through the executive leadership system (see Table 13-2).

THE BUREAUCRACY'S POWER IMPERATIVE

A common misperception is that the president, as the chief executive, has the sole claim on the bureaucracy's loyalty. In fact, each of the elected institutions has reason to claim proprietorship: the president as chief executive

TABLE 13-2 STRENGTHS AND WEAKNESSES OF MAJOR SYSTEMS FOR MANAGING THE BUREAUCRACY		
System	*Strengths*	*Weaknesses*
Patronage	Makes the bureaucracy more responsive to election outcomes by allowing the president to appoint some executive officials.	Gives executive authority to individuals chosen for their partisan loyalty rather than administrative or policy expertise; can favor interests that supported the president's election.
Merit	Provides for *competent* administration in that employees are hired on the basis of ability and allowed to remain on the job and thereby become proficient, and provides for *neutral* administration in that civil servants are not partisan appointees and are expected to work in an evenhanded way.	Can result in fragmented, unresponsive administration since career bureaucrats are secure in their jobs and tend to place the interests of their particular agency ahead of those of other agencies or the nation's interests as a whole.
Executive leadership	Provides for presidential leadership of the bureaucracy in order to make it more responsive and to coordinate and direct it (left alone, the bureaucracy tends toward fragmentation).	Can upset the balance between executive and legislative power and can make the president's priorities, not fairness or effective management, the basis for administrative action.

and Congress as the source of the authorization and funding of the bureaucracy's programs.

The U.S. system of separate institutions sharing power results in a natural tendency for each institution to guard its turf. In addition, the president and members of Congress differ in their constituencies and thus in the interests to which they are most responsive. For example, although the agricultural sector is just one of many concerns of the president, it is of vital interest to senators and representatives from farm states. Finally, because the president and Congress are elected separately, the White House and one or both houses of Congress may be in the hands of opposing parties. Since 1968, this source of executive–legislative conflict has been more often the rule than the exception.

If agencies are to operate successfully in this system, they must seek support where they can find it—if not from the president, then from Congress; if not today, then tomorrow. In other words, agencies must play politics.[17] Any agency that is content to sit idly by while new priorities for money and policy are determined is virtually certain to lose out to other agencies that are willing to fight for power.

The Agency Point of View

Administrators have little choice but to look out for their agency's interests, a perspective that is called the **agency point of view.**[18] This perspective comes naturally to most high-ranking civil servants. Their careers within the bureaucracy have taught them to do their part in making the organization effective. Many top bureaucrats are also personally committed to their agency's objectives as a result of having spent years working on its programs.[19] As one top administrator said when testifying before the House Appropriations Committee, "Mr. Chairman, you would not think it proper for me to be in charge of this work and not be enthusiastic about it . . . would you? I have been in it for thirty years, and I believe in it."[20]

Professionalism also cements agency loyalties. As public policymaking has become more complex, high-level administrative positions have increasingly been filled by scientists, engineers, lawyers, educators, physicians, and other professionals (see box: How the United States Compares). Most of them take jobs in an agency whose programs are consistent with their professional values.

Studies confirm that bureaucrats believe in the importance of their agency's work. One study found that social welfare administrators are three times as likely as other civil servants to believe that social welfare programs should be given a high budget priority.[21]

Sources of Bureaucratic Power

In promoting their agency's interests, bureaucrats rely on their specialized knowledge, the support of interests that benefit from the programs they run, and the backing of the president and Congress.

HOW THE UNITED STATES COMPARES

Educational Backgrounds of Bureaucrats

To staff its bureaucracy, the U.S. government tends to hire persons with specialized educations to hold specialized jobs. This approach heightens the tendency of bureaucrats to take the agency point of view. By comparison, Great Britain tends to recruit its bureaucrats from the arts and humanities, on the assumption that general aptitude is the best qualification for detached professionalism. The continental European democracies also emphasize detached professionalism, but in the context of the supposedly impartial application of rules. As a consequence, high-ranking civil servants in Europe tend to have legal educations. The college majors of senior civil servants in the United States and other democracies reflect these tendencies.

College Major of Senior Civil Servants	Denmark	Germany	Great Britain	Italy	Netherlands	United States
Natural science/ engineering	16%	8%	26%	10%	25%	32%
Social science/ humanities/ business	20	18	52	37	28	50
Law	60	63	3	53	45	18
Other	4	11	19	—	2	—
	100%	100%	100%	100%	100%	100%

From THE POLITICS OF BUREAUCRACY 4th ed. by B. Guy Peters. Copyright 1995 by Longman Publishers USA. Reprinted by permission of Addison-Wesley Educational Publishers Inc.

The Power of Expertise   Most of the policy problems that the federal government confronts do not lend themselves to simple solutions. Whether the issue is space travel or hunger in America, expert knowledge is essential to the development of effective public policy. Much of this expertise is held by bureaucrats. They spend their careers working in a particular policy area, and many of them have had scientific, technical, or other specialized training.[22]

By comparison, elected officials are generalists. To some degree, members of Congress do specialize through their committee work, but they rarely have the time or inclination to acquire a commanding knowledge of a particular issue. The president's understanding of policy issues is even more general. Not surprisingly, the president and members of Congress depend on the bureaucracy for policy advice and planning.

All agencies acquire some power through their careerists' expertise.[23] No matter how simple a policy issue may appear at first, it invariably involves more than meets the eye. A recognition that the United States has a trade deficit with Japan, for example, can be the premise for policy change, but this recognition does not begin to address such basic issues as the form that the new policy might take, its probable cost and effectiveness, and its connection to other trade issues. Among the officials most likely to understand these issues are the bureaucrats in the Commerce Department and the Federal Trade Commission.

The Power of Clientele Groups   Most agencies have **clientele groups,** which are special interests that benefit directly from an agency's programs. Clientele groups place pressure on Congress and the president to retain the programs from which they benefit.[24] A result is that agency programs, once started, are difficult to terminate. "Government activities," as public administration expert Herbert Kaufman says, "tend to go on indefinitely."[25]

The importance of clientele groups was evident in 1995 when House Speaker Newt Gingrich threatened to "zero out" funding for the Corporation for Public Broadcasting. The threat produced an immediate response (some of it orchestrated by public broadcasting stations) from audience members and from groups such as the Childrens Television Workshop. They wrote, called, faxed, and cajoled members of Congress, saying that programs like *Sesame Street* and *All Things Considered* were irreplaceable by anything available from commercial broadcasting. Within a few weeks, Gingrich had relented somewhat, saying that a phase-out plan for ending the funding would be preferable to an abrupt cessation and that it might be prudent to retain funding for some activities, such as support of stations in rural areas not adequately served by commercial broadcasters.

In general, agencies lead and are led by the clientele groups that depend on the programs they administer.[26] Many agencies were created for the purpose of promoting particular interests in society. For example, the Department of Agriculture's career bureaucrats are dependable allies of farm interests year after year. The same cannot be said of the president, Congress as a whole, or either political party; they must balance farmers' demands against those of other interests.

THE POWER OF FRIENDS IN HIGH PLACES   Although members of Congress and the president sometimes appear to be at war with the bureaucracy, they need it as much as it needs them. An agency's resources—its programs, expertise, and group support—can assist elected officials in their efforts to achieve their goals. When George Bush came to the White House, he made the problem of drug-related crime a top priority, and he needed the help of Justice Department careerists to make his efforts successful. At a time when other agencies were feeling the pinch of a tight federal budget, the Justice Department's personnel increased by 20 percent during Bush's term of office.

Bureaucrats also seek favorable relations with members of Congress. Congressional support is vital because agencies' funding and programs are

The popular children's program *Sesame Street* is produced through the Corporation for Public Broadcasting, a government agency that gains leverage in budgetary deliberations from its public support. The singer Garth Brooks is shown here with two muppets during his appearance on *Sesame Street*.

established through legislation. Agencies that offer benefits to major constituency interests are particularly likely to have close ties to Congress. In some policy areas, more or less permanent alliances—"iron triangles"— form among agencies, clientele groups, and congressional subcommittees.[27] In other policy areas, temporary "issue networks" form among bureaucrats, lobbyists, and members of Congress.[28] As we saw in Chapters 9 and 11, these alliances enable agencies and interest groups to promote the programs they want and provide members of Congress with electoral support.[29]

BUREAUCRATIC ACCOUNTABILITY

Bureaucratic politics raises the specter of a huge, permanent, and uncontrollable organization run by entrenched unelected officials. This image certainly characterizes the way that many Americans perceive the federal bureaucracy. Even though most Americans say that they have a favorable impression of their most recent personal experience with the bureaucracy (as, say, when a senior citizen applies for social security), they have an unfavorable impression of the bureaucracy as a whole (see Figure 13-3). This view is somewhat unfair—the effectiveness of the U.S. federal bureaucracy has been shown by studies to compare favorably with that of other governmental bureaucracies at home and abroad[30]—but is nonetheless easy to understand. For one thing, the news media rarely cover the bureaucracy except when it makes a colossal mistake, fostering the impression that bureaucratic incompetence is widespread. In addition, the bureaucracy is a faceless institution that is largely beyond the citizens' direct control. When combined with Americans' traditional mistrust of concentrated political power, it is no surprise that they have qualms about the federal bureaucracy and want it more closely controlled.

Adapting the requirements of the bureaucracy to those of democracy has been a persistent challenge for public administration.[31] The issue is **accountability:** the capacity of the public to hold officials responsible for their actions. In the case of the bureaucracy, accountability works primarily through other institutions: the presidency, Congress, and the courts.

Accountability through the Presidency

The president can only broadly influence, not directly control, the bureaucracy.[32] "We can outlast any president" is a maxim of bureaucratic politics. In recent years, with the emphasis on scaling down the bureaucracy, the

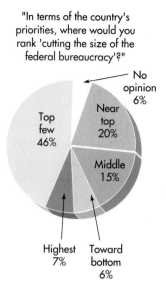

"In terms of the country's priorities, where would you rank 'cutting the size of the federal bureaucracy'?"

No opinion 6%

Near top 20%

Top few 46%

Middle 15%

Highest 7%

Toward bottom 6%

FIGURE 13-3   PUBLIC CONFIDENCE IN THE BUREAUCRACY
Americans generally have a low opinion of the federal bureaucracy even though by most indicators it is an effective organization of its type. Source: From *The American Democracy*, Fourth Edition, by Thomas Patterson, © 1999, reproduced with permission of The McGraw-Hill Companies.

saying seems more wishful than truthful. Nevertheless, each agency has its clientele and its congressional supporters, as well as statutory authority for its existence and activities. No president can unilaterally eliminate an agency or its funding and programs. Nor can the president be indifferent to the opinions of career civil servants—not without losing their support and expertise in developing and implementing his own policy objectives.

To encourage the bureaucracy to follow his lead, the president has important management tools that have developed out of the "executive leadership" concept discussed previously. These tools include reorganization, presidential appointees, and the executive budget.

REORGANIZATION   The bureaucracy's extreme fragmentation—its hundreds of separate agencies—makes presidential coordination of its activities difficult. Agencies operate independently of each other, resulting in an undetermined amount of waste and duplication of effort. For example, more than one hundred units are responsible for different pieces of education policy.

Although presidents have sometimes proposed large-scale reorganization plans, including elimination of whole departments, these efforts have usually failed because of opposition from the bureaucracy, interest groups, and Congress. Presidents have had more success with smaller changes, such as reducing the autonomy or number of employees of particular agencies. These changes serve to upgrade or downgrade programs but ordinarily have not greatly improved presidential control of the bureaucracy.[33]

PRESIDENTIAL APPOINTMENTS   Although there is almost no direct confrontation with a bureaucrat that a president cannot win, the president does not have time to deal personally with every troublesome careerist or make sure that the bureaucracy has complied with every presidential order. The president relies on political appointees in the agencies to ensure that directives are followed.

The power of presidential appointees is greatest in those agencies where wide latitude exists in the making of decisions. Although the Social Security Administration has a huge budget and gives monthly payments to more than forty million Americans, the eligibility of recipients is determined by relatively fixed rules. In contrast, most regulatory agencies have broad discretion over regulatory policy, and a change in leadership can have a substantial impact. For example, President Reagan's appointee to head the Federal Trade Commission, James Miller III, was a strong-willed economist who shared Reagan's belief that consumer protection policy had gone too far and was adversely affecting business interests. In Miller's first year as head of the FTC, the commission dropped one-fourth of its pending cases against business firms.[34] Overall, the number of enforcement actions during Miller's tenure was about 50 percent less that the comparable number in the previous period.

However, as we noted in Chapter 12, there are limits to what a president can accomplish through appointments.[35] High-level presidential appointees number in the hundreds, and their turnover rate is high: the average appointee remains in the administration for less than two years before moving on to other employment.[36] No president can keep track of all appointees, much less instruct them in detail. In addition, some presidential appointees will have a vested interest in the agencies they head. In choosing political appointees, the president is lobbied by groups that depend on agency programs. Rather than antagonize these groups, the president will accept their recommendations in some cases.

THE EXECUTIVE BUDGET   Faced with the difficulty of controlling the bureaucracy, presidents have come to rely heavily on their personal bureaucracy, the Executive Office of the President (EOP).

The Old Executive Office Building is adjacent to the west wing of the White House. Its occupants are part of the Executive Office of the President (EOP) and serve as contacts between the president and agency bureaucrats.

In terms of presidential management, the key unit within the EOP is the Office of Management and Budget (OMB). Funding, programs, and regulations are the mainstays of every agency, and the OMB has substantial influence on each of these areas. No agency can issue a major regulation without the OMB's verification that the regulation's benefits outweigh its costs, and no agency can propose legislation to Congress without the OMB's approval. However, the OMB's greatest influence over agencies derives from its budgetary role. At the start of the annual budget cycle, the OMB assigns each agency a budget limit in accord with the president's directives. The agency's tentative allocation requests are sent back to the OMB, which then conducts a final review of all requests before sending the full budget to Congress in the president's name.

In most cases, an agency's overall budget does not change much from year to year.[37] This fact indicates that a significant portion of the bureaucracy's activities persists regardless of who sits in the White House or

Congress. It must be noted, however, that the bulk of federal spending is for programs such as social security that, although enacted in the past, have the continuing support of the president, Congress, and the public.

Accountability through Congress

Congress has powerful means of influencing the bureaucracy. All agencies depend on Congress for their existence, authority, programs, and funding.

The most substantial control that Congress exerts on the bureaucracy is through its power to authorize and fund programs. Without authorization or funding, a program simply does not exist, regardless of the priority an agency claims it deserves. Congress can also void an administrative decision through legislation that prohibits it or mandates an alternative course of action. However, Congress lacks the institutional capacity to work out complex policies down to the last detail.[38] The bureaucracy would grind to a halt if it had to get congressional approval for all of its policy decisions. Congress has no option in most cases but to give the bureaucracy a general heading and then let it proceed along that course.

Congress also exerts some control through its oversight function, which involves monitoring the bureaucracy's work to ensure compliance with legislative intent.[39] As we noted in Chapter 11, however, oversight is a difficult and relatively unrewarding task, and members of Congress ordinarily place less emphasis on oversight than on their other major duties. Only when an agency has clearly stepped out of line is Congress likely to take decisive corrective action by holding hearings to ask tough questions and to warn of legislative punishment.

A dramatic example is environmental regulation during Reagan's presidency. Regulatory activity dropped sharply when Reagan took office. Then in 1983, the news media disclosed that the Environmental Protection Agency (EPA) had privately arranged lenient settlements for firms that had committed serious violations of toxic-waste disposal regulations. The ensuing congressional investigation resulted in the resignation, dismissal, or conviction in court of more than a half-dozen top EPA officials. EPA director Anne Burford was cited for contempt of Congress for her refusal to cooperate with the investigation. Because of congressional pressure, the EPA's toxic-waste inspection level more than tripled soon thereafter, and when Congress restored EPA's budget, it rose again. Within two years, the EPA's inspection rate was nearly six times higher (from about 325 inspections a year to 2,000). In their study of this case, B. Dan Wood and Richard W.

Waterman concluded: "Thus, for the EPA policy in which Congress was most directly involved, legislative influence was clearly manifest through the powers of oversight and appropriations."[40]

Of course, an awareness by bureaucrats that misbehavior can trigger a response from Congress helps to keep them in line.[41] Nevertheless, oversight cannot correct mistakes or abuses that have already occurred. Recognizing this limit on oversight, Congress has devised ways to constrain the bureaucracy *before* it acts. The simplest method is to draft laws that contain very specific provisions that limit bureaucrats' options when they implement policy. Another restrictive device is the "sunset law," which establishes a specific date when a law will expire unless it is reenacted by Congress. Advocates of sunset laws see them as a means to counter the bureaucracy's reluctance to give up programs that have outlived their usefulness. Since members of Congress usually want their policies to last far into the future, however, most legislation does not include a sunset provision.

Accountability through the Courts

The judiciary's influence on agencies is less direct than that of the elected branches, but the courts, too, can and do act to ensure the bureaucracy's compliance with Congress's requirements. Legally, the bureaucracy derives its authority from acts of Congress, and an injured party can bring suit against an agency on the grounds that it has failed to carry out the law properly. Judges can then order an agency to change its application of the law.[42]

However, the courts have tended to support administrators if their actions seem at all consistent with the laws they are administering. The Supreme Court has held that agencies can choose rule-making procedures that meet the minimal threshold set down by Congress, that agencies can apply any reasonable interpretation of statutes unless Congress has specifically stated something to the contrary, and that agencies in many instances have wide discretion in deciding whether to enforce statutes.[43] These positions reflect the need for flexibility in administration; the bureaucracy and the courts would both grind to a halt if judges routinely chose to substitute their interpretations of the law for those of administrators. The judiciary cannot conduct a decision-by-decision oversight of the bureaucracy. The judiciary has promoted bureaucratic accountability primarily by encouraging administrators to act responsibly in their dealings with the public and by protecting individuals and groups from the bureaucracy's worst abuses.

Accountability within the Bureaucracy Itself

A recognition of the difficulty of ensuring adequate accountability of the bureaucracy through the presidency, Congress, and the courts has led to the development of mechanisms of accountability within the bureaucracy itself. Two measures, whistle-blowing and demographic representativeness, are particularly noteworthy.

WHISTLE-BLOWING   Although the bureaucratic corruption that is rampant in some countries is relatively uncommon in the United States, a certain amount of waste, fraud, and abuse is inevitable in a bureaucracy as big as that of the federal government. **Whistle-blowing,** the act of reporting instances of corruption or mismanagement by other bureaucrats, is a potentially effective internal check.[44] Whistle-blowing, however, has not been highly successful. A survey conducted by a Senate subcommittee indicated that most federal employees will not report instances of mismanagement because they fear reprisals from their superiors. Their fears are not groundless. For example, the U.S. Air Force's top civilian safety official, Alan Diehl, was assigned to a lesser position after releasing a report indicating that Air Force investigators had routinely misrepresented the causes of military air crashes in order to save the Air Force and its top officers the embarrassment that would have occurred if the actual causes had been revealed.[45]

To encourage federal employees to come forward when they see instances of mismanagement, Congress enacted the Whistle Blower Protection Act to protect them from retaliation. Federal law also provides whistle-blowers with financial rewards in some cases.

DEMOGRAPHIC REPRESENTATIVENESS   Although the bureaucracy is an unrepresentative institution in the sense that its officials are not elected by the people, it can be representative in the demographic sense. If bureaucrats were a demographic microcosm of the general public, they presumably would treat the various groups and interests in society more fairly.[46]

At present, the bureaucracy is not demographically representative at its top levels (see Table 13-3). About 60 percent of managerial and professional positions are held by white males. Women and minorities hold proportionally few high-ranking posts. However, the employment status of women and, to a lesser extent, minorities has improved somewhat in recent years, and top officials in the bureaucracy include a greater proportion of women

TABLE 13-3   FEDERAL JOB RANKINGS (GS) OF VARIOUS
DEMOGRAPHIC GROUPS

Women and minority group members are underrepresented in the top jobs
of the federal bureaucracy.

Grade Level*	Women's Share		Hispanics' Share		Blacks' Share	
	1976	1999	1982	1997	1982	1997
GS 13–15 (highest ranks)	5%	29%	5%	8%	2%	4%
GS 9–12	20	43	10	14	4	6
GS 5–8	60	68	19	25	4	7
GS 1–4 (lowest ranks)	78	69	23	28	5	8

*In general, the higher-numbered grades are managerial and professional positions, and the lower-numbered grades are clerical and manual labor positions.
SOURCE: Office of Workforce Information, 1998, 2001.

and minorities than is found in private industry. Moreover, if all levels of the federal bureaucracy are considered, it comes reasonably close to being representative of the nation's population.

Demographic representativeness is only a partial answer to the problem of bureaucratic accountability. A fully representative civil service would still be required to play agency politics. The careerists in, say, defense agencies and welfare agencies are not very different in their demographic backgrounds, but they differ markedly in their opinions about policy. Each group believes that the goals of its agency should take priority. The inevitability of agency politics is the most significant of all political facts about the U.S. federal bureaucracy.[47]

REINVENTING GOVERNMENT

There have been numerous attempts during the twentieth century to enhance the bureaucracy's efficiency, responsiveness, and accountability. Another wave of this reform effort began in the 1990s and has aimed to improve the administration of government by the reduction of its size, cost, and lines of authority.

This effort is based in part on the notion that the bureaucracy would be more effective and responsive if it were made smaller. In *Reinventing Government*, David Osborne and Ted Gaebler argue that the bureaucracy of today was created in response to earlier problems, particularly those spawned by the Industrial Revolution and a rampant spoils system. They claim that the information age requires a different kind of administrative structure, one that is more flexible and less hierarchical. Instead of the provision of goods and services, the bureaucracy ought to be in the business of creating incentives that will encourage individuals to make their own way and ought to foster competition among and between agencies and private firms. This requires a less centralized form of administration that is oriented toward consumers and results. Osborne and Gaebler would empower lower-level employees to make decisions that previously were made at the top of the bureaucracy.[48]

This concept informed the Clinton administration's National Performance Review and is embedded in some laws and administrative practices. An example is a law that requires agencies to monitor their performance by standards such as efficiency, responsiveness, and outcomes. These standards have long been considered gauges of administrative effectiveness but have often been overlooked as bureaucrats went about their customary ways of doing business. The law seeks to overcome this inertia by *requiring* agencies to actively monitor their performance.

The downsizing of the federal bureaucracy has also been driven by political forces. Chronic budget deficits in the 1980s and early 1990s and the public's dissatisfaction with Washington helped to create political momentum to reduce the scope of the federal government through both program reductions and the devolution of power to states and localities (see Chapter 2; see also box: States in the Nation). The momentum intensified with the Republican takeover of Congress in 1995. One consequence was a cutback in federal control of welfare policy (see Chapter 16).

The new era will be one of smaller government, not small government. There are limits to how far the federal government can be trimmed. Some activities can be delegated to states and localities, and others can be privatized, but many, if not most, of Washington's programs cannot be reassigned. National defense, social security, and Medicare are but three examples, and they alone account for the bulk of federal spending (see Chapters 16 and 17).

Some analysts question the logic and presumed consequences of the changes that are taking place. They have asked, for example, whether the principles of decentralized management and market-oriented programs are as sound as their advocates claim. The delegation of control to lower-level administrators weakens the hierarchical connection between elected and administrative officials. A reason for hierarchy was to ensure that decisions made at the bottom of the bureaucracy were faithful to the laws made by Congress. Free to act on their own, lower-level administrators, as they did under the spoils system, might favor certain people and interests over others.[49] There is also the issue of the identity of the "customers" in a market-oriented administration.[50] Who are the Security and Exchange Commission's customers—firms, brokerage houses, or shareholders? Won't some agencies inevitably favor their more powerful customers at the expense of the less powerful ones?

A second objection to the changes taking place is that government may be "hollowed out" in the sense that it may not have the financial and human resources to adequately perform the missions it retains.[51] Even many of the strongest advocates of scaling down the federal government worry about this possibility in particular areas. For example, congressional Republicans, who have in most cases sought to reduce the scale of federal programs, have advocated increases in defense spending out of a belief that earlier cutbacks had reduced military readiness to an unacceptable level. Increased defense spending is also supported by Republican President George W. Bush, who, in other areas, has advocated a reduction in federal programs.

Thus, although the current wave of administrative reform is unique in its specific elements, it involves longstanding questions about the bureaucracy. How can it be made more responsive, and yet act fairly? How can it be made more efficient, and yet accomplish what Americans require of it? How can it be made more creative, and yet be held accountable? There are, as history makes clear, no easy or final answers to these questions.

SUMMARY

Bureaucracy is a method of organizing people and work; it is based on the principles of hierarchical authority, job specialization, and formalized rules. As a form of organization, bureaucracy is the most efficient means of getting people to work together on tasks of great magnitude and complexity. It is also a form of organization that is prone to waste and rigidity, which is why efforts are being made to "reinvent" it.

The United States could not be governed without a large federal bureaucracy. The day-to-day work of the federal government, from mail delivery to provision of social security to international diplomacy, is done by the bureaucracy. Federal employees work in roughly four hundred major agencies, including cabinet departments, independent agencies, regulatory agencies, government corporations, and presidential commissions. Yet the bureaucracy is more than simply an administrative giant. Administrators exercise considerable discretion in their policy decisions. In the process of implementing policy, they make important policy and political choices.

Each agency of the federal government was created in response to political demands on national officials. Because of its origins in political demands, the administration of government is necessarily political. An inherent conflict results from two simultaneous but incompatible demands on the bureaucracy: that it respond to the demands of partisan officials, but also that it administer programs fairly and competently. These tensions are evident in the three concurrent personnel management systems under which the bureaucracy operates: patronage, merit, and executive leadership.

Administrators are actively engaged in politics and policymaking. The fragmentation of power and the pluralism of the American political system result in a policy process that is continually subject to conflict and contention. There is no clear policy or leadership mandate in the American system, and hence government agencies must compete for the power required to administer their programs effectively. Accordingly, civil servants tend to have an agency point of view: they seek to advance their agency's programs and to repel attempts by others to weaken their position. In promoting their agency, civil servants rely on their policy expertise, the backing of their clientele groups, and support from the president and Congress.

Because administrators are not elected by the people they serve yet wield substantial independent power, the bureaucracy's accountability is a major issue. The major checks on the bureaucracy are provided by the president, Congress, and the courts. The president has some power to reorganize the bureaucracy and the authority to appoint the political head of each agency. The president also has management tools (such as the executive budget) that can be used to limit administrators' discretion. Congress has influence on bureaucratic agencies through its authorization and funding powers and through various devices (including sunset laws and oversight hearings) that hold administrators accountable for their actions. The judiciary's role in ensuring the bureaucracy's accountability is smaller than that of the elected branches, but the courts do have the authority to force agencies to act in accordance with legislative intent, established procedures, and constitutionally guaranteed rights. Nevertheless, administrators are not fully accountable. They exercise substantial independent power, a situation that is not easily reconciled with democratic values.

Efforts are currently under way to scale down the federal bureaucracy. This reduction includes cuts in budgets, staff, and organizational units, and also involves changes in the way the bureaucracy does its work. This process is a response to both political forces and new management theories.

MAJOR CONCEPTS

accountability	cabinet (executive) departments
agency point of view	clientele groups
bureaucracy	demographic representativeness

executive leadership system

formalized rules

government corporations

hierarchical authority

independent agencies

job specialization

merit (civil service) system

neutral competence

patronage system

policy implementation

presidential commissions

regulatory agencies

spoils system

whistle-blowing

SUGGESTED READINGS AND WEB SITES

Brehm, John, and Scott Gates. *Working, Shirking, and Sabotage: Bureaucratic Response to a Democratic Public.* Ann Arbor: University of Michigan Press, 1996. A generally favorable assessment of the bureaucracy's responsiveness to the public it serves.

Cook, Brian J. *Bureaucracy and Self-Government: Reconsidering the Role of Public Administration in American Politics.* Baltimore, Md.: Johns Hopkins University Press, 1996. A thorough history of public administration in American politics.

Gore, Albert. *Creating a Government That Works Better and Costs Less: The Report of the National Performance Review.* Washington, D.C.: U.S. Superintendent of Documents, 1993. The report of Vice President Gore's task force on streamlining government.

Kerwin, Cornelius M. *Rulemaking: How Government Agencies Write Law and Make Policy.* Washington, D.C.: Congressional Quarterly Press, 1994. Suggests that the most important function that government agencies perform is rulemaking.

Kettl, Donald F., Patricia W. Ingraham, Ronald P. Sanders, and Constance Horner. *Civil Service Reform: Building a Government That Works.* Washington, D.C.: Brookings Institution Press, 1996. A careful analysis of government management.

Osborne, David, and Ted Gaebler. *Reinventing Government: How the Entrepreneurial Spirit Is Transforming the Public Sector.* New York: Addison-Wesley, 1992. The book that Washington policymakers in the 1990s regarded as the guide to transforming the bureaucracy.

Wood, B. Dan, and Richard W. Waterman. *Bureaucratic Dynamics. The Role of Bureaucracy in a Democracy.* Boulder, Colo.: Westview Press, 1994. A penetrating analysis of bureaucratic agencies and their power relationships with the president, Congress, and constituent groups.

http://iccweb.com/federal   A site for those interested in finding employment with the federal government. The site provides job application and other information for the various federal agencies.

http://www.census.gov   The Census Bureau is the best source of statistical information on Americans and the government agencies that administer programs affecting them.

http://www.whistleblower.org   The Government Accountability Project is designed to protect and encourage whistle-blowers by providing information and support to federal employees.

http://www.whitehouse.gov/WH/Cabinet   This site lists the cabinet secretaries and provides links to each cabinet-level department.

READING 13

Reinventing Government

DAVID OSBORNE AND TED GAEBLER

Introduction

In their essay, David Osborne and Ted Gaebler argue for the "reinvention" of the federal bureaucracy. They contend that the bureaucracy developed in response to conditions of the past and needs to be reformulated to fit new circumstances. They envision a more flexible and adaptable bureaucracy that is better suited to today's fast-paced world. Bureaucratic reform, as was noted in Chapter 13, has been a periodic goal of public administration and, typically, has been a response to unintended consequences of previous reforms.

It is hard to imagine today, but one-hundred years ago the word *bureaucracy* meant something positive. It connoted a rational, efficient method of organization—something to take the place of the arbitrary exercise of power by authoritarian regimes. Bureaucracies brought the same logic to government work that the assembly line brought to the factory. With their hierarchical authority and functional specialization, they made possible the efficient undertaking of large, complex tasks. Max Weber, the great German sociologist, described them using words no modern American would dream of applying:

> The decisive reason for the advance of bureaucratic organization has always been its purely technical superiority over any other form of organization. . . .
>
> Precision, speed, unambiguity . . . reduction of friction and of material and personal costs—these are raised to the optimum point in the strictly bureaucratic administration. . . .

During times of intense crisis—the Depression and two world wars—the bureaucratic model worked superbly. In crisis, when goals were clear and widely shared, when tasks were relatively straightforward, and when virtually everyone was willing to pitch in for the cause, the top-down, command-and-control mentality got things done. The results spoke for themselves, and most Americans fell in step. By the 1950s, as William H. Whyte wrote, we had become a nation of "organization men."

But the bureaucratic model developed in conditions very different from those we experience today. It developed in a slower-paced society, when change proceeded at a leisurely gait. It developed in an age of hierarchy, when only those at the top of the pyramid had enough information to make informed decisions. It developed in a society of people who worked with their hands, not their minds. It developed in a time of mass markets, when most Americans had similar wants and needs. And it developed when we had strong geographic communities—tightly knit neighborhoods and towns.

Today all that has been swept away. We live in an era of breathtaking change. We live in a global marketplace, which puts enormous competitive pressure on our economic institutions. We live in an information society, in which people get access to information almost as fast as their leaders do. We live in a knowledge-based economy, in which educated workers bridle at commands and demand autonomy. We live in an age of niche markets, in which customers have become accustomed to high quality and extensive choice.

In this environment, bureaucratic institutions developed during the industrial era—public *and* private—increasingly fail us.

Today's environment demands institutions that are extremely flexible and adaptable. It demands institutions that deliver high-quality goods and services, squeezing ever more bang out of every buck. It demands institutions that are responsive to their customers, offering choices of nonstandardized services; that lead by persuasion and incentives rather than commands; that give their employees a sense of meaning and control, even ownership. It demands institutions that *empower* citizens rather than simply *serving* them.

Bureaucratic institutions still work in some circumstances. If the environment is stable, the task is relatively simple, every customer wants the same service, and the quality of performance is not critical, a traditional public bureaucracy can do the job. Social security still works. Local government agencies that provide libraries and parks and recreational facilities still work, to a degree.

But most government institutions perform increasingly complex tasks, in competitive, rapidly changing environments, with customers who want quality and choice. These new realities have made life very difficult for our public institutions—for our public education system, for our public health care programs, for our public housing authorities, for virtually every large, bureaucratic program created by American governments before 1970. It was no accident that during the 1970s we lost a war, lost faith in our national leaders, endured repeated economic problems, and experienced a tax revolt. In the years since, the clash between old and new has only intensified. The result has been a period of enormous stress in American government. . . .

Unfortunately, we do not know how to get what we want. Most of our leaders assume that the only way to cut spending is to eliminate programs, agencies, and employees. Ronald Reagan talked as if we could simply go into the bureaucracy with a scalpel and cut out pockets of waste, fraud, and abuse.

But waste in government does not come tied up in neat packages. It is marbled throughout our bureaucracies. It is embedded in the very way we do business. It is employees on idle, working at half speed—or barely working at all. It is people working hard at tasks that aren't worth doing, following regulations that should never have been written, filling out forms that should never have been printed. It is the *$100 billion* a year that Bob Stone estimates the Department of Defense wastes with its foolish overregulation.

Waste in government is staggering, but we cannot get at it by wading through budgets and cutting line items. As one observer put it, our governments are like fat people who must lose weight. They need to eat less and exercise more; instead, when money is tight they cut off a few fingers and toes.

To melt the fat, we must change the basic incentives that drive our governments. We must turn bureaucratic institutions into entrepreneurial institutions, ready to kill off obsolete initiatives, willing to do more with less, eager to absorb new ideas.

The lessons are there: our more entrepreneurial governments have shown us the way. Yet few of our leaders are listening. Too busy climbing the rungs to their next office, they don't have time to stop and look anew. So they remain trapped in old ways of looking at our problems, blind to solutions that lie right in front of them. This is perhaps our greatest stumbling block: the power of outdated ideas. As the great economist John Maynard Keynes once noted, the difficulty lies not so much in developing new ideas as in escaping from old ones.

The old ideas still embraced by most public leaders and political reporters assume that the important question is *how much* government we have—not *what kind* of government. Most of our leaders take the old model as a given, and either advocate more of it (liberal Democrats), or less of it (Reagan Republicans), or less of one program but more of another (moderates of both parties).

But our fundamental problem today is not too much government or too little government. We have debated that issue endlessly since the tax revolt of 1978, and it has not solved our problems. Our fundamental problem is that we have the *wrong kind of government.* We do not need more government or less government, we need *better* government. To be more precise, we need better *governance.*

Governance is the process by which we collectively solve our problems and meet our society's needs. Government is the instrument we use. The instrument is outdated, and the process of reinvention has begun.

SOURCE: From David Osborne and Ted Gaebler, "Reinventing government," *Reinventing Government: How the Entrepreneurial Spirit Is Transforming the Public Sector,* Addison-Wesley, 1992. Copyright © 1992 by David Osborne. Reprinted by permission of ICM.
David Osborne and Ted Gaebler are managing partners of the Reinventing Government Network. Osborne was chief author of the National Performance Review. Gaebler heads his own consulting firm.

CHAPTER FOURTEEN

The Judiciary

It is emphatically the province and duty of the judicial department to say what
the law is. Those who apply the rule to particular cases, must of necessity
expound and interpret that rule. If two laws conflict with each other,
the courts must decide on the operation of each.

JOHN MARSHALL[1]

T HROUGH ITS ruling in *Bush* v. *Gore*, the U.S. Supreme Court
effectively ended the 2000 presidential election. At issue was
whether the "undervotes" in Florida—ballots on which counting machines
had detected no vote for president—would be tabulated by hand. Florida's
top court had ordered a statewide manual recount, but the U.S. Supreme
Court by a narrow 5-4 margin had issued a rare emergency order halting
the action. Three days later, the Supreme Court's majority delivered its
ruling, saying that the manual recount violated the Constitution's equal
protection clause. Florida's high court had said that officials should base the
hand count on the "intent of the voter." The Supreme Court held that this
standard gave county officials in Florida too much leeway and violated the
right of citizens to have their votes counted fairly and equally.

The ruling brought charges that the Supreme Court had acted politically rather than on any strict interpretation of the law. In issuing a halt to
the recount, the Court had divided sharply along ideological lines. The majority consisted of its most conservative members, all of whom were Republican appointees: Chief Justice William Rehnquist and associate justices
Sandra Day O'Connor, Anthony Kennedy, Antonin Scalia, and Clarence
Thomas. In a dissenting opinion, Justice John Paul Stevens said: "Preventing the recount from being completed will inevitably cast a doubt upon the
legitimacy of the election." Stevens argued that the Florida high court's decision had properly reflected "the basic principle, inherent in our Constitution and our democracy, that every legal vote should be counted."[2]

Bush v. *Gore* was hardly the first time that the Supreme Court has been a center of controversy. If liberals were angered by its 2000 election decision, conservatives were outraged, for example, by a series of abortion rulings that began with *Roe* v. *Wade* in 1973.[3] The *Roe* decision touched off a heated debate within the legal community. Some legalists supported the decision, arguing that the judiciary must act to protect basic rights, even ones, including abortion, that are not explicitly provided by the Constitution.[4] Other legalists claimed that the Court has overstepped its authority. From their perspective, the problem with the *Roe* decision was that a right to abortion is not supported by any specific constitutional guarantee and therefore should not be established by judicial fiat.[5]

These examples illustrate three key points about court decisions. First, the judiciary is an extremely important policymaking body. Some of its rulings are as consequential as nearly any law passed by Congress or executive action taken by the president. Second, the judiciary has considerable discretion in its rulings. The *Bush* v. *Gore* and *Roe* v. *Wade* decisions were not based on any literal reading of the law: the justices in each case invoked *their* interpretation of the Constitution's provisions for individual rights. Third, the judiciary is a political as well as a legal institution, as illustrated by the conflict surrounding recent Supreme Court nominations. Once a

Demonstrators rally outside the U.S. Supreme Court building during hearings on the *Bush* v. *Gore* case that effectively brought the 2000 presidential election to an end. At times, the policy rulings of the judiciary are as significant as the decisions of the president or Congress.

law is established, it is expected to be administered in an evenhanded way; but the law itself is a product of contending political forces, is developed through a political process, has political content, and is applied by political appointees.

This chapter describes the federal judiciary and the work of its judges and justices. Like the executive and legislative branches, the judiciary is an independent branch of the U.S. government, but, unlike the two other branches, it is headed by officials who are not elected by the people. The judiciary is not a democratic institution, and its role is different from and, in some areas, more controversial than those of the executive and legislative branches. This chapter explores this issue in the process of discussing several main points:

* *The federal judiciary includes the Supreme Court of the United States, which functions mainly as an appellate court; courts of appeals, which hear appeals; and district courts, which hold trials. Each state has a court system of its own, which for the most part is independent of supervision by the federal courts.*

* *Judicial decisions are constrained by applicable constitutional law, statutory law, and precedent. Nevertheless, political factors have a major influence on judicial appointments and decisions; judges are political officials as well as legal ones.*

* *The judiciary has become an increasingly powerful policymaking body in recent decades, which has raised the question of the judiciary's proper role in a democracy.*

THE FEDERAL JUDICIAL SYSTEM

The writers of the Constitution were determined that the judiciary would be a separate and legitimate branch of the federal government but, for practical reasons, did not spell out the full structure of the federal court system. Article III of the Constitution establishes the Supreme Court of the United States and then grants Congress the authority to establish lower federal courts of its choosing.

Federal judges are nominated by the president, and if confirmed by the U.S. Senate, they are appointed by the president to the office. The Constitution states that judges "shall hold their offices during good behavior." However, the Constitution does not contain a precise definition of "good behavior," and no Supreme Court justice and only a very small number of lower-court judges have been removed from office through impeachment and conviction by Congress. In practice, federal judges and justices serve until they retire or die. Their lifetime tenure protects the judiciary's independence; without it, judges would be subject to intimidation by the elected officials who held power over their appointments.

Unlike the offices of president, senator, and representative, the federal judicial office has no age, residency, or citizenship qualifications placed on it by the Constitution. Nor does the Constitution require a judge to have legal training. Tradition alone dictates that federal judges have an educational or professional background in the law.

The Supreme Court of the United States

The Supreme Court of the United States is the nation's highest court. The chief justice of the United States presides over the Supreme Court and, like the eight associate justices, is selected by the president and is subject to Senate confirmation. The chief justice has the same voting power as the other justices but has usually exercised additional influence because of the position's leadership role.

The Constitution grants the Supreme Court both original and appellate jurisdiction. A court's **jurisdiction** is its authority to hear cases of a particular type. **Original jurisdiction** is the authority to be the first court to hear a case. The Supreme Court's original jurisdiction embraces legal disputes involving foreign diplomats and those in which the opposing parties are state governments. The Court in its entire history has convened as a court of original jurisdiction only a few hundred times and has rarely done so in recent years.

The Supreme Court does its most significant work as an appellate court. **Appellate jurisdiction** is the authority to review cases that have already been heard in lower courts and are appealed to the higher court by the losing party; such courts are called appeals courts, or appellate courts. The Supreme Court's appellate jurisdiction extends to cases arising under the Constitution, federal law and regulations, and treaties. The Court also hears appeals involving admiralty or maritime issues and legal controversies that cross state or national boundaries. Appellate courts, including the Supreme Court, do not retry cases; rather, they determine whether a trial court acted in accord with applicable law.

SELECTING CASES   The primary function of the judiciary is to interpret the law in such a way that rules made in the past (for example, the Constitution or legislation) can be applied reasonably in the present. This function gives the courts—all courts—a role in policymaking. Antitrust legislation, for example, is designed to prevent uncompetitive business practices, but like all such legislation, it is not self-enforcing. It is up to the courts to decide whether and how these laws apply to the case at hand.

As the nation's highest court, the Supreme Court is particularly important in establishing legal precedents that guide lower courts. A *precedent* is a judicial decision that serves as a rule for settling subsequent cases of a similar nature. Lower courts are expected to follow precedent—that is, to resolve cases of a like nature in ways consistent with upper-court rulings. However, for reasons that will be explained later, they do not always do so.

The Supreme Court's ability to set legal precedent is strengthened by its nearly complete discretion in choosing the cases it will hear. The large majority of cases reach the Supreme Court through a **writ of *certiorari***, which the Court may grant in response to a request from the losing party in a lower-court case. Four of the nine justices must agree to accept a particular case before it is granted a writ. Each year roughly seven thousand parties apply for *certiorari*, but the Court accepts only about one hundred cases for a full hearing and written opinion that explains the basis for the Court's decision. The Court issues another one hundred to two hundred *per curiam* (unsigned) decisions, which are made summarily without a hearing and simply state the facts of the case and the Court's decision. The Court is most likely to grant *certiorari* when the U.S. government through the solicitor general (the high-ranking Justice Department official, who serves as the government's lawyer in Supreme Court cases) requests it.[6]

The Court seldom accepts a routine case, even if the justices believe that a lower court has erred. The Supreme Court's job is not to correct every mistake of other courts, but to resolve broad legal questions. As a result, the justices usually choose cases that involve substantial legal issues. This criterion is vague, but essentially means that a case must center on an issue of significance not merely to the parties involved, but to the nation. As a result, most of the cases heard by the Court raise major constitutional issues, or affect the lives of many Americans, or address issues that are being decided inconsistently by the lower courts, or are in conflict with a previous Supreme Court ruling.[7] The last of these situations is particularly likely to propel a case to the Supreme Court, which naturally takes a keen interest in lower-court judgments that depart from its rulings.

DECIDING CASES   Once the Supreme Court accepts a case, it sets a date on which the attorneys for the two sides will present their oral arguments. Strict time limits, usually thirty minutes per side, are placed on these arguments, because each side has already submitted written arguments to the justices.

The open hearing is far less important than the **judicial conference** that follows, which is attended only by the nine justices. The conference's proceedings are kept strictly confidential. This secrecy allows the justices to speak freely and tentatively about a case. The chief justice presides over the conference and ordinarily speaks first.[8] The other justices then speak in order of their seniority (length of service on the Court). This arrangement enhances the senior members' ability to influence the discussion. After the discussion, the justices vote on the case.

ISSUING DECISIONS AND OPINIONS   After a case has been discussed and decided upon in conference, the Court prepares and issues its ruling, which consists of a decision and one or more opinions. The **decision** indicates which party the Court supports and by how large a margin. The **opinion** explains the reasons behind the decision. The opinion is the most important part of a Supreme Court ruling, because it informs others of the justices' interpretations of laws. When a majority of the justices agree on the legal basis of a decision, the result is a **majority opinion.**

In some cases there is no majority opinion, because a majority of the justices agree on the decision but cannot agree on the legal basis for it. The result is a **plurality opinion,** which presents the view held by most of the justices who side with the winning party. Another type of opinion is a **concurring opinion,** which is a separate view written by a justice who votes with the majority but disagrees with its reasoning.

Justices on the losing side can write a **dissenting opinion** to explain their reasons for disagreeing with the majority position. Sometimes these dissenting views become a later Court's majority position. In a 1942 dissenting opinion, Justice Hugo Black wrote that defendants in state felony trials should have legal counsel, even if they could not afford to pay for it. Two decades later, in *Gideon* v. *Wainwright* (1963), the Court adopted this position.[9]

Other Federal Courts

There are more than one hundred federal courts but there is only one Supreme Court, and its position at the top of the country's judicial system gives the Supreme Court unparalleled importance. It is a mistake, however, to conclude that the Supreme Court is the only court of consequence. Judge Jerome Frank once wrote of the "upper-court myth," which is the

Types of Supreme Court Opinions

Per curiam: Unsigned decision of the Court that states the facts of the case and the Court's ruling.

Majority opinion: A written opinion of the majority of the Court's justices stating the reasoning underlying their decision on a case.

Plurality opinion: A written opinion that in the absence of a majority opinion presents the reasoning of most of the justices who side with the winning party.

Concurring opinion: A written opinion of one or more justices who support the majority position but disagree with the majority's reasoning on a case. This opinion expresses the reasoning of the concurring justices.

Dissenting opinion: A written opinion of one or more justices who disagree with the majority's decision and opinion. This opinion provides the reasoning underlying the dissent.

view that appellate courts, and in particular the Supreme Court, are the only truly significant judicial arenas, and that lower courts dutifully follow the rulings handed down by those at the appellate level.[10] The reality is very different, as the following discussion will explain.

U.S. DISTRICT COURTS   The lowest federal courts are the district courts (see Figure 14-1). There are more than ninety federal district courts altogether—at least one in every state and as many as four in some states. District-court judges, who number about eight hundred in all, are appointed by the president with the consent of the Senate. Federal cases usually originate in district courts, which are trial courts, where the parties argue their sides. District courts are the only courts in the federal system in which juries hear testimony. Most cases at this level are presented before a single judge.

Lower federal courts unquestionably rely on and follow Supreme Court decisions in their own rulings. This requirement was reiterated in a 1982 case, *Hutto* v. *Davis:* "Unless we wish anarchy to prevail within the federal judicial system, a precedent of this Court must be followed by the lower federal courts no matter how misguided the judges of those courts may think it to be."[11]

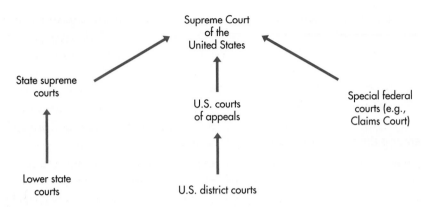

FIGURE 14-1   THE FEDERAL JUDICIAL SYSTEM
This simplified diagram shows the relationships among the various levels of federal courts and between state and federal courts. The losing party in a case can appeal a lower-court decision to the court at the next-highest level, as the arrows indicate. Decisions can be removed from state courts to federal courts only if they raise a constitutional question.

However, the idea that lower courts are guided strictly by Supreme Court rulings is part of the "upper-court myth." District-court judges may misunderstand the Supreme Court's position and deviate from it for that reason. In addition, the facts in a case being heard in a district court are seldom exactly the same as those of a previous case settled by the Supreme Court. The lower-court judge must decide whether the facts are sufficiently different to require the application of a different legal principle. Finally, it is not unusual for the Supreme Court to take a very broad legal position that is encompassing enough to allow lower courts to decide its exact meaning in practice. Trial-court judges then have a creative role in judicial decision making that rivals that of appellate court judges.

Most federal cases end with the district court's decision; the losing party does not appeal the decision to a higher court. This is another indication of the highly significant role of district-court judges.

U.S. COURTS OF APPEALS   When cases are appealed from district courts, they go to a federal court of appeals. These appellate courts make up the second level of the federal court system. Courts of appeals do not use juries. No new evidence is submitted in an appealed case; appellate courts base their decisions on a review of lower-court records. Appellate judges act as supervisors in the legal system, reviewing trial-court decisions and correcting what they consider to be legal errors. Facts (i.e., the circumstances of a case) found by district courts are presumed to be correct.

The United States has twelve general appeals courts, each of which serves a "circuit" that is composed of between three and nine states, except the one that serves the District of Columbia only. There is also the U.S. Court of Appeals for the Federal Circuit, which specializes in appeals of cases involving patents and international trade. Between four and twenty-six judges sit on each court of appeals, but each case is usually heard by a panel of three judges. On rare occasions, all the judges of a court of appeals sit as a body (*en banc*) in order to resolve difficult controversies, typically ones that have resulted in conflicting decisions within the same circuit.

Courts of appeals offer the only real hope of reversal for many appellants, since fewer than 1 percent of the cases they hear are later reviewed by the Supreme Court.

SPECIAL U.S. COURTS   The federal judiciary includes a few specialty courts. Among them are the U.S. Claims Court, which hears cases in which the U.S. government has been sued for damages; the U.S. Court of International Trade, which handles cases involving appeals of U.S. Customs Office rulings; and the U.S. Court of Military Appeals, which hears appeals of military courts-martial. Some federal agencies and commissions also have adjudicative powers, and their decisions can be appealed to a federal court of appeals.

The State Courts

The American states are separate governments within a federal system. Each state is protected in its sovereignty by the Tenth Amendment, and each state has its own court system. Like the federal courts, state court systems have trial courts at the bottom level and appellate courts at the top.

Each state decides for itself the structure of its courts and the method of judicial appointment. In some states, judges are appointed by the governor, but judgeships are *elective offices* in most states. The common form involves competitive elections of either a partisan or a nonpartisan nature, although some states use a system called the *merit plan* (also called the "Missouri Plan" because Missouri was the first state to use it), under which the governor selects a judge from a short list of acceptable candidates provided by a judicial selection commission. After a year or more on the bench, the judge selected must be approved by the voters in order to serve a longer term. Thereafter, the judge must face a periodic (usually every six years) "retention election" in which voters decide whether he or she will continue in the office (see box: States in the Nation).

★ STATES IN THE NATION ★

Principal Methods of Selecting State Judges

The states rely on a variety of methods for selecting the judicial officers of their highest court, including the merit plan, partisan election, non-partisan election, and political appointment. The states that appoint judges grant this power to the governor except in Virginia, Connecticut, and South Carolina, where the legislature makes the choice.

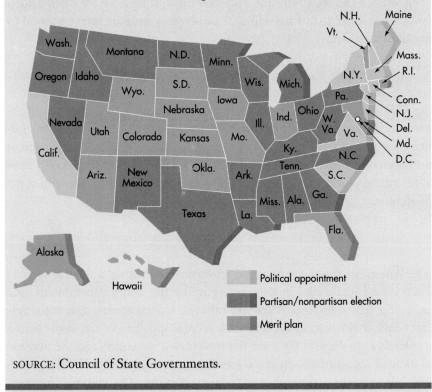

Political appointment

Partisan/nonpartisan election

Merit plan

SOURCE: Council of State Governments.

Besides the upper-court myth, there exists a "federal court myth," which holds that the federal judiciary is the most significant part of the judicial system and that state courts play a subordinate role. This view is inaccurate as well. More than 95 percent of the nation's legal cases are decided in state courts. Most felonies and misdemeanors (from traffic infractions to murder) and most civil controversies (such as divorces and corporate disputes) are defined by state or local law. Moreover, nearly all cases

The Florida Supreme Court hears the arguments that led it to order a statewide canvass of uncounted ballots in the Bush-Gore presidential contest. Less than a day after it was rendered, the court's order was blocked by the U.S. Supreme Court. It was a rare intervention. Upwards of 95 percent of the nation's legal cases are decided entirely within the state court system, an indication of the "federal-court myth."

that originate in state courts also end there; the federal courts never come into the picture, since the case does not involve a federal issue.

In state criminal cases, after a person has been convicted and after all avenues of appeal in the state court system have been exhausted, the defendant can seek a writ of habeas corpus from a federal district court (see Chapter 4). The federal court often confines itself to the federal aspects of the matter, such as whether the defendant in a criminal case received the protections guaranteed by the U.S. Constitution. In addition, the federal court must accept the facts determined by the state court unless such findings are clearly in error. In short, legal and factual determinations of state courts can bind the federal courts—a clear contradiction of the federal court myth.

However, cases traditionally within the jurisdiction of the states can become federal cases through rulings of federal courts. In *Roe* v. *Wade* (1973), for example, the Supreme Court concluded that women had a constitutional right to choose an abortion, thus making abortion rights, which had been a state issue, also a federal one.[12] (This situation is called "diversity of citizenship" jurisdiction, meaning that both state and federal courts have some jurisdiction over the issue.)

FEDERAL COURT APPOINTEES

The quiet setting of the courtroom, the dignity of its proceedings, and the lack of fanfare with which a court delivers its decisions give the impression that the judiciary is about as far removed from the world of politics as a governmental institution can possibly be. The reality, however, is different. Federal judges and justices are political officials who exercise the authority of a separate and powerful branch of government. All federal jurists bring their political views with them into the courtroom and have regular opportunities to promote their political beliefs through the cases they decide. Accordingly, the process by which federal judges are appointed is a partisan one.

Selecting Supreme Court Justices and Federal Judges

The formal mechanism for appointments to the Supreme Court and the lower federal courts is the same: the president nominates and the Senate confirms or rejects. Beyond that basic similarity, however, there are significant differences.

SUPREME COURT NOMINEES   A Supreme Court appointment is a critical choice for a president. The cases that come before the Court tend to be controversial and have far-reaching implications. And since the Court is a small body, each justice's vote can be crucial to the decisions it makes. As most justices retain their positions for many years, presidents can influence judicial policy through their appointments long after they have left office. The careers of some Supreme Court justices provide dramatic testimony to the enduring effects of judicial appointments. Franklin D. Roosevelt appointed William O. Douglas to the Supreme Court in 1939, and for thirty years after Roosevelt's death in 1945, Douglas remained a strong liberal influence on the Court.

Presidents have employed a variety of approaches in their efforts to select a Supreme Court nominee who will reflect their political philosophy. A president may choose to depend chiefly on his own counsel, ask the Justice Department for advice, or seek the views of interested parties who share his general philosophy. Nominees must also be acceptable to others. Every nominee is closely scrutinized by the legal community, interested groups, and the media, and must also undergo an extensive background check by the FBI.[13]

Within the Senate, a key body is the Judiciary Committee, whose members have responsibility for conducting hearings on judicial nominees and recommending their confirmation or rejection by the full Senate. Nearly 20 percent of presidential nominees have been rejected by the

The Justices of the U.S. Supreme Court pose for a photo. From left, they are Clarence Thomas, Antonin Scalia, Sandra Day O'Connor, Anthony Kennedy, David Souter, Stephen Breyer, John Paul Stevens, Chief Justice William Rehnquist, and Ruth Bader Ginsburg.

Senate on grounds of judicial qualification, political views, personal ethics, or partisanship. Most of these rejections in the country's history occurred before 1900, and partisan politics was the main reason. Today a nominee with strong professional and ethical credentials is less likely to be blocked for partisan reasons alone.

Presidents often take into account the Senate's probable reaction when choosing a nominee. In selecting Ruth Bader Ginsburg and Stephen Breyer as his first nominees, President Clinton eschewed the choice of more controversial judges who might have been closer to his own views on issues before the Court. In general, though, the burden of proof rests with the Senate. To avoid the charge of unprincipled partisanship, the Senate in most cases has unofficially accepted the premise that it must build an overwhelming case against confirmation before denying the president's nominee a seat on the nation's highest court. An exception was Robert Bork, whose nomination was rejected in 1987 primarily because of opposition from Senate Democrats who disagreed with his conservative judicial philosophy, which had been pointedly argued in his writings and public speeches.

LOWER-COURT NOMINEES The president normally gives the deputy attorney general the task of screening potential nominees for lower-court judgeships.[14] **Senatorial courtesy** is also a consideration in these appointments: this tradition, which dates back to the 1840s, holds that a senator from the state in which a vacancy has arisen should be given a say in the nomination if the senator is of the same party as the president.[15] If not consulted, the senator involved can request that confirmation be denied, and other senators will normally grant the request as a "courtesy" to a fellow senator.[16] Not surprisingly, presidents have preferred to give senators a voice in judicial appointments.

Although the president does not become as personally involved in selecting lower-court nominees as in naming potential Supreme Court justices, lower-court appointments are collectively a significant factor in the impact of a president's administration. Recent presidents have appointed about two hundred judges each term.

Justices and Judges as Political Officials

Presidents generally manage to appoint jurists who have a similar political philosophy. Although Supreme Court justices are free to make their own decisions, their legal positions can usually be inferred from their prior activities. A study by the judicial scholar Robert Scigliano found that about three of every four appointees have behaved on the Supreme Court approximately as presidents could have expected.[17] Of course, a president has no guarantee that a nominee will behave as expected. Justices Earl Warren and William Brennan proved more liberal than President Dwight D. Eisenhower would have liked. When he was asked whether he had made any mistakes as president, Eisenhower replied, "Yes, two, and they are both sitting on the Supreme Court."[18]

THE ROLE OF PARTISANSHIP   In nearly every instance, presidents have chosen members of their own party as Supreme Court nominees. Partisanship is also decisive in nominations to lower-court judgeships. More than 90 percent of recent district and appeals court nominees have been members of the president's own party.[19]

The fact that judges and justices are chosen through a partisan political process should not be interpreted to mean that they engage in blatant partisanship while on the bench. Judges and justices are officers of a separate branch and prize their judicial independence. All Republican appointees do not vote the same way on cases, nor do all Democrats. Nevertheless, the partisan backgrounds of judges are a significant influence on their decisions. A study of the voting records of appellate court judges, for example, found that Republican appointees tend to be more conservative than

Democratic appointees in their civil rights and civil liberties decisions.[20] In Supreme Court cases, Democratic and Republican appointees have often been on opposite sides, although other divisions also occur.

OTHER CHARACTERISTICS OF JUDICIAL APPOINTEES   In recent years, increasing numbers of federal justices and judges have had prior judicial experience; the assumption is that such individuals are best qualified for appointment to the federal bench. Most recent appellate court appointees have been district or state judges or have worked in the office of the attorney general. Elective office (particularly a seat in the U.S. Senate) was once the typical route to the Supreme Court,[21] but now justices have typically held appellate court judgeships before their appointment (see Table 14-1).

White males are greatly overrepresented on the federal bench, just as they dominate in Congress and at the top levels of the executive branch.[22] However, the number of women and minority-group judges increased substantially as a result of the appointments of President Clinton. Partisanship has been a significant factor in the appointment of women and minorities to the bench (see Table 14-2). Democratic presidents Carter and Clinton were more likely than Republican presidents Reagan and Bush to appoint such individuals, a reflection of the differences in the parties' coalitions (see Chapter 8).

The Supreme Court itself is also demographically unrepresentative. Thurgood Marshall in 1967 became the first black justice, and Sandra Day O'Connor in 1981 became the first woman. Antonin Scalia in 1986 became the Court's first justice of Italian descent. No person of Hispanic or Asian descent has ever been a member of the Court.

Judicial scholars disagree on the importance of the Court's demographic makeup. Henry J. Abraham dismisses concerns about it, claiming that the Court was never meant to be a representative body.[23] In contrast, Sheldon Goldman asserts that the judiciary's sensitivity to society's diverse interests depends to a degree on the social backgrounds that the justices bring with them to the Court.[24]

THE NATURE OF JUDICIAL DECISION MAKING

Federal judges and justices are political officials: they constitute one of three coequal branches of the national government (see box: How the United States Compares). Yet, unlike members of Congress or the president, judges

TABLE 14-1	JUSTICES OF THE SUPREME COURT, 1998		
Most recent appointees held an appellate-court position before being nominated to the Supreme Court.			
Justice	Year of Appointment	Nominating President	Position before Appointment
William Rehnquist*	1971	Nixon	Assistant attorney general, Department of Justice
John Paul Stevens	1975	Ford	Judge, U.S. Courts of Appeals
Sandra Day O'Connor	1981	Reagan	Judge, Arizona Courts of Appeals
Antonin Scalia	1986	Reagan	Judge, U.S. Courts of Appeals
Anthony Kennedy	1988	Reagan	Judge, U.S. Courts of Appeals
David Souter	1990	Bush	Judge, U.S. Courts of Appeals
Clarence Thomas	1991	Bush	Judge, U.S. Courts of Appeals
Ruth Bader Ginsburg	1993	Clinton	Judge, U.S. Courts of Appeals
Stephen Breyer	1994	Clinton	Judge, U.S. Courts of Appeals

*Appointed chief justice in 1986.

serve in a legal institution and make their decisions in a legal context. As a consequence, their discretionary power is less than that of elected officials. Article III of the Constitution bars the federal judiciary from issuing decisions except on actual cases before it. As federal judge David Bazelon noted, a judge "can't wake up one morning and simply decide to give a helpful little push to a school system, a mental hospital, or the local housing agency."[25]

The Legal Context of Judicial Decisions

The most substantial restriction on the courts is the law itself. Although a president or Congress can make almost any decision that is politically acceptable, the judiciary must justify its decision in terms of existing provisions of the law.[26] When asked by a friend to "do justice," Oliver Wendell

TABLE 14-2 BACKGROUND CHARACTERISTICS OF PRESIDENTS' JUDICIAL NOMINEES

The judicial nominees of recent presidents have differed in their gender and racial characteristics.

	Judicial Appointees of:			
	Carter	*Reagan*	*Bush*	*Clinton*
Men	85%	92%	81%	69%
Women	15	8	19	31
Whites	79%	93%	88%	75%
African Americans	14	2	7	17
Hispanics	6	4	4	6
Asians	1	1	1	2

SOURCE: From People for the American Way. Reprinted by permission.

Holmes, Jr., replied, "That is not my job. My job is to play the game according to the rules."[27] In playing according to the rules, judges engage in a creative legal process that requires them to identify the facts of the case, determine and sometimes formulate the relevant legal principles or rules, and then apply them to the case at hand.

THE CONSTRAINTS OF THE FACTS A basic distinction in any legal case is between "the facts" and "the laws." The **facts** of a case, as determined by trial courts, are the relevant circumstances of a legal dispute or offense. In the case of a person accused of murder, for example, key facts would include evidence that linked the accused to the crime, whether the killing was premeditated or committed in an act of momentary rage, and whether police respected the rights of the accused (for example, whether the accused was informed of the right to remain silent and to have an attorney present during interrogation).

The facts of a case are critical because they determine which law or laws are applicable to the case. The courts must respond to the facts of a dispute. This restriction is a very substantial one. A murder case cannot be used as an occasion for a judge to issue a ruling on freedom of religion.

THE CONSTRAINTS OF THE LAW In deciding cases, the judiciary is also constrained by existing **laws.** To use an obvious comparison, the laws governing a case of alleged murder differ from the laws that apply to a

HOW THE UNITED STATES COMPARES

Judicial Power

U.S. courts are highly political by comparison with the courts of most other democracies. First, U.S. courts operate within a common-law tradition, which makes judge-made law (through precedent) a part of the legal code. Many democracies have a civil-law tradition, in which nearly all law is defined by legislative statutes. Second, because U.S. courts operate in a constitutional system of divided power, they are required to rule on conflicts between state and nation or between the executive and legislative branches, which thrusts the judiciary into the middle of political conflicts. It should not be surprising, then, that federal judges and justices are appointed through an overtly political process in which partisan views and activities are major considerations. Many federal judges, particularly at the district level, have no significant prior judicial experience. In fact, the United States is one of the few countries that does not mandate formal training for judges.

The pattern is different in most European democracies. Judgeships there tend to be career positions. Individuals are appointed to the judiciary at an early age and then work their way up the judicial ladder largely on the basis of seniority. Partisan politics does not play a large role in appointment and promotion. By tradition, European judges see their job as the strict interpretation of statutes, not the creative application of them.

The power of U.S. courts is nowhere more evident than in the exercise of judicial review: the voiding of a legislative or executive action on the grounds that it violates the Constitution. Judicial review had its origins in European experience and thought, but it was first formally applied in the United States when, in *Marbury* v. *Madison* (1803), the Supreme Court declared an act of Congress unconstitutional. Some democracies, including Great Britain, still do not allow broadscale judicial review, but most democracies now provide for it.

traffic violation. Very different laws govern these two cases, and the judge must apply the law or laws that fit the particular case. A judge must treat a murder case as a murder case, applying to it the laws that define murder and the penalties that can be imposed when someone is found guilty of murder.

The laws of a case can include constitutional provisions, legislative statutes (and administrative regulations based on these statutes), and judicial precedents.

The Constitution and Its Interpretation The Constitution of the United States is the nation's highest law, and the judges and justices are sworn to uphold it. When a case arises that raises a constitutional issue, a court has the duty to apply the Constitution to the case. For example, the Constitution prohibits the states from printing their own currency. If a state decided that it would do so anyway, a federal judge would be obliged to rule against the practice.

Nevertheless, some constitutional provisions are open to interpretation in some cases. For example, the Fourth Amendment of the Constitution protects individuals against "unreasonable searches and seizures," but the meaning of "unreasonable" is not spelled out. Nevertheless, judges respect the Constitution's purpose and intent. The question for a judge is what the Framers had in mind by a particular provision. For example, in deciding whether wire-tapping and other electronic means of surveillance are covered by the prohibition against unreasonable searches and seizures, the issue is what rights the amendment was designed to protect. Electronic surveillance was not invented until 150 years after the Fourth Amendment was ratified. But the Fourth Amendment was intended to protect individuals against the government's intrusion into their private lives. For this reason, the courts have concluded that government cannot indiscriminately tap a person's telephone.

Statutes and Their Interpretation The vast majority of cases that arise in courts involve issues of statutory law rather than constitutional law. Most criminal acts (such as murder and assault) and civil actions (such as divorce and contract disputes) are covered by laws (statutes) created by legislative action or by regulations that have been developed by administrators on the basis of statutory law. There are thousands upon thousands of such laws and regulations, and they are usually at issue in a court case. There ordinarily is no constitutional provision at issue, for example, when a worker sues a company over a job-related injury or when a person is charged with burglary.

All federal courts are bound by federal statutes (laws passed by Congress) and by federal administrative regulations, as well as by treaties. When hearing a case involving statutory law or administrative regulation, judges must work within the limits of the applicable law or regulation. A company that is charged with violating federal environmental law will be judged within the context of that law—what it permits and what it prohibits, and the penalties that would apply if the company is found to have broken the law.

When hearing such a case, judges will often try to determine whether the meaning of the statute or regulation can be determined by common sense (the "plain meaning rule"). The question for the judge is what the law or regulation was intended to safeguard (such as a particular issue of environmental protection). In most instances the law or regulation is clear enough that when the facts of the case are judged against it, a reasonable decision can be reached. Not all cases, however, are clear-cut in their facts or in the applicable law or laws. In these instances, courts have no choice but to exercise their judgment.

Legal Precedents (Previous Rulings) and Their Interpretation The U.S. legal system developed from the English common-law tradition, which includes the principle that a court's decision on a case should be consistent with previous judicial rulings. This principle is known as **precedent** and reflects the philosophy of *stare decisis* (Latin for "to stand by things that have been settled"): the doctrine that principles of law, once established, should be accepted as authoritative in all subsequent similar cases. Judges and justices often cite past rulings as a justification for their decisions in the cases before them.

Precedent is important because it gives predictability to the application of law. If courts routinely ignored how similar cases had been decided in the past, they would create confusion and uncertainty among those who must make choices on the basis of their understanding of how the law has been applied in previous situations.[28] A business firm that is seeking to comply with environmental protection laws, for example, can develop company policies that will keep the company safely within the law if court decisions in this area are predictable. But if courts routinely ignore precedent, a firm might unintentionally engage in activity that a court could arbitrarily conclude was unlawful.

Government has an obligation to citizens and firms alike to make clear what its laws are and how they are being applied. Precedent is one of the means by which greater consistency in the application of the law can be achieved.

Sources of Law That Constrain the Federal Judiciary's Decisions

U.S. Constitution: The federal courts are bound by the provisions of the U.S. Constitution. The sparseness of its wording, however, requires the Constitution to be applied in the light of particular circumstances. Thus judges are accorded a substantial degree of discretion in their constitutional judgments.

Statutory law: The Supreme Court is constrained by statutes and by administrative regulations derived from the provisions of statutes. Most laws, however, are somewhat vague in their provisions and often have unanticipated applications. As a result, judges have some freedom in deciding cases based on statutes.

Precedent: Federal courts tend to follow precedent (or *stare decisis*), which is a legal principle developed in earlier court decisions. Because times change and not all cases have a clear precedent, judges have some discretion in their evaluation of the way earlier cases apply to a current case.

Political Influences on Judicial Decisions

Although judicial rulings are justified by reference to laws, judges nearly always have some degree of discretion in their decisions. The Constitution is a sparsely worded document and must be adapted to new and changing situations; as a result, federal judges must interpret the Constitution in the context of the issue at hand. The judiciary also has no choice at times but to apply its own judgment to statutory law. Congress often cannot anticipate or reach agreement on all the specific applications of a legislative act, and therefore uses general language to state the act's purpose. The judiciary must decide what this language means in the context of a specific case arising under the act. Precedent is even less precise as a guide to decision. Precedent is more a rule of thumb than a strict command; it must constantly be weighed against what Justice Oliver Wendell Holmes, Jr., described as the "felt necessities of the time."

The Supreme Court's rulings in two 1998 cases involving sexual harassment in the workplace illustrate the ambiguity that can exist in the written law. The Court developed its rulings in the context of the antidiscrimination provisions of the Civil Rights Act of 1964. The act itself, however, contains no description of, or even reference to, job-related sexual harassment. Nevertheless, the act does prohibit workplace discrimination, and the Court could not easily dismiss sexual harassment as an irrelevant form of job-related discrimination. In judging the two cases, however, the Court had no choice except to decide for itself which actions in the workplace are instances of harassment and which are not. In this sense, the Court was "making" law; it was deciding how legislation enacted by Congress applied to actions that Congress had not addressed when it wrote the legislation.[29] (The Court's rulings in the two cases are discussed in Chapter 5.)

In sum, judges have leeway in their decisions. As a consequence, their rulings reflect not only legal influences but political ones, which come from both outside and inside the judicial system.

"OUTSIDE" INFLUENCES ON COURT DECISIONS   The courts can make unpopular choices, but, in the long run, judicial decisions must be seen as fair if they are to be obeyed. In other words, the judiciary cannot ignore the expectations of the general public, interest groups, and elected representatives.

Judges are responsive to public opinion, although much less so than are elected officials. In some cases, for example, the Supreme Court has tailored its rulings in an effort to gain public support or dampen public resistance. In the *Brown* case, the justices, recognizing that school desegregation would be an explosive issue in the South, required only that desegregation take place "with all deliberate speed" rather than immediately or on a fixed timetable. The Supreme Court's apparent strategy has been to stay close enough to popular opinion to avoid seriously eroding public support for its decisions.[30]

Organized groups make their opinions known to the judiciary through the lawsuits they file. The range of interests that use lawsuits as a policy tactic includes traditional advocacy groups such as the American Civil Liberties Union (ACLU) and newer ones such as the Christian Legal Society's Center for Law and Religious Freedom. Groups also participate in cases brought by others through *amicus curiae* ("friend of the court") briefs, which they file in support of one of the parties to a case.[31]

The influence of groups and the general public on the judiciary also takes place indirectly, through the elected branches of government. In response to public and group pressure, elected officials try to persuade the judiciary to hand down rulings favored by their constituents. Both Congress and the president have powerful means of influencing the federal judiciary.

Congress is constitutionally empowered to establish the Supreme Court's size and appellate jurisdiction, and Congress can rewrite legislation that it feels the judiciary has misinterpreted. Although Congress seldom punishes the judiciary directly, its members have often expressed displeasure with judicial action. In a 1998 Senate speech, the chair of the Judiciary Committee, Orrin Hatch (R-Utah), lashed out at judges who he claimed were "making laws instead of interpreting the law." Such judges, Hatch asserted, "should resign to run for public office—at least they would be accountable for their actions."[32] Other Republicans on the Judiciary Committee shared Hatch's view, and they delayed confirmation of a number of President Clinton's judicial nominees on the grounds that they were unlikely to be "strict constructionists." (*Strict constructionism* holds that a judicial officer should apply a narrow interpretation of the laws, whereas *loose constructionism* holds that a judicial officer can apply an expansive interpretation.)

The president also has ways to influence the judiciary. The president is responsible for enforcing court decisions and has some influence on the types of cases that come before the courts. Under President Ronald Reagan, for instance, the Justice Department vigorously backed several suits challenging affirmative action programs and made no great attempt to push cases that would have expanded the application of such programs.

The judicial branch is increasingly an arena in which interest groups contend for influence. Many of these disputes have pitted environmental groups against business firms. Shown here are demonstrators on both sides of the issue of whether protection of the spotted owl, an endangered species, should take precedence over the interests of the timber industry.

Presidents can also influence the federal courts through their judicial appointments.[33] When Democrat Bill Clinton took office in 1993, more than a hundred federal judgeships were vacant. President Bush had expected to win reelection and had not moved quickly to fill vacancies as they arose. By the time it was apparent that Bush might lose the election, the Democrat-controlled Congress was able to delay action on the appointments. This enabled Clinton to fill the positions with loyal Democrats who could be expected to partially offset the influence of the Republican judges appointed during the previous twelve years by presidents Reagan and Bush. The tables were turned in 2001 when George W. Bush took office. Senate Republicans had slowed action on Clinton nominees, enabling Bush to appoint Republicans to existing vacancies.

"Inside" Influences: The Justices' Own Political Beliefs
The judiciary symbolizes John Adams's characterization of the U.S. political system as "a government of laws, and not of men." The characterization has value as myth, but as the judicial scholar John Schmidhauser noted, "laws are made, enforced, and interpreted by men."[34] As an inevitable result, the decisions of the courts bear the indelible imprint of judges' political beliefs.[35]

This influence is most evident in the case of the Supreme Court. The justices are frequently divided in their opinions, and the divisions often reflect the justices' political backgrounds. During the 1999 Supreme Court term, for example, sixteen cases were decided by a 5–4 decision. In fourteen of those cases, Chief Justice William Rehnquist and justices Antonin Scalia and Clarence Thomas, all of whom are Republican appointees, were opposed by justices Stephen Breyer and Ruth Bader Ginsburg, the two Democratic appointees on the Court.[36]

Most Supreme Court justices hold relatively stable political views during their tenure. As a result, major shifts in the Supreme Court's position usually occur in conjunction with changes in its membership. When the Court in the 1980s moved away from the criminal justice rulings of the 1960s, it was largely because the more recently appointed justices believed that government should have more leeway in its efforts to fight crime.

JUDICIAL POWER AND DEMOCRATIC GOVERNMENT

The issue of judicial power is heightened by the fact that federal judges are not elected. The principle of self-government asserts that lawmaking majorities have the power to decide society's policies. Because the United

States has a constitutional system that places checks on the will of the majority, there is obviously an important role in the system for a counter-majoritarian institution such as the judiciary (see Table 14-3). Yet court decisions often reflect the political philosophy of the judges, who constitute a tiny political elite that wields significant power.[37] A critical question is how far unelected judges ought to go in substituting their policy judgments for those of legislative and executive officials who are elected by the people.

The judiciary's power is most evident when it declares executive or legislative action to be unconstitutional. The power of the courts to make such determinations is called **judicial review** and was first asserted in the landmark *Marbury v. Madison* case of 1803, when the Supreme Court rebuked both the president and Congress (see Chapter 2). Without judicial review, the federal courts would be unable to restrain an elected official or institution that had gone out of control.

Yet judicial review places the judgment of the courts above that of elected officials when interpretation of the Constitution is at issue, creating the possibility of conflict between the courts and the elected branches. The imposing nature of judicial review has led the judiciary to apply judicial review somewhat sparingly, although the Supreme Court alone has invoked it in more than one thousand cases—the large majority of which have involved action by state and local officials rather than the president or Congress. Many of these cases, as we saw in Chapters 4 and 5, involved issues of civil liberties (e.g., free expression) and civil rights (e.g., racial discrimination).

Even in the area of statutory law, however, there is plenty of room for the exercise of judicial power. Most statutes (legislative acts) specify general goals, which judges then have to apply in particular situations. Often, a case reaches the courts precisely because the law in question is vague as to how it might apply to the case, which enables courts to make the determination.

The Debate over the Proper Role of the Judiciary

The question of judicial power centers on the basic issue of **legitimacy:** the proper authority of the judiciary in a political system based in part on the principle of majority rule. The judiciary's policymaking significance and discretion have been sources of controversy throughout the country's history, but the controversies have seldom been livelier than during recent decades.

The judiciary at times has acted almost legislatively by defining broad social policies, such as abortion, busing, affirmative action, church-state relations, and prison reform. In a recent year, for example, the prison systems

TABLE 14-3 SIGNIFICANT SUPREME COURT CASES
Included are some of the most influential cases decided by
the U.S. Supreme Court.

Selected Supreme Court Cases

Case	Ruling
Marbury v. Madison (1803)	Established principle of judicial review (Chapter 2)
McCullough v. Maryland (1819)	Strengthened national power over states (Chapter 3)
Dred Scott v. Sanford (1857)	Decided that slaves were property and not citizens (Chapter 3)
Plessy v. Ferguson (1896)	Established the "Separate but Equal" doctrine (Chapter 5)
Gitlow v. New York (1925)	Protected free expression from state action by 14th Amendment (Chapter 4)
Brown v. Topeka Board of Education (1954)	Abolished the "Separate but Equal" doctrine and banned segregation in public schools (Chapter 5)
Gideon v. Wainwright (1963)	Decided that states must provide an attorney for poor defendants accused of committing felonies (Chapter 4)
Miranda v. Arizona (1966)	Decided that the police must inform suspects of their rights when they are arrested (Chapter 4)
Roe v. Wade (1973)	Decided that women have full freedom to choose abortion during the first three months of pregnancy under the right of privacy (Chapter 4)

in forty-two states were operating under court orders that mandated improvements in health care or overcrowding. School prayer is an older example. Until the Supreme Court in 1962 prohibited the reciting of prayer in public schools, the practice was governed by state legislatures and, in some cases, by local school districts. Through such actions the judiciary has restricted the policymaking authority of the states, has narrowed legislative discretion, and has made judicial action an effective alternative to election victory for certain interests.[38]

The judiciary has become more extensively involved in policymaking for many of the same reasons that Congress and the president have been thrust into new policy areas and become more deeply involved in old ones. Social and economic changes have required government to play a larger role in society, and this development has generated a seemingly endless series of new legal controversies.

Judicial action raises an important question. How far should the judiciary go in asserting its authority when that authority collides with or goes beyond the action of elected institutions? There are two general schools of thought on this question: one advocates judicial restraint and the other supports judicial activism. Although these terms are somewhat imprecise and often misused, they are helpful in efforts to clarify opposing philosophical positions on the Court's proper role.[39]

THE DOCTRINE OF JUDICIAL RESTRAINT   The doctrine of **judicial restraint** holds that the judiciary should be highly respectful of precedent and should defer to the judgment of legislatures. The restraint doctrine emphasizes the consistency of law and rule through elected institutions. It holds that broad issues of the public good should be decided in nearly all cases by the majority through legislation enacted by elected officials. The judges' role is to discover the application of legislation and precedent to specific cases rather than to search for new principles that essentially change the meaning of the law.

Advocates of judicial restraint support their position with two major arguments. First, they contend that when the judiciary assumes policy functions that traditionally belong to elected institutions, it undermines the fundamental premise of self-government: the right of the majority to choose society's policies.[40] Second, judicial self-restraint is admired because it preserves the public support that is essential to the long-term authority of the courts. The judiciary must be concerned with **compliance**—with whether its decisions will be respected and obeyed. If the judiciary thwarts the majority's desires, public confidence in its legitimacy can be endangered, and popularly elected officials may act to undermine judicial decisions.[41]

Advocates of judicial restraint acknowledge that established law is never so precise as to provide exact answers to every question raised by every case and requires some degree of judicial discretion. And in rare circumstances, decisive judicial action may be both appropriate and necessary, as in the

The Supreme Court in 1996 struck down an amendment to the Colorado
constitution that would have barred civil rights protections for homosexuals. The
ruling was criticized by some advocates of judicial restraint.

historic *Brown* v. *Board of Education* decision (1954). Although the Constitution does not provide an explicit basis for school desegregation,
government-supported racial discrimination violates the principle of equal
justice under the law.[42]

Yet many advocates of judicial restraint see no constitutional justification for many of the Supreme Court's civil rights decisions. In *Romer* v.
Evans (1996), for example, the Court struck down an amendment to the
Colorado constitution that was adopted by majority vote in a statewide referendum. The amendment had nullified existing civil rights protections for
homosexuals in the state and had also barred the passage of new ones. In a
blistering dissent, Justice Antonin Scalia, an advocate of judicial restraint,
said the Court's decision to invalidate the Colorado amendment was "an act
not of judicial judgment but of political will." Scalia said that the statewide
referendum was "the most democratic of procedures" and that the decision
of Colorado voters should have been upheld.[43]

THE DOCTRINE OF JUDICIAL ACTIVISM   In contrast to the judicial
restraint position is the idea that the courts should take an expansive view
of judicial power. Although advocates of this doctrine, which is known as
judicial activism, acknowledge the principles of precedent and majority

rule, they claim that the courts should not be overly deferential to existing legal principles or to the judgments of elected officials.

Until recently, the doctrine of judicial activism was associated with liberal activists who contend that courts should resort to general principles of fairness when existing law is insufficient. Liberal judicial activists argue, for example, that fairness for African American children requires that in some circumstances children should be bused to achieve school integration. In areas where social justice depends substantially on protection of the rights of the individual, the judiciary is said to have a responsibility to act positively and decisively.[44]

Activists who emphasize the Court's obligation to protect civil rights and liberties find justification for their position in the U.S. Constitution's strong moral language and several of its provisions.[45] They view the Constitution as designed chiefly to protect people from unreasonable governmental interference in their lives—a goal that can be accomplished only by a judiciary that is willing to stand up to the lawmaking majority whenever the latter tries to restrict individual freedom or run roughshod over powerless minorities.

Judicial activism is not, however, confined to liberals. In the 1860s–1930s period conservative activists on the Supreme Court struck down most legislative efforts to regulate economic activity (see Chapter 3). Judicial activism from the right recently became an issue again when the Court overturned several precedents in the area of the rights of the accused. In 1990, Chief Justice William Rehnquist, in a rare action, asked Congress to restrict the right of those convicted in state courts to file habeas corpus appeals in federal courts. Congress rejected the proposal, and in 1991 a majority on the Rehnquist Court took action on its own to achieve the goal. In one ruling, the Court held that an inmate could not obtain a federal appeal simply because his or her lawyer had made a procedural mistake during the trial in a state court. Chief Justice Rehnquist wrote that precedent is not "an inexorable command."[46]

Conservative activism is also evident in recent Supreme Court cases on the issue of federalism. Since the late 1930s, the Court had deferred to Congress on commerce policy, but it has recently struck down several commerce-related statutes (see Chapter 3). The Court's four most conservative justices (Rehnquist, Scalia, Thomas, and Kennedy), joined by Justice O'Connor, supported the major decisions, each of which was decided by a 5-to-4 margin. In one of these cases, *Kimel v. Florida Board of Regents* (2000), the Court ruled that Congress did not have the power to require states to comply with a federal age-discrimination law because age is not among the forms of discrimination expressly prohibited by the Fourteenth Amendment's equal protection clause.[47] The various rulings reflected Chief Justice William Rehnquist's long-held goal of limiting Congress's authority over the states.[48] "[The Rehnquist Court] doesn't defer to government at any level," said Walter Dellinger, a former solicitor general. "The Court is confident it can come up with the right decisions, and it believes it is constitutionally charged with doing so."[49]

Arguably, conservative activism was never more evident than in the Supreme Court's *Bush* v. *Gore* (2000) decision. The five justices in the majority were the same justices who in previous decisions had upheld states' rights and had opposed expansive applications of the Fourteenth Amendment's equal protection clause. Yet they invoked the equal protection clause to block the statewide manual recount that has been ordered by Florida's high court because no uniform standard for counting the ballots existed. When the Court issued a rare stay order to stop the recount, Justice Antonin Scalia claimed that it was justified because the recount could cast doubt on the legitimacy of Bush's election. The fact was, Bush had not yet been officially elected. Some observers suggested that, if Bush had been trailing in the Florida vote, the Court's majority would have allowed the recount to continue. Justice John Paul Stevens, who thought the Florida high court had acted properly in ordering a manual count, basically accused his colleagues on the Supreme Court of devising a ruling based on their partisan desires rather than on the law. Stevens noted that different standards for casting and counting ballots were found throughout the United States. The Court's ruling in *Bush* v. *Gore*, said Stevens, "can only lend credence to the most cynical appraisal of the work of judges throughout the land."[50]

Whether from the right or the left, judicial activism is characterized by a willingness to pit the judgment and power of the courts against the judgment and power of other authorities. To a degree, all judges are activists in the sense that their decisions are necessarily creative ones. The law as expressed through the Constitution, statutes, and precedent is not precise enough to provide an automatic answer to every court case. Judges and justices have no choice but to exercise judgment when the text of the law is inexact. And, to a degree, all judges are restrained in the sense that their decisions must have roots in the law. Judges cannot simply make any decision they might choose; they are confined by the facts of a case and the laws that might reasonably be applied to it. But judges and justices vary in the degree to which they are willing to contest the judgment of other political institutions and the degree to which they are willing to depart from the wording of the law. These differences separate the judicial activists from the practitioners of judicial restraint.

The Judiciary's Proper Role: A Question of Competing Values

The dispute between advocates of judicial activism and advocates of judicial restraint is a philosophical one that involves opposing values. The debate is important because it addresses the central question of what role the judiciary ought to play in American democracy. Should unelected judges involve themselves deeply in policy by adopting a broad conception of their power, or should they give wide discretion to elective institutions? Should judges defer to precedent, or should they be willing to change course, even at the risk of sending the law down uncharted paths? These questions cannot be answered simply on the basis of whether one personally agrees or disagrees with a particular judicial decision. The answer necessarily depends on a value judgment about the role of the judiciary in a governing system based on the often-conflicting concepts of majority rule and individual rights.

The United States is a constitutional democracy that recognizes both the power of the majority to rule and the claim of the minority to protection of its rights. The judiciary was not established as the nation's moral conscience and does not have a monopoly on the issue of minority interests and rights. Yet the judiciary was established as a coequal branch of government and was charged with the responsibility for protecting individual rights and minority interests. In short, the constitutional question of how far the courts should be allowed to go in substituting their judgment for that of elected institutions and established law is open to interpretation. The trade-off is significant on all issues: minority rights versus majority rule, states' rights versus federal power, legislative authority versus judicial authority. The question of whether judicial restraint or judicial activism is more desirable is one that every student of American government should ponder.

SUMMARY

At the lowest level of the federal judicial system are the district courts, where most federal cases begin. Above them are the federal courts of appeals, which review cases appealed from the lower courts. The U.S. Supreme Court is the nation's highest court. Each state has its own court system, consisting of trial courts at the bottom, intermediate appellate courts (in some states), and a supreme court (in all states) at the top. Cases originating in state courts ordinarily cannot be appealed to the federal courts unless a federal issue is involved, and then the federal courts can choose to rule only on the federal aspects of the case. Federal judges at all levels are nominated by the president, and if confirmed by the Senate, they are appointed by the president to the office. Once on the federal bench, they serve until they die, retire, or are removed by impeachment and conviction.

The Supreme Court is unquestionably the most important court in the country. The legal principles it establishes are binding on lower courts, and its capacity to define the law is enhanced by the control it exercises over the cases it hears. However, it is inaccurate to assume that lower courts are inconsequential (the upper-court myth). Lower courts have considerable discretion, and the great majority of their decisions are not reviewed by a higher court. It is also inaccurate to assume that federal courts are far more significant than state courts (the federal court myth).

The courts have less discretionary authority than elected institutions. The judiciary's positions are constrained by the facts of a case and by the laws as defined through the Constitution, statutes and government regulations, and legal precedent. Yet existing legal guidelines are seldom so precise that judges have no choice in their decisions. As a result, political influences have a strong impact on the judiciary. It responds to national conditions, public opinion, interest groups, and elected officials, particularly the president and members of Congress. Another political influence on the judiciary is the personal beliefs of judges, who have individual preferences that are evident in the way they decide on issues that come before the courts. Not surprisingly, partisan politics plays a significant role in judicial appointments.

In recent decades, the Supreme Court has issued broad rulings on individual rights, some of which have required governments to take positive action on behalf of minority interests. As the Court has crossed into areas traditionally left to lawmaking majorities, the legitimacy of its policies has been questioned. Advocates of judicial restraint claim that the justices' personal values are inadequate justification for exceeding the proper judicial role. They argue that the Constitution entrusts broad issues of the public good to elective institutions and that judicial activism ultimately undermines public respect for the judiciary. Judicial activists counter that the courts were established as an independent branch and should not hesitate to promote new principles when they see a need, even if this action puts them into conflict with popularly elected officials who are beholden to electoral majorities.

MAJOR CONCEPTS

appellate jurisdiction	judicial conference
compliance	judicial restraint
concurring opinion	judicial review
decision	jurisdiction (of a court)
dissenting opinion	laws (of a court case)
facts (of a court case)	legitimacy (of judicial power)
judicial activism	majority opinion

opinion (of a court)

original jurisdiction

plurality opinion

precedent

senatorial courtesy

writ of *certiorari*

SUGGESTED READINGS AND WEB SITES

Carp, Robert A. *The Federal Courts,* 3d ed. Washington, D.C.: Congressional Quarterly Press, 1998. An overview of the federal judiciary system.

Maltz, Earl M. *Rethinking Constitutional Law: Originalism, Interventionism, and the Politics of Judicial Review.* Lawrence: University Press of Kansas, 1994. A critical and timely analysis of constitutional interpretation in the modern age.

O'Brien, David M. *Storm Center,* 5th ed. New York: Norton, 2000. An analysis of the Supreme Court in the context of the controversy surrounding the role of the judiciary in the U.S. political system.

Salokar, Rebecca Mae. *The Solicitor General: The Politics of Law.* Philadelphia, Pa.: Temple University Press, 1992. A study of the important and increasingly political role of the nation's top trial lawyer.

Scalia, Antonin. *A Matter of Interpretation: Federal Courts and the Law.* Princeton, N.J.: Princeton University Press, 1997. A critical assessment of how the Supreme Court interprets law.

Schwartz, Bernard. *Decision: How the Supreme Court Decides Cases.* New York: Oxford University Press, 1996. A behind-the-scenes look at Supreme Court justices' decisions.

Watson, George L., and John Alan Stookey. *Shaping America: The Politics of Supreme Court Appointments.* New York: Longman, 1995. An examination of the process by which Supreme Court justices are nominated and confirmed.

http://www.courttv.com/cases   This web site allows you to take the facts of actual court cases, examine the law and the arguments, and then decide each case for yourself.

http://www.fjc.gov   The home page of the Federal Judicial Center, an agency created by Congress to conduct research and provide education on the federal judicial system.

http://www.lib.umich.edu/libhome/Documents.center/fedjudi.html   A University of Michigan web page that provides detailed information on the federal judicial system.

http://www.rominger.com/supreme.htm   A vast site that provides links to the Supreme Court, pending cases, the state court systems, and other subjects.

READING 14

Judicial Interpretation

WILLIAM J. BRENNAN, JR.

Introduction

As a legal institution, the Supreme Court operates within the framework of laws. But how fully binding on the Court is the law? In this essay, the late Justice William Brennan discusses this issue in the context of his application of the words of the Constitution to Supreme Court cases. Brennan explains the difficulty of discerning the Framers' intentions, beginning with the fact that they frequently disagreed among themselves on the meaning of particular constitutional provisions. He argues that the Constitution cannot mean whatever a momentary majority wants it to mean and claims that some of its principles (such as checks and balances) are unmistakable. Nevertheless, he embraces the view that the Constitution was meant to be a flexible document that can, and must, be adapted to meet America's changing needs.

The Constitution is fundamentally a public text—the monumental charter of a government and a people—and a Justice of the Supreme Court must apply it to resolve public controversies. For, from our beginning, a most important consequence of the constitutionally created separation of powers has been the American habit, extraordinary to other democracies, of casting social, economic, philosophical and political questions in the form of lawsuits, in an attempt to secure ultimate resolution by the Supreme Court. . . . Not infrequently, these are the issues upon which contemporary society . . . is most deeply divided. They arouse our deepest emotions. The main burden of my twenty-nine terms on the Supreme Court has thus been to wrestle with the Constitution in this heightened public context, to draw meaning from the text in order to resolve public controversies.

Two other aspects of my relation to this text warrant mention. First, constitutional interpretation for a federal judge is, for the most part, obligatory. When litigants approach the bar of court to adjudicate a constitutional dispute, they may justifiably demand an answer. Judges cannot avoid a definitive interpretation because they feel unable to, or would prefer not to, penetrate to the full meaning of the Constitution's provisions. Unlike literary critics, judges cannot merely savor the tensions or revel in the ambiguities inhering in the text—judges must resolve them.

Second, consequences flow from a Justice's interpretation in a direct and immediate way. A judicial decision respecting the incompatibility of Jim Crow with a constitutional guarantee of equality is not simply a contemplative exercise in defining the shape of a just society. It is an order—supported by the full coercive power of the state—that the present society change in a fundamental aspect. . . . More than the litigants may be affected. The course of vital social, economic and political currents may be directed.

These . . . defining characteristics of my relation to the constitutional text—its public nature, obligatory character, and consequentialist aspect—cannot help but influence the way I read that text. When Justices interpret the Constitution they speak for their community, not for themselves alone. The act of interpretation must be undertaken with full consciousness that it is, in a very real sense, the community's interpretation that is sought. Justices are not platonic guardians appointed to wield authority according to their personal moral predilections. Precisely because coercive force must attend any judicial decision to countermand the will of a contemporary majority, the Justices must render constitutional interpretations that are received as legitimate. The source of legitimacy is, of course, a wellspring of controversy in legal and political circles. At the core of the debate is what the late Yale Law School Professor Alexander Bickel labeled "the countermajoritarian difficulty." Our commitment to self-governance in a representative democracy must be reconciled with vesting in electorally unaccountable Justices the power to invalidate the expressed desires of representative bodies on the ground of inconsistency with higher law. . . .

There are those who find legitimacy in fidelity to what they call "the intentions of the Framers." In its most doctrinaire incarnation, this view demands that Justices discern exactly what the Framers thought about the question under consideration and simply follow that intention in resolving the case before them. It is a view that feigns self-effacing deference to the specific judgments of those who forged our original social compact. But in truth it is little more than arrogance cloaked as humility.

It is arrogant to pretend that from our vantage we can gauge accurately the intent of the Framers on application of principle to specific, contemporary questions. All too often, sources of potential enlightenment such as records of the ratification debates provide sparse or ambiguous evidence of the original intention. Typically, all that can be gleaned is that the Framers themselves did not agree about the application or meaning of particular constitutional provisions, and hid their differences in cloaks of generality. Indeed, it is far from clear whose intention is relevant—that of the drafters, the congressional disputants, or the ratifiers in the state—or even whether the idea of an original intention is a coherent way of thinking about a jointly drafted document drawing its authority from a general assent of the states. And apart from the problematic nature of the sources, our distance of two centuries cannot but work a prism refracting all we perceive. One cannot help but speculate that the chorus of lamentations calling for interpretation faithful to "original intention"—and proposing nullification of interpretations that fail this quick litmus test—must inevitably come from persons who have no familiarity with the historical record. . . .

Another, perhaps more sophisticated, response to the potential power of judicial interpretation stresses democratic theory: because ours is a government of the people's elected representatives, substantive value choices should by and large be left to them. This view emphasizes not the transcendent historical authority of the Framers but the predominant contemporary authority of the elected branches of government. . . .

The view that all matters of substantive policy should be resolved through the majoritarian process has appeal under some circumstances, but I think it ultimately will not do. Unabashed enshrinement of majority would permit the imposition of a social caste system or wholesale confiscation of property so long as a majority of the authorized legislative body, fairly elected, approved. Our Constitution could not abide such a situation. It is the very purpose of a Constitution—and particularly of the Bill of Rights—to declare certain values transcendent, beyond the reach of temporary political majorities. The majoritarian process cannot be expected to rectify claims of minority right that arise as a response to the outcomes of that very majoritarian process. . . .

Faith in democracy is one thing, blind faith quite another. Those who drafted our Constitution understood the difference. One cannot read the text without admitting that it embodies substantive value choices; it places certain values beyond the power of any legislature. Obvious are the separation of powers; the privilege of the Writ of Habeas Corpus; prohibition of Bills of Attainder and *ex post facto* laws; prohibition of cruel and unusual punishments; the requirement of just compensation for official taking of property; the prohibition of laws tending to establish religion or enjoining the free exercise of religion; and, since the Civil War, the banishment of slavery and official race discrimination. With respect to at least such principles, we simply have not constituted ourselves as strict utilitarians. While the Constitution may be amended, such amendments require an immense effort by the People as a whole.

To remain faithful to the content of the Constitution, therefore, an approach to interpreting the text must account for the existence of these substantive value choices, and must accept the ambiguity inherent in the effort to apply them to modern circumstances. . . .

We current Justices read the Constitution in the only way that we can: as Twentieth Century Americans. We look to the history of the time of framing and to the intervening history of interpretation. But the ultimate question must be, what do the words of the text mean in our time? For the genius of the Constitution rests not in any static meaning it might have had in a world that is dead and gone, but in the adaptability of its great principles to cope with current problems and current needs.

SOURCE: From William J. Brennan, Jr., *"Judicial Interpretation."* Address to the Text and Teaching Symposium, Georgetown University, October 12, 1985. *William J. Brennan, Jr., served for three decades as an associate justice of the Supreme Court of the United States.*

CHAPTER FIFTEEN

Economic and Environmental Policy

We the people of the United States, in order to . . . insure domestic tranquility . . . .
PREAMBLE, U.S. CONSTITUTION

HE STOCK market had been on a dizzying ride upward. It had gained nearly 20 percent since the start of the year. Then, in early spring of 2000, investors got jittery. Signs of inflation were beginning to surface, the government was pursuing a hard line in its anti-trust suit with the software giant Microsoft, and the turnaround in the Asian economies looked shaky. The Dow Jones and Nasdaq indexes dropped sharply, knocking more than $3 trillion off the value of stocks. Would history repeat itself? Would the United States get swamped by another global economic depression like the one that followed the collapse of the stock market in 1929?

In fact, Wall Street and the rest of America reacted rather calmly to the market downturn in 2000. There was continued volatility in the Dow Jones, but there was no panic. Among the reasons was the fact that substantial government programs were in place to stabilize and stimulate the U.S. economy. When the Great Depression struck, no such programs had existed. Moreover, the response to the 1929 crash guaranteed that the economic crisis would worsen. Businesses cut back on production, investors fled the stock market, depositors withdrew their bank savings, and consumers slowed their spending. All these actions accelerated the downward spiral. In 2000, however, government programs were in place if need be to protect depositors' savings, to slow the drop in stock prices, and to steady the economy through adjustments in interest rates and spending programs.

This chapter examines the economic role of the government, focusing on its promotion and regulation of economic interests and its fiscal and monetary policies. Directly or indirectly, the federal government is a party to almost every economic transaction in which Americans engage.

448

Although the private decisions of firms and individuals are the main force in the American economic system, these decisions are influenced by government policy. Washington seeks to maintain high productivity, employment, and purchasing power; regulates business practices that would otherwise harm the environment or result in economic inefficiencies and inequities; and promotes economic interests. The main ideas presented in this chapter are the following:

* *Through regulation, the U.S. government imposes restraints on business activity that are designed to promote economic efficiency and equity.*
* *Through regulatory and conservation policies, the U.S. government seeks to protect and preserve the environment from the effects of business firms and consumers.*
* *Through promotion, the U.S. government helps private interests to achieve their economic goals.*
* *Through its taxing and spending decisions (fiscal policy), the U.S. government seeks to maintain a level of economic supply and demand that will keep the economy prosperous.*
* *Through its money-supply decisions (monetary policy), the U.S. government—through the "Fed"—seeks to maintain a level of inflation consistent with sustained controllable economic growth.*

REGULATING THE ECONOMY

An **economy** is a system of production and consumption of goods and services that are allocated through exchange. When a shopper gets groceries at a store and pays money in return, that transaction is one of the millions of economic exchanges that make up the economy. In *The Wealth of Nations* (1776), Adam Smith presented the case for the **laissez-faire doctrine,** which holds that private individuals and firms should be left alone to make their own production and distribution decisions. Smith reasoned that when there is a demand for a good (that is, when people desire a good and have the ability to buy it), private entrepreneurs will respond by producing the good and distributing it to places where demand exists. Smith argued that the desire for profit is the "invisible hand" that guides the system toward the greatest welfare for all.

Smith acknowledged that the doctrine of laissez-faire capitalism had a few limits. Certain areas of the economy, such as currency, roadways, and postal services, were natural monopolies and were better run by government than by private firms. Otherwise, Smith argued, the economy was best left in private hands.

In contrast, Karl Marx proposed a worker-controlled economy. In *Das Kapital* (*Capital*, 1867), Marx argued that a free market system is exploitative because producers, through their control of production and markets, can compel workers to labor at a wage below the value they add to production and can force consumers to pay higher prices for goods than are justified by the cost of production. To end the exploitation, Marx proposed a collective economy. When the workers owned the means of production, the economy would operate in the interest of all people.

Marx and Smith represent the extremes of economic theory. No country in the world has an economy that conforms fully to either the laissez-faire or the collectivist model. All national economies today are of "mixed" form in that they contain elements of both private and public control. However, the world's economies vary greatly in their mix. The United States tends toward private ownership, whereas China tends toward collective ownership. In between, but closer to the American type of economy, are certain European countries whose governments, on behalf of their people, own and operate a number of key industries, including steel, airlines, and oil.

Although the U.S. government itself owns only a few businesses (such as Amtrak), it plays a substantial economic role through **regulation** of privately owned businesses. U.S. firms are not free to act as they please, but must operate within production and distribution bounds set by federal regulations. Regulatory policy is generally intended to promote either economic *efficiency* or *equity* (see Table 15-1).

Efficiency through Government Intervention[1]

Economic efficiency results when firms fulfill as many of society's needs as possible while using as few of its resources as possible. **Efficiency** refers to the relationship of inputs (the labor and material that go into making a product or service) to outputs (the product or service itself). The greater the output for a given input, the more efficient the production process.

Adam Smith and other classical economists believed that the free market was the optimal means of achieving efficiency. Producers would try to use as few resources as possible in order to keep their prices low so that they could compete successfully for customers. Efficient producers would be able to underprice inefficient ones, who would thereby be driven out of business.

	TABLE 15-1 THE MAIN OBJECTIVES OF REGULATORY POLICY The government intervenes in the economy to promote efficiency and equity.	
Objective	Definition	Representative Actions by Government
Efficiency	Fulfillment of as many of society's needs as possible at the cost of as few of its resources as possible. The greater the output is for a given input, the more efficient is the process.	Preventing restraint of trade; requiring producers to pay the costs of damage to the environment; reducing restrictions on business that cannot be justified on a cost-benefit basis.
Equity	Fairness to each party of the outcome of an economic transaction.	Requiring firms to bargain in good faith with labor; protecting consumers in their purchases; protecting workers' safety and health.

PREVENTING RESTRAINT OF TRADE   The assumption that the market always determines price is flawed; the same incentive—the profit motive—that drives producers to respond to demand can drive them to corner the market on a good. If a producer gains a monopoly on a good or colludes with other producers to fix its price, consumers are forced to pay an artificially high price. Rather than selling at a low price in order to attract customers, the producer will charge as high a price as the market will bear.

Restraint of trade was prevalent in the United States in the late nineteenth century, when large trusts came to dominate many areas of the economy, including the oil, steel, railroad, and sugar markets. Railroad companies, for example, had no competition on short routes and gouged their customers. In 1887, Congress took its first step toward regulating the trusts by enacting the Interstate Commerce Act. The legislation created the Interstate Commerce Commission (ICC), which was charged with regulating railroad practices and fares.

Business competition today is regulated by several federal agencies, including, for example, the Federal Trade Commission (FTC) and the

Although corporate mergers decrease competition, the government generally has tolerated mergers in business sectors in which capital costs are high. Here, Steve Case (left) and Gerald Levin (right) announce the merger of America Online (AOL), and Time-Warner, which created the world's largest communications conglomerate.

Anti-trust Division of the Justice Department. There is no strict rule that governs this regulatory activity. In some cases, the government has prohibited mergers or required divestments in order to increase competition. In 1999, for example, the Federal Communications Commission (FCC) voided a proposed merger of Bell Atlantic and GTE, ruling that the companies had failed to show that the merger would not hurt consumers. In other cases, the government has pressured companies whose marketing practices threaten competition. An example is the Justice Department's recent suit against Microsoft for using its Windows Operating System to promote its Internet Explorer at the expense of other web browsers such as Netscape Navigator.

In most cases, however, the government tolerates business concentration, even permitting the merger of large firms, such as Time-Warner's merger with AOL in 2001. Although such mergers reduce competition, the government tolerates concentrated ownership in the oil, automobile, and other industries in which high capital costs make it difficult for smaller firms to compete successfully.[2] Government acceptance of corporate giants also reflects a realization that market competition no longer involves just domestic firms. For example, the "Big Three" U.S. automakers (General Motors, Ford, and Chrysler) face stiff competition from imports, particularly those from Japan and Germany. The recent merger of Chrysler and Germany's Daimler-Benz is testimony to the increased globalization of market competition.

MAKING BUSINESS PAY FOR INDIRECT COSTS   Economic inefficiencies can result not only from restraint of trade but also from the failure of businesses or consumers to pay the full costs of resources used in production. Classical economics assumes that market prices reflect all the costs of production, but this assumption is rarely warranted. Consider companies whose industrial wastes seep into lakes and rivers. The price of these companies' products does not reflect the water pollution, and hence customers do not pay all the costs that society has incurred in the making of the products. Economists label such unpaid costs **externalities.**

Until the 1960s, the federal government did not require firms to pay such costs. The impetus to begin doing so came not only from lawmakers but also from the scientific community and environmental groups. The Clean Air Act of 1963 and the Water Pollution Control Act of 1964 required industry to install antipollution devices to keep the discharge of air and water pollutants within specified limits. In 1970 Congress created the Environmental Protection Agency (EPA) to monitor compliance with federal regulations governing air and water quality and the disposal of toxic wastes. (Environmental policy is discussed more fully later in the chapter.)

CURBING OVERREGULATION   Although government intervention is intended to increase economic efficiency, the effect can be the opposite. Government regulation raises the cost of doing business. Firms have to expend work hours to monitor and implement government regulations, which in some instances (for example, pollution control) also require companies to buy and install expensive equipment. These costs are efficient to the degree that they produce commensurate benefits.

Yet if government places needless or excessive regulatory burdens, firms waste resources in the process of complying.[3] The result is higher-priced goods that are more expensive for consumers and less competitive in the domestic and global markets. In other words, too much regulation is a source of inefficiency. An example is a provision of the Safe Drinking Water Act that required communities to reduce contaminants in their water supply from the current level, whatever that level happened to be. In most communities, the effect was to improve the quality of the water supply. But in Anchorage, Alaska, the result was an absurd remedy. The city's water supply was so clean already that officials had to ask local fish-processing plants to dump their wastes into the sewer system so that Anchorage would have impurities to remove from its water.[4]

Situations of this kind have led to regulatory reform.[5] In 1995, Congress enacted legislation to tighten the regulatory process by requiring cost-benefit analysis and risk assessment (the severity of the problem) to be taken into account in certain regulatory decisions.

DEREGULATION Another response to regulatory excess is the policy of **deregulation:** the rescinding of regulations already in force for the purpose of improving efficiency. This process began in 1977 with passage of the Airlines Deregulation Act, which eliminated government-set air fares and, in some instances, government-mandated air routes. The change had the intended effect: air fares declined in price, and there was more competition between airlines on most routes. Congress followed airline deregulation with partial deregulation of the trucking, banking, energy, and communications industries, among others.

The free market principle has its limits, however, just as the regulatory principle can be carried too far. Deregulation has not been an unqualified success.[6] The savings and loan (S&L) industry is a prime example. S&Ls had been hit hard by the high inflation of the 1970s, and they hoped to restore their financial base through high-yield investments. Since existing regulations prevented them from pursuing riskier investments, the S&L industry successfully lobbied Congress for a change. When deregulation lifted restrictions on how S&Ls could invest depositors' savings, many of them began to engage in highly speculative ventures, such as commercial real estate. By 1989 the S&L industry was in crisis. Bad management, poor investments, and outright fraud had resulted in an industrywide loss of billions of dollars. In order to save what was left of the industry, President Bush and Congress developed a bailout plan that will eventually cost the taxpayers more than $100 billion.

The savings and loan crisis demonstrates that the issue of business regulation is not a simple question of whether or not to regulate. On the one hand, too much regulation can burden firms with bureaucratic red tape, costly implementation procedures, and limited options. On the other hand, too little regulation can give firms the leeway to exploit the public unfairly or recklessly. Either too little or too much regulation can result in economic inefficiency. The challenge for policymakers is to strike the proper balance between regulatory measures and free market mechanisms.

Equity through Government Intervention

As we noted earlier, the government intervenes in the economy to bring equity as well as efficiency to the marketplace. **Equity** occurs when an economic transaction is fair to each party.[7] While efficiency refers to the relationship of inputs to outputs, equity refers to *outcomes:* whether they are reasonable and mutually acceptable. A transaction can be considered fair if each party enters into it freely and is not unknowingly at a disadvantage (for example, if the seller knows a product is defective, equity requires that the buyer also know of the defect).

An early equity measure was the creation of the Food and Drug Administration (FDA) in 1907. Because consumers are often unable to tell whether foods and drugs are safe to use, the FDA works to keep adulterated foods and dangerous or ineffective drugs off the market. In the 1930s, financial reforms were among the equity measures enacted under the New Deal. The Securities and Exchange Act of 1934 and the Banking Act of 1934 were designed in part to protect investors and savers from dishonest or imprudent brokers and bankers. The New Deal also provided greater equity for organized labor, which previously had been in a weak position in its dealings with management. The Fair Labor Standards Act of 1938, for example, established minimum wages, maximum working hours, and constraints on the use of child labor.

The 1960s and 1970s produced the greatest number of equity reforms. From 1965 to 1977, ten federal agencies, such as the Consumer Product Safety Commission, were established to protect consumers, workers, and the public from harmful effects of business activity. Among the products declared to be unsafe in the 1960s and 1970s were the insecticide DDT, cigarettes, and leaded gasoline.[8] The rule eliminating lead in gasoline, for example, has given society a major benefit; the average level of lead in children's blood has decreased by 75 percent since the measure went into effect.[9]

The Politics of Regulatory Policy

Economic regulation has come in waves, as changes in national conditions have produced intermittent bursts of social consciousness.

THE REFORMS OF THE PROGRESSIVE AND NEW DEAL ERAS   The first wave of regulation came during the Progressive era, when reformers sought to break the power of the trusts by placing constraints on unfair business practices. The second wave came in the New Deal era, when reformers sought to stimulate economic recovery through regulatory policies that were designed as much to save business as to restrain it.

Although business fought Progressive and New Deal reforms, long-term opposition was lessened by the fact that most of the resulting regulation applied to a particular industry rather than to firms of all types. This pattern made it possible for an affected industry to gain influence with those officials who were responsible for regulating its activities. By cultivating close ties to the Federal Communications Commission (FCC), for example, the broadcast networks managed to obtain policies that protected their near monopoly on broadcasting and gave them high and sustained profits. Although not all industries have had as much leverage with their regulators as broadcasting, it is generally true that industries have not been greatly hampered by the older form of regulation, and in many cases have substantially benefited from it.

THE ERA OF NEW SOCIAL REGULATION   The third wave of regulatory reform, in the 1960s and 1970s, differed from the Progressive and New Deal phases in both its policies and its politics. The third wave has been called the era of "new social regulation" because of the social goals it addressed in three major policy areas: environmental protection, consumer protection, and worker safety.

Most of the regulatory agencies established during the third wave have much broader policy mandates than those created earlier. They are responsible not just for a single industry but for firms of all types, and their policy scope covers a wide range of activities. The Environmental Protection Agency (EPA), for example, is charged with regulating environmental pollution of almost any kind by almost any firm.

Because newer agencies such as the EPA have a wide-ranging clientele, no one firm or industry can easily influence agency policy to a great extent. There is also strong group competition in some of the newer regulatory 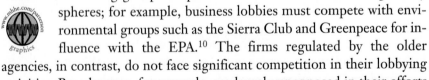 spheres; for example, business lobbies must compete with environmental groups such as the Sierra Club and Greenpeace for influence with the EPA.[10] The firms regulated by the older agencies, in contrast, do not face significant competition in their lobbying activities. Broadcasters, for example, are largely unopposed in their efforts to influence the Federal Communications Commission. Although television viewers and radio listeners have a stake in FCC decisions, they are not well enough organized to petition it effectively on a regular basis.

GOVERNMENT AS PROTECTOR
OF THE ENVIRONMENT

Few changes in public opinion and policy during recent decades have been as dramatic as those relating to the environment. Most Americans today recycle some of their garbage, and nearly two-thirds say they are either active environmentalists or sympathetic to environmental concerns. In the 1960s, few Americans bothered to sort their trash and it was a rare person who could have answered a polling question that asked whether he or she was an "environmentalist." The term was not commonly used, and people would not have understood its meaning.

The modern environmental movement gained impetus with the publication in 1962 of Rachel Carson's *The Silent Spring*.[11] Written at a time when the author was dying of breast cancer, *Silent Spring* revealed the threat of pesticides such as DDT to waterways and wildlife and challenged the notion that scientific progress was an unqualified benefit to society. Carson's appearance at a Senate hearing contributed to legislative action that produced the 1963 Clean Air Act and the 1965 Water Quality Act. It was the first time in the nation's history that the federal government had taken major steps to protect the nation's air, water, and ground from pollution. Today, this protection extends to nearly two hundred potentially harmful forms of emission.

Conservationism: The Older Wave

Although government policy aimed at protecting the ambient environment is relatively new, the government has been involved in land conservation for more than a century. The first national park was created at Yellowstone in 1872 and, like the later ones, was established to preserve the nation's natural heritage for generations to come. The national park system serves more than one hundred million visitors each year and covers a total of eighty million acres, an area larger than every state except Alaska, Texas, California, and Montana.

The national parks are run by the National Park Service, an agency within the Department of Interior. Another agency, the U.S. Forest Service, which is located within the Department of Agriculture, manages the national forests, which cover an area more than twice the size of the national parks. They, too, have been preserved in part to protect the nation's natural heritage.

The nation's parks and forests, however, are subject to a "dual use" policy. They are nature preserves and recreation areas, but they are also rich in natural resources: minerals, forests, and grazing lands. The federal government sells permits to ranchers, timber companies, and mining firms that give them the right to take some of these resources, a policy that can place their interests in conflict with those of conservationists.

A case in point is the spotted-owl controversy that erupted in the Pacific Northwest in the late 1980s. The spotted owl is an endangered species found in the region's virgin forests, which are also a mainstay of the region's timber industry. The issue of timber rights in the spotted owl's habitat pitted timber companies, loggers, and logging towns against conservationists in a bitter dispute that was waged through lawsuits, public demonstrations, and the lobbying of Congress and the White House. The timber interests eventually prevailed, but they did not get the extensive logging rights they had been seeking.

Environmentalism: The Newer Wave

As previously indicated, the decade of the 1960s was pivotal in the federal government's realization that Americans needed protection from the harmful effects of air, water, and ground pollutants. The period was capped by the first Earth Day. Held in the spring of 1970, it was the brainchild of

Environmental regulations restricting the level of automobile pollution have greatly improved air quality in America's cities.

Senator Gaylord Nelson (D-Wisconsin), who had devoted nearly ten years to finding ways to draw the public's attention to environmental issues. With the first Earth Day, Nelson succeeded to a degree not even he could have imagined: ten thousand grade schools and high schools, two thousand colleges, and one thousand communities participated in the event, which included public rallies and environmental cleanup efforts. Earth Day has been held every year since and is now a worldwide event.

The year 1970 also marked the creation of the Environmental Protection Agency. Within a few months, the EPA was issuing new regulations at such a rapid pace that business firms had difficulty keeping track of all the mandates, much less complying fully with them. They eventually found an ally in President Gerald Ford, who, in a 1975 speech to the National Federation of Industrial Business, claimed that business regulation was costing $150 billion annually, or $2,000 for every American family.[12] Although Ford's estimate exceeded that of economic analysts, his point was not lost on policymakers or the people. The economy was in a slump, and the costs of complying with the new regulations were impeding an economic recovery. Polls indicated a decline in public support for regulatory action.

Since then, environmental protection policy has not been greatly expanded, but neither has it greatly contracted. The emphasis has been on administering and amending the laws put into effect in the 1960s and 1970s.

Environmental regulation has had a dramatic effect on air and water quality. Pollution levels today are far below their levels in the 1960s, when yellowish-gray fog ("smog") hung over cities like Los Angeles and New York; when bodies of water like the Potomac River and Lake Erie were open sewers; and when communities like the Love Canal neighborhood of Niagara Falls, New York, sat atop contaminated ground that slowly poisoned its occupants.

The positive impact of environmental policy has not eliminated the conflict surrounding it. An ongoing issue is how far government should go in the efforts to reduce pollution. When the Clinton administration in 1997 announced tougher standards for ozone and tiny airborne particles, majorities in the House and Senate opposed the initiative. They claimed that existing standards were sufficient and that the changes were supported by questionable scientific research. The main effect of the new standards, they said, would be to saddle business with millions of dollars in compliance costs. "The choice here is not between clean air and dirty air," said Representative John Dingell (D-Michigan), an opponent of the new standards. "It is a choice between clean air and jobs."[13]

GOVERNMENT AS PROMOTER OF ECONOMIC INTERESTS

The U.S. government has always made important contributions to the nation's economy. The Constitution was written in part to provide for a national government strong enough to promote a sound economy. The Constitution stipulated that the government was to regulate commerce, create a strong currency, develop uniform commercial standards, and provide a stable credit system. The fledgling government also immediately demonstrated its concern for economic interests. Congress in 1789 gave a boost to the nation's shipping industry by placing a tariff on imported goods carried by foreign ships. Since that first boost, the U.S. government has awarded thousands of direct benefits to economic interests.

In Chapters 11 and 13 we described how congressional and bureaucratic politics results in the promotion of group interests. Here we will briefly examine a few illustrations of the scope of government's contribution to the interests of business, labor, and agriculture.

Promoting Business

American business is not opposed to all government regulation. It objects only to regulatory policies that are adverse to its interests. We have noted that, at various times and in differing ways, many federal regulatory agencies have primarily served the interests of the industries they are intended to regulate.

Loans and tax breaks are another way that government promotes business. Firms receive loan guarantees, direct loans, tax credits for capital investments, and tax deductions for capital depreciation. Over the past forty years the burden of federal taxation has shifted dramatically, from corporations to individuals. A few decades ago, the revenues raised from taxes on corporate income were roughly the same as the revenues raised from taxes on individual income. Today, individual taxpayers carry the heavier burden by a more than 4 to 1 ratio. Some analysts do not regard the change as particularly significant, arguing that higher corporate taxes would be passed along to the public anyway in the form of higher prices for goods and services.

The most significant contribution that government makes to business is the traditional services it provides, such as education, transportation, and defense. Colleges and universities, which are funded primarily by governments, furnish business with most of its professional and technical work force and with much of the basic research that goes into product development. The nation's public roadways, waterways, and airports are other government benefits without which business could not thrive. In short, America's business has no bigger booster than government.

Promoting Labor

Laissez-faire philosophy dominated government's approach to labor well into the twentieth century. The governing principle, developed by the courts in the early nineteenth century, held that workers had limited rights of collective action. Union activity was regarded as interference with the natural supply of labor and the free setting of wages. The extent of hostility toward labor is evident in the use of federal troops during the late 1800s to break up strikes.

The 1930s brought significant changes. The key legislation was the National Labor Relations Act of 1935, which guaranteed workers the right to bargain collectively and prohibited business from discriminating against union employees and from unreasonably interfering with union activities. Government has also aided labor over the years by legislating minimum wages and maximum work hours, unemployment benefits, safer and more healthful working conditions, and nondiscriminatory hiring practices.

Although government support for labor extends beyond these examples, it is not nearly so extensive as its assistance to business. America's individualistic culture has hindered the formulation of public policies that are as favorable to labor as those in European countries.

Promoting Agriculture

Until well into the twentieth century, most Americans still lived on farms and in small rural communities. Agriculture was America's dominant business and was assisted by government's land policies. The Homestead Act of 1862, for example, opened government-owned lands to settlement, creating spectacular "land rushes" by offering 160 free acres of government land to each family that staked a claim, built a house, and farmed the land for five years.

Farm programs today provide assistance to small farmers and commercial enterprises (agribusinesses) and cost the federal government billions of dollars annually. A major goal of this spending is to eliminate some of the risks associated with farming. Weather, world markets, and other factors can radically affect crop and livestock prices, and federal programs are designed to protect farmers from these adverse developments.

Striking janitors parade in Beverly Hills, California.
Although government provides support for labor through
a variety of policies, U.S. workers have less power and
fewer rights than their European counterparts, a
reflection of America's individualistic culture.

In 1996, Congress passed the Freedom to Farm Act. It trimmed the
crop allocation and price subsidy programs that had previously characterized U.S. farm policy. These programs had been designed to keep the price
of farm products relatively high even when the market was weak. The programs, however, were a huge expense to the taxpayers. The 1996 legislation
was designed to let the market largely determine the prices that farmers
would receive for their crops and to let farmers themselves decide on the
crops they would plant. However, the program has a safety net: a floor price
was set for commodities in case the market slumped (for example, the government guarantee for corn was set at roughly $1.90 a bushel). As it hap-
pened, crop prices fell sharply in 1998 and the prospect that they will soon
rise is dim. Subsidy payments to American farmers totaled $18 billion in fis-
cal year 1999. Most analysts believe that it will be many years before substantial federal assistance to farmers is a thing of the past.

FISCAL POLICY: GOVERNMENT AS MANAGER OF THE ECONOMY, I

Until the 1930s, the U.S. government adhered to the prevailing free market theory and made no attempt to maintain the stability of the economy as
a whole. The economy was regarded as largely self-regulating. The economy was fairly prosperous, but it periodically experienced economic depression that resulted in widespread joblessness and financial loss.

The greatest economic catastrophe in the nation's history—the Great Depression of the 1930s—finally brought an end to traditional economics. Franklin D. Roosevelt's emergency spending and job programs, designed to stimulate the economy and put Americans back to work, heralded the change. Roosevelt's efforts were controversial at the time, but today government is expected to have ongoing policies that will maintain high economic production, employment, and growth, and will control prices and interest rates.

Taxing and Spending Policy

The government's efforts to maintain a stable economy are made partly through its taxing and spending decisions, which together are referred to as its **fiscal policy** (see Table 15-2).

The annual federal budget is the foundation of fiscal policy. George Washington wrote his budget on a single sheet of paper, but the federal budget today is thousands of pages long and takes eighteen months to prepare and enact. The budget is a massive policy statement that allocates federal expenditures among thousands of government programs and provides for the revenues—taxes, social insurance receipts, and borrowed funds—to pay for these expenditures (see Figure 15-1). From one perspective, the budget is the national government's allocation of costs and benefits. Every federal program benefits some interest, whether it be farmers who get price supports, defense firms that obtain military contracts, or retirees who receive monthly social security checks.

From another standpoint, that of fiscal policy, the budget is a device for stimulating or dampening economic growth. Changes in overall levels of spending and taxing are means of keeping the economy's normal ups and downs from becoming extreme.

TABLE 15-2   FISCAL POLICY: A SUMMARY
Taxing and spending levels can be adjusted in order to affect economic conditions.

Problem	Fiscal Policy Actions
Low productivity and high unemployment	Demand side: increase spending Supply side: cut business taxes
Excess production and high inflation	Decrease spending Increase taxes

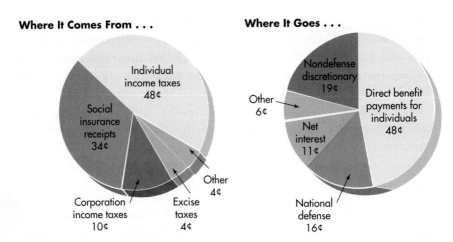

FIGURE 15-1 THE FEDERAL BUDGET DOLLAR, FISCAL YEAR 2001
Source: Office of Management and Budget.

Fiscal policy has its origins in the economic theories of John Maynard Keynes. In *The General Theory of Employment, Interest, and Money* (1936), Keynes noted that employers become overly cautious during a depression and will not expand production, even as wages drop. He also noted that consumers slow their spending out of concern they may lose their jobs. Challenging the traditional idea that government should draw back during depressions, Keynes claimed that severe economic downturns can be shortened only by increased government spending. Keynes said that government should engage in **deficit spending**—spending more than it gets in taxes—which can be accomplished by the borrowing and printing of money. By placing additional money in the hands of consumers and investors, government can stimulate spending, production, and employment, and thus promote recovery.[14]

According to Keynesian theory, the government's response should be commensurate with the severity of the problem. During an **economic depression**—an exceptionally steep and sustained downturn in the economy—the government should engage in massive new spending programs to hasten the recovery. During a less severe **economic recession**, new government spending should be less substantial.

DEMAND-SIDE STIMULATION AND THE DEFICIT PROBLEM

Keynes's theory focused on government's efforts to stimulate consumer spending. This **demand-side economics** emphasizes the consumer "demand" component of the supply-demand equation. When the economy is sluggish, the government can increase its spending, thus placing more money in consumers' hands. With additional money to spend, consumers buy more goods and services. This increased demand, in turn, fosters production and employment. In this way, government spending contributes to economic recovery.

Although heightened spending is a tool that government can employ during a severe economic crisis, it is not a sensible response to every economic dip.[15] Its application is affected by government's overall financial situation. In the early 1990s, for example, the U.S. economy was in its longest downturn since World War II, but policymakers chose not to boost federal spending temporarily as a means of blunting the recession. The reason was simple enough. During the previous two decades, there had been a **budget deficit:** each year, the federal government had spent more than it had received in tax and other revenues. The result was a huge **national debt,** which is the total cumulative amount that the U.S. government owes to creditors. By the early 1990s, the debt had reached $4 trillion, and an enormous amount of money was required each year merely to pay the interest on the national debt. Interest payments were larger than the entire federal budget as recently as 1970 and were roughly the total of all federal income taxes paid by Americans who lived west of the Mississippi River. This drain on the government's resources made it politically difficult for policymakers to increase the level of government spending in order to boost the economy.

The situation is much different today. In 1998, for the first time since 1969, the U.S. government had a **balanced budget:** revenues from taxes for the year were equal to government expenditures. Since then, there has been a **budget surplus:** the federal government has received more in tax and other revenues than it has spent. The surplus was attributable to a surging U.S. economy that was in the midst of its longest period of sustained growth in the country's history. With more people working and with the stock market moving even higher, tax revenues had increased and government welfare expenditures had declined. The rosy budget picture also reflected the fiscal discipline of the Clinton administration and the Republican Congress, which had slowed the growth in federal expenditures.

The economic turnaround has greatly changed the fiscal outlook (see Figure 15-2). The federal budget surplus exceeded $100 billion in 2000 and is projected to continue to grow for another decade. The bonanza has led policymakers to seek new spending programs and tax cuts, but it will also make it easier, when the economy recedes, as it inevitably will, for government to apply demand-side measures to hasten the economic recovery. An

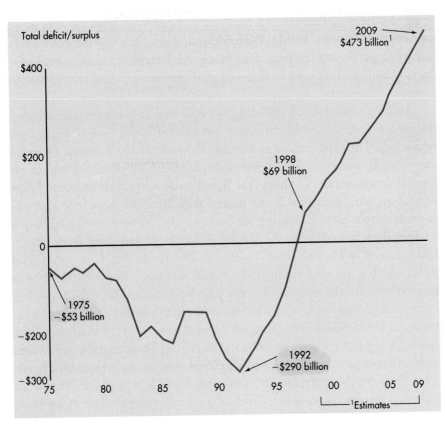

FIGURE 15-2 THE FEDERAL BUDGET DEFICIT/SURPLUS, 1975–2009
The Federal government ran a budget deficit until recently; it now has a budget surplus that is projected to last for many years. Source: Office of Management and Budget.

increase in federal spending is once again a tool that policymakers could employ during a recessionary period.

The importance of demand-side fiscal policy, however, cannot be measured only by its effect during economic downturns. Although the United States has had recessionary periods since the 1930s, none of these downturns has been anywhere near the severity of the Great Depression. One reason is that government spending is now at permanently high levels. Each month, for example, roughly forty million Americans receive a social security check from the government. In turn, they spend it on food, clothing, housing, entertainment, and other goods and services. They pump billions of dollars each month into the U.S. economy, which creates jobs and

★ STATES IN THE NATION ★

Federal Taxing and Spending

Federal spending and taxation are the basis of fiscal policy, which has an uneven effect on the states. Some states get a positive "balance of payments" in that their citizens pay less in federal taxes than the state and its citizens receive in federal spending. The biggest winners are New Mexico, which in 1999 had a positive balance of payments of $3,944 per person and Montana, North Dakota, and Virginia, which had balances just over $3,000. Fourteen other states had a positive balance of $1,000 or more. In contrast, some states have a negative balance of payments; their citizens pay more in federal taxes than they and the state get back through federal spending. New Jersey ($2,342) and Connecticut ($2,840) led this list in 1999. Twelve other states had a negative balance of $500 or more per capita. Most of the "winners" are in the South; most of the "losers" are in the Midwest and Northeast.

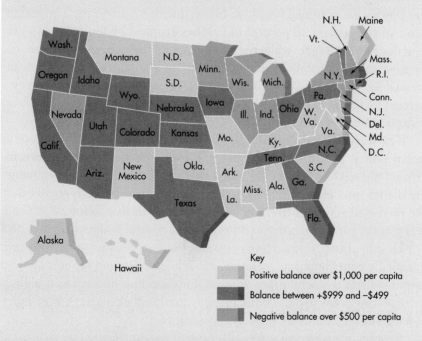

Key

Positive balance over $1,000 per capita

Balance between +$999 and −$499

Negative balance over $500 per capita

SOURCE: Created by author from data provided by Taubman Center for State and Local Government, John F. Kennedy School of Government, Harvard University, December, 2000.

income for millions of other Americans. And social security is only one—albeit the largest—of the federal spending programs. Every day, the federal government spends about $4 billion, which is more than the typical large corporation pumps into the economy during an entire year. The U.S. economy thus has a constant demand-side stimulus: government spending on an ongoing and massive scale.

SUPPLY-SIDE STIMULATION   A fiscal policy alternative to demand-side stimulation is **supply-side economics,** which emphasizes the business (supply) component of the supply-demand equation.[16] Supply-side theory was a cornerstone of President Reagan's economic program. He believed that economic growth would flow as easily from stimulation of the business sector as from stimulation of consumer demand. "Reaganomics" included substantial tax breaks for businesses and upper-income individuals.

Reagan contended that increased prosperity for wealthy Americans would "trickle down" to those at the bottom as production increased and more jobs were created. However, the benefits of the economic growth of the 1980s were confined largely to higher-income Americans. The real income of the poorest 20 percent of families dropped by more than 10 percent during the decade, while the real income of the richest 20 percent rose by roughly 30 percent. Meanwhile, taxes for the poorest 20 percent increased by 3 percent, while taxes for the highest 20 percent decreased by 5 percent.[17] The result was a widening of the "income gap" between America's poorer and richer families.

The Reagan administration also overestimated the stimulus effect of its tax-cut policy. It had estimated that the increased tax revenues from increased business activity would soon offset the loss of revenue from reducing the tax rate. However, the loss from the tax cuts was much greater than the increased revenues from the economic growth that followed. A result was that the tax cuts contributed to the rising federal budget deficit.

Despite these discouraging aspects, Reagan's supply-side measures eventually contributed to economic growth. The Reagan tax cuts allowed business firms to spend more on capital investments and enabled higher-income Americans to place more money into the stock markets, which provided additional funds for business investment.

Supply-side economics was also evident in some economic policies of the 1990s. After the Republicans assumed control of Congress in 1995, for example, they reduced the **capital-gains tax,** which is the tax that individuals pay on gains in capital investments, such as property and stocks. A reduction in the capital-gains tax increases the incentive for individuals to invest their money in capital markets. Firms use this money to expand their operations and markets, thereby creating jobs and increasing the supply of goods, each of which can stimulate consumer demand, which contributes to economic growth.

CONTROLLING INFLATION   High unemployment and low production are only two of the economic problems that government is called upon to solve. Another is **inflation,** which is an increase in the average level of prices of goods and services. Before the late 1960s, inflation was a minor irritant: prices rose by less than 4 percent annually. But inflation rose sharply during the last years of the Vietnam War and remained high throughout the 1970s, reaching a postwar record rate of 13 percent in 1979. Since then, inflation has moderated and concern about it has lessened.

To fight inflation, government can apply remedies opposite to those used to fight unemployment and low productivity. Inflation normally occurs when jobs are plentiful and people have extra money to spend. Demand is high in such periods, and prices are pulled up in what is known as "demand-pull" inflation. By reducing its spending or by raising personal income taxes, government takes money from consumers, thus reducing demand and dampening prices. (The main policy tool for addressing inflation is monetary policy, which is discussed later in the chapter.)

The Process and Politics of Fiscal Policy

The president and Congress jointly determine fiscal policy, mainly through the annual budgetary process. The Constitution grants Congress the power to tax and spend, but the president, as chief executive, has a major role in shaping the budget. The president's veto power also provides him a strong tool when negotiating the budget with Congress. In reality, the budgetary process involves give-and-take between Congress and the president, as each tries to exert influence over the final product.[18]

THE BUDGETARY PROCESS   The budgetary process is a very elaborate one, as could be expected when billions of dollars in federal spending are at issue. From beginning to end, the process lasts a year and a half (see Figure 15-3).

The budgetary process begins in the executive branch when, in consultation with the Office of Management and Budget (OMB), establishes general budget guidelines. The OMB is part of the Executive Office of the President (see Chapter 12) and takes its directives from the president. Hundreds of agencies and thousands of programs are covered by the budget, and the OMB uses the president's decisions to determine the instructions

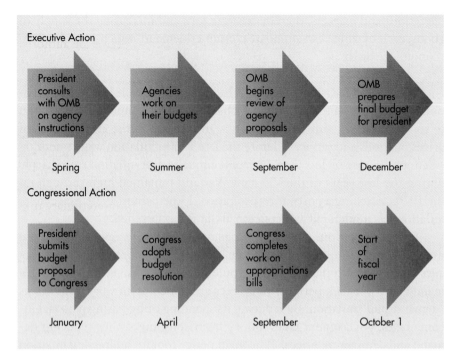

Executive Action

President consults with OMB on agency instructions → Agencies work on their budgets → OMB begins review of agency proposals → OMB prepares final budget for president

Spring   Summer   September   December

Congressional Action

President submits budget proposal to Congress → Congress adopts budget resolution → Congress completes work on appropriations bills → Start of fiscal year

January   April   September   October 1

FIGURE 15-3 FEDERAL BUDGETARY PROCESS
The budget begins with the president's instructions to the agencies and ends when Congress enacts the budget. The entire process spans about eighteen months.

that will govern each agency's budget preparations. For example, each agency is assigned a budget ceiling within which it must work.

The agencies receive these instructions in the spring and then work through the summer to develop a detailed agency budget, taking into account their existing programs and any new or proposed ones. These agency budgets then go to the OMB in September for a full review that invariably includes further consultation with each agency. Throughout, the OMB is in close touch with the White House to ensure that the budget items conform to the president's objectives.

The OMB usually acts to restrain the agencies, since they naturally tend to want more resources, while the OMB has the job of tailoring the budget to the president's priorities. In point of fact, however, the president does not have any real say over most of the budget. About two-thirds of the budget involves mandatory spending. The spending is authorized by current law, and the government must allocate and spend the money unless the law itself is rescinded, which is unlikely. Examples are social security and

Medicare, which provide mandatory benefits to all individuals who apply and meet the eligibility criteria. The president does not have the authority to suspend or redefine these programs. Interest on the national debt is also part of the budget and here, too, the president has no real option. The federal government is obligated to pay interest on money it has borrowed.

The OMB focuses on the third of the budget that involves discretionary spending, which includes such areas as defense, foreign aid, education, national parks, space exploration, public broadcasting, and highways. In reality, even a large part of this spending is truly not discretionary. No president would even consider slashing defense spending to almost nothing or closing the national parks, and even modest cuts in a discretionary program may encounter resistance in Congress.

The president, then, works on the margins of the budget, trying to push it in directions that are consistent with administration goals. The effort in many policy areas consists of a modest increase or decrease in spending compared with that of the previous year. There are also always a few areas where the president will attempt a more dramatic adjustment. During each year of his second term, for example, President Clinton asked for significant increases in education and health spending.

In January, the president transmits the full budget to Congress. This budget is only a proposal, because Congress has the constitutional power to appropriate funds. In reviewing the president's proposed budget, Congress relies heavily on the Congressional Budget Office (CBO), which, as discussed in Chapter 11, is the congressional equivalent to the OMB. The CBO carefully studies the items in the budget and also subjects the budget's revenue estimates and projected program costs to its own analysis. If the CBO believes that an agency has misjudged the amount of money that is needed to meet its legislatively required programs, it will bring this information to the attention of the appropriate members of Congress. Similarly, if the CBO concludes that the OMB has miscalculated how much the government can be expected to receive in taxes and other revenues, this information will be noted.

The key congressional committees in the budgetary process are the budget and the appropriations committees. The House and Senate Budget Committees are responsible for drafting a "budget resolution," which includes projections on total spending, total revenues, and allocation between the mandatory and discretionary spending categories. These guidelines are then submitted to the full House and Senate for approval. The budget ceilings that are part of the resolution place a tentative limit on how much money will be allocated for each spending area.

The House Appropriations Committee, through its subcommittees, then takes on the primary task of reviewing the budget items, which includes hearings with each federal agency. There are thirteen such subcommittees, and each has responsibility for a substantive area, such as defense or agriculture. Agency budgets are invariably changed at this stage. A subcommittee may cut an agency's budget because it believes that the agency's work is not very important or that the agency has asked for more funds that it needs to carry out its programs. Or the subcommittee may decide to increase an agency's budget beyond what the president has requested. Whichever occurs, each subcommittee leaves its own mark on each agency's budget. The subcommittees' recommendations are then submitted to the House Appropriations Committee for final review and submission to the full House for a vote. The Senate Appropriations Committee and its subcommittees conduct a similar process, but the Senate is a smaller body, and its review of agency requests is normally less thorough. To some degree, the Senate committee and its subcommittees serve as a "court of appeals" for agencies that have had their budget requests reduced by the process in the House.

During Congress's work on the budget, the president's recommendations undergo varying degrees of change. The priorities of a majority in Congress are never exactly those of the president, even when they are of the same party. When they are of opposite parties, their priorities may differ greatly.

After the work of the appropriations committees is completed and has been approved by the full House and Senate, differences in the Senate and House versions of the appropriations bills are reconciled in conference committee (see Chapter 11). The legislation is then sent to the president for approval or veto. The threat of a presidential veto is often enough to persuade Congress to restore some of its cuts in the president's original proposals. In the end, the budget inevitably reflects both presidential and congressional priorities. Neither branch ever gets everything that it wants, but each branch always gets some of what it wants.

Once the budget has been passed by both the House and the Senate and is signed by the president, it takes effect on October 1, which is the starting date of the federal government's fiscal year. If agreement on the budget has not been reached by October 1, temporary funding is required in order to maintain government operations. In late 1995, President Clinton and the Republican Congress deadlocked to such an extent on budgetary issues that they could not even agree on temporary funding. Their standoff twice forced a brief shutdown of nonessential government activities.

Partisan Differences

Politics plays a significant part in the making of fiscal policy because Democrats and Republicans often disagree over its direction. The Democratic coalition has traditionally included the majority of lower-income and working-class Americans. Accordingly, the party's leaders are sensitive to rising unemployment because blue-collar workers are usually the first and most deeply affected. Democrats in Washington have usually responded to a sluggish economy with increased government spending, which offers direct help to the unemployed and stimulates demand. Virtually every increase in federal unemployment benefits during the past fifty years, for example, has been initiated by Democratic officeholders.

Republican leaders are more likely than Democrats to be concerned about inflation. It attacks the purchasing power of all Americans, including higher-income individuals, who are less likely than lower-income persons to be affected by rising unemployment rates. Inflation also raises the cost of doing business, because firms must pay higher interest rates for the money they borrow. Since business and the middle class make up a significant chunk of its electoral base, the Republican party usually wants to hold government spending at a level where the inflationary effects are small.

Tax policy also has partisan dimensions. Democratic policymakers have typically sought tax policies that are more beneficial to working-class and lower-middle-class Americans. Democrats have favored a **graduated** (or progressive) **personal income tax,** in which the tax rate goes up substantially as income rises. Republicans have preferred to keep taxes on upper incomes at a relatively low level, contending that this policy encourages the savings and investment that foster economic growth. These differences were evident, for example, in the battle over the Taxpayer Refund and Relief Act of 1999, which President Clinton vetoed. The GOP-sponsored bill contained the largest tax cut since 1981; the chief beneficiaries would have been upper-income taxpayers. In the House of Representatives, 98 percent of Republicans and only 3 percent of Democrats supported the bill. In the Senate, 95 percent of Republicans and 11 percent of Democrats backed it.[19] (Tax policy is discussed further in Chapter 16.)

MONETARY POLICY: GOVERNMENT AS MANAGER OF THE ECONOMY, II

Fiscal policy is not the only instrument of economic management available to government; another is **monetary policy,** which is based on manipulation of the amount of money in circulation (see Table 15-3). Monetarists

TABLE 15-3 MONETARY POLICY: A SUMMARY
The money supply can be adjusted in order to affect economic conditions.

Problem	Monetary Policy Action by Federal Reserve
Low productivity and high unemployment (require an increase in the money supply)	Buys securities Lowers interest rate on loans to member banks Lowers cash reserve that member banks must deposit in Federal Reserve System
Excess productivity and high inflation (require a decrease in the money supply)	Sells securities Raises interest rate on loans to member banks Raises cash reserve that member banks must deposit in Federal Reserve System

such as the economist Milton Friedman hold that control of the money supply is the key to sustaining a healthy economy. Too much money in circulation contributes to inflation because too many dollars are chasing too few goods, which drives up prices. Too little money in circulation results in a slackening economy and rising unemployment, because consumers lack the ready cash and easy credit required to push spending levels up. Monetarists believe in tightening or loosening the money supply as a way of slowing or invigorating the economy.

The "Fed"

Control over the money supply rests not with the president or Congress but with the Federal Reserve System, which was created by the Federal Reserve Act of 1913. The Federal Reserve is directed by a board of governors (the "Fed") whose seven members serve for fourteen years, except for the chair and vice-chair, who serve for four years. All members are appointed by the president with the approval of the Senate. The Fed regulates the activities of all national banks and those state banks that choose to

HOW THE UNITED STATES COMPARES

Global Economic Competitiveness

The United States ranks second only to Singapore in global economic competitiveness, according to a survey by the World Economic Forum, a private economic research organization in Switzerland.

The ranking is based on eight different factors: institutional openness, internationalization, government, management, finance, infrastructure, science and technology, and labor. The United States is strong on its technology, management, and finance. Its weakest point was the people factor, where it was downgraded on education programs and welfare services (for example, the United States, unlike other advanced industrialized countries, does not have government-provided health care).

The United States is ranked substantially higher than its major economic rivals, Japan and Germany. They trailed by a wide margin.

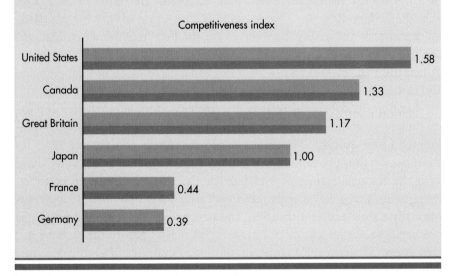

Competitiveness index

United States 1.58
Canada 1.33
Great Britain 1.17
Japan 1.00
France 0.44
Germany 0.39

become members of the Federal Reserve System—about six thousand banks in all.

The Fed decides how much money to add or to subtract from the economy, seeking a balance that will permit steady growth without causing an unacceptable level of inflation. The most visible way that the Fed affects the money supply is by lowering or raising the interest rates charged on money borrowed from the Federal Reserve by its member banks. When the Fed raises the interest rate, banks also tend to raise the rate they charge for new loans, which discourages borrowing and thus reduces the amount of money entering the economy. Conversely, by lowering the interest rate, the Fed encourages firms and individuals to borrow from banks, which increases the money supply.

The Fed's interest-rate decisions are closely watched by the financial markets, political leaders, and the media. Any increase or decrease is a sign that the Fed has concluded that the economy is growing too quickly or too slowly.

The Fed also affects the money supply by selling and buying government securities in the open market. By offering securities at an attractive price, the Fed encourages investors to exchange their cash for securities, thus taking money out of the economy. On the other hand, when the Fed buys securities that people hold, it puts cash into their hands, thus expanding the money supply.

The third and final way the Fed affects the money supply is by raising or lowering the cash reserve that member banks are required to deposit with the Federal Reserve. This reserve is a proportion of each member's total deposits. By increasing the reserve rate, the Fed takes money from member banks, which reduces the money available for loans and investments. When the Fed lowers the reserve rate, banks have more money available and can make more loans to consumers and investors.

Economists debate the relative effectiveness of monetary policy and fiscal policy, but monetary policy has one obvious advantage: it can be implemented more quickly. The Fed can adjust interest and reserve rates on short notice, thus providing the economy a psychological boost to go along with the financial effect of a change in the money supply. In contrast, changes in fiscal policy usually take much longer to implement; Congress is normally a slow-acting institution, and new taxing and spending programs ordinarily require a substantial preparation period before they can be put into effect. Moreover, Republicans and Democrats are often divided over which fiscal policy tool to use—taxing or spending—and may not be able to reach agreement on how to respond to a faltering economy.

The Politics of the "Fed"

The greater flexibility of monetary policy has positioned the Fed as the institution with primary policy responsibility for keeping the U.S. economy on a steady course. The Fed's power can easily be exaggerated. The U.S. economy is subject to a lot of influences, and the Fed's impact is relatively modest. Nevertheless, the Fed is a vital component of U.S. economic policy and has become increasingly so. Alan Greenspan, chair of the Federal Reserve Board, has been described by the *Washington Post* as "the Man Who Really Runs America."

The power of the Fed raises important questions. One is the issue of representation: Whose interests does the Fed serve—those of the public as a whole or those of the banking sector? The Fed is not a wholly impartial body. Although it makes decisions in the context of economic theories and projections, it is "the bankers' bank" and is protective of monied interests. The Fed is typically more concerned with rising inflation, which erodes the value of money (including banks' returns on loans and investments), than with rising unemployment, which has its greatest impact on those at the bottom of the economic ladder. The Fed tends to hike interest rates when signs of rising inflation appear. Higher rates have the effect of slowing inflation, but they also slow job and income growth.

A related issue is one of accountability: Should the Fed, an unelected body, have so much power? Although appointed by the president, members of the Federal Reserve Board are not subject to removal. They serve for fixed terms and are relatively insulated from political pressures, including the changes that take place through elections. Of course, the Fed, as a banking institution, has a vested interest in a healthy economy (too much inflation erodes banks' returns on loans; too much unemployment decreases demand for loans) and thus operates within its own system of "checks and balances." Nevertheless, the restraints on the Fed are much weaker than those on popularly elected institutions.

The Fed, as previously indicated, was created in 1914. At the time, economists had not "invented" the theory of monetary policy, and the Fed had no role in the management of the nation's economy. If the Fed were being created today, it would likely have a different structure, although there is general agreement, as in the case of Europe's central banks, that some degree of independence is desirable.

The Fed is a preeminent example of *elitist* politics at work. Congress at some future point may decide that an overly independent Fed can no longer be tolerated and may bring monetary policy more closely under the control of elected institutions. Whether this happens may hinge on the Fed's willingness to exercise power sparingly and in the broad interests of society. (The economic policies of the federal government in the areas of social welfare and national security are discussed in the next two chapters.)

SUMMARY

Although private enterprise is the main force in the American economic system, the federal government plays a significant role through its policies to regulate, promote, and stimulate the economy.

Regulatory policy is designed to achieve efficiency and equity, which require government to intervene, for example, to maintain competitive trade practices (an efficiency goal) and to protect vulnerable parties in economic transactions (an equity goal). Many of the regulatory decisions of the federal government, particularly those of older agencies, are made largely in the context of group politics. Business lobbies have an especially strong influence on the regulatory policies that affect them. In general, newer regulatory agencies have policy responsibilities that are broader in scope and apply to a larger number of firms than those of the older agencies. As a result, the policy decisions of newer agencies are more often made in the context of party politics. Republican administrations are less vigorous in their regulation of business than are Democratic administrations.

Business is the major beneficiary of the federal government's efforts to promote economic interests. A large number of programs, including those to provide loans and research grants, are designed to assist businesses, which are also protected from failure through such measures as tariffs and favorable tax laws. Labor, for its part, gets government assistance through laws concerning such matters as worker safety, the minimum wage, and collective bargaining. Yet America's individualistic culture tends to put labor at a disadvantage, keeping it less powerful than business in its dealings with the government. Agriculture is another economic sector that depends substantially on government's help, particularly in the form of income stabilization programs, such as those that provide subsidies and price supports.

The U.S. government pursues policies that are designed to protect and conserve the environment. A few decades ago, the environment was not a policy priority. Today, there are many programs in this area, and the public has become an active participant in efforts to conserve resources and prevent exploitation of the environment.

Through its fiscal and monetary policies, Washington attempts to maintain a strong and stable economy—one that is characterized by high productivity, high employment, and low inflation. Fiscal policy is based on government decisions in regard to spending and taxing, which are aimed at either stimulating a weak economy or dampening an overheated (inflationary) economy. Fiscal policy is worked out through Congress and the president and is consequently responsive to political pressures. However, since it is difficult to raise taxes or cut programs, the government's ability to apply fiscal policy as an economic remedy is limited. Monetary policy is based on the money supply and works through the Federal Reserve System, which is headed by a board whose members hold office for fixed terms. The Fed is a relatively independent body, a fact that has given rise to questions as to whether it should have such a large role in national economic policy.

MAJOR CONCEPTS

balanced budget	equity
budget deficit	externalities
budget surplus	fiscal policy
capital-gains tax	graduated personal income taxes
deficit spending	inflation
demand-side economics	laissez-faire doctrine
deregulation	monetary policy
economic depression	national debt
economic recession	regulation
economy	supply-side economics
efficiency	

SUGGESTED READINGS AND WEB SITES

Friedman, Milton, and Walter Heller. *Monetary vs. Fiscal Policy.* New York: Norton, 1969. Opposing arguments by a leading monetarist and a leading Keynesian.

Gould, Kenneth A., Allan Schnaiberg, and Adam S. Weinberg. *Local Environmental Struggles: Citizen Activism in the Treadmill of Production.* New York: Cambridge University Press, 1996. An analysis through case studies of opportunities and constraints on environmental action in the United States.

Harris, Richard A., and Sidney M. Milkis. *The Politics of Regulatory Change: A Tale of Two Agencies.* 2d ed. New York: Oxford University Press, 1996. An analysis of the Reagan, Bush, and Clinton administrations' approaches to regulatory policy.

Schick, Allen with Felix Lostracco. *The Federal Budget: Politics, Policy, Process,* revised ed. Washington, D.C.: Brookings Institution Press, 2000. A forward look at the federal budget.

Shaiko, Ronald G. *Voices and Echoes for the Environment.* New York: Columbia University Press, 1999. The representation and communication of environmental groups.

Streeter, Thomas. *Selling the Air: A Critique of the Policy of Commercial Broadcasting in the United States.* Chicago: University of Chicago Press, 1996. An analysis of the impact of government regulation on the broadcasting market.

Young, H. Peyton. *Equity: In Theory and Practice.* Princeton, N.J.: Princeton University Press, 1995. A systematic assessment of what economic equity entails in theory and actual situations.

http://www.bog.frb.fed.us   The Federal Reserve System's web site. It describes the "Fed," provides information about its current activities, and has links to some of the Fed's national and international information sources.

http://www.epa.gov   The Environmental Protection Agency (EPA) web site has information on environmental policy and regulations, EPA projects, and related subjects.

http://www.ftc.gov   The Federal Trade Commission is one of the older regulatory agencies. Its web site describes the range of its activities.

http://www.whitehouse.gov/WH/EOP/OMB   The home page of the Office of Management and Budget contains a summary of the annual federal budget and describes the OMB's operations and responsibilities.

READING 15

Long-Term Goals for the Economy
ALICE M. RIVLIN

Introduction
To Alice Rivlin, who was deputy chair of the "Fed," the real issue of economic policy is whether it contributes to sustainable growth. To some, sustainable economic growth is the narrow issue of wealth creation. To Rivlin, it is a much larger issue including, for example, whether wealth is shared widely enough to ensure the government's stability and whether the environment is protected vigorously enough to safeguard its resources for use by future generations.

What should Americans expect from their economy? How should they assess whether it is performing well or badly? Most questions about the health of the economy relate to the short-run ups and downs of the business cycle. If the economy is recovering from recession, people are generally optimistic. They are likely to return incumbent politicians to office. If unemployment is rising, or prices are soaring, people are gloomier and readier for a political change.

Preoccupation with the immediate, however, obscures the longer-term trends that determine how the economy will be performing in the future and whether the next generation will live better than this one. . . .

There is no obvious single measure of how well the economy is performing in the long run, and there is lots of room for argument about what aspects are important and how to measure them. At a minimum, Americans ought to want three things from their economy: the average standard of living should be rising; the improving level of living should be shared by all groups; and the rising standard should be sustainable. All three elements of this definition are important. . . .

A rising standard of living makes many choices less agonizing and contentious. A family whose income is rising does not always have to give up something when a new need arises. A society with increasing resources can afford both greater private well-being and improved public services. As incomes rise, constant tax rates generate higher revenues. It is possible to have better schools, roads, and other public services without actually raising tax rates. (Although, of course, demands for public services may still outrun the available public resources.) A society with rising income can assist the less fortunate without forcing the more fortunate to accept cuts in their income.

To be sure, just as money does not always buy happiness for individuals or families, rising incomes do not always lead to harmonious politics. Public choices remain difficult and contentious, even in affluent countries. One reason may be that rich countries, like rich people, have a huge set of choices about what goods and services to provide and how to pay for them, including options to borrow now and pay later. Poor countries have fewer options. They have to defend their borders and provide basic services. They have a hard time obtaining credit from international lenders. Moreover, according to one theory, rising incomes intensify political struggles because they escalate the competition for goods that are physically scarce (such as seashore property) or socially scarce (such as political power or access to the "best" universities).

Nevertheless, just as most people prefer more income to less, most would rather live in a society in which average incomes are rising, winners outnumber losers, and new initiatives do not have to be paid for by reducing some ongoing activity, public or private. . . .

Increases in the average standard of living do not indicate satisfactory economic performance if those increases are confined to the favored few or even the favored many. A rising average does not constitute success if substantial groups of people are being left out and falling further behind the rest of the population. The situation is especially worrisome if the people being left out of the general prosperity are clearly identifiable both to themselves and to others because of race, sex, ethnic origin, or some other visible characteristic. If those who lose out are disproportionately concentrated in identifiable groups, they are bound to feel resentment and to allege favoritism and discrimination. Moreover, separation of the disadvantaged groups from the rest of the society is likely to be self-reinforcing. If people with specific characteristics are perceived as less successful, this fact is likely to undermine their confidence, discourage them from investing in education, and perpetuate stereotypes that lead to both increased discrimination and further lack of success.

Broad sharing of prosperity in America, like average rising income and sustainability, has international as well as domestic importance. U.S. efforts to encourage other countries to assist their poor and minorities and to promote freer market systems are undermined if the U.S. market system is visibly failing identifiable groups at home.

Individuals often increase their immediate standard of living in ways that reduce it later—by piling up credit card debts that have to be repaid out of future income, for example. Nations can be shortsighted too, so it is important to make certain that increases in the national standard of living are not achieved by creating serious problems for the future.

Economic growth accompanied by high inflation, for example, is neither desirable nor sustainable. Inflation distorts the economy. It encourages people to put their money in real estate and art objects rather than in investments that enhance future productivity. It favors debtors over creditors and discourages savers.

Nations, like individuals, can borrow beyond their capacity to repay, default on obligations, and damage their creditworthiness. They can borrow to finance consumption or ill-conceived investments and end up with burdensome interest charges and repayment obligations that reduce their future standard of living.

Economic activity that fails to replace the capital it uses is also unsustainable. Accounting principles that apply to companies require recognition that capital assets wear out and must be replaced. However, public capital such as roads, bridges, schools, and government buildings is often allowed to wear out or fall into disrepair without people recognizing that the future national standard of living will be reduced by such shortsighted policies. The decay is often gradual and the cost spread widely. Deteriorating roads, for example, cause accidents, delays, excess fuel consumption, and repair bills paid by owners of cars and trucks, not the government. For taxpayers and vehicle users together, building a highway to a high standard of durability and keeping it in repair can be much less costly in the long run than building it cheaply and repairing it sooner.

Economic growth can also be unsustainable if it damages the environment in ways that lower the standard of living in the future. Shortsighted agricultural development in vast areas of the United States in the nineteenth and early twentieth centuries depleted the soil and created the dust bowl. Deforestation in the Himalayas is producing fuel short-ages, soil erosion, and flooding that threaten the livelihood of people in wide areas. The burning of tropical forests in the Amazon basin exposes poor soil that cannot support farming or ranching for long periods, as well as contributing to the buildup of greenhouse gases and destroying the treasures of the forests themselves. Development that pollutes lakes, rivers, and oceans or leads to buildup of toxic waste or mountains of trash and garbage cannot be sustained for long.

Most of the attention to sustainability and economic development in recent years has been focused on the environment and on less developed countries. Where people live at the margin of subsistence, there is great potential for famine and other disasters as a result of shortsighted prac-tices. Moreover, the loss of millions of species from rapid destruction of tropical rain forests, extinction of wild animals in Africa, and the squan-dering of other irreplaceable assets of developing countries has aroused concern around the world for the common heritage of the planet.

Taking a longer view of economic processes, however, is no less im-portant to the developed countries. Life in the United States could be far less attractive, healthy, and safe if economic growth destroys the natural beauty of the country, poisons the atmosphere, and pollutes the lakes and streams. Moreover, the United States cannot be effective in convincing developing countries to reform their practices if it fails to adhere to sus-tainable policies itself. American credibility in urging conservation of tropical forests is greatly undermined by our own rapid destruction of the ancient forests of the Pacific Northwest.

SOURCE: From *Reviving the American Dream: Congress, the States and the Federal Government* by Alice M. Rivlin, 1992. Reprinted by permission of The Brook-ings Institution.

Alice M. Rivlin is a former member of the Federal Reserve Board. She was previously director of the Office of Management and Budget (OMB) and director of the Congres-sional Budget Office (CBO). She is now Senior Fellow in the Economic Studies Pro-gram at the Brookings Institution.

CHAPTER SIXTEEN

Welfare and Education Policy

> We the people of the United States, in order to . . . promote
> the general welfare . . . .
>
> PREAMBLE, U.S. CONSTITUTION

IT HAPPENED with unpredicted suddenness. In just five years, the number of people on the welfare rolls had plummeted by 48 percent nationwide. Caseloads had peaked in 1994 but now were down in every state. What was surprising was the size of the drop. The number of families on welfare had declined by more than 80 percent in Wisconsin, Idaho, Wyoming, and by more than half in twenty-three other states. There were only three states—Hawaii, Rhode Island, and New Mexico—in which the drop was less than 20 percent (see "States in the Nation"). The trend defied what has been described as the welfare "reverse gravity" law: rolls that go up but do not come down.

Two factors were driving the change. One was the booming national economy. Unemployment had steadily declined, and as more Americans went into the work force, the demand for welfare decreased. The second factor was the 1996 Welfare Reform Act, which had shortened welfare eligibility and required that able-bodied recipients find work or risk loss of all benefits. The question on policymakers' minds was the proportion of the decline attributable to the change in the welfare system. Representative Clay Shaw, Jr. (R-Florida), who sponsored the reform law, declared that it was the primary reason for the dramatic drop: "It shows the faith we had in [the legislation] was well placed." Senator Daniel Patrick Moynihan (D-New York), who led the opposition to the bill, said; "It doesn't show anything yet." Moynihan claimed the real test would come when the economy turned downward, and he expressed doubt that the chronically unemployed would find jobs in that situation.[1]

These contrasting views typify views of social welfare policy. It is an area in which opposing philosophies of government collide. There are

481

those, like Moynihan, who believe the government must provide substantial and sustained assistance to those Americans who are less equipped to compete effectively in the marketplace. There are others, like Shaw, who believe that welfare payments, except to those who are unmistakably unfit to work, discourage personal effort and create welfare dependency.

Another source of conflict over welfare policy is the country's federal system of government. Welfare was traditionally a responsibility of state and local governments. Only since the 1930s has the federal government also played a significant role. Some welfare programs are jointly run by the federal and state governments. They are funded at different levels from one state to the next, but operate within guidelines set down by the national government and are partly funded by Washington. The strictness of federal guidelines and the amount that the federal government should contribute to the programs have long been deeply contentious issues.

This chapter examines the social problems that federal welfare programs are designed to alleviate and describes how these programs operate. It also addresses public education policies. A goal of this chapter is to provide an informed basis for understanding issues of social welfare and education and to show why disagreements in these areas are so substantial. They involve hard choices that almost inevitably require trade-offs between federal and state power and between the values of individual self-reliance and egalitarian compassion. The main points of the chapter are these:

* *Poverty is a large and persistent problem in America, affecting deeply about one in seven Americans, including many of the country's most vulnerable groups: children, female-headed families, and minorities.*

* *Welfare policy has been a partisan issue, with Democrats taking the lead on government programs to alleviate economic insecurity and Republicans acting to slow down or reverse these initiatives.*

* *Social welfare programs are designed to reward and foster self-reliance or, when this is not possible, to provide benefits only to those individuals who are truly in need.*

* *As a result of America's individualistic culture, public support for social insurance programs (such as social security) is far higher than that for public assistance programs (such as TANF).*

* *A prevailing principle in the United States is equality of opportunity, which in terms of public policy is most evident in the area of public education. No country invests more heavily in its public schools and colleges than does the United States.*

★ STATES IN THE NATION ★

The Declining Number of Families on Welfare

The welfare rolls in the United States peaked in March 1994. After that, the number of American families on welfare dropped precipitously, which analysts attributed to both the surge in the U.S. economy and the 1996 welfare reform bill that instituted new work rules. The decline in the welfare rolls was dramatic in all regions of the country. The biggest drop (89 percent) was in Wisconsin. The smallest (7 percent) was in Hawaii.

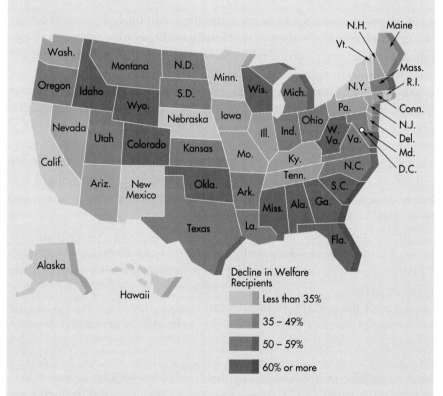

Decline in Welfare Recipients

Less than 35%

35 – 49%

50 – 59%

60% or more

SOURCE: Department of Health and Human Services. Period of change is January 1993 to March 1999.

POVERTY IN AMERICA: THE NATURE OF THE PROBLEM

In the broadest sense, social welfare policy encompasses all efforts by government to improve the social conditions of any and all citizens. In a narrower sense, which is the way the term will be used in most of this chapter, social welfare policy refers to those efforts by government to help individuals meet their basic human needs, including food, clothing, and shelter.

The Poor: Who and How Many?

America's social welfare needs are substantial. Although Americans are far better off economically than most of the world's peoples, poverty is a significant and persistent problem in the United States. The government defines the **poverty line** as the annual cost of a thrifty food budget for an urban family of four, multiplied by three to include the cost of housing, clothes, and other necessities. Families whose incomes fall below that line are officially considered poor. In 2000, the poverty line was set at an annual income of roughly $16,700 for a family of four. One in seven Americans, more than thirty-five million people, including nearly fifteen million children, live near or below the poverty line. If they could join hands, they would form a line that stretched from New York to Tokyo and back again.

America's poor include individuals of all ages, races, religions, and regions, but poverty is substantially more prevalent among some groups. Children are one of the largest groups of poor Americans. One in every five children lives in poverty. Most poor children live in single-parent families, usually with the mother. In fact, as can be seen from Figure 16-1, a high proportion of Americans residing in families headed by divorced, separated, or unmarried women live below the poverty line. These families are at a disadvantage because most women earn less than men for comparable work, especially in nonprofessional fields. Women without higher education or special skills often cannot find jobs that pay enough to justify the child care expenses they incur due to their work. In recent years, single-parent, female-headed families have been five times as likely as two-income families to fall below the poverty line. Poverty in America is mainly a women's problem, a situation referred to as "the feminization of poverty."

Poverty is also widespread among minority group members. About 30 percent of African Americans and Hispanics live below the poverty line, compared with 10 percent of whites.

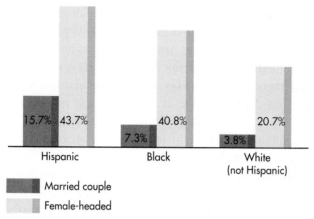

FIGURE 16-1 PERCENTAGE OF FAMILIES LIVING IN POVERTY, BY FAMILY COMPOSITION AND RACE/ETHNICITY
Poverty is far more prevalent among female-headed households and African American and Hispanic households. Source: U.S. Bureau of the Census, 2000.

Poverty is geographically concentrated. Although it is often portrayed as an urban problem, it is somewhat more prevalent in rural areas. About one in six rural residents—as compared with one in eight urban residents—live in families with incomes below the poverty line. The urban figure is misleading, however, in that the poverty rate is very high in inner-city areas. Suburbs are the safe haven from poverty. Because suburbanites are removed from it, many of them have no sense of the impoverished condition of what Michael Harrington called "the other America."[2]

The "invisibility" of poverty in America is evident in polls that show that most Americans substantially underestimate the number of poor in their country. There is certainly nothing in the daily lives of many Americans or what they see on television that would lead them to think that poverty rates are uncommonly high. Yet the United States has the highest level of poverty among the advanced industrialized nations, and its rate of child poverty is more than twice the average of the others (see box: How the United States Compares).

Living in Poverty: By Choice or Chance?

Many Americans hold to the idea that poverty is largely a matter of choice—that most low-income Americans are unwilling to make the effort to hold a responsible job and get ahead in life. In his book *Losing Ground*, Charles Murray argued that America has a permanent underclass of unproductive citizens who prefer to live on welfare and whose children receive little educational encouragement at home and grow up to be copies of their parents.[3] There are, indeed, such people in America. They likely number in the millions. They are the toughest challenge for policymakers because almost nothing about their lives equips them to escape from poverty and its attendant ills.

Yet most poor Americans are in their situation as a result of circumstance rather than choice. A ten-year study of American families by a University of Michigan research team found that most of the poor are poor only for a while and that they are poor for temporary reasons: loss of a job, desertion by the father, and so on.[4] When the U.S. economy goes into a tailspin the impact devastates many families. In the recessionary period of 1990–1992, more than four million Americans fell into poverty as a result of job loss.

It is also the case that holding a full-time job does not guarantee that a family will rise above the poverty line. A family of four with one employed adult who works forty hours a week at $6 an hour (which is roughly the minimum wage level) has an annual income of about $12,000, which is well below the poverty line. Millions of Americans—mostly household workers, service workers, unskilled laborers, and farm workers—are in this position. The U.S. Bureau of Labor Statistics estimates that roughly 7 percent of Americans who work full time do not earn enough to lift their families above the poverty line.[5]

THE POLITICS AND POLICIES OF SOCIAL WELFARE

Welfare policy has generally been debated along partisan lines, a reflection of differences in the coalitions and philosophies of the Republican and Democratic parties. With its ties to labor, the poor, and minorities, the Democratic party has initiated nearly all major federal welfare programs. The key House of Representatives vote on the Social Security Act of 1935, for example, found 85 percent of Democrats supporting it and 99 percent of Republicans against it.[6]

Republicans gradually came to accept the idea that the federal government has a role in social welfare, but argued that the role should be kept as small as practicable. Thus, in the 1960s, Republican opposition to President Lyndon Johnson's Great Society was substantial. His programs included federal initiatives in health care, education, public housing, nutrition, and other areas traditionally dominated by state and local government. More

HOW THE UNITED STATES COMPARES

Children Living in Poverty

The United States has the highest child poverty rate among industrialized nations. One in five American children live in poverty; in most other industrialized nations, fewer than one in ten does so.

One reason for the difference is that income in the United States is less evenly distributed. As a consequence, the United States has the highest percentage of both rich and poor children in the industrialized world. In addition, the United States spends less on government assistance for the poor. Without government help, for example, the child poverty rate in the United States and France would be about equal: 25 percent. Through its government programs, France reduces the ratio to less than 7 percent. Through its welfare programs, the United States cuts the rate only slightly.

Child poverty in the United States is made worse by the relatively large number of single-parent families, although Sweden, which has a similarly large number, has one of the world's lowest rates of child poverty.

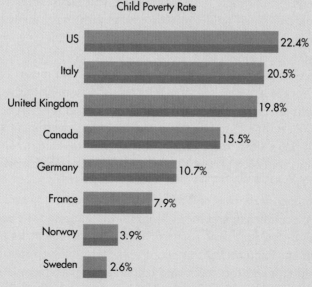

Child Poverty Rate

US	22.4%
Italy	20.5%
United Kingdom	19.8%
Canada	15.5%
Germany	10.7%
France	7.9%
Norway	3.9%
Sweden	2.6%

SOURCE: United Nations Children's Fund, 2001.

than 70 percent of congressional Republicans voted against the 1965 Medicare and Medicaid programs, which provide government-paid medical assistance for the elderly and the poor. In the 1980s, in the face of opposition from congressional Democrats, Republican president Reagan made social welfare spending the prime target of his effort to cut the domestic budget. Compared with the decade beginning in the late 1960s, when welfare spending per poor person nearly tripled, the 1980s saw a 20 percent decline in actual dollars spent on each welfare recipient. The 1996 Welfare Reform Act, which was designed to cut welfare rolls and costs, was passed largely with Republican support; a majority of congressional Democrats opposed it.

Although the Republican and Democratic parties have been at odds on the issue of social welfare, they have also had reason to work together. Social 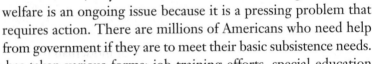 welfare is an ongoing issue because it is a pressing problem that requires action. There are millions of Americans who need help from government if they are to meet their basic subsistence needs. This help has taken various forms: job training efforts, special education programs, income redistribution measures, and individual-benefit policies.

JOB TRAINING   The government's social welfare effort has included attempts to provide jobs and job training. Employment policy and welfare policy have been loosely linked since the Great Depression, when Franklin Roosevelt combined public jobs programs with social security legislation. At one point during the depression, a fifth of the nation's entire work force was employed in public jobs.

Americans strongly favor work over welfare as a means of public assistance. Work is believed to foster initiative and responsibility, while welfare is thought to create dependency and irresponsibility. In a Los Angeles Times poll, respondents were asked what action government should take to help the poor. Only 6 percent said that the government should provide money or services, whereas 20 percent preferred public works jobs and 72 percent favored job training.

The history of work and job training programs, however, is an uneven one. For example, an ambitious program that began in the early 1970s under Republican president Richard Nixon, and which at its peak provided employment for four million people, was terminated a decade later amid charges that it was too costly and had failed to place people in permanent jobs, as opposed to subsidized temporary positions. Subsequent job-training programs were less ambitious and, if anything, even less successful in moving the unemployed into permanent jobs.

A New Beginning
Welfare to Work

President Clinton signs into law the 1996 welfare reform bill that ended the 61-year-old federal guarantee of aid to the poor. The new legislation limits federal welfare assistance to a period of five years.

The picture changed with passage of the 1996 Welfare Reform Act. The historic bill ended a six-decade federal guarantee of cash assistance to needy families, replacing it with a system of cash grants to the states, which have responsibility for caring for welfare recipients and getting them into jobs. The legislation's goal is to reduce long-term welfare dependency by limiting the time that recipients can receive welfare and by providing the states with incentives to prepare recipients for work. States may not let recipients receive federal welfare assistance for more than five years (although a fifth of recipients can be exempted from this requirement), and within two years on welfare, a recipient must find work or face the loss of benefits. States receive federal funds with which to provide benefits, community service jobs, and job training, but unless they meet the program's goals (for example, half of their welfare recipients must be moved from welfare to work by the year 2002), they will have their federal assistance reduced. In other words, the welfare reform act includes incentives to encourage both states and welfare recipients to create situations that will lead to employment.

The long-term effectiveness of the new program is yet to be determined. The trend so far is cause for optimism. The number of Americans on welfare has declined sharply since the 1996 Welfare Reform Act was passed. Nevertheless, the economy was strong and growing when the law took effect, and new jobs were plentiful. The real test of the new program will come when the economy goes into a prolonged slump. Another test will be whether the states can train welfare recipients who are severely lacking in job skills. Most of the welfare recipients who have found employment since 1996 had enough skills that they required little or, in most cases, no job training. Most of those who have been unable to find employment have limited education and few job-related skills.[7]

EDUCATION INITIATIVES: HEAD START   The social welfare effort also includes formal education programs, most notably Head Start. It provides preschool education for poor children in order to give them a better chance to succeed when they begin school. Head Start was established in the 1960s as part of President Lyndon Johnson's War on Poverty, which was designed to alleviate the problems of America's poor through initiatives in such areas as nutrition, job training, health care, and housing. Funding in some of these areas was cut sharply in the 1980s. Head Start's budget dropped to a level that allowed only 10 percent of eligible children to participate. As evidence mounted of poverty's devastating impact on children's development, President Bush and the Democratic Congress concluded that Head Start was the kind of social investment that the country could hardly afford not to make, and it became one of the few domestic programs to receive a substantial funding increase during the Bush administration. Additional funding was provided when Bill Clinton took office. Nevertheless, less than half of the eligible children are enrolled in Head Start, and many who complete the program do not sustain their advantage because their home situation provides no support for educational achievement.

INCOME AND TAX MEASURES   The income of the average American family exceeds $40,000, which is substantial enough to provide a reasonable standard of living. Of course, the average income is just that—an average. It hides other averages—for example, the average white family has an income that is more than $15,000 higher than the average black family's income—and it hides wide disparities in the income of those individuals at the top and the bottom of the income ladder.

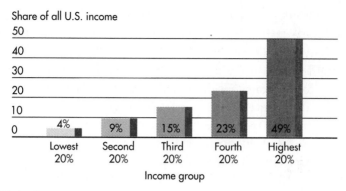

Share of all U.S. income

FIGURE 16-2 INCOME INEQUALITY
The United States has the highest degree of income inequality of any
industrialized democracy. Citizens in the top fifth get nearly half of all income;
those in the bottom fifth get less than one-twentieth of all income. Source: U.S.
Bureau of the Census, 2000.

In fact, the United States has substantial income inequality (see Figure
16-2). The top 20 percent of Americans receive half of the total income,
while the other 80 percent get the other half. The bottom 20 percent receive less than 5 percent of the total income, and many of them live in
poverty. In contrast, Americans at the top of the income ladder live very
well. The upper 5 percent have about as much total yearly income as the
bottom 50 percent. This 10 to 1 ratio is greater than that found in other industrialized democracies, and the gap between rich and poor in the United
States has widened in recent decades.

Income taxes in the United States have not been the instrument of redistribution that they are in other democracies. As of 2000, the top tax rate
in the United States was 39.5 percent, and it did not apply until taxable income reached the $250,000 level. An upper tax rate of 50 percent or more
is common in Europe, and there are fewer loopholes, such as the deduction
of home mortgage interest, that provide tax breaks for the more well-to-do.
In terms of the actual rate of taxes paid, middle-income and moderately
high-income Americans are in about the same situation. The higher marginal tax rate on higher-income people is offset by their additional deductions and the existence of nonprogressive taxes such as the social security
tax. (This tax is a flat rate that begins with the first dollar earned each year
and stops completely after about $65,000 in earnings.)

The net result is that the *effective tax rate* (the actual percentage of income that is spent to pay taxes) of high-income and middle-income Americans is not greatly different. When social security and personal income

taxes are combined, the average family's effective tax rate is about 25 percent. For families with an income of a million dollars or more, the effective tax rate is only a few points higher.[8]

Although well-to-do Americans pay relatively low taxes, the fact that they make a lot of money means, in absolute terms, that they contribute a sizable share of tax revenues. The top 10 percent of taxpayers in terms of income pay about half of the personal income taxes received by the federal government. Some of this tax revenue is redistributed downward to lower-income groups through social welfare programs.

The United States also has a policy designed to reallocate income directly to lower-income persons. This policy is the Earned Income Tax Credit (EITC). Low-income families with at least one child are eligible for EITC. About ten million American families receive EITC payments; the maximum payment to any one family is about $3,750. Eligibility for payment is determined when persons file their personal income taxes. Those with family incomes below a specified level receive the payment, which phases out as income rises.

INDIVIDUAL-BENEFIT PROGRAMS

EITC involves what is called a **transfer payment,** or a government benefit that is given directly to an individual. All spending to promote the general welfare is designed to help individuals, but much of it—such as federal funds for public school construction and hospital equipment—is not in the form of transfer payments. Many federal programs, however, do transfer benefits directly to individuals, such as social security payments to retired people. These individual-benefit programs are what most people have in mind when they speak of "social welfare."

Individual-benefit programs are designed to alleviate the personal hardships associated with such conditions as joblessness, poverty, and old age. For most of these programs, any individual who meets the established criteria of eligibility is entitled to the benefits. For this reason, such programs are termed **entitlement programs.** In this sense, they have the same force in law as taxes. Just as individuals are required by law to pay taxes to government on the income they earn, individuals are entitled by law to receive government benefits for which they qualify.

All told, individual-benefit programs are the major thrust of U.S. social welfare policy. The federal budget for such programs is roughly $900 billion, which is more money than is spent on any other government activity, including national defense.

At an earlier time in the nation's history, the federal government spent almost nothing on social welfare. Welfare policy was deemed to fall within the powers reserved to the states by the Tenth Amendment and to be adequately addressed by them, even though they did not offer substantial welfare services. Individuals were expected to fend for themselves, and those unable to do so were usually supported by relatives and friends. This approach reflected the idea of **negative government,** which holds that government governs best by staying out of people's lives, thus giving them as much freedom as possible to determine their own pursuits and encouraging them to become self-reliant.

The situation changed dramatically with the Great Depression. The unemployment level reached 25 percent, which prompted demands for help from the federal government. Franklin D. Roosevelt's New Deal brought economic relief in the form of public jobs and welfare programs, and helped to change opinions about the federal government's welfare role.[9] Americans came to look favorably upon Washington's help. This attitude reflected a faith in **positive government:** the idea that government intervention is necessary in order to enhance personal liberty and security when individuals are buffeted by economic and social forces beyond their control.

Since the 1930s, the federal government's welfare role has increased immeasurably, and individuals now expect the federal government to provide benefits to ease the loss of income caused by retirement, disability, unemployment, and the like. Not all individual-benefit programs are alike, however, in their philosophies or levels of public support. Individual-benefit programs fall into two general categories: *social insurance* and *public assistance.* Programs in the first category enjoy widespread public support and receive a higher level of funding; programs in the second category encounter substantial public opposition and receive less funding.

Social Insurance Programs

More than forty million Americans receive monthly benefits from social insurance programs—including social security, Medicare, unemployment insurance, and workers' compensation. The two major programs, social security and Medicare, cost the federal government more than $600 billion per year. Individuals who paid special payroll taxes when they were employed are eligible for benefits. This is why such programs are labeled **social insurance:** recipients get an insurance benefit under a program that they have helped fund. This self-financing feature of social insurance programs accounts for their strong public support.

SOCIAL SECURITY   The leading social insurance program is social security for retirees.[10] The program began with passage of the Social Security Act of 1935 and is funded through payroll taxes on employees and employers. Franklin D. Roosevelt emphasized that retiring workers would receive an insurance benefit that they had earned through their payroll taxes, not a handout from the government. Today, social security has Americans' full support. Public opinion polls indicate that upwards of 90 percent of Americans favor current or higher levels of social security benefits for the elderly. Social security is one of the few welfare programs run entirely by the federal government. Washington collects the payroll taxes that fund the program and sends monthly checks directly to the roughly forty million social security recipients, who each, on average, receive more than $650 a month.

Although many people believe that an individual's social security benefits are financed by his or her past contributions, they are actually funded largely through payroll taxes on the current work force. The typical social security recipient gets more money from the government than he or she has paid into the fund; thus it is necessary to use contributions from the current work force to finance the program.

Several social security reform bills have been introduced recently in Congress, and President Bush appointed a commission in 2001 to develop a plan for restructuring social security. A major reform of the system will likely occur in the near future. Because of medical and other advances, Americans live longer than they once did, and a social security crisis will occur during the twenty-first century unless the current system is changed. Roughly 20 percent of the U.S. population will be over sixty-five in the year 2030, and there will not be enough workers by then to fund the payout to retirees without adjustments to the current program.

The reason change is likely in the near future is that the longer the delay is, the more painful is the solution: higher taxes and lower benefits. There are a number of ways of ensuring the solvency of social security, and there are proponents for nearly every possibility, from investing social security taxes in stocks to raising the income level on which social security taxes are levied. The plan most likely to be enacted is one that preserves social security as a safety net for the elderly poor while creating opportunities for taxpayers to get a greater return on a portion of their social security payments through the stock market.

UNEMPLOYMENT INSURANCE   The 1935 Social Security Act provides for unemployment benefits for workers who have lost their jobs involuntarily. Unemployment insurance is a joint federal-state program. The federal government collects the payroll taxes that fund unemployment benefits, but states have the option of deciding whether the taxes will be paid by employers only or by both employees and employers (most states use the first option). Individual states also set the tax rate, conditions of eligibility, and benefit level, subject to minimum standards established by the federal government. Although unemployment benefits vary widely among states, they average about a third ($180 a week) of what an average worker makes while employed, and in most cases the benefits are terminated after twenty-six to thirty-nine weeks.

The unemployment program does not have the same high level of public support as social security. The situation reflects in part a common belief that the loss of a job, or the failure to find a new one right away, is somehow a personal failing. Unemployment statistics suggest otherwise. For example, U.S. Bureau of Labor statistics indicate that of those who lost their jobs in 1994, only 16 percent had made the decision to quit working or were fired. The others became unemployed because of either a temporary layoff or the permanent elimination of a job position.

MEDICARE   After World War II, most European democracies instituted systems of government-paid health care, and President Harry Truman, a Democrat, proposed a similar program for Americans. The American Medical Association (AMA) called Truman's plan "un-American," lobbied hard against it, and threatened to mobilize local physicians to campaign against members of Congress who supported "socialized medicine." Truman's proposal never came to a vote in Congress. In 1961, President John F. Kennedy, also a Democrat, proposed a health care program restricted to social security recipients, but the AMA, the insurance industry, and conservative members of Congress succeeded in blocking the plan.[11]

The 1964 elections swept a tide of liberal Democrats into Congress, and the result was Medicare. Enacted in 1965, the program provides medical assistance to retirees and is funded primarily through payroll taxes. Medicare, too, is based on the insurance principle, and therefore it has gained nearly the same high level of public support as social security.

Medicare provides for care in a hospital or nursing home, but the recipient pays part of the initial cost and pays most of the expenses after one hundred days. Medicare does not cover all physicians' fees, but enrollees in the program have the option of paying an insurance premium for fuller coverage of these fees. Enrollees who cannot afford the additional premium can apply to have the government pay it.

As with social security, a major reform of the Medicare program is likely in the near future. The rising cost of medical care and the growing number of elderly have combined to threaten the solvency of the Medicare program; it is projected within a decade to run out of money unless new revenues and cost-cutting measures are devised. Among the options under consideration are increased payroll taxes, more cost-sharing by recipients, more use of managed care options, and more substantial controls on government payments to doctors and hospitals.

Public Assistance Programs

Unlike social insurance programs, **public assistance** programs are funded through general tax revenues and are available only to the financially needy. Eligibility for such entitlement programs is established by a **means test,** a demonstration that the applicant is poor enough to qualify for the benefit. In other words, applicants must prove that they are poor. Public assistance programs are commonly referred to as "welfare" and the recipients as "welfare cases." Opinion polls show that public assistance programs have less public support than do social insurance programs.

About twenty-five million Americans receive public assistance, typically through programs established by the federal government, administered mainly by the states, and funded jointly by the state and federal governments. Most Americans have the mistaken impression that public assistance programs account for the lion's share of federal welfare spending. In fact, the federal government spends more than twice as much on its two major social insurance programs, social security and Medicare, as it does on all public assistance programs combined.

SUPPLEMENTAL SECURITY INCOME (SSI) A major public assistance program is Supplemental Security Income (SSI), which originated as federal assistance to the blind and elderly poor as part of the Social Security Act of 1935. By the 1930s, most states had begun or were considering such programs. Although the federal legislation was designed to replace their efforts, the states have retained a measure of control over benefits and eligibility and are required to provide some of the funding. Because SSI recipients (who now include the disabled in addition to the blind and elderly poor) have obvious reasons for their inability to provide for themselves, this public assistance program is not widely criticized.

AID TO NEEDY FAMILIES Perhaps the most controversial of the major public assistance programs was Aid for Families with Dependent Children (AFDC). Partly funded by the federal government but administered by the states, the AFDC program was created in the 1930s as survivors'

Supplemental Security Income (SSI) is a combined
federal-state program that provides public assistance to
blind and disabled people.

insurance to assist children whose fathers had died prematurely. Relatively
small and noncontroversial at inception, AFDC was the target of severe
criticism by the 1970s. Although some attacks on it were based on false
claims (for example, that most of the recipients were unwed teenage mothers when, in fact, less than 10 percent were in this category),[12] AFDC was
widely unpopular because it was linked in people's minds to welfare dependency and irresponsibility. It was an entitlement program, which meant that
any single parent (and, in some states, two parents) living in poverty could
claim the benefit and keep it for as long as a dependent child was in the
household. By 1995, AFDC was supporting fourteen million Americans at
an annual cost of more than $20 billion.

In 1996, AFDC was terminated as part of the Welfare Reform Act.
Funding for AFDC was replaced by the Temporary Assistance for Needy
Families block grant (TANF), which gives each state an annual cash grant
that is to be used to design its own program for assisting needy families and
getting welfare recipients into jobs. These programs must operate within
tight federal guidelines, including these:

- Americans' eligibility for federal cash assistance is limited to no more than five years in their lifetime.
- Within two years, the heads of most families on welfare will have to find work or risk the loss of benefits.
- Unmarried teenage mothers are qualified for welfare benefits only if they remain in school and live with a parent or legal guardian.
- Single mothers will lose a portion of their benefits if they refuse to cooperate in identifying the father of their children.

Although states are allowed to make some exceptions to some of the rules (for example, an unmarried teenage mother who faces sexual abuse at home is permitted to live elsewhere), the rules govern in most cases. States are also empowered in some areas to impose more restrictive rules. For example, a state can deny increased benefits to a mother who is already receiving assistance and has another child.

Within the limits, states can design a program of their choosing, and wide differences are expected. Even AFDC benefits varied widely, ranging from less than $300 in most southern and southwestern states to more than $450 in most northeastern and some midwestern states. Since the TANF grants that states will initially receive are roughly proportional to the amounts they were spending on AFDC, these regional differences are certain to persist.

The new welfare program is such a substantial departure from the past that the long-term picture is difficult to predict. Some observers believe it will have dire effects. The liberal Urban Institute estimates that within a decade the bill will push more than one million children into poverty as their family's eligibility for assistance expires. Other observers see it as the long-awaited answer to welfare dependency. They point, for example, to the higher-than-anticipated decline in welfare recipients during the program's first years. The conservative Heritage Foundation concluded in a report that the new program's tough rules had succeeded in forcing able-bodied unemployed to find gainful work.[13]

FOOD STAMPS   The food stamp program, which took its present form in 1961, is fully funded by the federal government. The program provides an **in-kind benefit**—not cash, but food stamps that can be spent only on grocery items.

Food stamps are available only to people who qualify on the basis of low income. The program is intended to improve the nutrition of poor families by enabling them to purchase qualified items, mainly foodstuffs, with food stamps. Some critics say that food stamps stigmatize their users by making it obvious to onlookers in the checkout line that they are "welfare cases." More prevalent criticisms are that the program is too costly and that too many undeserving people receive food stamps. The 1996 welfare reform bill restricts to three months in any three-year period the food-stamp eligibility of able-bodied adults with no children.

SUBSIDIZED HOUSING   Low-income persons are also eligible for subsidized housing. Most of the federal spending in this area is on housing vouchers rather than the construction of low-income housing units. Under the voucher system, the individual receives a monthly rent-payment voucher, which is given in lieu of cash to the landlord, who then hands the voucher over to the government in exchange for cash. The welfare recipient is given a voucher (an in-kind benefit) rather than cash in order to ensure that the funds are actually used to obtain housing. About five million households annually receive a federal housing subsidy.

The U.S. government spends much less on public housing than on tax breaks for homeowners, most of whom are middle- and upper-income Americans. Homeowners are allowed tax deductions for their mortgage

One of the many ironies of the U.S. social welfare policy is that tax deductions on home mortgages for the middle and upper classes are government subsidies, just as are rent vouchers for the poor, but only the latter are stigmatized as "welfare handouts."

interest payments and their local property tax payments. The total of these tax concessions is three times as much as is spent by the federal government on housing for low-income families.

MEDICAID   When it enacted Medicare in 1965, Congress also established Medicaid, which provides health care for poor people who are already on welfare. It is considered a public assistance program, rather than a social insurance program like Medicare, because it is based on need and funded by general tax revenues. Roughly 60 percent of Medicaid funding is provided by the federal government, and about 40 percent by the states. More than thirty million Americans receive Medicaid assistance.

Medicaid is controversial because of its costs. As health care costs have spiraled, far ahead of the inflation rate, so have the costs of Medicaid. It absorbs the biggest share of public assistance dollars spent by the U.S. government and has forced state and local governments to cut other services to meet the costs of their share. "It's killing us," was how one local official described the impact of Medicaid on his community's budget.[14] As is true of other public assistance programs, Medicaid has been criticized for supposedly serving too many people who could take care of themselves if they tried harder. The idea is contradicted, ironically, by the situation faced by many working Americans. There are roughly forty million working Americans who make too much money to qualify for Medicaid but who cannot afford health insurance.

EDUCATION AS EQUALITY OF OPPORTUNITY: THE AMERICAN WAY

All democratic societies promote economic security, but they do so to different degrees. European democracies have instituted such programs as government-paid health care for all citizens, compensation for all unemployed workers, and retirement benefits for all elderly citizens. As we have seen, the United States provides these benefits only to some citizens in each category. For example, not all elderly Americans are entitled to social security benefits. If they paid social security taxes for a long enough period when they were employed, they (including their spouses) qualify for benefits. Otherwise, they do not, even if they are in dire economic need.

Such policy differences between Europe and the United States stem from cultural and historical differences. Democracy developed in Europe in reaction to centuries of aristocratic rule, the inequities of which brought the issue of human equality to the forefront. When strong labor and socialist parties then emerged as a consequence of industrialization, European democracies initiated sweeping social welfare programs that brought about greater economic equality. In contrast, American democracy emerged out of a tradition of limited government that emphasized personal freedom. Equality was a lesser issue, and class consciousness was weak. No major labor or socialist party emerged in America during industrialization to represent the working class, and there was no persistent and strong demand for welfare policies that would bring about an economic leveling.

Equality, Inequality, and Public Opinion

These differing legacies are evident today in the opinions of Americans and Europeans toward freedom and equality. When asked in a Gallup poll which value they prized more highly, Americans chose freedom by 72 percent to 20 percent. Among Europeans, the margin was only 49 percent to 35 percent. On the basis of his study of political values, Karl Lamb concluded that most Americans "cannot really imagine a society that would provide substantial material equality."[15]

Americans' view of equality is best expressed by the term **equality of opportunity,** which is the idea that individuals should have an equal chance to succeed on their own. The concept embodies equality, in its emphasis on giving everyone a fair chance to get ahead. Yet equality of opportunity also embodies liberty, because it allows people to succeed or fail on their own as a result of what they do with their opportunities. The presumption is that people will end up differently—some rich, some poor. It is sometimes said that equality of opportunity offers individuals an equal chance to become unequal.

In practice, equality of opportunity works itself out primarily in the private sector, where Americans compete for jobs, promotions, and other advantages. However, a few public policies have the purpose of enhancing equality of opportunity. The most significant of these policies is public education.

Public Education: Leveling through the Schools

During the nation's first century, the question of a free education to all children divided the landed wealthy from the advocates of broad-based democracy. The wealthy feared that an educated public would challenge their power. The democrats wanted to provide more people with the foundation for economic advantage. The democrats won out. Public schools sprang up in nearly every community and were open free of charge to children who could attend.

The United States today invests more heavily in public education at all levels than does any other country. The curriculum in American schools is also relatively standardized. Unlike those countries that divide children even at the grade school level into different tracks that lead ultimately to different occupations, the United States aims to educate all children in much the same way. Of course, public education is not a uniform experience for American children. The quality of education depends significantly on the wealth of the community in which a child resides, since schools are funded primarily through local property taxes.

Nevertheless, the United States through its public schools educates a broad segment of the population. Arguably, no country in the world has made an equivalent effort to give children, whatever their parents' background, an equal opportunity in life through education. This spending level on public elementary and secondary schools averages roughly $6,000 per pupil, compared with less than $4,000 per pupil in western Europe.

America's commitment to broad-based education extends to college; the United States is far and away the world leader in terms of the proportion of adults receiving a college education.[16]

The nation's education system preserves both the myth and the reality of the American Dream. The belief that success can be had by anyone who works for it could not be sustained if the education system were tailored for a privileged elite. And educational attainment is related to personal success, at least as measured by annual incomes. In fact, the gap in income between those with and those without a college education is now greater than at any time in the country's history.

In part because the public schools have such a large role in creating an equal opportunity society, they have been heavily criticized in recent years. Violence in the schools is a major parental concern. So, too, is poor performance on standardized tests, such as the Scholastic Aptitude Test (SAT). The United States is not even in the top ten nations as judged by students' test scores in science or math.[17]

Disgruntled parents have demanded changes,[18] and these demands have led some communities to allow parents to choose the public schools their children will attend. Under this policy, the schools compete for students, and those that attract the most students are rewarded with the largest budgets. Polls indicate that Americans favor such a policy by more than a 2 to 1 margin. Advocates of the policy contend that it compels school administrators and teachers to do a better job and gives students the option of rejecting a school that is performing poorly. Opponents of the policy say that it creates a few well-funded schools and a lot of poorly funded ones, yielding no net gain in educational quality. Critics also claim that the policy discriminates against poor and minority group children, whose parents are less likely to be in a position to steer them toward the better schools.

A more contentious issue is a "voucher system" that would allow parents to use tax dollars to send their children even to private or parochial schools. The recipient school would receive a voucher redeemable from the government, and the student would get a corresponding reduction in his or her private or parochial school tuition. Polls indicate that Americans are narrowly opposed to vouchers, and ballot initiatives that would have created voucher systems were defeated in 2000 by voters in several states. The major argument against a voucher system is that it would weaken the public schools by draining them of money and students. Ninety percent of school-age children attend public schools and, for the moment at least, Americans are more intent on improving the public schools than on supporting policies that would benefit private schools.

The issue of school choice goes to the heart of the issue of equal opportunity. On the one hand, an elite-centered school system widens the gap between the country's richer and poorer groups. On the other hand, making students compete with one another for the best education conforms with the country's individualistic tradition.

The Federal Role in Education: Political Differences

Education is primarily a state and local responsibility. Most school policies—from length of the school year to teachers' qualifications—are set by state legislatures and local school boards. Over 90 percent of the funds spent on schools are provided through state and local tax revenues. Federal intervention in school policy has often been resisted by states and localities, as exemplified by their response to desegregation and busing directives (see Chapter 5). Less-affluent states and localities have sought federal aid for their schools but, as indicated by the limited scope of the federal program that provides aid to poorer schools, it is difficult to get congressional support for grant programs targeted at needy schools. Few members of Congress are willing to support large appropriations for education that do not include benefits for their constituents.

Indeed it was not until 1965 that Congress enacted the first general federal aid to education legislation: the Higher Education Act and the

Elementary and Secondary Education Act. The former became the foundation for Pell Grants, federal loans to college students, and federally subsidized college work-study programs. The latter provided funding for such items as school construction, textbooks, special education, and teacher training.

These acts were not the very first federal programs in the education area. A century earlier, for example, Congress had passed the Morrill Act, which provided states with free tracts of land if the land were used to establish colleges. America's great "land grant" universities are the consequence. The G.I. bill that was enacted after World War II and that enabled millions of service veterans to attend college was another. Yet a third was the National Defense Education Act of 1958, which provided loans and special institutes for students in science and related fields. But not until the 1965 legislation did the federal government assume a broader, ongoing role in public education.

Since then, federal assistance to public schools and colleges has been an important part of their financing, albeit a small part relative to the overall amount that the nation spends on public education. Federal funds during the past two decades have been split almost equally between support for college and for public school education.

As education has become increasingly an issue of national debate, Washington officials have been drawn into it. President Clinton rejected the idea of unrestricted school choice, arguing that it would weaken the nation's public schools and make them a repository of America's poorest and most difficult-to-educate children. But Clinton proposed standardized national testing as a means of evaluating schools' performance and advocated federal grants for the purpose of renovating the nation's most outmoded school buildings. Then in 1998, Clinton persuaded reluctant congressional Republicans to accept, as part of a budget compromise, a multibillion-dollar grant that would allow the nation's overcrowded schools to hire tens of thousands of new teachers. GOP lawmakers are philosophically less inclined to federal solutions to public school problems and are politically less responsive than Democratic lawmakers to the interests of less-affluent constituents. In other words, many of the partisan and philosophical differences that affect federal welfare policy also affect federal education policy.

Nevertheless, education has become such a large political issue that national leaders of both parties have favored an expanded federal role. In his 2000 presidential campaign, Republican George W. Bush proposed more than $15 billion in new federal spending in areas such as reading programs for disadvantaged students, teacher training and recruitment, charter

The Supreme Court has held that American children are entitled to an "adequate" education but do not have the right to an "equal" education. America's public schools differ greatly in quality primarily as a result of the differences in the wealth of the communities they serve. Some public schools are overcrowded and have few facilities and little equipment. Others are very well equipped, have spacious facilities, and have small class sizes.

schools, and technology equipment. His first budgetary address to Congress as president reiterated his commitment to education, and, soon thereafter, he submitted education proposals to Congress for its consideration.

CULTURE, POLITICS, AND SOCIAL WELFARE

Surveys have repeatedly indicated that a majority of Americans are convinced that most people on welfare could get along without it if they tried. Because public assistance programs have limited public support, there are constant political pressures to reduce welfare expenditures and to weed out undeserving recipients. The unwritten principle of social welfare in America, reflecting the country's individualistic culture, is that the individual must somehow earn any social welfare benefit, or, barring that, demonstrate a convincing need for the benefit. The result is a welfare system that is both *inefficient*, in that much of the money spent on welfare never reaches the recipients, and *inequitable*, in that most of the money spent on social welfare never gets to the people who are most in need of help.

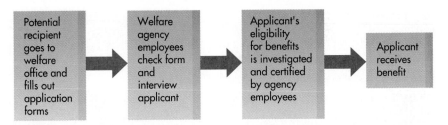

FIGURE 16-3 THE CUMBERSOME ADMINISTRATIVE PROCESS BY WHICH WELFARE RECIPIENTS GET THEIR BENEFITS

Inefficiency: The Welfare Web

The United States has by far the most intricate system of social welfare in the world. Scores of separate programs have been established to address different, often overlapping needs. A single individual in need of public assistance may qualify for many, none, or one of these programs, and the eligibility criteria are sometimes bizarre. Consider the case of Gary Myers of Springfield, Missouri, who declared bankruptcy because he could not afford to pay $1,400 in hospital bills that his family had incurred. Had Myers made exactly $4 less than his $509 monthly wage as a security guard, he would have qualified for government payment of his medical expenses. Because of the extra $4 Myers received nothing.

Beyond the question of the fairness of such rules is the question of their efficiency. The unwritten principle that the individual must somehow earn or deserve a particular benefit makes the U.S. welfare system highly labor-intensive. Consider, for example, the 1996 welfare reform bill, which limits eligibility to families with incomes below a certain level and, in most instances, to families with a single parent living in the home. Because of this requirement, the eligibility of each applicant must be periodically checked by a caseworker (see Figure 16-3). This procedure makes such programs doubly expensive; in addition to payments to the recipients, there are the costs of paying caseworkers, supervisors, and support staffs, as well as processing the extensive paperwork involved.

The administrative costs of welfare are substantially lower in Europe, since eligibility is either universal, as in the case of health care, or less stringently defined. There have been proposals to adopt a European-like system in the United States; President Nixon's attempt to establish a guaranteed annual income for every American family is an example. All of these proposals have failed to win broad support, mainly because they run counter to Americans' belief in individualism. Thus, it is not surprising that the 1996

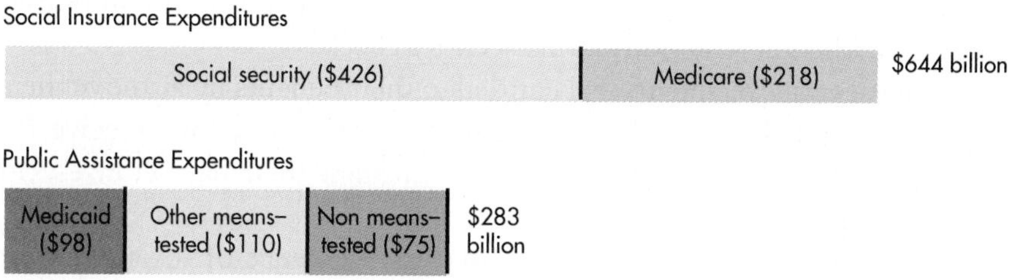

Social Insurance Expenditures

Social security ($426)	Medicare ($218)	$644 billion

Public Assistance Expenditures

Medicaid ($98)	Other means-tested ($110)	Non means-tested ($75)	$283 billion

FIGURE 16-4 FEDERAL SPENDING FOR SOCIAL INSURANCE AND PUBLIC ASSISTANCE PROGRAMS
Social insurance spending far exceeds public assistance spending. Source: U.S. Social Security Administration, 2001.

welfare bill created additional layers of welfare administration. Recipients' lifetime welfare histories have to be maintained, and states must maintain job placement and training programs. Whether the change will be cost-effective will be determined by whether large numbers of welfare recipients actually find permanent employment. Whether the change fits the American way of welfare is more easily judged: it clearly does. The reform gives the poor an incentive to succeed on their own.

Inequity: The Middle-Class Advantage

Most Americans hold to the traditional belief in individualism and self-reliance, which they generalize to other people. Although they recognize a need for programs for the poor and disadvantaged, they tend to minimize both the number of such individuals and the extent of their need. The situation means that less advantaged Americans cannot count on a great deal of political support from other sectors of society. Even the much-heralded War on Poverty of the 1960s was less a war than a skirmish. Weak middle-class support for the effort, reports that the programs were poorly administered and were not reaching the target audience, and the fiscal pressures of the Vietnam conflict combined to undermine the antipoverty effort. Congressional appropriations for the War on Poverty programs never totaled so much as $2 billion in a given year.

Social security and Medicare are another story entirely.[19] These two social insurance programs have broad public support, even though together they cost the federal government more than twice what is spent on all major public assistance programs (see Figure 16-4). A reason for the difference in public funding and approval for social security is that it benefits the majority. Most Americans are either actual or potential social security recipients.

It is good politics for elected officials to appeal to the forty million retired Americans who get a monthly social security check.

Social security recipients feel entitled to their benefits by virtue of their payroll tax contributions. As indicated earlier, however, they receive far greater benefits than they have "earned" through their payroll taxes. So they are, in a sense, getting public assistance.

It is important to note, however, that the existence of social security substantially lessens the demand for other forms of public assistance. Monthly social security keeps millions of Americans, mostly widows, out of poverty. About a fourth of social security recipients have no other significant source of income. Without social security, they would be completely dependent on public assistance programs.

Nevertheless, many social security recipients, while legally entitled to the benefits they receive, have no actual financial need for them. Only a third of social security recipients are in the lowest fifth of the population in income. Families in the top fifth of the income population receive more in federal social insurance benefits than is spent on TANF, food stamps, and housing subsidies combined.

The contradictions and difficulties of social welfare in America come together in the contrasting cases of social insurance and public assistance. Although the latter is targeted toward the truly needy, it is less acceptable politically and culturally and receives much less funding. The situation testifies to the strength of traditional American values of individualism and self-reliance and to the power of money and votes.

Social welfare, as we have seen, is the arena in which many of the conflicts of the American political system come together: individualism versus equality, Congress versus the president, national authority versus local authority, public sector versus private sector, Republicans versus Democrats, poorer versus richer, social insurance versus public assistance. The politics of welfare is a politics of contradictory values and competing interests, which ensures that it will be a contentious issue for years to come.

SUMMARY

The United States has a complex social welfare system of multiple programs addressing specific welfare needs. Each program applies only to those individuals who qualify for benefits by meeting the specific eligibility criteria. In general, these criteria are designed to reward and promote self-reliance or, when help is necessary, to ensure that laziness is not rewarded or fostered—in short, to limit benefits to those individuals who truly cannot help themselves. This approach to social welfare reflects Americans' traditional belief in individualism.

Poverty is a large and persistent problem in America. About one in seven people fall below the government-defined poverty line, and they include a disproportionate number of children, female-headed families, minority group members, and rural and inner-city dwellers. The ranks of the poor are increased by economic recessions and reduced through government welfare programs.

Welfare policy has been a partisan issue, with Democrats taking the lead on government programs to alleviate economic insecurity and Republicans acting to slow down or decentralize these initiatives. Changes in social welfare have usually occurred through presidential leadership in the context of majority support for the changes. Welfare policy has been worked out through programs to provide jobs and job training, education programs, income measures, and, especially, transfer payments through individual-benefit programs.

Individual-benefit programs fall into two broad categories: social insurance and public assistance. The former includes such programs as social security for retired workers and Medicare for the elderly. Social insurance programs are funded by payroll taxes on potential recipients, who thus, in a sense, earn the benefits they later receive. Because of this arrangement, social insurance programs have broad public support. Public assistance programs, in contrast, are funded by general tax revenues and are targeted toward needy individuals and families. These programs are not controversial in principle: most Americans believe that government should assist the truly needy. However, because of a widespread belief that most welfare recipients could get along without assistance if they tried, these programs do not have universal public support, are only modestly funded, and are politically vulnerable.

The balance between economic equality and individualism tilts more heavily toward individualism in the United States than in other advanced industrialized democracies. Entitlement to social security, for example, is not a universal right of the elderly in the United States, whereas it is elsewhere. Compared to other democracies, however, the United States attempts to more equally educate its children, a policy consistent with its cultural emphasis on equality of opportunity.

Social welfare is a contentious issue. A major reason is that opposing sides disagree fundamentally on the nature of the problem. In one view, social welfare is too costly and assists too many people who could help themselves; another view holds that social welfare is not broad enough and that too many disadvantaged Americans live in poverty. In light of these irreconcilable differences, in combination with federalism and the widely shared view that welfare programs should target specific problems, the existing system of multiple programs, despite its administrative complexity and inefficiency, has been the only politically feasible alternative.

MAJOR CONCEPTS

entitlement program	in-kind benefits
equality of opportunity	means test

negative government

positive government

poverty line

public assistance

social insurance

transfer payment

SUGGESTED READINGS AND WEB SITES

Chubb, John E., and Terry M. Moe. *Politics, Markets, and America's Schools*. Washington, D.C.: Brookings Institution, 1990. The authors recommend a new system of public education designed around parent-student choice and school competition.

Cook, Fay Lomax, and Edith J. Barrett. *Support for the American Welfare State: The Views of Congress and the Public*. New York: Columbia University Press, 1992. A thorough study of the views underlying welfare policy.

Gans, Herbert J. *The War against the Poor: The Underclass and Anti-Poverty Policy*. New York: Basic Books, 1996. A study of attitudes toward and policies affecting poverty.

Henig, Jeffrey R. *Rethinking School Choice: Limits of the Market Metaphor*. Princeton, N.J.: Princeton University Press, 1995. An argument against parental choice as the basis of public school enrollment.

Melnick, R. Shep. *Between the Lines: Interpreting Welfare Rights*. Washington, D.C.: Brookings Institution Press, 1994. An analysis of the intricate relationship between social welfare legislation and its interpretation in the courts.

Newman, Katherine S. *No Shame in My Game*. New York: Alfred A. Knopf and Russell Sage Foundation, 1999. A careful study of America's working poor.

Wilson, William Julius. *When Work Disappears: The World of the New Urban Poor*. New York: Knopf, 1996. An important analysis of jobs and poverty in the inner city.

http://wtw.doleta.gov   The U.S. Department of Labor's web site on the status of the Welfare-to-Work program, including state-by-state assessments.

http://www.nea.org   The home page of the National Education Association. It provides information on the organization's membership and policy goals.

http://www.os.dhhs.gov   The web site of the Department of Health and Human Services—the agency that is responsible for most federal social welfare programs.

http://www.ssw.umich.edu/poverty/mission.html   The web site of the University of Michigan's Program on Poverty and Social Welfare Policy. The program seeks to stimulate interest in policy issues and to transmit research findings to policymakers.

Reading 16

Saving Social Security

ROBERT D. REISCHAUER

Introduction

Social security has been one of the most successful programs ever undertaken by the federal government. For six decades, it has protected the nation's elderly from the poverty that once characterized old age. But will it do the same for today's young people when they retire? Social security recipients are paid through reserves created by payroll taxes on the current work force. But the ratio of workers to retirees will decline sharply in the coming decades and, at some point, the reserves will be exhausted. The prospect of a bankrupt social security system has prompted officials and policy analysts to consider ways to guarantee its long-term solvency. A controversial option is to invest a portion of social security reserve funds in the stock and bond markets, which could increase the rate of return on these funds but would also increase the risk that the funds would be depleted by a market crash or political manipulation. In his essay, Robert Reischauer, a prominent economist who once headed the Congressional Budget Office (CBO), argues in support of a market option that would include safeguards on the investments. President George W. Bush included a market option among his reform criteria when he set up a presidential commission on social security in 2001.

It is an unpleasant yet inescapable reality that there are three, and only three, ways to close Social Security's long run fiscal deficit. Taxes can be raised, benefits can be reduced, or the return on the trust fund's reserves can be increased. . . .

Because neither the public nor lawmakers have greeted the prospect of higher taxes or reduced spending with any enthusiasm, the option of boosting the returns on Social Security's reserves is worth close examination. While higher returns can not solve the program's long run financing problem alone, they can make the remaining problem more manageable.

Since the program's inception, the law has required that Social Security reserves be invested exclusively in securities guaranteed as to principal and interest by the federal government. Most trust fund holdings consist of special nonmarketable Treasury securities that carry the average interest rate of government notes and bonds that mature in four or more years and are outstanding at the time the special securities are issued. In addition to their low risk, these special issues have one clear advantage. They can be sold back to the Treasury at par at any time—a feature not available on publicly held notes or bonds, whose market prices fluctuate from day to day. They also have one big disadvantage—they yield relatively low rates of return.

The restriction that has been placed on Social Security's investments is unfair to program participants, both workers paying payroll taxes and beneficiaries. [The average return on social security reserve funds has been less than half the return on private investment. . . .]

In 1935, Congress ruled out trust fund investments in private stocks and bonds for good reasons. First, policymakers were concerned that the fund's managers might, on occasion, have to sell the assets at a loss, a move that would engender public criticism. Second, they feared that if the fund had to liquidate significant amounts of securities, these sales might destabilize markets, depressing the value of assets held in private portfolios and upsetting individual investors. An even more important consideration was that they feared that politicians—like themselves—might be tempted to use reserve investment policy to interfere with markets or meddle in the activities of private businesses.

The concerns that Congress had in 1935 were certainly legitimate ones. But conditions have changed over the past 64 years in ways that reduce their saliency. Stock and bond markets are far larger, less volatile, and more efficient now than they were in the 1930s. . . .

On the other hand, the pressures special interests place on lawmakers and the stresses imposed by reelection are probably greater now than they were in the past. For these reasons, many justifiably continue to be concerned about possible political interference in trust fund investment activities. Chairman Greenspan of the Federal Reserve Board has stated that he does not "believe that it is politically feasible to insulate such huge funds from government direction."

If there were no effective way to shield trust fund investment decisions from political pressures, the advantage of higher returns that a diversified investment strategy would yield would not be worth the price that would have to be paid. However, experience suggests both that concerns about political interference are exaggerated and that institutional safeguards can be constructed that would reduce the risk of interference to a de minimis level.

A number of federal government pension funds now invest in private securities. They include the Thrift Saving Plan for government workers and the pension plans of the Federal Reserve Board, the U.S. Air Force and the Tennessee Valley Authority. The managers of these pension funds have not been subject to political pressures. They have pursued only financial objectives in selecting their portfolios and have not tried to exercise any control over the companies in which they have invested.

Of course, the fact that the managers of smaller government pension funds have not been subject to political pressures provides no guarantee that the much larger and more visible Social Security system would enjoy a similar fate. Special interests might seek Congressional sponsors for resolutions restricting investments more for the publicity such limits would provide their cause than for any economic impact the directive might have if carried out. In addition, some Members might feel obliged to propose restrictions against investing in corporations that have been found to violate antitrust laws, trade restrictions, workplace health and safety regulations, or other federal limits. Political pressures might cause others to pressure the trustees to exclude investments in companies that have closed a plant in their district and moved their production facilities and jobs abroad.

For these reasons, it would be essential to enact legislation that would create a multi-tiered firewall to protect trust fund investment decisions from political pressures, one that would forestall efforts by Members of Congress or the executive branch from using trust fund investments to influence corporate policy. The first tier of such an institutional structure should be the creation of an independent agency charged with managing the trust fund's investments. This board—which could be called the Social Security Reserve Board (SSRB)—could be modeled after the Federal Reserve Board, which for over eight decades has successfully performed two politically charged tasks—controlling growth of the money supply and regulating private banks—without succumbing to political pressures. Like the governors of the Federal Reserve, the members of the SSRB should be appointed by the president and confirmed by the Senate. To ensure their independence, they should serve staggered terms of at least ten years in length. . . .

A second tier of protection should be provided by limiting the discretion given to the SSRB. The primary responsibility of the board should be to select, through competitive bids, several private sector fund managers, each of whom would be entrusted with investing a portion of the fund's reserves. . . .

A third tier of insulation from political pressures should be provided by authorizing fund managers only to make passive investments. They would be charged with investing in securities—bonds or stocks—of companies chosen to represent the broadest of market indexes, indexes that reflect all of the shares sold on the three major exchanges. In other words, the trust fund's investment would be in a total stock market index such as the Wilshire 5,000 or Wilshire 7,000 index. . . . Unlike actively managed mutual funds, there would be no discretion to pick and choose individual stocks and, therefore, no window through which political or social considerations could enter. . . .

Allowing the Social Security system to invest a portion of its growing reserves in private assets will increase the returns on the trust fund balances and reduce the size of the unavoidable payroll tax increases and benefit reductions that will be needed to eliminate the program's long-run deficit. Concerns that political interests might attempt to influence trust fund investment decisions are legitimate but institutional safeguards can be enacted into law that would reduce the possibility of such interference to a de minimis level.

SOURCE: Testimony before the House of Representatives Subcommittee on Social Security, March 3, 1999, Washington, D.C.
Robert D. Reischauer is Senior Fellow in Economic Studies at the Brookings Institution and former director of the Congressional Budget Office.

CHAPTER SEVENTEEN

Foreign and Defense Policy

We the people of the United States, in order to . . . provide for the common
defense . . . .

PREAMBLE, U.S. CONSTITUTION

I N 2000, the leaders of the world's most powerful industrial nations met for their seventh annual summit meeting. They discussed global economic stability, including a rebound in the Asian economies. They urged several lagging countries to get their banking systems in order. They also tackled issues thrust on them by recent events, including the change in leadership in Russia.

The G-7 summit meeting sharply dramatized the changing nature of world politics and the role of the United States in it. America's once bitter enemy, Russia, was no longer a military threat. It was a struggling nation, trying with only a small amount of success to shed its communist past. In fact, two of the countries at the summit, Germany and Japan, were closer to the position of rivals of the United States than was Russia. The rivalry, however, was economic in nature; Germany and Japan had trade surpluses with the United States and were competitors in the global marketplace.

Yet the focus of the summit was cooperation rather than competition. The underlying assumption was that the world's most powerful nations could all gain if they set aside their differences and worked together to promote economic growth and limit political instability.

As the economic summit illustrates, national security is an issue of economic vitality as well as one of military strength.[1] The primary goal of U.S. foreign policy is the preservation of the American state. This objective requires military readiness in order to protect the territorial integrity and international interests of the United States. But the American state also represents a society of more than 250 million people, whose livelihood depends in significant part upon the nation's position in the international economy.[2] Through participation in global policies that foster economic

511

Since the end of the Cold War, U.S. national security
policy has increasingly been defined in the context of
America's position in the global economy. Pictured here
is the Seattle harbor, one of the nation's busiest ports.
Of the fifty states, Washington is the most economically
dependent on international trade.

growth, the United States can secure the jobs and trade that are essential to
the maintenance of a high standard of living.

The national security policies of the United States embrace an extraordinary array of activities—so many, in fact, that they could not possibly be
addressed adequately in an entire book, much less a single chapter. There
are some 160 countries in the world, and the United States has relations of
one kind or another—military, diplomatic, economic—with all of them.
This chapter narrows the subject by focusing on a few main ideas:

★ *Since World War II, the United States has acted in the role of world leader, which has substantially affected its military, diplomatic, and economic policies.*

★ *The United States maintains a high degree of defense preparedness, which mandates a substantial level of defense spending and a worldwide deployment of U.S. conventional and strategic forces.*

★ *Changes in the international marketplace have led to increased economic interdependence among nations, which has had a marked influence on the U.S. economy and on its security planning; increasingly, national security has been defined in economic rather than military terms.*

THE ROOTS OF U.S. FOREIGN AND DEFENSE POLICY

For nearly half a century, U.S. defense policy was defined mostly by conflict with the Soviet Union. From the Berlin airlift in 1948 to the Vietnam escalation in 1965 to the Star Wars initiative in 1983, the United States seemed willing to pay any price to halt the spread of communism. Then, in the late 1980s, the Soviet empire suddenly and dramatically began to fall apart. In December 1991, the Soviet Union itself ceased to exist. For decades, there had been two superpowers, the Soviet Union and the United States. Now there is only one.

With the end of the cold war, the United States has had to redefine its foreign and defense policies. The country is still at the center of world politics, but its challenges have changed: they are less military and more economic.[3] A strong domestic base, more than a mighty military arsenal, has become the key to global success.

Although the age of superpower conflict is over, the changes in foreign and defense policy that lie ahead will take shape within a context defined by that era. Decisions made in the past carry into the future, both informing and channeling new ones.

The United States as Global Superpower

Before World War II, the United States was an **isolationist** country, deliberately avoiding a large role in world affairs. A different America emerged from the war. It had more land, sea, and air power than any other country in the world, a huge military-industrial base, and several hundred overseas military bases. The United States had become an **internationalist** country, deeply involved in the affairs of other nations.

U.S. national security policy after World War II was built upon a concern with the power and intentions of the Soviet Union.[4] At the Yalta Conference in 1945, U.S. president Franklin Roosevelt and Soviet leader Josef Stalin had agreed that East European nations were entitled to self-determination within a Soviet zone of influence, but Stalin breached the agreement. After the war, Soviet occupation forces assisted the communist parties in eastern Europe in capturing state power, usually by coercive means. In the words of Britain's wartime prime minister, Winston Churchill, an "iron curtain" had fallen across Europe.

THE DOCTRINE OF CONTAINMENT   The Soviet Union's aggressive action led U.S. policymakers to assess Soviet aims.[5] Particularly noteworthy was the evaluation of George Kennan, a U.S. diplomat and expert on Soviet affairs. Kennan concluded that invasions from the West in World Wars I and II had made the Soviet Union (which had lost twenty-five million lives in World War II, compared with U.S. losses of five hundred thousand) almost paranoid in its concern for regional security. Although Kennan believed that the USSR would someday mature into a responsible world power, he contended that it was an immediate threat to neighboring countries. He counseled a policy of "long-term, patient but firm, and vigilant containment."[6] Kennan's analysis contributed to the formulation of the doctrine of **containment,** which was based on the idea that the Soviet Union was an aggressor nation that had to be stopped from achieving its territorial ambitions.

Harry S Truman, who became president after Roosevelt's death in 1945, rejected Kennan's view that the USSR was motivated by a concern for *regional* security. Truman saw the Soviet Union as an aggressive ideological foe that was bent on *global* domination and that could be stopped only by the forceful use of U.S. power. Truman's view was based on assumptions derived from territorial concessions made to Germany's Adolf Hitler by Britain and France at a conference in Munich in 1938; rather than appeasing Hitler, these concessions convinced him that Germany could bully its way to further gains. The idea that appeasement only encourages further aggression was the *lesson of Munich*, and it became the dominant view of U.S. policymakers in the postwar period.

THE COLD WAR   Developments in the late 1940s embroiled the United States in a **cold war** with the Soviet Union. The term refers to the fact that the two countries were not directly engaged in actual combat (a "hot war") but were locked into a deep-seated hostility, which lasted forty-five years. From the United States' perspective, the cold war was an extension of containment policy and included support for governments threatened by communist takeovers. In June 1950, when the Soviet-backed North Koreans invaded South Korea, President Truman immediately committed U.S. troops to the conflict, which ended in stalemate and the loss of thirty-five thousand American lives.

The Limits of American Power: The Vietnam War

For the United States, a major turning point in foreign policy was the Vietnam War. It was the most costly application of the containment doctrine: fifty-eight thousand American soldiers lost their lives.

Vietnam was part of France's colonial empire until the French army was defeated in 1954 by guerrilla forces, which were led by Ho Chi Minh, a nationalist with communist sympathies. The Geneva conference that ended the war resulted in a partitioning of Vietnam: the northern region was placed under Ho Chi Minh's leadership and the southern region under anticommunist leaders. The United States provided economic assistance to South Vietnam, anticipating that its government would quickly develop the public support that would enable it to prevail in a Vietnam unification election that was scheduled for 1956. When it became apparent that Ho Chi Minh would easily win the election, the United States helped to get it canceled and began to increase its military assistance to the South Vietnamese army. By the time of President John F. Kennedy's assassination in 1963, the United States had about seventeen thousand military advisers in South Vietnam. Lyndon Johnson sharply escalated the war in 1965 by committing U.S. combat units to the conflict. By the late 1960s, 550,000 Americans were fighting in South Vietnam.

U.S. forces in Vietnam were technically superior in combat to the communist fighters, but they were fighting an enemy they could not easily identify in a society they did not fully understand.[7] Vietnam was a guerrilla war, with no front lines and few set battles. As the conflict dragged on, American public opinion, most visibly among the young, turned against the war, which contributed to President Johnson's decision not to run for reelection in 1968. Public opinion forced Richard Nixon, who became president in 1969, to aim not for victory but for a gradual disengagement. U.S. combat troops left Vietnam in 1973 and, two years later, North Vietnamese forces concluded their takeover of the country.

In the jungle warfare of Vietnam, American soldiers had difficulty finding the enemy and adapting to guerrilla tactics.

DÉTENTE   America's defeat in Vietnam forced U.S. policymakers to reconsider the country's international role. The *lesson of Vietnam* was that there were limits to the country's ability to assert its will in the world. Nixon claimed that the United States could no longer act as the "Lone Ranger" for the free world and sought to reduce tensions with communist countries.[8] The new philosophy was reflected by the Helsinki Accords of 1971, in which the United States accepted the territorial boundaries of eastern Europe that had been established at the end of World War II. Then Nixon took a historic journey to the People's Republic of China in 1972, the first official contact with that country since the communists had taken power in 1949.

Another indication of a change in policy was the Strategic Arms Limitation Talks (SALT), which began in 1969. The SALT talks presumed that the United States and the Soviet Union each had an interest in retaining enough nuclear weapons to deter the other from an attack, but that neither side had an interest in mutual destruction. Along with the lowering of East-West trade barriers, these efforts marked the start of a new era of communication and cooperation, or **détente** (a French word meaning "a relaxing"), between the United States and the Soviet Union.[9]

DISINTEGRATION OF THE "EVIL EMPIRE"   Although the period of détente during the 1970s marked a major shift in U.S.–Soviet relations, it did not last. The Soviet invasion of Afghanistan in 1979 convinced U.S. leaders that the USSR was still bent on expansion and threatened Western interests in the oil-rich Middle East. Ronald Reagan, elected president in 1980, called for a renewed hard line toward the Soviet Union, which he described as the "evil empire."[10]

U.S. policymakers did not fully realize it at the time, but the Soviet Union was collapsing under its isolation from Western technology and markets, its inefficient centralized command economy, and its efforts to keep up with the Reagan administration's arms spending. In March 1985, Mikhail Gorbachev became the Soviet leader and proclaimed a need to restructure the Soviet society, an initiative known as *perestroika*. He also ordered the withdrawal of Soviet troops from Afghanistan (which had become his country's Vietnam) and sought to reduce tensions with the United States.

Gorbachev's efforts came too late to save the Soviet Union. In 1989, the withdrawal of Soviet troops from eastern Europe accelerated a prodemocracy movement that was already under way in the region. Poland initiated major reforms. Hungary dismantled the "iron curtain" that had blocked free travel to Austria. Then, in November, the Berlin Wall between East and West Germany—the most visible symbol of the separation of East and West—came down. On December 8, 1991, the leaders of the Russian, Belarus, and Ukrainian republics declared that the Soviet Union no longer existed.

A New World Order

The end of the cold war prompted President George Bush to call for a "new world order." His formulation abandoned the assumption that world affairs are a zero-sum game, in which for one nation to gain something, another nation has to lose. Bush contended that nations can move forward together. The concept emphasized **multilateralism:** the idea that major nations should act together in response to problems and crises.[11]

Multilateralism characterized the U.S. response to Iraq's invasion of Kuwait in August 1990. President Bush worked through the United Nations, which passed resolutions demanding the unconditional withdrawal of Iraqi forces and imposed a trade embargo on Iraqi oil. The military force arrayed against Iraq was also nominally a UN force, although it was led by a U.S. commander and consisted mostly of U.S. troops. Several countries, including Germany and Japan, supported the effort with money instead of troops.

The Gulf operation was successful from a strictly military perspective. Despite the size and combat readiness of Iraq's army, the shooting war ended quickly, prompting President Bush to claim that the United States had "kicked the Vietnam syndrome [the legacy of America's defeat in Vietnam] once and for all." But the outcome of the Gulf War was much less successful from another perspective. Bush's decision to stop the war short of a march on Baghdad left Saddam Hussein in power, and he responded by repressing ethnic and religious minorities in Iraq and by defying UN directives that called for the destruction of Iraq's weapons of mass destruction. The United States has been forced to conduct periodic air strikes on Iraqi installations, including attacks in 2001, which have helped to contain Hussein but have not dislodged him from power.

Multilateralism has also been applied in the Balkans. In 1992, the Bosnian Serbs, supported by the Serb-dominated Yugoslav government, attacked Muslims and Croats in Bosnia. Forced evacuations and mass executions were part of the Serbs' effort to rid areas of Bosnia of rival ethnic and religious groups. Finally, in 1995, after UN economic sanctions and limited air strikes had failed to deter Serb aggression, planes of the United States and its Western allies undertook a bombing campaign that led to U.S.-negotiated peace talks (the Dayton Accords). The talks brought an end to hostilities and the deployment to Bosnia of sixty thousand peacekeeping troops (including twenty thousand from the United States). Whether this action will result in lasting peace in Bosnia is yet to be determined; the peacekeeping force, which was scheduled to remain in Bosnia for two years, is still there, serving as a buffer between the contending parties.

War in the Balkans flared again in 1999, after the Yugoslav Serbs began a campaign of "ethnic cleansing" in the Serbian province of Kosovo, which had a population that was 90 percent ethnic Albanian. After failed attempts at a negotiated settlement, planes from the NATO countries (North Atlantic Treaty Organization, discussed below) attacked Serbia. (Yugoslavia is a federation that includes Serbia and Montenegro.) The mountainous terrain made air power less effective than it had been in the Iraqi desert, and the Serb army and militia units intensified their campaign against the ethnic Albanians, which created a refugee problem on a scale not seen in Europe since World War II. The refugees fled into neighboring Macedonia and Albania, which lacked the resources to handle the influx. The conflict also increased tensions between Russia and the West; Russia is a traditional ally of the Serbs and vehemently opposed the NATO action. The war with Serbia threatened to destabilize the entire region, and some foreign policy analysts concluded that NATO's military intervention had worsened an already bleak situation. Others argued that "Operation Allied Force" (as the NATO operation was officially labeled) was the only option left to Western leaders. Serbian president Slobodan Milosevic had blatantly pursued his campaign of ethnic cleansing, even in the face of Western economic sanctions and the threat of indictment by an international war crimes tribunal. After weeks of intensive bombing, Milosevic pulled his troops out of Kosovo. Ethnic Albanians moved back in, and despite the presence of UN peacekeeping troops, commenced revenge attacks on some of the Serbs who remained.

As these examples indicate, multilateralism has been only somewhat successful as a strategy for resolving international conflicts. With the deployment of enough resources, the world's major powers can intervene with some success in many parts of the developing world. However, these interventions are not always popular at home and offer no guarantee of long-term success. Regional and internal conflicts typically stem from enduring ethnic, religious, factional, or national hatreds, or from chronic problems such as government corruption, famine, and overcrowding. Even if these hatreds or problems can be momentarily eased, they are often too deep-seated to be permanently resolved. This fact contributed to President George W. Bush's declaration that his administration would in most instances refrain from intervening in regional conflicts.

THE PROCESS OF FOREIGN AND MILITARY POLICYMAKING

National security is unlike other areas of government policy because it rests on relations with powers outside rather than within a country. Nations have sovereignty within their recognized territory; each nation is the ultimate governing authority over this territory and the people within it. In reality, of course, the world is not composed of equal sovereign states. Some are more powerful than others, and the strong sometimes bully the weak. Nevertheless, there is no international body that is recognized by all nations as the final (sovereign) authority on disputes between them.

As a result, the chief instruments of national security policy—diplomacy, military force, economic exchange, and intelligence gathering—differ from those of domestic policy.

The Policymaking Instruments

Diplomacy is the process of negotiation between countries. In most cases, nations prefer to settle their differences by talking rather than by fighting. Through negotiation, countries can usually reach agreement on common (mutual) problems. By definition, acts of diplomacy involve negotiation between two (*bilateral*) or more (*multilateral*) nations.

Military power is a second instrument of foreign policy, and it can be used *unilaterally*—that is, by a single nation acting alone. Most countries use military power as a defensive measure; they maintain forces, or enter into military alliances with other countries, in order to protect themselves from potential aggressors. Throughout the history of nations, however, there have always been a few countries that use military force more actively. The United States is such a nation. In the nineteenth century, it used force to take territory from the Indian tribes and from Mexico and Spain. Although the United States has not pursued territorial goals since then, it has otherwise made frequent use of its military power. Recent examples include the unilateral invasions of Grenada in 1983, Panama in 1989, Haiti in 1994, and the multilateral war against Iraq in 1991 and bombing of Serbs in 1995 and 1999.

Economic exchange is a third instrument of world politics. This form of international relations usually takes one of two forms: trade or assistance. Trade among nations is the more important form. Nearly all countries aspire to a strong trading position so as to have access to outside products and markets for their products. Some countries, however, are so weak economically that they require assistance from more prosperous countries. This assistance is typically also designed to help the stronger partner by providing it a market for its goods.

A fourth instrument of world politics is intelligence gathering, which is the process of monitoring other countries' activities. For many reasons, but primarily because all nations pursue their individual self-interest, each nation keeps a watchful eye on the others.

The Policymaking Machinery

In the case of the United States, the lead actor in the application of these four instruments of foreign policy is the president. As we indicated in Chapter 12 and will discuss later in this chapter, the president shares power and responsibility for foreign and military policy with Congress, but the president has the stronger claim to leadership because of the constitutional roles of commander in chief, chief diplomat, and chief executive.

The president has an executive agency, the National Security Council (NSC), that provides advice on foreign and military issues. The NSC is chaired by the president; it includes the vice-president and the secretaries of state and defense as full members and the director of the Central Intelligence

In a ceremony symbolizing America's role as world leader, President Clinton brought Palestinian leader Yasser Arafat (left) and Israeli prime minister Benjamin Netanyahu together for a historic handshake after the signing of an interim Mideast peace accord in 1998. (In this photo, King Hussein of Jordan—second from left and now deceased—looks on.) However, the peace process fell apart in 2000 as Palestinians and Israelis engaged in bitter fighting.

Agency (CIA) and the chairman of the Joint Chiefs of Staff as advisory members. Since State, Defense, and the CIA often have conflicting and self-centered views of national security, the NSC acts to keep the president in charge by providing a broader perspective. The NSC's staff of experts is directed by the president's national security adviser, who, with an office in the White House and access to defense, diplomatic, and intelligence sources, has become influential in the formulation of U.S. policy.

The complexity of international politics makes it impossible for the president or any government agency to fully control U.S. policy. Moreover, as a world power, the United States relies upon outside institutions, such as the United Nations, to pursue some of its policy objectives. The key organizational units in the foreign policy area can be categorized according to their primary functions—defense, intelligence, diplomacy, and trade.

DEFENSE ORGANIZATIONS The Department of Defense (DOD), which has roughly 1.3 million uniformed personnel and seven hundred thousand civilian employees, is responsible for the military security of the United States. DOD was created in 1947 when the three military services— the army, navy, and air force—were placed under the secretary of defense.

Each service has its own secretary, but they all report to the defense secretary, who represents all the services in relations with Congress and the president. Each service naturally regards its mission and budget as more important than those of the other services. The defense secretary helps reduce the adverse effects of these interservice rivalries.

Of the country's military alliances, the North Atlantic Treaty Organization (NATO) is the most important. NATO was created as a "forward defense" against a possible Soviet invasion of western Europe. The NATO forces, which include troops of the United States, Canada, and most western European countries, conduct joint military exercises and engage in joint strategic and tactical military planning. After the demise of the Soviet Union, NATO was restructured as a smaller, more flexible force that might deal with new risks, such as international terrorism and ethnic rivalries. NATO's attack on Serbia in 1999 was the first-ever military campaign for the alliance.

In 1997, NATO expanded its membership to include three countries of eastern Europe, a change Russia opposed. Poland, Hungary, and the Czech Republic were once part of the Soviet military alliance (the Warsaw Pact countries), and Russia views NATO expansion as a threat to its interests. NATO leaders see an expanded European alliance as the best guarantee of lasting peace on the continent. (In 1999, European nations decided to create their own collective military force; the long-term implications for NATO are unclear.)

INTELLIGENCE ORGANIZATIONS　Foreign and military policy require a high level of knowledge about what is happening in the world.[12] Responsibility for gathering such information falls on specialized federal agencies, including the Central Intelligence Agency; the National Security Agency, which specializes in electronic communications analysis; and intelligence agencies within the Departments of State and Defense.

With the decline of the Soviet threat, intelligence agencies are giving increased attention to drug trafficking, industrial espionage, and terrorism. These efforts are a deterrent but cannot prevent all such activities. The U.S. embassies in Kenya and Tanzania, for example, had no advance warning when terrorist bombs destroyed them in 1998, killing several hundred people, including twelve Americans.

DIPLOMATIC ORGANIZATIONS　The U.S. Department of State conducts most of the country's day-to-day business with foreign countries through its embassies, headed by U.S. ambassadors. State's traditional duties include negotiating political agreements with other nations, protecting U.S. citizens and interests abroad, promoting U.S. economic interests, gathering foreign intelligence, and representing the United States abroad.

American diplomatic efforts also take place through international organizations, such as the Organization of American States (OAS) and the United Nations. The breakdown of the Soviet bloc in 1989 renewed the possibility that the world's great powers could work together to achieve common goals. Some analysts believe that the UN may finally be able to play the prominent role in international affairs that was envisioned for it when it was chartered. International terrorism, famine, peacekeeping, and drug trafficking are among the problems that the UN has recently addressed.

ECONOMIC ORGANIZATIONS   The shift in emphasis in global affairs from military forces to economic markets has brought to the fore a new set of government agencies, those representing economic sectors. The agriculture, commerce, labor, and treasury departments are playing increasingly important roles in foreign affairs. In addition, some specialty agencies, such as the Federal Trade Commission and the Export-Import Bank of the United States, are involved in international trade and finance.

The United States also works through major international organizations that promote goals, such as economic development and free trade, that are consistent with U.S. policy objectives. The newest of these international organizations is the World Trade Organization (WTO), which was created in 1995 and is the formal institution through which most nations negotiate general rules of international trade. The WTO also adjudicates disputes over these rules. In 1998, for example, U.S.–based Kodak films lost a dispute with the Japanese film company Fuji. Kodak had charged that Fuji was involved in unfair marketing practices that prevented Kodak from gaining a significant share of film sales in Japan. The WTO sided with Fuji's argument that its sales volume was a result of customer preference and the quality of its film.

The World Bank and the International Monetary Fund (IMF) are older institutions. Created at the 1944 Bretton Woods Conference by the United States and Great Britain, they are designed to assist developing countries. The World Bank makes long-term loans to poor countries for capital investment projects, such as the construction of dams, power plants, highways, and factories, that will promote economic growth. In contrast, the IMF makes short-term loans so that countries experiencing temporary problems will not collapse economically or resort to ruinous practices, such as the imposition of high tariffs. In 1997 and 1998, for example, the IMF made multi-billion-dollar loans to Korea, Thailand, and other Asian countries whose economies had gone into a tailspin from poor investment practices and currency devaluation.

THE MILITARY DIMENSION OF NATIONAL SECURITY POLICY

The dissolution of the Soviet Union brought about the first significant scaling back of U.S. defense spending since the end of the Vietnam War. Nevertheless, the United States spends far more on defense, in both relative and absolute terms, than its allies. On a per capita basis, U.S. military spending is more than twice that of other members of the NATO alliance (see box: How the United States Compares). The U.S. defense budget is second to none in the world, but so is the military power it buys. During the Gulf War, the world's fourth largest army, Iraq's, was no match for the United States' superior military equipment and technology. The war lasted about six weeks, with fewer than two hundred U.S. casualties, but left an estimated fifty thousand to one hundred thousand Iraqi dead.

Defense Capability

The United States owes its status as the world's only superpower in part to the strength of its conventional forces. The U.S. Navy has a dozen aircraft carriers, nearly one hundred attack submarines, and hundreds of other fighting and supply ships. The U.S. Air Force has thousands of high-performance aircraft. The U.S. Army has more than five hundred thousand troops on active duty, and they are amply supported by tanks, artillery pieces, armored personnel carriers, and attack helicopters.

Assessments of military power have traditionally been based on the number of planes, tanks, and other weapons a nation possesses, and how they compare to those of potential adversaries. But, increasingly, these assessments must also account for the ability of a nation to connect these weapons to information. Surveillance devices (such as satellites), high-speed computers, and sophisticated software give military commanders the ability to gather, process, and disseminate information about tactical and strategic situations and thus to direct the use of available weaponry in the most efficient and effective way. The United States has a substantial lead in this technology and will retain it for years to come.

Even though there is a "revolution in military power," older weapons systems are still a part of the American arsenal. The nuclear weapons that

HOW THE UNITED STATES COMPARES

The Burden of Military Spending

The United States bears a disproportionate share of the defense costs of the NATO alliance. The U.S. military establishment is huge and is deployed all over the world, and the taxpayers spend more than $250 billion per year to maintain it. These expenditures directly account for roughly 5 percent of the U.S. gross national product (GNP). By comparison, defense spending by Germany, Italy, and Canada accounts for 3 percent or less of their GNPs. The percentages for Britain and France are higher but not as high as for the United States. Japan, which is not part of NATO, spends only 1 percent of its GNP on defense.

The United States has pressured its allies to carry a larger share of the defense burden, but these countries have resisted, contending that the cost would be too high and that their security would not be substantially improved. A partial exception to this situation was the Persian Gulf War. U.S. troops and equipment accounted for the bulk of the military strength arrayed against Iraq, but the financial cost of the war effort was borne by other countries. Germany, Japan, Saudi Arabia, and Kuwait were among the countries that helped fund the war.

The chart below indicates the approximate per capita level of defense spending in the United States and countries with which it is closely allied.

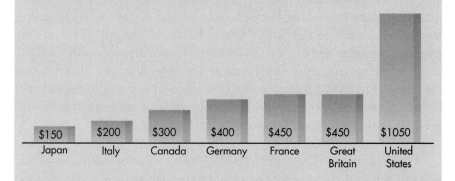

$150	$200	$300	$400	$450	$450	$1050
Japan	Italy	Canada	Germany	France	Great Britain	United States

SOURCE: OECD and Defense Department statistics.

starkly defined the nation's cold war with the Soviet Union are an example. During the cold war, the United States followed a policy of **deterrence,** based on the notion that the Soviet Union could be prevented from launching a nuclear attack by the knowledge that the United States would retaliate in kind.[13] Nuclear deterrence remains a part of America's defense capability.

The Uses of Military Power

U.S. military forces have been trained for or called upon for six types of military action.

UNLIMITED NUCLEAR WARFARE   The idea of an all-out nuclear war was always too horrible to imagine, but the fear of nuclear holocaust has diminished since the cold war ended. The United States and Russia have reduced their nuclear arsenals and have created monitoring systems that are designed to reduce the possibility that either side could launch a surprise attack. Nevertheless, both sides retain their capacity for a full-scale nuclear war. America's nuclear weapons are deployed in what is called the "nuclear triad," which refers to the three ways in which these weapons can be launched—by land-based missiles, submarine-based missiles, and bombers. The triad provides a "second-strike capability": the ability to absorb a first-strike nuclear attack and survive with enough nuclear power for massive retaliation (second strike).

LIMITED NUCLEAR WARFARE   Some experts believe that while the risk of an all-out nuclear attack on the United States diminished with the end of the cold war, the possibility that a single nuclear weapon might be used against the United States may have increased. A major concern arising from the breakup of the Soviet Union has been control of its nuclear weapons, strategic and tactical. In addition, terrorist groups and "outlaw" regimes, such as Iraq, are a threat because the technology and materials that are required to build nuclear weapons are more widely accessible than ever before. Accordingly, the United States, Russia, and other nuclear powers are cooperating to reduce the spread of nuclear weapons.

UNLIMITED CONVENTIONAL WARFARE   The end of the cold war has also reduced the prospect of an unlimited conventional war. A great part of U.S. military preparedness and strategy in the past half century was based on the scenario of an invasion of western Europe by the Soviet Union and its allies. Even if the cold war should begin anew, Russia or any other part of the former Soviet Union would require years to build its military capacity to the point where it could pose a credible threat to Europe. Since the end of the cold war, U.S. policy has aimed to prevent a resurgence of aggressive Russian nationalism. Through economic and other forms of assistance and encouragement, the United States in conjunction with other industrialized nations has sought to assist Russia in a transition toward a more open and democratic political system.

LIMITED CONVENTIONAL WARFARE   Recent conflicts in the Gulf and the Balkans have demonstrated that the United States has the military capacity to punish a well-armed foe. These conflicts have not demonstrated, however, that limited conventional wars routinely produce satisfactory results over the longer term. The reason is simple enough. If a political problem can be easily resolved, there is almost never a reason to apply military force. Diplomatic, economic, and other forms of intervention are normally sufficient to achieve a resolution. Limited conventional warfare comes into play when other methods fail—that is, when the division between the contending parties is too deep to be resolved peacefully or when an aggressor is unrelenting. However, military force is unlikely to correct the problem that triggered the military response. Thus, in the Persian Gulf and Kosovo, military intervention by the United States punished the aggressor party but did not settle the underlying dispute.

Before the 1970s, limited conventional warfare was seen as an instrument of containment policy. Since then, some analysts have questioned whether the United States has a coherent strategy for the limited use of its military power. They argue that U.S. intervention has been sporadic and restricted by a determination to avoid casualties, which results in a reliance on air power even in those situations where military objectives would require the full use of ground forces. They cite the continuing threat that Iraq poses in the Gulf region and that Serbs pose in the Balkans as evidence of the lack of a coherent strategy.

U.S. policymakers have defended the tendency to rely on air power by saying that the American public, since Vietnam, has been unwilling to support military operations that would incur high casualties and that, in any event, the strategic goal did not include total victory. Said a Bush administration official about the Gulf War: "The President was not prepared to pay the political price that increased American casualties would have involved or to take responsibility for putting Iraq back together after an unconditional surrender or to figure out how to contain the power of Iran and Syria once the Iraqi regime was destroyed."[14]

COUNTERINSURGENCY   The Vietnam conflict was an **insurgency,** an uprising by irregular forces against an established government. In most Third World countries, insurgencies originate in the grievances of people who are struggling against the monopoly of economic and political power by a ruling elite. In the past, the insurgents often received support in the form of military equipment from the Soviet Union. Most insurgencies were therefore seen by the United States as a threat to its political and economic interests.

U.S. involvement in Third World insurgencies dropped sharply after Vietnam and diminished even further with the end of the cold war. Neither the American public nor U.S. officials have wanted to involve the nation deeply in such wars, although more limited activities, such as the training and equipping of foreign troops, are a part of U.S. defense policy.

POLICE-TYPE ACTION   With the end of the cold war, U.S. policy-makers have begun to pay closer attention to other global problems, including drug trafficking, political instability, population movement, and terrorism. The U.S. military has become increasingly involved with these problems. U.S. peacekeeping missions in Somalia, the Balkans, and Haiti are examples, as is the use of U.S. military advisers in drug-interdiction operations in Latin America. U.S. military personnel have also been used to stop "boat people" from Cuba, Haiti, and other Caribbean islands from entering the United States illegally.

U.S. military commanders have been reluctant to expand their mission to include police-type actions, such as immigration control, that traditionally have been a civilian responsibility. But given the high cost of keeping a large defense force, the absence of a highly visible and dangerous enemy such as the former Soviet Union, and the increase in the types of problems that require police-type action, it is likely that the pressure to use U.S. troops in unconventional ways will continue.

The Politics of National Defense

All Americans would agree that the physical security of the United States is of paramount concern. The consensus breaks down, however, on specific issues. The Vietnam conflict created deep and lasting divisions of opinion over the proper uses of America's military capacity. In contrast, U.S. policy in the Persian Gulf crisis had majority support from start to end.

PUBLIC OPINION AND ELITE CONFLICT   Defense policy is a mix of *majoritarian* and *elite* politics. On issues of broad national concern, majority opinion is a vital component.[15] It was public opinion, for example, that ultimately forced U.S. policymakers to withdraw American troops from Vietnam and Somalia.

Debates over foreign and defense policy, however, typically take place among political elites.[16] Most citizens are not interested enough to contribute to most of these debates. Few Americans, for example, can name even half the countries in Africa, much less speak knowledgeably about their politics. This situation gives foreign policy experts and officials wide latitude in determining policy.

THE MILITARY-INDUSTRIAL COMPLEX   Political disputes over defense policy are more than honest differences of opinion among people. They also involve billions of dollars in jobs and contracts. In fiscal year 2000, the U.S. defense budget was roughly $250 billion, or nearly 5 percent of the gross national product. A high level of defense spending has been justified by reference to the nation's security needs. However, an alternative explanation for high defense spending points to the demands of the U.S. armed services and defense firms. In his 1961 Farewell Address, President Dwight D. Eisenhower warned against the "unwarranted influence" and "misplaced power" of what he termed "the military-industrial complex."

The **military-industrial complex** has three components: the military establishment, the industries that manufacture weapons, and the members of Congress from states and districts that depend heavily on the arms industry. In other words, the military-industrial complex is an aggregation of interests that benefit from a high level of defense spending, regardless of whether these expenditures can be justified from the standpoint of national security. Many members of Congress are eager to approve arms contracts (or at least reluctant to oppose them) because of the economic impact such contracts have on constituents. The B-1 bomber, for example, was built with the help of 5,200 subcontractors located in forty-eight states and in all but a handful of congressional districts.

Without doubt, some proportion of U.S. defense spending reflects the workings of the military-industrial complex.[17] The problem is that no one knows exactly what this proportion is, and the estimates vary widely.

THE ECONOMIC DIMENSION OF NATIONAL SECURITY POLICY

Economic considerations are a vital component of national security policy. In the simplest sense, economic strength is a prerequisite of military strength: a powerful defense establishment can only be maintained by a country that is economically well-off. However, in a broader and more important sense, economic prosperity enables a people to "secure" their way of life. As President Eisenhower said, it is folly to weaken at home what one is trying to strengthen abroad.

The cold war sometimes hid the essential truth of this observation. Global power, in addition to being a means by which nations achieved other goals, became an end in itself. The Soviet Union paid the highest price. In the end, its status as a military superpower was achieved at the expense of economic growth and development, and ultimately led to its collapse.[18] The United States may also have paid a substantial price. In a widely read book, *The Rise and Fall of the Great Powers*, Paul Kennedy concluded that the United States had succumbed to "imperial overstretch" by straining its resources to maintain its global military presence and, in the process, weakening its domestic economic base.[19]

A Changing World Economy

However, some aspects of U.S. superpower policy had clear economic benefits. The best example is the European Recovery Plan, better known as the Marshall Plan. Proposed in 1947 and named after one of its chief architects,

Microsoft's Bill Gates speaks to an audience about his firm's international scope. Global trade opportunities for American business firms have become an increasingly important objective of U.S. foreign policy.

the widely respected General George Marshall, it is perhaps the boldest and most successful U.S. foreign policy initiative of the twentieth century. It called for $3 billion in immediate aid for the postwar rebuilding of Europe, with an additional $10 billion or so to follow. The Marshall Plan was unprecedented both in its scope (today, the equivalent cost would be more than $100 billion) and in its implications—for the first time, the United States had committed itself to a continuing major role in European affairs. Through the Marshall Plan, the countries of western Europe regained economic and political stability in a relatively short time.

Apart from enabling the countries of western Europe to better confront the perceived Soviet military and political threat, the Marshall Plan was also designed to meet the economic needs of the United States. Wartime production had lifted the country out of the Great Depression, but the end of the war in 1945 brought a recession and renewed fears of hard times. A rejuvenated western Europe furnished a market for U.S. goods. In effect, western Europe became a junior partner within a system of global trade that worked to the advantage of the United States.

Since then, major changes have taken place in the world economy. Germany and Japan have become economic rivals of the United States. Trade with these countries has resulted in a deficit for the United States, particularly in the case of trade with Japan. The United States imports billions more annually in goods and services from Japan than it exports to that country. In addition, western Europe, including Germany, has become a less receptive market for U.S. goods. European countries are now each other's best customers, trading among themselves through the European Union (EU).

In economic terms, the world can best be described as tripolar—in other words, economic power is concentrated in three centers. One center is the United States, which produces roughly 20 percent of the world's goods and services. Another center is Japan, which accounts for 10 percent of the world's economy; China and its fast-growing economy can also be located in this center. The third and largest economic center, with more than 25 percent of the world's gross product, is the EU, which includes Belgium, Denmark, France, Germany, Great Britain, Greece, Ireland, Italy, Luxembourg, the Netherlands, Portugal, Spain, Sweden, Finland, and Austria.

By a few indicators, the United States is the weakest of the three economic centers: it has the largest national debt and the worst trade imbalance. In other ways, however, the United States is the strongest of the three economic powers. Its economy is more well-rounded. Like the EU and Japan, the United States has a strong industrial base, but, unlike Japan, it also has a strong agricultural sector and, unlike both Japan and the EU, it has abundant natural resources. Its vast fertile plains have made it the world's leading agricultural producer. The United States ranks among the top three countries worldwide in production of wheat, corn, potatoes, peanuts, cotton, eggs, cattle, and pigs. As for natural resources, the United States ranks among the top five nations in copper, uranium, lead, sulfur, zinc, coal, gold, iron ore, natural gas, silver, and magnesium.[20]

As we discussed in Chapter 15, the United States also ranks highest in the world in terms of its global economic competitiveness. This ranking was assigned by the Switzerland-based Institute for Management Development, which bases its competitiveness surveys on countries' capacity to generate wealth. The United States owes its position to such factors as the strength of its domestic economy and its technical know-how.[21]

This competitive advantage has been evident since the early 1990s. As Asia and parts of Europe have struggled with slow growth rates, the United States has enjoyed prolonged high employment and steady economic growth without the accelerated inflation that normally accompanies such a period. The gloomy economic forecasts of Paul Kennedy and others in the late 1980s have proven inaccurate, and other countries have increasingly looked to the United States, and particularly its high-flying technology sector, for policy and market innovations that could spark their own economic expansion.

One area where the United States has struggled is its balance of trade. In terms of total goods and services, the United States is the world's leading exporting nation. U.S. firms export roughly $1 trillion in goods and services each year. The problem is that imports to the United States are even greater. The effect is a substantial trade deficit. The United States has not had a trade surplus in any year since 1975, and recently has had annual deficits of $100 billion or more (see Figure 17-1).

American Goals in the Global Economy

The United States depends on other countries for raw materials, finished goods, and capital to meet Americans' production and consumption demands. Meeting this objective requires the United States to have influence on world markets. The broad goals of the United States in the world economy include these:

- Sustaining a stable and open system of trade that will promote prosperity at home

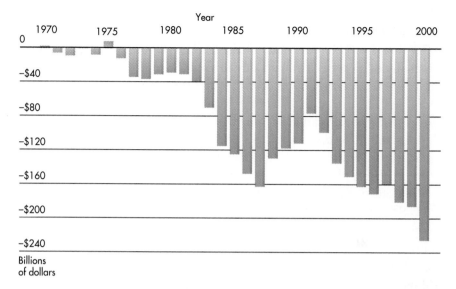

FIGURE 17-1   THE TRADE DEFICIT
Not since 1975 has the United States exported more goods and services than it imports. Source: U.S. Census Bureau, 2001.

- Maintaining access to energy and other resources that are vital to the regular functioning of the U.S. economy
- Keeping the widening gap between the rich and poor countries from destabilizing the world's economy[22]

GLOBAL TRADE   Since the end of the cold war, U.S. foreign policy has centered on the global economy. International commerce is not only more competitive than in the past; it is more important. Nations' economies are increasingly interconnected as a result of the transportation and communication revolution. Because of it, **multinational corporations** (firms with major operations in more than one country) now find it easy to manage worldwide operations. From a headquarters in New York, a firm has no difficulty directing a production facility in Thailand that is filling orders for markets in Europe and South America. Money, goods, and services now flow freely and quickly across national borders, and large firms increasingly think about markets in global rather than national terms. And as firms have adjusted their behavior, nations have also had to adjust. U.S. presidents once went abroad primarily to strengthen security alliances. Presidents Bush and Clinton traveled primarily for the purpose of strengthening trade relations and negotiating international economic agreements.

Economic globalization is a term that describes the increased interdependence of nations' economies. This development is both an opportunity and a threat to U.S. economic interests. The opportunity rests with the possibility of increased demand abroad for U.S. goods and services as a result of open trade with other countries and economic growth within these countries. The threat lies in the fact that foreign firms also compete in the global marketplace and may use their competitive advantages, such as cheaper labor, to outposition U.S. firms. In addition, as nations' economies become more interdependent, instability in one market can spread quickly to others, causing a broad decline in the global economy.

The effect of interdependency was evident in the summer of 1998, when the U.S. stock market dropped sharply in response to adverse economic developments in Asia and Latin America. The economic downturn in these regions also affected the U.S. balance of trade. As their economies slowed, their demand for goods declined, and U.S. exports declined accordingly. In addition, as the value of currency in these regions dropped, U.S. firms had to compete at home with foreign goods that were suddenly lower in price. The net effect was a record trade deficit in 1998 of $180 billion.

Not surprisingly, global economic stability has been a high priority for the U.S. officials. Working unilaterally and through international organizations such as the World Bank and the IMF, the U.S. government has provided financial and other assistance when economic instability occurs elsewhere in the world. The United States has also pressured other nations to reform their economic policies to meet the demands of a global marketplace. Banking reforms in Japan, Thailand, and Indonesia are examples of the type of changes the United States has sought. New international financial institutions that would be tailored to the demands of the new global economy have also been part of the U.S. policy agenda.

If U.S. policymakers are generally in agreement on the need for stable international markets, they are divided over a second issue: free trade. Although the principle of free trade is widely embraced as a linchpin of the global economy, it is a contentious issue in specific contexts. To oversimplify, the opposing sides on trade issues can be described as the protectionism and the free-trade positions. **Protectionism** emphasizes the immediate interests of domestic producers and includes measures designed to enable them to compete successfully in the domestic market with foreign competitors. For some protectionists, the issue is simply a matter of defending domestic firms against the actions of their foreign competitors. For others, the issue is one of "fair trade." They become protectionist in those instances where foreign firms have an unfair competitive advantage, as, for example, when they are subsidized by their governments, which allows them to market their goods at artificially low prices.

The Congress is a center of protectionist sentiment in the United States. Many members of Congress are determined to protect locally operating firms that are adversely affected by foreign competitors. In fact, most Americans believe that free trade results in a loss of jobs to low-wage countries. But there is a paradoxical aspect to this opinion: most Americans also say that they favor free trade among nations, as long as it is fair to all sides.

The **free-trade** position assumes that the long-term economic interests of all countries are advanced when tariffs and other trade barriers are kept to a minimum. Most free-trade advocates couple their advocacy with fair-trade demands, but they are committed philosophically and in practice to the idea that free trade fuels economic growth and results in a net gain for U.S. business.

The political leadership on free trade has usually come from the White House, although it is fair to say that most members of Congress, except on vital interests affecting their constituencies, support the principle of global free trade. But presidents have been stronger advocates of free trade as a result of their tendency to take a national view of issues. All recent presidents have embraced the notion that free trade promotes growth and produces a net gain for U.S. firms and workers. And since their political fortunes tend to rise and fall with the overall strength of the nation's economy, presidents have typically pursued free-trade policies.

Opposing views on global trade clashed in 1993 over the issue of the North American Free Trade Agreement (NAFTA), which aims to create an EU-type market among the United States, Canada, and Mexico. Opponents of the agreement, who included organized labor, most environmental groups, and a majority of the Democrats in Congress, argued that it would result in the loss of countless jobs to Mexico. Its proponents, who included President Clinton, most large U.S. corporations, and most congressional Republicans, contended that the agreement would boost the economies of all three countries and was necessary if the United States were to maintain a leading position in global trade. The measure obtained majority support in Congress, but only after side agreements were worked out to protect some American producers from the adverse effects of open trade in North America.

In 1997, NAFTA was once again a focus of debate in Congress, but this time in the context of a proposal to extend the president's "fast-track" trade negotiation authority. This authority allows the president to negotiate trade agreements with other countries and then submit them to Congress for an up or down vote. Congress can defeat but cannot amend such agreements. Labor, environmental groups, and a majority of Democrats in Congress opposed the extension, saying that trade agreements routinely fail to protect workers and the environment and that Congress ought to retain authority to amend any agreement negotiated by the president. They argued that NAFTA had been an environmental and employment nightmare; for example, recently constructed factories on the Mexican side of the border were dumping tons of pollutants into the Rio Grande. This time, the opponents of free trade prevailed; the proposal to extend the president's fast-track authority was defeated.

In general, however, momentum is on the side of free-trade advocates. A prime example is the General Agreement on Tariffs and Trade (GATT), which received congressional approval in 1994 and was also ratified by most other countries. GATT established rules aimed at creating a nearly global free market: the rules lower worldwide tariffs by a third, strengthen protection of intellectual property (such as patents and copyrights), and create panels that will arbitrate trade disputes and establish standards in areas such as the environment, securities, and worker safety. This multilateral trading system is coordinated by the World Trade Organization (WTO), which was established in 1995 as the successor to GATT. The WTO's 124 member nations have basically committed themselves to an open trade policy buttressed by regulations that are designed to ensure fair play among the participants.

The WTO, however, is certain to be the target of intense criticism. Some Americans oppose, in principle, any international organization with the power to set policy that is binding on the United States. The WTO will be no different in this respect than the UN has been. The WTO will also be subject to more precise forms of pressure, as was evident when mass protests disrupted the 1999 WTO Conference in Seattle. To gain support among member nations, the WTO has focused on trade barriers and has shied from issues that are more contentious, such as a country's labor laws. The Seattle protests, which drew international activists as well as ones from the United States, were aimed at forcing the WTO to take environmental and labor practices (for example, child labor) into account in its trade agreements. It is generally conceded that the Seattle protests were but one round in what is sure to be protracted struggle over the shape of global trade policy.

ACCESS TO NATURAL RESOURCES   Although the United States is rich in natural resources, it is not self-sufficient. The major deficiency is oil; domestic production provides for only about half the nation's use.

★ STATES IN THE NATION ★

Foreign Exports and State Economies

The states differ considerably in the extent to which their economies depend on foreign exports. The state of Washington, with its aerospace, fishing, and logging industries and proximity to Canada and Asia, is the leading exporter. Trade with foreign countries accounts for 22 percent of the state's economy. Louisiana (16%), Alaska (11%), and Vermont (11%) are the only other states whose exports exceed 10 percent of the total state economy.

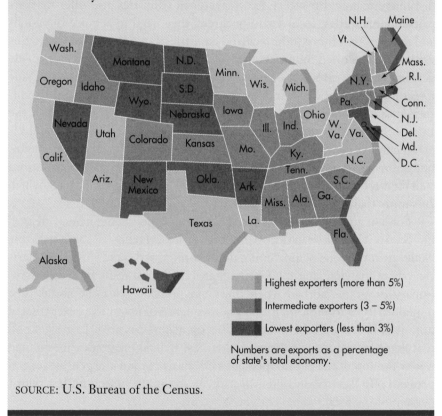

Highest exporters (more than 5%)

Intermediate exporters (3 – 5%)

Lowest exporters (less than 3%)

Numbers are exports as a percentage of state's total economy.

SOURCE: U.S. Bureau of the Census.

Outside the United States, most of the world's oil is found in the Middle East, Latin America, and Russia. Access to this oil has occurred mainly through the marketplace, but U.S. military force has also been instrumental. The 1990–1991 war in the Persian Gulf is an example. Iraq's invasion of oil-rich Kuwait threatened Western supplies, and its defeat quelled the threat.

In general, however, military power has increasingly become a less-effective means of preserving economic leverage.[23] Economic interdependence has made military intervention mostly counterproductive. For example, when Iranian fundamentalists took over the U.S. embassy in Teheran in 1979, one of the reasons the United States refrained from attacking Iran's oil fields was that the action would have substantially reduced the Middle East's oil-producing capacity.

Relations with the Developing World   Political instability in the less developed countries, as in the case of Iraq's invasion of Kuwait, is disruptive to world markets. Less developed countries also offer marketplace opportunities. In order to progress, they need to acquire the goods and services that more industrialized countries can provide. To foster this demand, the United States and the other industrialized countries provide developmental assistance to poorer countries. These contributions include direct foreign aid and also indirect assistance through international organizations such as the IMF and the World Bank. Since World War II, the United States has been far and away the leading source of aid to the developing countries of the world. The United States is still a major contributor, but is now far down the list in terms of its per capita annual contributions (see Figure 17-2). The primary recipient of U.S. foreign aid is Israel, which gets more than a fourth of the total.

Foreign aid is a prime target of politicians. Upon being named chair of the Senate Foreign Relations Committee, Jesse Helms (R-N.C.) said he would trim millions in aid "going down foreign ratholes."[24] Many Americans share the view that the United States ought not to be funding discretionary programs abroad when there are pressing needs at home. The unpopularity of foreign aid is also a consequence of the public's exaggerated notion of how much the United States spends in this area. In a 1994 poll that asked respondents to name the largest federal programs, foreign aid was at the top of the list (27 percent said it was the most expensive federal program). In fact, foreign aid is near the bottom, accounting for less than 1 percent of the total federal budget.[25]

Foreign aid accounts for only some of the funds that flow from the United States to developing countries; private investment is another source. The United States is the country whose firms invest most heavily abroad. In 1998, U.S. multinational corporations invested roughly $50 billion abroad. Foreign investment by U.S.–based multinationals works to America's advantage in at least two important ways. First, it sends a flow of overseas profits back to the United States, which strengthens the country's

Per capita foreign aid

Sweden	$185
France	$143
Japan	$120
Germany	$115
Canada	$70
Britain	$56
Italy	$33
United States	$29

FIGURE 17-2   PER CAPITA ASSISTANCE TO DEVELOPING COUNTRIES
The United States ranks relatively high (though not the highest) in terms of total amount spent on foreign aid to developing countries, but ranks low in terms of per capita expenditures. Source: OECD (Organization for Economic Cooperation and Development), 1998.

financial base. Second, it makes other nations dependent on the prosperity of the United States; their economies are linked to U.S. businesses.

Economic development and foreign aid were the focus of President Clinton's 1998 trip to sub-Saharan Africa, the first such trip by an American president. In Johannesburg, South Africa, Clinton said that economic development was the long-term goal, but it was not a substitute for short-term assistance. "Trade cannot replace aid when there is still so much poverty," the president said.[26] During the cold war, the United States had been willing to back almost any type of regime in Africa as long as it was aligned against the Soviet Union. Since then, the United States has had a different view of Africa, much as its view of Asia, eastern Europe, and South America has changed. The emphasis has been on economic trade, human rights, and democratic institutions. These objectives, more clearly now than at any time since World War I, are the foundation of U.S. foreign policy.

Some critics suggest that the United States has placed too much emphasis on trade issues and not enough on issues of human rights and democracy. Trade with China, in particular, has been a point of contention.

President George W. Bush has described free trade as
"a forward strategy for freedom." Like other presidents
recently, Bush has said free trade promotes liberty
and democracy throughout the world.

The Chinese government's brutal crackdown on prodemocracy demonstrators in Beijing's Tiananmen Square in 1989 and subsequent treatment of political dissidents led some U.S. policymakers and activists to conclude that China's trade with the United States should be contingent on a dramatic improvement in its human rights record. And in fact, the United States has pressured China and other countries to improve their human rights policies. But the pressure in most instances has stopped at the point where trade relations would be seriously jeopardized. Free trade has been seen as a key to political liberalization. According to this view, improved trade raises living standards, which gradually creates a demand for individual rights and democratic institutions. President George W. Bush describes free trade as "a forward strategy for freedom."

The Politics of Global Economic Policy

The global economy has changed a great deal since America's halcyon days in the period immediately following World War II. It is much more competitive and less responsive to military power. The United States depends more heavily than in the past on the strength of its own economy to forge a favorable position in world trade. This situation has caused U.S.

corporations in recent years to launch cost-cutting measures in order to make their products more competitive in the global market.[27] The changes have also led U.S. policymakers to alter their approaches to business regulation, public education, and many other policies that affect the country's competitive position. Another indicator of a new approach is the emphasis that the United States has placed on the WTO, whose member nations are committed to lowering trade barriers so as to promote the type of world trading system that can benefit all participating countries.

Public opinion in recent years has consistently supported the idea that the United States should turn its attention away from military priorities toward economic ones. This opinion seems to reflect the lesson that American elites and officials have drawn from international experiences during the last half-century, particularly during the past decade or so. The consensus is broad enough to suggest that economic priorities will continue to be a driving factor in American foreign policy.

SUMMARY

From 1945 to 1990, U.S. foreign and defense policies were dominated by a concern with the Soviet Union. During most of this period the United States pursued a policy of containment based on the premise that the Soviet Union was an aggressor nation bent on global conquest. Containment policy led the United States into wars in Korea and Vietnam and to maintain a large defense establishment. U.S. military forces are deployed around the globe, and the nation has a large nuclear arsenal. The end of the cold war, however, made some of this weaponry and much of the traditional military strategy less relevant to maintaining America's security. Cutbacks in military spending and a redefinition of the military's role are under way.

With the end of the cold war, the United States has taken a new approach to foreign affairs, which President George Bush labeled as a "new world order." It proposes that nations work together toward common goals and includes efforts to address global problems, such as drug trafficking, environmental pollution, and regional conflicts. The NATO intervention in Kosovo is a recent example of the multilateralism that is a characteristic of the new world order.

Increasingly, national security is being defined in economic terms. After World War II, the United States helped establish a global trading system within which it was the leading partner. The nation's international economic position, however, has gradually weakened, owing to domestic problems and to the emergence of strong competitors, particularly Japan and Germany. Many analysts believe that a revitalized economic sector rather than military power holds the key to America's future position in international affairs.

The chief instruments of national security policy are diplomacy, military force, economic exchange, and intelligence gathering. These are exercised through specialized agencies of the U.S. government, such as the Departments of State and Defense, which are largely responsive to presidential leadership. Increasingly, national security policy has also relied on international organizations, such as the UN and the World Trade Organization, which are responsive to the global concerns of major nations.

MAJOR CONCEPTS

cold war

containment

détente

deterrence

economic globalization

free trade

insurgency

internationalist

isolationist

military-industrial complex

multilateralism

multinational corporations

protectionism

SUGGESTED READINGS AND WEB SITES

Barnet, Richard J., and John Cavanagh. *Global Dreams: Imperial Corporations and the New World Order.* New York: Simon & Schuster, 1994. Argues that the key players in today's world are large multinational corporations.

Dumbrell, John. *American Foreign Policy: Carter to Clinton.* New York: St. Martin's Press, 1996. A thorough history of United States foreign policy since the Vietnam War.

Greider, William. *One World, Ready or Not: The Manic Logic of Global Capitalism.* New York: Simon & Schuster, 1997. A critical analysis of the global economy, and its effect on Americans' lives.

Holsti, Ole. *Public Opinion and American Foreign Policy.* Ann Arbor: University of Michigan Press, 1996. An analysis that concludes public opinion has had a significant and positive impact on U.S. foreign policy.

Johnson, Loch K. *Secret Agencies: U.S. Intelligence Agencies in a Hostile World.* New Haven, Conn.: Yale University Press, 1996. A nuanced assessment of the record of U.S. intelligence agencies.

Kirshner, Jonathan. *Currency and Coercion: The Political Economy of International Monetary Power.* Princeton, N.J.: Princeton University Press, 1997. A study of how states use currency and coercion to advance their security.

Lindsay, James M. *Congress and the Politics of U.S. Foreign Policy.* Baltimore, Md.: Johns Hopkins University Press, 1994. An analysis of Congress's increasingly assertive role in foreign policy.

http://www.defenselink.mil   The U.S. Department of Defense's web site provides information on each of the armed services, daily news from the American Forces Information Service, and other material.

http://www.foreignrelations.org   This site includes reports and assessments of the Council of Foreign Relations and transcripts of speeches by U.S. and world political leaders on topics of international interest.

http://www.igc.org/igc   The Institute for Global Communications (IGC) provides information and services to organizations and activists on a broad range of international issues, including human rights.

http://www.wto.org   The World Trade Organization (WTO) web site contains information on the organization's activities and has links to related sites.

READING 17

A Borderless World

KENICHI OHMAE

Introduction

In his essay, Kenichi Ohmae analyzes the implications of global economic change for nations, citizens, and policies. If Ohmae overstates the degree to which governments and people have lost control of their economies, he nonetheless captures the spirit of political change inherent in a world shadowed by giant multinational corporations whose first loyalty is to financiers and stockholders. In doing so, he drives home a theme of Chapter 17: that the challenges of foreign policy today are primarily economic rather than military in nature.

A funny—and, to many observers, a very troubling—thing has happened on the way to former U.S. President Bush's so-called "new world order": the old world has fallen apart. Most visibly, with the ending of the Cold War, the long-familiar pattern of alliances and oppositions among industrialized nations has fractured beyond repair. Less visibly, but arguably far more important, the modern nation state itself—that artifact of the 18th and 19th centuries—has begun to crumble.

For many observers, this erosion of the long-familiar building blocks of the political world has been a source of discomfort at least and, far more likely, of genuine distress. They used to be confident that they could tell with certainty where the boundary lines ran. These are our people; those are not. These are our interests; those are not. These are our industries; those are not. It did not matter that little economic activity remained truly domestic in any sense that an Adam Smith or a David Ricardo would understand. Nor did it matter that the people served or the interests protected represented a small and diminishing fraction of the complex social universe within each set of established political borders.

The point, after all, was that everyone knew—or could talk and act as if he or she knew—where the boundary lines ran. Everyone's dealings could rest, with comfortable assurance, on the certain knowledge, as Robert Reich has put it, of who was "us" and who was "them." The inconvenient fact that most of the guns pointed in anger during the past two decades were pointed by national governments at some segment of the people those governments would define as "us"—well, that really did not matter, either. Boundaries are boundaries.

Politics, runs the time-worn adage, is the art of the possible. Translated, that means it is also the art of ignoring or overlooking discordant facts: guns pointed the wrong way, democratic institutions clogged to the point of paralysis by minority interests defended in the name of the majority—and, perhaps most important, domestic economies in an increasingly borderless world of economic activity. So what if average GNP per capita in China is $317 but, in Shenzhen, whose economy is closely linked with that of Hong Kong, it is $5,695? Boundaries are boundaries, and political dividing lines mean far more than demonstrable communities of economic interest.

No, they don't. Public debate may still be hostage to the outdated vocabulary of political borders, but the daily realities facing most people in the developed and developing worlds—both as citizens and as consumers—speak a vastly different idiom. Theirs is the language of an increasingly borderless economy, a true global marketplace. But the references we have—the maps and guides—to this new terrain are still largely drawn in political terms. Moreover, as the primary features on this landscape—the traditional nation states—begin to come apart at the seams, the overwhelming temptation is to redraw obsolete, U.N.-style maps to reflect the shifting borders of those states. The temptation is understandable, but the result is pure illusion. No more than the work of early cartographers do these new efforts show the boundaries and linkages that matter in the world now emerging. . . .

The uncomfortable truth is that, in terms of the global economy, nation states have become little more than bit actors. They may originally have been, in their mercantilist phase, independent, powerfully efficient engines of wealth creation. More recently, however, as the downward-ratcheting logic of electoral politics has placed a death grip on their economies, they have become—first and foremost—remarkably inefficient engines of wealth distribution. Elected political leaders gain and keep power by giving voters what they want, and what they want rarely entails a substantial decrease in the benefits, services, or subsidies handed out by the state.

Moreover, as the workings of genuinely global capital markets dwarf their ability to control exchange rates or protect their currency, nation states have become inescapably vulnerable to the discipline imposed by economic choices made elsewhere by people and institutions over which they have no practical control. Witness, for example, the recent, Maastricht-related bout of speculation against the franc, the pound, and the kronor. Witness, also, the unsustainable but self-imposed burden of Europe's various social programs. . . .

Second, and more to the point, the nation state is increasingly a nostalgic fiction. It makes even less sense today, for example, than it did a few years ago to speak of Italy or Russia or China as a single economic unit. Each is a motley combination of territories with vastly different needs and vastly different abilities to contribute. . . .

Third, when you look closely at the goods and services now produced and traded around the world, as well as at the companies responsible for them, it is no easy matter to attach to them an accurate national label. Is an automobile sold under an American marquee really a U.S. product when a large percentage of its components comes from abroad? Is the performance of IBM's foreign subsidiaries or the performance of its R&D operations in Europe and Japan really a measure of U.S. excellence in technology? For that matter, are the jobs created by Japanese plants and factories in the Mississippi Valley really a measure of the health of the Japanese, and not the U.S., economy? The barbershop on the corner may indisputably be a part of the domestic American economy. But it is just not possible to make the same claim, with the same degree of confidence, about the firms active on the global stage. . . .

An arresting, if often overlooked, fact about today's borderless economy is that people often have better access to low-cost, high-quality products when they are not produced "at home." Singaporeans, for example, enjoy better and cheaper agricultural products than do the Japanese, although Singapore has no farmers—and no farms—of its own. Much the same is true of construction materials, which are much less expensive in Singapore, which produces none of them, than in Japan, which does. . . .

For more than a decade, some of us have been talking about the progressive globalization of markets for consumer goods like Levi's jeans, Nike athletic shoes, and Hermés scarves—a process, driven by global exposure to the same information, the same cultural icons, and the same advertisements, that I have elsewhere referred to as the "California-ization" of taste. Today, however, the process of convergence goes faster and deeper. It reaches well beyond taste to much more fundamental dimensions of worldview, mindset, and even thought process. There are now, for example, tens of millions of teenagers around the world who, having been raised in a multimedia-rich environment, have a lot more in common with each other than they do with members of older generations in their own cultures. For these budding consumers, technology-driven convergence does not take place at the sluggish rate dictated by yesterday's media. It is instantaneous—a nanosecond migration of ideas and innovations.

The speed and immediacy of such migrations take us over an invisi-ble political threshold. In the post–Cold War world, the information flows underlying economic activity in virtually all corners of the globe simply cannot be maintained as the possession of private elites or public officials. They are shared, increasingly, by all citizens and consumers. This sharing does not, of course, imply any necessary similarity in how local economic choices finally get made. But it does imply that there is a powerful centripetal force at work, counteracting and counterbalancing all the centrifugal forces noted above.

The emotional nexus of culture, in other words, is not the only web of shared interest able to contain the processes of disintegration un-leashed by the reappearance of older fault lines. Information-driven par-ticipation in the global economy can do so, too, ahead of the fervid but empty posturing of both cheap nationalism and cultural messianism. The well-informed citizens of a global marketplace will not wait pas-sively until nation states or cultural prophets deliver tangible improve-ments in lifestyle. They no longer trust them to do so. Instead, they want to build their own future, now, for themselves and by themselves. They want their own means of direct access to what has become a genuinely global economy.

SOURCE: Kenichi Ohmae, *The End of the Nation State: The Rise of Regional Economies*, Copyright ©1995 by McKinsey & Company, Inc. Reprinted with the permission of the Free Press, a Division of Simon & Schuster, Inc. *Dr. Kenichi Ohmae heads a citizens' political reform movement in Japan and was formerly a director of an international management consulting firm.*

Appendixes

In Congress, July 4, 1776,

THE UNANIMOUS DECLARATION OF THE THIRTEEN UNITED STATES OF AMERICA

When, in the course of human events, it becomes necessary for one people to dissolve the political bands which have connected them with another, and to assume, among the powers of the earth, the separate and equal station to which the laws of nature and of nature's God entitle them, a decent respect to the opinions of mankind requires that they should declare the causes which impel them to the separation.

We hold these truths to be self-evident, that all men are created equal; that they are endowed by their Creator with certain unalienable rights; that among these, are life, liberty, and the pursuit of happiness. That, to secure these rights, governments are instituted among men, deriving their just powers from the consent of the governed; that, whenever any form of government becomes destructive of these ends, it is the right of the people to alter or to abolish it, and to institute a new government, laying its foundation on such principles, and organizing its powers in such form, as to them shall seem most likely to effect their safety and happiness. Prudence, indeed, will dictate that governments long established, should not be changed for light and transient causes; and, accordingly, all experience hath shown, that mankind are more disposed to suffer, while evils are sufferable, than to right themselves by abolishing the forms to which they are accustomed. But, when a long train of abuses and usurpations, pursuing invariably the same object, evinces a design to reduce them under absolute despotism, it is their right, it is their duty, to throw off such government and to provide new guards for their future security. Such has been the patient sufferance of these colonies, and such is now the necessity which constrains them to alter their former systems of government. The history of the present King of Great Britain is a history of repeated injuries and usurpations, all having, in direct object, the establishment of an absolute tyranny over these States. To prove this, let facts be submitted to a candid world:

He has refused his assent to laws the most wholesome and necessary for the public good.

He has forbidden his governors to pass laws of immediate and pressing importance, unless suspended in their operation till his assent should be obtained; and, when so suspended, he has utterly neglected to attend to them.

He has refused to pass other laws for the accommodation of large districts of people, unless those people would relinquish the right of representation in the legislature; a right inestimable to them, and formidable to tyrants only.

He has called together legislative bodies at places unusual, uncomfortable, and distant from the depository of their public records, for the sole purpose of fatiguing them into compliance with his measures.

He has dissolved representative houses repeatedly for opposing, with manly firmness, his invasions on the rights of the people.

He has refused, for a long time after such dissolutions, to cause others to be elected; whereby the legislative powers, incapable of annihilation, have returned to the people at large for their exercise; the state remaining, in the meantime, exposed to all the danger of invasion from without, and convulsions within.

He has endeavored to prevent the population of these States; for that purpose, obstructing the laws for naturalization of foreigners, refusing to pass others to encourage their migration hither, and raising the conditions of new appropriations of lands.

He has obstructed the administration of justice, by refusing his assent to laws for establishing judiciary powers.

He has made judges dependent on his will alone, for the tenure of their offices, and the amount and payment of their salaries.

He has erected a multitude of new offices, and sent hither swarms of officers to harass our people, and eat out their substance.

He has kept among us, in time of peace, standing armies, without the consent of our legislatures.

He has affected to render the military independent of, and superior to, the civil power.

He has combined, with others, to subject us to a jurisdiction foreign to our Constitution, and unacknowledged by our laws; giving his assent to their acts of pretended legislation:

For quartering large bodies of armed troops among us:

For protecting them by a mock trial, from punishment, for any murders which they should commit on the inhabitants of these States:

For cutting off our trade with all parts of the world:

For imposing taxes on us without our consent:

For depriving us, in many cases, of the benefit of trial by jury:

For transporting us beyond seas to be tried for pretended offences:

For abolishing the free system of English laws in a neighboring province, establishing therein an arbitrary government, and enlarging its boundaries, so as to render it at once an example and fit instrument for introducing the same absolute rule into these colonies:

For taking away our charters, abolishing our most valuable laws, and altering, fundamentally, the powers of our governments:

For suspending our own legislatures, and declaring themselves invested with power to legislate for us in all cases whatsoever.

He has abdicated government here, by declaring us out of his protection, and waging war against us.

He has plundered our seas, ravaged our coasts, burnt our towns, and destroyed the lives of our people.

He is, at this time, transporting large armies of foreign mercenaries to complete the works of death, desolation, and tyranny, already begun, with circumstances of cruelty and perfidy scarcely paralleled in the most barbarous ages, and totally unworthy the head of a civilized nation.

He has constrained our fellow citizens, taken captive on the high seas, to bear arms against their country, to become the executioners of their friends, and brethren, or to fall themselves by their hands.

He has excited domestic insurrections amongst us, and has endeavored to bring on the inhabitants of our frontiers, the merciless Indian savages, whose known rule of warfare is an undistinguished destruction of all ages, sexes, and conditions.

In every stage of these oppressions, we have petitioned for redress, in the most humble terms; our repeated petitions have been answered only by repeated injury. A prince, whose character is thus marked by every act which may define a tyrant, is unfit to be the ruler of a free people.

Nor have we been wanting in attention to our British brethren. We have warned them, from time to time, of attempts made by their legislature to extend an unwarrantable jurisdiction over us. We have reminded them of the circumstances of our emigration and settlement here. We have appealed to their native justice and magnanimity, and we have conjured them, by the ties of our common kindred, to disavow these usurpations, which would inevitably interrupt our connections and correspondence. They, too, have been deaf to the voice of justice and consanguinity. We must, therefore, acquiesce in the necessity which denounces our separation, and hold them as we hold the rest of mankind, enemies in war, in peace, friends.

We, therefore, the representatives of the United States of America, in general Congress assembled, appealing to the Supreme Judge of the world for the rectitude of our intentions, do, in the name, and by the authority of the good people of these colonies, solemnly publish and declare, that these united colonies are, and of right ought to be, free and independent states: that they are absolved from all allegiance to the British Crown, and that all political connection between them and the state of Great Britain is, and ought to be, totally dissolved; and that, as free and independent states, they have full power to levy war, conclude peace, contract alliances, establish commerce, and to do all other acts and things which independent states may of right do. And, for the support of this declaration, with a firm reliance on the protection of Divine Providence, we mutually pledge to each other our lives, our fortunes, and our sacred honor.

The foregoing Declaration was, by order of Congress, engrossed, and signed by the following members:

John Hancock

New Hampshire
Josiah Bartlett
William Whipple
Matthew Thornton

Massachusetts Bay
Samuel Adams
John Adams
Robert Treat Paine
Elbridge Gerry

Rhode Island
Stephen Hopkins
William Ellery

Connecticut
Roger Sherman
Samuel Huntington
William Williams
Oliver Wolcott

New York
William Floyd
Philip Livingston
Francis Lewis
Lewis Morris

New Jersey
Richard Stockton
John Witherspoon
Francis Hopkinson
John Hart
Abraham Clark

Pennsylvania
Robert Morris
Benjamin Rush
Benjamin Franklin
John Morton
George Clymer
James Smith
George Taylor
James Wilson
George Ross

Delaware
Caesar Rodney
George Read
Thomas M'Kean

Maryland
Samuel Chase
William Paca
Thomas Stone
Charles Carroll, of
  Carrollton

Virginia
George Wythe
Richard Henry Lee
Thomas Jefferson
Benjamin Harrison
Thomas Nelson, Jr.
Francis Lightfoot Lee
Carter Braxton

North Carolina
William Hooper
Joseph Hewes
John Penn

South Carolina
Edward Rutledge
Thomas Heyward, Jr.
Thomas Lynch, Jr.
Arthur Middleton

Georgia
Button Gwinnett
Lyman Hall
George Walton

Resolved, That copies of the Declaration be sent to the several assemblies, conventions, and committees, or councils of safety, and to the several commanding officers of the continental troops; that it be proclaimed in each of the United States, at the head of the army.

THE CONSTITUTION OF THE UNITED STATES[1]

We the People of the United States, in Order to form a more perfect Union, establish Justice, insure domestic Tranquility, provide for the common defence, promote the general Welfare, and secure the Blessings of Liberty to ourselves and our Posterity, do ordain and establish this CONSTITUTION for the United States of America.

Article I

Section 1.
All legislative Powers herein granted shall be vested in a Congress of the United States, which shall consist of a Senate and House of Representatives.

Section 2.
The House of Representatives shall be composed of Members chosen every second Year by the People of the several States, and the Electors in each State shall have the Qualifications requisite for Electors of the most numerous Branch of the State Legislature.

No Person shall be a Representative who shall not have attained to the Age of twenty-five Years, and been seven Years a Citizen of the United States, and who shall not, when elected, be an Inhabitant of that State in which he shall be chosen.

[Representatives and direct Taxes[2] shall be apportioned among the several States which may be included within this Union, according to their respective Numbers, which shall be determined by adding to the whole Number of free Persons, including those bound to Service for a Term of Years, and excluding Indians not taxed, three fifths of all other Persons.][3] The actual Enumeration shall be made within three Years after the first Meeting of the Congress of the United States, and within every subsequent Term of ten Years, in such Manner as they shall by Law direct. The Number of Representatives shall not exceed one for every thirty Thousand, but each State shall have at Least one Representative; and until such enumeration shall be made, the State of New Hampshire shall be entitled to chuse three, Massachusetts

---

[1]This version, which follows the original Constitution in capitalization and spelling, was published by the United States Department of the Interior, Office of Education, in 1935.

[2]Altered by the Sixteenth Amendment.

[3]Negated by the Fourteenth Amendment.

eight, Rhode-Island and Providence Plantations one, Connecticut five, New York six, New Jersey four, Pennsylvania eight, Delaware one, Maryland six, Virginia ten, North Carolina five, South Carolina five, and Georgia three.

When vacancies happen in the Representation from any State, the Executive Authority thereof shall issue Writs of Election to fill such Vacancies.

The House of Representatives shall chuse their Speaker and other Officers; and shall have the sole Power of Impeachment.

Section 3.

The Senate of the United States shall be composed of two Senators from each State, chosen by the Legislature thereof, for six Years; and each Senator shall have one Vote.

Immediately after they shall be assembled in Consequence of the first Election, they shall be divided as equally as may be into three Classes. The Seats of the Senators of the first Class shall be vacated at the Expiration of the second Year, of the second Class at the Expiration of the fourth Year, and of the third Class at the Expiration of the sixth Year, so that one-third may be chosen every second Year; and if Vacancies happen by Resignation, or otherwise, during the Recess of the Legislature of any State, the Executive thereof may make temporary Appointments until the next Meeting of the Legislature, which shall then fill such Vacancies.

No Person shall be a Senator who shall not have attained to the Age of thirty Years, and been nine Years a Citizen of the United States, and who shall not, when elected, be an Inhabitant of that State for which he shall be chosen.

The Vice President of the United States shall be President of the Senate, but shall have no vote, unless they be equally divided.

The Senate shall chuse their other Officers, and also a President pro tempore, in the absence of the Vice President, or when he shall exercise the Office of President of the United States.

The Senate shall have the sole Power to try all Impeachments. When sitting for that purpose they shall be on Oath or Affirmation. When the President of the United States is tried, the Chief Justice shall preside: And no person shall be convicted without the Concurrence of two thirds of the Members present.

Judgment in Cases of Impeachment shall not extend further than to removal from Office, and disqualification to hold and enjoy any Office of honor, Trust, or Profit under the United States: but the Party convicted shall nevertheless be liable and subject to Indictment, Trial, Judgment, and Punishment, according to Law.

Section 4.

The Times, Places and Manner of holding Elections for Senators and Representatives, shall be prescribed in each State by the Legislature thereof; but the Congress may at any time by Law make or alter such Regulations, except as to the Places of Chusing Senators.

The Congress shall assemble at least once in every Year, and such Meeting shall be on the first Monday in December, unless they shall by Law appoint a different Day.

Section 5.

Each House shall be the Judge of the Elections, Returns and Qualifications of its own Members, and a Majority of each shall constitute a Quorum to do Business; but a smaller number may adjourn from day to day, and may be authorized to compel the Attendance of absent Members, in such Manner, and under such Penalties, as each House may provide.

Each House may determine the Rules of its Proceedings, punish its Members for disorderly Behaviour, and, with the Concurrence of two thirds, expel a Member.

Each House shall keep a Journal of its Proceedings, and from time to time publish the same, excepting such Parts as may in their Judgment require Secrecy; and the Yeas and Nays of the Members of either House on any question shall, at the Desire of one fifth of those Present, be entered on the Journal.

Neither House, during the Session of Congress, shall, without the Consent of the other, adjourn for more than three days, nor to any other Place than that in which the two Houses shall be sitting.

Section 6.

The Senators and Representatives shall receive a Compensation for their Services, to be ascertained by Law, and paid out of the Treasury of the United States. They shall in all Cases, except Treason, Felony, and Breach of the Peace, be privileged from Arrest during their Attendance at the Session of their respective Houses, and in going to and returning from the same; and for any Speech or Debate in either House, they shall not be questioned in any other Place.

No Senator or Representative shall, during the Time for which he was elected, be appointed to any civil Office under the Authority of the United States, which shall have been created, or the Emoluments whereof shall have been increased, during such time; and no Person holding any Office under the United States shall be a Member of either House during his continuance in Office.

Section 7.

All Bills for raising Revenue shall originate in the House of Representatives; but the Senate may propose or concur with Amendments as on other bills.

Every Bill which shall have passed the House of Representatives and the Senate, shall, before it becomes a Law, be presented to the President of the United States; If he approve he shall sign it, but if not he shall return it, with his Objections, to that House in which it shall have originated, who shall enter the Objections at large on their Journal, and proceed to reconsider it. If after such Reconsideration two thirds of that House shall agree to pass the bill, it shall be sent, together with the objections, to the other House, by which it shall likewise be reconsidered, and if approved by two thirds of that House, it shall become a Law. But in all such Cases the Votes of both Houses shall be determined by Yeas and Nays, and the Names of the Persons voting for and against the Bill shall be entered on the Journal of each House respectively. If any Bill shall not be returned by the President within ten Days (Sundays excepted) after it shall have been presented to him, the Same shall be a Law, in like Manner as if he had signed it, unless the Congress by their Adjournment prevent its Return, in which Case it shall not be a Law.

Every Order, Resolution, or Vote to which the Concurrence of the Senate and House of Representatives may be necessary (except on a question of Adjournment) shall be presented to the President of the United States; and before the Same shall take Effect, shall be approved by him, or being disapproved by him, shall be repassed by two thirds of the Senate and House of Representatives, according to the Rules and Limitations prescribed in the Case of a Bill.

Section 8.

The Congress shall have Power To lay and collect Taxes, Duties, Imposts and Excises, to pay the Debts and provide for the common Defence and general Welfare of the United States; but all Duties, Imposts and Excises shall be uniform throughout the United States;

To borrow money on the credit of the United States;

To regulate Commerce with foreign Nations, and among the several States, and with the Indian Tribes;

To establish an uniform rule of Naturalization, and uniform Laws on the subject of Bankruptcies throughout the United States;

To coin Money, regulate the Value thereof, and of foreign Coin, and fix the Standard of Weights and Measures;

To provide for the Punishment of counterfeiting the Securities and current Coin of the United States;

To establish Post Offices and post Roads;

To promote the Progress of Science and useful Arts, by securing for limited Times to Authors and Inventors the exclusive Right to their respective Writings and Discoveries;

To constitute Tribunals inferior to the Supreme Court;

To define and punish Piracies and Felonies committed on the high Seas, and Offenses against the Law of Nations;

To declare War, grant Letters of Marque and Reprisal, and make Rules concerning Captures on Land and Water;

To raise and support Armies, but no Appropriation of Money to that Use shall be for a longer Term than two Years;

To provide and maintain a Navy;

To make Rules for the Government and Regulation of the land and naval forces;

To provide for calling forth the Militia to execute the Laws of the Union, suppress Insurrections and repel Invasions;

To provide for organizing, arming, and disciplining the Militia, and for governing such Part of them as may be employed in the Service of the United States, reserving to the States respectively, the Appointment of the Officers, and the Authority of training the Militia according to the discipline prescribed by Congress;

To exercise exclusive Legislation in all Cases whatsoever, over such District (not exceeding ten Miles square) as may, by Cession of particular States, and the acceptance of Congress, become the Seat of the Government of the United States, and to exercise like Authority over all Places purchased by the Consent of the Legislature of the State in which the Same shall be, for the Erection of Forts, Magazines, Arsenals, Dock-yards, and other needful Buildings;—And

To make all Laws which shall be necessary and proper for carrying into Execution the foregoing Powers, and all other Powers vested by this Constitution in the Government of the United States, or in any Department or Officer thereof.

Section 9.

The Migration or Importation of such Persons as any of the States now existing shall think proper to admit, shall not be prohibited by the Congress prior to the Year one thousand eight hundred and eight, but a tax or duty may be imposed on such Importation, not exceeding ten dollars for each Person.

The privilege of the Writ of Habeas Corpus shall not be suspended, unless when in Cases of Rebellion or Invasion the public Safety may require it.

No bill of Attainder or ex post facto Law shall be passed.

No capitation, or other direct, Tax shall be laid unless in Proportion to the Census or Enumeration herein before directed to be taken.

No Tax or Duty shall be laid on Articles exported from any State.

No Preference shall be given by any Regulation of Commerce or Revenue to the Ports of one State over those of another: nor shall Vessels bound to, or from, one State, be obliged to enter, clear, or pay Duties in another.

No Money shall be drawn from the Treasury, but in Consequence of Appropriations made by Law; and a regular Statement and Account of the Receipts and Expenditures of all public Money shall be published from time to time.

No Title of Nobility shall be granted by the United States: And no Person holding any Office of Profit or Trust under them, shall, without the Consent of the Congress, accept of any present, Emolument, Office, or Title, of any kind whatever, from any King, Prince, or foreign State.

Section 10.

No State shall enter into any Treaty, Alliance, or Confederation; grant Letters of Marque and Reprisal; coin Money; emit Bills of Credit; make any Thing but gold and silver Coin a Tender in Payment of Debts; pass any Bill of Attainder, ex post facto Law, or Law impairing the Obligation of Contracts, or grant any Title of Nobility.

No State shall, without the Consent of the Congress, lay any Imposts or Duties on Imports or Exports, except what may be absolutely necessary for executing its inspection Laws; and the net Produce of all Duties and Imposts, laid by any State on Imports or Exports, shall be for the use of the Treasury of the United States; and all such Laws shall be subject to the Revision and Control of the Congress.

No state shall, without the Consent of Congress, lay any duty of Tonnage, keep Troops, or Ships of War in time of Peace, enter into any Agreement or Compact with another State, or with a foreign Power, or engage in War, unless actually invaded, or in such imminent Danger as will not admit of delay.

Article II

Section 1.

The executive Power shall be vested in a President of the United States of America. He shall hold his Office during the Term of four years, and, together with the Vice President, chosen for the same Term, be elected, as follows:

Each State shall appoint, in such Manner as the Legislature thereof may direct, a Number of Electors, equal to the whole Number of Senators and Representatives to which the State may be entitled in the Congress: but no Senator or Representative, or Person holding an Office of Trust or Profit under the United States, shall be appointed an Elector.

[The Electors shall meet in their respective States, and vote by Ballot for two persons, of whom one at least shall not be an Inhabitant of the same State with themselves. And they shall make a List of all the Persons voted for, and of the Number of Votes for each; which List they shall sign and certify, and transmit sealed to the Seat of the Government of the United States, directed to the President of the Senate. The President of the Senate shall, in the Presence of the Senate and House of Representatives, open all the Certificates, and the Votes shall then be counted. The Person having the greatest Number of Votes shall be the President, if such Number be a Majority of the whole Number of Electors appointed; and if there be more than one who have such Majority, and have an equal Number of Votes, then the House of Representatives shall immediately chuse by Ballot one of them for President; and if no Person have a Majority, then from the five highest on the List the said House shall in like Manner chuse the President. But in chusing the President, the Votes shall be taken by States, the Representation from each State having one Vote; a quorum for this Purpose shall consist of a Member or Members from two-thirds of the States, and a Majority of all the States shall be necessary to a Choice. In every Case, after the Choice of the President, the Person having the greatest Number of Votes of the Electors shall be the Vice President. But if there should remain two or more who have equal votes, the Senate shall chuse from them by Ballot the Vice President.]⁴

The Congress may determine the Time of chusing the Electors, and the Day on which they shall give their Votes; which Day shall be the same throughout the United States.

No person except a natural-born Citizen, or a Citizen of the United States, at the time of the Adoption of this Constitution, shall be eligible to the Office of President; neither shall any Person be eligible to that Office who shall not have attained to the Age of thirty-five years, and been fourteen Years a Resident within the United States.

In Case of the Removal of the President from Office, or of his Death, Resignation, or Inability to discharge the Powers and Duties of the said Office, the same shall devolve on the Vice President, and the Congress may by Law provide for the

⁴Revised by the Twelfth Amendment.

Case of Removal, Death, Resignation, or Inability, both of the President and Vice President, declaring what Officer shall then act as President, and such Officer shall act accordingly, until the disability be removed, or a President shall be elected.

The President shall, at stated Times, receive for his Services a Compensation, which shall neither be increased nor diminished during the Period for which he shall have been elected, and he shall not receive within that Period any other Emolument from the United States, or any of them.

Before he enter on the execution of his Office, he shall take the following Oath or Affirmation:—"I do solemnly swear (or affirm) that I will faithfully execute the Office of President of the United States, and will, to the best of my Ability, preserve, protect, and defend the Constitution of the United States."

Section 2.

The President shall be Commander in Chief of the Army and Navy of the United States, and of the Militia of the several States, when called into the actual Service of the United States; he may require the Opinion, in writing, of the principal Officer in each of the executive Departments, upon any subject relating to the Duties of their respective Offices, and he shall have Power to Grant Reprieves and Pardons for Offenses against the United States, except in Cases of Impeachment.

He shall have Power, by and with the Advice and Consent of the Senate, to make Treaties, provided two-thirds of the Senators present concur; and he shall nominate, and by and with the Advice and Consent of the Senate, shall appoint Ambassadors, other public Ministers and Consuls, Judges of the supreme Court, and all other Officers of the United States, whose Appointments are not herein otherwise provided for, and which shall be established by Law: but the Congress may by Law vest the Appointment of such inferior Officers, as they think proper, in the President alone, in the Courts of Law, or in the Heads of Departments.

The President shall have Power to fill up all Vacancies that may happen during the Recess of the Senate, by granting Commissions which shall expire at the End of their next Session.

Section 3.

He shall from time to time give to the Congress Information of the State of the Union, and recommend to their Consideration such Measures as he shall judge necessary and expedient; he may, on extraordinary occasions, convene both Houses, or either of them, and in Case of Disagreement between them, with respect to the Time of Adjournment, he may adjourn them to such Time as he shall think proper; he shall receive Ambassadors and other public Ministers; he shall take care that the Laws be faithfully executed, and shall Commission all the Officers of the United States.

Section 4.

The President, Vice President and all civil Officers of the United States, shall be removed from Office on Impeachment for, and Conviction of, Treason, Bribery, or other high Crimes and Misdemeanors.

Article III

Section 1.

The judicial Power of the United States, shall be vested in one supreme Court, and in such inferior Courts as the Congress may from time to time ordain and establish. The Judges, both of the supreme and inferior Courts, shall hold their Offices during good Behaviour, and shall, at stated Times, receive for their Services, a Compensation, which shall not be diminished during their Continuance in Office.

Section 2.

The judicial Power shall extend to all Cases, in Law and Equity, arising under this Constitution, the Laws of the United States, and Treaties made, or which shall be made, under their Authority;—to all Cases affecting ambassadors, other public ministers and consuls;—to all cases of admiralty and maritime Jurisdiction;—to Controversies to which the United States shall be a Party;—to Controversies between two or more states;—between a State and Citizens of another State;[5]— between Citizens of different States—between Citizens of the same State claiming Lands under Grants of different States, and between a State, or the Citizens thereof, and foreign States, Citizens, or Subjects.

In all Cases affecting Ambassadors, other public Ministers and Consuls, and those in which a State shall be Party, the supreme Court shall have original Jurisdiction. In all the other Cases before mentioned, the supreme Court shall have appellate Jurisdiction, both as to Law and Fact, with such Exceptions, and under such Regulations as the Congress shall make.

The trial of all Crimes, except in Cases of Impeachment, shall be by Jury; and such Trial shall be held in the State where the said Crimes shall have been committed; but when not committed within any State, the Trial shall be at such Place or Places as the Congress may by Law have directed.

Section 3.

Treason against the United States, shall consist only in levying War against them, or in adhering to their Enemies, giving them Aid and Comfort. No Person shall be convicted of Treason unless on the Testimony of two Witnesses to the same overt Act, or on Confession in open Court.

The Congress shall have power to declare the Punishment of Treason, but no Attainder of Treason shall work Corruption of Blood, or Forfeiture except during the Life of the Person attained.

Article IV

Section 1.

Full Faith and Credit shall be given in each State to the public Acts, Records, and judicial Proceedings of every other State. And the Congress may by general Laws

[5]Qualified by the Eleventh Amendment.

prescribe the Manner in which such Acts, Records and Proceedings shall be proved, and the Effect thereof.

Section 2.

The Citizens of each State shall be entitled to all Privileges and Immunities of Citizens in the several States.

A Person charged in any State with Treason, Felony, or other Crime, who shall flee from Justice, and be found in another State, shall on demand of the executive Authority of the State from which he fled, be delivered up, to be removed to the State having Jurisdiction of the crime.

No Person held to Service or Labour in one State, under the Laws thereof, escaping into another, shall, in Consequence of any Law or Regulation therein, be discharged from such Service or Labour, but shall be delivered up on Claim of the Party to whom such Service or Labour may be due.

Section 3.

New States may be admitted by the Congress into this Union; but no new State shall be formed or erected within the Jurisdiction of any other State; nor any State be formed by the Junction of two or more States, or parts of States, without the Consent of the Legislatures of the States concerned as well as of the Congress.

The Congress shall have Power to dispose of and make all needful Rules and Regulations respecting the Territory or other Property belonging to the United States; and nothing in this Constitution shall be so construed as to Prejudice any Claims of the United States, or of any particular State.

Section 4.

The United States shall guarantee to every State in this Union a Republican Form of Government, and shall protect each of them against Invasion; and on Application of the Legislature, or of the Executive (when the Legislature cannot be convened) against domestic Violence.

Article V

The Congress, whenever two-thirds of both Houses shall deem it necessary, shall propose Amendments to this Constitution, or, on the Application of the Legislatures of two-thirds of the several States, shall call a Convention for proposing Amendments, which, in either Case, shall be valid to all Intents and Purposes, as part of this Constitution, when ratified by the Legislatures of three-fourths of the several States, or by Conventions in three-fourths thereof, as the one or the other Mode of Ratification may be proposed by the Congress; Provided that no Amendment which may be made prior to the Year One thousand eight hundred and eight shall in any Manner affect the first and fourth Clauses in the Ninth Section of the first Article; and that no State, without its Consent, shall be deprived of its equal Suffrage in the Senate.

Article VI

All Debts contracted and Engagements entered into, before the Adoption of this Constitution, shall be as valid against the United States under this Constitution, as under the Confederation.

This Constitution, and the Laws of the United States which shall be made in Pursuance thereof; and all Treaties made, or which shall be made, under the Authority of the United States, shall be the supreme Law of the Land; and the Judges in every State shall be bound thereby, any Thing in the Constitution or Laws of any State to the Contrary notwithstanding.

The Senators and Representatives before mentioned, and the Members of the several State Legislatures, and all executive and judicial Officers, both of the United States and of the several States, shall be bound by Oath or Affirmation to support this Constitution; but no religious Tests shall ever be required as a qualification to any Office or public Trust under the United States.

Article VII

The Ratification of the Conventions of nine States shall be sufficient for the Establishment of this Constitution between the States so ratifying the same.

Done in Convention by the Unanimous Consent of the States present the Seventeenth Day of September in the Year of our Lord one thousand seven hundred and Eighty seven, and of the Independence of the United States of America the Twelfth. In Witness whereof We have hereunto subscribed our Names.[6]

George Washington
President and deputy from Virginia

New Hampshire
John Langdon
Nicholas Gilman

Massachusetts
Nathaniel Gorham
Rufus King

Connecticut
William Samuel
   Johnson
Roger Sherman

New York
Alexander Hamilton

New Jersey
William Livingston
David Brearley
William Paterson
Jonathan Dayton

Pennsylvania
Benjamin Franklin
Thomas Mifflin
Robert Morris
George Clymer
Thomas FitzSimons
Jared Ingersoll
James Wilson
Gouverneur Morris

[6]These are the full names of the signers, which in some cases are not the signatures on the document.

Delaware	Virginia	South Carolina
George Read	John Blair	John Rutledge
Gunning Bedford, Jr.	James Madison, Jr.	Charles Cotesworth
John Dickinson	*North Carolina*	Pinckney
Richard Bassett		Charles Pinckney
Jacob Broom	William Blount	Pierce Butler
	Richard Dobbs Spaight	
Maryland	Hugh Williamson	*Georgia*
James McHenry		William Few
Daniel of St. Thomas		Abraham Baldwin
Jenifer		
Daniel Carroll		

Articles in Addition to, and Amendment of, the Constitution of the United States of America, Proposed by Congress, and Ratified by the Legislatures of the Several States, Pursuant to the Fifth Article of the Original Constitution.[7]

Amendment I

Congress shall make no law respecting an establishment of religion, or prohibiting the free exercise thereof; or abridging the freedom of speech, or of the press; or the right of the people peaceably to assemble, and to petition the Government for a redress of grievances.

Amendment II

A well regulated Militia, being necessary to the security of a free State, the right of the people to keep and bear Arms shall not be infringed.

Amendment III

No Soldier shall, in time of peace, be quartered in any house, without the consent of the Owner, nor in time of war, but in a manner to be prescribed by law.

Amendment IV

The right of the people to be secure in their persons, houses, papers, and effects, against unreasonable searches and seizures, shall not be violated, and no Warrants

[7]This heading appears only in the joint resolution submitting the first ten amendments.

shall issue, but upon probable cause, supported by Oath or affirmation, and particularly describing the place to be searched, and the persons or things to be seized.

Amendment V

No person shall be held to answer for a capital or otherwise infamous crime, unless on a presentment or indictment of a Grand Jury, except in cases arising in the land or naval forces, or in the Militia, when in actual service in time of War or public danger; nor shall any person be subject for the same offence to be twice put in jeopardy of life or limb; nor shall be compelled in any criminal case to be a witness against himself, nor be deprived of life, liberty, or property, without due process of law; nor shall private property be taken for public use, without just compensation.

Amendment VI

In all criminal prosecutions, the accused shall enjoy the right to a speedy and public trial, by an impartial jury of the State and district wherein the crime shall have been committed, which district shall have been previously ascertained by law, and to be informed of the nature and cause of the accusation; to be confronted with the witnesses against him; to have compulsory process for obtaining witnesses in his favour, and to have the Assistance of Counsel for his defense.

Amendment VII

In suits at common law, where the value in controversy shall exceed twenty dollars, the right of trial by jury shall be preserved, and no fact tried by a jury, shall be otherwise reexamined in any Court of the United States, than according to the rules of the common law.

Amendment VIII

Excessive bail shall not be required, nor excessive fines imposed, nor cruel and unusual punishments inflicted.

Amendment IX

The enumeration of the Constitution, of certain rights, shall not be construed to deny or disparage others retained by the people.

Amendment X

The powers not delegated to the United States by the Constitution, nor prohibited by it to the States, are reserved to the States respectively, or to the people. [Amendments I–X, in force 1791.]

Amendment XI [1798]

The Judicial power of the United States shall not be construed to extend to any suit in law or equity, commenced or prosecuted against one of the United States by Citizens of another State, or by Citizens or Subjects of any Foreign State.

Amendment XII [1804]

The Electors shall meet in their respective States and vote by ballot for President and Vice-President, one of whom, at least, shall not be an inhabitant of the same State with themselves; they shall name in their ballots the person voted for as President, and in distinct ballots the person voted for as Vice-President, and they shall make distinct lists of all persons voted for as President, and of all persons voted for as Vice-President, and of the number of votes for each, which lists they shall sign and certify, and transmit sealed to the seat of the government of the United States, directed to the President of the Senate;—The President of the Senate shall, in the presence of the Senate and House of Representatives, open all the certificates and the votes shall then be counted;—The person having the greatest number of votes for President, shall be the President, if such number be a majority of the whole number of Electors appointed; and if no person have such majority, then from the persons having the highest numbers not exceeding three on the list of those voted for as President, the House of Representatives shall choose immediately, by ballot, the President. But in choosing the President, the votes shall be taken by states, the representation from each state having one vote; a quorum for this purpose shall consist of a member or members from two-thirds of the states, and a majority of all the states shall be necessary to a choice. And if the House of Representatives shall not choose a President whenever the right of choice shall devolve upon them, before the fourth day of March next following, then the Vice-President shall act as President, as in the case of the death or other constitutional disability of the President.—The person having the greatest number of votes as Vice-President, shall be the Vice-President, if such number be a majority of the whole number of Electors appointed, and if no person have a majority, then from the two highest numbers on the list, the Senate shall choose the Vice-President; a quorum for the purpose shall consist of two-thirds of the whole number of Senators, and a majority of the whole number shall be necessary to a choice. But no person constitutionally ineligible to the office of President shall be eligible to that of Vice-President of the United States.

Amendment XIII [1865]

Section 1.
Neither slavery nor involuntary servitude, except as a punishment for crime where-of the party shall have been duly convicted, shall exist within the United States, or any place subject to their jurisdiction.

Section 2.
Congress shall have power to enforce this article by appropriate legislation.

Amendment XIV [1868]

Section 1.
All persons born or naturalized in the United States, and subject to the jurisdiction thereof, are citizens of the United States and of the State wherein they reside. No State shall make or enforce any law which shall abridge the privileges or immunities of citizens of the United States; nor shall any State deprive any person of life, liberty, or property, without due process of law; nor deny to any person within its jurisdiction the equal protection of the laws.

Section 2.
Representatives shall be apportioned among the several States according to their respective numbers, counting the whole number of persons in each State, excluding Indians not taxed. But when the right to vote at any election for the choice of electors for President and Vice-President of the United States, Representatives in Congress, the Executive and Judicial officers of a State, or the members of the Legislature thereof, is denied to any of the male inhabitants of such State, being twenty-one years of age, and citizens of the United States, or in any way abridged, except for participation in rebellion, or other crime, the basis of representation therein shall be reduced in the proportion which the number of such male citizens shall bear to the whole number of male citizens twenty-one years of age in such State.

Section 3.
No person shall be a Senator or Representative in Congress, or elector of President and Vice-President, or hold any office, civil or military, under the United States, or under any State, who, having previously taken an oath, as a member of Congress, or as an officer of the United States, or as a member of any State legislature, or as an executive or judicial officer of any State, to support the Constitution of the United States, shall have engaged in insurrection or rebellion against the same, or given aid or comfort to the enemies thereof. But Congress may by a vote of two-thirds of each House, remove such disability.

Section 4.
The validity of the public debt of the United States, authorized by law, including debts incurred for payment of pensions and bounties for services in suppressing insurrection or rebellion, shall not be questioned. But neither the United States nor any State shall assume or pay any debts or obligation incurred in aid of insurrection or rebellion against the United States, or any claim for the loss or emancipation of any slave; but all such debts, obligations, and claims shall be held illegal and void.

Section 5.
The Congress shall have the power to enforce, by appropriate legislation, the provisions of this article.

Amendment XV [1870]

Section 1.
The right of citizens of the United States to vote shall not be denied or abridged by the United States or by any State on account of race, color, or previous condition of servitude—

Section 2.
The Congress shall have power to enforce this article by appropriate legislation.

Amendment XVI [1913]

The Congress shall have power to lay and collect taxes on incomes, from whatever source derived, without apportionment among the several States, and without regard to any census or enumeration.

Amendment XVII [1913]

The Senate of the United States shall be composed of two Senators from each State, elected by the people thereof, for six years; and each Senator shall have one vote. The electors in each State shall have the qualifications requisite for electors of the most numerous branch of the State legislatures.

When vacancies happen in the representation of any State in the Senate, the executive authority of such State shall issue writs of election to fill such vacancies: *Provided,* That the legislature of any State may empower the executive thereof to make temporary appointments until the people fill the vacancies by election as the legislature may direct.

This amendment shall not be so construed as to affect the election or term of any Senator chosen before it becomes valid as part of the Constitution.

Amendment XVIII [1919]

Section 1.
After one year from the ratification of this article the manufacture, sale, or transportation of intoxicating liquors within, the importation thereof into, or the exportation thereof from the United States and all territory subject to the jurisdiction thereof for beverage purposes is hereby prohibited.

Section 2.
The Congress and the several States shall have concurrent power to enforce this article by appropriate legislation.

Section 3.
This article shall be inoperative unless it shall have been ratified as an amendment to the Constitution by the legislatures of the several States, as provided in the Constitution, within seven years from the date of the submission hereof to the States by the Congress.

Amendment XIX [1920]

The right of citizens of the United States to vote shall not be denied or abridged by the United States or by any State on account of sex.
Congress shall have power to enforce this article by appropriate legislation.

Amendment XX [1933]

Section 1.
The terms of the President and Vice-President shall end at noon on the 20th day of January, and the terms of Senators and Representatives at noon on the 3d day of January, of the years in which such terms would have ended if this article had not been ratified; and the terms of their successors shall then begin.

Section 2.
The Congress shall assemble at least once in every year, and such meeting shall begin at noon on the 3d day of January, unless they shall by law appoint a different day.

Section 3.

If, at the time fixed for the beginning of the term of the President, the President elect shall have died, the Vice-President elect shall become President. If a President shall not have been chosen before the time fixed for the beginning of his term or if the President elect shall have failed to qualify, then the Vice-President elect shall act as President until a President shall have qualified; and the Congress may by law provide for the case wherein neither a President elect nor a Vice-President elect shall have qualified, declaring who shall then act as President, or the manner in which one who is to act shall be selected, and such person shall act accordingly until a President or Vice-President shall have qualified.

Section 4.

The Congress may by law provide for the case of the death of any of the persons from whom the House of Representatives may choose a President whenever the right of choice shall have devolved upon them, and for the case of the death of any of the persons from whom the Senate may choose a Vice-President whenever the right of choice shall have devolved upon them.

Section 5.

Sections 1 and 2 shall take effect on the 15th day of October following the ratification of this article.

Section 6.

This article shall be inoperative unless it shall have been ratified as an amendment to the Constitution by the legislatures of three-fourths of the several States within seven years from the date of its submission.

Amendment XXI [1933]

Section 1.

The eighteenth article of amendment to the Constitution of the United States is hereby repealed.

Section 2.

The transportation or importation into any State, Territory, or possession of the United States for delivery or use therein of intoxicating liquors, in violation of the laws thereof, is hereby prohibited.

Section 3.

This article shall be inoperative unless it shall have been ratified as an amendment to the Constitution by conventions in the several States, as provided in the Constitution, within seven years from the date of the submission hereof to the States by the Congress.

Amendment XXII [1951]

No person shall be elected to the office of the President more than twice, and no person who has held the office of President, or acted as President, for more than two years of a term to which some other person was elected President shall be elected to the office of the President more than once.

But this Article shall not apply to any person holding the office of President when this Article was proposed by the Congress, and shall not prevent any person who may be holding the office of President, or acting as President, during the term within which this Article becomes operative from holding the office of President or acting as President during the remainder of such term.

This article shall be inoperative unless it shall have been ratified as an amendment to the Constitution by the legislatures of three-fourths of the several states within seven years from the date of its submission to the states by the Congress.

Amendment XXIII [1961]

Section 1.
The District constituting the seat of Government of the United States shall appoint in such manner as the Congress may direct:

A number of electors of President and Vice-President equal to the whole number of Senators and Representatives in Congress to which the District would be entitled if it were a State, but in no event more than the least populous State; they shall be in addition to those appointed by the States, but they shall be considered, for the purposes of the election of President and Vice-President, to be electors appointed by a State; and they shall meet in the District and perform such duties as provided by the twelfth article of amendment.

Section 2.
The Congress shall have power to enforce this article by appropriate legislation.

Amendment XXIV [1964]

Section 1.
The right of citizens of the United States to vote in any primary or other election for President or Vice President, for electors for President or Vice President, or for Senator or Representative in Congress, shall not be denied or abridged by the United States or any state by reason of failure to pay any poll tax or other tax.

Section 2.
The Congress shall have the power to enforce this article by appropriate legislation.

Amendment XXV [1967]

Section 1.
In case of the removal of the President from office or of his death or resignation, the Vice President shall become President.

Section 2.
Whenever there is a vacancy in the office of the Vice President, the President shall nominate a Vice President who shall take office upon confirmation by a majority vote of both Houses of Congress.

Section 3.
Whenever the President transmits to the President Pro Tempore of the Senate and the Speaker of the House of Representatives his written declaration that he is unable to discharge the powers and duties of his office, and until he transmits to them a written declaration to the contrary, such powers and duties shall be discharged by the Vice President as Acting President.

Section 4.
Whenever the Vice President and a majority of either the principal officers of the executive departments or of such other body as Congress may by law provide, transmit to the President Pro Tempore of the Senate and the Speaker of the House of Representatives their written declaration that the President is unable to discharge the powers and duties of his office, the Vice President shall immediately assume the powers and duties of the office as Acting President.

Thereafter, when the President transmits to the President Pro Tempore of the Senate and the Speaker of the House of Representatives his written declaration that no inability exists, he shall resume the powers and duties of his office unless the Vice President and a majority of either the principal officers of the executive departments or of such other body as Congress may by law provide, transmit within four days to the President Pro Tempore of the Senate and the Speaker of the House of Representatives their written declaration that the President is unable to discharge the powers and duties of his office. Thereupon Congress shall decide the issue, assembling within forty-eight hours for that purpose if not in session. If the Congress, within twenty-one days after receipt of the latter written declaration, or, if Congress is not in session, within twenty-one days after Congress is required to assemble, determines by two-thirds vote of both Houses that the President is unable to discharge the powers and duties of his office, the Vice President shall continue to discharge the same as Acting President; otherwise, the President shall resume the powers and duties of his office.

Amendment XXVI [1971]

Section 1.
The right of citizens of the United States, who are eighteen years of age or older, to vote shall not be denied or abridged by the United States or by any State on account of age.

Section 2.
The Congress shall have the power to enforce this article by appropriate legislation.

Amendment XXVII [1992]

No law varying the compensation for the services of Senators and Representatives shall take effect until an election of Representatives shall have intervened.

Notes

CHAPTER ONE

[1]Alexis de Tocqueville, *Democracy in America (1835–1840)*, ed. J. P. Mayer and A. P. Kerr (Garden City, N.Y.: Doubleday/Anchor, 1969), 640.

[2]McElroy, John Harmon. American Beliefs: *What Keeps a Big Country and a Diverse People United*. (Chicago, I.R. Dec, 1999).

[3]Clinton Rossiter, *Conservativism in America* (New York: Vintage, 1962), 67.

[4]James Bryce, *The American Commonwealth*, vol. 2 (New York: Macmillan, 1960), 247–254. First published in 1900.

[5]Ralph Barton Perry, *Puritanism and Democracy* (New York: Vanguard, 1944), 124–125; see also Peter D. Salins, *Assimilation, American Style* (New York: Basic Books, 1996); Philip L. Fetzer, *The Ethnic Moment* (Armonk, N.Y.: M.E. Sharpe Publishers, 1996).

[6]See Gabriel Almond and Sidney Verba, *The Civic Culture* (Boston: Little, Brown, 1965); Richard Merelman, *Making Something of Ourselves: On Culture and Politics in the United States* (Berkeley: University of California Press, 1984).

[7]Paul Gagnon, "Why Study History?" *Atlantic Monthly*, November 1988, 47.

[8]Louis Hartz, *The Liberal Tradition in America* (New York, Harcourt, Brace, 1953), 12.

[9]Tocqueville, *Democracy in America*, 310.

[10]Times Mirror Center for the People and the Press survey, 1990–1991.

[11]See Douglas Muzzio and Richard Behn, "Thinking about Welfare," *The Public Perspective*, February/March 1995, 35–38; Stanley Feldman and John Zaller, "The Political Culture of Ambivalence: Ideological Responses to the Welfare State," *American Journal of Political Science*, 36 (1992): 268–307.

[12]See Seymour Martin Lipset, *American Exceptionalism: A Double-Edged Sword* (New York: Norton, 1996); Claude Levi-Strauss, *Structural Anthropology* (Chicago: University of Chicago Press, 1983); Clifford Geertz, *Myth, Symbol, and Culture* (New York: Norton, 1974).

[13]U.S. Census Bureau figures.

[14]Quoted in Ralph Volney Harlow, *The Growth of the United States*, vol. 2 (New York: Henry Holt, 1943), 497.

[15]Survey of American Political Culture, James Davison Hunter and Carol Bowman, directors, University of Virginia, 1996.

[16]Harold D. Lasswell, *Politics: Who Gets What, When, How* (New York: McGraw-Hill, 1938).

[17]Theodore Lowi and Benjamin Ginsberg, *American Government: Freedom and Power* (New York: Norton, 1990), 8.

[18]Harold D. Lasswell and Abraham Kaplan, *Power and Society* (New Haven, Conn.: Yale University Press, 1950), 75–77.

[19]*Federalist* No. 47.

[20]See Charles H. McIlwain, *Constitutionalism: Ancient and Modern* (Ithaca, N.Y.: Cornell University Press, 1983).

[21]Alan S. Rosenbaum, ed., *Constitutionalism: The Philosophical Dimension* (Westport, Conn.: Greenwood, 1988), 4.

[22]Benjamin I. Page and Robert Shapiro, "Effects of Public Opinion on Policy," *American Political Science Review* 77 (March, 1983): 178; see also Urie Bronfenbrenner, Peter McClelland, Stephen Leci, Phyllis Moen, and Elaine Wethington, *The State of Americans* (New York: Free Press, 1996).

[23]See Robert Dahl, *Democracy and Its Critics* (New Haven, Conn.: Yale University Press, 1989).

[24]C. Wright Mills, *The Power Elite* (New York: Oxford University Press, 1965).

[25]William Domhoff, *The Power Elite and the State: How Policy Is Made in America* (New York: Aldine de Gruyter, 1990).

[26]Roberto Michels, *Political Parties* (New York: Collier Books, 1962). First published in 1911.

[27]David Easton, *The Political System* (New York: Knopf, 1965), 97.

[28]E. E. Schattschneider, *Two Hundred Million Americans in Search of a Government* (New York: Holt, Rinehart & Winston, 1969), 42.

CHAPTER TWO

[1]Quoted in Charles S. Hyneman, "Republican Government in America," in George J. Graham, Jr., and Scarlett G. Graham, eds., *Founding Principles of American Government*, rev. ed. (Chatham, N.J.: Chatham House, 1984), 19.

[2]Tape of White House Conversation, March 22, 1973.

[3]John Locke, *The Two Treatises of Government*, ed. Thomas I. Cook (New York: Hafner, 1947), 159–186, 228–247; see also A. John Simmons, *The Lockean Theory of Rights* (Princeton, N.J.: Princeton University Press, 1994).

[4]Winthrop D. Jordon and Leon F. Litwack, *The United States*, 6th ed. (Englewood Cliffs, N.J.: Prentice-Hall, 1987), 72–74.

[5]George Bancroft, *History of the Formation of the Constitution of the United States of America*, 3d ed., vol. 1 (New York: D. Appleton, 1883), 166.

[6]Catherine Drinker Bowen, *Miracle at Philadelphia* (Boston: Little, Brown, 1986), 10.

[7]Alfred H. Kelly, Winifred A. Harbison, and Herman Belz, *The American Constitution*, 7th ed. (New York: Norton, 1991), 122.

[8]Max Weber, "Politics as a Vocation," in Hans H. Gerth and C. Wright Mills, eds., *From Max Weber: Essays in Sociology* (New York: Oxford University Press, 1958), 78.

[9]Gaillard Hunt, ed., *The Writings of James Madison* (New York: Putnam, 1904), 274.

[10]*Federalist* No. 47.

[11]See *Federalist* Nos. 47 and 48.

[12]Richard Neustadt, *Presidential Power* (New York: Macmillan, 1986), 33.

[13]*Marbury* v. *Madison*, 1 Cranch 137 (1803).

[14]Martin Diamond, *The Founding of the Democratic Republic* (Itasca, Ill.: Peacock, 1981), 62–71.

[15]*Federalist* No. 10.

[16]Leslie F. Goldstein, "Judicial Review and Democratic Theory: Guardian Democracy vs. Representative Democracy," *Western Political Quarterly* 40 (1987): 391–412.

[17]Benjamin Ginsberg, *The Consequences of Consent* (New York: Random House, 1982), 22.

[18]Robert Dahl, *Pluralist Democracy in the United States* (Chicago: Rand McNally, 1967), 92.

[19]This interpretation is taken from Walter Lippmann, *Public Opinion* (New York: Free Press, 1965), 178–179; for a general discussion of the uncertain meaning of the Constitution, see Lawrence H. Tribe and Michael C. Dorf, *On Reading the Constitution* (Cambridge, Mass.: Harvard University Press, 1991).

[20]Charles S. Beard, *An Economic Interpretation of the Constitution* (1913: New York, Macmillan, 1941).

CHAPTER THREE

[1]Woodrow Wilson, *Constitutional Government in the United States* (New York: Columbia University Press, 1908), 173.

[2]Thomas E. Patterson, *The 1996 Election and Other Recent Developments* (New York: McGraw-Hill, 1997), 29.

[3]See Samuel Beer, *To Make a Nation: The Rediscovery of American Federalism* (Cambridge, Mass.: The Belknap Press of Harvard University, 1993).

[4]*Federalist* No. 2.

[5]*Federalist* No. 45.

[6]*McCulloch* v. *Maryland*, 4 Wheaton 316 (1819).

[7]*Gibbons* v. *Ogden*, 22 Wheaton 1 (1824).

[8]Oliver Wendell Holmes, Jr., *Collected Legal Papers* (New York: Harcourt, Brace, 1920), 295–296.

[9]John C. Calhoun, *The Works of John C. Calhoun* (New York: Russell & Russell, 1968).

[10]See *Cooley* v. *Board of Wardens of the Port of Philadelphia*, 53 Howard 299 (1851).

[11]*Dred Scott* v. *Sanford*, 19 Howard 393 (1857).

[12]*U.S.* v. *Cruikshank*, 92 U.S. 452 (1876).

[13]*Santa Clara County* v. *Southern Pacific Railroad Co.*, 118 U.S. 394 (1886).

[14]*U.S.* v. *E. C. Knight Co.*, 156 U.S. 1 (1895).

[15]*Hammer* v. *Dagenhart*, 247 U.S. 251 (1918).

[16]*Lochner* v. *New York*, 198 U.S. 25 (1905).

[17]Alfred H. Kelly, Winfred A. Harbison, and Herman Belz, *The American Constitution*, 7th ed. (New York: Norton, 1991), 529; see also William G. Ross, *A Muted Fury* (Princeton, N.J.: Princeton University Press, 1993).

[18]James E. Anderson, *The Emergence of the Modern Regulatory State* (Washington, D.C.: Public Affairs Press, 1962), 2–3.

[19]*Schechter Poultry Co.* v. *United States*, 295 U.S. 495 (1935).

[20]*NLRB* v. *Jones and Laughlin Steel*, 301 U.S. 1 (1937).

[21]*American Power and Light* v. *Securities and Exchange Commission*, 329 U.S. 90 (1946); see also Richard A. Maidment, *The Judicial Response to the New Deal* (New York: Manchester University Press, 1992).

[22]Louis Fisher, *American Constitutional Law* (New York: McGraw-Hill, 1990), 384.

[23]Richard A. Maidment, *The Judicial Response to the New Deal: The U.S. Supreme Court and Economic Regulation* (New York: Manchester University Press, 1992).

[24]*Garcia* v. *San Antonio Transit Authority*, 469 U.S. 528 (1985).

[25]See Thomas Anton, *American Federalism and Public Policy* (Philadelphia: Temple University Press, 1989).

[26]Morton Grodzins, *The American System: A New View of Government in the United States* (Chicago: Rand McNally, 1966).

[27]See Paul A. Peterson, *The Price of Federalism* (Washington, D.C.: The Brookings Institution, 1995).

[28]Rosella Levaggi, *Fiscal Federalism and Grants-in-Aid* (Brookfield, Vt.: Avebury, 1991).

[29]See David L. Shapiro, *Federalism: A Dialogue* (Evanston, Ill.: Northwestern University Press, 1995). See also Douglas D. Rose, "National and Local Forces in State Politics," *American Political Science Review* 67 (December 1973): 1162– 1163.

[30]Charles Schultze, "Federal Spending: Past, Present and Future," in Henry Owen and Charles Schultze, eds., *Setting National Priorities: The Next Ten Years* (Washington, D.C.: Brookings Institution, 1976), 323–369.

[31]Richard Nathan and Fred Doolittle, *Reagan and the States* (Princeton, N.J.: Princeton University Press, 1987); Timothy J. Conlan, *From New Federalism to Devolution* (Washington, D.C.: Brookings Institution, 1998).

[32]*Garcia* v. *San Antonio Authority*, 469 U.S. 528 (1985).

[33]*United States* v. *Lopez*, 514 U.S. 549 (1995).

[34]*Printz* v. *United States*, 117 S. Ct. 2157 (1997).

[35]*Kimel* v. *Florida Board of Regents*, No. 98-791 (2000).

[36]*Reno* v. *Condon*, No. 98-1464 (2000).

[37]Andrew W. Dobelstein, *Politics, Economics, and Public Welfare* (Englewood Cliffs, N.J.: Prentice-Hall, 1980), 5.

[38]Lloyd A. Free and Hadley Cantril, *The Political Beliefs of Americans* (New York: Simon & Schuster, 1968), 21; see also William Lunch, *The Nationalization of American Politics* (Berkeley: University of California Press, 1987).

[39]Survey for the Times Mirror Center for the People and the Press by Princeton Survey Research Associates, July 12–27, 1994; see also, Tommy Thompson, *Power to the People* (New York: HarperCollins, 1996).

[40]Daniel J. Boorstin, *The Americans: the Democratic Experience* (New York: Vintage Books, 1974).

CHAPTER FOUR

[1]Julian P. Boyd, ed., *The Papers of Thomas Jefferson*, vol. 12 (Princeton, N.J.: Princeton University Press, 1955), 440.

[2]*Anderson v. Creighton*, 483 U.S. 635 (1987).

[3]*Schenck v. Pro-Choice Network*, No. 95-106 (1997).

[4]*Schenck v. United States*, 249 U.S. 47 (1919).

[5]*Dennis v. United States*, 341 U.S. 494 (1951).

[6]See, for example, *Yates v. United States*, 354 U.S. 298 (1957); *Noto v. United States*, 367 U.S. 290 (1961); *Scales v. United States*, 367 U.S. 203 (1961).

[7]*United States v. Carolene Products Co.*, 304 U.S. 144 (1938).

[8]*United States v. O'Brien*, 391 U.S. 367 (1968).

[9]*United States v. Eichman*, 496 U.S. 310 (1990).

[10]*Texas v. Johnson*, 109 S. Ct. at 2544 (1989).

[11]*Buckley v. Valeo*, 424 U.S. 1 (1976).

[12]*New York Times Co. v. United States*, 403 U.S. 713 (1971).

[13]*Nebraska Press Assn. v. Stuart*, 427 U.S. 539 (1976).

[14]*Barron v. Baltimore*, 7 Peters 243 (1833).

[15]*Gitlow v. New York*, 268 U.S. 652 (1925).

[16]*Fiske v. Kansas*, 274 U.S. 30 (1927) (speech); *Near v. Minnesota*, 283 U.S. 697 (1931) (press); *Cantwell v. Connecticut*, 310 U.S. 296 (1940) (religion); and *DeJonge v. Oregon*, 299 U.S. 253 (1937) (assembly and petition).

[17]*Near v. Minnesota*.

[18]*Brandenburg v. Ohio*, 395 U.S. 444 (1969).

[19]*R.A.V. v. St. Paul*, No. 90-7675 (1992).

[20]*Wisconsin v. Mitchell*, No. 92-515 (1993).

[21]*National Socialist Party v. Skokie*, 432 U.S. 43 (1977).

[22]*Forsyth County v. Nationalist Movement*, No. 91-538 (1992).

[23]*New York Times Co. v. Sullivan*, 376 U.S. 254 (1964).

[24]*Milkovich v. Lorain Journal*, 497 U.S. 1 (1990); see also *Masson v. The New Yorker*, No. 89-1799 (1991).

[25]*National Endowment for the Arts v. Karen Finley*, No. 97-371 (1998).

[26]*Roth v. United States*, 354 U.S. 476 (1957).

[27]*Barnes v. Glen Theatre*, No. 90-26 (1991).

[28]*Stanley v. Georgia*, 394 U.S. 557 (1969).

[29]*Osborne v. Ohio*, 495 U.S. 103 (1990).

[30]*Denver Area Consortium v. FCC*, No. 95-124 (1996).

[31]*Reno v. American Civil Liberties Union*, No. 96-511 (1997).

[32]See Michael J. Perry, *Religion in Politics* (New York: Oxford University Press, 1997).

[33]*Lemon v. Kurtzman*, 403 U.S. 602 (1971).

[34]Ibid.

[35]*Mitchell v. Helms*, No. 98-1648 (2000).

[36]*Engel v. Vitale*, 370 U.S. 421 (1962).

[37]*Abington School District v. Schempp*, 374 U.S. 203 (1963).

[38]*Wallace v. Jaffree*, 472 U.S. 38 (1985).

[39]*Santa Fe Independent School District v. DOE*, No. 99-62 (2000).

[40]*City of Boerne v. Flores*, No. 95-2074 (1997).

[41]*Wisconsin v. Yoder*, 406 U.S. 295 (1972); see also *Church of the Lukumi Babalu Aye v. City of Hialeah*, No. 91-948 (1993).

[42]*Griswold v. Connecticut*, 381 U.S. 479 (1965).

[43]*Roe v. Wade*, 401 U.S. 113 (1973).

[44]*Webster v. Reproductive Health Services*, 492 U.S. 490 (1989); see also *Rust v. Sullivan*, No. 89-1391 (1991).

[45]*Planned Parenthood v. Casey*, No. 91-744 (1992).

[46]*Stenberg v. Carhart*, No. 99-830 (2000).

[47]*Bowers v. Hardwick*, 478 U.S. 186 (1986).

[48]*Vacco v. Quill*, 117 S.C. 36 (1996); *Washington v. Glucksberg*, No. 96-110 (1997).

[49]*Powell v. Alabama*, 287 U.S. 45 (1932).

[50]*Mapp v. Ohio*, 367 U.S. 643 (1961).

[51]*Gideon v. Wainwright*, 372 U.S. 335 (1963).

[52]*Malloy v. Hogan*, 378 U.S. 1 (1964).

[53]*Miranda v. Arizona*, 384 U.S. 436 (1966); see also *Escobedo v. Illinois*, 378 U.S. 478 (1964).

[54]*Pointer v. Texas*, 380 U.S. 400 (1965).

[55]*Klopfer v. North Carolina*, 386 U.S. 213 (1967).

[56]*Duncan v. Louisiana*, 391 U.S. 145 (1968).

[57]*Benton v. Maryland*, 395 U.S. 784 (1969).

[58]*Dickerson v. United States*, No. 99-5525 (2000).

[59]*Weeks v. United States*, 232 U.S. 383 (1914).

[60]*Nix v. Williams*, 467 U.S. 431 (1984); see also *United States v. Leon*, 468 U.S. 897 (1984).

[61]*Michigan v. Sitz*, No. 88-1897 (1990).

[62]*Keeney v. Tamaya-Reyes*, No. 90-1859 (1992); see also *Coleman v. Thompson*, No. 89-7662 (1991).

[63]*Chicago v. Morales*, No. 97-1121 (1999).

[64]*Richards v. Wisconsin*, No. 96-5955 (1997).

[65]*Townsend v. Sain*, 372 U.S. 293 (1963).

[66] *Keeney* v. *Tamaya-Reyes*, No. 90-1859 (1992); see also *Coleman* v. *Thompson*, No. 89-7662 (1991).

[67] *Brecht* v. *Abrahamson*, No. 91-7358 (1993); see also *McCleskey* v. *Zant*, No. 89-7024 (1991).

[68] *Felker* v. *Turpin*, No. 95-8836 (1996); but see *Stewart* v. *Martinez-Villareal*, No. 97-300 (1998).

[69] *Williams* v. *Taylor*, No. 99-6615 (2000).

[70] Kurt Heine, "Philadelphia Cops Beat One of Their Own," *Syracuse Herald-American*, January 15, 1995, A13; see also Richard H. Uviller, *Virtual Justice* (New Haven, Conn.: Yale University Press, 1996).

[71] *Wilson* v. *Seiter*, No. 89-7376 (1991).

[72] *Harmelin* v. *Michigan*, No. 89-7272 (1991).

[73] See Alpheus T. Mason, *The Supreme Court: Palladium of Freedom* (Ann Arbor: University of Michigan Press, 1962); see also Henry J. Abraham, *Freedom and the Court* (New York: Oxford University Press, 1998); Robert F. Nagel, *Judicial Power and American Character* (New York: Oxford University Press, 1996).

CHAPTER FIVE

[1] Speech of Martin Luther King, Jr., in Washington, D.C., August 2, 1963.

[2] *Washington Post* wire story, May 14, 1991.

[3] Reported on *CBS Evening News*, January 16, 1989.

[4] Robert Nisbet, "Public Opinion versus Popular Opinion," *Public Interest* 41 (1975): 171.

[5] The classic analysis of this system of legalized segregation is C. Vann Woodward, *The Strange Career of Jim Crow*, 3d rev. ed. (New York: Oxford University Press, 1974).

[6] *Plessy* v. *Ferguson*, 163 U.S. 537 (1896).

[7] See, for example, *Missouri ex rel. Gaines* v. *Canada*, 305 U.S. 57 (1938).

[8] See Richard Kugler, *Simple Justice: The History of Brown v. Board of Education and Black America's Struggle for Equality* (New York: Knopf, 1977).

[9] *Brown* v. *Board of Education of Topeka*, 347 U.S. 483 (1954).

[10] See Taylor Branch, *Parting the Waters* (New York: Simon & Schuster, 1988).

[11] See Steven A. Shull, *The President and Civil Rights Policy: Leadership and Change* (Westport, Conn.: Greenwood, 1989).

[12] See Donald M. Kinder and Lynn M. Sanders, *Divided by Color* (Chicago: University of Chicago Press, 1996).

[13] See Derrick Bell, *And We Are Not Saved: The Elusive Quest for Racial Justice* (New York: Basic Books, 1987); Robert C. Smith and Richard S. Hzer, *Race, Class, and Culture* (Albany: State University of New York Press, 1992).

[14] See Keith Reeves, *Voting Hopes or Fears?* (New York: Oxford University Press, 1997).

[15]See Carol M. Swain, *Black Faces, Black Interests* (Cambridge, Mass.: Harvard University Press, 1993).

[16]*Tinker* v. *Colwell*, 193 U.S. 473 (1904).

[17]See Ellen Carol DuBois, *Feminism and Suffrage: The Emergence of an Independent Women's Movement in America, 1848–1869* (Ithaca, N.Y.: Cornell University Press, 1978).

[18]See Jane Mansbridge, *Why We Lost the ERA* (Chicago: University of Chicago Press, 1986).

[19]See Kathleen Hall Jamieson, *Beyond the Double Bind* (New York: Oxford University Press, 1995).

[20]Linda Witt, Karen M. Paget, and Glenna Matthews, *Running as a Woman* (New York: Free Press, 1994).

[21]Mary Lou Kendrigan, *Political Equality in a Democratic Society: Women in the United States* (Westport, Conn.: Greenwood, 1984).

[22]Timothy Bledsoe and Mary Herring, "Victims of Circumstance: Women in Pursuit of Political Office," *American Political Science Review* 84 (1990): 213–224.

[23]"The Gender Story," *The Public Perspective*, August/September 1996, 1–33; Sue Tolleson Rinehart, *Gender Consciousness and Politics* (New York: Routledge, 1992).

[24]See, for example, "The Gender Gap at the State Level," *The Public Perspective*, January/February 1993, 100.

[25]*County of Washington* v. *Gunther*, No. 80-429 (1981).

[26]*Faragher* v. *City of Boca Raton*, No. 97-282 (1998); *Burlington Industries* v. *Ellerth*, No. 97-569 (1998).

[27]*Davis* v. *Monroe County*, No. 97-843 (1999); *United States* v. *Morrison et al*, No. 99-5 (2000).

[28]Hans Stavans, *The Hispanic Condition* (New York: HarperPerennial, 1996).

[29]*De Canas* v. *Bica*, 424 U.S. 351 (1976).

[30]Nancy Gibbs, "Keep Out, You Tired, You Poor . . . ," *Time*, October 3, 1994, 46–47.

[31]James Truslow Adams, *The March of Democracy*, vol. 4 (New York: Scribner's, 1933), 284–285; see also, Charles J. McClain, *In Search of Equality: The Chinese Struggle against Discrimination in Nineteenth-Century America* (Berkeley: University of California Press, 1994).

[32]*Lau* v. *Nichols*, 414 U.S. 563 (1974).

[33]*Sutton* v. *United Air Lines*, No. 97-1943 (1999); *Murphy* v. *United Parcel Service*, No. 97-1992 (1999).

[34]*Boy Scouts of America* v. *Dale*, No. 99-699 (2000).

[35]*Romer* v. *Evans*, No. 94-1039 (1996).

[36]See *Reed* v. *Reed*, 404 U.S. 71 (1971); see also Joseph Ignagni and Thomas R. Marshall, "Gender Equality and the Supreme Court: Taking Another Look," *American Review of Politics* 16 (Fall/Winter 1995): 239–252.

[37]*Craig* v. *Boren*, 429 U.S. 190 (1976).

[38]*Rostker* v. *Goldberg*, 453 U.S. 57 (1980).

[39]*United States* v. *Virginia*, No. 94-1941 (1996).

[40]U.S. Conference of Mayors, 1998.

[41]See J. Morgan Kousser, *The Shaping of Southern Politics: Suffrage Restriction and the Establishment of the One-Party South, 1880–1910* (New Haven, Conn.: Yale University Press, 1974).

[42]V. O. Key, Jr., *Southern Politics* (New York: Knopf, 1949), 495.

[43]*Smith* v. *Allwright*, 321 U.S. 649 (1944).

[44]*Bush* v. *Verg*, No. 94-805 (1996); *Shaw* v. *Hunt*, No. 94-923 (1996); *Muller* v. *Johnson*, No. 94-631 (1995).

[45]*Hunt* v. *Cromartie*, No. 98-85 (1999).

[46]See Terry Eastland, *Ending Affirmative Action* (New York: Basic Books, 1997); but see also Barbara A. Bergmann, *In Defense of Affirmative Action* (New York: Basic Books, 1997); John David Skrentny, *The Ironies of Affirmative Action* (Chicago: University of Chicago Press, 1996).

[47]*University of California Regents* v. *Bakke*, 438 U.S. 265 (1978).

[48]*Steelworkers* v. *Weber*, 443 U.S. 193 (1979); *Fullilove* v. *Klutnick*, 448 U.S. 448 (1980).

[49]*Local No. 28, Sheet Metal Workers* v. *Equal Employment Opportunity Commission*, 478 U.S. 421 (1986); see also *Local No. 93, International Association of Firefighters* v. *Cleveland*, 478 U.S. 501 (1986); *Firefighters* v. *Stotts*, 459 U.S. 969 (1984); *Wygant* v. *Jackson*, 476 U.S. 238 (1986).

[50]*Adarand* v. *Pena*, No. 94-310 (1995).

[51]Jodi Wilgoren, "New Law in Texas Preserves Racial Mix in State's Colleges," *The New York Times*, November 24, 1999, A1.

[52]Gunnar Myrdal, *An American Dilemma: The Negro Problem and Modern Democracy* (New York: Harper, 1944).

[53]*Swann* v. *Charlotte-Mecklenburg County Board of Education*, 402 U.S. 1 (1971).

[54]*Milliken* v. *Bradley*, 418 U.S. 717 (1974).

[55]Christopher Jencks and Meredith Phillips, eds., *The Black-White Test Score Gap* (Washington, D.C.: Brookings Institution Press, 1998).

[56]Quoted in Megan Twohey, "Desegregation Is Dead," *National Journal* 31, no. 38 (September 18, 1999), 2614.

[57]*Board of Education of Oklahoma City* v. *Dowell*, 498 U.S. 237 (1991).

[58]*Missouri* v. *Jenkins*, 515 U.S. 70 (1995).

[59]*Sheff* v. *O'Neill*, No. 95-2071 (1996).

[60] Linda Darling-Hammond, "Black America: Progress and Prospects," Brookings Institution, 1998.

[61] Quoted in Twohey, "Desegregation Is Dead."

CHAPTER SIX

[1]V. O. Key, Jr., *Public Opinion and American Democracy* (New York: Knopf, 1961), 8.

[2]See Benjamin I. Page and Robert Shapiro, *The Rational Public* (Chicago: University of Chicago Press, 1992), 285–288.

[3]Jerry L. Yeric and John R. Todd, *Public Opinion*, 2d ed. (Itasca, Ill.: Peacock, 1989), 3.

[4]Elisabeth Noelle-Neumann, *The Spiral of Silence*, 2d ed. (Chicago: University of Chicago Press, 1993), ch. 1.

[5]Sidney Verba and Norman H. Nie, *Participation in America: Political Democracy and Social Equality* (New York: Harper & Row, 1972), 281–284.

[6]See Michael W. Traugott and Paul J. Lavrakas, *The Voters' Guide to Election Polls* (Chatham, N.J.: Chatham House, 1996).

[7]Ibid.

[8]Steven A. Peterson, *Political Behavior: Patterns in Everyday Life* (Newbury Park, Calif.: Sage Publications, 1990), 28–29.

[9]Ibid.

[10]See Murray Edelman, *Politics as Symbolic Action* (Chicago: Markham, 1971).

[11]See M. Kent Jennings and Richard Niemi, "The Transmission of Political Values from Parent to Child," *American Political Science Review* 62 (March 1968): 169–184.

[12]M. Kent Jennings and Richard G. Niemi, *Generations and Politics* (Princeton, N.J.: Princeton University Press, 1981), 91.

[13]See David Easton and Jack Dennis, *Children in the Political System* (New York: McGraw-Hill, 1969); Gabriel Almond and Sidney Verba, *The Civic Culture* (Boston: Little, Brown, 1965), 276.

[14]Orit Ichilov, *Political Socialization, Citizenship Education, and Democracy* (New York: Teachers College Press, 1990).

[15]Noelle-Neumann, *The Spiral of Silence*.

[16]See Shanto Iyengar, *Is Anyone Responsible? How Television Frames Political Issues* (Chicago: University of Chicago Press, 1991); Shanto Iyengar and Donald Kinder, *News That Matters: Television and American Opinion* (Chicago: University of Chicago Press, 1987).

[17]Thomas E. Patterson, *Out of Order* (New York: Vintage, 1994), ch. 2; see also Marion R. Just, Ann N. Crigler, Dean E. Alger, Timothy E. Cook, Montague Kern, and Darrell M. West, *Crosstalk: Citizens, Candidates, and the Media in a Presidential Campaign* (Chicago: University of Chicago Press, 1996).

[18]See John R. Zaller, *The Nature and Origins of Mass Opinion* (New York: Cambridge University Press, 1992).

[19]See Richard Merelman, *Making Something of Ourselves* (Berkeley: University of California Press, 1984); John White, *The New Politics of Old Values* (Hanover, N.H.: University Press of New England, 1988); Richard J. Ellis, *American Political Cultures* (New York: Oxford University Press, 1993).

[20]Philip Converse, "The Nature of Belief Systems in Mass Publics," in David Apter, ed., *Ideology and Discontent* (New York: Free Press, 1965), 206; John L. Sullivan, James E. Pierson, and George E. Marcus, "Ideological Constraint in the Mass Public," *American Journal of Political Science* 22 (May 1978): 233–249; Eric R. A. N. Smith, *The Unchanging American Voter* (Berkeley: University of California Press, 1989).

[21]See E. J. Dionne, *Why Americans Hate Politics* (New York: Simon & Schuster, 1992); E. J. Dionne, *They Only Look Dead* (New York: Simon & Schuster, 1996); David Frum, *What's Right?* (New York: Basic Books, 1996).

[22]CNN/USA Today poll conducted by the Gallup Organization, 1997.

[23]"The Gender Story," *The Public Perspective*, August/September 1996, 1–33; Sue Tolleson Rinehart, *Gender Consciousness and Politics* (New York: Routledge, 1992).

[24]Susan A. MacManus, *Young v. Old: Generational Combat in the 21st Century* (Boulder, Colo.: Westview Press, 1996).

[25]See Angus Campbell, Philip Converse, Warren Miller, and Donald Stokes, *The American Voter* (New York: Wiley, 1960), chs. 3–4.

[26]Martin P. Wattenberg, *The Decline of American Political Parties, 1952–1984* (Cambridge, Mass.: Harvard University Press, 1990).

[27]See E. E. Schattschneider, *The Semisovereign People* (New York: Holt, Rinehart & Winston, 1980), ch. 8.

[28]See William Domhoff, *The Power Elite and the State* (New York: Aldine de Gruyter, 1990); but see also Paul Brace and Barbara Hinckley, *Follow the Leader* (New York: Basic Books, 1992).

[29]Benjamin I. Page and Robert Y. Shapiro, "Effects of Public Opinion on Policy," *American Political Science Review* 77 (March 1983): 178.

[30]See Benjamin Ginsberg, *The Consequences of Consent* (New York: Random House, 1982); but also see Samuel L. Popkin, *The Reasoning Voter: Communication and Persuasion in Presidential Campaigns* (Chicago: University of Chicago Press, 1991); Arthur Lupia and Mathew McCubbins, *The Democratic Dilemma* (New York: Cambridge University Press, 1998).

[31]See Paul Brace and Barbara Hinckley, *Follow the Leader: Opinion Polls and Modern Presidents* (New York: Basic Books, 1992).

CHAPTER SEVEN

[1]Walter Lippmann, *Public Opinion* (New York: Free Press, 1965), 36.

[2]Sidney Verba, Kay Schlozman, and Henry Brady, *Voice and Equality* (Cambridge, Mass.: Harvard University Press, 1995); see also Steven J. Rosenstone and John Mark Hansen, *Mobilization, Participation and Democracy in America* (New York: Macmillan, 1993).

[3]Quoted in Ralph Volney Harlow, *The Growth of the United States* (New York: Henry Holt, 1943), 312.

[4]See William H. Flanigan and Nancy Zingale, *The Political Behavior of the American Electorate*, 9th ed. (Washington, D.C.: Congressional Quarterly Press, 1998), 24–26.

[5]Example from Gus Tyler, "One Cheer for the Democrats," *New Leader*, November 3, 1986, 6.

[6]Turnout figures provided by Washington, D.C., embassies of the respective countries, 1998.

[7]Ivor Crewe, "Electoral Participation," in David Butler, Howard R. Penniman, and Austin Ranney, eds., *Democracy at the Polls* (Washington, D.C.: American Enterprise Institute, 1981), 249.

[8]Philip E. Converse with Richard Niemi, "Non-Voting among Young Adults in the United States," in William J. Crotty et al., eds., *Political Parties and Political Behavior* (Boston: Allyn & Bacon, 1971), 456.

[9]Richard Boyd, "Decline of U.S. Voter Turnout," *American Politics Quarterly* 9 (April 1981): 142.

[10]Ruy A. Teixeira, *The Disappearing American Voter* (Washington, D.C.: Brookings Institution, 1992).

[11]Crewe, "Electoral Participation," 251–253.

[12]G. Bingham Powell, "Voting Turnout in Thirty Democracies," in Richard Rose, ed., *Electoral Participation: A Comparative Analysis* (Beverly Hills, Calif.: Sage, 1980), 6.

[13]M. Margaret Conway, Gertrude A. Steuernagel, and David Ahern, *Women and Political Participation: Cultural Change in the Political Arena* (Washington, D.C.: Congressional Quarterly Press, 1997).

[14]Sidney Verba, Kay Schlozman, and Henry Brady, *Voice and Equality* (Cambridge, Mass.: Harvard University Press, 1995).

[15]See Joseph Nye, David King, and Philip Zelikow, *Why People Don't Trust Government* (Cambridge, Mass.: Harvard University Press, 1997).

[16]See, for example, Norman H. Nie, G. Bingham Powell, and Kenneth Prewitt, "Social Structure and Political Participation," *American Political Science Review* 63 (September 1969).

[17]John M. Strate, Charles J. Parrish, Charles D. Elder, and Coit Ford III, "Life Span Civic Development and Voting Participation," *American Political Science Review* 83 (June 1989): 443–465.

[18]Norma Nie, Jane Junn, and Kenneth Stehlik-Barry, *Education and Democratic Citizenship in America* (Chicago: University of Chicago Press, 1996).

[19]M. Margaret Conway, *Political Participation in the United States*, 2d ed. (Washington, D.C.: Congressional Quarterly Press, 1991), 23–25.

[20]Verba, Schlozman, and Brady, *Voice and Equality*.

[21]Mark Kesselman and Joel Kreiger, *European Politics in Transition* (Lexington, Mass.: Heath, 1987), 87.

[22]Edie N. Goldenberg and Michael W. Traugott, *Campaigning for Congress* (Washington, D.C.: Congressional Quarterly Press, 1984), ch. 9.

[23]Thomas E. Patterson, *The Mass Media Election* (New York: Praeger, 1980), chs. 7–10.

[24]D. Roderick Kiewiet, *Macro-Economics and Micro-Politics* (Chicago: University of Chicago Press, 1983), 154–158; Gallup Reports, (1936–1996).

[25]V. O. Key, Jr., *The Responsible Electorate* (Cambridge, Mass.: Belknap Press of Harvard University Press, 1966), ch. 1.

[26]Verba, Schlozman, and Brady, *Voice and Equality*.

[27]Joseph Schumpeter, *Capitalism, Socialism, and Democracy* (New York: Harper Torchbooks, 1950), 269.

[28]Craig A. Rimmerman, *The New Citizenship* (Boulder, Colo.: Westview Press, 1997).

[29]W. Russell Neuman, *The Paradox of Mass Politics* (Cambridge, Mass.: Harvard University Press, 1986), 176.

[30]Samuel H. Barnes et al., eds., *Political Action* (Beverly Hills, Calif.: Sage, 1979), 541–542.

[31]Russell J. Dalton, *Citizen Politics in Western Democracies*, 3d ed. (Chatham, N.J.: Chatham House, 1996), 43.

[32]Barnes et al., *Political Action*, 541–542.

[33]Robert Putnam, *Bowling Alone* (New York: Simon and Schuster, 2000).

[34]For example, interest-group membership has risen.

[35]Robert Putnam, *Making Democracy Work* (Princeton, N.J.: Princeton University Press, 1994).

[36]Patterson, *Mass Media Election*, ch. 4.

[37]Survey of Pew Center for People and the Press, 1998.

[38]See Benjamin Ginsberg, *The Consequences of Consent* (New York: Random House, 1982), ch. 2.

[39]Lee Bruce Stokes, "New Players in the Trade Game," *National Journal*, December 18, 1999, 3630.

[40]Dalton, *Citizen Politics in Western Democracies*, 38.

[41]Ibid., 68.

[42]Ronald Inglehart, "Post-Materialism in an Environment of Insecurity," *American Political Science Review* 75 (1981): 880–900; Edward N. Mueller and Mitchell A. Seligson, "Inequality and Insurgency," *American Political Science Review* 81 (1987): 425–451.

[43]William Watts and Lloyd A. Free, eds., *The State of the Nation* (New York: University Books, Potomac Associates, 1967), 97.

[44]Robert E. Lane, "Market Justice, Political Justice," *American Political Science Review* 80 (1986): 383; see also Jennifer Nedelsky, *Private Property and the Limits of American Constitutionalism* (New York: Oxford University Press, 1990).

[45]Ginsberg, *Consequences of Consent*, 49.

[46]Stephen Earl Bennett and David Resnick, "The Implications of Nonvoting for Democracy in the United States," *American Journal of Political Science* (August 1990): 771–802.

CHAPTER EIGHT

[1]E. E. Schattschneider, *Party Government* (New York: Rinehart, 1942), 1.

[2]E. E. Schattschneider, *The Semisovereign People: A Realist's View of Democracy in America* (New York: Holt, Rinehart & Winston, 1961), 140.

[3]See John Aldrich, *Why Parties? The Origin and Transformation of Political Parties in America* (Chicago: University of Chicago Press, 1995).

[4]L. Sandy Maisel, *Parties and Elections in America*, 2d ed. (New York: McGraw-Hill, 1993), 27.

[5]Aldrich, *Why Parties?*

[6]See Richard P. McCormick, *The Second American Party System: Party Formation in the Jacksonian Era* (Chapel Hill: University of North Carolina Press, 1966).

[7]Alexis de Tocqueville, *Democracy in America (1835–1840)*, ed. J. P. Mayer and A. P. Kerr (Garden City, N.Y.: Doubleday/Anchor, 1969), 60.

[8]Aldrich, *Why Parties?*, 151.

[9]See Kristi Andersen, *The Creation of a Democratic Majority, 1928-1936* (Chicago: University of Chicago Press, 1979).

[10]See Kevin Phillips, *The Emerging Republican Majority* (New Rochelle, N.Y.: Arlington House, 1969).

[11]See Harold W. Stanley, "Southern Partisan Changes: Dealignment, Realignment or Both?" *Journal of Politics* 50 (1988): 64–88; Earl Black and Merle Black, *Politics and Society in the South* (Cambridge, Mass.: Harvard University Press, 1987); Robert H. Swansbrough and David M. Brodsky, eds., *The South's New Politics: Realignment and Dealignment* (Columbia: University of South Carolina Press, 1988); Dewey L. Grantham, *The Life and Death of the Solid South* (Lexington: University of Kentucky Press, 1988).

[12]William H. Flanigan and Nancy Zingale, *Political Behavior of the American Electorate*, 9th ed. (Washington, D.C.: Congressional Quarterly Press, 1998), 58–63.

[13]Frederick G. Dutton, *Changing Sources of Power* (New York: McGraw-Hill, 1971), ch. 6.

[14]See E. J. Dionne, Jr., *Why Americans Hate Politics* (New York: Simon & Schuster, 1992).

[15]The classic account of the relationship of electoral and party systems is Maurice Duverger, *Political Parties* (New York: Wiley, 1954), bk. II, ch. 1; see also Arend Lijphardt, *Electoral Systems and Party Systems* (New York: Oxford University Press, 1994).

[16]Clinton Rossiter, *Parties and Politics in America* (Ithaca, N.Y.: Cornell University Press, 1960), 11.

[17]Nancy Gibbs and Michael Duffy, "Fall of the House of Newt," *Time*, November 16, 1998, 47.

[18]Gerald M. Pomper, *Passions and Interests: Political Party Concepts of American Democracy* (Lawrence: University of Kansas Press, 1992), ch. 1.

[19]Ibid, ch. 1.

[20]John F. Bibby, *Politics, Parties, and Elections in America*, 2d ed. (Chicago: Nelson-Hall, 1992), 275–283.

[21]Steven J. Rosenstone, Roy L. Behr, and Edward H. Lazarus, *Third Parties in America*, 2d ed. (Princeton, N.J.: Princeton University Press, 1996).

[22]Daniel A. Mazmanian, *Third Parties in Presidential Elections* (Washington, D.C.: Brookings Institution, 1984), 143–144.

[23]See Lawrence Goodwyn, *The Populist Movement* (New York: Oxford University Press, 1978).

[24]Anthony King, *Running Scared* (New York: Free Press, 1997).

[25]See Alan Ehrenhalt, *The United States of Ambition* (New York: Times Books, 1991).

[26]See Paul S. Herrnson, *Party Campaigning in the '80s* (Cambridge, Mass.: Harvard University Press, 1988); Aldrich, *Why Parties?*

[27]See James L. Gibson, John P. Frendreis, and Laura L. Vertz, "Party Dynamics in the 1980s: Change in County Party Organizational Strength, 1980–1984," *American Journal of Political Science* 33 (1989): 67–90.

[28]James L. Gibson, Cornelius Cotter, John Bibby, and Robert Huckshorn, "Assessing Party Organizational Strength," *American Journal of Political Science* 27 (May 1983): 200.

[29]See Sarah McCally Morehouse, "Money Versus Party Effort," *American Journal of Political Science* 34 (1990): 706–724.

[30]David Adamany, "Political Parties in the 1980s," in Michael J. Malbin, ed., *Money and Politics in the United States* (Chatham, N.J.: Chatham House, 1984), 114.

[31]Gibson et al., "Assessing Party Organizational Strength," 206.

[32]Joseph Napolitan, *The Election Game and How to Win It* (New York: Doubleday, 1972).

[33]David B. Magleby and Candice J. Nelson, *The Money Chase: Congressional Campaign Finance Reform* (Washington, D.C.: Brookings Institution, 1990).

[34]John F. Bibby, *Politics, Parties, and Elections in America*, 3d ed. (Chicago: Nelson-Hall, 1996), 205.

[35]Federal Elections Commission data, 1999.

[36]David Chagall, *The New King-Makers* (New York: Harcourt Brace Jovanovich, 1981).

[37]Michael W. Traugott and Paul J. Lavrakas, *The Voters' Guide to Election Polls* (Chatham, N.J.: Chatham House, 1996).

[38]Kiku Adatto, "Sound Bite Democracy," Joan Shoronstein Center on the Press, Politics, and Public Policy, Research Paper R-2, Harvard University, Cambridge, Mass., June 1990.

[39]Darrell M. West, *Air Wars: Television Advertising in Election Campaigns, 1952–1992* (Washington, D.C.: Congressional Quarterly Press, 1993), 140–146.

[40]Ibid.

[41]Stephen Ansolabehere and Shanto Iyengar, *Going Negative* (New York: Free Press, 1995), ch. 5.

[42]West, *Air Wars*, 12.

[43]Ibid., 143.

[44]Thomas E. Patterson, *Out of Order* (New York: Vintage, 1994), ch. 2.

[45] Associated Press Wire, "Candidates Try E-mail Route to Election: Presidential Hopefuls All Using Web Sites," November 26, 1999.

[46]David E. Price, *Bringing Back the Parties* (Washington, D.C.: Congressional Quarterly Press, 1984), 116.

[47]See James P. Pfiffner, *The Modern Presidency* (New York: St. Martin's Press, 1994), ch. 6.

CHAPTER NINE

[1]E. E. Schattschneider, *The Semisovereign People: A Realist's View of Democracy in America* (New York: Holt, Rinehart & Winston, 1960), 35.

[2]Quoted in Norman J. Ornstein and Shirley Elder, *Interest Groups, Lobbying, and Policymaking* (Washington, D.C.: Congressional Quarterly Press, 1978), 11.

[3]Alexis de Tocqueville, *Democracy in America (1835–1840)*, ed. J. P. Mayer and A. P. Kerr (Garden City, N.Y.: Doubleday/Anchor, 1969), bk. II, ch. 4.

[4]See Jack L. Walker, Jr., *Mobilizing Interest Groups in America* (Ann Arbor: University of Michigan Press, 1991).

[5]E. Pendleton Herring, *Group Representation before Congress* (Washington, D.C.: Brookings Institution, 1929), 78.

[6]Kay Lehman Schlozman and John T. Tierney, *Organized Interests and American Democracy* (New York: Harper & Row, 1986), 41.

[7]See Robert H. Salisbury, John P. Heinz, Edward O. Leumann, and Robert L. Nelson, "Who Works with Whom? Interest Group Alliances and Opposition," *American Political Science Review* 81 (December 1987): 1217–1234.

[8]See Walker, *Mobilizing Interest Groups in America.*

[9]See Lawrence Rothenberg, *Linking Citizens to Government: Interest Group Politics at Common Cause* (New York: Cambridge University Press, 1992).

[10]Mancur Olson, *The Logic of Collective Action* (Cambridge, Mass.: Harvard University Press, 1965), 64.

[11]See Ernest Wittenberg and Elisabeth Wittenberg, *How to Win in Washington* (Cambridge, Mass.: Blackwell, 1989), 81.

[12]Walker, *Mobilizing Interest Groups in America*, ch. 1.

[13]Christopher J. Bosso, "The Color of Money: Environmental Groups and the Pathologies of Fund Raising," in Allan J. Cigler and Burdett Loomis, *Interest Group Politics*, 4th ed. (Washington, D.C.: Congressional Quarterly Press, 1995), 101–103.

[14]See Steve Bruce, *The Rise and Fall of the New Christian Right* (New York: Oxford University Press, 1988).

[15]Schlozman and Tierney, *Organized Interests and American Democracy*, 54; see also Ronald J. Hrebenar and Ruth K. Scott, *Interest Group Politics in America* (Englewood Cliffs, N.J.: Prentice-Hall, 1990), 167.

[16]Ornstein and Elder, *Interest Groups, Lobbying, and Policymaking*, 82–86.

[17]See John Mark Hansen, *Gaining Access* (Chicago: University of Chicago Press, 1991).

[18]Robert H. Salisbury and Paul Johnson, "Who You Know versus What You Know," *American Journal of Political Science* 33 (February 1989): 175–195; see also William P. Brown, *Cultivating Congress* (Lawrence: University Press of Kansas, 1995).

[19]Ornstein and Elder, *Interest Groups, Lobbying, and Policymaking*, 70.

[20]Quoted in ibid, 77.

[21]Bruce C. Wolfe and Bertram J. Levine, *Lobbying Congress*, 2d ed. (Washington, D.C.: Congressional Quarterly Press, 1996).

[22]See Marver Bernstein, *Regulating Business by Independent Commission* (Princeton, N.J.: Princeton University Press, 1955).

[23]Paul J. Quirk, *Industry Influence in Federal Regulatory Agencies* (Princeton, N.J.: Princeton University Press, 1981).

[24]John E. Chubb, *Interest Groups and the Bureaucracy: The Politics of Energy* (Stanford, Calif.: Stanford University Press, 1983), 200–201.

[25]Charles T. Goodsell, *The Case for Bureaucracy*, 3d ed. (Chatham, N.J.: Chatham House, 1994), 55–60.

[26]Lee Epstein and C. K. Rowland, "Interest Groups in the Courts," *American Political Science Review*, 85 (1991): 205–217.

[27]See John Mark Hansen, *Gaining Access* (Chicago: University of Chicago Press, 1991); but see William P. Browne, *Cultivating Congress* (Lawrence: University of Kansas Press, 1995).

[28]Hugh Heclo, "Issue Networks and the Executive Establishment," in Anthony King, ed., *The New American Political System* (Washington, D.C.: American Enterprise Institute, 1978), 87–124.

[29]Ornstein and Elder, *Interest Groups, Lobbying, and Policymaking*, 88–93; see also Paul S. Herrnson, Ronald Shaiko, and Clyde Wilcox, eds., *The Interest Group Connection* (Chatham, N.J.: Chatham House, 1998).

[30]Wittenberg and Wittenberg, *How to Win in Washington*, 81.

[31]Quoted in Mark Green, "Political PAC-Man," *The New Republic*, December 13, 1982, 20.

[32]Frank J. Sorauf, *Inside Campaign Finance* (New Haven, Conn.: Yale University Press, 1992).

[33]Quoted in Larry Sabato, *PAC Power: Inside the World of Political Action Committees* (New York: Norton, 1984), 72.

[34]Federal Elections Commission (FEC) Report, April 29, 1993.

[35]"Tobacco Industry Courts the Hill with Compromise, Conciliation," *Congressional Quarterly Weekly Report: Guide to American Government* (Washington, D.C.: Congressional Quarterly Press, 1998), 51–57.

[36]See Michael J. Malbin, "Of Mountains and Molehills," in Michael J. Malbin, *Parties, Interest Groups, and Campaign Finance Laws* (Washington, D.C.: American Enterprise Institute, 1981), 157–177.

[37]See Dan Clawson, Alan Neustadtl, and Denise Scott, *Money Talks* (New York: Basic Books, 1992); Thomas L. Gatz, *Improper Influence* (Ann Arbor: University of Michigan Press, 1996).

[38]V. O. Key, Jr., *Public Opinion and American Democracy* (New York: Knopf, 1961), 428.

[39]See Robert Dahl, *Who Governs?* (New Haven, Conn.: Yale University Press, 1961); Robert Dahl, *Dilemmas of Pluralist Democracy* (New Haven, Conn.: Yale University Press, 1982).

[40]Walker, *Mobilizing Interest Groups in America*, 112.

[41]Theodore J. Lowi, *The End of Liberalism: The Second Republic of the United States* (New York: Norton, 1979).

[42]Jeffrey Berry, *The Interest Group Society* (Boston: Little, Brown, 1984), 172.

[43]See William Domhoff, *The Power Elite and the State* (New York: Aldine de Gruyter, 1990).

[44]See Lawrence S. Rothenberg, *Linking Citizens to Government* (New York: Cambridge University Press, 1992).

[45]Benjamin Ginsberg, *The Consequences of Consent* (New York: Random House, 1982), 214.

[46]See, for example, Andrew S. McFarland, *Common Cause* (Chatham, N.J.: Chatham House, 1984), 48–49.

[47]Jonathan Rauch, *Demosclerosis: The Silent Killer of American Government* (New York: Times Books, 1994).

CHAPTER TEN

[1]Theodore H. White, *The Making of the President, 1972* (New York: Bantam Books, 1973), 327.

[2]See Richard Davis, *The Press and American Politics*, 2d ed. (Upper Saddle River, N.J.: Prentice Hall, 1996), 24–27.

[3]Comment at the annual meeting of the American Association of Political Consultants, Washington, D.C., 1977.

[4]Culver H. Smith, *The Press, Politics, and Patronage* (Athens: University of Georgia Press, 1977), 2, 15, 39–55.

[5]Frank Luther Mott, *American Journalism, a History: 1690–1960* (New York: Macmillan, 1962), 114–115.

[6]Smith, *Press, Politics, and Patronage*, 163–168.

[7]Doris A. Graber, *Mass Media and American Politics*, 4th ed. (Washington, D.C.: Congressional Quarterly Press, 1993), 36; Mark Wahlgren Summers, *The Press Gang* (Chapel Hill: University of North Carolina Press, 1994).

[8]See Michael Schudson, *Discovering the News* (New York: Basic Books, 1978).

[9]Commission on Freedom of the Press, *A Free and Responsible Press* (Chicago: University of Chicago Press, 1974), 62–63.

[10]Mott, *American Journalism*, 220–227, 241, 243.

[11]Edwin Emery, *The Press and America: An Interpretive History of the Mass Media* (Englewood Cliffs, N.J.: Prentice-Hall, 1977), 350.

[12]Quoted in Mott, *American Journalism*, 529.

[13]See Dean A. Alger, *The Media and Politics*, 2d ed. (Belmont, Calif.: Wadsworth, 1996), 122–123.

[14]Quoted in David Halberstam, *The Powers That Be* (New York: Knopf, 1979), 208–209.

[15]Leo Bogart, *The Age of Television* (New York: Unger, 1956), 213.

[16]Theodore H. White, *America in Search of Itself: The Making of the President, 1956–1980* (New York: Harper & Row, 1982), 172–173.

[17]Quoted in Michael Robinson and Margaret Sheehan, *Over the Wire and on TV* (New York: Russell Sage Foundation, 1983), 226.

[18]William Cole, ed., *The Most of A. J. Leibling* (New York: Simon, 1963), 7.

[19]Figures from *Standard Rate and Data Service and Electronic Media*, various dates.

[20]Ibid.

[21]Graber, *Mass Media and American Politics*, 36.

[22]See Ben Bagdikian, *The Media Monopoly*, 5th ed. (Boston: Beacon, 1997).

[23]Edward J. Epstein, *News from Nowhere: Television and the News* (New York: Random House, 1973), 37.

[24]White, *The Making of the President, 1972*, 346–348.

[25]See John Chancellor and Walter R. Mears, *The News Business* (New York: Harper & Row, 1983).

[26]David L. Paletz and Robert M. Entman, *Media Power Politics* (New York: Free Press, 1981), 16.

[27]Dean Alger, *Megamedia* (Lanham, Md.: Rowman & Littlefield, 1998), 13–14.

[28]Study for Committee of Concerned Journalists, 1998.

[29]James David Barber, "Characters in the Campaign: The Literary Problem," in James David Barber, ed., *Race for the Presidency* (Englewood Cliffs: N.J.: Prentice-Hall, 1978), 114–115.

[30]See Kenneth T. Walsh, *Feeding the Beast* (New York: Free Press, 1996).

[31]Bernard C. Cohen, *The Press and Foreign Policy* (Princeton, N.J.: Princeton University Press, 1963), 13.

[32]See John Anthony Maltese, *Spin Control* (Chapel Hill: University of North Carolina Press, 1994); Howard Kurtz, *Spin Cycle* (New York: Free Press, 1998).

[33]S. Robert Lichter and Richard E. Noyes, *Good Intentions Make Bad News*, updated ed. (Lanham, Md.: Rowman & Littlefield, 1997), ii.

[34]Thomas Patterson, *Out of Order* (New York: Vintage, 1994), ch. 3.

[35]Thomas E. Patterson, "Bad News, Bad Governance," *ANNALS* 546 (July 1996): 97–108; James Fallows, *Breaking the News* (New York: Pantheon, 1996).

[36]Data from Center for Media and Public Affairs, Washington, D.C., 1996.

[37]Doreen Carvajal, "For News Media, Some Introspection," the *New York Times*, April 5, 1998, 28.

[38]Quoted in Max Kampelman, "The Power of the Press," *Policy Review* 6 (1978): 19.

[39]Ibid.

[40]Quoted in Epstein, *News from Nowhere*, ix.

[41]"Internal Affairs: TV News Coverage of the White House Sex Scandals," *Media Monitor*, Center for Media and Public Affairs, Washington, D.C., March/April 1998.

[42]Lippmann, *Public Opinion*, 221; see also Timothy E. Cook, *Governing with the News* (Chicago: University of Chicago Press, 1997).

CHAPTER ELEVEN

[1]Roger H. Davidson and Walter J. Oleszek, *Congress and Its Members*, 2d ed. (Washington, D.C.: Congressional Quarterly Press, 1985), 7.

[2]See Paul S. Herrnson, *Congressional Elections: Campaigning at Home and in Washington* (Washington, D.C.: Congressional Quarterly Press, 1995).

[3]See Gary C. Jacobson, *The Politics of Congressional Elections*, 4th ed. (New York: Longman, 1996).

[4]See Jonathan S. Krasno, *Challenges, Competition, and Reelection* (New Haven, Conn.: Yale University Press, 1995).

[5]David R. Mayhew, *Congress: The Electoral Connection* (New Haven, Conn.: Yale University Press, 1974), 16; Richard F. Fenno, Jr., *Home Style: House Members in Their Districts* (Boston: Little, Brown, 1978), 167.

[6]James L. Payne, "The Personal Electoral Advantage of House Incumbents, 1936–1976," *American Politics Quarterly* 8 (October 1980): 465–482.

[7]Lawrence C. Dodd, "A Theory of Congressional Cycles," in Gerald Wright, Leroy Rieselbach, and Lawrence C. Dodd, *Congress and Policy Change* (New York: Agathon, 1986).

[8]Bruce Cain, John Ferejohn, and Morris P. Fiorino, *The Personal Vote* (Cambridge, Mass.: Harvard University Press, 1987).

[9]Information provided by Clerk of the House, 1999.

[10]Harold W. Stanley and Richard G. Niemi, *Vital Statistics on American Politics*, 5th ed. (Washington, D.C.: Congressional Quarterly Press, 1995), 217.

[11]See Diana Evans Yiannakis, "House Members' Communication Styles," *Journal of Politics* 44 (November 1982): 1049–1073.

[12]*Congressional Quarterly Guide to Congress*, 3d ed. (Washington, D.C.: Congressional Quarterly Press, 1982), 666; see also Frank J. Sorauf, *Inside Campaign Finance* (New Haven, Conn.: Yale University Press, 1992), 67, 86.

[13]Federal Elections Commission data, 1999.

[14]See Gary C. Jacobson, *The Electoral Origins of Divided Government* (Boulder, Colo.: Westview Press, 1990).

[15]Quoted in "A Tale of Myths and Measures: Who Is Truly Vulnerable?" *Congressional Quarterly Weekly Report*, December 4, 1993, 7; see also Dennis F. Thompson, *Ethics in Congress* (Washington, D.C.: Brookings Institution Press, 1995).

[16]James E. Campbell, *The Presidential Pulse of Congressional Elections* (Lexington: University Press of Kentucky, 1993).

[17]Linda L. Fowler and Robert D. McClure, *Political Ambition* (New Haven, Conn.: Yale University Press, 1989); see also Jonathan S. Krasno and Donald Philip Green, "Preempting Quality Challengers in House Elections," *Journal of Politics* 50 (November 1988): 878.

[18]Thomas Kazee, "Recruiting Challengers in U.S. House Elections," *Legislative Studies Quarterly* (August 1983): 469–480.

[19]Keith R. Poole and Howard Rosenthal, "Patterns of Congressional Voting," *American Journal of Political Science*, 35 (February 1991): 228.

[20]Linda Witt, Karen M. Paget, and Glenna Matthews, *Running as a Woman: Gender and Power in American Politics* (New York: Free Press, 1993); see also Sue Thomas, *How Women Legislate* (New York: Oxford University Press, 1994).

[21]Ronald M. Peters, Jr., *The American Speakership* (Baltimore: Johns Hopkins University Press, 1990).

[22]Fred R. Harris, *Deadlock or Decision: The U.S. Senate and the Rise of National Politics* (New York: Oxford University Press, 1993), 182.

[23]See, for example, Donald Matthews, *U.S. Senators and Their World* (Chapel Hill: University of North Carolina Press, 1960).

[24]See Barbara Sinclair, *Transformation of the U.S. Senate* (Baltimore, Md.: Johns Hopkins University Press, 1989).

[25]See Barbara Sinclair, *Legislators, Leaders, and Lawmaking* (Baltimore, Md.: Johns Hopkins University Press, 1995).

[26]See David W. Rohde, *Parties and Leaders in the Postreform House* (Chicago: University of Chicago Press, 1991).

[27]Jonathan D. Salant, "New Chairman Swing to Right: Freshmen Get Choice Posts," *Congressional Quarterly Weekly Report*, December 10, 1994, 3493.

[28]See Steven H. Haeberle, "The Institutionalization of the Subcommittee in the United States House of Representatives," *Journal of Politics* 40 (November 1978): 1054–1065.

[29]Ibid.

[30]David W. Rhode and Kenneth A. Shepsle, "Domestic Committee Assignments in the House of Representatives," *American Political Science Review*, September 1973, 889–905.

[31]Steven S. Smith, *The American Congress* (Boston: Houghton Mifflin, 1995), 189–198.

[32]See Stephen E. Frantzich and Steven E. Schier, *Congress: Games and Strategies* (Dubuque, Iowa: Brown & Benchmark, 1995), 127.

[33]See Gerald S. Strom, *The Logic of Lawmaking* (Baltimore: Johns Hopkins University Press, 1990).

[34]See Barbara Sinclair, *Unorthodox Lawmaking* (Washington, D.C.: Congressional Quarterly Press, 1997).

[35]See Robert Spitzer, *President & Congress* (New York: McGraw-Hill, 1993).

[36]See Paul C. Light, *The President's Agenda*, rev. ed. (Baltimore: Johns Hopkins University Press, 1991).

[37]Walter J. Oleszek, *Congressional Procedures and the Policy Process*, 4th ed. (Washington, D.C.: Congressional Quarterly Press, 1995), ch. 10.

[38]See Gary Orfield, *Congressional Power: Congress and Social Change* (New York: Harcourt Brace Jovanovich, 1975).

[39]James L. Sundquist, "Congress and the President: Enemies or Partners?" in Lawrence C. Dodd and Bruce I. Oppenheimer, eds., *Congress Reconsidered* (New York: Praeger, 1977), 240.

[40]See Paul C. Light, *Forging Legislation* (New York: Norton, 1992).

[41]See Gary W. Cox and Mathew D. McCubbins, *Legislative Leviathan* (Berkeley: University of California Press, 1993).

[42]Eric M. Uslaner, *The Decline of Comity in Congress* (Ann Arbor: University of Michigan Press, 1994).

[43]Joel A. Aberbach, *Keeping a Watchful Eye* (Washington, D.C.: Brookings Institution, 1990); William T. Gormley, *Taming the Bureaucracy* (Princeton, N.J.: Princeton University Press, 1989).

[44]Mathew D. McCubbins and Thomas Schwartz, "Congressional Oversight Overlooked," *American Journal of Political Science* 2 (February 1984): 165–179.

[45]Davidson and Oleszek, *Congress and Its Members*, 2d ed., 7.

CHAPTER TWELVE

[1]Woodrow Wilson, *Constitutional Government in the United States* (New York: Columbia University Press, 1908), 67.

[2]Charles O. Jones, *The Presidency in a Separated System* (Washington, D.C.: Brookings Institution, 1994).

[3]James W. Davis, *The American Presidency* (New York: Harper & Row, 1987), 13.

[4]See Barry M. Blechman and Stephen S. Kaplan, *Force without War* (Washington, D.C.: Brookings Institution, 1978).

[5]*United States* v. *Belmont*, 57 U.S. 758 (1937).

[6]Robert DiClerico, *The American President*, 4th ed. (Englewood Cliffs, N.J.: Prentice-Hall, 1995), 47.

[7]Quoted in Wilfred E. Binkley, *President and Congress*, 3d ed. (New York: Vintage, 1962), 142.

[8]Theodore Roosevelt, *An Autobiography* (New York: Scribner's, 1931), 383.

[9]See Richard M. Pious, *The American Presidency* (New York: Basic Books, 1979), 83.

[10]Robert J. Spitzer, *President and Congress* (New York: McGraw-Hill, 1993), 35–37. Raymond Tatalovich and Byron W. Daynes, *Presidential Power in the United States* (Monterey, Calif.: Brooks/Cole, 1984), 322–323.

[11]Kenneth A. Oye, Robert J. Lieber, and Donald Rothchild, *Eagle in a New World* (New York: HarperCollins, 1992).

[12]Spitzer, *President and Congress*, 137–232.

[13]James Bryce, *The American Commonwealth* (New York: Commonwealth Edition, 1908), 230.

[14]Davis, *The American Presidency*, 20.

[15]Hugh Heclo, "Introduction: The Presidential Illusion," in Hugh Heclo and Lester M. Salamon, eds., *The Illusion of Presidential Government* (Boulder, Colo.: Westview Press, 1981), 6.

[16]Thomas R. Marshall, *Presidential Nominations in a Reform Age* (New York: Praeger, 1981); James W. Ceaser, *Presidential Selection: Theory and Development* (Princeton, N. J. Princeton University Press, 1979).

[17]Thomas E. Patterson, *Out of Order* (New York: Vintage, 1994).

[18]See Michael Nelson, ed., *The Elections of 1992* (Washington, D.C.: Congressional Quarterly Press, 1993), 2–4.

[19]See Hugh Winebrenner, *The Iowa Precinct Caucuses* (Ames: Iowa State University Press, 1987); Gary R. Orren and Nelson W. Polsby, eds., *Media and Momentum: The New Hampshire Primary and Nomination Politics* (Chatham, N.J.: Chatham House, 1987).

[20]Myron A. Levine, *Presidential Campaigns and Elections* (Itasca, Ill.: Peacock, 1995), 30.

[21]Kiku Adatto, "Sound Bite Democracy," Joan Shorenstein Center on the Press, Politics, and Public Policy, Research Paper R-2, Harvard University, Cambridge, Mass., June 1990.

[22]Sidney Kraus, ed., *The Great Debates* (Bloomington: Indiana University Press, 1962), 190.

[23]Stephen Ansolabehere and Shanto Iyengar, *Going Negative: How Attack Ads Shrink and Polarize the Electorate* (New York: Free Press, 1995).

[24]John P. Burke, *The Institutional Presidency* (Baltimore: Johns Hopkins University Press, 1992); Charles E. Walcott and Karen M. Hult, *Governing the White House* (Lawrence: University Press of Kansas, 1995).

[25]Davis, *The American Presidency*, 240; see also Bradley Patterson, *The Ring of Power* (New York: Basic Books, 1988), 90–91.

[26]James Pfiffner, *The Modern Presidency* (New York: St. Martin's Press, 1994), 91–96.

[27]Quoted in Stephen J. Wayne, *Road to the White House, 1992* (New York: St. Martin's Press, 1992), 143; see also Timothy Welch, ed., *At the President's Side* (Columbia: University of Missouri Press, 1997).

[28]See Shirley Anne Warshaw, *Powersharing: White House–Cabinet Relations in the Modern Presidency* (Albany: State University of New York Press, 1995).

[29]See Jeffrey E. Cohen, *The Politics of the United States Cabinet* (Pittsburgh: University of Pittsburgh Press, 1988).

[30]Pfiffner, *The Modern Presidency*, 123.

[31]Quoted in James MacGregor Burns, "Our Super-Government—Can We Control It?" the *New York Times*, April 24, 1949, 32.

[32]See Paul C. Light, *Thickening Government: Federal Hierarchy and the Diffusion of Accountability* (Washington, D.C.: Brookings Institution, 1995).

[33]James Pfiffner, "The President's Chief of Staff: Lessons Learned," *Presidential Studies Quarterly* 22 (Winter 1993): 77–102.

[34]See Richard Rose, *The Postmodern Presidency*, 2d ed. (Chatham, N.J.: Chatham House, 1991).

[35]Pfiffner, *The Modern Presidency*, 117–122.

[36]Michael Mezey, *Congress, the President, and Public Policy* (Boulder, Colo.: Westview Press, 1989), 110–115.

[37]George Edwards III, *At the Margins* (New Haven, Conn.: Yale University Press, 1989), 39–46.

[38]Erwin Hargrove, *The Power of the Modern Presidency* (New York: Knopf, 1974).

[39]James P. Pfiffner, *The Strategic Presidency: Hitting the Ground Running*, 2d ed. (Chicago: Dorsey Press, 1996).

[40]Aaron Wildavsky, "The Two Presidencies," *Trans-action*, December 1966, 7.

[41]See Lance T. LeLoup and Steven A. Shull, "Congress versus the Executive: The Two Presidencies Reconsidered," *Social Science Quarterly*, March 1979, 707.

[42]Pfiffner, *The Modern Presidency*, ch. 6.

[43]Wildavsky, "The Two Presidencies."

[44]Thomas P. (Tip) O'Neill, with William Novak, *Man of the House: The Life and Political Memoirs of Speaker Tip O'Neill* (New York: Random House, 1987), 297.

[45]Fred I. Greenstein, ed., *Leadership in the Modern Presidency* (Cambridge, Mass.: Harvard University Press, 1988), ch. 10.

[46]Robert J. Spitzer, *The Presidential Veto: Touchstone of the American Presidency* (Albany: State University of New York Press, 1988).

[47]Richard E. Neustadt, *Presidential Power and the Modern Presidents* (New York: Free Press, 1990), 71–72.

[48]*Clinton v. City of New York*, 97-1374 (1998).

[49]Neustadt, *Presidential Power*, 33.

[50]Mary E. Stuckey, *The President as Interpreter-in-Chief* (Chatham, N.J.: Chatham House, 1991).

[51]Harvey G. Zeidenstein, "Presidents' Popularity and Their Wins and Losses on Major Issues: Does One Have a Greater Influence over the Other?" *Presidential Studies Quarterly*, Spring 1985, 287–300; see also Richard Brody, *Assessing the President* (Stanford, Calif.: Stanford University Press, 1991).

[52]Gallup Polls, November 2–5, 1979, and November 30–December 3, 1979.

[53]John E. Mueller, "Presidential Popularity from Truman to Johnson," *American Political Science Review* 64 (March 1970): 18–34; Kathleen Frankovic, "Public Opinion in the 1992 Campaign," in Gerald M. Pomper, ed., *The Election of 1992* (Chatham, N.J.: Chatham House, 1993).

[54]See John Anthony Maltese, *Spin Control* (Chapel Hill: University of North Carolina Press, 1994); Howard Kurtz, *Spin Cycle* (New York: Basic Books, 1998).

[55]Samuel Kernell, *Going Public: New Strategies of Presidential Leadership* (Washington, D.C.: Congressional Quarterly Press, 1986), 1.

[56]Jeffrey Tulis, *The Rhetorical Presidency* (Princeton, N.J.: Princeton University Press, 1987); Craig Allen Smith, *The White House Speaks* (Westport, Conn.: Greenwood, 1994); but see also Kenneth Walsh, *Feeding the Beast* (New York: Random House, 1996).

[57]Stuckey, *The President as Interpreter-in-Chief.*

[58]Heclo, "Introduction: The Presidential Illusion," 2.

[59]Theodore J. Lowi, *The "Personal" Presidency: Power Invested, Promise Unfulfilled* (Ithaca, N.Y.: Cornell University Press, 1985); see also Jeffrey E. Cohen, *Presidential Responsiveness and Public Policymaking* (Ann Arbor: University of Michigan Press, 1997).

CHAPTER THIRTEEN

[1]Norman Thomas, *Rule 9: Politics, Administration, and Civil Rights* (New York: Random House, 1966), 6.

[2]James P. Pfiffner, "The National Performance Review in Perspective," working paper, 94-4, The Institute of Public Policy, George Mason University, 1994, 2.

[3]Quoted in Albert Gore, Jr., *From Red Tape to Results* (Washington, D.C.: U.S. Superintendent of Documents, 1993), 1.

[4]See John J. DiIulio, ed., *Deregulating the Public Service* (Washington, D.C.: Brookings Institution, 1994).

[5]*Rutan v. Republican Party of Illinois*, 497 U.S. 62 (1990).

[6]Sar A. Levitan and Alexandra B. Noden, *Working for the Sovereign* (Baltimore: Johns Hopkins University Press, 1983), 28–29, 39.

[7]See Cornelius M. Kerwin, *Rulemaking* (Washington, D.C.: Congressional Quarterly Press, 1994).

[8]Michael Lipsky, *Street-Level Bureaucracy* (New York: Russell Sage Foundation, 1980); see also George Serra, "Citizen-Initiated Contact and Satisfaction with Bureaucracy," *Journal of Public Administration* 5 (April 1995): 175–188.

[9]Jay M. Shafritz, *Personnel Management in Government* (New York: Marcel Dekker, 1981), 9–13.

[10]James Q. Wilson, "The Rise of the Bureaucratic State," *Public Interest* 41 (Fall 1975): 77–103.

[11]David Nachmias and David H. Rosenbloom, *Bureaucratic Government: U.S.A.* (New York: St. Martin's Press, 1980), 39; U.S. Bureau of the Census, *Historical Statistics of the United States: Colonial Times to 1970*, pt. 2 (Washington, D.C.: U.S. Government Printing Office, 1975), 1102.

[12]David H. Rosenbloom, *Federal Service and the Constitution* (Ithaca, N.Y.: Cornell University Press, 1971), 83.

[13]For insights on this and other civil service mechanisms, see Patricia Ingraham and David Rosenbloom, *The Promise and Paradox of Civil Service Reform* (Pittsburgh: University of Pittsburgh Press, 1992); Donald F. Kettl, Patricia W. Ingraham, Ronald P. Sanders, and Constance Horner, *Civil Service Reform* (Washington, D.C.: Brookings Institution Press, 1996).

[14]Herbert Kaufman, "Emerging Conflicts in the Doctrine of Public Administration," *American Political Science Review* 50 (December 1956): 1060.

[15]Ibid., 1062.

[16]See Richard W. Waterman, *Presidential Influence and the Administrative State* (Knoxville: University of Tennessee Press, 1989).

[17]Norton E. Long, "Power and Administration," *Public Administration Review* 10 (Autumn 1949), 269.

[18]See Herbert Kaufman, *The Administrative Behavior of Federal Bureaucrats* (Washington, D.C.: Brookings Institution, 1981), 4.

[19]See John Brehon and Scott Gates, *Working, Shirking and Sabotage* (Ann Arbor: University of Michigan Press, 1996).

[20]Quoted in Aaron Wildavsky, *The Politics of the Budgetary Process*, 4th ed. (Boston: Little, Brown, 1984), 19.

[21]Joel D. Aberbach and Bert A. Rockman, "Clashing Beliefs within the Executive Branch," *American Political Science Review* 70 (June 1976): 461.

[22]See B. Dan Wood and Richard W. Waterman, *Bureaucratic Dynamics* (Boulder, Colo.: Westview Press, 1994).

[23]Jonathan Bendor, Serge Taylor, and Roland Van Gaalen, "Stacking the Deck: Bureaucratic Missions and Policy Design," *American Political Science Review* 81 (September 1987): 873–896.

[24]See Brehon and Gates, *Working, Shirking and Sabotage.*

[25]Herbert Kaufman, *Are Government Organizations Immortal?* (Washington, D.C.: Brookings Institution, 1976), 76.

[26]Long, "Power and Administration," 269.

[27]See John Mark Hansen, *Gaining Access* (Chicago: University of Chicago Press, 1991).

[28]Hugh Heclo, "Issue Networks and the Executive Establishment," in Anthony King, ed., *The New American Political System* (Washington, D.C.: American Enterprise Institute, 1978), 102.

[29]Joel D. Aberbach and Bert A. Rockman, "Bureaucrats and Client Groups: A View from Capitol Hill," *American Journal of Political Science* 22 (November 1978): 821.

[30] See B. Guy Peters, *The Politics of Bureaucracy*, 4th ed. (New York: Longman, 1995).

[31]See Martin Laffin, "Reinventing the Federal Government," in Christopher Peele, Christopher J. Bailey, Bruce Cain, and B. Guy Peters, eds., *Developments in American Politics* 2 (Chatham, N.J.: Chatham House, 1995), 172–176; Harry W. Reynolds, Jr., ed., *Ethics in American Public Service* (Philadelphia: Annals of the American Academy, 1995).

[32]Phillip B. Heymann, *The Politics of Public Management* (New Haven, Conn.: Yale University Press, 1988).

[33]James G. March and Johan P. Olson, "Organizing Political Life: What Administrative Reorganization Tells Us about Government," *American Political Science Review* 77 (June 1983): 281–296.

[34]Kenneth J. Meier, *Regulation* (New York: St. Martin's Press, 1985), 110–111.

[35]See Richard P. Nathan, *The Plot That Failed: Nixon and the Administrative Presidency* (New York: Wiley, 1975).

[36]See Hugh Heclo, *A Government of Strangers* (Washington, D.C.: Brookings Institution, 1977), 117–118.

[37]Quoted in Aaron Wildavsky, *The Politics of the Budgetary Process,* 4th ed. (Boston: Little, Brown, 1984).

[38]See Donald Kettl, *Deficit Politics* (New York: Macmillan, 1992).

[39]See Joel D. Aberbach, *Keeping a Watchful Eye* (Washington, D.C.: Brookings Institution, 1990).

[40]B. Dan Wood and Richard W. Waterman, "Political Control of the Bureaucracy," *American Political Science Review* 85 (September 1991): 820–821.

[41]Cathy Marie Johnson, *The Dynamics of Conflict between Bureaucrats and Legislators* (Armonk, N.Y.: Sharpe, 1992).

[42]David Rosenbloom, "The Evolution of the Administrative State, and Transformations of Administrative Law," in David Rosenbloom and Richard Schwartz, eds., *Handbook of Regulation and Administrative Law* (New York: Marcel Dekker, 1994), 3–36.

[43]See *Vermont Yankee Nuclear Power Corp.* v. *National Resources Defense Council, Inc.,* 435 U.S. 519 (1978); *Chevron* v. *National Resources Defense Council,* 467 U.S. 837 (1984); *Heckler* v. *Chaney,* 470 U.S. 821 (1985).

[44]Roberta Ann Johnson and Michael E. Kraft, "Bureaucratic Whistleblowing and Policy Change," *Western Political Quarterly* 43 (December 1990): 849–874.

[45]"Way, Way Off in the Wild Blue Yonder," *Time,* May 29, 1995, 32–33.

[46]See Brian J. Cook, *Bureaucracy and Self-Government* (Baltimore, Md.: Johns Hopkins University Press, 1996).

[47]See Wood and Waterman, *Bureaucratic Dynamics.*

[48]David Osborne and Ted Gaebler, *Reinventing Government: How the Entrepreneurial Spirit Is Transforming the Public Sector* (New York: Addison-Wesley, 1992); see also Michael Barzelay and Babak J. Armajani, *Breaking through Bureaucracy* (Berkeley: University of California Press, 1992); Robert D. Behn, *Leadership Counts* (Cambridge, Mass.: Harvard University Press, 1991).

[49]Ronald C. Moe, "The 'Reinventing Government' Exercise: Misinterpreting the Problem, Misjudging the Results," *Public Administration Review* (March/April, 1994): 125–136.

[50]Tom Shoop, "From Citizens to Customers," *Government Executive* (May 1994): 27–30.

[51]See Mark Goldstein, *America's Hollow Government: How Washington Has Failed the People* (Homewood, Ill.: Business One Irwin, 1992); but see also James Pinkerton, *What Comes Next?* (New York: Hyperion, 1995).

CHAPTER FOURTEEN

[1]*Marbury* v. *Madison*, 1 Cranch 137 (1803).
[2]*Bush* v. *Gore*, No. 00-949 (2000).
[3]*Roe* v. *Wade*, 401 U.S. 113 (1973).
[4]See Michael J. Perry, *The Constitution and the Courts* (New York: Oxford University Press, 1994).
[5]Raoul Berger, *Government by Judiciary: The Transformation of the Fourteenth Amendment* (Cambridge, Mass.: Harvard University Press, 1977).
[6]Rebecca Mae Salokar, *The Solicitor General: The Politics of Law* (Philadelphia: Temple University Press, 1992); see also Cornell W. Clayton, *The Politics of Justice: The Attorney General and the Making of Legal Policy* (Armonk, N.Y.: Sharpe, 1992).
[7]See Bernard Schwartz, *How the Supreme Court Decides Cases* (New York: Oxford University Press, 1996).
[8]Lawrence Baum, *The Supreme Court*, 4th ed. (Washington, D.C.: Congressional Quarterly Press, 1996), 117.
[9]*Gideon* v. *Wainwright*, 372 U.S. 335 (1963).
[10]From a letter to the author by Frank Schwartz of Beaver College. This section reflects substantially Professor Schwartz's recommendations to the author, as does the later section that addresses the "federal-court myth."
[11]*Hutto* v. *Davis*, 370 U.S. 256 (1982).
[12]*Roe* v. *Wade*, 410 U.S. 113 (1973).
[13]David M. O'Brien, *Storm Center: The Supreme Court in American Politics*, 4th ed. (New York: Norton, 1996), 69–76.
[14]Robert A. Carp, *The Federal Courts*, 3d ed. (Washington, D.C.: Congressional Quarterly Press, 1998).
[15]Stephen L. Wasby, *The Supreme Court in the Federal Judicial System*, 4th ed. (Chicago: Nelson-Hall, 1993), 75.
[16]Henry J. Abraham, *The Judicial Process*, 7th ed. (New York: Oxford University Press, 1998), 24–26.
[17]Robert Scigliano, *The Supreme Court and the Presidency* (New York: Free Press, 1971), 146; see also David Savage, *Turning Right: The Making of the Rehnquist Supreme* Court (New York: Wiley, 1992).
[18]Quoted in Baum, *The Supreme Court*, 37.
[19]See John C. Hughes, *The Federal Courts, Politics, and the Rule of Law* (New York: Longman, 1995).
[20]John Gottschall, "Reagan's Appointments to the U.S. Courts of Appeals," 70 *Judicature* 48 (1986): 54.

[21]Joseph B. Harris, *The Advice and Consent of the Senate* (Berkeley: University of California Press, 1953), 313.

[22]Office of Public Affairs, Department of Justice, 1999.

[23]Henry J. Abraham, "The Judicial Function under the Constitution," *News for Teachers of Political Science* 41 (Spring 1984): 14.

[24]Sheldon Goldman, "Should There Be Affirmative Action for the Judiciary?" *Judicature* 62 (May 1979): 494.

[25]Quoted in Louis Fisher, *American Constitutional Law* (New York: McGraw-Hill, 1990), 5.

[26]Baum, *The Supreme Court*, 117.

[27]Quoted in Charles P. Curtis, *Law and Large as Life* (New York: Simon & Schuster, 1959), 156–157.

[28]See Joan Biskupic and Elder Witt, *The Supreme Court and the Powers of the American Government* (Washington, D.C.: Congressional Quarterly Press, 1996), ch. 1.

[29]*Faragher* v. *City of Boca Raton*, No. 97-282 (1998); *Burlington Industries* v. *Ellerth*, No. 97-569 (1998).

[30]Wasby, *The Supreme Court in the Federal Judicial System*, 53.

[31]See Lee Epstein, *Conservatives in Court* (Knoxville: University of Tennessee Press, 1985), 80–88.

[32]Linda Greenhouse, "Sure Justices Legislate. They Have To." *The New York Times*, July 5, 1998, 4–1.

[33]See George L. Watson and John Alan Stookey, *Shaping America: The Politics of Supreme Court Appointments* (New York: Longman, 1995).

[34]John Schmidhauser, *The Supreme Court* (New York: Holt, Rinehart & Winston, 1964), 6.

[35]Jeffrey A. Segal and Harold J. Spaeth, *The Supreme Court and the Attitudinal Model* (New York: Cambridge University Press, 1993).

[36]Linda Greenhouse, "The Justices Decide Who's in Charge," *The New York Times*, June 27, 1999, sec. 4, p. l.

[37]O'Brien, *Storm Center*, 14–15.

[38]Ibid., 59–61.

[39]Some of the references cited in the following sections are taken from Abraham, "The Judicial Function," 12–14; see also Harry H. Wellington, *Interpreting the Constitution* (New Haven, Conn.: Yale University Press, 1990).

[40]Abraham, "The Judicial Function under the Constitution," 14.

[41]See Antonin Scalia, *A Matter of Interpretation* (Princeton, N.J.: Princeton University Press, 1997).

[42]Louis Lusky, *By What Right? A Commentary on the Supreme Court's Power to Revise the Constitution* (Charlottesville, Va.: Michie, 1975), 214–216.

[43]*Romer* v. *Evans*, No. 94-1039 (1996).

[44]Abraham, "The Judicial Function," 13.

[45]See Larry W. Yackle, *Reclaiming the Federal Courts* (Cambridge, Mass.: Harvard University Press, 1994).

[46]"Good for the Left, Now Good for the Right," *Newsweek*, July 8, 1991, 22.

[47]*Kimel v. Florida Board of Regents*, No. 98-791 (2000).

[48]Greenhouse, "The Justices Decide Who's in Charge," p. 1.

[49]Quoted in ibid.

[50]*Bush v. Gore*, No. 00-949 (2000).

CHAPTER FIFTEEN

[1]This section relies substantially on Alan Stone, *Regulation and Its Alternatives* (Washington, D.C.: Congressional Quarterly Press, 1982).

[2]See Marc Allen Eisner, *Regulatory Politics in Transition* (Baltimore: Johns Hopkins University Press, 1993).

[3]See Walter A. Rosenbaum, *Environmental Politics and Policy*, 3d ed. (Washington, D.C.: Congressional Quarterly Press, 1994).

[4]Paul Portney, "Beware of the Killer Clauses inside the GOP's 'Contract,' " *The Washington Post National Weekly Edition*, January 23–29, 1995, 21.

[5]See Richard A. Harris and Sidney M. Milkis, *The Politics of Regulatory Change* (New York: Oxford University Press, 1996).

[6]Donald F. Kettl, "The Savings and Loan Bailout: The Mismatch between the Headlines and the Issues," *PS: Political Science and Politics* 23 (September 1991): 441–447.

[7]H. Peyton Young, *Equity: In Theory and Practice* (Princeton, N.J.: Princeton University Press, 1995).

[8]David E. Vogel, "The 'New' Social Regulation in Historical and Comparative Perspective," in Thomas McGraw, ed., *Regulation in Perspective* (Cambridge, Mass.: Harvard University Press, 1981), 162.

[9]Molly Ivins, "GOP Job Bill Is Truly Bad," *Syracuse Post-Standard*, February 15, 1995, A10.

[10]See Ronald Shaiko, "Greenpeace, U.S.A.," *ANNALS* 528 (July 1993), 89–103.

[11]Rachel Carson, *The Silent Spring* (Boston: Houghton Mifflin, 1962).

[12]*U.S. News & World Report*, June 30, 1975, 25.

[13]"Hill Foes of New Clean Air Rules Unite Behind Moratorium Bill," *Congressional Quarterly Weekly Report, Spring 1998* (Washington, D.C.: Congressional Quarterly Press, 1998), 61.

[14]See Robert Lekachman, *The Age of Keynes* (New York: Random House, 1966).

[15]See Donald F. Kettl, *Deficit Politics* (New York: Macmillan, 1992).

[16]See Bruce Bartlett, *Reaganomics: Supply-Side Economics* (Westport, Conn.: Arlington House, 1981); Kenneth Hoover and Raymond Plant, *Conservative Capitalism in Britain and the United States* (New York: Routledge, 1989).

[17]House Ways and Means Committee data, 1991.

[18]See Aaron Wildavsky, *The New Politics of the Budgetary Process* (New York: HarperCollins, 1992); Allen Schick, *The Federal Budget* (Washington, D.C.: Brookings Institution Press, 1995).

[19]See Richard E. Cohen, "Rating Congress—A Guide Separating the Liberals from the Conservatives," *National Journal,* May 8, 1982, 800–810.

CHAPTER SIXTEEN

[1]Jason DeParle, "Welfare Reform, One Year Later," *Syracuse Herald American,* January 4, 1998, D1.

[2]Michael Harrington, *The Other America: Poverty in the United States* (New York: Macmillan, 1962); see also Sheldon H. Danziger, Gary D. Sandefur, and Daniel H. Weinberg, eds., *Confronting Poverty* (Cambridge, Mass.: Harvard University Press, 1994).

[3]Charles Murray, *Losing Ground: American Social Policy, 1950–1980* (New York: Basic Books, 1984).

[4]*Five Thousand American Families* (Ann Arbor: University of Michigan Institute for Social Research, 1977); also see William Julius Wilson, *When Work Disappears* (New York: Knopf, 1996).

[5]See Katherine Newman, *No Shame in My Game* (New York: Alfred A. Knopf and Russell Sage Foundation, 1999), 41.

[6]Everett Carll Ladd, *American Political Parties* (New York: Norton, 1970), 205.

[7]DeParle, "Welfare Reform."

[8]Kevin Phillips, *Boiling Point* (New York: Random House, 1993), 109–111. Phillips indicates a 26.7 percent effective tax rate on wealthy Americans. It is slightly higher today as a result of the 1993 tax law changes.

[9]V. O. Key, Jr., *The Responsible Electorate* (Cambridge, Mass.: Belknap Press of Harvard University, 1966), 43.

[10]See Jill Quadrangle, *The Transformation of Old Age Security* (Chicago: University of Chicago Press, 1988).

[11]For a general overview of 1950s and 1960s policy disputes, see James Sundquist, *Politics and Policy* (Washington, D.C.: Brookings Institution, 1968).

[12]"Welfare: Myths, Reality," Knight-Ridder News Service story, *Syracuse Post-Standard,* December 5, 1994, A1, A6.

[13]Judith Havemann, "Tough Steps Credited for Welfare Dip," *Washington Post,* May 10, 1999, A2.

[14]Quoted in Malcolm Gladwell, "The Medicaid Muddle," *The Washington Post National Weekly Edition,* January 16–22, 1995, 31.

[15]Karl A. Lamb, *As Orange Goes: Twelve California Families and the Future of American Politics* (New York: Norton, 1974), 178.

[16]Based on Organization for Economic Co-Operation and Development (OECD) data, 2001.

[17]Laurel Shaper Walters, "World Educators Compare Notes," *Christian Science Monitor,* September 7, 1994, 8.

[18]See John E. Chubb and Terry M. Moe, *Politics, Markets, and America's Schools* (Washington, D.C.: Brookings Institution, 1990); but see also Jeffrey R.

Henig, *Rethinking School Choice* (Princeton, N.J.: Princeton University Press, 1995). [19]See Phillip Longman, *Return of Thrift: How the Collapse of the Middle Class Welfare System in the United States Will Reawaken Values in America* (New York: Free Press, 1996).

CHAPTER SEVENTEEN

[1]William Greider, *One World, Ready or Not* (New York: Simon & Schuster, 1994). [2]See Peter B. Kenen, ed., *Understanding Interdependence: The Macroeconomics of the Open Economy* (Princeton, N.J.: Princeton University Press, 1995). [3]American Assembly Report (cosponsored by the Council on Foreign Relations), *Rethinking America's Security* (New York: Harriman, 1991), 8. [4]For an overview of Soviet policy, see Alvin Z. Rubenstein, *Soviet Foreign Policy since World War II*, 4th ed. (New York: HarperCollins, 1992); for an assessment of U.S. policy, see Robert Dallek, *The American Style of Foreign Policy* (New York: Oxford University Press, 1990). [5]See John Lewis Gaddis, *Strategies of Containment* (New York: Oxford University Press, 1982). [6]Mr. X. (George Kennan), "The Sources of Soviet Conduct," *Foreign Affairs* 25 (July 1947): 566–582. [7]See Stanley Karnow, *Vietnam: A History* (New York: Penguin, 1983); David M. Barrett, *Uncertain Warriors: Lyndon Johnson and His Vietnam Advisors* (Lawrence: University of Kansas, Press 1993). [8]Charles Kegley and Eugene Wittkopf, *American Foreign Policy*, 2d ed. (New York: St. Martin's Press, 1982), 48. [9]See Keith L. Nelson, *The Making of Détente* (Baltimore: Johns Hopkins University Press, 1995). [10]See Russell J. Ling, "Reagan and the Russians," *American Political Science Review* 78 (June 1984): 338–355. [11]For a general view of America's new world role, see Kenneth A. Oye, Robert J. Lieber, and Donald Rothchild, *Eagle in a New World: American Grand Strategy in the Post-Cold War Era* (New York: HarperCollins, 1992). [12]Loch K. Johnson, *Secret Agencies* (New Haven, Conn.: Yale University Press, 1996). [13]See Robert Jervis, *The Illogic of American Nuclear Strategy* (Ithaca, N.Y.: Cornell University Press, 1984). [14]Richard J. Barnet, "Reflections: The Disorders of Peace," *The New Yorker*, January 20, 1992, 61. [15]See Ole Holsti, *Public Opinion and American Foreign Policy* (Ann Arbor: University of Michigan Press, 1996). [16]See James M. Lindsay, *Congress and the Politics of U.S. Foreign Policy* (Baltimore: Johns Hopkins University Press, 1994); William Conrad Gibbons, *The U.S.*

Government and the Vietnam War (Washington, D.C.: U.S. Government Printing Office, 1994).

[17]Seymour Melman, *Pentagon Capitalism* (New York: McGraw-Hill, 1970), 175; Paul A. Koistinen, *The Military-Industrial Complex* (New York: Praeger, 1980).

[18]See Elie Abel, *The Shattered Bloc: Beyond the Upheaval in Eastern Europe* (Boston: Houghton Mifflin, 1990).

[19]Paul Kennedy, *The Rise and Fall of the Great Powers* (New York: Random House, 1988); for an alternative view, see Joseph Nye, *Bound to Lead: The Changing Nature of American Power* (New York: Basic Books, 1990).

[20]U.S. government data, various agencies, 1998.

[21]*The World Competitiveness Yearbook* (Lausanne, Switzerland: International Institute for Management Development, 1999).

[22]American Assembly, *Rethinking America's Security*, 9; see also Robert O. Keohane, Joseph S. Nye, and Stanley Hoffmann, eds., *After the Cold War* (Cambridge, Mass.: Harvard University Press, 1993).

[23]See Robert O. Keohane and Joseph S. Nye, *Power and Interdependence: World Politics in Transition*, 2d ed. (Boston: Little, Brown, 1989).

[24]Tom Masland, "Going Down the Aid 'Rathole'?" *Newsweek*, December 5, 1994, 39.

[25]Hobart Rowen, "The Budget: Fact and Fiction," *The Washington Post National Weekly Edition*, January 16–22, 1995, 5.

[26]Associated Press, "Clinton Remembers Those Who Fought Apartheid," *Syracuse Herald American*, March 29, 1998, A5.

[27]See Richard J. Barnet and John Cavanagh, *Global Dreams* (New York: Simon & Schuster, 1994).

Glossary

accountability   The ability of the public to hold government officials responsible for their actions.

affirmative action   A term that refers to programs designed to ensure that women, minorities, and other traditionally disadvantaged groups have full and equal opportunities in employment, education, and other areas of life.

age-cohort tendency   The tendency for a significant break in the pattern of political socialization to occur among younger citizens, usually as the result of a major event or development that disrupts preexisting beliefs.

agency point of view   The tendency of bureaucrats to place the interests of their agency ahead of other interests and ahead of the priorities sought by the president or Congress.

agenda setting   The power of the media through news coverage to focus the public's attention and concern on particular events, problems, issues, personalities, and so on.

agents of socialization   Those agents, such as the family and the media, that have significant impact on citizens' political socialization.

air wars   A term that refers to the fact that modern campaigns are often a battle of opposing televised advertising campaigns.

alienation   A feeling of personal powerlessness that includes the notion that government does not care about the opinions of people like oneself.

Anti-Federalists   A term used to describe opponents of the Constitution during the debate over ratification.

apathy   A feeling of personal noninterest or unconcern with politics.

appellate jurisdiction   The authority of a given court to review cases that have already been tried in lower courts and are appealed to it by the losing party; such a court is called an appeals court or appellate court. (See also **original jurisdiction.**)

authority   The recognized right of an individual or institution to exercise power. (See also **power.**)

balanced budget   Situation when the government's tax revenues for the year are equal to its expenditures.

bicameral legislature   A legislature having two chambers.

bill   A proposed law (legislative act) within Congress or another legislature. (See also **law.**)

Bill of Rights   The first ten amendments to the Constitution. They include such rights as freedom of speech and trial by jury.

block grants Federal grants-in-aid that permit state and local officials to decide how the money will be spent within a general area, such as education or health. (See also **categorical grants.**)

budget deficit Situation when the government's expenditures for the year exceed its tax revenues.

budget surplus Situation when the government's tax and other revenues for the year exceed its expenditures.

bureaucracy A system of organization and control based on the principles of hierarchical authority, job specialization, and formalized rules. (See also **formalized rules; hierarchical authority; job specialization.**)

cabinet A group consisting of the heads of the (cabinet) executive departments, who are appointed by the president, subject to confirmation by the Senate. The cabinet was once the main advisory body to the president but no longer plays this role. (See also **cabinet departments.**)

cabinet (executive) departments The major administrative organizations within the federal executive bureaucracy, each of which is headed by a secretary (cabinet officer) and has responsibility for a major function of the federal government, such as defense, agriculture, or justice. (See also **cabinet; independent agencies.**)

candidate-centered politics Election campaigns and other political processes in which candidates, not political parties, have most of the initiative and influence. (See also **party-centered politics.**)

capital-gains tax A tax that individuals pay on money gained from the sale of a capital asset, such as property or stocks.

capitalism An economic system based on the idea that government should interfere with economic transactions as little as possible. Free enterprise and self-reliance are the collective and individual principles that underpin capitalism.

categorical grants Federal grants-in-aid to states and localities that can be used only for designated projects. (See also **block grants.**)

charter The chief instrument by which a state governs its local units; it spells out in detail what a local government can and cannot do.

checks and balances The elaborate system of divided spheres of authority provided by the U.S. Constitution as a means of controlling the power of government. The separation of powers among the branches of the national government, federalism, and the different methods of selecting national officers are all part of this system.

citizens' (noneconomic) groups Organized interests formed by individuals drawn together by opportunities to promote a cause in which they believe but that does not provide them significant individual economic benefits. (See also **economic groups; interest group.**)

city manager system Form of municipal government that entrusts the executive role to a professionally trained manager, who is chosen, and can be fired, by the city council.

civic duty The belief of an individual that civic and political participation is a responsibility of citizenship.

civil liberties The fundamental individual rights of a free society, such as freedom of speech and the right to a jury trial, which in the United States are protected by the Bill of Rights.

civil rights (equal rights) The right of every person to equal protection under the laws and equal access to society's opportunities and public facilities.

civil service system See **merit system.**

clear-and-present-danger test A test devised by the Supreme Court in 1919 to define the limits of free speech in the context of national security. According to the test, government cannot abridge political expression unless it presents a clear and present danger to the nation's security.

clientele groups Special-interest groups that benefit directly from the activities of a particular bureaucratic agency and are therefore strong advocates of the agency.

cloture A parliamentary maneuver that, if a three-fifths majority votes for it, limits Senate debate to thirty hours and has the effect of defeating a filibuster. (See also **filibuster.**)

cold war The lengthy period after World War II when the United States and the USSR were not engaged in actual combat (a "hot war") but were nonetheless locked in a state of deep-seated hostility.

collective (public) goods Benefits that are offered by groups (usually citizens' groups) as an incentive for membership but that are nondivisible (e.g., a clean environment) and therefore are available to nonmembers as well as members of the particular group. (See also **free-rider problem; private goods.**)

commerce clause The clause of the Constitution (Article I, Section 8) that empowers the federal government to regulate commerce among the states and with other nations.

commission system Form of municipal government that invests executive and legislative authority in a commission, with each commissioner serving as a member of the local council but also having a specified executive role, such as police commissioner or public works commissioner.

common-carrier role The media's function as an open channel through which political leaders can communicate with the public. (See also **public representative role; signaler role; watchdog role.**)

comparable worth The idea that women should get pay equal to men for work that is of similar difficulty and responsibility and that requires similar levels of education and training.

compliance The issue of whether a court's decisions will be respected and obeyed.

concurring opinion A separate opinion written by a Supreme Court justice who votes with the majority in the decision on a case but who disagrees with the majority's reasoning. (See also **dissenting opinion; majority opinion; plurality opinion.**)

confederacy A governmental system in which sovereignty is vested entirely in subnational (state) governments. (See also **federalism; unitary system.**)

conference committee A temporary committee that is formed to bargain over the differences in the House and Senate versions of a bill. The committee's members are usually appointed from the House and Senate standing committees that originally worked on the bill.

conservatives Those who emphasize the marketplace as the means of distributing economic benefits but look to government to uphold traditional social values. (See also **liberals; libertarians; populists.**)

constituency The individuals who live within the geographical area represented by an elected official. More narrowly, the body of citizens eligible to vote for a particular representative.

constitution The fundamental law that defines how a government will legitimately operate.

constitutional democracy A government that is democratic in its provisions for majority influence through elections and constitutional in its provisions for minority rights and rule by law.

constitutional initiative The process by which a citizen or group can petition to place a proposed amendment on the ballot at the next election by obtaining the signatures of a certain number of registered voters, and if the amendment gets majority support, it becomes part of the constitution.

constitutionalism The idea that there are definable limits on the rightful power of a government over its citizens.

containment A doctrine, developed after World War II, based on the assumptions that the Soviet Union was an aggressor nation and that only a determined United States could block Soviet territorial ambitions.

Cooley's rule The term used to describe the idea that cities should be self-governing, articulated in an 1871 ruling by Michigan judge Thomas Cooley.

cooperative federalism The situation in which the national, state, and local levels work together to solve problems.

de facto discrimination Discrimination on the basis of race, sex, religion, ethnicity, and the like that results from social, economic, and cultural biases and conditions. (See also **de jure discrimination.**)

de jure discrimination Discrimination on the basis of race, sex, religion, ethnicity, and the like that results from a law. (See also **de facto discrimination.**)

dealignment A situation in which voters' partisan loyalties have been substantially and permanently weakened. (See also **party identification; realignment.**)

decision A vote of the Supreme Court in a particular case that indicates which party the justices side with and by how large a margin.

deficit spending Situation when the government spends more than it collects in taxes and other revenues.

delegates Elected representatives whose obligation is to act in accordance with the expressed wishes of the people whom they represent. (See also **trustees.**)

demand-side economics A form of fiscal policy that emphasizes "demand" (consumer spending). Government can use increased spending or tax cuts to place more money in consumers' hands and thereby increase demand. (See also **fiscal policy; supply-side economics.**)

democracy A form of government in which the people govern, either directly or through elected representatives.

demographic representativeness The idea that the bureaucracy will be more responsive to the public if its employees at all levels are demographically representative of the population as a whole.

denials of power A constitutional means of limiting governmental action by listing those powers that government is expressly prohibited from using.

deregulation The rescinding of excessive government regulations for the purpose of improving economic efficiency.

descriptive reporting The style of reporting that aims to describe *what* is taking place or has occurred.

détente A French word meaning "a relaxing" and used to refer to an era of improved relations between the United States and the Soviet Union that began in the early 1970s.

deterrence The idea that nuclear war can be discouraged if each side in a conflict has the capacity to destroy the other with nuclear weapons.

devolution The passing down of authority from the national government to states and localities.

Dillon's rule The term used to describe relations between state and local government; it holds that local governments are creatures of the State, which in theory even has the power to abolish them.

direct primary See **primary election.**

dissenting opinion The opinion of a justice in a Supreme Court case that explains the reasons for disagreeing with the majority's decision. (See also **concurring opinion; majority opinion; plurality opinion.**)

diversity The principle that individual differences should be respected, are a legitimate basis of self-interest, and are a source of strength for the American nation.

dual federalism A doctrine based on the idea that a precise separation of national power and state power is both possible and desirable.

due process clause (of the Fourteenth Amendment) The clause of the Constitution that has been used by the judiciary to apply the Bill of Rights to the action of state government.

economic depression A very severe and sustained economic downturn. Depressions are rare in the United States: the last one was in the 1930s.

economic globalization The increased interdependence of nations' economies. The change is a result of technological, transportation, and communication advances that have enabled firms to deploy their resources across the globe.

economic groups Interest groups that are organized primarily for economic reasons but that engage in political activity in order to seek favorable policies from government. (See also **citizens' groups; interest group.**)

economic recession A moderate but sustained downturn in the economy. Recessions are part of the economy's "normal" cycle of ups and downs.

economy A system of production and consumption of goods and services that are allocated through exchange among producers and consumers.

efficiency An economic principle that holds that firms should fulfill as many of society's needs as possible while using as few of its resources as possible. The greater the output (production) for a given input (for example, an hour of labor), the more efficient the process.

elastic clause See **"necessary and proper" clause.**

electoral college An unofficial term that refers to the electors who cast the states' electoral votes.

electoral mastery A strong base of popular support that frees a congressional incumbent from constant worry over reelection.

electoral votes The method of voting that is used to choose the U.S. president. Each state has the same number of electoral votes as it has members in Congress (House and Senate combined). By tradition, electoral voting is tied to a state's popular voting; thus, the presidential candidate with the most popular votes overall has usually also had the most electoral votes.

elitism The view that the United States is essentially run by a tiny elite (composed of wealthy or well-connected individuals) who control public policy through both direct and indirect means.

entitlement program Any of a number of individual benefit programs, such as social security, that require government to provide a designated benefit to any person who meets the legally defined criteria for eligibility.

enumerated (expressed) powers The seventeen powers granted to the national government under Article I, Section 8 of the Constitution. These powers include taxation and the regulation of commerce as well as the authority to provide for the national defense.

equal protection clause A clause of the Fourteenth Amendment that forbids any state to deny equal protection of the laws to any individual within its jurisdiction.

equal rights See **civil rights.**

equality The principle that all individuals have moral worth and are entitled to fair treatment under the law.

equality of opportunity The idea that all individuals should be given an equal chance to succeed on their own.

equality of result The objective of policies intended to reduce or eliminate the effects of discrimination so that members of traditionally disadvantaged groups will have the same benefits of society as do members of advantaged groups.

equity (in relation to economic policy) The situation in which the outcome of an economic transaction is fair to each party. An outcome can usually be considered fair if each party enters into a transaction freely and is not knowingly at a disadvantage.

establishment clause The First Amendment provision that government may not favor one religion over another or favor religion over no religion, and that prohibits Congress from passing laws respecting the establishment of religion.

exclusionary rule The legal principle that government is prohibited from using in trials evidence that was obtained by unconstitutional means (for example, illegal search and seizure).

executive departments See **cabinet departments.**

executive leadership system An approach to managing the bureaucracy that is based on presidential leadership and presidential management tools, such as the president's annual budget proposal. (See also **merit system; patronage system.**)

expressed powers See **enumerated powers.**

externalities Burdens that society incurs when firms fail to pay the full cost of resources used in production. An example of an externality is the pollution that results when corporations dump industrial wastes into lakes and rivers.

facts (of a court case) The relevant circumstances of a legal dispute or offense as determined by a trial court. The facts of a case are crucial because they help to determine which law or laws are applicable in the case.

federalism A governmental system in which authority is divided between two sovereign levels of government: national and regional. (See also **confederacy; unitary system.**)

Federalists A term used to describe supporters of the Constitution during the debate over ratification.

filibuster A procedural tactic in the U.S. Senate whereby a minority of legislators prevents a bill from coming to a vote by holding the floor and talking until the majority gives in and the bill is withdrawn from consideration. (See also **cloture.**)

fiscal federalism A term that refers to the expenditure of federal funds on programs run in part through state and localities.

fiscal policy A tool of economic management by which government attempts to maintain a stable economy through its taxing and spending decisions. (See also **demand-side economics;**

monetary policy; supply-side economics.)

formalized rules   A basic principle of bureaucracy that refers to the standardized procedures and established regulations by which a bureaucracy conducts its operations. (See also **bureaucracy.**)

free-exercise clause   A First Amendment provision that prohibits the government from interfering with the practice of religion or prohibiting the free exercise of religion.

free-rider problem   The situation in which the benefits offered by a group to its members are also available to nonmembers. The incentive to join the group and to promote its cause is reduced because nonmembers (free riders) receive the benefits (e.g., a cleaner environment) without having to pay any of the group's costs. (See also **collective goods.**)

free trade   The view that the long-term economic interests of all countries are advanced when tariffs and other trade barriers are kept to a minimum. (See also **protectionism.**)

freedom of expression   Americans' freedom to communicate their views, the foundation of which is the First Amendment rights of freedom of conscience, speech, press, assembly, and petition.

gender gap   The tendency of women and men to differ in their political attitudes and voting preferences.

gerrymandering   The process by which one party draws district boundaries to its advantage.

government   The institutions, processes, and rules that facilitate control of a particular area and its inhabitants.

government corporations   Bodies, such as the U.S. Postal Service and Amtrak, that are similar to private corporations in that they charge for their services, but different in that they receive federal funding to help defray expenses. Their directors are appointed by the president with Senate approval.

graduated personal income tax   A tax on personal income in which the tax rate increases as income increases; in other words, the tax is higher for higher income levels.

grants-in-aid   Federal cash payments to states and localities for programs they administer.

grants of power   The method of limiting the U.S. government by confining its scope of authority to those powers expressly granted in the Constitution.

grassroots lobbying   A form of lobbying designed to persuade officials that a group's policy position has strong constituent support.

grassroots party   A political party organized at the level of the voters and dependent on their support for its strength.

Great Compromise   The agreement of the constitutional convention to create a two-chamber Congress with the House apportioned by population and the

Senate apportioned equally by state.

hard money Campaign funds given directly to candidates to spend as they choose.

hierarchical authority A basic principle of bureaucracy that refers to the chain of command within an organization whereby officials and units have control over those below them. (See also **bureaucracy.**)

hired guns The professional consultants who run campaigns for high office.

home rule A device designed to give local governments more leeway in their policies; it allows a local government to design and amend its own charter, subject to the laws and constitution of the state and also subject to veto by the state.

honeymoon period The president's first months in office, a time when Congress, the press, and the public are more inclined than usual to support presidential initiatives.

ideology A consistent pattern of opinion on particular issues that stems from a core belief or set of beliefs.

Imminent Lawless Action Test A legal test that says government cannot lawfully suppress advocacy that promotes lawless action unless such advocacy is aimed at producing, and is likely to produce, imminent lawless action.

implied powers The federal government's constitutional authority (through the "necessary and proper" clause) to take action that is not expressly authorized by the Constitution but that supports actions that are so authorized. (See also **"necessary and proper" clause.**)

in-kind benefits Government benefits that are cash equivalents, such as food stamps or rent vouchers. This form of benefit ensures that recipients will use public assistance in a specified way.

inalienable (natural) rights Those rights that persons theoretically possessed in the state of nature, prior to the formation of governments. These rights, including those of life, liberty, and property, are considered inherent and as such are inalienable. Since government is established by people, government has the responsibility to preserve these rights.

independent agencies Bureaucratic agencies that are similar to cabinet departments but usually have a narrower area of responsibility. Each such agency is headed by a presidential appointee who is not a cabinet member. An example is the National Aeronautics and Space Administration. (See also **cabinet departments.**)

individual goods See **private goods.**

individualism A philosophical belief that stresses the values of hard work and self-reliance and holds that the individual should be left to succeed or fail on his or her own.

individualistic subculture American subculture oriented toward private life and economic gain, with politics largely an extension of this perspective; characterizes middle, western, and southwestern states.

inflation A general increase in the average level of prices of goods and services.

initiative The process by which citizens can place legislative measures on the ballot through signature petitions, and if the measure receives a majority vote, it becomes law.

inside lobbying Direct communication between organized interests and policymakers, which is based on the assumed value of close ("inside") contacts with policymakers.

insurgency A type of military conflict in which irregular soldiers rise up against an established regime.

interest group A set of individuals who are organized to promote a shared political interest. (See also **citizens' groups; economic groups.**)

interest-group liberalism The tendency of public officials to support the policy demands of self-interested groups (as opposed to judging policy demands according to whether or not they serve a larger conception of "the public interest").

intermediate-scrutiny test A test applied by courts to laws that attempt a gender classification. In effect, the test eliminates gender as a legal classification unless it serves an important objective and is substantially related to the objective's achievement.

internationalism The view that the country should involve itself deeply in world affairs. (See also **isolationism.**)

interpretive reporting The style of reporting that aims to explain *why* something is taking place or has occurred.

iron triangle A small and informal but relatively stable group of well-positioned legislators, executives, and lobbyists who seek to promote policies beneficial to a particular interest. (See also **issue network.**)

isolationism The view that the country should deliberately avoid a large role in world affairs and, instead, concentrate on domestic concerns. (See also **internationalism.**)

issue network An informal network of public officials and lobbyists who have a common interest and expertise in a given area and who are brought together temporarily by a proposed policy in that area. (See also **iron triangle.**)

job specialization A basic principle of bureaucracy that holds that the responsibilities of each job position should be explicitly defined and that a precise division of labor within the organization should be maintained. (See also **bureaucracy.**)

judicial activism The doctrine that the courts should develop new legal principles when judges see a compelling need, even if this action places them in conflict with the policy decisions of elected officials. (See also **judicial restraint.**)

judicial conference A closed meeting of the justices of the U.S.

Supreme Court to discuss the points of the cases before them; the justices are not supposed to discuss conference proceedings with outsiders.

judicial restraint The doctrine that the judiciary should be highly respectful of precedent and should defer to the judgment of legislatures. The doctrine claims that the job of judges is to work within the confines of laws set down by tradition and law-making majorities. (See also **judicial activism**.)

judicial review The power of courts to decide whether a governmental institution has acted within its constitutional powers and, if not, to declare its action null and void.

jurisdiction (of a congressional committee) The policy area in which a particular congressional committee is authorized to act.

jurisdiction (of a court) A given court's authority to hear cases of a particular kind. Jurisdiction may be original or appellate.

laissez-faire doctrine A classic economic philosophy that holds that owners of businesses should be allowed to make their own production and distribution decisions without government regulation or control.

law (as enacted by Congress) A legislative proposal, or bill, that is passed by both the House and Senate and is either signed or not vetoed by the president. (See also **bill**.)

lawmaking function The authority (of a legislature) to make the laws necessary to carry out the government's powers. (See also **oversight function; representation function**.)

laws (of a court case) The constitutional provisions, legislative statutes, or judicial precedents that apply to a court case.

legitimacy (of election) The idea that the selection of officeholders should be based on the will of the people as reflected through their votes.

legitimacy (of judicial power) The issue of the proper limits of judicial authority in a political system based in part on the principle of majority rule.

libel Publication of material that falsely damages a person's reputation.

liberals Those who favor activist government as an instrument of economic security and redistribution but reject the notion that government should favor a particular set of social values. (See also **conservatives; libertarians; populists**.)

libertarians Those who oppose government as an instrument of traditional values and of economic security. (See also **conservatives; liberals; populists**.)

liberty The principle that the people should be free to act and think as they choose, provided they do not infringe unreasonably on others' freedom.

limited government A government that is subject to strict limits on its lawful uses of powers and hence on its ability to deprive people of their liberty.

lobbying The process by which interest-group members or lobbyists attempt to influence public policy through contacts with public officials.

logrolling The trading of votes between legislators so that each gets what he or she most wants.

majoritarianism The idea that the majority prevails not only in elections but also in determining policy.

majority opinion A Supreme Court opinion that results when a majority of the justices are in agreement on the legal basis of the decision. (See also **concurring opinion; dissenting opinion; plurality opinion.**)

material incentive An economic or other tangible benefit that is used to attract group members.

means test The requirement that applicants for public assistance must demonstrate they are poor in order to be eligible for the assistance. (See also **public assistance.**)

merit (civil service) system An approach to managing the bureaucracy whereby people are appointed to government positions on the basis of either competitive examinations or special qualifications, such as professional training. (See also **executive leadership system; patronage system.**)

metropolitan government Form of local government created when local governments join together and assign it responsibility for a range of activities so as to reduce the waste and duplication that results when every locality in a densely populated area has its own police force, its own sanitation department, and so on.

military-industrial complex The three components (the military establishment, the industries that manufacture weapons, and the members of Congress from states and districts that depend heavily on the arms industry) that mutually benefit from a high level of defense spending.

momentum A strong showing by a candidate in early presidential nominating contests, which leads to a buildup of public support for the candidate.

monetary policy A tool of economic management, available to government, based on manipulation of the amount of money in circulation. (See also **fiscal policy.**)

money chase A term used to describe the fact that U.S. campaigns are very expensive and that candidates must spend a great amount of time raising funds in order to compete successfully.

moralistic subculture American subculture, characterized by an emphasis on the public interest, honesty, and public participation; typical of states in the northern tier of the nation.

multilateralism The situation in which nations act together in response to problems and crises.

multinational corporations Business firms with major operations in more than one country.

multiparty system A system in which three or more political parties have the capacity to gain control of government separately or in coalition.

national debt   The total cumulative amount that the U.S. government owes to creditors.

natural rights   See **inalienable rights.**

"necessary and proper" clause (elastic clause)   The authority granted Congress in Article I, Section 8 of the Constitution "to make all laws which shall be necessary and proper" for the implementation of its enumerated powers. (See also **implied powers.**)

negative government   The philosophical belief that government governs best by staying out of people's lives, thus giving individuals as much freedom as possible to determine their own pursuits. (See also **positive government.**)

neutral competence   The administrative objective of a merit-based bureaucracy. Such a bureaucracy should be "competent" in the sense that its employees are hired and retained on the basis of their expertise and "neutral" in the sense that it operates by objective standards rather than partisan ones.

New Jersey (small-state) Plan   A constitutional proposal for a strengthened Congress, but one in which each state would have a single vote, thus granting a small state the same legislative power as a larger state.

news   The news media's version of reality, usually with an emphasis on timely, dramatic, and compelling events and developments.

news media   See **press.**

nomination   The designation of a particular individual to run as a political party's candidate (its "nominee") in the general election.

noneconomic groups   See **citizens' groups.**

North-South Compromise   The agreement over economic and slavery issues that enabled northern and southern states to settle differences that threatened to defeat the effort to draft a new constitution.

objective journalism   A model of news reporting that is based on the communication of "facts" rather than opinions and that is "fair" in that it presents all sides of partisan debate. (See also **partisan press.**)

open party caucuses   Meetings at which a party's candidates for nomination are voted upon and that are open to all of the party's rank-and-file voters who want to attend.

open-seat election   An election in which there is no incumbent in the race.

opinion (of a court)   A court's written explanation of its decision, which serves to inform others of the legal basis for the decision. Supreme Court opinions are expected to guide the decisions of other courts. (See also **concurring opinion; dissenting opinion; majority opinion; plurality opinion.**)

ordinance   A law issued by a local government under authority granted by the state government.

original jurisdiction   The authority of a given court to be the first court to hear a case. (See also **appellate jurisdiction.**)

outside lobbying A form of lobbying in which an interest group seeks to use public pressure as a means of influencing officials.

oversight function A supervisory activity of Congress that centers on its constitutional responsibility to see that the executive carries out the laws faithfully and spends appropriations properly. (See also **lawmaking function; representation function.**)

packaging (of a candidate) A term of modern campaigning that refers to the process of recasting a candidate's record into an appealing image.

partisan press Newspapers and other communication media that openly support a political party and whose news in significant part follows the party line. (See also **objective journalism.**)

party caucus A group that consists of a party's members in the House or Senate and that serves to elect the leadership, set policy goals, and determine party strategy.

party-centered politics Election campaigns and other political processes in which political parties, not individual candidates, hold most of the initiative and influence. (See also **candidate-centered politics.**)

party coalition The groups and interests that support a political party.

party competition A process in which conflict over society's goals is transformed by political parties into electoral competition in which the winner gains the power to govern.

party discipline The willingness of a party's House or Senate members to act together as a cohesive group and thus exert collective control over legislative action.

party identification The personal sense of loyalty that an individual may feel toward a particular political party. (See also **dealignment; realignment.**)

party leaders Members of the House and Senate who are chosen by the Democratic or Republican caucus in each chamber to represent the party's interests in that chamber and who give some central direction to the chamber's deliberations.

party organizations The party organizational units at national, state, and local levels; their influence has decreased over time because of many factors. (See also **candidate-centered politics; party-centered politics; primary election.**)

party realignment An election or set of elections in which the electorate responds strongly to an extraordinarily powerful issue that has disrupted the established political order. A realignment has a lasting impact on public policy, popular support for the parties, and the composition of the party coalitions.

patronage system An approach to managing the bureaucracy whereby people are appointed to important government positions as a reward for political services they have rendered and because of their partisan loyalty. (See also executive leadership system; merit system; spoils system.)

pluralism A theory of American politics that holds that society's interests are substantially represented through the activities of groups.

plurality opinion A court opinion that results when a majority of justices agree on a decision in a case but do not agree on the legal basis for the decision. In this instance, the legal position held by most of the justices on the winning side is called a plurality opinion. (See also **concurring opinion; dissenting opinion; majority opinion.**)

police power A term that refers to the broad power of government to regulate the health, safety, and morals of the citizenry.

policy Generally, any broad course of governmental action; more narrowly, a specific government program or initiative.

policy implementation The primary function of the bureaucracy; it refers to the process of carrying out the authoritative decisions of Congress, the president, and the courts.

political action committee (PAC) The organization through which an interest group raises and distributes funds for election purposes. By law, the funds must be raised through voluntary contributions.

political culture The characteristic and deep-seated beliefs of a particular people.

political movements See **social movements.**

political participation A sharing in activities designed to influence public policy and leadership, such as voting, joining political parties and interest groups, writing to elected officials, demonstrating for political causes, and giving money to political candidates.

political party An ongoing coalition of interests joined together to try to get their candidates for public office elected under a common label.

political socialization The learning process by which people acquire their political opinions, beliefs, and values.

political system The various components of American government. The parts are separate, but they connect with each other, affecting how each performs.

politics The process through which society makes its governing decisions.

population In a public opinion poll, the people (for example, the citizens of a nation) whose opinions are being estimated through interviews with a sample of these people.

populists Those who favor activist government as a means of promoting both economic security and traditional values. (See also **conservatives; liberals; libertarians.**)

pork barrel projects Legislative acts whose tangible benefits are targeted at a particular legislator's constituency.

positive government The philosophical belief that government intervention is necessary in order to enhance personal liberty when individuals are buffeted by economic and social forces beyond their control. (See also **negative government.**)

poverty line As defined by the federal government, the annual cost of a thrifty food budget for an urban family of four, multiplied by three to allow also for the cost of housing, clothes, and other expenses. Families below the poverty line are considered poor and are eligible for certain forms of public assistance.

power The ability of persons or institutions to control policy. (See also **authority.**)

precedent A judicial decision in a given case that serves as a rule of thumb for settling subsequent cases of a similar nature; courts are generally expected to follow precedent.

presidential approval rating A measure of the degree to which the public approves or disapproves of the president's performance in office.

presidential commissions Organizations within the bureaucracy that are headed by commissioners appointed by the president. An example is the Commission on Civil Rights.

press (news media) Those print and broadcast organizations that are in the news-reporting business.

primacy tendency The tendency for early learning to become deeply embedded in one's mind.

primary election A form of election in which voters choose a party's nominees for public office. In most states, eligibility to vote in a primary election is limited to voters who designated themselves as party members when they registered to vote. A primary is direct when it results directly in the choice of nominee; it is indirect (as in the case of presidential primaries) when it results in the selection of delegates who then choose the nominee.

prior restraint Government prohibition of speech or publication before the fact, which is presumed by the courts to be unconstitutional unless the justification for it is overwhelming.

private (individual) goods Benefits that a group (most often an economic group) can grant directly and exclusively to the individual members of the group. (See also **collective goods.**)

probability sample A sample for a poll in which each individual in the population has a known probability of being selected randomly for inclusion in the sample. (See also **public opinion poll.**)

procedural due process The constitutional requirement that government must follow proper legal procedures before a person can be legitimately punished for an alleged offense.

proportional representation A form of representation in which seats in the legislature are allocated proportionally according to each political party's share of the popular vote. This system enables smaller parties to compete successfully for seats. (See also **single-member districts.**)

prospective voting A form of electoral judgment in which voters choose the candidate whose policy promises most closely match their own preferences. (See also **retrospective voting.**)

protectionism The view that the immediate interests of domestic producers should have a higher priority (through, for example, protective tariffs) than free trade between nations has. (See also **free trade.**)

public assistance A term that refers to social welfare programs funded through general tax revenues and available only to the financially needy. Eligibility for such a program is established by a means test. (See also **means test; social insurance.**)

public goods See **collective goods.**

public opinion Those opinions held by ordinary citizens that they express openly.

public opinion poll A device for measuring public opinion whereby a relatively small number of individuals (the sample) is interviewed for the purpose of estimating the opinions of a whole community (the population). (See also **probability sample.**)

public representative role A role whereby the media attempt to act as the public's representatives. (See also **common-carrier role; signaler role; watchdog role.**)

purposive incentive An incentive to group participation based on the cause (purpose) that the group seeks to promote.

realignment See **party realignment.**

reapportionment The reallocation of House seats among states after each census as a result of population changes.

reasonable-basis test A test applied by courts to laws that treat individuals unequally. Such a law may be deemed unconstitutional if its purpose is held to be "reasonably" related to a legitimate government interest.

recall The process by which citizens can petition for the removal from office of an elected official before the scheduled completion of his or her term.

redistricting The process of altering election districts in order to make them as nearly equal in population as possible. Redistricting takes place every ten years, after each population census.

referendum The process through which the legislature may submit proposals to the voters for approval or rejection.

registration The practice of placing citizens' names on an official list of voters before they are eligible to exercise their right to vote.

regulation Government restrictions on the economic practices of private firms.

regulatory agencies Administrative units, such as the Federal Communications Commission and the Environmental Protection Agency, that have responsibility for the monitoring and regulation of ongoing economic activities.

representation function The responsibility of a legislature to represent various interests in society. (See also **lawmaking function; oversight function.**)

representative democracy A system in which the people participate in the decision-making process of government not directly but indirectly, through the election of officials to represent their interests.

republic Historically, the form of government in which representative officials met to decide on policy issues. These representatives were expected to serve the public interest but were not subject to the people's immediate control. Today, the term *republic* is used interchangeably with *democracy*.

reserved powers The powers granted to the states under the Tenth Amendment to the Constitution.

retrospective voting A form of electoral judgment in which voters support the incumbent candidate or party when their policies are judged to have succeeded and oppose the candidate or party when their policies are judged to have failed. (See also **prospective voting.**)

rider An amendment to a bill that deals with an issue unrelated to the content of the bill. Riders are permitted in the Senate but not in the House.

sample In a public opinion poll, the relatively small number of individuals interviewed for the purpose of estimating the opinions of an entire population. (See also **public opinion poll.**)

sampling error A measure of the accuracy of a public opinion poll. It is mainly a function of sample size and is usually expressed in percentage terms. (See also **probability sample.**)

selective incorporation The absorption of certain provisions of the Bill of Rights (for example, freedom of speech) into the Fourteenth Amendment so that these rights are protected from infringement by the states.

self-government The principle that the people are the ultimate source and proper beneficiary of governing authority; in practice, a government based on majority rule.

senatorial courtesy The tradition that a U.S. senator from the state in which a federal judicial vacancy has arisen should have a say in the president's nomination of the new judge if the senator is of the same party as the president.

seniority A member of Congress's consecutive years of service on a particular committee.

separated institutions sharing power The principle that, as a way to limit government, its powers should be divided among separate branches, each of which also shares in the power of the others as a means of checking and balancing them. The result is that no one branch can exercise power decisively without the support or acquiescence of the others.

separation of powers The division of the powers of government among separate institutions or branches.

service relationship The situation where party organizations assist candidates for office but have no power to require them to accept or campaign on the party's main policy positions.

service strategy Use of personal staff by members of Congress to perform services for constituents in order to gain their support in future elections.

signaler role The accepted responsibility of the media to alert the public to important developments as soon as possible after they happen or are discovered. (See also **common-carrier role; public representative role; watchdog role.**)

single-issue politics The situation in which separate groups are organized around nearly every conceivable policy issue and press their demands and influence to the utmost.

single-member districts The form of representation in which only the candidate who gets the most votes in a district wins office. (See also **proportional representation.**)

slander Spoken words that falsely damage a person's reputation.

social capital The sum of face-to-face interactions among citizens in a society.

social insurance Social welfare programs based on the "insurance" concept, so that individuals must pay into the program in order to be eligible to receive funds from it. An example is social security for retired people. (See also **public assistance.**)

social (political) movements Active and sustained efforts to achieve social and political change by groups of people who feel that government has not been properly responsive to their concerns.

soft money Campaign contributions that are not subject to legal limits and are given to parties rather than directly to candidates.

sovereignty The ultimate authority to govern within a certain geographical area.

split-ticket voting The pattern of voting in which the individual voter in a given election casts a ballot for one or more candidates of each major party. (See also **straight-ticket voting.**)

spoils system The practice of granting public office to individuals in return for political favors they have rendered. (See also **patronage system.**)

standing committee A permanent congressional committee with responsibility for a particular area of public policy. An example is the Senate Foreign Relations Committee.

state constitutional convention A state convention convened to amend the state constitution or draft a new one.

stewardship theory A theory that argues for a strong, assertive presidential role, with presidential authority limited only at points specifically prohibited by law. (See also **Whig theory.**)

straight-ticket voting The pattern of voting in which the individual voter in a given election supports only candidates of one party. (See also **split-ticket voting.**)

strict-scrutiny test A test applied by courts to laws that attempt a racial or ethnic classification. In effect, the strict-scrutiny test eliminates race or ethnicity as legal classification when it places minority group members at a disadvantage. (See also **suspect classifications.**)

strong mayor-council system The most common form of municipal government, consisting of the mayor as chief executive and the local council as the legislative body, in which the mayor has veto power and a prescribed responsibility for budgetary and other policy actions.

structuring tendency The tendency of earlier political learning to structure (influence) later learning.

suffrage The right to vote.

sunset laws Legislative acts that have a specific expiration date unless reenacted.

supply-side economics A form of fiscal policy that emphasizes "supply" (production). An example of supply-side economics would be a tax cut for business. (See also **demand-side economics; fiscal policy.**)

supremacy clause Article VI of the Constitution, which makes national law supreme over state law when the national government is acting within its constitutional limits.

suspect classifications Legal classifications, such as race and national origin, that have invidious discrimination as their purpose and are therefore unconstitutional. (See also **strict-scrutiny test.**)

symbolic speech Action (for example, the waving or burning of a flag) for the purpose of expressing a political opinion.

traditionalistic subculture American subculture reflecting the stratified society out of which it grew, which is conservative in its focus and elitist in its leadership; typifies states of the old Confederacy and those on its borders.

transfer payment A government benefit that is given directly to an individual, as in the case of social security payments to a retiree.

trustees Elected representatives whose obligation is to act in accordance with their own consciences as to what policies are in the best interests of the public. (See also **delegates.**)

two-party system A system in which only two political parties have a real chance of acquiring control of the government.

tyranny of the majority The potential of a majority to monopolize power for its own gain and to the detriment of minority rights and interests.

unitary system A governmental system in which the national government alone has sovereign (ultimate) authority. (See also **confederacy; federalism.**)

unit rule The rule that grants all of a state's electoral votes to the candidate who receives most of the popular votes in the state.

unity The principle that Americans are one people who form an indivisible union.

veto The refusal of the president to sign a bill, thereby keeping it from becoming law unless Congress overrides the veto.

Virginia (large-state) Plan A constitutional proposal for a strong Congress with two chambers, both of which would be based on numerical representation, thus granting more power to the larger states.

voter turnout The proportion of persons of voting age that actually votes in a given election.

watchdog role The accepted responsibility of the media to protect the public from deceitful, careless, incompetent, and corrupt officials by standing ready to expose any official who violates accepted legal, ethical, or performance standards. (See also **common-carrier role; public representative role; signaler role.**)

weak mayor-council system A form of municipal government in which the mayor's policymaking powers are less substantial than the council's; the mayor has no power to veto the council's actions and often has no formal role in such activities as budget making.

Whig theory A theory that prevailed in the nineteenth century and held that the presidency was a limited or restrained office whose occupant was confined to expressly granted constitutional authority. (See also **stewardship theory.**)

whistle-blowing An internal check on the bureaucracy whereby individual bureaucrats report instances of mismanagement that they observe.

writ of *certiorari* Permission granted by a higher court to allow a losing party in a legal case to bring the case before it for a ruling; when such a writ is requested of the U.S. Supreme Court, four of the Court's nine justices must agree to accept the case before it is granted *certiorari*.

Credits

Chapter 1   Page 3: Joseph Sohm/Stock Boston; p. 10: Newhouse News Service; p. 15: Walter Hodges/Stone; p. 21: John Neubauer/PhotoEdit; p. 24: AP/Wide World Photos.

Chapter 2   Page 28: Jim Wells/Archive Photos; p. 32: Library of Congress; p. 35, 51: The Granger Collection.

Chapter 3   Pages 61, 69: The Granger Collection; p. 72: "Home, Sweet Home," by Winslow Homer/Christie's Images; p. 74: Library of Congress; p. 79: AP/Wide World Photos.

Chapter 4   Page 92: Robert Brenner/PhotoEdit; p. 95: AP/Wide World Photos; p. 101: Bonnie Kamin/PhotoEdit; p. 103: Donna Binder/Impact Visuals; p. 111: Alan Klehr/Stone; p. 115: Stephen Ferry/Liaison Agency.

Chapter 5   Page 125: Charles Moore/Black Star; p. 131: Chip Henderson/Stone; p. 135: Tony Freeman/PhotoEdit; p. 142: Karim-Shamsi-Basha/Saba; p. 151: Kim Kulish/Saba.

Chapter 6   Page 157: Staddart/Katz/Saba; p. 166: Charles Gupton/Corbis Stock Market; p. 180: Bettmann/CORBIS.

Chapter 7   Page 187: Culver Pictures; p. 197: Reuters NewMedia Inc./CORBIS; p. 200: Bettmann/CORBIS; p. 203: Michael Newman/PhotoEdit; p. 208: Loren Callahan/ Liaison Agency.

Chapter 8   Page 219: Bettmann/CORBIS; p. 228: AFP/Corbis; p. 236 (left): Democratic National Committee; p. 236(right): Republican National Committee; p. 238: Allen Tannenbaum/Corbis Sygma.

Chapter 9   Page 256: Jim Sulley/The Image Works; p. 260: AP/Wide World Photos; p. 266: Frederic Neema/Corbis Sygma; p. 274: Davis Barber/PhotoEdit.

Chapter 10   Page 280: AP/Wide World Photos; p. 287(left): U.S. House of Representatives; p. 287(right): U.S. Senate; p. 294: Les Stone/Corbis Sygma; p. 301: Reuters NewMedia Inc./CORBIS.

Chapter 11   Page 313: Win McNamee/Reuters/Archive; p. 322: Vanessa Vick/Photo Researchers; p. 337: Bettmann/CORBIS.

Chapter 12   Page 345: AP/Wide World Photos; p. 349: Bruce Hoertel/Liaison Agency; p. 376: Diana Walker/Liaison Agency.

Chapter 13   Page 382: Paul Chesley/Stone; p. 390: Bob Daemmrich/Stock Boston; p. 394: Bettmann/CORBIS; p. 401: Don Perdue/Liaison Agency; p. 405: Wally McNamee/Woodfin Camp & Assoc.

Chapter 14   Pages 416, 425: AP/Wide World Photos; p. 427: Ken Heinen/AP/Wide World Photos; p. 437: Joe Cempa/Black Star; 442: Karl Gehring/Liaison Agency.

Chapter 15   Page 452: Chris Hondros/Liaison Agency; 458: Jim Pickerell/Stock Boston; 462: Damien Dovarganes/AP/Wide World Photos.

Chapter 16   Page 489: Stephen Jaffe/Reuters/Archive Photos; 497: Dan Fineman-Appel/Corbis Sygma; 499(left): Sally Weigand/Index Stock Imagery; 499(right): Glenn Kulbako/Index Stock Imagery; 505(left): Bob Daemmrich/The Image Works; 505(right): David Young-Wolff/PhotoEdit.

Chapter 17   Page 512: Vince Streano/Stone; p. 516: Bettmann/CORBIS; p. 521: Dirck Halstead/Liaison Agency; 530: Najlah Feanny/Saba; p. 540: AP/Wide World Photos.

Index

Abortion, 13, 14, 199, 207, 213, 220, 227, 259, 264, 270, 273, 345, 377, 416, 425
  protesting, 91–92
  woman's right of, 106
Accommodations, discrimination in, 141
Accountability, 402
  within bureaucracy, 408–409
  bureaucratic, 402–409
  through Congress, 406–407
  through courts, 407–408
  through presidency, 403–405
Activism
  unconventional, 206–208
Acts of Toleration, 102
Adams, John, 46, 52, 92, 216
Adarand v. *Pena*, 148
Administrative organizations, types of, 384–388
Affirmative action, 12, 273
  defined, 146
  differing views of, 146
  key decisions of, 148
  Supreme Court position on, 147–149
AFL-CIO, 253, 254
Africa, 539
African Americans. *See also* Affirmative action; Civil rights movement; National Association for the Advancement of Colored People (NAACP); Slavery
  affirmative action and, 146–150, 174
  attitudes of, 174
  busing, 150–152, 174

African Americans—*Cont.*
  civil rights movement, 124–126
  college enrollment of, 130
  criminal justice and, 125
  discrimination against, 114, 121–122, 125, 139, 140, 141, 142, 153, 170, 220
  education of, 150–152
  elections and, 125
  historical discrimination, 1, 8, 36, 65, 70, 123–134
  poverty and, 8, 484, 485
  public schools and, 123, 152
  representation of, 126, 143, 144, 408–409, 429
  state population of, 36–37
  suffrage and, 143, 187, 195
Age-cohort tendency, 166
Age Discrimination Act, 138
Age Discrimination in Employment Act, 138
Agency point of view, 398–399
Agenda setting, 295
Agents of political socialization, 167–169
Agricultural groups, 255
Agriculture, 461–462
Aid to Families with Dependent Children (AFDC), 496–497, 498
Ailes, Roger, 241
Air Force, U.S., 524
Airlines Deregulation Act, 454
Air wars, 242–243
Alabama, 99, 104, 124
Alaska, 453–454
Alienation, 195, 196

Amendments. *See* Bill of Rights; *individual amendments*
America. *See under* United States
American Association of Retired Persons (AARP), 267
American Association of University Professors, 255
American Bar Association, 255
American Civil Liberties Union (ACLU), 264
American Creed, 5
American Farm Bureau Federation, 255
American flag, burning, 94–95, 99
American Independent party, 229
American Indians. *See* Native Americans
American Medical Association (AMA), 255, 495
American Nazi party, 99
American Petroleum Institute, 261
American Revolution, 30–33
Americans for Democratic Action (ADA), 259
Americans with Disabilities Act, 137
Amicus curiae briefs, 436
Annapolis Convention, 34
Anti-Federalists, 38, 64–65, 67
AOL, 452
Apathy, 190
Appellate jurisdiction, 418
Appointees, presidential, 360–361
Arizona, 110, 133
Arkansas, 243
Army, U.S., 524
Articles of Confederation, 33, 34, 38, 61, 65
Asian Americans, 122, 136–137. *See also* Affirmative action; Civil rights movement
demographic pattern of, 136–137
discrimination against, 136–137, 142
economic status of, 137
education and, 137

Asian Americans—*Cont.*
immigration of, 136
representation of, 137
Associated Press (AP), 285
Authority, 14
Authority of government, dividing, 42–44

Baker, Howard, 271
Bakke, Alan, 147
Balanced budget, 465
Balkins, 518
Banking Act, 455
Barbour, Haley, 271
Barron v. *Baltimore*, 96
Bay of Pigs, 367
Bazelon, David, 431
Beard, Charles S., 54, 55
Beard's economic theory of Constitution, 54–55
Berlin Wall, 517
Bernstein, Carl, 296
Bias in news media, 297
Bicameral Congress, 44
Bilateral diplomacy, 520
Bill, 323–326
Bill of Rights, 45, 46, 90, 105, 108–109, 114, 118. *See also* *individual amendments*
Black, Hugo, 420
Blacks. *See* African Americans
Blair, Tony, 245
Block grants, 80, 83
Bork, Robert, 427
Bosnia, 518
Boston Tea Party, 30, 207
Bowers v. *Hardwick*, 107, 138
Boxer, Barbara, 128
Boy Scouts, 138
Brandenburg v. *Ohio*, 93, 97
Breckinridge, John C., 217
Bretton Woods Conference, 523
Breyer, Stephen, 438
Broadcast media development, 273–275

Brown v. *Board of Education of Topeka,* 124, 140, 436, 442
Bryan, William Jennings, 228
Bryce, James, 3, 349
Buchanan, Pat, 230
Buckley v. *Valeo,* 95
Budget, executive, 404–406
Budget and Accounting Act, 349
Budgetary process, 469–472
Budget Committees, 471
Budget deficit, 465
Budget Impoundment and Control Act, 330–331, 373
Budget resolution, 471
Budget surplus, 465–466
Bull Moose party, 228, 229
Bureaucracy, 383. *See* Federal bureaucracy
Bureaucratic accountability, 402–409
Bureaucratic power, sources of, 398–402
Burke, Edmund, 49
Bush, George, 83, 213, 242, 264, 343, 352, 369, 370, 375, 401, 429, 438, 454, 517
Bush, George W., 1, 16, 53, 178, 213, 224, 227, 229, 239, 244, 342, 354, 356, 358, 359, 361, 362, 375, 438, 444, 494, 504, 519, 540
Bush v. *Gore,* 415–416, 444
Business
 judicial protection of, 72–73
 promoting, 460–461
Business groups, 253–254
Busing, 150–152, 443
 course and impact of, 150–151

Cabinet, 362
Cabinet departments, 386–387
Cable television, 102
Calhoun, John C., 70
California, 101, 133, 134, 135, 147, 310, 328, 459

California Civil Rights Initiative, 149
Campaign
 for election, 239–244
 for nomination, 341–343
Campaign activities, 201–202
Campaign spending, 95
Candidate-centered campaigns, 239–244
Candidate-centered politics, 214
Capital gains tax, 468
Capitalism, 17–18
Capture theory, 263
Carson, Rachel, 457
Carter, Jimmy, 370, 375, 429
Carville, James, 241
Cash grants, 79–82
Castro, Fidel, 279, 367
Categorical grants, 80, 83
Catholics, 173
Central Intelligence Agency (CIA), 387, 522
Certiorari, writ of, 419
Chavez, Cesar, 134
Checks and balances, 14–15, 43–45, 48
Cheney, Dick, 315, 361
Chicago v. *Morales,* 112
Child labor, 73
Children, poverty and, 484, 487
Children's Television Workshop, 400
China, 539–540
Chinese Americans. *See* Asian Americans
Christian Coalition, 228, 259
Christian Moral Government Fund, 270
Christians, fundamentalist, 173
Chrysler Corporation, 453
Churches, as agents of socialization, 169
Churchill, Winston, 514
Citadel, 140
Citizens groups, 255–256
 defined, 255
Citizenship, 188

Citizens party, 228
Civic duty, 195
Civil liberties, 89–118
  defined, 90
Civil rights, 370
  defined, 122
Civil Rights Act of 1964, 124–125,
  127, 133, 136, 140–141, 435
Civil Rights Act of 1968, 140,
  141–142
Civil Rights Act of 1991, 127
Civil rights movement, 109, 123, 220
Civil Service Commission, 394
Civil Service system, 389, 393–395
Civil War, 70–71
Claims Court, U.S., 423
Class, guiding public opinion,
  173–174
Clay, Henry, 361
Clean Air Act, 453, 457
Clear-and-present-danger test, 93
Cleveland, Grover, 218
Clientele groups, power of, 400–401
Clinton, Hillary, 238, 239, 322
Clinton, William, 104, 149,
  156–157, 164, 200, 224, 241,
  264, 310, 333, 334, 337, 343,
  345, 363, 369, 371, 373, 375,
  377, 381, 389, 427, 429, 438,
  465, 472, 489, 533, 535, 539
Closed rule, 325
Cloture, 326
Cold war, 93, 348, 369–370,
  514–515
Collective action, 256–257
Collective economy, 450
Collective goods, 256
Colonial constitutions, 29–30
Colorado, 138, 442
Columbia School of Journalism, 283
Commerce clause, 70, 72–73, 75
Commission on Civil Rights, 389
Commission on Fine Arts, 389
Committee chairpersons, 317–318
Committee membership, 321–322

Committee system, 319–323
Common-carrier role, 295–296
Common Cause, 258
Common law, 29
Communications Act, 286
Communications Decency Act, 102
Community activities, 202–203
Comparable worth, 130
Compliance, 441
Concurring opinion, 420
Confederacy, 63
Conference committees, 320–321,
  327, 472
Congress, U.S., 304–338. See also
  House of Representatives, U.S.;
  Senate, U.S.
  accountability through, 245,
    406–407
  bicameral, 35–36
  bills in, 323–327
  as career, 305–312
  checks and balances and, 44
  committee chairpersons in,
    316–319
  committee jurisdiction, 322–323
  committee membership, 321–322
  committee system in, 319–323
  election to, 305–312
  fiscal policy and, 471–472
  foreign policy and, 535
  fragmentation in, 331–332
  incumbents in, 305–312
  lawmaking function of, 327–332
  leadership in, 312–315, 326–327
  lobbying, 262
  NAFTA and, 535–536
  oversight function of, 335–338
  party leaders in, 312–316
  party unity and fragmentation in,
    326–329, 333–335
  personal misconduct in, 309–310
  pluralism in, 338
  policymaking role of, 327–337
  presidency and, 330
  presidency colliding with, 371–374

Congress, U.S.—*Cont.*
  presidents and, 371–376
  protectionism and, 534
  representation function of,
    332–334
  seniority principle in, 318
  standing committees of, 319–321
  using incumbency to stay in,
    307–308
  women in, 312
Congressional Budget Office
  (CBO), 330, 471
Congressional Budget Schedule,
  471–472
Congressional Research Service
  (CRS), 331
Connecticut, 39, 65, 105, 243
Connor, Eugene, 124
Conservationism, 457–458
Conservatives, 171–172
  by state, 175
Constituency, 307
Constituency politics, 332–333
Constitution, defined, 39
Constitution, U.S., 1, 32, 67–68,
  460. *See also* Bill of Rights;
  individual amendments.
  alterations to, 51–55
  amending the, 41
  interpretation of, 430–432
  negotiating toward, 34–38
  presidency requirements in, 344
  process of writing, 34
  ratification of, 36–37
  slavery and, 36
Constitutional democracy, 27–57, 55
Constitutional government, 55
Constitutionalism, 17
Constitutional restraints on political
  power, 40–47
Consumer Product Safety
  Commission, 455
Containment, 514
  doctrine of, 514
Contract with America, 224, 411

Conventional warfare, 526–527
Cooperative federalism, 76–78
Corporation for Public
  Broadcasting, 400
Council of Economic Advisers
  (CEA), 360
Counterinsurgency, 528
Court decisions
  "inside" influences on, 435–436
  "outside" influences on, 436–437
Court of International Trade,
  U.S., 423
Court of Military Appeals, U.S., 423
Court-packing plan, 75
Courts. *See also* Supreme Court, U.S.
  accountability through, 407–408
  federal, 417–423
  lobbying of, 264
  state, 423–426
Courts of appeal, U.S., 422–423
Craig v. *Boren*, 140
Crane, Phil, 318
Creationism, 105
Crime, 107–116
Cross-cutting cleavages, public
  opinion and, 177
Cuba, 279
Cuban Americans. *See* Hispanic
  Americans
Cultural beliefs, 2–3
Cultural thinking guiding public
  opinion, 170
Culture, 3–12

Dahmer, Jeffrey, 289
Davis, John W., 354
Dayton peace agreement, 518
Dealignment, 220–221
Death penalty, 109, 113
Debt, national, 465
De Canas v. *Bica*, 134
Decision, 420
Declaration of Independence, 1, 5,
  31–33, 122
De facto discrimination, 145

Defense capability, 507
Defense organizations, 521
Defense policy. *See also* Foreign and
  defense policy
Defense spending, 525
Deficit spending, 464
De jure discrimination, 145
Delaware, 35, 39
Delegates, 53
Demand-side economics, 449,
  464–465
Democracy, 16, 27–57
Democratic National Committee
  (DNC), 235
Democratic party, 199, 216, 219,
  220, 221, 225–227
Demographic groups, federal job
  rankings in, 409
Demographic representativeness,
  408–409
Demosclerosis, 276
Denials of power, 41, 46
Dennis v. *United States*, 93
Department of Agriculture,
  393, 457
Department of Defense (DOD),
  336, 387, 521–522
Department of Health and Human
  Services, 387
Department of Interior, 457
Department of Justice, 386, 401
Department of State, 387, 522–523
Deregulation, 454
Descriptive reporting, 283
Détente, 516
Deterrence, 526
Developing world, 538–540
Devolution, 76, 81–83, 84
Dewey, Thomas E., 164
Dickerson v. *United States*, 110
Dingell, John, 459
Diplomacy, 519–520
Diplomatic organizations, 522–523
Direct primary, 232
Disabled Americans, 137–138

Discrimination. *See also* African
  Americans, Asian Americans,
  Hispanic Americans, Native
  Americans, Women.
  in accommodations, 140
  de facto, 145
  de jure, 145
  in health care, 153
  in housing, 141–142
  in jobs, 141
  by private parties, 141
Dissenting opinion, 420
District courts, U.S., 421–422
District of Columbia, 356
Diversity, 5
Doctrine of nullification, 70
Dole, Robert, 164, 200, 242
Domhoff, G. William, 21
"don't ask, don't tell" policy, 138
double jeopardy, 108
Douglas, Stephen A., 217
Dred Scott decision, 70, 71
Drudge, Matt, 287
Dual federalism, 71–75
Dual use policy, 458
Due process clause (of Fourteenth
  Amendment), 96–97, 109

Earned Income Tax Credit
  (EITC), 492
Earth Day, 458
Easton, David, 22
Economic class, 173–174
Economic competitiveness, global,
  475, 531–532
Economic dimension of national
  security policy, 529–541
Economic exchange, 449
Economic globalization, 534
Economic groups, 253–254
Economic interest groups, 253
Economic interests, government
  promoting, 460–463
Economic organizations,
  523–524

Economic policy, 448–470
Economics
  demand-side, 449, 464–465
  supply-side, 468–469
Economy, 449
  global, 475, 531–536
  mixed, 450
  regulating, 455–456
Education, 500–505
  college, 8, 9
  equality of opportunity through, 500–505
  federal role in, 503–505
  public, 13, 501–503
  special, 490
  spending on, 333–334
  voting and, 181
Education for All Handicapped Children Act, 137–138
Effective tax rate, 491
Efficiency, 450, 455
  promoting, 450–456
Eighth Amendment, 108, 115
Eisenhower, Dwight, 219, 428, 529
Elastic clause, 66–67, 68, 69
Elderly, 138, 176, 249
Elections, 46. See also Voting
  frequency of, 193
  midterm House of Representatives and, 310
  presidential. See Presidential elections
  primary. See Primary elections
Election strategy, 242–243, 355–356
Electoral College, 16, 50, 53, 351
Electoral votes in states, 355–356, 357, 358
Electors, 352
Elementary and Secondary Education Act, 504
Elitism, 20–22, 180, 477, 528
Emily's List, 241
Employees, federal, 389–391
Employment, federal, 389–391
Engel v. Vitale, 104

Entitlement program, 492
Enumerated powers, 66
Environment, government as protector of, 457–459
Environmental groups, 259
Environmentalism, 458–459
Environmental Protection Agency (EPA), 387, 406–407, 453, 459
Equal Credit Act, 127
Equality, 4
  under the law, 138–144
  struggle for, 122–138
Equality of opportunity, 501
Equality of result, 144–150
Equal Pay Act, 127
Equal protection clause, 139–141, 144
Equal rights, 121–153
  defined, 122
Equal Rights Amendment (ERA), 127
Equity, 455
Era of Good Feeling, 216
Espionage Act, 93
Establishment clause, 103–104, 105
European Recovery Plan, 530
European Union (EU), 531–532
"Evil Empire," 516–517
Excessive entanglement, 103–104
Exclusionary rule, 110–112
  weakening, 111
Executive. See Presidency.
Executive agencies, lobbying, 262–263
Executive agreements, 345
Executive branch, checks and balances and, 44
Executive budget, 404–405
Executive departments, 386
Executive leadership systems, 395–396
Executive Office of the President (EOP), 360–361, 396, 404–405
Executive power, 345
Executive privilege, 336

Expertise, power of, 400
Export-Import Bank of the
U.S., 523
Ex post facto laws, 41
Expressed powers, 66
Expression, freedom of, 91–107
Externalities, 453

Factional parties, 228–229
Facts (of a court case), 431
Fair Labor Standards Act, 454
Families
as agents of political
socialization, 167
Family and Medical Leave Act, 127,
130–131
Farm Bureau, 255
Farmers Union, 255
Farm program, 462
Fast track authority, 535
"Fed," 474–477
Federal administration, 383–392
Federal bureaucracy, 381–411
development of, 392–396
policy responsibilities of, 391–392
power imperative of, 396–402
Federal Bureau of Investigation, 392
Federal Communications
Commission (FCC), 263, 286,
391, 452, 456
Federal court appointees, 426–430
Federal courts, 417–423
Federal Deposit Insurance
Corporation (FDIC), 75, 389
Federal Election Campaign Act, 354
Federal employment, 389–390
Federal government, employees of,
389–391
Federal grants-in-aid, 78–81, 82
Federalism, 40, 46, 59–86
argument for, 63–65
contemporary, 75–84
cooperative, 76–78
defined, 62
dual, 71–75
fiscal, 78–80

Federalism—*Cont.*
in historical perspective, 67–75
national and state sovereignty and,
60–67, 85
new, 83–84
system of, 60–66
Federalist No. 10, 42, 49, 65, 253
Federalist No. 28, 63–64
Federalist No. 51, 28
Federalist No. 69, 344
Federalist Papers, 38
Federalists, 38, 46, 67, 216
Federal judges, selecting, 51
Federal judicial system, 417–423
Federal Reserve Act, 474
Federal Reserve Bank, 474–475
Federal Reserve System, 474–477
Federal-state power, boundaries
of, 85
Federal system, 60
Federal Trade Commission (FTC),
404, 451, 523
Feinstein, Dianne, 128, 310
Felker v. *Turpin*, 114
Female. *See* Women
Ferraro, Geraldine, 128
Fifteenth Amendment, 143, 187
Fifth Amendment, 108, 127
Filibuster, 326
First Amendment, 91, 93, 94, 97–98,
101, 102–104, 207, 288
First Bank of the United States, 68
First Continental Congress, 31
Fiscal Federalism, 78–80
Fiscal policy, 462–473
nature of, 462–469
partisan differences and, 473
process and politics of, 469–472
summary, 463
Flag, burning American, 94–95, 99
Florida, 110, 133, 279
election of 2000, 1, 16, 178, 342,
355, 358, 415–416
Food and Drug Administration
(FDA), 455
Food stamps, 498–499

Forbes, Steve, 244
Ford, Gerald, 459
Foreign aid, 538–539
Foreign and defense policy,
511–541
instruments for making, 520–524
politics of, 528–529
process of making, 519–520
roots of, 513–519
Formalized rules, 384
Fourteenth Amendment, 72, 73, 90,
96–97, 103, 104, 107, 108, 109,
139–141, 144
selective incorporation and,
96–97
Fourth Amendment, 90, 108, 111,
112, 433
Fragmentation, 331–332
Framers, of Constitution, 28, 45,
48–50, 85, 344, 351
goals of, 28, 32–40
Frank, Jerome, 420–421
Frank, Reuven, 285
Franked mail, 307
Franklin, Benjamin, 34
Free assembly, 93–95, 98
Freedman, Milton, 474
Freedom
of expression, 91–102, 117
of the press, 95–96, 288–289
of religion, 102–105
Freedom to Farm Act, 462
Free-exercise clause, 103, 104–105
Free-rider problem, 256
Free speech, 90, 93–95
Free trade, 535
French and Indian War, 30
Fuji films, 523
Fullilove v. *Klutnik*, 147
Fundamentalist Christians, 226, 227

Gaebler, Ted, 409
Gallup Poll, 164
Garcia v. *San Antonio Authority*, 84
Garfield, James, 394
Gender gap, 128, 176, 226

General Accounting Office
(GAO), 331
General Agreement on Tariffs and
Trade (GATT), 536
Georgia, 39, 61, 107, 144
Gerrymandering, 311
Gibbons v. *Ogden*, 70
GI Bill, 504
Gideon v. *Wainwright*, 110, 420
Gingrich, Newt, 81, 224, 338, 400
Ginsberg, Ruth Bader, 438
Gitlow v. *New York*, 96–97
Global economic competitiveness,
475, 531–532
Global economic policy, politics of,
540–541
Global economy, 475, 531–536
Global superpower, United States
as, 513
Global trade, 533–536
Glorious Revolution, 102
Goldwater, Barry, 222
Gonzalez, Elian, 279–280
GOP. *See* Republican party
Gorbachev, Mikhail, 517
Gore, Al, 1, 16, 213, 226, 229, 342,
355, 358, 381
Government, 13, 14, 63, 64, 259
Government corporations, 389
Government employees, 77
Government licensing, news media
and, 285–286
Government loans, 460
Government revenues, 78
Government tax revenue, shares
of, 78
Graduated personal income tax, 473
Grants
block, 80, 83
categorical, 80, 83
Grants-in-aid, federal, 78–80,
81, 82
Grants of power, 41, 46
Grassroots lobbying, 267–268
Grassroots party, 216–217
Great Compromise, 34–35

Great Depression, 73–74, 166, 218, 350, 463, 498
Great Society, 76, 79, 85, 486
Green Party (Germany), 222
Green Party (U.S.), 229, 230, 355
Greenpeace U.S.A., 259
Greenspan, Alan, 477
Griswold v. *Connecticut*, 105–106
Group politics, 252
Group thinking, guiding public opinion, 173–177
GS (Graded Service) job ranking, 390
G-7 summit, 511
Guerrilla war, 528
Gulf war. *See* Persian Gulf war
Gun control, 332, 377

Habeas corpus, 41, 108, 112–114, 443
Haiti, 377
Hamilton, Alexander, 38, 52, 63, 68, 215, 282, 344
Hammer v. *Dagenhart*, 73
Handgun Violence Control Act, 84
Harassment, sexual, in workplace, 130–131
Hard money, 237
Harrington, Michael, 485
Harrison, Benjamin, 53, 352
Hastert, Dennis, 224, 313
Hatch, Orrin, 437
Hatch Act, 391
Hate speech, 98
Hawaii, 481
Hayes, Rutherford B., 53, 352
Head Start, 15, 490
Health care, 495–496, 500
Hearst, William Randolph, 282
Helms, Jesse, 538
Helsinki Accords, 516
Henry, Patrick, 61
Heritage Foundation, 498
Hierarchical authority, 383
Higher Education Act, 503

Hired guns (political consultants), 241–242
Hispanic Americans, 121, 133–136, 272. *See also* Affirmative action; Civil rights movement
affirmative action and, 148
attitudes of, 174
college enrollment of, 130
demographic pattern of, 133
differences among, 133
discrimination against, 121, 134–135, 142
economic status of, 484, 485
education and, 130, 137, 152–153
growing political power of, 135–136, 144
immigration and, 10, 133
migrant worker strikes and, 133–134
party identification by national origin, 134
political action of, 133–134
in public office, 136
representation of, 126, 135–136, 144
rights of, 133–134
voting pattern of, 134, 135–136
Hitler, Adolf, 514
Ho Chi Minh, 515
Holmes, Oliver Wendell, Jr., 70, 93, 430–431, 435
Homestead Act, 461
Homosexuals, 107, 122, 138, 207
Honeymoon period, 366–367
Hoover, Herbert, 218, 219, 347
House Appropriations Committee, 472
House Commerce Committee, 323
House International Relations Committee, 335
House of Representatives, U.S., 35. *See also* Congress, U.S.
committee chairpersons in, 316–319
committee system in, 319–323

House of Representatives—*Cont.*
constitutional qualifications for
serving in, 309
incumbents in, 305–312
midterm elections and, 310
party leaders in, 312–314
redistricting and, 311
selection of, 50, 55
Speaker of, 313–314
standing committees of, 320
women in, 312
House Rules Committee, 314, 325
House Ways and Means
Committee, 322
Housing
discrimination in, 141–142
subsidized, 499–500
Huffington, Michael, 310
Human rights, trade and, 539–540
Humphrey, Hubert, 353
Hunt v. *Cromartie*, 144
Hussein, Saddam, 518

Idaho, 481
Ideals, 1–24
limits of, 8, 10, 12
power of, 6
Ideological groups, 259
Ideological parties, 229–230
Ideological thinking, guiding public
opinion, 171–173
Ideology, 171
Illinois, 98–99
Immigration, 4
Chinese, 10
Immigration Reform and Control
Act, 134
Imminent lawless action, 98
Impeachment, 371–372
Implied powers, 66–67, 68–69
Inalienable rights, 31
Income, 490–491
Income taxes, 473, 491–492
Incumbency, 245, 246
pitfalls of, 308–311

Incumbency—*Cont.*
safe, 311–312
using, 307–308
Independent agencies, 387
Independents, 177
Indians, American. *See* Native
Americans
Individual-benefit programs,
492–500
Individual goods, 253
Individualism, 4, 6, 18, 209
public opinion and, 170
Individual rights, 17, 45, 117
Industrial Revolution, 71–72
Inflation, 469
Influence, organizing for, 260–272
Initiative, 53, 54
In-kind benefits, 498
Inputs to political system, 23
Inside lobbying, 260–267
Insurgency, 528
Integration
school, 152–153
social, 150–153
Intelligence organizations, 522
Interdependency, 76–78
Interest-group liberalism, 274
Interest groups, 249–276
agricultural, 255
business, 253–254
categories of, 253–260
citizens', 255–256
defined, 250
economic, 253–254
government as, 259–260
ideological, 259
labor, 254
professional, 255
public, 257–258
single issue, 259
Interest rates, 476–477
Intergovernmental relations,
76–78
Intermediate scrutiny test, 140
Internationalism, 514

International Monetary Fund (IMF), 369, 523–524
Internet, 205–206, 244, 255, 257, 286–287
Interpretive reporting, 283
Interstate commerce, 68, 73
Interstate Commerce Commission (ICC), 452
Intrastate commerce, 68, 73
Iowa, 354
Iran, 375, 538
Iraq, 524
Iron triangles, 264, 265, 266, 402
Isolationist, 513
Israel, 538
Issue networks, 265–266, 402

Jackson, Andrew, 53, 70, 216, 242, 346–347, 352, 393
Jacksonian democracy, 53, 216
Japan, 531–532
Jay, John, 38
Jefferson, Thomas, 5, 31, 32, 33, 41, 45, 46, 47, 52, 89, 92, 122–123, 215, 282
Jeffersonian democracy, 52
Jews, 173
Jim Crow era, 8
Job-related issues for women, 130–131
Jobs, discrimination in, 146
Job specialization, 383
Job training, 498–500
Johnson, Andrew, 371
Johnson, Gregory Lee, 94–95
Johnson, Lyndon, 76, 79, 85, 342, 366, 373, 486, 490, 515
Joint Chiefs of Staff (JCS), 521
Joint committees, 320
Journalism, 289–290
Judges as political officials, 428–430
Judicial activism, 442–444
Judicial appointees, 429
Judicial conference, 420
Judicial decisions, 429
  legal context of, 430–432

Judicial decisions—Cont.
  political influences on, 84, 435–438
Judicial power, 432
  democratic government and, 445
  shared, 44–45
Judicial protection of business, 72–73
Judicial restraint, 441–442
Judicial review, 47, 433, 439
Judicial system, federal, 415–445
Judiciary, 415–445. See also Courts; Supreme Court, U.S.
  debate over proper role of, 442–445
  proper role of, 445
Judiciary Act of 1789, 47
Judiciary branch, checks and balances and, 44
Jurisdiction (of a congressional committee), 323
Jurisdiction (of a court), 418
Justices as political officials, 428–430

Kefauver, Estes, 353
Kennan, George, 514
Kennedy, Anthony, 415
Kennedy, John, 346, 367, 495
Kennedy, Robert, 213
Keynes, John Maynard, 464
Kimel v. Florida Board of Regents, 84, 443
King, Martin Luther, Jr., 121, 124–125, 167
King George III, 30, 31
Kodak, 523
Korean war, 515
Kosovo, 156–157, 518–519
Ku Klux Klan, 97
Kuwait, 517

Labor, 461
Labor groups, 254–255
Laissez-faire capitalism, 71–75, 461
Laissez-faire doctrine, 449–450

Latin Americans. *See* Hispanic Americans
Lau v. *Nichols*, 137
Law, bill into, 323–327
Lawmaking function (of Congress), 327–332
League of Nations, 348
League of Women Voters, 258
Legal context of judicial decisions, 430–432
Legislative branch, checks and balances and, 44
Legislative devices for restraining bureaucracy, 406–407
Legislative oversight, 335–338
Legislative powers, shared, 44
Legislative Reorganization Act, 322
Legislative veto, 336
Legislatures, national, 369. *See also* Congress, U.S.; House of Representatives, U.S.; Senate, U.S.
Legitimacy (of court decision), 439
Legitimacy (of election), 350
Lesson of Munich, 514
Lesson of Vietnam, 516
Lewinsky, Monica, 298, 371
Libel, 99, 288
Liberals, 172
  by state, 175
Libertarian party, 228
Libertarians, 172
Liberty, 3
  concept of, 17
  protection of, 63–64
Limbaugh, Rush, 285
Limited conventional warfare, 527
Limited government, 28–29, 40, 45, 46, 51
  providing for, 40–47
  roots of, 29–31
Limited nuclear warfare, 526
Limited popular rule, 49–50
Lincoln, Abraham, 71, 167, 217
Line-item veto, 370–371

Lippmann, Walter, 185, 300
Livingston, Craig, 363
Lobbying, 261
  Congress, 262
  courts, 264
  executive agencies, 262–263
  grassroots. *See* Grassroots lobbying
  inside. *See* Inside lobbying
  outside. *See* Outside lobbying
Lobbying groups, 260–272
Local governments, employees of, 77
Local party organizations, 233–234
Lochner v. *New York*, 73
Locke, John, 31, 63, 102
Loitering, 112
Loose construction, 437
Lott, Trent, Sen., 59
Louisiana, 105
Love Canal, 459
Lower-court myth, 423

McCain, John, 244
McCulloch, Edwin, 69
McCulloch v. *Maryland*, 68–70
McGovern, George, 355
Madison, James, 28, 34, 38, 41–42, 45, 49, 65, 67, 215, 253, 275
Maine, 190
Majoritarianism, 19–20, 528
Majority, tyranny of the, 17, 47
Majority leader of the House, 314
Majority leader of the Senate, 314–315
Majority opinion, 159, 420
Majority rule, 16, 28–29, 180
Mandamus, writ of, 46–47
Mandates, 83
Mapplethorpe, Robert, 100
Mapp v. *Ohio*, 109–110, 111
Marbury, William, 46–47
Marbury v. *Madison*, 47, 439
March on Washington for Jobs and Freedom 1963, 124

Marshall, George C., 531
Marshall, John, 47–48, 69, 415
Marshall, Thurgood, 429
Marshall Plan, 530–531
Marx, Karl, 450
Maryland, 68–69, 115
Mason, George, 62
Massachusetts, 33–35, 65
Mass media. *See* News media
Material incentive, 253
Means test, 496
Medicaid, 76, 500
Medicare, 495–496
Mercedes Benz, 453
Merit plan (for judges), 423
Merit Service Protection Board, 394
Merit system. *See* Civil Service system
Michels, Roberto, 22
Michigan, 115, 253
Microsoft, 452
Midterm elections, 189
Military-industrial complex, 529
Military power, uses of, 526–531
Military spending, 529
Miller, James, 404
Miller v. *California*, 101
Mills, C. Wright, 21
Milosevic, Slobodan, 519
Minnesota, 97, 190, 230
Minority groups, 109, 114, 121–122, 128, 139, 144, 146–147, 174, 226, 272, 275, 359, 409–410
Miranda v. *Arizona*, 110
Mississippi, 59
Missouri, 106
Missouri Compromise of 1820, 71
Missouri Plan, 423–424
Mitchell, John, 296
Mixed economy, 17–18
Momentum, 354
Monetary policy, 473–477
Money chase, 239–240

Monroe, James, 216
Montesquieu, 42, 63
Morrill Act, 504
Morris, Dick, 241
"Motor Voter" registration law, 190, 192
Mott, Lucretia, 127
Moynihan, Daniel Patrick, 59, 481
Multilateral diplomacy, 520
Multilateralism, 517–519
Multinational corporations, 533
Multiparty system, 221, 223
Munich Conference, 516
Murray, Charles, 485

Nader, Ralph, 229, 230, 355
Napolitan, Joe, 241
National Aeronautics and Space Administration (NASA), 387
National Association for the Advancement of Colored People (NAACP), 259, 264
National Association of Auto Dealers, 273–274
National authority, 73–76
National debt, 465
National Defense Education Act, 504
National Economic Council, 362
National Endowment for the Arts (NEA), 100
National Farmers Union, 255
National Industry Recovery Act (NIRA), 74
National Labor Relations Act, 461
National leaders, methods of choosing, 50
National Organization for Women (NOW), 259
National Park Service, 457
National party conventions, 354–355
National Performance Review (NPR), 381–382, 410
National power, 66

National Railroad Passenger
  Corporation (Amtrak), 389
National Rifle Association (NRA),
  259, 268
National security advisor, 360
National Security Council (NSC),
  360, 520–521
National security policies, 511–541
National sovereignty, 60–66
National Welfare Rights
  Organization, 275
Native Americans, 121–122,
  132–133
  civil rights movement and, 132
  discrimination against, 12
  militant, 132
Natural resources, access to,
  536–537
Natural rights, 31
Navy, U.S., 524
Nazi party, American, 99
Near, Jay, 97
Near v. Minnesota, 97
"Necessary and proper" clause,
  66–67, 68, 69, 70
Negative government, 493
Nelson, Gaylord, 458
Neutral competence, 394–395
New Deal, 73–75, 79, 166, 350,
  455, 456
New federalism, 83–84
New Hampshire, 33, 39, 353
New Jersey, 39, 66, 115, 243
New Jersey Plan, 35–36
New Mexico, 133, 481
News, 279–302
  defined, 280
  values and imperatives of,
    289–291, 292
News media, 279–302
  affecting public opinion,
    300–302
  as agents of political
    socialization, 168
  broadcast development, 273–276

News media—*Cont.*
  defined, 281
  development of, 281–282
  election campaigns and,
    242–243, 298
  following politics in, 204–205
  freedom and conformity in,
    287–291
  government licensing and,
    285–287
  lack of accountability of, 299–301
  as link, 291–300
  watchdog role of, 296–298
News production, domination of,
  289–290
New world order, 517–519
New York, 66, 70, 96, 107, 243
New York Times, The, 283,
  289, 373
New York Times Co. v. Sullivan,
  99–100
*New York Times Co. v. United
  States*, 95
Nineteenth Amendment, 127,
  143, 186
Ninth Amendment, 105
Nixon, Richard, 27–28, 83, 296, 342,
  371, 373, 396, 498, 506, 515
Nominations, 232–239
Noneconomic groups, 255–256
North American Free Trade
  Agreement (NAFTA), 257
North Atlantic Treaty Organization
  (NATO), 156–157, 518–519,
  522, 524, 535–536
North Carolina, 38, 61, 143
North Dakota, 190, 328
North-South constitutional
  compromise, 36
Nuclear warfare, 526

Objective journalism, 282–283
Obscenity, Supreme Court and,
  100–102
Ochs, Adolph, 283

O'Connor, Sandra Day, 128, 415, 429
Office of Management and Budget (OMB), 331, 360, 394, 395, 469–471
Office of Personnel Management (OPM), 394
Ohio, 97, 100, 101, 109–110
"Open Door" policy, 348
Open Party caucuses, 353
Open-rule, 325
Opinion (of a court), 420, 421
Opinion-poll respondents, sampling error by number of, 162
Opinion polls, 162–165
Opinion polls, government by, 180–181
Oregon, 107, 190
Organization of American States (OAS), 523
Original jurisdiction, 418
Osborne, David, 409
Otis, James, 30
Outcomes (economic), 455
Outputs from political system, 23
Outside lobbying, 267–272
Overregulation, curbing, 453–454
Oversight
  legislative, 335–338
  obstacles to, 330–331
  process of, 335–338
Oversight function, of Congress, 335–338

Packaging (of candidates), 242–243
PACs. See Political action committees
Paine, Thomas, 186
Panama, 369
Parliamentary system, 43–44, 56, 319
Partisan differences, in fiscal policy, 473
Partisan press, 282
Partisanship, 177–179
Partisan support in Congress, 371

Partisan thinking, 177–179
Party caucuses, 312
Party-centered politics, 214
Party coalition, 222–227
Party competition, 215
Party democracy, 244–245
Party differences, 226
Party discipline, 326
Party identification, 177–178, 219
Party leaders (in Congress), 312–316
Party-line voting, 333–335
Party organizations, 231–238
  local, 233–234
  national, 235–236
  state, 235
  weakening of, 232–234
Party realignment, 216–218
Paterson, William, 35
Patronage system, 392, 393
Peers as agents of political socialization, 168
Pendleton Act, 394
Pennsylvania, 42, 106, 243
Pentagon Papers, 95, 373
People for the American Way, 260
Per curiam decisions, 419
Perestroika, 517
Perot, Ross, 230
Persian Gulf war, 96, 207, 517–518, 524, 527, 537–538
Personal income tax, 473
Philadelphia constitutional convention, 34–37, 60–62
Physically impaired, 137–138
Physician-assisted suicide, 107
Planned Parenthood v. *Casey*, 106
"Pledge of Allegiance," 167
Plessy v. *Ferguson*, 123
Pluralism, 19, 20, 249–250, 272–275
Pluralist democracy, 159
Pluralist theory, 272–273
  questionable aspects, 273–276
Plurality opinion, 420
Pocket veto, 327
Police-type actions, 528

Policy, 15
  influence of public opinion on, 180–182
Policy implementation, 391–392
Policymaking, 264–266, 520–524
Policy responsibilities of federal bureaucracy, 391–392
Political action committees (PACs), 268–272, 307–308, 309
Political culture, 3–12
Political leaders and institutions as agents of political socialization, 168
Political machines, big-city, decline of, 233–234
Political movements, 206–208
Political officials, justices and judges as, 428–429
Political participation, 185–210
Political parties, 213–246, 250. *See also individual parties*
  advantages of, 214, 215
  American, origins of, 215–216
  candidate-centered campaigns in, 239–246
  coalition formation in, 222–223, 225–227
  competition and collective action in, 215–223
  competitive, number of, 221
  controlling nominations, 232–233
  decline of control by, elections and, 232–238
  factional, 228
  first, 215–216
  ideological, 228
  local organizations, 233–234
  minor, 227–229
  money and media and, 236–237
  national conventions, 235
  national organizations, 235–236
  organization of, 233–236
  policy formulation in, 222–223
  realignments and, 218–221
  single issue, 227

Political parties—*Cont.*
  state organizations, 235
  systems of, 221–224
Political power, constitutional restraints on, 40–47
Political socialization, 156–181
  agents of, 167–171
  process of, 165–166
Political system, 22–24
  in United States, 22–24
Politics, process of, 12–22
Politics of global economic policy, 540–541
Polk, James K., 282
Polling error, sources of, 164–165
Pollution, 457, 459
Popular rule, limited, 49–51
Population (in polling), 162
Populist party, 228
Populists, 172
Pork barrel projects, 307
Pornography, 101–102
Positive government, 493
Poverty, 484–486
  children and, 484, 487
  minority groups and, 485, 486
  percentage living in, 484
  in United States, 484–486
  War on, 507
  women and, 484
Poverty line, 484
Powell, Colin, 362
Power, 14–15
Power, theories of, 18–22
Power elite, 20
Power imperative of federal bureaucracy, 396–402
Powers of the nation, 66–67
Powers of the states, 66–67
Prayer, school, 104, 440
Precedent, 419, 434
Presidency, 342–378. *See also individual presidents*
  accountability through, 403–405
  bureaucracy and, 403
  campaign for election, 355–359

Presidency—*Cont.*
  campaign for nomination,
    353–355
  checks and balances and, 44
  colliding with Congress, 371–374
  Congress and, 369–374
  congressional support of, 371
  election of, 350–358
  fiscal policy and, 469–471
  force of circumstance in, 365–366
  foreign policy and, 367, 369,
    520–521
  free trade and, 535–536
  increase in power of, 346–350
  modern foundation of, 346–350
  news media and, 350–352
  policy leadership and, 364–377
  problem of appointee control,
    363–364
  public support of, 375–379
  requirements in Constitution, 359
  staffing, 360–362
  televised, 376–377
Presidential appointees, 360–364,
  404–405
Presidential approval rating, 375
Presidential commissions, 389
Presidential debates, 358
Presidential elections, 350–358
Presidential leadership, 378,
  395–396
  factors in, 364–377
  need for, 347–350
  support for, 374–378
Presidential primary, 353–355
Presidential selection system,
  development of, 50–51, 55,
  350–353
Presidential veto, 370
President *pro tempore* of Senate, 315
President's cabinet, 362
Press, 281. *See also* News media
Press skepticism, 296
Pressure groups. *See* Interest groups
Primacy tendency, 165

Primary elections, 51, 55, 193, 232
Print media. *See* News media
Printz v. *United States*, 84
Prior restraint, 95–96
Prisons, 115–117
Privacy, right of, 105–106
Private (individual) goods, 253
Private parties, discrimination by, 138
Probability sample, 164
Probable cause, 89, 108, 111, 112
Procedural due process, 107–108
Procedural rights, selective
  incorporation of, 109
Professional groups, 255
Progressive income tax, 473
Progressive reforms, 228, 352
Progressives, 53, 232
  reforms of, 53
Prohibition party, 228
Proportional representation, 222
Proposition 187, California,
  134–135
Proposition 209, California, 149
Proposition 227, 137
Prospective voting, 199
Protectionism, 534
Protestants, 173
Protest politics, 207–208
Public affairs, awareness of,
  159–160, 161
Public assistance, 496, 507
Public assistance programs,
  496–500, 507
Public education, 12–13, 77
Public goods, 256
Public interest groups, 257–258
Public opinion, 156–181
  cross-cutting cleavages and, 177
  defense policy and, 528–529
  defining, 158–159
  environmentalism and, 457
  federal-state power and, 81
  frames of reference guiding,
    170–179
  government by, 180–181

Public opinion—*Cont.*
  influence of, on policy, 180
  information and, 159–160, 161
  measurement of, 160–161
  nature of, 158–164
  press skepticism and, 299
  role of, 180–181
Public opinion poll, 162–166
Public representative role, 299–302
Public support of presidency,
  375–378
Puerto Ricans. *See* Hispanic
  Americans
Pulitzer, Joseph, 282, 283
Purposive incentive, 255
Putnam, Robert, 203

Quakers, 42

Race, guiding public opinion, 174
Race-based redistricting, 140
Racial profiling, 114–115
Racial segregation, 123
Radio, 283–285
Ratification of Constitution, 36–39
Reagan, Ronald, 83, 127, 168, 264,
  345, 366, 376, 404, 406, 437,
  468, 517
Realignments, 217–219
Reapportionment, 311
Reasonable-basis test, 139, 140
Reconstruction, 123
Redistricting, 144, 311
Redlining, 142
Referendum, 53, 54
Reform party, 230
*Regents of the University of California
  v. Bakke*, 147
Region, guiding public opinion, 174
Registration, 190
Registration requirements, 190–191
Regulation, 450
Regulatory agencies, 387
Regulatory policy
  objectives of, 455–456

Regulatory policy—*Cont.*
  politics of, 456
Rehnquist, William, 84, 85, 415, 444
Reinventing government, 409–410
Religion
  freedom of, 29
  "free exercise" of, 104–105
  guiding public opinion, 169, 173
  opinions on, 173
Religious Freedom Restoration
  Act, 104
Reno v. ACLU, 102
Reno v. Condon, 85
Rent vouchers, 499
Reporting
  descriptive, 283
  interpretive, 283
Representation function (of
  Congress), 321
Representative democracy, 49
Republic, 49
Republican National Committee
  (RNC), 235–236
Republican party, 199, 217–219,
  225–227
Reserved powers, 67
Reserve rate, 476
Restraint of trade, preventing,
  451–453
Result, equality of. *See* Equality
Retrospective voting, 200–201
Revenues, government, 78
Reverse discrimination, 121, 147
Revolutionary War, 30–31, 34
Revolution of 1800, 52
Rhode Island, 35, 38, 49, 51, 481
Rider (to Senate bill), 326
Right-to-Life party, 227
Roberts, Owen, 75
Roe v. Wade, 106, 416, 425
Rollins, Ed, 241
Romer v. Evans, 138–139, 442
Roosevelt, Franklin, 73, 75, 85, 166,
  218–219, 343, 350, 366, 367,
  463, 494, 514

Roosevelt, Theodore, 228, 230, 348, 364, 376
Rostenkowski, Dan, 310
Rostker v. *Goldberg*, 140
Roth v. *United States*, 100
Rulemaking (in bureaucracy), 391–392
Rules Committee, House, 325
Rules of politics, 12–22
Rutledge, John, 36

Safe Drinking Water Act, 453
Salant, Richard, 299
Sample, 162
Sampling error, 162–163
Savings and loan (S&L) industry, 454
Scalia, Antonin, 415, 442, 444
Schechter v. *United States*, 74
Schenck v. *United States*, 74
School choice, 502–503
School prayer, 270
Schools
    as agents of political socialization, 167–168
Scott, Dred, 71
Second Bank of the United States, 68
Second-strike capability, 526
Securities and Exchange Act, 455
Securities and Exchange Commission (SEC), 387
Sedition Act of 1798, 92
Select committees, 320
Selective incorporation, 96–98
    Fourteenth Amendment and, 96–98
    of procedural rights, 108–110
Self-government, 4, 28–29, 52
    democracy and, 47–56
    providing for, 47–55
Self-incrimination, 108
Senate, U.S., 35. *See also* Congress, U.S.
    committee chairpersons in, 316–319

Senate—*Cont.*
    committee system in, 319–323
    constitutional qualifications for serving in, 309
    incumbents in, 305–312
    majority leader of, 314–315
    party leaders in, 314–315
    president *pro tempore*, 315
    selection of, 50, 53
    special problem of strong challengers in, 310–311
    standing committees of, 319–321
Senate Appropriations Committee, 472
Senate Budget Committee, 471
Senate Foreign Relations Committee, 335
Senate Judiciary Committee, 426
Senatorial courtesy, 427–428
Seniority, 318
Seniority principle in Congress, 318
Sentencing policies, 117
Separated institutions sharing power, 43–46
Separation of church-state, 103–104
Separation of powers, 42, 55
Serbia, 156–157, 518–519, 522
Service relationship, 238
Service strategy, 307
Seventeenth Amendment, 53
Sexual harassment in workplace, 131
Shaw, Jr., Clay, 481
Shays' Rebellion, 33–35
Sherman Antitrust Act, 73
Sierra Club, 259
Signaler role, 294–296
Simpson, O. J, 299–300
Simpson-Mizzoli Act, 134
Single-issue groups, 259
Single-issue parties, 227–228
Single-issue politics, 250
Single-member districts, 221–222
Sixth Amendment, 108
Slander, 99

Slavery, 1, 8, 65, 70, 123, 217
  Constitution and, 36
Smith, Adam, 449–450
Smith, Howard, 318
Social capital, 203
Social insurance, 493, 507
Social insurance programs,
  493–496, 507
Social integration, 150–152
Socialism, 17, 18
Social movements, 206–208
Social regulation, new, 456
Social security, 494
Social Security Act, 486, 494, 496
Social welfare
  culture and politics and, 505–508
  politics of, 486, 488
Social welfare policy, 6, 76, 85,
  481–508
Soft money, 237
Sound bites, 296
South Africa, 539
South Carolina, 52, 70, 140
South-North constitutional
  compromise, 36
Sovereignty, 62
Soviet Union, 93, 369, 513, 514,
  516, 517, 526, 527, 530
Spanish-American War, 282–283
Spanish speakers. See Hispanic
  Americans
Speaker of House of
  Representatives, 312–314
Special (U.S.) courts, 423
Special interests. See interest groups
Speech
  free, 93–95, 97–98
  hate, 98
Spending policy, 463–464
Spin, 243, 295–296
Split-ticket voting, 220
Spoils system, 393
Spotted owl controversy, 458
Stalin, Josef, 514
Stamp tax, 30

Standing committees, 319–321
Stanton, Elizabeth Cady, 127
Stare decisis, philosophy of, 434
Starr, Kenneth, 337, 371
State courts in federal system,
  423–425
State governments
  employees of, 77
  free expression and, 96–99
State judges, methods of
  selecting, 424
State party organizations, 235
State powers, national powers and,
  62–63
States
  Bill of Rights applied to, 97
  in constitutional system, 62–63
State sovereignty, 60–66
States' rights, 70–71
States' Rights party, 229
Statutes, interpretation of, 433–434
Stenberg v. Carhart, 106–107
Stevens, John Paul, 89, 415, 444
Stewardship theory, 346–347
Stone, Harlan Fiske, 94
Straight-ticket voting, 220
Strategic Arms Limitation Talks
  (SALT), 516
Strict construction, 437
Strict-scrutiny test, 139
Structuring tendency, 165–166
Subsidized housing, 499–500
Suffrage, 186
Sunset law, 336–337, 407
Supplemental Security Income
  (SSI), 496
Supply-side economics, 468–469
Supply-side stimulation, 468
Supremacy clause, 66, 68, 69
Supreme Court, U.S., 418–421. See
  also individual cases
  accountability through, 407
  affirmative action and, 147–149
  African Americans and, 123
  checks and balances and, 44

Supreme Court—*Cont.*
  deciding cases, 419–420
  election of 2000, 178, 342, 358,
    415–416
  freedom of religion and, 103–105
  free expression and, 91–102
  issuing decisions and opinions,
    420–421
  nominees, 426–428
  opinions of, 420
  right of privacy, 105–107
  rights of persons accused of
    crimes, 109–116
  selecting cases, 418–419
  sexual discrimination and,
    129–131, 140–141
Supreme Court justices, selecting,
  426–427
Suspect classifications, 139
Swann v. *Charlotte-Mecklenburg*
  County Board of Education, 150
Symbolic speech, 94–95

Taft, William Howard, 228
Taft-Hartley Act, 390–391
Taney, Roger B., 71
Taxation, federal, 463
Taxes. *See* personal income tax
Taxpayer Refund and Relief Act, 473
Tax revenue, government, shares
  of, 78
Televised presidency, 376–377
Television viewing, 204
Temporary Assistance for Needy
  Families (TANF), 83, 497, 498
Tenth Amendment, 67, 73
Terrorism, 522
  in Kenya, 522
  in Tanzania, 522
Texas, 94, 99, 106, 133, 134,
  144, 149
Texas v. *Johnson*, 94–95
Thomas, Bill, 318
Thomas, Clarence, 415
Three-fifths compromise, 36

Tiananmen Square, 540
Time-Warner, 452
Title IX of the Education
  Amendment of 1972, 127
Tobacco lobby, 271
Tocqueville, Alexis de, 1, 5, 217, 251
Townshend Act, 30
Toxic waste, 458–459
Trade
  free, 535–536
  global, 533–538
  human rights and, 538–540
  restraint of, preventing, 451–452
Trade deficit, 532
Transfer payments, 492
Transportation bill, 304
"Trickle-down" theory, 468
Truman, Harry, 164, 229, 363
Trustees, 49
Turf wars, 323
Turnout, voter, 189, 310
Twelfth Amendment, 356
Twenty-fourth Amendment,
  143, 187
Twenty-sixth Amendment, 187
Two-party system, 221, 223
Tyranny of the majority, 17, 47

Unconventional activism, 206–208
Unemployment insurance, 494–495
Unitary governments, 63
Unitary system, 63
United Auto Workers (UAW), 253
United Nations, 523
United States Forest Service, 457
United States v. *Lopez*, 84
United States v. *O'Brien*, 94
United States v. *Virginia*, 140
Unit rule, 356
Unity, 5
University of California Regents v.
  Bakke, 147
University of Missouri, 283
Unlimited conventional warfare,
  526–527

Unlimited nuclear warfare, 526
Upper-court myth, 422
Urban Institute, 498
U.S. Chamber of Commerce, 254
U.S. Postal Service, 389

Ventura, Jesse, 231
Veto, 327, 346, 469
Vice-president, 314, 360
Vietnam war, 17, 95, 196, 207, 373,
    515–516, 528
  public opposition to, 94, 515
Violence Against Women Act, 131
Virginia, 39, 140
Virginia Plan, 34–35
Virginia Military Institute, 140
Virtual political participation,
    205–206
Voter participation, 185–201
Voter turnout, 189–201, 310
Voting, 193–194, 197–206. See also
    Elections
Voting Rights Act, 125,
    143–144, 187
Voucher system, 503

Wallace, George, 229
War on Poverty, 490, 507
War Powers Act, 373
Warren, Earl, 124
Warsaw Pact countries, 522
Washington (state), 107
Washington, George, 33, 34, 39, 52,
    68, 215, 346
Washington Post, 296
Watchdog role, 296–297
Watergate affair, 27–28, 196,
    296, 371
Water Pollution Control Act, 453
Water Quality Act, 457
Weaver, James B., 228
Webster, Daniel, 361
Webster v. Reproductive Health
    Services, 106
Welfare, 505–508

Welfare policy, 481–508
Welfare reform, 59–60
Welfare Reform Act of 1996, 59–60,
    83, 481, 486, 489, 490, 497
Welfare system, 507
Welfare web, 506–507
Whig party, 217
Whig theory, 346–347
Whistle Blower Protection Act, 408
Whistle-blowing, 408
White House Office (WHO), 360,
    361, 363
White House Office of
    Communications, 295
White House Press Office, 295
Whren v. United States, 111–112
Williams, Jody, 255, 257
Wilson, Woodrow, 59, 160, 218,
    228, 342, 347, 348
Wisconsin, 105, 481
Women, 1, 12, 121, 127–131, 275.
    See also Affirmative action; Civil
    rights movement; National
    Organization for Women
    (NOW)
  abolitionist movement and, 127
  affirmative action and,
    146–147, 174
  attitudes of, 174–175
  college enrollment of, 130
  comparable worth issue and, 130
  discrimination against, 127, 139,
    140–141
  economic status of, 130
  education level of, 130
  Equal Rights Amendment
    and, 127
  family leave issue and, 127, 130
  as federal judges, 429
  "gender gap" in voting, 128,
    176, 227
  glass ceiling and, 130
  legal status of, 127–133
  organizations and, 259
  party coalitions and, 226

Women—*Cont.*
  political action and, 128, 241, 275
  representation of, 128–130, 312,
    359, 408–409, 429
  reproductive rights of, 106, 425
  sexual harassment of, 130, 131
  suffrage, 127, 143, 187, 195
  as Supreme Court justices,
    128, 429
  violence against, 131
Woodward, Bob, 296
World Bank, 523

World economy, changing, 531–533
World Trade Organization (WTO),
  207, 208, 523, 536
Wounded Knee, 132
Writ of *certiorari*, 419
Writ of *mandamus*, 46–47
Wyoming, 481

Yalta Conference, 514
Yellow journalism, 282–283
Yellowstone National Park, 457